NOTES

ON THE

NEW TESTAMENT

EXPLANATORY AND PRACTICAL

BY

ALBERT BARNES

ENLARGED TYPE EDITION

EDITED BY

ROBERT FREW, D.D.

THESSALONIANS, TIMOTHY, TITUS and PHILEMON

BAKER BOOK HOUSE
Grand Rapids, Michigan

ISBN: 0-8010-0556-6

First Printing, August 1949
Second Printing, February 1951
Third Printing, March 1955
Fourth Printing, October 1958
Fifth Printing, April 1961
Sixth Printing, December 1963
Seventh Printing, September 1966
Eighth Printing, April 1969
Ninth Printing, October 1971
Tenth Printing, August 1973
Eleventh Printing, February 1975
Twelfth Printing, November 1976
Thirteenth Printing, January 1977
Fourteenth Printing, February 1978

PHOTOLITHOPRINTED BY CUSHING - MALLOY, INC.
ANN ARBOR, MICHIGAN, UNITED STATES OF AMERICA
1978

THE FIRST

EPISTLE TO THE THESSALONIANS.

INTRODUCTION.

§ 1. *The situation of Thessalonica.*

THESSALONICA was a city and seaport of Macedonia. It was at the head
of the bay Thermaicus, or the Gulf of Thessalonica (see the map prefixed to
the Notes on the Acts of the Apostles), and was, therefore, favourably situated for commerce. It was on the great Egnatian Way; was possessed of
an excellent harbour, and had great advantages for commerce through the
Hellespont, and with Asia Minor and the adjacent countries. It was south-
west of Philippi and Amphipolis, and a short distance north-east of Berea.
Macedonia was an independent country until it was subdued by the Romans.
The occasion of the wars which led to its conquest by the Romans was an
alliance which was formed by Philip II. with Carthage, during the second
Punic war. The Romans delayed their revenge for a season; but Philip
having laid siege to Athens, the Athenians called the Romans to their aid,
and they declared war against the Macedonians. Philip was compelled to
sue for peace, to surrender his vessels, to reduce his army to 500 men, and
to defray the expenses of the war. Perseus, the successor of Philip, took up
arms against the Romans, and was totally defeated at Pydna by Paulus
Æmilius, and the Romans took possession of the country. Indignant at
their oppression, the Macedonian nobility and the whole nation rebelled under
Andriscus; but after a long struggle they were overcome by Quintus Cæcil-
ius, surnamed, from his conquest, Macedonius, and the country became a
Roman province, B.C. 148. It was divided into four districts, and the city
of Thessalonica was made the capital of the second division, and was the
station of a Roman governor and questor. At the time, therefore, that the
gospel was preached there, this whole country was subject to Roman authority.
The city, called, when Paul visited it, Thessalonica, was anciently called
Therme, and by this name was known in the times of Herodotus, Thucydides,
and Æschines. We are informed by Strabo that Cassander changed the
name of Therme to Thessalonica, in honour of his wife, who was a daughter
of Philip. Others have said that the name was given to it by Philip himself,
in memory of a victory which he obtained over the armies of Thessaly. In
the time of Brutus and Cassius it was a city of so much importance that the
promise of being permitted to plunder the city, as the reward of victory, infused new courage into their armies.
The city was inhabited by Greeks, Romans, and Jews. It adored many
gods, but particularly Jupiter, as the father of Hercules, the alleged founder
of its ancient royal family. It had a celebrated amphitheatre, where gladia-
torial shows were exhibited for the amusement of the citizens, and a circus
for public games. The Roman part of the population was, of course, introduced after the conquest, and it is impossible now to estimate the relative
number of the Greeks and the Romans in the time when the gospel was
preached there. In common with most of the other cities of Greece, a considerable number of Jews resided there, who had a synagogue at the time when
the city was visited by Paul, Acts xvii. 1. Little is known of the *morals* of
the place, but there is reason to believe that it was somewhat distinguished

for dissoluteness of manners. "The females, particularly, could claim little credit on the score of modest retiring demeanour; for this virtue was in so low estimation in the city that the place was selected as the scene of the wanton fancies of the satirist" (Lucian). See Hug, *Intro.*
The name of the place now is Saloniki. It is a Turkish commercial town, and contains about 70,000 inhabitants. Its situation and appearance are thus described by Dr. Clarke:—"The walls of Salonica give a very remarkable appearance to the town, and cause it to be seen at a great distance, being white-washed; and what is still more extraordinary, they are painted. They extend in a semicircular manner from the sea, enclosing the whole of the buildings within a *peribolus*, whose circuit is five or six miles; but a great part of the space within the walls is void. It is one of the few remaining cities which has preserved the ancient form of its fortifications; the mural turrets yet standing, and the walls that support them, being entire. Their antiquity is perhaps unknown, for, though they have been ascribed to the Greek emperors, it is very evident they were constructed in two distinct periods of time; the old Cyclopean masonry remaining in the lower parts of them, surmounted by an upper structure of brickwork. Like all the ancient and modern cities of Greece, its wretched aspect within is forcibly contrasted with the beauty of its external appearance. The houses are generally built of unburnt bricks, and, for the most part, they are no better than so many hovels." It is, however, a flourishing commercial town, from which is exported the corn, cotton, wool, tobacco, bees'-wax, and silk of Macedonia. It is the seat of a Pasha, and has still among its population a considerable proportion of Jews. Rabbi Benjamin of Tudela, who visited it in A.D. 1160, describes it under the name of *Salunki*, and says that it was built by Seleucus, one of the four Greek nobles who arose after Alexander, and that when he visited it, it was "a large city containing about five hundred Jewish inhabitants." "The Jews," says he, "are much oppressed in this place, and live by the exercise of handicrafts" (*Itinerary*, vol. i. 49, 50, ed. 1840). He describes it as having at that time more Jewish inhabitants than any other town in Greece, Thebes alone excepted. It is said at present to contain about 20,000 Jewish inhabitants. Its favourable situation for commerce is probably the cause of the numerous assemblage of the Jews there. See Asher's ed. of Benjamin of Tudela, vol. ii. p. 42.

§ 2. *The establishment of the church in Thessalonica.*

The gospel was first preached in Thessalonica by Paul and Silas. After their release from imprisonment at Philippi they passed through Amphipolis and Apollonia, and came to Thessalonica. For some cause they appear not to have paused to preach in either of the first two places, but went at once to the city of Thessalonica. That was a much more important place, and they may have been attracted there particularly because many Jews resided there. It was customary for the apostle Paul, when he came to a place where there were Jews, to preach the gospel first to them; and as there was a synagogue in Thessalonica he entered it, and for three Sabbath-days reasoned with the Jews in regard to the Messiah. The points on which he endeavoured to convince them were, that, according to the Scriptures, it was necessary that the Messiah should be put to death, and that he would rise from the dead, and that all the predictions on these points were completely fulfilled in Jesus of Nazareth, Acts xvii. 2, 3. A few of the Jews believed, and a much larger number of the "devout Greeks," and also a considerable number of females of the more elevated ranks. From these converts the church was organized, and the number at the organization would seem to have been large. It is not quite certain how long Paul and Silas remained at Thessalonica. It is known only that they preached in the synagogue for three Sabbaths, and if that were all the time that they remained there, it could not have been more than about three weeks. But it is not certain that they did not remain in the city a longer time. It is possible that they may have been excluded from the synagogue, but still may have found some other place in which to preach. This would seem probable from one or two circumstances referred to in the history and in the Epistle. In the history (Acts xvii. 5), it appears that Paul and Silas, for a time at least, made the house of Jason their home, and that so large numbers attended on their ministry as to give occasion to great excitement among the Jews. In the epistle (1 Thes. ii. 9), Paul says that when he was among them he "laboured night and day, because he would not be chargeable unto any of them, and preached unto them the gospel of God" (comp. 2 Thes. iii. 8), which looks as if he had been with them a longer time than the "three Sabbaths," and as if he had laboured at his usual occupation for support before he shared the hospitality of Jason. It appears also, from Phil. iv. 16, that he was there long enough to receive repeated supplies from the church at Philippi. "For even in Thessalonica ye sent once and again unto my necessity."

Paul and Silas were driven away from Thessalonica by the opposition of the Jews. A mob was created by them; the house of Jason was assailed; he and "certain brethren," who were supposed to have harboured and secreted Paul and Silas, were dragged before the magistrates and accused of receiving those who "had turned the world upside down," and who were guilty of treason against the Roman emperor, Acts xvii. 5-7. So great was the tumult, and such would be the danger of Paul and Silas if they remained there, that the members of the church judged it best that they should go to a place of safety, and they were conveyed by night to the neighbouring city of Berea. There the gospel was received with more favour, and Paul preached without opposition until the Jews from Thessalonica, hearing where he was, came thither and excited the people against him, Acts xvii. 13. It became necessary again that he should be removed to a place of safety, and he was conducted to Athens, while Silas and Timothy remained at Berea. Timothy, it appears, had accompanied Paul, and had been with him as well as Luke at Philippi and Thessalonica, though he is not mentioned as present with them until the arrival at Berea. When Paul went to Athens he gave commandment to those who conducted him that Silas and Timothy should come to him as soon as possible; and while he waited for them at Athens he delivered the memorable speech on Mars' hill, recorded in Acts xvii. Their actual arrival at Athens is not mentioned by Luke (Acts xvii.), but that Timothy came to him there appears from 1 Thes. iii. 1, 2, "Wherefore when we could no longer forbear, we thought it good to be left at Athens alone, and sent Timotheus our brother, &c., to comfort you concerning your faith." Timothy appears, therefore, to have been with Paul at Athens but a short time, for he sent him back to Thessalonica, and before his return Paul had gone to Corinth, whither Timothy followed him, Acts xviii. 5.

§ 3. *The time and place of writing the Epistle.*

The subscription at the close of this epistle affirms that it was written at Athens. But these subscriptions are of no authority whatever (see Notes at the close of 1 Corinthians), and in this case, as in several others, the subscription is false. Paul remained but a short time at Athens, and there is internal evidence that the epistle was not written there. In 1 Thes. iii. 1, 2, Paul says that such was his anxiety for them that he had concluded to remain at Athens alone, and that he had sent Timothy to them from that place to impart to them consolation. In the same epistle (chap. iii. 6) he speaks of Timothy's return to him *before* the epistle was written. But from Acts xvii. and xviii. 5 it is evident that Timothy did not return to Paul at Athens, but that he and Silas came to him after he had left Athens and had gone to Corinth. To that place Paul had gone after his short visit to Athens, and there he remained a year and a half, Acts xviii. 11. It is further evident that the epistle was not written to the Thessalonians *so soon* as it would be necessary to suppose if it were written from Athens. In chap. ii. 17, 18, the author says, "But we, brethren, being taken from you a short time in presence, not in heart, endeavoured the more abundantly to see your face with great desire. Wherefore we would have come unto you, even I Paul, *once and again;* but Satan hindered us." From this it is evident that the apostle had repeatedly endeavoured to visit them, but had been hindered. But it is not reasonable to suppose that he had attempted this during the short time that he was in Athens, and so soon after having been driven away from Berea. It is more probable that this had occurred during his residence at Corinth, and it would seem also from this that the epistle was written towards the close of his residence there. At the time of writing the epistle, Silas and Timothy were with the apostle (chap. i. 1), and we know that they were with him when he was at Corinth, Acts xviii. 5.

If this epistle was written at the time supposed, at Corinth, it must have been about the 13th year of the reign of Claudius, and about A.D. 52. That this was the time in which it was written is the opinion of Mill, of Lardner, of Hug, and is indeed generally admitted. It was the *first* epistle written by the apostle Paul, and, in some respects, may be allowed to excite a deeper interest on that account than any others of his. The Second Epistle to the Thessalonians is supposed to have been written at the same place, and probably in the same year. See Lardner, vol. vi. 4–6. Grotius, indeed, supposes that the order of the epistles has been inverted, and that that which is now called the "Second Epistle to the Thessalonians" was in fact first sent. But there is no evidence of this.

§ 4. *The character of the church at Thessalonica, and the design of the Epistle.*

The church at Thessalonica at first was composed of the following classes of persons:—(1) Jews. To them Paul preached first, and though the mass of them opposed him and rejected his message, yet some of them believed, Acts xvii. 4. (2) Greeks who had been proselyted to the Jewish faith, and who seem to have been in attendance on the synagogue, Acts xvii. 4. They are called "devout Greeks"—σεβομένοι Ἑλλήνοι—that is, religious Greeks, or those who had renounced the worship of idols, and who attended on the worship of the synagogue. They were probably what the Jews called "proselytes of the gate;" persons who were admitted to many privileges, but who were not proselytes in the fullest sense. There were many such persons usually where a synagogue was established among the Gentiles. (3) Females of the more elevated rank and standing in the community, Acts xvii. 4. They were women of influence, and were connected with distinguished families. Possibly they also may have been of the number of the proselytes. (4) Not a few members of the church appear to have been converted from idolatry by the preaching of the apostle, or had connected themselves with it after he had left them. Thus, in chap. i. 9, it is said, "For they themselves show of us what manner of entering in we had unto you, *and how ye turned to God from idols,* to serve the living and true God."

Though the apostle had been much opposed when there, and the gospel had been rejected by the great body of the inhabitants of Thessalonica, yet it had been most cordially embraced by these different classes (chap. ii. 13), and they were entirely harmonious in the belief of it. They forgot all their former differences in the cordiality with which they had embraced the gospel.

The characteristics of the church there, and the circumstances existing, which gave occasion for the two epistles to the Thessalonians, appear to have been, so far as can be gathered from the history (Acts xvii.), and the epistles themselves, the following:—

1. The members of the church had very cordially embraced the gospel; they were the warm friends of the apostle; they greatly desired to receive his instruction; and these things prompted him to the earnest wish which he had cherished to visit them (chap. ii. 17), and now led him to write to them; comp. chap. i. 5, 6; ii. 8, 9, 13, 19, 20. Paul had for them the strong affection which a nurse has for the children committed to her charge (chap. ii. 7), or a father for his children (chap. ii. 11), and hence the interest shown for them by writing these epistles.

2. They were disposed not only to embrace the gospel, but to spread it abroad (chap. i. 8), and Paul was evidently desirous of commending them for this, and of exciting them to greater love and zeal in doing it.

3. They had at first embraced the gospel amidst scenes of strife (chap. ii. 2); they were now opposed, as they had been there, by the Jews, and by their own countrymen (chap. ii. 14); and they appear to have been called to some peculiar trials, by the loss of some valued members of the church—friends who were peculiarly dear to their hearts, chap. ii. 3, 5; iii. 13. To console them in view of these afflictions was one design of the first epistle, and in doing it the apostle states one of the most interesting views of the resurrection to be found in the Scriptures, chap. iv. 14–18.

4. They had been instructed in reference to the future coming of the Saviour; the day of judgment, and the fact that the appearing of the "day of the Lord" would be like a thief in the night, chap. v. 2. But they seem to have inferred that that day was near, and they were looking for the immediate advent of the Redeemer, and the close of the world. To this view they seem to have been led by two things. One was, a misinterpretation of what the apostle says, chap. iv. 14–18; v. 2, 3, about the advent of the Redeemer, which they seem to have understood as if it meant that it would be "soon;" and the other was, probably, the fact that certain letters had been forged in the name of Paul which maintained this doctrine, 2 Thes. ii. 2. To correct this view was one of the leading objects of the second epistle, and accordingly the apostle in that shows them that events must occur preceding the coming of the Lord Jesus which would occupy a long time, and that the end of the world, therefore, could not be near, 2 Thes. ii. 3–12.

5. An error seems also to have prevailed among them in regard to the resurrection, which was the cause of great uneasiness to those who had lost Christian friends by death, 1 Thes. iv. 13. They seem to have supposed that when the Lord Jesus appeared, they who were alive would have great advantages over those who were deceased; that the living would be allowed to behold his glory, and to participate in the splendours of his personal reign, while those who were in their graves would slumber through these magnificent scenes. To correct these views, appears to have been one design of the first epistle. The apostle shows them that at the coming of the Saviour all the redeemed, whether living or dead, would participate alike in his glory. They who were alive would not anticipate those who were in their graves. In fact, he says, those who were dead would rise *before* the change would take place in the living that was to fit them to dwell with the Lord, and then all would be taken up to be for ever with him, 1 Thes. iv. 15–18.

6. It would appear to be not improbable that after the departure of the

apostle from Thessalonica, he had been accused by the enemies of the gospel there of a want of courage, and that they had urged this as proof that he was conscious that the gospel was an imposture. Besides, his leaving the church there without any instructors in a time when they greatly needed them, may have been urged as a proof that he had no real affection for them, or concern for their welfare. To meet this charge, the apostle urges several things, vindicating his conduct, and showing the strength of his attachment for them. He says, (1) That, as they knew, so far from being deterred by persecution from preaching, after a violent persecution at Philippi, he and his fellow-labourers had at once preached the same gospel at Thessalonica, and they had done it there amidst the same kind of opposition, chap. ii. 2. (2) That they themselves were witnesses that it had been done without any appearance of fraud or of guile. They had given them all possible proofs of sincerity, chap. ii. 3–5. (3) That they had given every proof possible that they did not seek glory from men, and that their aims were not selfish. They were willing to have imparted, not the gospel only, but also their own lives; and to show that they had no selfish aim while with them, they had supported themselves by the labour of their own hands, chap. ii. 6–9. (4) That so far from not feeling any interest in them, he had repeatedly sought to visit them, but had in every instance been prevented (chap. ii. 17, 18); and, (5) That, since *he* was prevented from going to them, he had submitted to the personal sacrifice of parting with Timothy at Athens, and of being left alone there, in order that he might go to them and comfort their hearts, chap. iii. 1, 2.

7. In common with other churches, gathered in part or in whole from the heathen, they were in danger of falling into the sins to which they had been addicted before their conversion, and one object of the first epistle is to put them on their guard against the leading vices to which they were exposed, chap. iv. 1–7.

8. It would seem, also, that there were some in the church who had a spirit of insubordination towards their religious teachers, and who, under pretence of edifying others, were guilty of disorder. To correct this was also one object of the epistle, 1 Thes. v. 12–14.

From these views, the design of this epistle, and also of the second epistle to the same church, which seems to have been written soon after this, will be apparent. They were the effusions of warm attachment towards a church which the apostle had founded, but from which he had been soon driven away, and which he had been prevented from revisiting when he had earnestly desired it. They are filled with expressions of tender regard; they remind the members of the church of the ardour with which they had at first embraced the gospel; caution them against the dangers to which they were exposed; commend them for their fidelity hitherto, and encourage them in their trials and persecutions. They present some most interesting views of the nature of the gospel, and especially contain statements about the resurrection of the saints which are not found elsewhere in the New Testament, and views in relation to the great apostasy, and the "man of sin," which demonstrate that the writer was inspired, and which are of inestimable importance in guarding the true church from the power of Antichrist. No one could have drawn the picture of the Papacy in the second chapter of the second epistle who was not under the inspiration of the Holy Ghost; and no true Christian can be sufficiently grateful that the apostle was thus inspired to reveal the features of that great apostasy, to put the church on its guard against the wiles and the power of him who "exalteth himself above all that is called God."

EPISTLE TO THE THESSALONIANS.

CHAPTER I.

PAUL, and *a*Silvanus, and Timotheus, unto the church of the *b*Thessalonians *which is* in God the Father, and *in* the Lord Jesus

CHAPTER I.

ANALYSIS OF THE CHAPTER.

The first chapter of this epistle embraces the following subjects:—

(1) The inscription by Paul, Silas, and Timothy, to the Thessalonians, and the usual salutations, ver. 1.

(2) An expression of thanks for their fidelity in the gospel, ver. 2-4. The apostle says that he made mention of them continually in his prayers; that he remembered their faith, and love, and patience, for by these things they had shown that they were among the elect of God.

(3) He reminds them of the manner in which they received the gospel when it was first preached to them, ver. 5, 6. The power of God had been manifested among them in a remarkable manner; they had embraced the gospel with strong assurance, and though in the midst of deep afflictions, they had received the word with joy.

(4) The effect of the establishment of the church in Thessalonica had been felt far abroad, and had been of the most happy character, ver. 7-10. They had become examples to all that believed in Macedonia and Achaia. From them the gospel had been sounded abroad throughout Greece, and indeed in all places with which they had connection by their commercial relations. Those who dwelt in distant places bore witness to the influence of the gospel on them, and to the power of that religion which had turned them from idols to serve the living God. These verses contain a beautiful illustration of the effect of the gospel in a place favourably situated for commerce, and

Christ: *c*Grace *be* unto you, and peace, from God our Father, and the Lord Jesus Christ.

2 We give thanks to God always

a 1 Pe.5.12.　　*b* Ac.17.1,&c.　　*c* Ep.1.2.

having extensive intercourse with other regions.

1. *Paul, and Silvanus, and Timotheus.* On the reasons why Paul associated other names with his in his epistles, see Notes on 1 Cor. i. 1, and 2 Cor. ii. 1. Silvanus, or Silas, and Timothy were properly united with him on this occasion, because they had been with him when the church was founded there, Acts xvii., and because Timothy had been sent by the apostle to visit them after he had himself been driven away, chap. ii. 1, 2. Silas is first mentioned in the New Testament as one who was sent by the church at Jerusalem with Paul to Antioch (Notes, Acts xv. 22); and he afterwards became his travelling companion. ¶ *Which is in God the Father, and* in *the Lord Jesus Christ.* Who are united to the true God and to the Redeemer; or who sustain an intimate relation to the Father and the Lord Jesus. This is strong language, denoting that they were a true church; comp. 1 John v. 20. ¶ *Grace* be *unto you,* &c. See Notes, Rom. i. 7.

2. *We give thanks to God always for you all.* See Notes, Rom. i. 9. ¶ *Making mention of you in our prayers.* Notes, Eph. i. 16. It may be observed here, (1) That the apostle was in the habit of constant prayer. (2) That he was accustomed to extemporary prayer, and not to written prayer. It is not credible that "forms" of prayer had been framed for the churches at Thessalonica and Ephesus, and the other churches for which Paul says he prayed, nor would it have been possible to have adapted such forms to the varying circum-

for you all, making mention of you in our prayers;

3 Remembering without ceasing your *d* work of faith, and *e* labour of love, and *f* patience of hope in

d Jn.6.29; 2 Th.1.11.

stances attending the organization of new churches.

3. *Remembering without ceasing.* Remembering your faith and love whenever we pray. This is not to be understood literally, but it is language such as we use respecting anything that interests us much. It is constantly in our mind. Such an interest the apostle had in the churches which he had established. ¶ *Your work of faith.* That is, your *showing* or *evincing* faith. The reference is probably to acts of duty, holiness, and benevolence, which *proved* that they exercised *faith* in the Lord Jesus Christ. Works of faith are those to which faith prompts, and which show that there *is* faith in the heart. This does not mean, therefore, a work of their own *producing* faith, but a work which showed that they *had* faith. ¶ *And labour of love.* Labour *produced* by love, or showing that you are actuated by love. Such would be all their kindness toward the poor, the oppressed, and the afflicted, and all their acts which showed that they loved the *souls* of men. ¶ *And patience of hope.* Patience in your trials, showing that you have such a hope of future blessedness as to sustain you in your afflictions. It was the hope of heaven through the Lord Jesus that gave them patience. See Notes on Rom. viii. 24. "The phrases here are Hebraisms, meaning *active faith,* and *laborious love,* and patient hope, and might have been so translated" (Doddridge). ¶ *In our Lord Jesus Christ.* That is, your hope is founded only on him. The only hope that we have of heaven is through the Redeemer. ¶ *In the sight of God and our Father.* Before God, even our Father. It is a hope which we have *through* the merits of the Redeemer, and which we are permitted to cherish *before* God; that is, in his very presence. When we think of God; when

our Lord Jesus Christ, in the sight of God and our Father;

4 Knowing, brethren [1] beloved, your election of God.

e He.6.10.   *f* Ro.12.12.
1 or, *beloved of God, your election.*

we reflect that we must soon stand before him, we are permitted to cherish this hope. It is a hope which will be found to be genuine even in the presence of a holy and heart-searching God. This does not mean that it had been merely *professed* before God, but that it was a hope which they might dare to entertain even in the presence of God, and which would bear the scrutiny of his eye.

4. *Knowing, brethren beloved, your election of God.* The margin here reads, "beloved of God, your election." The difference depends merely on the pointing, and that which would require the marginal reading has been adopted by Hahn, Tittman, Bloomfield, and Griesbach. The sense is not materially varied, and the common version may be regarded as giving the true meaning. There is no great difference between "being *beloved* of God," and "being *chosen* of God." The sense then is, "knowing that you are chosen by God unto salvation." Comp. Notes on Eph. i. 4, 5, 11. The word "knowing" here refers to Paul himself, and to Silas and Timothy, who united with him in writing the epistle, and in rendering thanks for the favours shown to the church at Thessalonica. The meaning is, that they had so strong confidence that they had been chosen of God as a church unto salvation, that they might say they *knew* it. The *way* in which they knew it seems not to have been by direct revelation or by inspiration, but by the *evidence* which they had furnished, and which constituted such a proof of piety as to leave no doubt of the fact (Calvin). What this evidence was, the apostle states in the following verses. It was shown by the manner in which they embraced the gospel, and by the spirit which they had evinced under its influence. The meaning here seems to be, not that all the members of the church at

5 For our gospel *came not unto you in word only, but also in

g Is.55.11; Mar.16.20.

h power, and in *i* the Holy Ghost, and in *k* much assurance; as ye

h 1 Co.2.4. *i* 2 Co.6.6. *k* He.2.3.

Thessalonica were certainly chosen of God to salvation — for, as in other churches, there might have been those there who were false professors—but that *the church, as such,* had given evidence that it was a true church—that it was founded on Christian principles—and that, as a church, it had furnished evidence of its "election by God." Nor can it mean, as Clarke and Bloomfield suppose, that God "had *chosen* and *called* the Gentiles to the same privileges to which he chose and called the Jews; and that as they (the Jews) had *rejected* the gospel, God had now *elected* the Gentiles in their stead;" for a considerable portion of the church was composed of *Jews* (see Acts xvii. 4, 5), and it cannot, therefore, mean that the *Gentiles* had been selected in the place of the Jews. Besides, the election of the *Gentiles*, or any portion of the human family, to the privileges of salvation, to the neglect or exclusion of any other part, would be attended with all the difficulties which occur in the doctrine of personal and individual election. Nothing is gained on this subject in removing the difficulties, by supposing that God chooses *masses* of men instead of *individuals.* How can the one be more proper than the other? What difficulty in the doctrine of election is removed by the supposition? Why is it not as right to choose an individual as a nation? Why not as proper to reject an individual as a whole people? If this means that the church at Thessalonica had shown that it was a true church of Christ, chosen by God, then we may learn, (1) That a true church owes what it has to the "election of God." It is because God has chosen it; has called it out from the world; and has endowed it in such a manner as to be a true church. (2) A church *may* give evidence that it is chosen of God, and is a true church. There are things which it may do, which will show that it is undoubtedly such a church as God has chosen, and such

as he approves. There *are* just principles on which a church should be organized, and there *is* a spirit which may be manifested by a church which will distinguish it from any other association of men. (3) It is not improper to speak with strong confidence of such a church as undoubtedly chosen of God. There *are* churches which, by their zeal, self-denial, and deadness to the world, show beyond question their "election of God," and the world may see that they are founded on other principles and manifest a different spirit from other organizations of men. (4) Every church *should* evince such a spirit that there may be no doubt of its "election of God." It should be so dead to the world; so pure in doctrine and in practice, and so much engaged in spreading the knowledge of salvation, that the world will see that it is governed by higher principles than any worldly association, and that nothing could produce this but the influence of the Holy Spirit of God.

5. *For our gospel came not unto you.* When first preached, Acts xvii. 1–3. Paul speaks of it as "*our* gospel," because it was the gospel *preached* by him and Silas and Timothy; comp. 2 Thes. ii. 14; 2 Tim. ii. 8. He did not mean to say that the gospel had been *originated* by him, but only that he had delivered the good news of salvation to them. He is here stating the *evidence* which had been given that they were a church "chosen by God." He refers, *first*, to the manner in which the gospel was received by them (ver. 5–7), and, *secondly*, to the spirit which they themselves manifested in sending it abroad, ver. 8–10. ¶ *In word only.* Was not merely *spoken;* or was not merely *heard.* It produced a powerful effect on the heart and life. It was not a mere empty sound that produced no other effect than to entertain or amuse; comp. Ezek. xxxiii. 32. ¶ *But also in power.* That is, in such power as to convert the soul. The apostle

know what manner of men we were among you for your sake.

6 And ye *became followers of us, and of the Lord, having re-

*2 Co.8.5.

evidently refers not to any miracles that were wrought there, but to the effect of the gospel on those who heard it. It is *possible* that there were miracles wrought there, as there were in other places, but there is no mention of such a fact, and it is not necessary to suppose it, in order to see the full meaning of this language. There was great *power* manifested in the gospel in its leading them to break off from their sins, to abandon their idols, and to give their hearts to God; see this more fully explained in the Notes on 1 Cor. ii. 4. ¶ *And in the Holy Ghost.* Comp. Notes on 1 Cor. ii. 4. It is there called the "demonstration of the Spirit." ¶ *And in much assurance.* That is, with firm conviction, or full persuasion of its truth. It was not embraced as a doubtful thing, and it did not produce the effect on the mind which is caused by anything that is uncertain in its character. Many seem to embrace the gospel as if they only *half* believed it, or as if it were a matter of very doubtful truth and importance; but this was not the case with the Thessalonians. There was the firmest conviction of its truth, and they embraced it "heart and soul;" comp. Col. ii. 2; Heb. vi. 11. From all that is said in this verse, it is evident that the power of God was remarkably manifested in the conversion of the Thessalonians, and that they embraced the gospel with an uncommonly strong conviction of its truth and value. This fact will account for the subsequent zeal which the apostle so much commends in them —for it is usually true that the character of piety in a church, as it is in an individual, is determined by the views with which the gospel is first embraced, and the purposes which are formed at the beginning of the Christian life. ¶ *As ye know what manner of men,* &c. Paul often appeals to those among whom he had laboured as competent witnesses with respect to his own conduct and character; see chap. ii. 9,

10; Acts xx. 33–35. He means here that he and his fellow-labourers had set them an example, or had shown what Christianity was by their manner of living, and that the Thessalonians had become convinced that the religion which they taught was real. The holy life of a preacher goes far to confirm the truth of the religion which he preaches, and is among the most efficacious means of inducing them to embrace the gospel.

6. *And ye became followers of us.* "You became *imitators—μιμηταί—* of us." This does not mean that they became *followers* of Paul, Silas, and Timothy, in the sense that they had set themselves up as *teachers,* or as the head of a sect, but that they *imitated* their manner of living; see Notes on 1 Cor. iv. 16; xi. 1. ¶ *And of the Lord.* The Lord Jesus. You also learned to *imitate* him. From this it is evident that the manner in which the Saviour lived was a prominent topic of their preaching, and also that it was one of the means of the conversion of the Thessalonians. It is probable that preaching on the pure and holy life of the Lord Jesus might be made a much more important means of the conversion of sinners than it is. Nothing is better adapted to show them the evil of their own guilty lives than the contrast between their lives and his; and nothing can be conceived better fitted to *win* them to holy living than the contemplation of his pure and holy deportment. ¶ *Having received the word in much affliction.* That is, amidst much opposition from others; see Acts xvii. 5–8. It was in the midst of these trials that they had become converted—and they seem to have been all the better Christians for them. In *this* they were imitators of the Saviour, or shared the same lot with him, and thus became his followers. Their embracing and holding fast the truths of religion amidst all this opposition, showed that they were controlled by the same

ceived the word in much affliction, with *m* joy of the Holy Ghost;

m Ac.13.52.

principles that he was, and that they were truly his friends. ¶ *With joy of the Holy Ghost.* With happiness produced by the Holy Ghost. Though they were much afflicted and persecuted, yet there was joy. There was *joy* in their conversion—in the evidence of pardoned sin—in the hope of heaven; see Notes, Acts viii. 8. However great may be the trials and persecutions experienced in receiving the gospel, or however numerous and long the sufferings of the subsequent life in consequence of having embraced it, there is a joy in religion that more than overbalances all, and that makes religion the richest of all blessings.

7. *So that ye were ensamples to all that believe.* Examples in reference to the firmness with which you embraced the gospel, the fidelity with which you adhered to it in trials, and the zeal which you showed in spreading it abroad. These things are specified in the previous and subsequent verses as characterizing their piety. The word here rendered *ensamples—τύπους—*is that from which the word *type* is derived. It properly denotes anything caused or produced by the means of *blows* (from τύπτω), and hence a mark, print, or impression, made by a stamp or die; and then a resemblance, figure, pattern, exemplar—a model after which anything is made. This is the meaning here. They became, as it were, a model or pattern after which the piety of others should be moulded, or showed what the piety of others ought to be. ¶ *In Macedonia.* Thessalonica was an important city of Macedonia (see the Intro.; comp. Notes, Acts xvi. 9), and of course their influence would be felt on the whole of the surrounding region. This is a striking instance of the effect which a church in a city may have on the country. The influence of a city church may be felt, and will usually be felt, afar on the other churches of a community—just as, in all other

7 So that ye were ensamples to all that believe in Macedonia and Achaia.

respects, a city has an important influence on the country at large. ¶ *And Achaia.* Achaia proper was the part of Greece of which Corinth was the capital. The word, however, was sometimes so used as to comprehend the whole of Greece, and in this sense it seems to be employed here, as there is no reason to suppose that their influence would be felt *particularly* in the province of which Corinth was the centre. Koppe observes that Macedonia and Achaia were the two provinces into which all Greece was divided when it was brought under the Roman yoke, the former of which comprehended Macedonia proper, Illyricum, Epirus, and Thessaly, and the other Greece properly so called. The meaning here is, therefore, that their influence was felt on all the parts of Greece; that their piety was spoken of, and the effect of their conversion had been felt in all those places. Thessalonica was a commercial city, and a seaport. It had intercourse with all the other parts of Macedonia, with Greece, and with Asia Minor. It was partly owing to the advantages of its situation that its influence was thus felt. Its own merchants and mariners who went abroad would carry with them the spirit of the religion of the church there, and those who visited it from other ports would see the effect of religion there. This is just an instance, therefore, of the influence which a commercial town and a seaport may have in religion on other parts of the world. A revival of religion in such a place will extend its influence afar to other places, and appropriate zeal among the friends of the Redeemer there may have an important effect on seaports, and towns, and lands far remote. It is impossible to over-estimate the importance of such places in regard to the spread of the gospel; and Christians who reside there—be they merchants, mechanics, lawyers, physicians, mariners, or ministers of the gospel, should feel that on them God

8 For from you ⁿsounded out the word of the Lord not only in Macedonia and Achaia, but also in ° every

ⁿ Ro.10.18.   o 2 Th.1.4.

has placed the responsibility of using a vast influence in sending the gospel to other lands. He that goes forth from a commercial town should be imbued with the spirit of the gospel, and churches located there should be so under the influence of religion, that they who come among them from abroad shall bear to their own lands honourable testimony of the power of religion there.

8. *For from you sounded out the word of the Lord.* The truths of religion were thus spread abroad. The word rendered "sounded out "— ἐξήχηται—refers to the sounding of a trumpet (Bloomfield), and the idea is, that the gospel was proclaimed like the sonorous voice of a trumpet echoing from place to place; comp. Isa. lviii. 1; Rev. i. 10. Their influence had an effect in diffusing the gospel in other places, *as if* the sound of a trumpet echoed and reechoed among the hills and along the vales of the classic land of Greece. This seems to have been done (1) *involuntarily;* that is, the necessary result of their conversion, even without any direct purpose of the kind of their own, would be to produce this effect. Their central and advantageous commercial position; the fact that many of them were in the habit of visiting other places; and the fact that they were visited by strangers from abroad, would naturally contribute to this result. But (2) this does not appear to be all that is intended. The apostle commends them in such a way as to make it certain that they were *voluntary* in the spread of the gospel; that they made decided efforts to take advantage of their position to send the knowledge of the truth abroad. If so, this is an interesting instance of one of the first efforts made by *a church* to diffuse the gospel, and to send it to those who were destitute of it. There is no improbability in the supposition that they sent out members of their

place your faith to God-ward is spread abroad; so that we need not to speak any thing.

9 For they themselves show

church—messengers of salvation—to other parts of Macedonia and Greece that they might communicate the same gospel to others. See Doddridge. ¶ *But also in every place.* Thessalonica was connected not only with Macedonia and Greece proper, in its commercial relations, but also with the ports of Asia Minor, and not improbably with still more remote regions. The meaning is, that in all the places with which they trafficked the effect of their faith was seen and spoken of. ¶ *Faith to God-ward.* Fidelity toward God. They showed that they had a true belief in God and in the truth which he had revealed. ¶ *So that we need not to speak anything.* That is, wherever we go, we need say nothing of the fact that you have been turned to the Lord, or of the character of your piety. These things are sufficiently made known by those who come from you, by those who visit you, and by your zeal in spreading the true religion.

9. *For they themselves.* They who have visited you, and they whom you have sent out; all persons testify of your piety. The apostle seems to refer to all whom he had met or had heard of "in all places," who said anything about the Thessalonians. They were unanimous in bearing testimony to their fidelity and piety. ¶ *Show of us what manner of entering in we had unto you.* The testimony which they bear of *you* is, *in fact,* testimony of the manner in which *we* preached the gospel, and demeaned ourselves when we were with you. It shows that we were intent on our Master's work, and that we were not actuated by selfish or sinister motives. The argument is that such effects could not have been produced among them if Paul, Silas, and their fellow-labourers had been impostors. Their sound conversion to God; their change from idolatry to the true religion, and the zeal which had been the result of

of us what manner of entering in we had unto you, and how ye turned *p* to God from idols, to serve the living and true God;

10 And to *q*wait for his Son from heaven, whom he raised from the dead, *even* Jesus, which delivered us from the *r*wrath to come.

their conversion, was an argument to which Paul and his fellow-labourers might appeal in proof of their sincerity and their being sent from God. Paul often makes a similar appeal; comp. Notes on 2 Cor. iii. 2, 3. It is certain that many of the Jews in Thessalonica, when Paul and his fellow-labourers were there, regarded them as impostors (Acts xvii. 6, 8), and there is every reason to suppose that after they left the city they would endeavour to keep up this impression among the people. To meet this, Paul now says that their own undoubted conversion to a life of holiness and zeal under their ministry, was an unanswerable argument that this was not so. How could impostors and deceivers have been the means of producing such effects? ¶ *And how ye turned to God from idols.* That is, under our preaching. This proves that the church was to a considerable extent composed of those who were converted from idolatry under the preaching of Paul; comp. Intro. § 4. The meaning here is, that they who came from them, or they who had visited them, bore abundant testimony to the fact that they had turned from idols to the worship of the true God; comp. Notes 1 Cor. xii. 2; Gal. iv. 8. ¶ *To serve the living and true God.* He is called the "*living* God" in opposition to idols—who are represented as dead, dumb, deaf, and blind; comp. Ps. cxxxv. 15–17; Notes, Isa. xliv. 10–17; Mat. xvi. 16; Jn. v. 26; Ac. xiv. 15.

10. *And to wait for his Son from heaven.* It is clear from this and from other parts of these two epistles that the return of the Lord Jesus to this world was a prominent subject of the preaching of Paul at Thessalonica. No small part of these epistles is occupied with stating the true doctrine on this point (1 Thes. iv. v.), and in correcting the errors which prevailed in regard to it after the departure of

Paul. Perhaps we are not to infer, however, that this doctrine was made *more* prominent there than others, or that it had been inculcated there more frequently than it had been elsewhere, but the apostle adverts to it here particularly because it was a doctrine so well fitted to impart comfort to them in their trials (chap. iv. 13–18), and because, in that connection, it was so well calculated to rouse them to vigilance and zeal, chap. v. 1–11. He makes it prominent in the second epistle, because material errors prevailed there in reference to it which needed to be corrected. In the passage before us he says that the return of the Son of God from heaven was an important point which had been insisted on when he was there, and that their conduct, as borne witness to by all, had shown with what power it had seized upon them, and what a practical influence it had exerted in their lives. They lived *as if* they were "*waiting*" for his return. They fully believed in it; they expected it. They were looking out for it, not knowing when it might occur, and *as if* it might occur at any moment. They were, therefore, dead to the world, and were animated with an earnest desire to do good. This is one of the instances which demonstrate that the doctrine that the Lord Jesus will return to our world, is fitted, when understood in the true sense revealed in the Scriptures, to exert a powerful influence on the souls of men. It is eminently adapted to comfort the hearts of true Christians in the sorrows, bereavements, and sicknesses of life (Jn. xiv. 1–3; Acts i. 11; 1 Thes. iv. 13–18; 2 Pet. iii. 8, 9); to lead us to watchfulness and to an earnest inquiry into the question whether we are prepared to meet him (Mat. xxiv. 37–44; xxv. 13); to make us dead to the world, and to lead us to act as becomes the children of light (1 Thes.

v. 5-9); to awaken and arouse
impenitent and careless sinners (1
Thes. v. 2, 3; 2 Pet. iii. 3-7); and
to excite Christians to self - deny -
ing efforts to spread the gospel in
distant lands, as was the case at
Thessalonica. Every doctrine of the
gospel is adapted to produce some
happy practical effects on mankind,
but there are few that are more full of
elevated and holy influences than that
which teaches that the Lord Jesus
will return to the earth, and which
leads the soul to wait for his appearing; comp. Notes, 1 Cor. i. 7; Phil.
iii. 20. ¶ *Whom he raised from the
dead.* Notes, Acts ii. 24-32; 1 Cor.
xv. 4-9. Paul probably means to intimate here that this was one of the
great truths which they had received,
that the Lord Jesus had been raised
from the dead. We know it was a
prominent doctrine wherever the gospel was preached. ¶ *Which delivered
us from the wrath to come.* Another
of the prominent doctrines of Christianity, which was undoubtedly always
inculcated by the first preachers of
religion. The "wrath to come" is
the divine indignation which will come
upon the guilty, Mat. iii. 7. From
that Christ delivers us by taking our
place, and dying in our stead. It was
the great purpose of his coming to
save us from this approaching wrath.
It follows from this, (1) that there
was wrath which man had to dread—
since Jesus came to deliver us from
something that was *real*, and not from
what was *imaginary;* and (2) that
the same wrath is to be dreaded now
by all who are not united to Christ,
since in this respect they are now just
as all were before he died; that is,
they are exposed to fearful punishment, from which He alone can deliver. It may be added that the existence of this wrath is *real*, whether
men believe it or not, for the fact of
its existence is not affected by our belief or unbelief.

REMARKS.

This chapter teaches—

(1) That it is right to commend
those who do well, ver 3. Paul was
never afraid of injuring anyone by
commending him when he deserved it;

nor was he ever afraid to rebuke when
censure was due.

(2) Christians are chosen to salvation, ver. 4. Their hope of heaven
depends on the "election of God."

(3) It is possible for *a people* to
know that they are chosen of God,
and to give such evidence of it that
others shall know it also, ver. 4. It
is possible for *a church* to evince such
a spirit of piety, self-denial, love, and
holiness, and such a desire to spread
the gospel, as to show that they are
"chosen of God," or that they are a
true church. This question is not to
be determined by their adherence to
certain rites and forms; by their holding to the sentiments of an orthodox
creed; or by their zeal in defence of
the "apostolic succession," but by
their bringing forth "the fruits of
good living." In determining that
the church at Thessalonica was
"chosen of God," Paul does not refer to its external organization, or to
the fact that it was founded by apostolic hands, or that it had a true ministry and valid ordinances, but to the
fact that it evinced the true spirit of
Christian piety; and particularly that
they had been zealous in sending the
gospel to others. There were three
things to which he referred: 1. That
the gospel had power over themselves,
inducing them to abandon their sins;
2. That it had such influence on their
lives that others recognized in them
the evidence of true religion; and 3.
That it made them benevolent, and excited them to make efforts to diffuse
its blessings abroad.

(4) If a *church* may know that it is
chosen or elected of God, it is true of
an individual also that *he* may know
it. It is not by any direct revelation
from heaven; not by an infallible communication of the Holy Spirit; not by
any voice or vision; but it is in the
same way in which this may be evinced
by a church. The conversion of an
individual, or his "election of God,"
may be certainly known by himself, if,
1. The gospel is received as "the word
of God," and induces him to abandon
his sins; 2. If it leads him to pursue
such a life that others shall see that
he is actuated by Christian principles;

and, 3. If he makes it his great aim in life to do good, and to diffuse abroad, as far as he can, that religion which he professes to love. He who finds in his own heart and life evidence of these things, need not doubt that he is among the "chosen of God."

(5) The character of piety in the life of an individual Christian, and in a church, is often determined by the manner in which the gospel is embraced at first, and by the spirit with which the Christian life is entered on; see Notes on ver. 5, 6. If so, then this fact is of immense importance in the question about organizing a church, and about making a profession of religion. If a church is so organized as to have it understood that it shall be to a considerable extent the patron of worldly amusements—a "half-way house" between the world and religion, that purpose will determine all its subsequent character—unless it shall be counteracted by the grace of God. If it is organized so as to look with a benignant and tolerant eye on gaiety, vanity, self-indulgence, ease, and what are called the amusements and pleasures of life, it is not difficult to see what will be its character and influence. How can such a church diffuse far and near the conviction that it is "chosen of God," as the church at Thessalonica did? And so of an individual. Commonly, the whole character of the religious life will be determined by the views with which the profession of religion is made. If there is a purpose to enjoy religion and the world too; to be the patron of fashion as well as a professed follower of Christ; to seek the flattery or the plaudits of man as well as the approbation of God, *that* purpose will render the whole religious life useless, vacillating, inconsistent, *miserable*. The individual will live without the enjoyment of religion, and will die leaving little evidence to his friends that he has gone to be with God. If, on the other hand, there be singleness of purpose, and entire dedication to God at the commencement of the Christian life, the religious career will be one of usefulness, respec-

tability, and peace. The most important period in a man's life, then, is that when he is pondering the question whether he shall make a profession of religion.

(6) A church in a city should cause its influence to be felt afar, ver. 7-9. This is true, indeed, of all other churches, but it is especially so of a church in a large town. Cities will be centres of influence in fashion, science, literature, religion, and morals. A thousand ties of interest bind them to other parts of a land, and though in fact there may be, as there often is, much more *intelligence* in a country neighbourhood than among the same number of inhabitants taken promiscuously from a city; and though there may be, as there often is, far more good sense and capability to appreciate religious truth in a country congregation than in a congregation in a city, yet it is true that the city will be the radiating point of influence. This, of course, increases the responsibility of Christians in a city, and makes it important that, like those of Thessalonica, they should be models of self-denial and of efforts to spread the gospel.

(7) A church in a commercial town should make use of its peculiar influence to spread the gospel abroad, ver. 7-9. Such a place is connected with remote lands, and those who, for commercial purposes, visit distant ports from that place, should bear with them the spirit of the gospel. Such, too, should be the character of piety in the churches in such a city, that all who visit it for any purpose, should see the reality of religion, and be led to bear the honourable report of it again to their own land.

(8) Such, too, should be the piety of any church. The church at Thessalonica evinced the true spirit of religion, ver. 7-9. Its light shone afar. It sent out those who went to spread the gospel. Its members, when they went abroad, showed that they were influenced by higher and purer principles than those which actuated them before conversion, and than were evinced by the heathen

world. Those who visited them, also, saw that there was a reality in religion, and bore an honourable report of it again to their own lands. Let any church evince *this* spirit, and it will show that it is "chosen of God," or a true church; and wherever there is a church formed after the primitive model, these traits will always be seen.

(9) It is *our* duty and privilege to "wait for the Son of God to return from heaven." We know not when his appearing, either to remove us by death, or to judge the world, will be —and we should therefore watch and be ready. The hope of his return to our world to raise the dead, and to convey his ransomed to heaven, is the brightest and most cheering prospect that dawns on man, and we should be ready, whenever it occurs, to hail him as *our* returning Lord, and to rush to his arms as *our* glorious Redeemer. It should be always the characteristic of *our* piety, as it was that of John, to say, "Even so, come, Lord Jesus," Rev. xxii. 20.

CHAPTER II.

ANALYSIS OF THE CHAPTER.

The principal *subjects* embraced in this chapter are the following:—

I. A statement of the conduct of Paul and his fellow-labourers when they first preached the gospel at Thessalonica, ver. 1–12. In this statement, the apostle specifies particularly the following things. (1) That he and his fellow-labourers had been shamefully treated at Philippi, and had been obliged to encounter much opposition at Thessalonica, ver. 1, 2. (2) That in their efforts to convert the Thessalonians they had used no deceit, corruption, or guile, ver. 3, 4. (3) That they had not sought the praise of men, and had not used the weight of *authority* which they might have done as the apostles of Christ, ver. 6. (4) That they had been gentle and mild in all their intercourse with them, ver. 7, 8. (5) That, in order not to be burdensome, or to subject themselves to the charge of selfishness, they had supported themselves by labouring night and day,

ver. 9. (6) That the Thessalonians themselves were witnesses in what a holy and pure manner they had lived when there, and how they had exhorted them to a holy life, ver. 10–12.

II. The apostle refers to the manner in which the Thessalonians had received the truth at first, as undoubtedly the word of God, and not as the word of men, ver. 13.

III. He reminds them of the fact that they had met with the same opposition from the Jews which the churches in Judea had, for that everywhere the Jews had made the same opposition to the messengers of God, killing the Lord Jesus and their own prophets, and forbidding the apostles everywhere to speak to the Gentiles, ver. 14–16.

IV. In the conclusion of the chapter, the apostle expresses the earnest desire which he had to visit them, and the reason why he had not done it. It was because he had been prevented by causes beyond his control, and now his earnest and sincere wish was that he might be permitted to see them—for they were his hope, and joy, and crown, ver. 17–20.

It is reasonable to suppose that the statements in this chapter were designed to meet a certain condition of things in the church there, and if so, we may learn something of the difficulties which the Thessalonians had to encounter, and of the objections which were made to Paul and to the gospel. It is often in this way that we can get the best view of the internal condition of a church referred to in the New Testament—not by direct *statement* respecting difficulties and errors in it, but by the character of the epistle sent to it. Judging by this rule, we should infer that there were those in Thessalonica who utterly denied the divine origin of the gospel. This general charge the apostle meets in the first chapter, by showing that the *power* of the gospel evinced in their conversion, and its *effects* in their lives, demonstrated it to be of heavenly origin.

In reference to the state of things

CHAPTER II.

FOR yourselves, brethren, know our entrance in unto you, that it was not in vain :

as referred to in this chapter, we should also infer the following things:—

(1) That it was represented by some that the apostle and his fellow-labourers sought influence and power; that they were dictatorial and authoritative; that they were indisposed to labour; and were, in fact, impostors. This charge Paul refutes abundantly by his appeal to what *they* knew of him, and what they had *seen* of him when he was there, ver. 1-12.

(2) That the church at Thessalonica met with severe and violent opposition from the Jews who were there, ver. 14-17. This appears to have been a formidable opposition; comp. Acts xvii. 5, *seq.* They would not only be likely to use violence, but it is not improbable that they employed the semblance of *argument* that might perplex the church. They might represent that they were from the same country as Paul and his fellow-labourers; that they, while pretending to great zeal for religion, were, in fact, apostates, and were engaged in overturning the revealed doctrines of God. It would be easy to represent them as men who, from this cause, were worthy of no confidence, and to urge the fact that those who thus acted in opposition to the religion of their own country, and to the sacred rites of the temple at Jerusalem, could be entitled to no regard. These charges, if they were made, the apostle meets, by assuring the Thessalonians that they were suffering precisely the same things which the churches in Judea did; that the Jews manifested the same spirit there which they did in Thessalonica; that they had killed alike the Lord Jesus and their own undoubted prophets, and that it was a characteristic of them that they were opposed to all other men. Their opposition, there-

2 But even after that we had suffered before, and were shamefully entreated, as ye know, *a*at Philippi, *b*we were bold in our

a Ac.16.12,&c.   b Ac.17.2,3.

fore, was not to be wondered at, nor was it to be regarded as any argument that the apostles, though Jews, were unworthy of confidence, ver. 15, 16.

(3) It was very probably represented by the enemies of Paul and his fellow-labourers, that they had fled from Thessalonica on the slightest danger, and had no regard for the church there, or they would have remained there in the time of peril, or, at least, that they would have returned to visit them. Their continued absence was probably urged as a proof that they had no concern for them. The apostle meets this by stating that they had been indeed "taken from them" for a little time, but that their hearts were still with them, and by assuring them that he had often endeavoured to visit them again, but that "Satan had hindered" him, ver. 17-20. He had, however, given them the highest proof of interest and affection that he could, for when he was unable to go himself, he had, at great self-denial, sent Timothy to establish them in the faith, and to comfort their hearts, chap. iii. 1-3. His absence, therefore, should not be urged as a proof that he had no regard for them.

1. *For yourselves, brethren, know our entrance in unto you.* Notes, chap. i. 9. Paul appeals to themselves for proof that they had not come among them as impostors. They had had a full opportunity to see them, and to know what influenced them. Paul frequently appeals to his own life, and to what they, among whom he laboured, knew of it, as a full refutation of the slanderous accusations of his enemies; comp. Notes, 1 Cor. iv. 10-16; ix. 19-27; 2 Cor. vi. 3-10. Every minister of the gospel ought so to live as to be able, when slanderously attacked, to make such an appeal to his people. ¶ *That it was not in vain—κενὴ.* This word

God to speak unto you the gospel of God *c*with much contention.

3 For our exhortation *was* not

of *d*deceit, nor of uncleanness, nor in guile:

c Jude 3.   *d* 2 Pe.1.16.

means (1) *empty, vain, fruitless,* or without success; (2) that in which there is no truth or reality—*false, fallacious,* Eph. v. 6; Col. ii. 8. Here it seems, from the connection (ver. 3–5), to be used in the latter sense, as denoting that they were not deceivers. The object does not appear to be so much to show that their ministry was *successful* as to meet a charge of their adversaries that they were impostors. Paul tells them that from their own observation they knew that this was not so.

2. *But even after that we had suffered before.* Before we came among you. ¶ *And were shamefully entreated, as ye know, at Philippi.* Acts xvi. 19, *seq.* By being beaten and cast into prison. The *shame* of the treatment consisted in the fact that it was wholly undeserved; that it was contrary to the laws; and that it was accompanied with circumstances *designed* to make their punishment as ignominious as possible. The Thessalonians knew of this, and Paul was not disposed to palliate the conduct of the Philippians. What was "shameful treatment" he speaks of as such without hesitation. It is not wrong to call things by their right names, and when we have been abused, it is not necessary that we should attempt to smooth the matter over by saying that it was not so. ¶ *We were bo'd in our God.* By humble dependence on the support of our God. It was only *his* powerful aid that could have enabled them to persevere with ardour and zeal in such a work after such treatment. The meaning here is, that they were not deterred from preaching the gospel by the treatment which they had received, but at the very next important town, and on the first opportunity, they proclaimed the same truth, though there was no security that they might not meet with the same persecution there. Paul evidently appeals to this in order to show them that they were not impostors, and that they were not in-

fluenced by the hope of ease or of selfish gains. Men who were not sincere and earnest in their purposes would have been deterred by such treatment as thy had received at Philippi. ¶ *With much contention.* Amidst much opposition, and where great *effort* was necessary. The Greek word here used is ἀγών (*agony*), a word referring usually to the Grecian games; Notes, Col. ii. 1. It means the course, or place of contest; and then the contest itself, the strife, the combat, the effort for victory; and the apostle here means that, owing to the opposition there, there was need of an effort on his part like the desperate struggles of those who contended for the mastery at the Grecian games; comp. Notes on 1 Cor. ix. 24-27. The triumph of the gospel there was secured only by an effort of the highest kind, and by overcoming the most formidable opposition.

3. *For our exhortation.* That is, the exhortation to embrace the gospel. The word seems to be used here so as to include *preaching* in general. The sense is, that the means which they used to induce them to become Christians were not such as to delude them. ¶ Was *not of deceit.* Was not founded on sophistry. The apostle means to say that the Thessalonians knew that his manner of preaching was not such as was adopted by the advocates of error. ¶ *Nor of uncleanness.* Not such as to lead to an impure life. It was such as to lead to holiness and purity. The apostle appeals to what they knew to be the *tendency* of his doctrine as an evidence that it was true. Most of the teaching of the heathen philosophers led to a life of licentiousness and corruption. The tendency of the gospel was just the reverse. ¶ *Nor in guile.* Not by the arts of deceit. There was no *craftiness* or *trick,* such as could not bear a severe scrutiny. No point was carried by art, cunning, or stratagem. Everything was done on the

4 But as we were allowed of God to be *put in trust with the gospel, even so we speak ; not as

e 1 Ti.1.11,12.

most honourable and fair principles. It is much when a man can say that he has never endeavoured to accomplish anything by mere *trick, craft,* or *cunning.* Sagacity and shrewdness are always allowable in ministers as well as others ; trick and cunning never. Yet stratagem often takes the place of sagacity, and trick is often miscalled shrewdness. Guile, craft, cunning, imply deception, and can never be reconciled with that entire honesty which a minister of the gospel, and all other Christians, ought to possess ; see Notes on 2 Cor. xii. 16 ; comp. Ps. xxxii. 2 ; xxxiv. 13 ; John i. 47 ; 1 Pet. ii. 1, 22 ; Rev. xiv. 5.

4. *But as we were allowed of God to be put in trust with the gospel.* Comp. 1 Tim. i. 11, 12. Since there had been committed to us an office so high and holy, and so much demanding sincerity, fidelity, and honesty, we endeavoured to act in all respects in conformity to the trust reposed in us. The gospel is a system of truth and sincerity, and we evinced the same. The gospel is concerned with great realities, and we did not resort to trick and illusion. The office of the ministry is most responsible, and we acted in view of the great account which we must render. The meaning is, that Paul had such a sense of the truth, reality, and importance of the gospel, and of his responsibility, as effectually to keep him from anything like craft or cunning in preaching it. An effectual restrainer from mere management and trick will always be found in a deep conviction of the truth and importance of religion. Artifice and cunning are the usual accompaniments of a bad cause—and, when adopted by a minister of the gospel, will usually, when detected, leave the impression that *he* feels that he is engaged in such a cause. If an object cannot be secured by sincerity and straightforward dealing, it is not desirable that

pleasing men, but God, which trieth our hearts.
5 For neither *at any time used

f 2 Co.2.17.

it should be secured at all. ¶ *Even so we speak.* In accordance with the nature of the gospel ; with the truth and sincerity which such a cause demands. ¶ *Not as pleasing men.* Not in the manner of impostors, who make it their object to please men. The meaning of the apostle is, that he did not aim to teach such doctrines as would flatter men ; as would win their applause ; or as would gratify their passions or their fancy. We are not to suppose that he *desired* to offend men ; or that he regarded their esteem as of no value ; or that he was indifferent whether they were pleased or displeased ; but that it was not the direct object of his preaching to please them. It was to declare the truth, and to obtain the approbation of God whatever men might think of it ; see Notes on Gal. i. 10. ¶ *Which trieth our hearts.* It is often said to be an attribute of God that he tries or searches the hearts of men, 1 Chr. xxviii. 9 ; xxix. 17 ; Jer. xi. 20 ; xvii. 10 ; Ps. xi. 4 ; Rom. viii. 27. The meaning here is, that the apostle had a deep conviction of the truth that God knew all his motives, and that all would be revealed in the last day.

5. *For neither at any time used we flattering words.* See Notes on Job xxxi. 21, 22 ; and on 2 Cor. ii. 17. The word here rendered "flattering " —κολακεία—occurs nowhere else in the New Testament. The meaning is, that the apostle did not deal in the language of adulation ; he did not praise them for their beauty, wealth, talent, or accomplishments, and conceal from them the painful truths about their guilt and danger. He stated simple truth—not refusing to commend men if truth would admit of it, and never hesitating to declare his honest convictions about their guilt and danger. One of the principal arts of the deceiver on all subjects is flattery ; and Paul says, that when preaching to the Thessalonians he had carefully avoided it. He now appeals

we flattering words, as ye know, nor a cloke of covetousness; God *is* witness:

6 Nor *g* of men sought we

g Jn.5.41,44; Ga.1.10.

glory, neither of you, nor *yet* of others, when we might have ¹been *ʰ*burdensome, as the apostles of Christ.

1 or, *used authority.*   *h* 2 Co.12.13–15.

to that fact as a proof of his own integrity. They knew that he had been faithful to their souls. ¶ *Nor a cloke of covetousness.* The word rendered "*cloke*" here—πρόφασις—means, properly, "what is shown or appears before anyone;" *i.e. show, pretence, pretext,* put forth in order to cover one's real intent, Mat. xxii. 14; Mark xii. 40; Luke xx. 47. The meaning here is, that he did not put on a *pretence* or *appearance* of piety for the sake of promoting the schemes of covetousness. The *evidence* of that was not only what they observed of the general spirit of the apostle, but also the fact that when with them he had actually laboured with his own hands for a support, ver. 9. It is obvious that there were those there, as sometimes there are now, who, under the pretence of great zeal for religion, were really seeking wealth, and it is possible that it may have been alleged against Paul and his fellow-labourers that they were such persons. ¶ *God is witness.* This is a solemn appeal to God for the truth of what he had said. He refers not only to their own observation, but he calls God himself to witness his sincerity. God knew the truth in the case. There could have been no imposing on him; and the appeal, therefore, is to one who was intimately acquainted with the truth. Learn hence, (1) That it is right, on important occasions, to appeal to God for the truth of what we say. (2) We should always so live that we *can* properly make such an appeal to him.

6. *Nor of men sought we glory.* Or *praise.* The love of applause was not that which influenced them; see Notes on Col. i. 10. ¶ *Neither of you, nor yet of others.* Nowhere has this been our object. The love of fame is not that which has influenced us. The particular idea in this verse seems to be, that though they had uncommon

advantages, as the apostles of Christ, for setting up a dominion or securing an ascendency over others, yet they had not availed themselves of it. As an apostle of Christ; as appointed by him to found churches; as endowed with the power of working miracles, Paul had every advantage for securing authority over others, and turning it to the purposes of ambition or gain. ¶ *When we might have been burdensome.* Marg., "or, *used authority.*" Some understand this as meaning that they might have demanded *a support* in virtue of their being apostles; others, as Calvin, and as it is in the margin, that they might have used authority, and have governed them wholly in that manner, exacting unqualified obedience. The Greek properly refers to that which is *weighty* —ἐν βάρει—heavy, burdensome. Anything that *weighs down* or *oppresses* —as a burden, sorrow, or authority— would meet the sense of the Greek. It seems probable, from the context, that the apostle did not refer either to authority or to support exclusively, but may have included both. In their circumstances it might have been somewhat burdensome for them to have maintained him and his fellow-labourers, though as an apostle he *might* have required it; comp. 1 Cor. ix. 8–15. Rather than be oppressive in this respect, he had chosen to forego his right, and to maintain himself by his own labour. As an apostle also he might have exerted his *authority,* and might have made use of his great office for the purpose of placing himself at the head of churches, and giving them laws. But he chose to do nothing that would be a burden; he treated them with the gentleness with which a nurse cherishes her children (ver. 7), or a father his sons (ver. 11), and employed only the arts of persuasion; comp. Notes on 2 Cor. xii. 13–16. ¶ *As the apostles of Christ.*

7 But we were gentle among you, even as a nurse cherisheth her children:

8 So, being affectionately desirous of you, we were willing to have *im-

---

Though the writer uses the word *apostles* here in the plural number, it is not certain that he means to apply it to Silas and Timothy. He often uses the plural number where he refers to himself only; and though Silas and Timothy are joined with him in this epistle (chap. i. 1), yet it is evident that he writes the letter as if he were alone and that they had no part in the composition or the instructions. Timothy and Silas are associated with him for the mere purpose of salutation or kind remembrance. That this is so, is apparent from chap. iii. In ver. 1 of that chapter, Paul uses the plural term also, "When *we* could no longer forbear, we thought it good to be left at Athens alone;" comp. ver. 5, "For this cause, when *I* could no longer forbear, *I* sent to know your faith." Neither Silas nor Timothy were apostles in the strict and proper sense, and there is no evidence that they had the "authority" which Paul here says might have been exerted by an apostle of Christ.

7. *But we were gentle among you.* Instead of using authority, we used only the most kind and gentle methods to win you and to promote your peace and order. The word here rendered "nurse," may mean any one who nurses a child, whether a mother or another person. It seems here to refer to a mother (comp. ver. 11), and the idea is, that the apostle felt for them the affectionate solicitude which a mother does for the child at her breast.

8. *So, being affectionately desirous of you.* The word here rendered "being affectionately desirous"— ἱμείρω—occurs nowhere else in the New Testament. It means *to long after, to have a strong affection for.* The sense here is, that Paul was so strongly attached to them that he would have been willing to lay down his life for them. ¶ *We were willing*

parted unto you, not the gospel of God only, but also our own souls, because ye were dear unto us.

9 For ye remember, brethren,

i Ro.1.11.

---

to have imparted unto you. To have given or communicated, Rom. i. 11. ¶ *Not the gospel of God only.* To be willing to communicate the knowledge of the gospel was in itself a strong proof of love, even if it were attended with no self-denial or hazard in doing it. We evince a decided love for a man when we tell him of the way of salvation, and urge him to accept of it. We show strong interest for one who is in danger, when we tell him of a way of escape, or for one who is sick, when we tell him of a medicine that will restore him; but we manifest a much higher love when we tell a lost and ruined sinner of the way in which he may be saved. There is no method in which we can show so strong an interest in our fellow-men, and so much true benevolence for them, as to go to them and tell them of the way by which they may be rescued from everlasting ruin. ¶ *But also our own souls.* Or rather *lives* —ψυχὰς; Mat. vi. 25; xx. 28; Luke xii. 22, 23; Mark iii. 4. This does not mean that the apostle was willing to be *damned*, or to lose his *soul* in order to save them, but that if it had been necessary he would have been ready to lay down his life; see 1 John iii. 16, "We ought to lay down our lives for the brethren;" comp. Notes, John xv. 13. His object seems to be to assure them that he did not leave them from any want of love to them, or from the fear of being put to death. It was done from the strong conviction of duty. He appears to have left them because he could no longer remain without exposing others to danger, and without the certainty that there would be continued disturbances; see Acts xvii. 9, 10.

9. *Ye remember, brethren, our labour.* Doubtless in the occupation of a tent-maker; Notes, Acts xx. 34; 1 Cor. iv. 12. ¶ *And travail.* See Notes on 2 Cor. xi. 27. The word means *wearisome labour.* ¶ *For la-*

our *k*labour and travail: for labouring night and day, because we would not be chargeable unto any of you, we preached unto you the gospel of God.

10 Ye *are* witnesses, and God *also*, how holily and justly and unblameably we behaved ourselves among you that believe:

k Ac.20.34,35; 2 Th.3.7,8.

11 As ye know how we exhorted, and comforted, and charged every one of you, as a father *doth* his children,

12 That ye would *l* walk worthy of God, *m* who hath called you unto his kingdom and glory.

13 For this cause also thank we God without ceasing, because, when

l Ep.4.1.   *m* 1 Co.1.9.

bouring night and day. That is, when he was not engaged in preaching the gospel. He appears to have laboured through the week and to have preached on the Sabbath; or if engaged in preaching in the day time during the week, he made it up *by night labour.* ¶ *We preached unto you the gospel of God.* That is, I supported myself when I preached among you. No one, therefore, could say that I was disposed to live in idleness; no one that I sought to make myself rich at the expense of others.

10. *Ye are witnesses.* They had a full opportunity of knowing his manner of life. ¶ *And God* also. Notes on ver. 5. ¶ *How holily.* Piously—observing all the duties of religion. ¶ *And justly.* In our intercourse with men. I did them no wrong. ¶ *And unblameably.* This seems to refer to his duties *both* to God and man. In reference to all those duties no one could bring a charge against him. Every duty was faithfully performed. This is not a claim to absolute *perfection*, but it is a claim to consistency of character, and to faithfulness in duty, which every Christian should be enabled to make. Every man professing religion should so live as to be able to appeal to all who have had an opportunity of knowing him, as witnesses that he was consistent and faithful, and that there was nothing which could be laid to his charge.

11. *How we exhorted.* That is, to a holy life. ¶ *And comforted.* In the times of affliction. ¶ *And charged.* Gr. *testified.* The word *testify* is used here in the sense of *protesting*, or making an earnest and solemn appeal. They came as *witnesses* from God of the truth of religion, and of the importance of living in a holy manner.

They did not *originate* the gospel themselves, or teach its duties and doctrines as their own, but they came in the capacity of those who bore *witness* of what God had revealed and required, and they did this in the earnest and solemn manner which became such an office. ¶ *As a father* doth *his children.* With an interest in your welfare, such as a father feels for his children, and with such a method as a father would use. It was not done in a harsh, dictatorial, and arbitrary manner, but in tenderness and love.

12. *That ye would walk worthy of God,* &c. That you would live in such a manner as would honour God, who has chosen you to be his friends; Notes, Eph. iv. 1. A child "walks worthy of a parent" when he lives in such a way as to reflect honour on that parent for the method in which he has trained him; when he so lives as to bring no disgrace on him, so as not to pain his heart by misconduct, or so as to give no occasion to any to speak reproachfully of him. This he does, when (1) he keeps all his commands; (2) when he leads a life of purity and virtue; (3) when he carries out the principles of the family into his own life; (4) when he honours a father by evincing a profound respect for his opinions; and (5) when he endeavours to provide for his comfort and to promote his welfare. In a manner similar to this, a true Christian honours God. He lives so as not to bring a reproach upon him or his cause, and so as to teach the world to honour him who has bestowed such grace upon him. ¶ *Who hath called you.* Notes, 1 Cor. i. 9.

13. *For this cause also thank we God.* In addition to the reasons for

ye received the word of God which ye heard of us, ye received it [n] not as the word of men, but as it is in truth, the word of God, which [o] effectually worketh also in you that believe.

14 For ye, brethren, became followers of the churches of God which in Judea are in Christ Jesus : for ye also have suffered like things of

n Mat.10.40; 2 Pe.3.2.   o Ja.1.18; 1 Pe.1.23.

thankfulness already suggested, the apostle here refers to the fact that they received the truth, when it was preached, in such a way as to show that they fully believed it to be the word of God. ¶ *Not as the word of men.* Not of human origin, but as a divine revelation. You were not led to embrace it by human reasoning, or the mere arts of persuasion, or from personal respect for others, but by your conviction that it was a revelation from God. It is only when the gospel is embraced in this way that religion will show itself sufficient to abide the fiery trials to which Christians may be exposed. He who is convinced by mere human reasoning may have his faith shaken by opposite artful reasoning; he who is won by the mere arts of popular eloquence will have no faith which will be proof against similar arts in the cause of error; he who embraces religion from mere respect for a pastor, parent, or friend, or because others do, may abandon it when the popular current shall set in a different direction, or when his friends shall embrace different views; but he who embraces religion as the truth of God, and from the love of the truth, will have a faith, like that of the Thessalonians, which will abide every trial. ¶ *Which effectually worketh also in you that believe.* The word rendered "which" here—ὅς —may be referred either to "truth" or to "God." The grammatical construction will admit of either, but it is not material which is adopted. Either of them expresses a sense undeniably true, and of great importance. The meaning is, that the truth was made efficacious in the minds of all who became true Christians. It induced them to abandon their sins, to devote themselves to God, to lead pure and holy lives, and enabled them to abide the trials and temptations of life. Comp. Notes on Phil. ii. 12, 13; Heb. xiii. 21. The particular *illustration*

here is, that when they embraced the gospel it had such an efficacy on their hearts as to prepare them to meet all the terrors of bitter persecution without shrinking.

14. *For ye, brethren, became followers of the churches of God which in Judea are in Christ Jesus.* Which are *united* to the Lord Jesus, or which are founded on his truth; that is, which are true churches. Of those churches they became *imitators* — μιμηταί—to wit in their sufferings. This does not mean that they were founded on the same model; or that they professed to be the followers of those churches, but that *they had been treated in the same way*, and thus were *like* them. They had been persecuted in the same manner, and by the same people—the Jews; and they had borne their persecutions with the same spirit. The *object* of this is to comfort and encourage them, by showing them that others had been treated in the same manner, and that it was to be expected that a true church would be persecuted by the Jews. They ought not, therefore, to consider it as any evidence that they were not a true church that they had been persecuted by those who claimed to be the people of God, and who made extraordinary pretensions to piety. ¶ *For ye also have suffered like things of your own countrymen.* Literally, " of those who are of your *fellow-tribe*, or *fellow-clansmen* "—συμφυλετῶν. The Greek word means "one of the same tribe," and then a fellow-citizen, or fellow-countryman. It is not elsewhere used in the New Testament. The particular reference here seems not to be to the heathen who were the *agents* or *actors* in the scenes of tumult and persecutions, but to the Jews by whom they were led on, or who were the prime movers in the persecutions which they had endured. It is necessary to suppose that they were principally Jews who were the *cause* of the

your own countrymen, even as they *have* of the Jews;

15 Who both killed the Lord

Jesus and *p* their own prophets, and have [2] persecuted us; and

persecution which had been excited against them in order to make the parallelism between the church there and the churches in Palestine exact. At the same time there was a propriety in saying that, though the parallelism was exact, it was by the "hands *of their own countrymen*" that it was done; that is, they were the visible agents or actors by whom it was done—the instruments in the hands of others. In Palestine, the Jews persecuted the churches *directly;* out of Palestine they did it by means of others. They were the real *authors* of it, as they were in Judea, but they usually accomplished it by producing an excitement among the heathen, and by the plea that the apostles were making war on civil institutions. This was the case in Thessalonica. "The Jews which believed not, moved with envy, set all the city on an uproar;" "they drew Jason and certain brethren *unto the rulers of the city*, crying, Those that have turned the world upside down have come hither also," Acts xvii. 5, 6. The same thing occurred a short time after at Berea. "When the Jews of Thessalonica had knowledge that the word of God was preached of Paul at Berea, they came thither also *and stirred up the people*," Acts xvii. 13; comp. Acts xiv. 2, "The unbelieving Jews stirred up the Gentiles, and made their minds evil-affected against the brethren." "The epistle, therefore, represents the case accurately as the history states it. It was the Jews always who set on foot the persecutions against the apostles and their followers" (Paley, *Hor. Paul. in loco*). It was, therefore, strictly true, as the apostle here states it, (1) that they were subjected to the same treatment from the Jews as the churches in Judea were, since they were the *authors* of the excitement against them; and (2) that it was carried on, as the apostle states, "by their own countrymen;" that is, that they were the agents or instruments by which it was done.

This kind of *undesigned coincidence* between the epistle and the history in the Acts of the Apostles is one of the arguments from which Paley (*Hor. Paul.*) infers the genuineness of both. ¶ *As they* have *of the Jews.* Directly. In Palestine there were no others but Jews who could be excited against Christians, and they were obliged to *appear* as the persecutors themselves.

15. *Who both killed the Lord Jesus.* See the Notes on Acts ii. 23. The meaning here is, that it was characteristic of the Jews to be engaged in the work of persecution, and that they should not regard it as strange that they who had put their own Messiah to death, and slain the prophets, should now be found persecuting the true children of God. ¶ *And their own prophets.* See Notes on Mat. xxi. 33-40; xxiii. 29-37; Acts vii. 52. ¶ *And have persecuted us.* As at Iconium (Acts xiv. 1), Derbe, and Lystra (Acts xiv. 6), and at Philippi, Thessalonica, and Berea. The meaning is, that it was characteristic of them to persecute, and they spared no one. If they had persecuted the apostles themselves, who were their own countrymen, it should not be considered strange that they should persecute those who were Gentiles. ¶ *And they please not God.* Their conduct is not such as to please God, but such as to expose them to his wrath, ver. 16. The meaning is not that they did not aim to please God—whatever may have been the truth about that—but that they had shown by all their history that their conduct could not meet with the divine approbation. They made extraordinary pretensions to being the peculiar people of God, and it was important for the apostle to show that their conduct demonstrated that they had no such claims. *Their* opposition to the Thessalonians, therefore, was no proof that *God* was opposed to them, and they should not allow themselves to be troubled by such opposition. It was rather proof that they were the friends of God—

they please not God, and are contrary to all men;

16 Forbidding[q] us to speak to

since those who now persecuted them had been engaged in persecuting the most holy men that had lived. ¶ *And are contrary to all men.* They do not merely *differ* from other men in customs and opinions—which might be harmless—but they keep up *an active opposition* to all other people. It was not opposition to one nation only, but to all; it was not to one form of religion only, but to all—even including God's last revelation to mankind; it was not opposition evinced in their own country, but they carried it with them wherever they went. The truth of this statement is confirmed, not only by authority of the apostle and the uniform record in the New Testament, but by the testimony borne of them in the classic writers. This was universally regarded as their national characteristic, for they had so demeaned themselves as to leave this impression on the minds of those with whom they had intercourse. Thus Tacitus describes them as "cherishing hatred against all others"—adversus omnes alios hostile odium (*Hist.* v. 5). So Juvenal (*Sat.* xiv. 103, 104), describes them:

Non monstrare vias eadem nisi sacra colenti,
Quæsitum ad fontem solos deducere verpos.

"They would not even point out the way to any one except of the same religion, nor, being asked, guide any to a fountain except the circumcised." So they are called by Appollonius "atheists and misanthropes, and the most uncultivated barbarians"—ἄθεοι καὶ μισανθρώποι καὶ ἀφύεστατοι τῶν βάρβαρων (Josephus, *Con. Ap.* ii. 14). So Diodorus Siculus (xxxiv. p. 524), describes them as "those alone among all the nations who were unwilling to have any intercourse [or intermingling—ἐπιμιξίας] with any other nation, and who regarded all others as enemies" — καὶ πολεμίους ὑπολαμβάνειν πάντας. Their history had given abundant occasion for these charges.

16. *Forbidding us to speak to the Gentiles.* See Acts xvii. 5, 13. No particular instance is mentioned in

the life of Paul *previous* to this, when they had formally commanded him not to preach to the heathen, but no one can doubt that this was one of the leading points of difference between him and them. Paul maintained that the Jews and Gentiles were now on a level with regard to salvation; that the wall of partition was broken down; that the Jew had no advantages over the rest of mankind in this respect, and that the heathen might be saved without becoming Jews, or being circumcised, Rom. ii. 25–29; iii. 22–31; Notes, Col. i. 24. The Jews did not hold it unlawful "to speak to the Gentiles," and even to offer to them eternal life (Mat. xxiii. 15), but it was only on condition that they should become proselytes to *their* religion, and should observe the institutions of Moses. If saved, they held that it would be *as Jews*—either originally such, or such by becoming proselytes. Paul maintained just the opposite opinion, that heathens might be saved *without* becoming proselytes to the Jewish system, and that, in fact, salvation was as freely offered to them as to the children of Abraham. Though there are no express *instances* in which they prohibited Paul from speaking to the Gentiles recorded *before* the date of this epistle, yet events occurred *afterwards* which showed what were their feelings, and such as to make it in the highest degree probable that they had attempted to restrain him. See Acts xxii. 21, 22, "And he [Christ] said unto me [Paul], Depart, for I will send thee far hence unto the Gentiles. And they [the Jews] gave him audience unto this word, and then lifted up their voices and said, Away with such a fellow from the earth, for it is not fit that he should live." ¶ *That they might be saved.* That is, as freely as others, and on the same terms; not by conversion to Judaism, but by repentance and faith. ¶ *To fill up their sins alway.* At all times— πάντοτε —in every generation. That is, to do now as they

for the wrath is come upon them to ⁸the uttermost.

8 Re.22.11.

have always done, by resisting God and exposing themselves to his wrath. The idea is, that it had been a characteristic of the nation, at all times, to oppose God, and that they did it now in this manner in conformity with their fixed character. Comp. Acts vii. 51-53, and Notes on Mat. xxiii. 32, on the expression, "Fill ye up then the measure of your fathers." ¶ *For the wrath is come upon them.* This cannot mean that the wrath of God had been then *actually* poured out upon them in the extreme degree referred to, or that they had *experienced* the full expressions of the divine displeasure, for this epistle was written before the destruction of their city and temple (see the Introduction); but that the cup of their iniquity was full; that they were in fact abandoned by God; that they were the objects *even then* of his displeasure, and that their destruction was so certain that it might be spoken of as an indubitable fact. The "wrath of God" may be said to have come upon a man when he abandons him, even though there may not be *as yet* any *external* expressions of his indignation. It is not *punishment* that constitutes the wrath of God. That is the mere *outward expression* of the divine indignation, and the wrath of God may in fact have come upon a man when as yet there are no external tokens of it. The overthrow of Jerusalem and the temple were but the outward expressions of the divine displeasure at their conduct. Paul, inspired to speak of the feelings of God, describes that wrath as already existing in the divine mind; comp. Rom. iv. 17. ¶ *To the uttermost.* Gr. εἰς τέλος — *to the end;* that is, until wrath shall be *complete* or *exhausted;* or wrath in the extremest degree. It does not mean "to the end of their race or history," nor necessarily to the remotest periods of time, but to that which constitutes *completion,* so that there should

17 But we, brethren, being taken from you for a short time in presence, not in heart, endeavoured

be nothing *lacking* of that which would make indignation perfect: "εἰς τέλος — gantz und gar — thoroughly, entirely, through and through" (Passow). Some have understood this as meaning *at the last,* or *at length,* as Macknight, Rosenmüller, Koppe, and Wetstein; others as referring to *duration,* meaning that it would follow them everywhere; but the more correct interpretation seems to be to refer it to that *extremity* of calamity and woe which was about to come upon the nation. For an account of this, see Notes on Mat. xxiv. 21.

17. *But we, brethren, being taken from you.* There is more implied in the Greek word here rendered, "being taken from you"—ἀπορφανισθέντες—than appears from our translation. It properly has relation to the condition of an *orphan* (comp. Notes on Jn. xiv. 18), or one who is bereaved of parents. Then it is used in a more general sense, denoting *to be bereaved of;* and in this place it does not mean merely that he was "taken from them," but there is included the idea that it was like a painful bereavement. It was such a state as that of one who had lost a parent. No word, perhaps, could have expressed stronger attachment for them. ¶ *For a short time.* Gr., "For the time of an hour;" that is, for a brief period. The meaning is, that when he left them he supposed it would be only for a short time. The *fact* seems to have been (Acts xvii. 10), that it was supposed, when Paul was sent to Berea, that things would soon be in such a state that he could safely return to Thessalonica. He was "sent" there by those who thought it was necessary for the safety of some of his friends at Thessalonica, and he evidently purposed to return as soon as it could properly be done. It had, in fact, however, turned out to be a long and painful absence. ¶ *In presence, not in heart.* My heart was still with you. This is an elegant and touch-

the more abundantly to see your face with great desire.

18 Wherefore we would have come unto you, even I Paul, once and again; but Satan hindered us.

19 For what *is* our hope, or joy, or crown of ³rejoicing? *Are*

ing expression, which we still use to denote affection for an absent friend. ¶ *Endeavoured the more abundantly to see your face.* Made every endeavour possible. It was from no want of affection that I have not done it, but from causes beyond my control. ¶ *With great desire.* Comp. Notes, Luke xxii. 15.

18. *Wherefore we would have come unto you, even I Paul.* The phrase "even I Paul," seems to be used by way of emphasis. He had a special desire to go himself. He had sent Timothy to them (chap. iii. 2, 5), and perhaps, some might have been disposed to allege that Paul was afraid to go himself, or that he did not feel interest enough in them to go, though he was willing to *send* one to visit them. Paul, therefore, is at much pains to assure them that his long separation from them was unavoidable. ¶ *But Satan hindered us.* Comp. Notes on 2 Cor. xii. 7. In what way this was done is unknown, and conjecture would be useless. The apostle recognized the hand of *Satan* in frustrating his attempt to do good, and preventing the accomplishment of his strong desire to see his Christian friends. In the obstacles, therefore, to the performance of our duty, and in the hindrances of our enjoyment, it is not improper to trace the hand of the great enemy of good. The agency of Satan may, for aught we can tell, often be employed in the embarrassments that we meet with in life. The hindrances which we meet with in our efforts to do good, when the providence of God seems to favour us, and his word and Spirit seem to call us to a particular duty, often look very much like the work of Satan. They are just such obstructions as a very wicked being would be glad to throw in our way.

19. *For what* is *our hope.* That

not *ᵗ*even ye in *ᵘ*the presence of our Lord Jesus Christ *ᵛ*at his coming?

20 For ye are our glory and joy.

<small>³ or, *glorying.*   *t* 2 Co 1.14; Phi.4 1.
u Jude 24.   *v* Re 1.7.</small>

is, "I had a strong desire to see you; to assist you; to enjoy your friendship; for you are my hope and joy, and my absence does not arise from a want of affection." The meaning, when he says that they were his "*hope*," is, that their conversion and salvation was one of the *grounds* of his hope of future blessedness. It was an evidence that he was a faithful servant of God, and that he would be rewarded in heaven. ¶ *Or joy.* The source of joy here and in heaven. ¶ *Or crown of rejoicing.* Marg., as in Gr., *glorying;* that is, boasting, or exulting. The allusion is, probably, to the victors at the Grecian games; and the sense is, that he rejoiced in their conversion as the victor there did in the garland which he had won; Notes, 1 Cor. ix. 24–27. ¶ *Are not even ye?* Or, *will* not you be? ¶ *In the presence of our Lord Jesus Christ at his coming.* "When the Lord Jesus appears at the end of the world, then our highest source of happiness and honour will be your conversion and salvation." Then their salvation would be a proof of his fidelity. It would fill his soul with the highest happiness, that he had been the means of saving them from ruin.

20. *For ye are our glory and joy.* The meaning is, that the source of happiness to a minister of the gospel in the day of judgment will be the conversion and salvation of souls. The *object* of the apostle in dwelling on this in a manner so tender and affectionate is, to show them that his leaving them, and his long absence from them, were not caused by any want of affection for them.

REMARKS.

(1) Ministers of the gospel should be entirely sincere, and without guile. They should attempt to carry no measure—not even the conversion of sinners—by *trick* or *management*, ver. 3–5.

(2) They should not make it a point to please men, ver. 4. If they *do* please men, or if their ministry is acceptable to men, they should not regard it, indeed, as proof that they are unfaithful, for they "should have a good report of them that are without;" nor should they make it a point to *displease* men, or consider it a proof that because men are offended, *therefore* they are faithful; but it should not be their leading aim or purpose to gratify men. They should preach the truth; and if they do this, God will take care of their reputation, and give them just as much as they ought to have. The same principle should operate with all Christians. They should do *right*, and leave their reputation with God.

(3) Ministers of the gospel should be gentle, tender, and affectionate. They should be kind in feeling, and courteous in manner—like a father or a mother, ver. 7, 11. Nothing is ever gained by a sour, harsh, crabbed, dissatisfied manner. Sinners are never *scolded* either into duty or into heaven. "Flies are not caught with vinegar." No man is a better or more faithful preacher because he is rough in manner, coarse or harsh in his expressions, or sour in his intercourse with mankind. Not thus was the Master or Paul. There is no *crime* in being polite and courteous; none in observing the rules of good breeding, and paying respect to the sensibilities of others; and there is no piety in outraging all the laws which society has found necessary to adopt to promote happy intercourse. What is *wrong* we should indeed oppose—but it should be in the kindest manner towards *the persons* of those who do wrong; what is true and right we should maintain and defend—and we shall always do it more effectually if we do it kindly.

(4) Ministers should be willing to labour in any proper calling, if it is necessary for their own support or to do good, ver. 9. It is, indeed, the duty of a people to support the gospel, but there may be situations where they are not able to do it, and a minister should be *able* to earn something,

in some other way, and should be *willing* to do it. Paul made tents; and if he was willing to do that, a minister should not feel himself degraded if he is obliged to make shoes, or to hoe corn, or to plough, or to keep cattle. He had better *not* do it, if he can avoid it well—for he needs his time for his more important work; but he should feel it no dishonour if he is obliged to do it—and should feel that it is a privilege to preach the gospel even if he *is* obliged to support himself by making either tents or shoes. It is no dishonour for a minister to work hard; and it is not well for a man to enter the ministry wholly unacquainted with every other way of procuring an honest living.

(5) Every minister should be able to appeal to the people among whom he has laboured in proof that he is an honest man, and lives consistently with his profession, ver. 1, 9, 10, 11. The same remark applies to all other Christians. They should so live that they may at once refer to their neighbours in proof of the uprightness of their lives, and their consistent walk. But to be enabled to do this, a man should live as he ought—for the world generally forms a very correct estimate of character.

(6) The joy of a minister in the day of judgment will be measured by the amount of good which he has done, and the number of souls which he has been the means of converting and saving, ver. 19. It will not be the honour which he has received from men; the titles which they have conferred on him; the commendation which he has received for eloquence or talent, or the learning which he has acquired, but it will be found in the number of those who have been converted from the error of their ways, and in the evidence of the good which he did on the earth. And will not the same thing be substantially true of all others who bear the Christian name? Will it then be a source of joy to them that they were richer than their neighbours; or that they were advanced to higher honours; or that they had a more splendid mansion, or were able to fare more "sumptuously?" The good that we do will be remembered

certainly with pleasure in the day of judgment: of how many other things which now interest us so much can the same thing be said?

(7) Paul expected evidently to *recognize* the Thessalonian Christians at the day of judgment, for he said that they would be then his "joy and crown of rejoicing," ver. 19. But this could not be, unless he should be able to know those who had been converted by his instrumentality. If he expected then to recognize them, and to rejoice with them, then we also may hope to know our pious friends in that happy world. Nothing in the Bible forbids this hope, and we can hardly believe that God has created the strong ties which bind us to each other, to endure for the present life only. If Paul hoped to meet those who had been converted by his instrumentality, and to rejoice with them there, then the parent may hope to meet the child over whose loss he mourned; the husband and wife will meet again; the pious children of a family will be reassembled; and the pastor and his flock will be permitted to rejoice together before the Lord. This hope, which nothing in the Bible forbids us to entertain, should do much to alleviate the sorrow of the parting pang, and may be an important and powerful inducement to draw our own thoughts to a brighter and a better world. Of many of the living it is true that the best and dearest friends which they have are already in heaven—and how should their own hearts pant that they may meet them there!

CHAPTER III.

ANALYSIS OF THE CHAPTER.

This chapter is a continuation of the course of thought pursued in the previous chapter, and seems designed to meet the same state of feeling existing in Thessalonica, and the same objection which some there urged against the apostle. The objection seems to have been, that he had really no attachment for them, and no regard for their welfare; that he had fled from them on the slightest danger, and that when the danger was passed he had not returned, but had left them to bear their afflictions alone. It appears to have been inferred from his long absence, that he had no solicitude for their welfare, and had brought them into difficulties, to escape from which, or to bear which, he was now indisposed to render any assistance. It was important, therefore, for him to remind them of what he had actually done, and to state his real feelings towards them. He refers them, therefore, to the following things as proof of his interest in them, and his affection for them :—

(1) He had sent Timothy to them at great personal inconvenience, when he *could not* go himself, ver. 1–5.

(2) He had been greatly comforted by the report which Timothy had brought of their steadfastness in the faith, ver. 6–8. Every expression of their attachment to him had gone to his heart, and their faith and charity had been to him in his trials the source of unspeakable consolation. His very *life* depended, as it were, on their fidelity, and he says he should live and be happy if they stood fast in the Lord, ver. 8.

(3) He expresses again the earnest desire which he had to see them ; says that it had been to him the subject of unceasing prayer night and day, and beseeches God again now that he would be pleased to direct his way to them, ver. 9–11.

(4) As a proof of affection, the chapter is closed with a fervent prayer that God would cause them to abound more and more in love, and would establish their hearts unblameable before him, ver. 12, 13. The Thessalonians well knew the apostle Paul. They had had abundant proof of his love when he was with them; and if his enemies there had succeeded in any degree in causing their affection towards him to become cool, or to excite suspicions that he was not sincere, their love must have been rekindled and their suspicions must have been entirely allayed by the expressions of attachment in this chapter. Language of warmer love, or of deeper interest in the welfare of others, it would not be possible to find anywhere.

CHAPTER III.

WHEREFORE when we could no longer forbear, we

1. *Wherefore.* See chap. ii. 18. This particle (διὸ) is designed here to refer to another proof of his affection for them. One evidence had been referred to in his strong desire to visit them, which he had been unable to accomplish (chap. ii. 18), and he here refers to another—to wit, the fact that he had sent Timothy to them. ¶ *We could no longer forbear.* That is, when *I* could not (ver. 5), for there is every evidence that Paul refers to himself only though he uses the plural form of the word. There was no one with him at Athens after he had sent Timothy away (Acts xvii. 15; xviii. 5); and this shows that when, in chap. ii. 6, he uses the term *apostles* in the plural number, he refers to himself only, and does not mean to give the name to Timothy and Silas. If this be so, Timothy and Silas are nowhere called "apostles" in the New Testament. The word rendered here *could forbear* (στέγοντες), means, properly, *to cover, to conceal;* and then to hide or conceal anger, impatience, weariness, &c.; that is, to hold out as to anything, to bear with, to endure. It is rendered *suffer* in 1 Cor. ix. 12; *beareth,* 1 Cor. xiii. 7; and *forbear,* 1 Thes. iii. 1, 5. It is not elsewhere used in the New Testament. It means that he could no longer bear up under, hide, or suppress his impatience in regard to them—his painful emotions—his wish to know of their state; and he therefore sent Timothy to them. ¶ *We thought it good.* I was willing to suffer the inconvenience of parting with him in order to show my concern for you. ¶ *To be left at Athens alone.* Paul had been conducted to Athens from Berea, where he remained until Silas and Timothy could come to him, Acts xvii. 15. It appears from the statement here that Timothy *had* joined him there, but such was his solicitude for the church at Thessalonica, that he very soon after sent him there, and chose to remain

thought it good to be left at Athens alone;

2 And sent Timotheus, our

himself alone at Athens. Why he did not *himself* return to Thessalonica, is not stated. It is evidently implied here that it was a great personal inconvenience for him thus to part with Timothy, and to remain alone at Athens, and that he evinced the strong love which he had for the church at Thessalonica by being willing to submit to it. What that inconvenience consisted in, he has not stated, but it is not difficult to understand. (1) He was among total strangers, and, when Timothy was gone, without an acquaintance or friend. (2) The aid of Timothy was needed in order to prosecute the work which he contemplated. He had requested that Timothy should join him as soon as possible when he left Berea (Acts xvii. 15), and he evidently felt it desirable that in preaching the gospel in that city he should have all the assistance he could obtain. Yet he was willing to forego those comforts and advantages in order to promote the edification of the church at Thessalonica.

2. *And sent Timotheus.* That is, evidently, he sent him *from* Athens —for this is the fair construction of the passage. But in the history (Acts xvii.) there is no mention that Timothy came to Athens at all, and it may be asked how this statement is reconcilable with the record in the Acts? It is mentioned there that "the brethren sent away Paul [from Berea], to go as it were to the sea: but Silas and Timotheus abode there still. And they that conducted Paul brought him unto Athens," Acts xvii. 14, 15. The history further states, that after Paul had remained some time at Athens, he went to Corinth, where he was joined by Timothy and Silas, who came to him "*from Macedonia,*" Acts xviii. 5. But in order to reconcile the account in the Acts with the statement before us in the epistle, it is necessary to suppose that Timothy *had* come to Athens.

brother, and minister of God, and our ^afellow-labourer in the gospel of Christ, to establish you, and

to comfort you concerning your faith;

a Ac.17.15.

In reconciling these accounts, we may observe, that though the history does not expressly mention the arrival of Timothy at Athens, yet there are circumstances mentioned which render this extremely probable. First, as soon as Paul reached Athens, he sent a message back to Silas and Timothy to come to him as soon as possible, and there is every probability that this request would be obeyed, Acts xvii. 15. Secondly, his stay at Athens was on purpose that they might join him there. "Now whilst *Paul waited for them at Athens*, his spirit was stirred within him," Acts xvii. 16. Thirdly, his departure from Athens does not appear to have been in any sort hastened or abrupt. He had an opportunity of seeing the city (Acts xvii. 23); he disputed in the synagogue and in the market "daily" (Acts xvii. 17); he held a controversy with the philosophers (Acts xvii. 18 – 22); he made converts there (Acts xvii. 24), and "after these things" he calmly went to Corinth. There was no tumult or excitement, and it is not suggested that he was driven away, as in other places, because his life was in danger. There was, therefore, ample *time* for Timothy to come to him there—for Paul was at liberty to remain as long as he pleased, and as he stayed there *for the express purpose* of having Timothy and Silas meet him, it is to be presumed that his wish was in this respect accomplished. Fourthly, *the sending back of Timothy to Macedonia*, as mentioned in the epistle, is a circumstance which will account for the fact mentioned in Acts xviii. 5, that Timothy came to him "*at Corinth*," instead of at Athens. He had given directions for him to meet him *at Athens* (Acts xvii. 15), but the history mentions only that he met him, after a long delay, at *Corinth*. This delay, and this change of place, when they rejoined each other for the purpose of labouring together, can only be accounted for

by the supposition that Timothy *had* come to him at Athens, and had been immediately sent back to Macedonia, with instructions to join him again at Corinth. This is one of the "undesigned coincidences" between the history in the Acts of the Apostles and the epistles of Paul, of which Paley (*Hor. Paul.*) has made so good use in demonstrating the genuineness of both. "The epistle discloses a fact which is not preserved in the history; but which makes what is said in the history more significant, probable, and consistent. The history bears marks of an omission; the epistle furnishes a circumstance which supplies that omission." ¶ *Our brother.* Notes, Col. i. 1. The mention of his being a "*brother*" is designed to show his interest in the church there. He did not send one whose absence would be no inconvenience to him, or for whom he had no regard. He sent one who was as dear to him as a brother. ¶ *And minister of God.* Another circumstance showing his affection for them. He did not send a layman, or one who could not be useful with him or to them, but he sent one fully qualified to preach to them, and to break to them the bread of life. One of the richest tokens of affection which can be shown to any people, is to send to them a faithful minister of God. ¶ *And our fellow-labourer in the gospel of Christ.* A third token of affectionate interest in their welfare. The meaning is, "I did not send one whom I did not want, or who could be of no use here, but one who was *a fellow-labourer* with me, and whose aid would have been of essential service to me. In parting with him, therefore, for your welfare, I showed a strong attachment for you. I was willing to endure personal inconvenience, and additional toil, in order to promote your welfare." ¶ *To establish you.* To strengthen you; to make you firm — στηρίξαι. This was to be done by presenting such considerations as would enable

3 That [b] no man should be moved
by these afflictions : for yourselves
know that [c] we are appointed thereunto.

4 For verily, when we were

with you, we told you before
that we should suffer tribulation;
even as it came to pass, and ye
know.

5 For this cause, [d] when I could

them to maintain their faith steadfastly in their trials. ¶ *And to comfort you concerning your faith.* It
is evident that they were suffering
persecution on account of their faith
in the Lord Jesus; that is, for their
belief in him as a Saviour. The object of sending Timothy was to suggest such topics of consolation as
would sustain them in their trials—
that is, that he was the Son of God;
that the people of God had been persecuted in all ages; that God was able
to support them, &c.

3. *That no man should be moved.*
The word rendered *moved* (σαίνω) occurs nowhere else in the New Testament. It properly means to wag, to
move to and fro, as of dogs which
wag their tails in fondness (Hom. *Od.*
K. 216; Æl. *A. N.* x. 7; Ovid, xiv.
258); then to caress, to fawn upon, to
flatter; then to move or *waver* in
mind — as from fear; to dread, to
tremble. See Passow and Wetstein.
Here the sense is, to be so moved or
agitated by fear, or by the terror of
persecution, as to forsake their religion. The object of sending Timothy
was, that they might not be thus
moved, but that amidst all opposition
they might adhere steadfastly to their
religion. ¶ *These afflictions.* Notes,
chap. ii. 14. ¶ *For yourselves know
that we are appointed thereunto.* It is
not quite certain whether by the word
"*we*" here the apostle refers to himself; or to himself *and* the Thessalonians; or to Christians in general.
On either supposition what he says is
true, and either would meet the case.
It would be most to the purpose, however, to suppose that he means to state
the general idea that *all* Christians are
exposed to persecution and could not
hope to avoid it. It would then appear that the Thessalonians had partaken only of the common lot. Still
there may have been a special refer-

ence to the fact that Paul and his
fellow-labourers there were subjected
to trials; and if this be the reference,
then the idea is, that the Thessalonians should not be "moved" by their
trials, for even their teachers were
not exempt. Even their enemies
could not say that the apostle and his
co-workers were impostors, for they
had persevered in preaching the gospel when they knew that these trials
were coming upon them. The phrase,
"we are appointed thereunto," means
that such was the divine arrangement. No one who professed Christianity could hope to be exempted
from trial, for it was the common lot
of all believers. Comp. Notes on 1
Cor. iv. 9; 2 Tim. iii. 12.

4. *For verily, when we were with
you, we told you before,* &c. It is not
mentioned in the history (Acts xvii.)
that Paul thus predicted that peculiar
trials would come upon them, but
there is no improbability in what is
here said. He was with them long
enough to discourse to them on a great
variety of topics, and nothing can be
more probable than that, in their circumstances, the subjects of persecution and affliction would be prominent
topics of discourse. There was every
reason to apprehend that they would
meet with opposition on account of
their religion, and nothing was more
natural than that Paul should endeavour to prepare their minds for it
beforehand. ¶ *That we should suffer
tribulation.* We who preached to you;
perhaps also including those to whom
they preached. ¶ *Even as it came to
pass, and ye know.* When Paul, Silas,
and Timothy were driven away, and
when the church was so much agitated, by the opposition of the Jews,
Acts xvii. 5–8.

5. *For this cause.* Since I knew that
you were so liable to be persecuted,
and since I feared that some might

no longer forbear, I sent to know your faith, *e*lest by some means the tempter have tempted you, and our *f*labour be in vain.

6 But now when Timotheus came from you unto us, and brought us good tidings of your faith and charity, and that ye have good remembrance of us always, *g*desiring greatly to see us, as we also *to see* you;

7 Therefore, brethren, *h*we were comforted over you, in all our affliction and distress, by your faith:

8 For now we live, if ye *i*stand fast in the Lord.

e 2 Co.11.2,3.   *f* Ga.4.11.   *g* Phi.1.8.   *h* 2 Co.7.6,7.   *i* Ep.6.13,14; Phi.4.1.

be turned from the truth by this opposition. ¶ *When I could no longer forbear.* Notes, ver. 1. ¶ *I sent to know your faith.* That is, your *fidelity*, or your steadfastness in the gospel. ¶ *Lest by some means.* Either by allurements to apostasy, set before you by your former heathen friends; or by the arts of false teachers; or by the severity of suffering. Satan has *many* methods of seducing men from the truth, and Paul was fearful that by some of his arts he might be successful there. ¶ *The tempter.* Satan; for though the Jews were the immediate actors in those transactions, yet the apostle regarded them as being under the direction of Satan, and as accomplishing his purposes. He was, therefore, the real author of the persecutions which had been excited. He is here called the "*Tempter*," as he is often (comp. Mat. iv.), and the truths taught are: (1) that Satan is the great author of persecution; and, (2) that in a time of persecution—or of trial of any kind—he endeavours to *tempt* men to swerve from the truth, and to abandon their religion. In persecution, men are tempted to apostatize from God in order to avoid suffering. In afflictions of other kinds, Satan often tempts the sufferer to murmur and complain; to charge God with harshness, partiality, and severity, and to give vent to expressions that will show that religion has none of its boasted power to support the soul in the day of trial; comp. Job i. 9 11. In all times of affliction, as well as in prosperity, we may be sure that "the Tempter" is not far off, and should be on our guard against his wiles. ¶ *And our labour be in vain.* By your being turned from the faith; Notes, Gal. iv. 11.

6. *But now when Timotheus came*

from you unto us. To Corinth, after he had been sent to Thessalonica, Acts xviii. 5; comp. Notes on ver. 2. ¶ *And brought us good tidings.* A cheerful or favourable account. Gr., "evangelizing;" that is, bringing good news. ¶ *Of your faith.* Of your faithfulness or fidelity. Amidst all their trials they evinced fidelity to the Christian cause. ¶ *And charity.* Love; Notes, 1 Cor. xiii. 1. ¶ *And that ye have good remembrance of us always.* That is, probably, they showed their remembrance of Paul by obeying his precepts, and by cherishing an affectionate regard for him, notwithstanding all the efforts which had been made to alienate their affections from him. ¶ *Greatly desiring to see us, as we also* to see *you.* There was no disposition to blame him for having left them, or because he did not return to them. They would have welcomed him again as their teacher and friend. The meaning of this is, that there was between him and them a strong mutual attachment.

7. *We are comforted over you.* See Notes, 2 Cor. i. 3–7; vii. 6, 7. The sense here is, that their steadfastness was a great source of comfort to him in his trials. It was an instance where the holy lives and the fidelity of a people did much, as will always be the case, to lighten the burdens and cheer the heart of a minister of the gospel. In the inevitable trials of the ministerial office there is no source of comfort more rich and pure than this.

8. *For now we live, if ye stand fast in the Lord.* This is equivalent to saying, "My life and comfort depend on your stability in the faith, and your correct Christian walk." Comp. Martial, vi. 70, Non est vivere, sed valere, vita—"Life consists not merely in

9 For what thanks can we render to God again for you, for all the joy wherewith we joy for your sakes before our God;

10 Night and day praying exceedingly that we might see your living, but in the enjoyment of health." See also Seneca, Epis. 99, and Manilius, iv. 5, as quoted by Wetstein. The meaning here is, that Paul now *enjoyed* life; he had that which constituted real life, in the fact that they acted as became Christians, and so as to show that his labour among them had not been in vain. The same thing here affirmed is true of all faithful ministers of the gospel. They feel that they have something that may be called life, and that is worth living for, when those to whom they preach maintain a close walk with God.

9. *For what thanks can we render to God again.* That is, what expression of thanksgiving can we render to God that shall be an *equivalent* for the joy which your holy walk has furnished, or which will suitably express our gratitude for it.

10. *Night and day.* Constantly. ¶ *Praying exceedingly.* Gr., abundantly; that is, there was much more than ordinary prayer. He made this a special subject of prayer; he urged it with earnestness, and without intermission; comp. chap. ii. 17. ¶ *And might perfect that which is lacking in your faith.* Might render it *complete*, or fill up anything which is wanting. The word here used (καταρτίσαι), means, properly, *to make fully ready, to put full in order, to make complete.* See Notes, Rom. ix. 22; 2 Cor. xiii. 9; Gal. vi. 1. It is rendered *mending*, Mat. iv. 21; Mark i. 19; *perfect* and *perfected*, Mat. xxi. 19; Luke vi. 40; 2 Cor. xiii. 11; 1 Thes. iii. 10; Heb. xiii. 21; 1 Pet. v. 10; *fitted*, Rom. ix. 22; *perfectly joined together*, 1 Cor. i. 10; *restore*, Gal. vi. 1; *prepared*, Heb. x. 5; and *framed*, Heb. xi. 3. It is not elsewhere used in the New Testament. The meaning here is, that whatever was deficient in their views of religious doctrine the apostle desired to supply. It is to be remembered that

face, and might *k* perfect that which is lacking in your faith?

11 Now God himself and our Father, and our Lord Jesus Christ, [1] direct our way unto you.

k 2 Co.13.9,11; Col.4.12.   [1] or, *guide.*

he was with them but a comparatively short time before he was compelled to depart to Berea, and it is reasonable to suppose that there were many subjects on which he would be glad to have an opportunity to instruct them more fully.

11. *Now God himself.* This is evidently *a prayer.* He earnestly sought of God that he might be permitted to visit them, and that he would so prepare the way that he might do it. ¶ *And our Father.* Even our Father. The reference is particularly to the "Father," the First Person of the Trinity. It does not refer to the divine nature in general, or to God *as such*, but to God as the Father of the Lord Jesus. It is a distinct prayer offered to *him* that he would direct his way to them. It is right, therefore, to offer prayer to God as the First Person of the Trinity. ¶ *And our Lord Jesus Christ.* This also is a prayer, as much as the former was, for it can be understood in no other way. What can be its meaning, unless the apostle believed that the Lord Jesus had power to direct his way to them, and that it was proper for him to express this wish to him; that is, to *pray* to him? If this be so, then it is right to pray to the Lord Jesus, or to worship him. See Notes on Jn. xx. 28; Acts i. 24. Would Paul have prayed to an *angel* to direct his way to the church at Thessalonica? ¶ *Direct our way unto you.* Marg., *guide.* The Greek word — κατευθύνω — means, to guide straight towards or upon anything. It is rendered *guide* in Luke i. 79, and *direct* here and in 2 Thes. iii. 5. It does not elsewhere occur in the New Testament. The idea is that of conducting one *straight* to a place, and not by a roundabout course. Here the petition is that God would remove all obstacles so that he could come directly to them.

12 And the Lord make you to increase and *abound in love one toward another, and toward all *men*, even as we *do* toward you:

13 To the end he may *stablish your hearts unblameable in holiness before God, even our Father,

l 1 Jn.4.7-12.   *m* 2 Th.2.17; 1 Jn.3.20,21.
n Zec.14.5; Jude 14.

12. *And the Lord make you to increase and abound in love.* Comp. Notes, 2 Cor. ix. 8. The word "Lord" here probably refers to the Lord Jesus, as this is the name by which he is commonly designated in the New Testament; see Notes on Acts i. 24. If this be so, then this is a petition to the Lord Jesus as the fountain of all grace and goodness.

13. *To the end he may establish your hearts.* That is, "May the Lord cause you to increase in love (ver. 12), *in order* that you may be established, and be without blame in the day of judgment." The idea is, that if charity were diffused through their hearts, they would abound in every virtue, and would be at length found blameless. ¶ *Unblameable.* See Notes on chap. i. 10; Phil. ii. 15; iii. 6; Heb. viii. 7; comp. Luke i. 6; 1 Thes. v. 23. The meaning is, so that there could be no *charge* or *accusation* against them. ¶ *In holiness.* Not in outward conduct merely, or the observance of rites and forms of religion, but in purity of heart. ¶ *At the coming of our Lord Jesus Christ.* To judge the world ; Notes, chap. i. 10. As we are to appear before him, we should so live that our judge will find nothing in us to be *blamed.* ¶ *With all his saints.* With all his *holy ones*—τῶν ἀγίων. The word includes his *angels*, who will come with him (Mat. xxv. 31), and all the redeemed, who will then surround him. The idea is, that before that holy assemblage it is desirable that we should be prepared to appear *blameless.* We should be fitted to be welcomed to the "goodly fellowship" of the angels, and to be regarded as worthy to be numbered with the redeemed who "have washed their robes and have made them pure in the blood of the Lamb." When we

*n*at the coming of our Lord Jesus Christ with all his saints.

CHAPTER IV.

FURTHERMORE then we [1]beseech you, brethren, and [2]exhort *you* by the Lord Jesus, that as ye have received of us how ye

1 or, *request*.   2 or, *beseech*.

come to appear amidst that vast assemblage of holy beings, the honours of the world will appear to be small things ; the wealth of the earth will appear worthless, and all the pleasures of this life beneath our notice. Happy will they be who are prepared for the solemnities of that day, and who shall have led such a life of holy love—of pure devotion to the Redeemer—of deadness to the world—and of zeal in the cause of pure religion—of universal justice, fidelity, honesty, and truth, as to be without reproach, and to meet with the approbation of their Lord.

CHAPTER IV.
ANALYSIS OF THE CHAPTER.

This chapter, properly, comprises two parts :—First, various practical exhortations, ver. 1–12; and secondly, suggestions designed to console those who have been bereaved, ver. 13–18.

The first part embraces the following topics :—

(1) An exhortation to increase and abound in the Christian virtues which they had already manifested, ver. 1, 2.

(2) A particular exhortation on the subject of sanctification (ver. 3–8), in which two points are specified, probably as *illustrations* of the general subject, and embracing those in regard to which they were exposed to special danger. The first was fornication, the other was fraud.

(3) An exhortation to brotherly love, ver. 9, 10.

(4) An exhortation to quiet industry, and to honesty in their dealings, particularly with those who were Christians, ver. 11, 12.

The second part is designed to comfort the Thessalonians who had been bereaved, ver. 13–18. Some of their number had died. They appear to

ought to ^awalk and to please God, so ye would ^babound more and more.

2 For ye know what command-

a Col.1.10.   b 1 Co.15.58.   c 1 Co.6.15,18.

have been beloved members of the church, and dear friends of those to whom the apostle wrote. To console them he brings into view the doctrine of the second coming of the Saviour, and the truth that they would be raised up to live with him for ever. He reminds them that those who had died were "*asleep*"—reposing in a gentle slumber, *as if* they were to be awakened again (ver. 13); that they should not sorrow as they did who have no hope (ver. 13); that if they believed that Jesus died and rose again, they ought to believe that God would raise up all those who sleep in Jesus (ver. 14); that in the last day they would rise *before* the living should be changed, and that the living would not be taken up to heaven and leave their departed friends in their graves (ver. 15, 16), and that both the living and the dead would be raised up to heaven, and would be for ever with the Lord, ver. 17. With this prospect, they had every ground of comfort which they could desire, and they should sustain each other in their trials by this bright hope, ver. 18.

1. *Furthermore then*—Τὸ λοιπὸν. "As to what remains." That is, all that remains is to offer these exhortations; see Notes, 2 Cor. xiii. 11; Gal. vi. 17; Eph. vi. 10; Phil. iv. 8. The phrase is a formula appropriate to the *end* of an argument or discourse. ¶ *We beseech you.* Marg., *request.* The Greek is, "We *ask* you"—ἐρωτῶμεν. It is not as strong a word as that which follows. ¶ *And exhort* you. Marg., *beseech.* This is the word which is commonly used to denote earnest exhortation. The use of these words here implies that Paul regarded the subject as of great importance. He might have *commanded* them— but kind exhortation usually accomplishes more than a command. ¶ *By the Lord Jesus.* In his name and by his authority. ¶ *That as ye have received of us.* As you were taught by

ments we gave you by the Lord Jesus.

3 For this is the will of God, *even* your sanctification, ^cthat ye should abstain from fornication :

us. Paul doubtless had given them repeated instructions as to their duty as Christians. ¶ *How ye ought to walk.* That is, how ye ought to live. Life is often represented as a journey, Rom. vi. 4; viii. 1; 1 Cor. v. 7; Gal. vi. 16; Eph. iv. 1. ¶ So *ye would abound more and more.* "That is, follow the directions which they had received more and more fully" (Abbott).

2. *For ye know what commandments.* It was but a short time since Paul was with them, and they could not but recollect the rules of living which he had laid down. ¶ *By the Lord Jesus.* By the authority of the Lord Jesus. Some of those rules, or commandments, the apostle refers to, probably, in the following verses.

3. *For this is the will of God,* even *your sanctification.* It is the will or command of God that you should be holy. This does not refer to the *purpose* or *decree* of God, and does not mean that he intended to make them holy—but it means that it was his *command* that they should be holy. It was also true that it was agreeable to the divine will or purpose that they *should be* holy, and that he meant to use such an influence as to secure this; but this is not the truth taught here. This text, therefore, should not be brought as a proof that God intends to make his people holy, or that they *are* sanctified. It is a proof only that he *requires* holiness. The word here rendered *sanctification*—ἁγιασμὸς—is not used in the Greek classics, but is several times found in the New Testament. It is rendered *holiness,* Rom. vi. 19, 22; 1 Thes. iv. 7; 1 Tim. ii. 15; Heb. xii. 14; and *sanctification,* 1 Cor. i. 30; 1 Thes. iv. 3, 4; 2 Thes. ii. 13, and 1 Pet. i. 2; see Notes, Rom. vi. 19; 1 Cor. i. 30. It means here *purity* of life, and particularly abstinence from those vices which debase and degrade the soul.

4 That every one of you should know how to possess his vessel in sanctification and honour;

5 Not in the lust of concupis-

cence, even as [d]the Gentiles which know not God:

6 That no *man* go beyond and

d Ep.4.17,18.

Sanctification consists in two things: (1) in "ceasing to do evil;" and (2) in "learning to do well." Or in other words, the first work of sanctification is in overcoming the propensities to evil in our nature, and checking and subduing the unholy *habits* which we had formed before we became Christians; the second part of the work consists in cultivating the positive principles of holiness in the soul. ¶ *That ye should abstain from fornication.* A vice which was freely indulged among the heathen, and to which, from that fact, and from their own former habits, they were particularly exposed. On the fact that they were thus exposed, and on the reasons for these solemn commands on the subject, see Notes on Acts xv. 20, and 1 Cor. vi. 18.

4. *That every one of you should know how to possess his vessel.* The word *vessel* here (σκεῦος), probably refers to the body. When it is so used, it is either because the body is frail and feeble, like an earthen vessel easily broken (2 Cor. iv. 7), or because it is that which contains the soul, or in which the soul is lodged (Lucret. lib. iii. 441). The word *vessel* also (Heb. כְּלִי, Gr. σκεῦος) was used by the later Hebrews to denote a wife, as the vessel of her husband (Schœttg. *Hor. Heb.* p. 827; comp. Wetstein, *in loco*). Many, as Augustine, Wetstein, Schœttgen, Koppe, Robinson (*Lex.*), and others, have supposed that this is the reference here; comp. 1 Pet. iii. 7. The word *body*, however, accords more naturally with the usual signification of the word, and as the apostle was giving directions to the whole church, embracing both sexes, it is hardly probable that he confined his direction to those who had *wives*. It was the duty of females, and of the unmarried among the males, as well as of married *men*, to observe this command. The injunction then is, that we should preserve the body pure;

see Notes on 1 Cor. vi. 18–20. ¶ *In sanctification and honour.* Should not debase or pollute it; that is, that we should honour it as a noble work of God, to be employed for pure purposes; Notes, 1 Cor. vi. 19.

5. *Not in the lust of concupiscence.* In gross gratifications. ¶ *Even as the Gentiles.* This was, and *is*, a common vice among the heathen; see Notes, Acts xv. 20; Rom. i. 29; Eph. iv. 17, 18, and the reports of missionaries everywhere. ¶ *Which know not God.* See Notes, Rom. i. 21, 28; Eph. ii. 12.

6. *That no* man *go beyond*—ὑπερβαίνειν. This word means, *to make to go over*, as, *e.g.*, a wall or mountain; then, to *overpass*, to wit, certain limits, to transgress; and then to *go too far*, *i.e.* to go beyond right—hence to cheat or defraud. It is not used elsewhere in the New Testament. The idea of *overreaching* is that which is implied in its use here. ¶ *And defraud*—πλεονεκτεῖν. Marg., *oppress*, or *overreach*. This word properly means, to have more than another; then to *have* an advantage; and then to *take* advantage of anyone, to circumvent, defraud, cheat. It is rendered *got an advantage*, 2 Cor. ii. 11; *defraud*, 2 Cor. vii. 2; 1 Thes. iv. 6; *make a gain*, 2 Cor. xii. 17, 18. Comp. for the use of the *adjective*, 1 Cor. v. 10, 11; vi. 10; Eph. v. 5; and the *noun*, Mark vii. 22; Luke xii. 15; Rom. i. 29; 2 Cor. ix. 5; Eph. v. 3; Col. iii. 5; 1 Thes. ii. 5; 2 Pet. ii. 3, 14. It is the word commonly used to denote *covetousness*. *Taking advantage of*, is the idea which it conveys here. ¶ *In any matter.* Marg., "or *the*." According to the reading in the margin, this would refer to the particular matter under discussion (ver. 3–5), to wit, concupiscence, and the meaning then would be, that no one should be guilty of illicit intercourse with the wife of another. Many expositors — as Hammond

defraud[3] his brother in [4]*any* matter; because that the Lord *is* the avenger of all such, as we also have forewarned you and testified.

7 For God hath not called us unto uncleanness, *e*but unto holiness.

[3] or, *oppress;* or, *overreach.*　　[4] or, *the.*
e Le.11.44; He.12.14; 1 Pe.1.14-16.

Whitby, Macknight, Rosenmüller, and others—suppose that this is a prohibition of adultery, and there can be no doubt that it *does* include this. But there is no reason why it should be confined to it. The Greek is so general that it may prohibit all kinds of *fraud, overreaching,* or *covetousness,* and may refer to *any* attempt to deprive another of his rights, whether it be the right which he has in his property, or his rights as a husband, or his rights in any other respect. It is a general command not to defraud; in no way to take advantage of another; in no way to deprive him of his rights. ¶ *Because that the Lord* is *the avenger of all such.* Of all such as are guilty of fraud; that is, he will punish them ; comp. Notes on Rom. xii. 19; Eph. vi. 9. ¶ *As we have also forewarned.* Doubtless when he was with them.

7. *For God hath not called us unto uncleanness.* When he called us to be his followers, it was not that we should lead lives of impurity, but of holiness. We should, therefore, fulfil the purposes for which we were called into his kingdom. The word *uncleanness* (ἀκαθαρσία), means, properly, *impurity, filth;* and then, in a moral sense, *pollution, lewdness,* as opposed to chastity, Rom. i. 24; vi. 19; 2 Cor. xii. 21; Gal. v. 19; Eph. iv. 19; v. 3; Col. iii. 5.

8. *He therefore that despiseth.* Marg., *rejecteth.* That is, he who disregards such commands as these which call him to a holy life, is really rejecting and disobeying God. Some might be disposed to say that these were merely the precepts of man, and that therefore it was not important whether they were obeyed or not. The apostle assures them in the most solemn manner that, though

8 He therefore that [5]despiseth, despiseth not man, but God, who hath also given unto us his Holy Spirit.

9 But as touching brotherly love, ye need not that I write unto you ; for ye yourselves are *f*taught of God to love one another.

[5] or, *rejecteth.*　　*f* Jn.15.12,17.

communicated to them *by* man, yet they were really the commands of God. ¶ *Who hath also given unto us his Holy Spirit.* This is a claim to inspiration. Paul did not give these commands as his own, but as taught by the Spirit of God; comp. Notes on 1 Cor. vii. 40.

9. *But as touching brotherly love.* The "peculiar charity and affection which one Christian owes to another " (Doddridge); see Notes on John xiii. 34. ¶ *Ye need not that I write unto you.* That is, "as I have done on the other points." They were so taught of God in regard to this duty, that they did not need any special instruction. ¶ *For ye yourselves are taught of God.* The word here rendered "taught of God "—θεοδίδακτοί—occurs nowhere else in the New Testament. It is correctly translated, and must refer here to some *direct* teaching of God on their own hearts, for Paul speaks of their being so taught by him as to need no special precepts in the case. He probably refers to that influence exerted on them when they became Christians, by which they were led to love all who bear the divine image. He calls this being "taught of God," not because it was of the nature of *revelation* or *inspiration,* but because it was in fact the *teaching* of God in this case, though it was secret and silent. God has many ways of *teaching* men. The lessons which we learn from his providence are a part of his instructions. The same is true of the decisions of our own consciences, and of the secret and silent influence of his Spirit on our hearts, disposing us to love what is lovely, and to do what ought to be done. In this manner all true Christians are taught to love those who bear the image of their

10 And indeed ye do it toward all the brethren which are in all Macedonia: but we beseech you, brethren, that ye increase more and more;

11 And that ye study to be quiet, *and to do your own business, and to work with your own hands, as we commanded you;

g 1 Pe.4.15.

Saviour. They feel that they are brethren; and such is their strong attachment to them, from the very nature of religion, that they do not need any express command of God to teach them to love them. It is one of the first, the elementary effects of religion on the soul, to lead us to love "the brethren"—and to do this is one of the evidences of piety about which there need be no danger of deception; comp. 1 John iii. 14.

10. *And indeed ye do it.* See Notes on chap. i. 7. ¶ *But we beseech you, brethren, that ye increase more and more.* Notes, chap. iii. 12. Here, as elsewhere, the apostle makes the fact that they deserved commendation for what they had done, a stimulus to arouse them to still higher attainments (Bloomfield).

11. *And that ye study to be quiet.* Orderly, peaceful; living in the practice of the calm virtues of life. The duty to which he would exhort them was that of being subordinate to the laws; of avoiding all tumult and disorder; of calmly pursuing their regular avocations, and of keeping themselves from all the assemblages of the idle, the restless, and the dissatisfied. No Christian should be engaged in a *mob;* none should be identified with the popular excitements which lead to disorder and to the disregard of the laws. The word rendered "ye study" (φιλοτιμέομαι), means properly, *to love honour, to be ambitious;* and here means the same as when we say "*to make it a point of honour* to do so and so" (Robinson, *Lex.*). It is to be regarded as a sacred duty; a thing in which our honour is concerned. Every man should regard himself as *disgraced* who is concerned in a mob. ¶ *And to do your own business.* To attend to their own concerns, without interfering with the affairs of others. See Notes on Phil. ii. 4; comp. 2 Thes. iii. 11; 1 Tim. v. 13; 1 Pet. iv. 13.

The injunction here is one of the beautiful precepts of Christianity so well adapted to promote the good order and the happiness of society. It would prevent the impertinent and unauthorized prying into the affairs of others to which many are so prone, and produce that careful attention to what properly belongs to our calling in life, which leads to thrift, order, and competence. Religion teaches no man to neglect his business. It requires no one to give up an honest calling and to be idle. It asks no one to forsake a useful occupation, unless he can exchange it for one more useful. It demands, indeed, that we shall be willing so far to suspend our ordinary labours as to observe the Sabbath, to maintain habits of devotion, to improve our minds and hearts by the study of truth, to cultivate the social affections, and to do good to others as we have an opportunity; but it makes no one idle, and it countenances idleness in no one. A man who is habitually idle can have very slender pretensions to piety. There is enough in this world for every one to do, and the Saviour set such an example of untiring *industry* in *his* vocation as to give each one occasion to doubt whether he is his true follower if he is not disposed to be employed. ¶ *And to work with your own hands, as we commanded you.* This command is not referred to in the history (Acts xvii.), but it is probable that the apostle saw that many of those residing in Thessalonica were disposed to spend their time in indolence, and hence insisted strongly on the necessity of being engaged in some useful occupation; comp. Acts xvii. 21. Idleness is one of the great evils of the heathen world in almost every country, and the parent of no small part of their vices. The effect of religion everywhere is to make men industrious; and every man, who is

12 That ye may *h*walk honestly toward them that are without,

h Ro. 13. 13.   6 or, *no man.*

able, should feel himself under sacred
obligation to be employed. God made
man to work (comp. Gen. ii. 15; iii.
19), and there is no more benevolent
arrangement of his government than
this. No one who has already enough
for himself and family, but who can
make money to do good to others, has
a right to retire from business and to
live in idleness (comp. Acts xx. 34;
Eph. iv. 27); no one has a right to
live in such a relation as to be wholly
dependent on others, if he can support
himself; and no one has a right to
compel others to labour for him, and
to exact their unrequited toil, in order
that he may be supported in indolence
and ease. The application of this rule
to all mankind would speedily put
an end to slavery, and would convert
multitudes, even in the church, from
useless to useful men. If a man has
no *necessity* to labour for himself and
family, he should regard it as an inestimable *privilege* to be permitted to
aid those who cannot work—the sick,
the aged, the infirm. If a man has
no need to add to what he has for his
own temporal comfort, what a privilege it is for him to toil in promoting
public improvements; in founding col-
leges, libraries, hospitals, and asylums,
and in sending the gospel to those
who are sunk in wretchedness and
want! No man understands fully the
blessings which God has bestowed on
him, if he has hands to work and will
not work.

12. *That ye may walk honestly toward them that are without.* Out of
the church; comp. Notes on Col. iv.
5. The word rendered *honestly*, means
*becomingly, decorously, in a proper
manner,* Rom. xiii. 13; 1 Cor. xiv. 40.
It does not refer here to mere honesty
in the transaction of business, but to
their *general treatment* of those who
were not professing Christians. They
were to conduct themselves towards
them in all respects in a becoming
manner—to be honest with them; to
be faithful to their engagements; to
be kind and courteous in their inter-

and *that* ye may have lack of
6 nothing.

13 But I would not have you

course; to show respect where it was
due, and to endeavour in every way
to do them good. There are few precepts of religion more important than
those which enjoin upon Christians
the duty of a proper treatment of
those who are not connected with the
church. ¶ *And* that *ye may have
lack of nothing.* Marg., *no man.* The
Greek will bear either construction,
but the translation in the text is probably the correct one. The phrase is
to be taken in connection not merely
with that which immediately precedes
it—as if "their walking honestly towards those who were without" would
preserve them from want — but as
meaning that their industrious and
quiet habits, their patient attention to
their own business, and upright dealing with every man, would do it. They
would, in this way, have a competence, and would not be beholden to
others. Learn hence, that it is the
duty of a Christian so to live as not
to be dependent on others, unless he
is made so by events of divine providence which he cannot foresee or control. No man should be dependent
on others as the result of idle habits;
of extravagance and improvidence; of
the neglect of his own business, and
of intermeddling with that of others.
If by age, losses, infirmities, sickness,
he is made dependent, he cannot be
blamed, and he should not repine at
his lot. One of the ways in which a
Christian may always do good in society, and honour his religion, is by
quiet and patient industry, and by
showing that religion prompts to those
habits of economy on which the happiness of society so much depends.

13. *But I would not have you to be
ignorant.* I would have you fully informed on the important subject which
is here referred to. It is quite probable from this, that some erroneous
views prevailed among them in reference to the condition of those who
were dead, which tended to prevent
their enjoying the full consolation
which they might otherwise have

to be ignorant, brethren, concerning them which are asleep, that ye

done. Of the prevalence of these views it is probable the apostle had been informed by Timothy on his return from Thessalonica, chap. iii. 6. What they were we are not distinctly informed, and can only gather from the allusions which Paul makes to them, or from the opposite doctrines which *he* states, and which are evidently designed to correct those which prevailed among them. From these statements it would appear that they supposed that those who had died, though they were true Christians, would be deprived of some important advantages which those would possess who should survive to the coming of the Lord. There seems some reason to suppose, as Koppe conjectures (comp. also Saurin, *Serm.* vol. vi. 1), that the case of their grief was twofold; one, that some among them doubted whether there would be any resurrection (comp. 1 Cor. xv. 12), and that they supposed that they who had died were thus cut off from the hope of eternal happiness, so as to leave their surviving friends to sorrow "as those who had no hope;" the other, that some of them believed that, though those who were dead would indeed rise again, yet it would be long after those who were living when the Lord Jesus would return had been taken to glory, and would be always in a condition inferior to them. See Koppe, *in loco.* The effect of such opinions as these can be readily imagined. It would be to deprive them of the consolation which they might have had, and should have had, in the loss of their pious friends. They would either mourn over them as wholly cut off from hope, or would sorrow that they were to be deprived of the highest privileges which could result from redemption. It is not to be regarded as wonderful that such views should have prevailed in Thessalonica. There were those even at Corinth who wholly denied the doctrine of the resurrection (1 Cor. xv. 12); and we are to remember that those to whom the apostle now wrote had been recently converted from heathenism; that they

sorrow not, even as others which have no hope.

had enjoyed his preaching but a short time; that they had few or no books on the subject of religion; and that they were surrounded by those who had *no* faith in the doctrine of the resurrection at all, and who were doubtless able — as sceptical philosophers often are now—to urge their objections to the doctrine in such a way as greatly to perplex Christians. The apostle, therefore, felt the importance of stating the *exact truth* on the subject, that they might not have unnecessary sorrow, and that their unavoidable grief for their departed friends might not be aggravated by painful apprehensions about their future condition. ¶ *Concerning them which are asleep.* It is evident from this that they had been recently called to part with some dear and valued members of their church. The word *sleep* is frequently applied in the New Testament to the death of saints. For the reasons why it is, see the Notes on Jn. xi. 11; 1 Cor. xi. 30; xv. 51. ¶ *That ye sorrow not, even as others which have no hope.* That is, evidently, as the heathen, who had no hope of future life; comp. Notes on Eph. ii. 12. Their sorrow was caused not only by the fact that their friends were removed from them by death, but from the fact that they had no evidence that their souls were immortal; or that, if they still lived, that they were happy; or that their bodies would rise again. Hence, when they buried them, they buried their hopes in the grave, and so far as they had any evidence, they were never to see them again. Their grief at parting was not mitigated by the belief that the soul was now happy, or by the prospect of again being with them in a better world. It was on this account, in part, that the heathens indulged in expressions of such excessive grief. When their friends died, they hired men to play in a mournful manner on a pipe or trumpet, or women to howl and lament in a dismal manner. They beat their breasts; uttered loud shrieks; rent their garments; tore off their hair; cast dust on their heads, or sat down in ashes. It is not improbable that some among the Thessalonians, on the death of their pious friends, kept up these expressions of excessive sorrow. To prevent this, and to mitigate their sorrow, the apostle refers them to the bright hopes which Christianity had revealed, and points them to the future glorious reunion with the departed pious dead. Learn hence, (1) That the world without religion is destitute of hope. It is just as true of the heathen world now as it was of the ancient pagans, that they have no hope of a future state. They have no *evidence* that there is any such future state of blessedness; and *without* such evidence there can be no *hope;* comp. Notes on Eph. ii. 12. (2) That the excessive sorrow of the children of this world, when they lose a friend, is not to be wondered at. They bury their hopes in the grave. They part, for all that they know or believe, with such a friend for ever. The wife, the son, the daughter, they consign to silence — to decay — to dust, not expecting to meet them again. They look forward to no glorious resurrection when that body shall rise, and when they shall be reunited to part no more. It is no wonder that they weep—for who would *not* weep when he believes that he parts with his friends *for ever?* (3) It is only the hope of future blessedness that can mitigate this sorrow. Religion reveals a brighter world—a world where all the pious shall be reunited; where the bonds of love shall be made stronger than they were here; where they shall never be severed again. It is only *this* hope that can soothe the pains of grief at parting; only when we can look forward to a better world and feel that we shall see them again—love them again—love them for ever—that our tears are made dry. (4) The Christian, therefore, when he loses a Christian friend, should not sorrow as others do. He will feel, indeed, as keenly as they do, the loss of their society; the absence of their well-known faces; the want of the sweet voice of friend-

ship and love; for religion does not blunt the sensibility of the soul, or make the heart unfeeling. Jesus wept at the grave of Lazarus, and religion does not prevent the warm gushing expressions of sorrow when God comes into a family and removes a friend. But this sorrow should not be like that of the world. It should not be (*a*) such as arises from the feeling that there is to be no future union; (*b*) it should not be accompanied with repining or complaining; (*c*) it should not be excessive, or beyond that which God designs that we should feel. It should be calm, submissive, patient; it should be that which is connected with steady confidence in God; and it should be mitigated by the hope of a future glorious union in heaven. The eye of the weeper should look up through his tears to God. The heart of the sufferer should acquiesce in him even in the unsearchable mysteries of his dealings, and feel that all is right. (5) It is a sad thing to die without hope —so to die as to have no hope for ourselves, and to leave none to our surviving friends that we are happy. Such is the condition of the whole heathen world; and such the state of those who die in Christian lands, who have no evidence that their peace is made with God. As I love my friends—my father, my mother, my wife, my children—I would not have them go forth and weep over my grave as those who have no hope in my death. I would have their sorrow for my departure alleviated by the belief that my soul is happy with my God, even when they commit my cold clay to the dust; and were there no other reason for being a Christian, this would be worth all the effort which it requires to become one. It would demonstrate the unspeakable value of religion, that my living friends may go forth to my grave and be comforted in their sorrows with the assurance that my soul is already in glory, and that my body will rise again! No eulogium for talents, accomplishments, or learning; no pæans of praise for eloquence, beauty, or martial deeds; no remembrances of

14 For if we believe that Jesus died and rose again, *even so them*

i 1 Co.15.20,&c.

also which sleep in Jesus will God bring with him.

---

wealth and worldly greatness, would then so meet the desires which my heart cherishes, as to have them enabled, when standing round my open grave, to sing the song which only Christians can sing:—

Unveil thy bosom, faithful tomb,
Take this new treasure to thy trust;
And give these sacred relics room
To seek a slumber in the dust.

Nor pain, nor grief, nor anxious fear
Invade thy bounds. No mortal woes
Can reach the peaceful sleeper here,
While angels watch the soft repose.

So Jesus slept: God's dying Son
Pass'd thro' the grave, and blest the bed;
Rest here, blest saint, till from his throne
The morning break, and pierce the shade.

Break from his throne, illustrious morn;
Attend, O Earth, his sovereign word;
Restore thy trust—a glorious form—
Call'd to ascend, and meet the Lord.
                WATTS.

14. *For if we believe that Jesus died and rose again.* That is, if we believe this, we ought also to believe that those who have died in the faith of Jesus will be raised from the dead. The meaning is not that the *fact* of the resurrection depends on our *believing* that Jesus rose, but that the death and resurrection of the Saviour were connected with the resurrection of the saints; that the one followed from the other, and that the one was as certain as the other. The doctrine of the resurrection of the saints so certainly follows from that of the resurrection of Christ, that, if the one is believed, the other ought to be also; see Notes on 1 Cor. xv. 12–14. ¶ *Which sleep in Jesus.* A most beautiful expression. It is not merely that they have calm repose—like a gentle slumber—in the hope of awaking again, but that this is " *in Jesus* "—or "through" (διὰ) him; that is, his death and resurrection are the cause of their quiet and calm repose. They do not "sleep" in heathenism, or in infidelity, or in the gloom of atheism —but in the blessed hope which Jesus has imparted. They lie, *as he did,* in the tomb—free from pain and sor-

row, and with the certainty of being raised up again.

They sleep in Jesus, and are bless'd,
How kind their slumbers are;
From sufferings and from sin released,
And freed from every snare.

When, therefore, we think of the death of saints, let us think of what Jesus was in the tomb of Joseph of Arimathea. Such is the sleep of our pious friends now in the grave; such will be our own when we die. ¶ *Will God bring with him.* This does not mean that God will bring them with him *from heaven* when the Saviour comes—though it will be true that their spirits will descend with the Saviour; but it means that he will bring them from their graves, and will conduct them with him to glory, to be with him; comp. Notes, John xiv. 3. The declaration, as it seems to me, is designed to teach the general truth that the redeemed are so united with Christ that they shall share the same destiny as he does. As the head was raised, so will all the members be. As God brought Christ from the grave, so will he bring them; that is, his resurrection made it certain that they would rise. It is a great and universal truth that God will bring all from their graves who "sleep in Jesus;" or that they shall all rise. The apostle does not, therefore, refer so much to the *time* when this would occur—meaning that it would happen *when* the Lord Jesus should return—as to the fact that there was an established connection between him and his people, which made it certain that if they died united with him by faith, they would be as certainly brought from the grave as he was. If, however, it means, as Prof. Bush (*Anastasis,* pp. 266, 267) supposes, that they will be brought with him from heaven, or will accompany him down, it does not prove that there must have been a previous resurrection, for the full force of the language would be met by the supposition that their *spirits* had ascended

15 For this we say unto you by the word of the Lord, that we which are alive, *and* remain unto the coming of the Lord,

to heaven, and would be brought with him to be united to their bodies when raised. If this be the correct interpretation, then there is probably an allusion to such passages as the following, representing the coming of the Lord accompanied by his saints: "The Lord my God shall come, and all the saints with thee," Zec. xiv. 5; "And Enoch, the seventh from Adam, prophesied of these, saying, Behold, the Lord cometh, with ten thousand of his saints," Jude 14. "Who," says President Dwight (*Serm.* 164), "are those whom God will bring with Him at this time? Certainly not the *bodies* of his saints. . . . The only answer is, he will bring with him 'the spirits of just men made perfect.'"

15. *For this we say unto you by the word of the Lord.* By the command or inspired teaching of the Lord. Prof. Bush (*Anastasis*, p. 265) supposes that the apostle here alludes to what the Saviour says in Mat. xxiv. 30, 31, "And they shall see the Son of man coming in the clouds of heaven," &c. It is possible that Paul may have designed a general allusion to *all* that the Lord had said about his coming, but there cannot have been an exclusive reference to that passage, for in what he says here there are several circumstances mentioned to which the Saviour in Matthew does not allude. The probability, therefore, is, that Paul means that the Lord Jesus had made a special communication to him on the subject. ¶ *That we which are alive.* See this fully explained in the Notes on 1 Cor. xv. 51. From this expression, it would seem that some of the Thessalonians supposed that Paul meant to teach that he himself, and many of the living, would survive until the coming of the Lord Jesus, and, of course, that that event was near at hand. That this was *not* his meaning, however, he is at special pains to show in 2 Thes. ii. 1-10. ¶ And *remain unto the coming*

shall not prevent them which are asleep.

16 For [k] the Lord himself shall

[k] Mat.24.30,31; Ac.1.11; 2 Th.1.7.

of the Lord. Those Christians who shall then be alive. ¶ *Shall not prevent them which are asleep.* Shall not precede; anticipate; go before. The word *prevent* with us is now commonly used in the sense of *hinder*, but this is never its meaning in the Scriptures. The word, in the time of the translators of the Bible, was used in its primitive and proper sense (*prævenio*), meaning to precede, or anticipate: Job iii. 12, "Why did the knees *prevent* me?" that is, why did they anticipate me, so that I did not perish? Ps. lxxix. 8, "Let thy tender mercies speedily *prevent* us;" that is, go before us in danger. Ps. cxix. 147, "I *prevented* the dawning of the morning and cried;" that is, I *anticipated* it, or I prayed *before* the morning dawned. Mat. xvii. 25, "Jesus *prevented* him, saying;" that is, Jesus anticipated him; he commenced speaking before Peter had told him what he had said. Comp. Ps. xvii. 13; lix. 10; lxxxviii. 13; xcv. 2; 2 Sam. xxii. 6,19; Job xxx. 27; xli.11. The meaning here is, that they who would be alive at the coming of the Lord Jesus, would not be "changed" and received up into glory *before* those who were in their graves were raised up. The object seems to be to correct an opinion which prevailed among the Thessalonians, that they who should survive to the coming of the Lord Jesus would have great advantages over those who had died. What they supposed those advantages would be—whether the privilege of *seeing* him come, or that they would be raised to higher honours in heaven, or that they who had died would not rise at all, does not appear, nor is the origin of this sentiment known. It is clear, however, that it was producing an increase of their sorrow on the death of their pious friends, and hence it was very important to correct the error. The apostle, therefore, states that no such disadvantage could follow, for the matter of fact was, that the dead would rise first.

16. *For the Lord himself shall de-*

descend from heaven with a shout, with the voice of the archangel,

and with the trump of God: and [l] the dead in Christ shall rise first:

l Re.20.5,6.

scend from heaven. Notes, Acts i. 11. ¶ *With a shout.* The word here used (κέλευσμα), does not elsewhere occur in the New Testament. It properly means a *cry* of excitement, or of urging on; an outcry, clamour, or shout, as of sailors at the oar, Luc. *Catapl.* 19; of soldiers rushing to battle, Thuc. iii. 14; of a multitude of people, Diod. Sic. iii. 15; of a huntsman to his dogs, Xen. *Ven.* vi. 20. It does not mean here, that the Lord would himself make such a shout, but that he would be attended with it; that is, with a multitude who would lift up the voice like that of an army rushing to the conflict. ¶ *With the voice of the archangel.* The word archangel occurs nowhere else in the New Testament, except in Jude 9, where it is applied to Michael. It properly means a *chief* angel; one who is first, or who is over others—ἄρχων. The word is not found in the Septuagint, and the only archangel, therefore, which is *named* in the Scriptures, is Michael, Jude 9; comp. Rev. xii. 7. Seven angels, however, are referred to in the Scriptures as having an eminence above others, and these are commonly regarded as archangels, Rev. viii. 2, "And I saw the seven angels which stood before God." One of these is supposed to be referred to in the Book of Tobit, xii. 15, "I am Raphael, one of the seven holy angels, which present the prayers of the saints, and which go in and out before the glory of the Holy One." The names of three only of the seven are mentioned in the Jewish writings—Michael, the patron of the Jewish nation, Dan. x. 13, 21; xii. 1: Gabriel, Dan. viii. 16; ix. 21; comp. Luke i. 19, 26: Raphael, Tobit iii. 17; v. 4; viii. 2; ix. 1, 5; xii. 15. The Book of Enoch adds that of Uriel, pp. 187, 190, 191, 193. Michael is mentioned as one "of the chief princes," Dan. x. 13; and as "the great prince," Dan. xii. 1; comp. Notes on Eph. i. 21, and see an article by Prof. Stuart in the *Bibliotheca Sacra*, No. 1, on "Angel-

ology." It seems evident from the Scriptures, that there is one or more among the angels to whom the name archangel properly belongs. This view is in accordance with the doctrine in the Scriptures that the heavenly beings are divided into ranks and orders, for if so, it is not unreasonable to suppose that there should be one or more to whom the most exalted rank appertains; comp. Rev. xii. 7. Whether there is more than one to whom this name appropriately belongs, it is impossible now to determine, and is not material. The word here (in Greek) is without the article, and the phrase might be rendered, "with the voice of *an* archangel." The Syriac renders it, "with the voice of the prince of the angels." On an occasion so august and momentous as that of the coming of the final Judge of all mankind—the resurrection of the dead, and the solemn transactions before the tribunal of the Son of God deciding the destiny of countless millions for ever—it will not be inappropriate that the highest among the heavenly hosts should be present and take an important part in the solemnities of the day. It is not quite certain what is meant here by "the *voice* of the archangel," or for what purpose that voice will be heard. It cannot be that it will be to raise the dead—for that will be by the "voice of the Son of God" (John v. 28, 29), and it seems most probable that the meaning is, that this will be a part of the loud shout or cry which will be made by the descending hosts of heaven; or perhaps it may be for the purpose of summoning the world to the bar of judgment; comp. Mat. xxiv. 31. ¶ *And with the trump of God.* The trump which God appoints to be sounded on that solemn occasion. It does not mean that it will be sounded by God himself; see Notes on Mat. xxiv. 31. ¶ *And the dead in Christ.* Christians. ¶ *Shall rise first.* That is, before the living shall be changed. A doctrine similar to this was held by

17 Then we which are alive *and* remain, shall be caught up together

with them *ᵐ*in the clouds, to meet

m Re. 11. 12.

---

the Jews. "Resch Lachisch said, Those who die in the land of Israel, shall rise first in the days of the Messiah." See Wetstein, *in loco*. It is implied in all this description that the interval between their resurrection and the change which will occur to the living will be brief, or that the one will rapidly succeed the other; comp. Notes, 1 Cor. xv. 23, 51, 52.

17. *Then we which are alive.* Those who shall then be alive; see ver. 15. The word here rendered *then* (ἔπειτα), does not necessarily mean that this would occur *immediately*. It properly marks *succession in time*, and means *afterwards, next*, next in the order of events, Luke xvi. 7; Gal. i. 21; Jam. iv. 14. There may be a considerable interval between the resurrection of the pious and the time when the living shall be caught up to meet the Lord, for the change is to take place in them which will fit them to ascend with those who have been raised. The meaning is, that *after* the dead are raised, or the next thing *in order*, they and the living will ascend to meet the Lord. The proper meaning of the word, however, denotes a succession so close as to exclude the idea of a *long* interval in which other important transactions would occur, such an interval, for example, as would be involved in a long personal reign of the Redeemer on earth. The word demands *this* interpretation—that the *next* thing in order after the resurrection of the righteous, will be their being caught up with the living, with an appropriate change, into the air—though, as has been remarked, it will admit of the supposition of such a brief, momentary interval (ἐν ἀτόμῳ, ἐν ῥιπῇ ὀφθαλμοῦ, 1 Cor. xv. 51, 52) as shall be necessary to prepare for it. ¶ *Shall be caught up.* The word here used implies that there will be the application of external force or power by which this will be done. It will not be by any power of ascending which they will themselves have; or by any tendency of their raised or

changed bodies to ascend of their own accord, or even by any effort of their own will, but by *a power* applied to them which will cause them to rise. Comp. the use of the word ἁρπάζω in Mat. xi. 12, "the violent *take* it by force;" xiii. 19, "then cometh the wicked one and *snatcheth away;*" John vi. 15, "that they would come and take him *by force;*" x. 12, "the wolf *catcheth them;*" Acts viii. 39, "the Spirit of the Lord *caught away* Philip;" 2 Cor. xii. 2, "such an one *caught up* to the third heaven;" also, John xii. 28, 29; Acts xxiii. 10; Jude 23; Rev. xii. 5. The verb does not elsewhere occur in the New Testament. In all these instances there is the idea of either foreign force or violence effecting that which is done. What *force* or *power* is to be applied in causing the living and the dead to ascend, is not expressed. Whether it is to be by the ministry of angels, or by the direct power of the Son of God, is not intimated, though the latter seems to be most probable. The word should not be construed, however, as implying that there will be any reluctance on the part of the saints to appear before the Saviour, but merely with reference to the physical fact that power will be necessary to elevate them to meet him in the air. Will their bodies then be such that they will have the power of locomotion at will from place to place? ¶ *In the clouds.* Gr., "in clouds"— ἐν νεφέλαις—without the article. This may mean "in clouds;" that is, in such numbers and in such grouping as to resemble clouds. So it is rendered by Macknight, Koppe, Rosenmüller, Bush (*Anasta*. 266), and others. The absence of the article here would rather seem to demand this interpretation. Still, however, the other interpretation may be true, that it means that they will be caught up into the region of the clouds, or to the clouds which shall accompany the Lord Jesus on his return to our world, Mat. xxiv. 30; xxvi. 64; Mark xvi.

the Lord in the air: *n* and so shall we ever be with the Lord.

n Jn.14.3.

18 Wherefore [7] comfort one another with these words.

[7] or, exhort.

26; xiv. 62; Rev. i. 7; comp. Dan. vii. 13. In whichever sense it is understood, the expression is one of great sublimity, and the scene will be immensely grand. Some doctrine of this kind was held by the ancient Jews. Thus Rabbi Nathan (*Midras Tillin*, xlviii. 13) says, "What has been done before will be done again. As he led the Israelites from Egypt in the clouds of heaven, so will he do to them in the future time." ¶ *To meet the Lord in the air.* In the regions of the atmosphere—above the earth. It would seem from this, that the Lord Jesus, in his coming, would not descend *to* the earth, but would remain at a distance from it in the air, where the great transactions of the judgment will occur. It is, indeed, nowhere said that the transactions of the judgment will occur *upon* the earth. The world would not be spacious enough to contain all the assembled living and dead, and hence the throne of judgment will be fixed in the ample space above it. ¶ *And so shall we ever be with the Lord.* This does not mean that they will always remain with him *in the air* —for their final home will be heaven—and after the trial they will accompany him to the realms of glory, Mat. xxv. 34, "*Come,* ye blessed of my Father, inherit the kingdom," &c. The *time* during which they will remain with him "in the air" is nowhere mentioned in the Bible. It will be as long as will be necessary for the purposes of judging a world and deciding the eternal doom of every individual "according to the deeds done in the body." There is no reason to suppose that this will be accomplished in a single day of twenty-four hours; but it is impossible to form any conjecture of the period which will be occupied.

18. *Wherefore comfort one another.* Marg., *exhort.* The word *comfort* probably best expresses the meaning. They were to bring these glorious

truths and these bright prospects before their minds, in order to alleviate the sorrows of bereavement. The topics of consolation are these: first, that those who had died in the faith would not always lie in the grave; second, that when they rose they would not occupy an inferior condition because they were cut off before the coming of the Lord; and third, that all Christians, living and dead, would be received to heaven and dwell for ever with the Lord. ¶ *With these words.* That is, with these truths.

REMARKS.

1. This passage (ver. 13–18) contains a truth which is to be found in no heathen classic writer, and nowhere else, except in the teachings of the New Testament. For the elevated and glorious view which it gives of future scenes pertaining to our world, and for all its inestimable consolations, we are wholly indebted to the Christian religion. Reason, unassisted by revelation, never dared to *conjecture* that such scenes would occur; if it had, it would have had no arguments on which the conjecture could be supported.

2. The death of the Christian is a calm and gentle slumber, ver. 13. It is not annihilation; it is not the extinction of hope. It is like gentle repose when we lie down at night, and when we hope to awake again in the morning; it is like the quiet, sweet slumber of the infant. Why, then, should the Christian be afraid to die? Is he afraid to close his eyes in slumber? Why dread the night —the stillness of death? Is he afraid of the darkness, the silence, the chilliness of the midnight hour, when his senses are locked in repose? Why should death to him appear so terrible? *Is the slumbering of an infant an object of terror?*

3. There are magnificent scenes before us. There is no description anywhere which is more sublime than that in the close of this chapter. Great events are brought together

here, any one of which is more grand than all the pomp of courts, and all the sublimity of battle, and all the grandeur of a triumphal civic procession. The glory of the descending Judge of all mankind; the attending retinue of angels, and of the spirits of the dead; the loud shout of the descending host; the clangour of the archangel's trumpet; the bursting of graves and the coming forth of the millions there entombed; the rapid, sudden, glorious change on the millions of living men; the consternation of the wicked; the ascent of the innumerable host to the regions of the air, and the solemn process of the judgment there—what has ever occurred like these events in this world? And how strange it is that the thoughts of men are not turned away from the trifles—the show—the shadow—the glitter—the empty pageantry here—to these bright and glorious realities!

4. In those scenes we shall all be personally interested. If we do not survive till they occur, yet we shall have an important part to act in them. We shall hear the archangel's trump; we shall be summoned before the descending Judge. In these scenes we shall mingle, not as careless spectators, but as those whose eternal doom is there to be determined, and with all the intensity of emotion derived from the fact that the Son of God will descend to judge *us*, and to pronounce *our* final doom! Can we be too much concerned to be prepared for the solemnities of that day?

5. We have in the passage before us, an interesting view of the *order* in which these great events will occur. There will be (1) the descent of the judge with the attending hosts of heaven; (2) the raising up of the righteous dead; (3) the change which the living will undergo (comp. 1 Cor. xv. 52); (4) the ascent to meet the Lord in the air; and (5) the return with him to glory. What place in this series of wonders will be assigned for the resurrection of the *wicked*, is not mentioned here. The object of the apostle did not lead him to advert to that, since his purpose was to comfort the afflicted by the assurance that

their pious friends would rise again, and would suffer no disadvantage by the fact that they had died before the coming of the Redeemer. From John v. 28, 29, however, it seems most probable that they will be raised at the same time with the righteous, and will ascend with them to the place of judgment in the air.

6. There is no intimation here of a "personal reign" of Christ upon the earth. Indeed, there is no evidence that he will return *to* the earth at all. All that appears is, that he will descend "from heaven" to the regions of "the air," and there will summon the living and the dead to his bar. But there is no intimation that he will set up a visible kingdom then on earth, to continue a thousand or more years; that the Jews will be re-collected in their own land; that a magnificent city or temple will be built there; or that the saints will hover in the air, or reign personally with the Lord Jesus over the nations. There are two considerations, in view of this passage, which, to my mind, are conclusive proof that all this is romance—splendid and magnificent, indeed, as an Arabian tale—but wholly unknown to the apostle Paul. The one is, that *if* this were to occur, it is inconceivable that there should have been no allusion to it here. It would have been such a magnificent conception of the design of the Second Advent, that it could not have failed to have been adverted to in a description like this. The other consideration is, that such a view would have been exactly *in point* to meet the object of the apostle here. What could have been more appropriate in comforting the Thessalonian Christians respecting those who had died in the faith, than to describe the gorgeous scenes of the "personal reign" of Christ, and the important part which the risen saints were to play in that great drama? How can it be accounted for that the apostle did not advert to it? *Would a believer in the "personal reign" now be likely to omit so material a point in a description of the scenes which are to occur at the "Second Advent?"*

7. The saints will be for ever with the Lord. They will dwell with him in his own eternal home, John xiv. 3. This expression comprises the sum of all their anticipated felicity and glory. To be with Christ will be, in itself, the perfection of bliss; for it will be a security that they will sin no more, that they will suffer no more, and that they will be shielded from danger and death. They will have realized the object of their long, fond desire — that of seeing their Saviour; they will have suffered the last pang, encountered the last temptation, and escaped for ever from the dominion of death. What a glorious prospect is this! Assuredly we should be willing to endure pain, privation, and contempt here for the brief period of our earthly pilgrimage, if we may come at last to a world of eternal rest. What trifles are all earthly sorrows compared with the glories of an endless life with our God and Saviour!

8. It is possible that even the prospect of the judgment-day should be a source of consolation, ver. 18. To most men it is justly an object of dread — for *all* that they have to fear is concentrated on the issues of that day. But why should a Christian fear it? In the descending Judge he will hail his Redeemer and friend; and just in proportion as he has true religion here, will be the certainty of his acquittal there. Nay, his feelings in anticipation of the judgment may be more than the *mere* absence of fear and alarm. It may be to him the source of positive joy. It will be the day of his deliverance from death and the grave. It will confirm to him all his long-cherished hopes. It will put the seal of approbation on his life spent in endeavouring to do the will of God. It will reunite him to his dear friends who have died in the Lord. It will admit him to a full and glorious view of that Saviour whom "having not seen he has loved;" and it will make him the companion of angels and of God. If there is anything, therefore, which ought to cheer and sustain our hearts in the sorrows and bereavements of this life, it is the anticipation of the glorious scenes connected with the Second Advent of our Lord, and the prospect of standing before him clothed in the robes of salvation, surrounded by all those whom we have loved who have died in the faith, and with the innumerable company of the redeemed of all ages and lands.

CHAPTER V.

ANALYSIS OF THE CHAPTER.

This chapter consists of two parts: I. The continuation of the subject of the coming of the Lord, ver. 1–11; and, II. Various practical exhortations.

In the first part, the apostle states, (1) that it was well understood by the Thessalonians that the coming of the Lord would be sudden, and at an unexpected moment, ver. 1, 2; (2) he refers to the effect of his coming on the wicked and the righteous, and says that it would be attended with the sudden and inevitable destruction of the former, ver. 3; but that the result of his coming would be far different on the righteous, ver. 4–11. The prospect of his coming was fitted to make them watchful and sober, ver. 6–8; and his advent would be attended with their certain salvation, ver. 9–11.

In the second part of the chapter, he exhorts them to show proper respect for their spiritual teachers and rulers, ver. 12, 13; to endeavour to restrain the unruly, to support the feeble, and to evince towards all the spirit of patience and forbearance, ver. 14; to manifest a meek and benevolent manner of life, ver. 15; to rejoice always, ver. 16; to pray constantly, ver. 17; to render thanks to God in every situation, ver. 18; to cherish the influences of the Holy Ghost on their souls, ver. 19; to show respect for all the divine prophetic communications, ver. 20; to consider and examine carefully everything submitted to them for belief; to adhere steadfastly to all that was good and true, ver. 21; and to avoid the very appearance of evil, ver. 22. The epistle closes with a fervent prayer that God would sanctify them

CHAPTER V.

BUT of the times and the seasons, brethren, ye have no need that I write unto you.

2 For yourselves know per-

fectly that the day of the Lord so *a* cometh as a thief in the night.

3 For when they shall say, Peace and safety; then sudden

a Lu.12.39,40; 2 Pe.3.10; Re.16.15.

entirely; with an earnest entreaty that they would pray for him; with a command that the epistle should be read to all the churches, and with the benediction, ver. 22-28.

1. *But of the times and the seasons.* See Notes, Acts i. 7. The reference here is to the coming of the Lord Jesus, and to the various events connected with his advent; see the close of chap. iv. ¶ *Ye have no need that I write unto you.* That is, they had received all the information on the particular point to which he refers, which it was necessary they should have. He seems to refer particularly to the *suddenness* of his coming. It is evident from this, as well as from other parts of this epistle, that this had been, from some cause, a prominent topic which he had dwelt on when he was with them; see Notes on chap. i. 10.

2. *For yourselves know perfectly.* That is, they had been fully taught this. There could be no doubt in their minds respecting it. ¶ *The day of the Lord so cometh.* Of the Lord Jesus—for so the word "Lord" in the New Testament commonly means; see Notes, Acts i. 24. The "day of the Lord" means that day in which he will be manifested, or in which he will be the prominent object in view of the assembled universe. ¶ *As a thief in the night.* Suddenly and unexpectedly, as a robber breaks into a dwelling. A thief comes without giving any warning, or any indications of his approach. He not only gives none, but he is careful that none shall be given. It is a point with him that, if possible, the man whose house he is about to rob shall have no means of ascertaining his approach until he comes suddenly upon him; comp. Notes on Mat. xxiv. 37-43; Luke xii. 39, 40. In this way the Lord Jesus will return to judgment; and this *proves* that all the attempts to determine the day,

the year, or the *century* when he will come, must be fallacious. He intends that his coming to this world shall be sudden and unexpected, "like that of a thief in the night;" that there shall be no such indications of his approach that it shall *not* be sudden and unexpected; and that no warning of it shall be given so that men may know the time of his appearing. If this be not the point of the comparison in expressions like this, what is it? Is there anything else in which his coming will resemble that of a thief? And if this *be* the true point of comparison, how *can* it be true that men can ascertain *when* that is to occur? Assuredly, if they *can*, his coming will *not* be like that of a thief; comp. Notes on Acts i. 7.

3. *For when they shall say, Peace and safety.* That is, when the wicked shall say this, for the apostle here refers only to those on whom "sudden destruction" will come; comp. Notes on Mat. xxiv. 36-42; 2 Pet. iii. 3, 4. It is clear from this, (1) That when the Lord Jesus shall come the world will not all be converted. There will be some to be "destroyed." How large this proportion will be, it is impossible now to ascertain. This supposition, however, is not inconsistent with the belief that there will be a general prevalence of the gospel before that period. (2) The impenitent and wicked world will be sunk in carnal security when he comes. They will regard themselves as safe. They will see no danger. They will give no heed to warning. They will be unprepared for his advent. So it has always been. It seems to be a universal truth in regard to all the visitations of God to wicked men for punishment, that he comes upon them at a time when they are not expecting him, and that they have no faith in the predictions of his advent. So it was in the time of the flood; in the destruction of Sodom,

destruction cometh upon them, as *b*travail upon a woman with child; and they shall not escape.

4 But*c* ye, brethren, are not in

Gomorrah, and Jerusalem; in the overthrow of Babylon: so it is when the sinner dies, and so it will be when the Lord Jesus shall return to judge the world. One of the most remarkable facts about the history of man is, that he takes no warning from his Maker; he never changes his plans, or feels any emotion, *because* his Creator "thunders damnation along his path," and threatens to destroy him in hell. ¶ *Sudden destruction.* Destruction that was unforeseen (αἰφνίδιος) or unexpected. The word here rendered *sudden*, occurs nowhere else in the New Testament, except in Luke xxi. 34, "Lest that day come upon you *unawares.*" The word rendered *destruction*—ὄλεθρος—occurs in the New Testament only here and in 1 Cor. v. 5; 2 Thes. i. 9; 1 Tim. vi. 9, in all of which places it is correctly translated *destruction.* The word *destruction* is familiar to us. It means, properly, demolition; pulling down; the annihilation of the form of anything, or that form of parts which constitutes it what it is; as the destruction of grass by eating; of a forest by cutting down the trees; of life by murder; of the soul by consigning it to misery. It does not necessarily mean annihilation—for a house or city is not annihilated which is pulled down or burnt; a forest is not annihilated which is cut down; and a man is not annihilated whose character and happiness are destroyed. In regard to the destruction here referred to, we may remark, (1) it will be *after* the return of the Lord Jesus to judgment; and hence it is not true that the wicked experience all the punishment which they ever will in the present life; (2) that it seems fairly implied that the destruction which they will then suffer will not be annihilation, but will be connected with conscious existence; and (3) that they will then be cut off from life and hope and salvation. How can the solemn affirmation that they will be "destroyed suddenly," be

darkness, that that day should overtake you as a thief.

5 Ye are all the children of light,

b Je.13.21.　　　*c* Ep.5.8; 1 Jn.2.8.

consistent with the belief that all men will be saved? Is it the same thing to be *destroyed* and to be *saved?* Does the Lord Jesus, when he speaks of the salvation of his people, say that he comes to *destroy* them? ¶ *As travail upon a woman with child.* This expression is sometimes used to denote great consternation, as in Ps. xlviii. 6; Jer. vi. 24; Mic. iv. 9, 10; great pain, as Isa. liii. 11; Jer. iv. 31; John xvi. 21; or the *suddenness* with which anything occurs, Jer. xiii. 21. It seems here to be used to denote two things: first, that the coming of the Lord to a wicked world will be sudden; and, secondly, that it will be an event of the most distressing and overwhelming nature. ¶ *And they shall not escape.* That is, the destruction, or punishment. They calculated on impunity, but now the time will have come when none of these refuges will avail them, and no rocks will cover them from the "wrath to come."

4. *But ye, brethren, are not in darkness, that that day should overtake you as a thief.* The allusion here is to the manner in which a thief or robber accomplishes his purpose. He comes in the night, when men are asleep. So, says the apostle, the Lord will come to the wicked. They are like those who are asleep when the thief comes upon them. But it is not so with Christians. They are, in relation to the coming of the day of the Lord, as men are who are awake when the robber comes. They could see his approach, and could prepare for it, so that it would not take them by surprise.

5. *Ye are all the children of light.* All who are Christians. The phrase "children of light" is a Hebraism, meaning that they were the enlightened children of God. ¶ *And the children of the day.* Who live as if light always shone round about them. The meaning is, that in reference to the coming of the Lord they are as men would be in reference to the coming of a thief, if there were no night and no necessity of slum-

and the children of the day : we are not of the night, nor of darkness.

6. Therefore[d] let us not sleep, as

d Mat.25.5; Ro.13.12,13.

ber. They would always be wakeful and active, and it would be impossible to come upon them by surprise. Christians are always to be wakeful and vigilant; they are so to expect the coming of the Redeemer, that he will not find them off their guard, and will not come upon them by surprise.

6. *Therefore let us not sleep, as* do *others.* As the wicked world does; comp. Notes, Mat. xxv. 5. ¶ *But let us watch.* That is, for the coming of the Lord. Let us regard it as an event which is certainly to occur, and which *may* occur at any moment; Notes, Mat. xxv. 13. ¶ *And be sober.* The word here used (νήφω) is rendered *sober* in 1 Thes. v. 6, 8; 1 Pet. i. 13; v. 8; and *watch* in 2 Tim. iv. 5, and 1 Pet. iv. 7. It does not elsewhere occur in the New Testament. It properly means, to be temperate or abstinent, especially in respect to wine (Josephus, *Jewish Wars,* 5. 5, 7; Xenophon, *Cyr.* 7. 5, 20); and then it is used in a more general sense, as meaning to be sober-minded, watchful, circumspect. In this passage there is an allusion to the fact that persons not only *sleep* in the night, but that they are frequently *drunken* in the night also. The idea is, that the Lord Jesus, when he comes, will find the wicked sunk not only in carnal security, but in sinful indulgences, and that those who are Christians ought not only to be awake and to watch as in the day-time, but to be temperate. They ought to be like persons engaged in the sober, honest, and appropriate employments of the day, and not like those who waste their days in sleep, and their nights in revelry. A man who expects soon to see the Son of God coming to judgment, ought to be a sober man. No one would wish to be summoned from a scene of dissipation to his bar. And who would wish to be called there from the ball-room; from the theatre; from the scene of brilliant worldly amusement? The most gay votary

do others; but let us watch and [e] be sober.

7 For they that sleep, sleep in the

e 1 Pe.5.8.

of the world; the most accomplished and flattered and joyous patron of the ball-room; the most richly-dressed and admired daughter of vanity, would tremble at the thought of being summoned from those brilliant halls, where pleasure is now found, to the judgment bar. They would wish to have at least a little time that they might prepare for so solemn a scene. But if so, as this event may at any moment occur, why should they not be habitually sober-minded? Why should they not aim to be always in that state of mind which they know would be appropriate to meet him? Especially should Christians live with such vigilance and soberness as to be always prepared to meet the Son of God. What Christian can think it appropriate for him to go up to meet his Saviour from the theatre, the ball-room, or the brilliant worldly party? A Christian *ought* always so to live that the coming of the Son of God in the clouds of heaven would not excite the least alarm.

7. *For they that sleep, sleep in the night.* Night is the time for sleep. The day is the time for action, and in the light of day men should be employed. Night and sleep are made for each other, and so are the day and active employment. The meaning here is, that it is in accordance with the character of those who are of the night, that is, sinners, to be sunk in stupidity and carnal security as if they were asleep; but for the children of the day, that is, for Christians, it is no more appropriate to be inactive than it is for men to sleep in the day-time. "It is not to be wondered at that wicked men are negligent and are given to vice, for they are ignorant of the will of God. Negligence in doing right, and corrupt morals, usually accompany ignorance" (Rosenmüller). ¶ *And they that be drunken are drunken in the night.* The night is devoted by them to revelry and dissipation. It is in accordance with the

night; and they that be drunken, are drunken in the night.

8 But let us, who are of the day, be sober, putting on ᶠthe breast-

ᶠ Is.59.17.   g Ro.9.22; 1 Pe.2.8.

usual custom in all lands and times, that the night is the usual season for riot and revelry. The leisure, the darkness, the security from observation, and the freedom from the usual toils and cares of life, have caused those hours usually to be selected for indulgence in intemperate eating and drinking. This was probably more particularly the case among the ancients than with us; and much as drunkenness abounded, it was much more rare to see a man intoxicated in the daytime than it is now. To be drunk then in the day-time was regarded as the greatest disgrace. See Polyb. *Exc. Leg.* 8, and Apul. viii., as quoted by Wetstein. Comp. Notes, Acts ii. 15; Isa. v. 11. The object of the apostle here is, to exhort Christians to be sober and temperate, and the meaning is, that it is as disgraceful for them to indulge in habits of revelry, as for a man to be drunk in the day-time. The propriety of this exhortation, addressed to Christians, is based on the fact that intoxication was hardly regarded as a crime, and, surrounded as they were with those who freely indulged in drinking to excess, they were then, as they are now, exposed to the danger of disgracing their religion. The actions of Christians ought always to be such that they may be performed in open day and in the view of all the world. Other men seek the cover of the night to perform their deeds; the Christian should do nothing which may not be done under the full blaze of day.

8. *But let us, who are of the day, be sober.* Temperate, as men usually are in the day-time. ¶ *Putting on the breast-plate of faith and love.* This is a favourite comparison of the apostle Paul; see it explained at length in the Notes on Eph. vi. 14. ¶ *And for an helmet, the hope of salvation.* Notes, Eph. vi. 17.

9. *For God hath not appointed us to wrath.* This is designed as an encour-

plate of faith and love; and for an helmet, the hope of salvation.

9 For God ᵍhath not appointed us to wrath, but to obtain salvation by our Lord Jesus Christ,

agement to effort to secure our salvation. The wish of God is to save us, and therefore we should watch and be sober; we should take to ourselves the whole of the Christian armour, and strive for victory. If he had appointed us to wrath, effort would have been in vain, for we could do nothing but yield to our inevitable destiny. The hope of a final triumph should animate us in our efforts, and cheer us in our struggles with our foes. How much does the hope of victory animate the soldier in battle! When morally certain of success, how his arm is nerved! When everything conspires to favour him, and when he seems to feel that God fights for him, and intends to give him the victory, how his heart exults, and how strong is he in battle! Hence, it was a great point among the ancients, when about entering into battle, to secure evidence that the gods favoured them, and meant to give them the victory. For this purpose they offered sacrifices, and consulted the flight of birds and the entrails of animals; and for this armies were accompanied by soothsayers and priests, that they might interpret any signs which might occur that would be favourable, or to propitiate the favour of the gods by sacrifice. See Homer, *passim;* Arrian's *Expedition of Alexander,* and the classic writers generally. The apostle alludes to something of this kind here. He would excite us to maintain the Christian warfare manfully, by the assurance that God intends that we shall be triumphant. This we are to learn by no conjectures of soothsayers; by no observation of the flight of birds; by no sacrifice which *we* can make to propitiate his favour, but by the unerring assurance of his holy word. If we are Christians, we know that he intends our salvation, and that victory will be ours; if we are willing to become Christians, we know that the Almighty arm will be stretched out to

10 Who died for us, that, [h] whether we wake or sleep, we should live together with him.

11 Wherefore [1]comfort yourselves together, and edify one another, even as also ye do.

12 And we beseech you, brethren, to [i] know them which labour among you, and are over you in the Lord, and admonish you;

h Ro.14.8,9; 2 Co.5.15.　　　[1] or, *exhort.*
i He.13.7,17.

---

aid us, and that the "gates of hell" cannot prevent it.

10. *Who died for us.* That is, to redeem us. He designed by his death that we should ultimately live with him; and this effect of his death could be secured only as it was an atoning sacrifice. ¶ *Whether we wake or sleep.* Whether we are found among the living or the dead when he comes. The object here is to show that the one class would have no advantage over the other. This was designed to calm their minds in their trials, and to correct an error which seems to have prevailed in the belief that those who were found alive when he should return would have some priority over those who were dead; see Notes on chap. iv. 13-18. ¶ *Should live together with him.* Notes, John xiv. 3. The word rendered "together" (ἁμα) is not to be regarded as connected with the phrase " with him "—as meaning that he and they would be "together," but it refers to those who "wake and those who sleep"—those who are alive and those who are dead—meaning that they would be *together* or would be with the Lord *at the same time;* there would be no priority or precedence (Rosenmüller).

11. *Wherefore comfort yourselves.* Notes, chap. iv. 18. ¶ *And edify one another.* Strive to build up each other, or to establish each other in the faith by these truths; Notes, Rom. xiv. 19. ¶ *Even as also ye do.* Continue to do it. Let nothing intervene to disturb the harmony and consolation which you have been accustomed to derive from these high and holy doctrines.

12. *And we beseech you, brethren, to know them which labour among you.* Who they were is not mentioned. It is evident, however, that the church was not left without appointed persons to minister to it when its founders should be away. We

know that there were presbyters ordained over the church at Ephesus, and over the churches in Crete (Acts xx. 17; Titus i. 5), and that there were bishops and deacons at Philippi (Phil. i. 1), and there is every reason to believe that similar officers would be appointed in every newly organized church. The word *"know"* seems to mean that they were not to make themselves strangers to them—to be cold and distant towards them — to be ignorant of their wants, or to be indifferent to them. While a people are not obtrusively to intermeddle with the business of a minister, any more than they are with that of any other man, yet there *are* things in regard to him with which they should be acquainted. They should seek to be personally acquainted with him, and make him their confidant and counsellor in their spiritual troubles. They should seek his friendship, and endeavour to maintain all proper intercourse with him. They should not regard him as a distant man, or as a stranger among them. They should so far understand his circumstances as to know what is requisite to make him comfortable, and should be on such terms that they may readily and cheerfully furnish what he needs. And they are to "know" or regard him as their spiritual teacher and ruler; not to be strangers to the place where he preaches the word of life, and not to listen to his admonitions and reproofs as those of a stranger, but as those of a pastor and friend. ¶ *Which labour among you.* There is no reason to suppose, as many have done, that the apostle here refers to different classes of ministers. He rather refers to different parts of the work which the same ministers perform. The first is, that they "labour"—that is, evidently, in preaching the gospel. For the use of the word, see John iv. 38, where it occurs twice; 1 Cor. xv.

13 And to esteem them very highly in love for their work's sake. *And*[k] be at peace among yourselves.

k Mar.9.50.　　2 or, *beseech*.　　l He.12.12.

10; xvi. 16. The word is one which properly expresses wearisome toil, and implies that the office of preaching is one that demands constant industry. ¶ *And are over you in the Lord.* That is, by the appointment of the Lord, or under his direction. They are not absolute sovereigns, but are themselves subject to one who is over them—the Lord Jesus. On the word here rendered "are over you" (προϊ-σταμένους), see Notes on Rom. xii. 8, where it is translated *ruleth*. ¶ *And admonish you.* The word here used (νουθετέω) is rendered *admonish*, and *admonished*, in Rom. xv. 14; Col. iii. 16; 1 Thes. v. 12; 2 Thes. iii. 15; and *warn*, and *warning*, 1 Cor. iv. 14; Col. i. 28; 1 Thes. v. 14. It does not elsewhere occur in the New Testament. It means, to put in mind; and then to warn, entreat, exhort. It is a part of the duty of a minister to put his people in mind of the truth; to warn them of danger; to exhort them to perform their duty; to admonish them if they go astray.

13. *And to esteem them very highly in love.* To cherish for them an affectionate regard. The *office* of a minister of religion demands respect. They who are faithful in that office have a claim on the kind regards of their fellow-men. The very nature of the office requires them to do good to others, and there is no benefactor who should be treated with more affectionate regard than he who endeavours to save us from ruin; to impart to us the consolations of the gospel in affliction; and to bring us and our families to heaven. ¶ *For their work's sake.* Not primarily as a personal matter, or on their own account, but on account of the work in which they are engaged. It is a work whose only tendency, when rightly performed, is to do good. It injures no man, but contributes to the happiness of all. It promotes intelligence, industry, order, neat-

14 Now we [2] exhort you, brethren, warn [l] them that are [3] unruly, comfort the feeble-minded,[m] support the weak, [n] be patient toward all *men*.

3 or, *disorderly*.　　m Ro.15.1.　　n Ep.4.2.

ness, economy, temperance, chastity, charity, and kindness in this world, and leads to eternal blessedness in the world to come. A man who sincerely devotes himself to such a work has a claim on the kind regards of his fellow-men. ¶ *And be at peace among yourselves.* Notes, Mark ix. 50; Rom. xii. 18; xiv. 19.

14. *Now we exhort you, brethren.* Marg., *beseech.* This earnest entreaty is evidently addressed to the whole church, and not to the ministers of the gospel only. The duties here enjoined are such as appertain to all Christians in their appropriate spheres, and should not be left to be performed by ministers only. ¶ *Warn them.* The same word which in ver. 12 is rendered *admonish.* It is the duty of every church member, as well as of the ministers of the gospel, affectionately to admonish those whom they know to be living contrary to the requirements of the gospel. One reason why there is so little piety in the church, and why so many professors of religion go astray, is, that the great mass of church members feel no responsibility on this subject. They suppose that it is the duty *only* of the officers of the church to admonish an erring brother, and hence many become careless and cold and worldly, and no one utters a kind word to them to recall them to a holy walk with God. ¶ *That are unruly.* Marg., *disorderly.* The word here used (ἄτακτος), is one which properly means *not keeping the ranks*, as of soldiers; and then irregular, confused, neglectful of duty, disorderly. The reference here is to the members of the church who were irregular in their Christian walk. It is not difficult, in an army, when soldiers get out of the line, or leave their places in the ranks, or are thrown into confusion, to see that little can be accomplished in such a state of irregularity and confusion. As little

15 See*o* that none render evil for evil unto any *man;* but ever *p*follow that which is good, both among yourselves, and to all *men.*

difficult is it, when the members of a church are out of their places, to see that little can be accomplished in such a state. Many a church is like an army where half the soldiers are out of the line; where there is entire insubordination in the ranks, and where not half of them could be depended on for efficient service in a campaign. Indeed, an army would accomplish little if as large a proportion of it were irregular, idle, remiss, or pursuing their own aims to the neglect of the public interest, as there are members of the church who can never be depended on in accomplishing the great purpose for which it was organized. ¶ *Comfort the feeble - minded.* The dispirited; the disheartened; the downcast. To do this is also the duty of each church member. There are almost always those who are in this condition, and it is not easy to appreciate the value of a kind word to one in that state. Christians are assailed by temptation; in making efforts to do good they are opposed and become disheartened; in their contests with their spiritual foes they are almost overcome; they walk through shades of spiritual night, and find no comfort. In such circumstances, how consoling is the voice of a friend! How comforting is it to feel that they are not alone! How supporting to be addressed by one who has had the same conflicts, and has triumphed! Every Christian—especially every one who has been long in the service of his Master—has a fund of experience which *is the property of the church*, and which may be of incalculable value to those who are struggling now amidst many embarrassments along the Christian way. He who has that experience should help a weak and sinking brother; he should make his own experience of the efficacy of religion in *his* trials and conflicts, the means of sustaining others in their struggles. There is no one who would not reach out his

hand to save a child borne down a rapid stream; yet how often do experienced and strong men in the Christian faith pass by those who are struggling in the "deep waters, where the proud waves have come over their souls!" ¶ *Support the weak.* Notes, Rom. xv. 1. ¶ *Be patient toward all* men. See the Greek word here used, explained in the Notes on 1 Cor. xiii. 4; comp. Eph. iv. 2; Gal. v. 22; Col. iii. 12.

15. *See that none render evil for evil.* See Notes on Mat. v. 39, 44. The meaning here is, that we are not to take *vengeance;* comp. Notes on Rom. xii. 17, 19. This law is positive, and is universally binding. The moment we feel ourselves acting from a desire to "return evil for evil," that moment we are acting wrong. It may be right to defend our lives and the lives of our friends; to seek the protection of the law for our persons, reputation, or property, against those who would wrong us; to repel the assaults of calumniators and slanderers, but in no case should the motive be to do *them* wrong for the evil which they have done *us.* ¶ *But ever follow that which is good.* Which is benevolent, kind, just, generous; see Notes, Rom. xii. 20, 21. ¶ *Both among yourselves, and to all* men. The phrase "to all men," seems to have been added to avoid the possibility of misconstruction. Some might possibly suppose that this was a good rule to be observed towards those of their own number, but that a greater latitude in avenging injuries might be allowable towards their enemies out of the church. The apostle, therefore, says that the rule is universal. It relates to the heathen, to infidels, sceptics, and persecutors, as well as to the members of the church. To every man we are to do good as we are able—no matter what they do to us. This is the rule which God himself observes towards the evil and unthankful (Notes, Mat. v. 45), and

16 Rejoice[q] evermore.
17 Pray[r] without ceasing.
18 In[s] every thing give thanks:

q Phi.4.4.　　　r Ro.12.12.　　　s Ep.5.20.

for this is the will of God in Christ
Jesus concerning you.
19 Quench[t] not the Spirit.

t Ep.4.30.

is one of the original and beautiful laws of our holy religion.

16. *Rejoice evermore.* See Notes on Phil. iii. 1; iv. 4.

17. *Pray without ceasing.* See Notes on Rom. xii. 12. The direction here may be fairly construed as meaning, (1) That we are to be regular and constant in the observance of the *stated* seasons of prayer. We are to observe the duty of prayer in the closet, in the family, and in the assembly convened to call on the name of the Lord. We are not to allow this duty to be interrupted or intermitted by any trifling cause. We are so to act that it may be said we pray *regularly* in the closet, in the family, and at the usual seasons when the church prays to which we belong. (2) We are to maintain an uninterrupted and constant *spirit* of prayer. We are to be in such a frame of mind as to be ready to pray publicly if requested; and when alone, to improve any moment of leisure which we may have when we feel ourselves strongly inclined to pray. That Christian is in a bad state of mind who has suffered himself, by attention to worldly cares, or by light conversation, or by gaiety and vanity, or by reading an improper book, or by eating or drinking too much, or by late hours at night among the thoughtless and the vain, to be brought into such a condition that he cannot engage in prayer with proper feelings. There has been evil done to the soul if it is not prepared for, communion with God at all times, and if it would not find pleasure in approaching his holy throne.

18. *In every thing give thanks.* Notes, Eph. v. 20; Phil. iv. 6. We can always find *something* to be thankful for, and there may be reasons why we *ought* to be thankful for even those dispensations which appear dark and frowning. Chrysostom, once the Archbishop of Constantinople, and then driven into exile, persecuted, and despised, died

far away from all the splendours of the capital, and all the comforts and honours which he had enjoyed, uttering his favourite motto—δόξα τῷ Θεῷ πάντων ἕνεκεν—*glory to God for all things* (*Bibliotheca Sacra*, i. 700). So we may praise God for everything that happens to us under his government. A man owes a debt of obligation to him for *anything* which will recall him from his wanderings, and which will prepare him for heaven. Are there *any* dealings of God towards men which do not contemplate such an end? Is a man ever made to drink the cup of affliction when *no* drop of mercy is intermingled? Is he ever visited with calamity which does not in some way contemplate his own temporal or eternal good? Could we see all, we should see that we are never placed in circumstances in which there is not much for which we should thank God. And when, in his dealings, a cloud seems to cover his face, let us remember the good things without number which we *have* received, and especially remember that we are in the world of redeeming love, and we shall find enough for which to be thankful. ¶ *For this is the will of God.* That is, that you should be grateful. This is what God is pleased to require you to perform in the name of the Lord Jesus. In the gift of that Saviour he has laid the foundation for that claim, and he requires that you should not be unmindful of the obligation; see Notes, Heb. xiii. 15.

19. *Quench not the Spirit.* This language is taken from the way of putting out a fire, and the sense is, we are not to extinguish the influences of the Holy Spirit in our hearts. Possibly there may be an allusion here to fire on an altar, which was to be kept constantly burning. This fire may have been regarded as emblematic of devotion, and as denoting that that devotion was never to become extinct. The Holy

20 Despise[u] not prophesyings.

21 Prove[v] all things; [w]hold fast that which is good.

Spirit is the source of true devotion, and hence the enkindlings of piety in the heart, by the Spirit, are never to be quenched. Fire may be put out by pouring on water; or by covering it with any incombustible substance; or by neglecting to supply fuel. If it is to be made to burn, it must be nourished with proper care and attention. The Holy Spirit, in his influences on the soul, is here compared with *fire* that might be made to burn more intensely, or that might be extinguished. In a similar manner the apostle gives this direction to Timothy, "I put thee in remembrance that thou *stir up* (ἀναζωπυρεῖν, *kindle up, cause to burn*) the gift of God," 2 Tim. i. 6. Anything that will tend to damp the ardour of piety in the soul; to chill our feelings; to render us cold and lifeless in the service of God, may be regarded as "quenching the Spirit." Neglect of cultivating the Christian graces, or of prayer, of the Bible, of the sanctuary, of a careful watchfulness over the heart will do it. Worldliness, vanity, levity, ambition, pride, the love of dress, or indulgence in an improper train of thought, will do it. It is a great rule in religion that all the piety which there is in the soul is the fair result of culture. A man has no more religion than he intends to have; he has no graces of the Spirit which he does not seek; he has no deadness to the world which is not the object of his sincere desire, and which he does not aim to have. Anyone, if he will, may make elevated attainments in the divine life; or he may make his religion merely a religion of form, and know little of its power and its consolations.

20. *Despise not prophesyings.* On the subject of prophesyings in the early Christian church, see Notes on 1 Cor. xiv. 1, *seq.* The reference here seems to be to *preaching.* They were not to undervalue it in comparison with other things. It is possible that in Thessalonica, as appears to have been the case subsequently in Corinth (comp. 1 Cor. xiv. 19), there were

those who regarded the power of working miracles, or of speaking in unknown tongues, as a much more eminent endowment than that of stating the truths of religion in language easily understood. It would not be unnatural that comparisons should be made between these two classes of endowments, much to the disadvantage of the latter; and hence may have arisen this solemn caution not to disregard or despise the ability to make known divine truth in intelligible language. A similar counsel may not be inapplicable to us now. The office of setting forth the truth of God is to be the permanent office in the church; that of speaking foreign languages by miraculous endowment, was to be temporary. But the office of addressing mankind on the great duties of religion, and of publishing salvation, is to be God's great ordinance for converting the world. It should not be *despised*, and no man commends his own wisdom who contemns it; for, (1) It is God's appointment — the means which he has designated for saving men. (2) It has too much to entitle it to respect to make it proper to despise or contemn it. There is nothing else that has so much power over mankind as the preaching of the gospel; there is no other institution of heaven or earth among men that is destined to exert so wide and permanent an influence as the Christian ministry. (3) It is an influence which is wholly good. No man is made the poorer, or the less respectable, or more miserable in life or in death, by following the counsels of a minister of Christ when he makes known the gospel. (4) He who despises it contemns that which is designed to promote his own welfare, and which is indispensable for his salvation. It remains yet to be shown that any man has promoted his own happiness, or the welfare of his family, by affecting to treat with contempt the instructions of the Christian ministry.

21. *Prove all things.* Subject everything submitted to you to be be-

22 Abstain[z] from all appearance of evil.

z Is.33.15.

23 And the very God of peace sanctify you wholly: and *I pray*

---

lieved to the proper test. The word here used (δοκιμάζετε), is one that is properly applicable to metals, referring to the art of the assayer, by which the true nature and value of the metal is tested; see Notes, 1 Cor. iii. 13. This trial was usually made by fire. The meaning here is, that they were carefully to examine everything proposed for their belief. They were not to receive it on trust; to take it on assertion; to believe it because it was urged with vehemence, zeal, or plausibility. In the various opinions and doctrines which were submitted to them for adoption, they were to apply the appropriate tests from reason and the word of God, and what they found to be true they were to embrace; what was false they were to reject. Christianity does not require men to disregard their reason, or to be credulous. It does not expect them to believe anything because others say it is so. It does not make it a duty to receive as undoubted truth all that synods and councils have decreed; or all that is advanced by the ministers of religion. It is, more than any other form of religion, the friend of free inquiry, and would lead men everywhere to understand the reason of the opinions which they entertain; comp. Acts xvii. 11, 12; 1 Pet. iii. 15. ¶ *Hold fast that which is good.* Which is in accordance with reason and the word of God; which is adapted to promote the salvation of the soul and the welfare of society. This is just as much a duty as it is to "prove all things." A man who has applied the proper tests, and has found out what is truth, is bound to embrace it and to hold it fast. He is not at liberty to throw it away, as if it were valueless; or to treat truth and falsehood alike. It is a duty which he owes to himself and to God to adhere to it firmly, and to suffer the loss of all things rather than to abandon it. There are few more important rules in the New Testament than the one in this passage. It shows

what is the true nature of Christianity, and it is a rule whose practical value cannot but be felt constantly in our lives. Other religions require their votaries to receive everything upon trust; Christianity asks us to examine everything. Error, superstition, bigotry, and fanaticism attempt to repress free discussion, by saying that there are certain things which are too sacred in their nature, or which have been too long held, or which are sanctioned by too many great and holy names, to permit their being subjected to the scrutiny of common eyes, or to be handled by common hands. In opposition to all this, Christianity requires us to examine *everything*—no matter by whom held; by what councils ordained; by what venerableness of antiquity sustained; or by what sacredness it may be invested. We are to receive no opinion until we are *convinced* that it is true; we are to be subjected to no pains or penalties for not believing what we do *not* perceive to be true; we are to be prohibited from examining no opinion which our fellow-men regard as true, and which they seek to make others believe. No popular current in favour of any doctrine; no influence which name and rank and learning can give it, is to commend it to us as certainly worthy of our belief. By whomsoever held, we are to examine it freely before we embrace it; but *when* we are convinced that it is true, it is to be held, no matter what current of popular opinion or prejudice may be against it; no matter what ridicule may be poured upon it; and no matter though the belief of it may require us to die a martyr's death.

22. *Abstain from all appearance of evil.* Not only from evil itself, but from that which *seems* to be wrong. There are many things which are *known* to be wrong. They are positively forbidden by the laws of heaven, and the world concurs in the sentiment that they are wicked. But there are also many things about which there

God your whole spirit and soul and body be *^y*preserved blameless

y 1 Co.1.8,9.

unto the coming of our Lord Jesus Christ.

---

may be some reasonable doubt. It is not quite easy to determine in the case what is right or wrong. The subject has not been fully examined, or the question of its morality may be so difficult to settle, that the mind may be nearly or quite balanced in regard to it. There are many things which, in themselves, may not appear to us to be positively wrong, but which are so considered by large and respectable portions of the community; and for us to do them would be regarded as inconsistent and improper. There are many things, also, in respect to which there is great variety of sentiment among mankind—where one portion would regard them as proper, and another as improper. There are things, also, where, whatever may be our motive, we may be certain that our conduct will be regarded as improper. A great variety of subjects, such as those pertaining to dress, amusements, the opera, the ball-room, games of chance and hazard, and various practices in the transaction of business, come under this general class; which, though on the supposition that they cannot be proved to be in themselves positively wrong or forbidden, have much the *"appearance"* of evil, and will be so interpreted by others. The safe and proper rule is to *lean always* to the side of virtue. In these instances it may be certain that there will be no sin committed by abstaining; there *may be* by indulgence. No command of God, or of propriety, will be violated if we decline complying with these customs; but on the other hand we *may* wound the cause of religion by yielding to what possibly is a mere temptation. No one ever does injury or wrong by abstaining from the pleasures of the ball-room, the theatre, or a glass of wine; who can indulge in them without, in the view of large and respectable portions of the community, doing that which has the "appearance" at least of "evil?"

23. *And the very God of peace.* The God who gives peace or happi-

ness; comp. Notes, Rom. i. 7. ¶ *Sanctify you.* Notes, John xvii. 17. ¶ *Wholly*—ὁλοτελεῖς. In every part; completely. It is always proper to pray that God would make his people entirely holy. A *prayer* for perfect sanctification, however, should not be adduced as a *proof* that it is in fact attained in the present life. ¶ *Your whole spirit and soul and body.* There is an allusion here, doubtless, to the popular opinion in regard to what constitutes man. We have a body; we have animal life and instincts in common with the inferior creation; and we have also a rational and immortal soul. This distinction is one that appears to the mass of men to be true, and the apostle speaks of it in the language commonly employed by mankind. At the same time, no one can demonstrate that it is *not* founded in truth. The *body* we see, and there can be no difference of opinion in regard to its existence. The *soul* (ἡ ψυχή—*psyche*), the vital principle, the animal life, or the seat of the senses, desires, affections, appetites, we have in common with other animals. It appertains to the nature of the animal creation, though more perfect in some animals than in others, but is in all distinct from the soul as the seat of conscience, and as capable of moral agency. See the use of the word in Mat. xxii. 37; Mark xii. 30; Luke x. 27; xii. 20; Acts xx. 10; Heb. iv. 12; Rev. viii. 9, *et al.* In the Pythagorean and Platonic philosophy this was distinguished from the higher rational nature (ὁ νοῦς, τὸ πνεῦμα), as this last belonged to man alone. This *psyche* (ψυχή), "soul," or life, it is commonly supposed, becomes extinct at death. It is so connected with the bodily organization, that when the tissues of the animal frame cease their functions, this ceases also. This was not, however, the opinion of the ancient Greeks. Homer uses the term to denote that which leaves the body with the breath, as escaping from the ἕρκος ὀδόντων—*the fence or sept of the*

24 Faithful *is* [z]he that calleth you, who also will do *it*.

25 Brethren, pray for us.

z 1 Co.10.13; 2 Th.3.3.

teeth—and as also passing out through a wound. This ψυχὴ—*psyche*—continued to exist in Hades, and was supposed to have a definite form there, but could not be seized by the hands (*Ody.* ii. 207). See Passow, 2; comp. Prof. Bush, *Anasta.* pp. 72, 73. Though this word, however, denotes the vital principle or the animal life, in man it may be connected with *morals*—just as the body may be—for it is a part of himself in his present organization; and whatever may be true in regard to the inferior creation, it is his duty to bring *his whole nature* under law, or so to control it that it may not be an occasion of sin. Hence the apostle prays that the "whole *body* and *soul*"—or animal nature—may be made holy. This distinction between the animal life and the mind of man (the *anima* and *animus*, the ψυχὴ and the πνεῦμα), was often made by the ancient philosophers. See Plato, *Timœ.* p. 1048; A. Nemesius, *de Nat. Hom.* 1 Cit. Glyca, p. 70; Lucretius, iii. 94; 116, 131; Juvenal, xv. 146; Cicero, *de Divinat.* 129, as quoted by Wetstein *in loco*. A similar view prevailed also among the Jews. Rabbi Isaac (Zohar in Lev. fol. 29, 2), says, "Worthy are the righteous in this world and the world to come, for, lo, they are all holy; their *body* is holy, their *soul* is holy, their *spirit* and their *breath* is holy." Whether the apostle meant to sanction this view, or merely to speak in common and popular language, may indeed be questioned, but there seems to be a foundation for the language in the nature of man. The word here rendered *spirit* (πνεῦμα), refers to the intellectual or higher nature of man; that which is the seat of reason, of conscience, and of responsibility. This is immortal. It has no *necessary* connection with the body, as animal life or the *psyche* (ψυχὴ) has, and consequently will be unaffected by death. It is this which distinguishes man from the brute creation; this which allies him with higher intelligences around the throne of God. ¶ *Be preserved blameless un-*

to the coming of our Lord Jesus Christ. The apostle does not intimate here that either the body or the vital principle will be admitted to heaven, or will be found in a future state of being, whatever may be the truth on that subject. The prayer is, that they might be entirely holy, and be kept from transgression, until the Lord Jesus should come; that is, until he should come either to remove them by death, or to wind up the affairs of this lower world. See Notes on chap. i. 10. By his praying that the "body and the soul"—meaning here the animal nature, the seat of the affections and passions — might be kept holy, there is reference to the fact that, connected as they are with a rational and accountable soul, they may be *the occasion* of sin. The same natural propensities, the same excitability of passion, the same affections which in a brute would involve no responsibility, and have nothing moral in their character, may be a very different thing in *man*, who is placed under a moral law, and who is bound to restrain and govern *all* his passions by a reference to that law, and to his higher nature. For a cur to snarl and growl; for a lion to roar and rage; for a hyena to be fierce and untamable; for a serpent to hiss and bite, and for the ostrich to leave her eggs without concern (Job xxxix. 14), involves no blame, no guilt for them, for they are not accountable; but for *man* to evince the same temper, and the same want of affection, *does* involve guilt, for he has a higher nature, and all these things should be subject to the law which God has imposed on him as a moral and accountable being. As these things may, therefore, in man be the *occasion* of sin, and *ought* to be subdued, there was a fitness in praying that they might be "preserved blameless" to the coming of the Saviour; comp. Notes on 1 Cor. ix. 27.

24. *Faithful* is *he that calleth you.* That is, your sanctification after all depends on him, and as he has begun a work of grace in your hearts, you

26 Greet all the brethren with an holy kiss.

27 I [4]charge you by the Lord, that this epistle be read unto all the holy brethren.

[4] or, *adjure.*

28 The grace of our Lord Jesus Christ *be* with you. Amen.

The first *epistle* unto the Thessalonians was written from Athens.

---

may depend on his faithfulness to complete it; see Notes on chap. iv. 3; Phil. i. 6; 1 Cor. i. 9.

25. *Brethren, pray for us.* A request which the apostle often makes; Notes on Heb. xiii. 18. He was a man of like passions as others; liable to the same temptations; engaged in an arduous work; often called to meet with opposition, and exposed to peril and want, and he peculiarly needed the prayers of the people of God. A minister, surrounded as he is by temptations, is in great danger if he has not the prayers of his people. Without those prayers, he will be likely to accomplish little in the cause of his Master. His own devotions in the sanctuary will be formal and frigid, and the word which he preaches will be likely to come from a cold and heavy heart, and to fall also on cold and heavy hearts. There is no way in which a people can better advance the cause of piety in their own hearts than by praying much for their minister.

26. *Greet all the brethren with an holy kiss.* See Notes on Rom. xvi. 16.

27. *I charge you by the Lord.* Marg., *adjure.* Gr., "I put you under oath by the Lord"—ὁρκίζω ὑμᾶς τὸν Κύριον. It is equivalent to binding persons by an oath; see Notes on Mat. xxvi. 63; comp. Gen. xxi. 23, 24; xxiv. 3, 37; i. 25. ¶ *That this epistle be read unto all the holy brethren.* To all the church; comp. Notes on Col. iv. 16. The meaning is, that the epistle was to be read to the whole church on some occasion on which it was assembled together. It was not merely designed for the individual or individuals into whose hands it might happen to fall, but as it contained matters of common interest, and was designed for the whole body of believers at Thessalonica, the apostle gives a solemn charge that it should

not be suppressed or kept from them. Injunctions of this kind occurring in the epistles, look as if the apostles regarded themselves as under the influence of inspiration, and as having authority to give infallible instructions to the churches.

28. *The grace of our Lord Jesus Christ,* &c. Notes, Rom. xvi. 20.

REMARKS.

In regard to the subscription at the close of the epistle, purporting that it was written from Athens, see the Intro. § 3. These subscriptions are of no authority, and the one here, like several others, is probably wrong.

From the solemn charge in ver. 27 of this chapter, that "this epistle should be read to *all* the holy brethren," that is, to the church at large, we may infer that it is in accordance with the will of God that all Christians should have free access to the Holy Scriptures. What was the particular reason for this injunction in Thessalonica, is not known, but it is possible that an opinion had begun to prevail even then that the Scriptures were designed to be kept in the hands of the ministers of religion, and that their common perusal was to be prohibited. At all events, whether this opinion prevailed then or not, it is not unreasonable to suppose that the Holy Spirit, by whom this epistle was dictated, foresaw that the time *would* come when this doctrine would be defended by cardinals and popes and councils; and that it would be one of the means by which the monstrous fabric of the Papacy would be sustained and perpetuated. It is worthy of remark, also, that the apostle Paul, in his epistles to the Thessalonians, has dwelt more fully on the fact that the great apostasy would occur under the Papacy, and on the characteristics of that grand usurpation over the rights of men, than he has anywhere else in his epistles; see 2 Thes. ii. 11. It is no improbable supposition that with reference to that, and to counteract one of its leading dogmas, his mind was supernaturally directed to give this solemn injunction, that the contents of the epistle which he had written should be communicated without reserve to *all* the Christian brethren in Thessalonica. In view of this injunction, therefore, at the close of this epistle, we may remark, (1) That it is a subject of express divine command that the people should have access to the Holy Scriptures. So important was this considered, that it was deemed necessary to enjoin those who should receive the word of God, under the solemnities of an oath, and by all the force of apostolic authority, to communicate what they had received to others. (2) This injunction had reference to *all* the members of the church, for they were *all* to be made acquainted with the word of God. The command is, indeed, that it be "read" to them, but by parity of reasoning it would follow that it was to be in their hands; that it was to be accessible to them; that it was in no manner to be withheld from them. Probably many of them could not read, but *in some way* the contents of revelation were to be made known to them—and not by *preaching* only, but by *reading* the words of inspiration. No part was to be kept back; nor were they to be denied such access

that they could fully understand it; nor was it to be insisted on that there should be an authorized expounder of it. It was presumed that all the members of the church were qualified to understand what had been written to them, and to profit by it. It follows therefore, (3) That there is great iniquity in all those decisions and laws which are designed to keep the Scriptures from the common people. This is true (*a*) in reference to the Papal communion, and to all the ordinances there which prohibit the free circulation of the Sacred Volume among the people; (*b*) it is true of all those laws in slave-holding communities which prohibit slaves from being taught to read the Scriptures; and (*c*) it is true of all the opinions and dogmas which prevail in *any* community where the right of "private judgment" is denied, and where free access to the volume of inspiration is forbidden. The richest blessing of Heaven to mankind is the Bible; and there is no book ever written so admirably adapted to the common mind, and so fitted to elevate the sunken, the ignorant, and the degraded. There is no more decided enemy of the progress of the human race in intelligence, purity, and freedom, than he who prevents the free circulation of this holy volume; and there is no sincerer friend of the species than he who "causes it to be read by all," and who contributes to make it accessible to all the families and all the inhabitants of the world.   5

THE SECOND
EPISTLE TO THE THESSALONIANS.

INTRODUCTION.

For a general view of Thessalonica; of the establishment of the church there; of the character of the church, and of the design for which the apostle addressed these letters to it, see the Introduction to the First Epistle.

This epistle appears to have been written soon after the first, and from the same place—Corinth. See Intro. to the First Epistle, § 3. The proof of this indeed is not certain, for there are no marks of time or place *in* the epistle by which these points can be determined. The probability rests upon these grounds: (1) That the same persons—Paul, Silas, and Timothy—are associated in both epistles, and are mentioned as being together at the time when they were written (1 Thes. i. 1; 2 Thes. i. 1); but as there is reason to believe that they did not continue long together, it is to be presumed that one epistle was written soon after the other. (2) Paul refers to an error which had grown up, apparently in consequence of a misunderstanding of his first epistle (chap. ii. 1, 2); an error which he regarded as of great magnitude, and which was producing very unhappy results (chap. iii. 11, 12), and it was natural that he should hasten to correct that error as soon as possible. (3) There is some probability, as Benson has remarked, that the epistle was written *before* the troubles came upon him at Corinth under the administration of Gallio (Acts xviii. 12–16), and yet that he saw that the storm was approaching, and hints at it in chap. ii. 2, "And that we may be delivered from unreasonable and wicked men." If so, this epistle was written but a few months at farthest after the first. We may regard the evidence, therefore, as sufficiently clear, that this epistle was written at Corinth some time during the latter part of A.D. 53, or the beginning of A.D. 54.

There is little doubt as to the design for which it was written. Either by a false interpretation of his former epistle, or by an epistle forged in his name and sent to them, the opinion had become prevalent in the church at Thessalonica that the Saviour was about to appear, and that the end of the world was at hand; see chap. ii. 2; comp. Hug's *Intro.* § 94, and Stuart's Notes on the same, pp. 741, *seq.* To correct this impression was the leading design of this epistle. Some had become alarmed, and were suffering from unnecessary apprehension (chap. ii. 2); and some, under the natural belief that labour then was useless, and that property was of no value, had given up all attention to their worldly concerns (chap. iii. 10, 11); and it was of the utmost importance that the error should be corrected. This was done in this second epistle, and in doing it, Paul, as was usual, intermingled several other topics of importance, adapted to the condition of those to whom he wrote.

This epistle, though short, has great permanent value, and is indispensable to a proper understanding of the great doctrine of the Second Advent of the Redeemer. It was written, indeed, to correct an error in a single church, and at a particular time, but history has shown there is a tendency to that same error in all ages, and that there was need of some permanent inspired statement to check it. It was inferred from the First Epistle of Paul to the Thessalonians, that *he* meant to teach that the day of judgment was not far off. Had not this second epistle been written to correct that false interpretation, and to show what *was* his belief, it would have been charged on him that he was mistaken, and *then* the inference would have been naturally made that *all* the prophecies respecting that event were false. The distance between this and absolute infidelity, it is easy to see, is very small. Paul, by his prompt explanation, arrested that danger, and showed that he intended to teach no such doctrine as had been drawn from his first letter to them. This epistle, therefore, is of importance to show, (1) That the apostle did not believe, or mean to teach, that the end of the world was near. There are many expressions, indeed, which, like those in First Thessalonians, would *seem* to imply that the apostle held that belief, *but the explanation of an inspired apostle of his own sentiments at the time, settled that matter*. No one has now a right to charge that belief on him, or on others who then used the same language. No one can pretend that they held the opinion that the end of the world was near. There is no stronger language on that subject in any of their writings than occurs in the First Epistle to the Thessalonians, and Paul in the Second Epistle expressly says that he held no such opinion, and meant to teach no such thing. (2) This epistle is a standing rebuke of the kind of interpretation which attempts to determine the time when the Saviour will come, and of all those theories which represent "the day of Christ as at hand." The declarations in the Scriptures are positive and abundant that the time of his appearing is not made known to mortals (Notes on Acts i. 7), and it is not possible now to make out a *stronger* argument to prove that that time is near, than could have been made out from the First Epistle to the Thessalonians; and yet Paul deemed it necessary to write them a second letter, expressly to show them that the interpretation which they put on his language was unauthorized. The truth is, that it was not the design of God to make known to men the exact time when the Lord Jesus will return to judgment; and all attempts since the time of Paul to settle that have failed, and all will doubtless continue to fail, as they always have done.

THE SECOND
EPISTLE TO THE THESSALONIANS.

CHAPTER I.

PAUL, and Silvanus, and Timotheus, ^aunto the church of the Thessalonians in God our Father and the Lord Jesus Christ.

2 Grace^b unto you, and peace, from God our Father and the Lord Jesus Christ.

3 We are bound to thank God always for you, brethren, as it is

<small>a 1 Th.1.1,&c.   b 1 Co.1.3.</small>

CHAPTER I.
ANALYSIS OF THE CHAPTER.

This chapter comprises the following points:—

(1) The salutation, ver. 1, 2.

(2) An expression of thanks for the progress which the Thessalonians had made in piety, and especially for the manner in which they had been enabled to bear their trials, ver. 3, 4.

(3) An assurance that the manner in which they had been enabled to bear their trials was an evidence that they were true Christians, ver. 5.

(4) A declaration that those who had persecuted them, and all others who were wicked, would be punished when the Lord Jesus should come, and that when this should occur the righteous would appear in glory and honour, ver. 6–10.

(5) The expression of an earnest desire that they might be prepared for the solemn scenes of that day, ver. 11, 12.

1, 2. *Paul, and Silvanus, and Timotheus.* See Notes on 1 Thes. i. 1.

3. *We are bound to thank God always for you.* Notes on 1 Thes. i. 2. ¶ *As it is meet.* As it is fit or proper. ¶ *Because that your faith groweth exceedingly.* It would seem probable from this that Paul had heard from them since his first epistle

meet, because that your faith groweth exceedingly, and the charity of every one of you all toward each other aboundeth:

4 So that ^cwe ourselves glory in you in the churches of God, for your patience and faith in all your persecutions and tribulations that ^dye endure;

5 *Which is* ^ea manifest token

<small>c 2 Co.9.2; 1 Th.2.19,20.
d Ja.5.11.   e Phi.1.28.</small>

was written. He had doubtless received intelligence of the error which prevailed among them respecting his views of the coming of the Lord Jesus, and of the progress which the truth was making, at the same time. ¶ *And the charity of every one of you all toward each other.* Your mutual love.

4. *So that we ourselves glory in you in the churches of God.* That is, we mention your example to other churches, and glory in it, as an evidence of what the gospel is fitted to do; see Notes on 1 Thes. ii. 19, 20; comp. Notes on 2 Cor. ix. 2. ¶ *For your patience.* Your patient endurance of trials. ¶ *And faith.* Fidelity, or constancy. You have shown unwavering confidence in God in your afflictions. ¶ *In all your persecutions and tribulations that ye endure.* See Notes on 1 Thes. ii. 14; iv. 13. It would seem from this that the persecutions and trials to which the apostle referred in his first epistle were still continued.

5. *Which is a manifest token of the righteous judgment of God.* The word "*which*" is supplied by our translators, and there may be some doubt to what the apostle has reference as being "a manifest token of the righteous judgment of God." The general sense seems to be, that the fact that they

of the righteous judgment of God, that ye may be counted worthy of the kingdom of God, *f*for which ye also suffer:

were thus persecuted was an evidence that there would be a future judgment, when the righteous who were persecuted would be rewarded, and the wicked who persecuted them would be punished. The manner in which they bore their trials was an indication also of what the result would be in regard to them. Their patience and faith under persecutions were constantly showing that they would "be counted worthy of the kingdom of God, for which they were called to suffer." It is evident that a *relative* must be supplied here, as our translators have done, but there has been a difference of view as to what it refers. Some suppose that it is to "*patience*," others to "*persecutions and tribulations*," and others to the *whole sentence* preceding. The latter is probably the true construction, and the sense is, that the endurance of affliction in a proper manner by the righteous is a proof that there will be a righteous judgment of God in the last day. (1) It is evidence that there *will be* a future judgment—since the righteous here suffer so much, and the wicked triumph. (2) These things are now permitted *in order* that the character may be developed, and that the reason of the sentence in the last day may be seen. (3) The manner in which these afflictions are borne is an *evidence*—an *indication* (ἔνδειγμα) of what the results of the judgment will be. The word rendered "manifest token" (ἔνδειγμα), occurs nowhere else in the New Testament. It means an indication, token, proof—anything that *shows* or *points out* how a thing *is*, or *is to be* (from ἐνδείκνυμι, to show, to point out). The meaning here is, therefore, that the course of events referred to—the persecutions which they endured, and the manner in which they were borne—furnished a proof that there would be a righteous judgment, and also afforded an indication of what the result of that judgment would be. We may, in general, learn

6 Seeing*g* it *is* a righteous thing with God to recompense tribulation to them that trouble you;

f 1 Th.2.14; He.10.32,33.　　*g* Re.6.10.

what will be the issues of the judgment in the case of an individual from the manner in which he bears trials. ¶ *Of the righteous judgment of God.* That there will be a just judgment hereafter. The crimes of the wicked who go unpunished on the earth, and the sufferings of the good who are unavenged, are a demonstration that there will be a judgment, when all these inequalities will be adjusted. ¶ *That ye may be counted worthy.* As the result of your affliction, that you may be *fitted* for the kingdom of God. This does not mean that Christians will *merit* heaven by their sufferings, but that they may show that they have such a character that there is a *fitness* or *propriety* that they should be admitted there. They may evince by their patience and resignation, by their deadness to the world and their holy lives, that they are not disqualified to enter into that kingdom where the redeemed are to dwell. No true Christian will ever feel that he is *worthy* on his own account, or that he has any *claim* to eternal life, yet he may have evidence that he has the characteristics to which God has promised salvation, and is fitted to dwell in heaven. ¶ *Of the kingdom of God.* In heaven; see Notes on Mat. iii. 2. ¶ *For which ye also suffer.* The sufferings which you now endure are because you are professed heirs of the kingdom; that is, you are persecuted because you are Christians; see 1 Thes. ii. 14.

6. *Seeing* it is *a righteous thing with God to recompense tribulation to them that trouble you.* The sense is, "There will be a future judgment, because it is proper that God should punish those who now persecute you. It is not right that they should go unpunished, and triumph for ever. It is not an *arbitrary* thing, a thing which is indifferent, a thing which may or may not be done; it is a *just* and *proper* thing that the wicked should

7 And[h] to you who are troubled, rest with us; [i] when the Lord Jesus

h Re.14.13.   i 1 Th.4.16; Jude 14.

shall be revealed from heaven with [1] his mighty angels,

1 the angels of his power.

be punished." The doctrine is, that the future punishment of the wicked is *just* and *proper;* and that, *being* just and proper, it will be inflicted. Many suppose that there would be no justice in the eternal punishment of the wicked; that the threatening of that punishment is wholly arbitrary; that it might easily be dispensed with; and that *because* it is unjust it will *not* be inflicted, and need not be dreaded. But that it is just and proper, a very slight degree of reflection must show. For, (1) It is inconceivable that God should *threaten* such punishment unless it were just. How can it be reconciled with his perfections that he can hold up before mankind the assurance that any of them will be punished for ever, unless it be right that it should be so? Can we believe that he deliberately threatens what is wrong, or that, in the face of the universe, he publicly declares his intention to do what is wrong? (2) Men themselves believe that it is *just* that the wicked should be punished. They are constantly making laws, and affixing penalties to them, and executing them, under the belief that it is right. Can they regard it as wrong in God to do the same thing? Can that be wrong in him which is right in themselves? (3) If it is right to punish wickedness here, it is not wrong to punish it in the future world. There is nothing in the two *places* which can change the nature of what is done. If it is right for God to visit the sinner here with the tokens of his displeasure, there is nothing which can make it wrong to visit him in like manner in the future world. Why should that be wrong in another world which is right and proper in this? (4) It will be a righteous thing for God to punish the wicked in a future state, for they are *not* always punished here as they deserve. No one can seriously maintain that there is an equal distribution of rewards and punishments on the earth. Many a man goes to the grave having received *no* adequate punishment for his crimes. Many a murderer, pirate, robber, traitor, and plunderer of nations under the name of a conqueror, thus dies. No one can doubt that it would be a "just" thing to punish them here if they could be arrested. Why should it be any the less "just" to punish them when they enter another world? In like manner, many a man lives a life of profligacy; or is an open scoffer; or aims to cast off the government of God; or is a seducer of innocence; and yet lives in the midst of wealth, and goes down in calmness and peace to the grave, Ps. lxxiii. 3–5; Job xxi. 23–33. Why is it not "just" that such an one should be punished in the future world? comp. Ps. lxxiii. 16–20. But, if it is right that God should punish the wicked in the future world, it will be done. For, (1) There is nothing to hinder him from doing it. He has all power, and has all necessary means of inflicting punishment, entirely at his disposal. (2) It would not be right not to do it. It is not right for a magistrate to treat the righteous and the wicked alike, or to show that he has as much regard to the one as to the other. (3) It cannot be believed that God has uttered a threatening which he never *meant* to execute, or to appear before the universe as having held up before men the terror of the most awful punishment which *could* be inflicted, but which he never intended to carry into effect. Who could have confidence in such a Being? Who could know what to believe when he makes the most solemn declaration? (4) The Judge of all the earth "will do right;" and if it is right to *declare* that "the wicked shall be turned into hell," it will not be wrong to *inflict* the sentence. And if, on the whole, it is *right* that the sinner should be punished, *it will be done.* ¶ *Them that trouble you.* Those who persecute you; see 1 Thes. ii. 14.

7. *And to you who are troubled.*

8 In*k* flaming fire, ²taking*l* vengeance on *m*them that know not God, and *n*that obey not the gospel of our Lord Jesus Christ:

k He.10.27; 2 Pe.3.7.   ² or, *yielding.*
l De.32.41,43.   *m* Ps.79.6; Zep.1.6.
      n Ro.2.8.

That is, "It will be a righteous thing for God to give to you who are persecuted *rest* in the last day." As it will be right and proper to punish the wicked, so it will be right to reward the good. It will not, however, be in precisely the same sense. The wicked will *deserve* all that they will suffer, but it cannot be said that the righteous will *deserve* the reward which they will receive. It will be right and proper, because (1) there is a fitness that they who are the friends of God should be treated as such, or it is proper that he should show himself to be their friend; and (2) because in this life this is not always clearly done. They are often less prospered, and less happy in their outward circumstances than the wicked. There is, therefore, a propriety that in the future state God should manifest himself as their friend, and show to assembled worlds that he is not indifferent to character, or that wickedness does not deserve his smiles, and piety incur his frown. At the same time, however, it will be owing wholly to his grace that any are ever admitted to heaven. ¶ *Rest.* The future happiness of believers is often represented under the image of *rest.* It is rest like that of the weary labourer after his day of toil; rest, like that of the soldier after the hardships of a long and perilous march; rest, like the calm repose of one who has been racked with pain; see Notes on Heb. iv. 9. The word *rest* here (ἄνεσις) means a letting loose, a remission, a relaxation; and hence composure, quiet, 2 Cor. ii. 12; vii. 5. ¶ *With us.* That is, with Paul, Silas, and Timothy, ver. 1. It would increase the comfort of the Thessalonians derived from the anticipation of the future world, to reflect that they would meet their religious teachers and friends there. It always augments

9 Who shall be *o*punished with everlasting destruction from the presence of the Lord, and *p*from the glory of his power;

o Phi.3.19; 2 Pe.3.7.
p Is.2.19.

the anticipated joy of heaven to reflect that we are to share its blessedness with them. There is no envy among those who anticipate heaven; there will be none there. They who desire heaven at all, desire that it may be shared in the highest degree by all who are dear to them. ¶ *When the Lord Jesus shall be revealed from heaven.* Shall appear; shall come from heaven; Notes, 1 Thes. iv. 6. ¶ *With his mighty angels.* Marg., *angels of his power.* So the Greek. The sense is, that angels of exalted rank and glory will accompany him; Notes on 1 Thes. iv. 16; Mat. xxiv. 31; xxv. 31.

8. *In flaming fire.* This is a circumstance which is not noticed in the account of his appearing in the parallel place in 1 Thes. iv. 16. The object of the apostle here seems to be to represent him as coming amidst vivid flashes of lightning. He is commonly described as coming in clouds, and to that common description there is here added the image of incessant lightnings, as if the whole heavens were illuminated with a continued blaze. ¶ *Taking vengeance.* Marg., *yielding.* Gr., *giving.* The word *vengeance* is used in the sense of *punishment,* for there cannot be in God what literally corresponds with the passion of *revenge;* comp. Notes on Rom. xii. 19. ¶ *On them that know not God.* On all who are strangers to him; that is, who are living in heathenish darkness, or who, having heard of him, have no practical acquaintance with him. ¶ *And that obey not the gospel of our Lord Jesus Christ.* Who do not embrace it, and practise its precepts in their lives; comp. Notes on Rom. ii. 9.

9. *Who shall be punished with everlasting destruction.* See Notes on Mat. xxv. 41, 46. The word which is here rendered *destruction* (ὄλεθρον), is dif-

10 When he shall come *q* to be glorified in his saints, and *r* to be

q Mat. 25. 31.　　*r* Ps. 68. 35.

admired in all them that believe (because our testimony among you was believed) in that day.

---

ferent from that which occurs in Mat. xxv. 46, and which is there rendered *punishment, κόλασις.* The word ὄλεθρον —*olethron*—occurs only here and in 1 Cor. v. 5; 1 Thes. v. 3; 1 Tim. vi. 9; in each of which places it is rendered *destruction.* It does not denote annihilation, but is used in the same sense in which we use the word when we say that a thing is *destroyed.* Thus health is destroyed when it fails; property is destroyed when it is burned or sunk in the ocean; a limb is destroyed that is lost in battle; life is destroyed when one dies. In the case before us, the destruction, whatever it be, is (1) to be continued for ever; and (2) is to be of the nature of punishment. The meaning then must be, that the soul is destroyed as to the great purposes of its being—its enjoyment, dignity, honour, holiness, happiness. It will not be annihilated, but will live and linger on *in* destruction. It seems difficult to conceive how any one can profess to hold that this passage is a part of the word of God, and yet deny the doctrine of future eternal punishment. It would not be possible to state that doctrine in clearer language than this. It never *is* stated in clearer language in any creed or confession of faith, and if it be not true that the wicked will be punished for ever, it must be admitted that it would not have been *possible* to reveal the doctrine in human language. ¶ *From the presence of the Lord.* That is, a part of their punishment will consist in being banished from the immediate presence of the Lord. There is a sense in which God is everywhere present, and in that sense he will be in the world where the wicked will dwell, to punish them. But the phrase is also used to denote his more immediate presence; the place where are the symbols of his majesty and glory; the home of the holy and the blessed. It is in that sense that the word is used here, and the idea is, that it will be one of the

circumstances contributing to the deeper woe of the place of punishment, that those who dwell there will be banished from that holy abode, and will never be permitted to enter there. ¶ *And from the glory of his power.* The meaning seems to be, that they will not be able to endure the manifestation of his power and majesty when he shall appear, but will be driven away by it into outer darkness; see chap. ii. 8. The Saviour, in describing his Second Advent, uses this language: "They shall see the Son of man coming in the clouds of heaven, with power and great glory," Mat. xxiv. 30. There will be a great exhibition of both. The *power* will be seen in the convulsions of nature which will precede or attend him; in the resurrection of the dead; and in the bringing of all to judgment: and the *glory* will be seen in his own person; the dignity and number of his attendants; and the honour that shall then be conferred on him as the final Judge of all mankind. By the manifestation of that power and glory the wicked will be driven away into eternal ruin. They will not be able to stand before it, and though, in common with the righteous, they may see the majesty of the Redeemer in the last day, yet they will be driven away to witness it no more.

10. *When he shall come to be glorified in his saints.* That is, the redeemed in that day will be the means of promoting his glory, or the universe will see his glory manifested in their redemption. His chief glory as seen in that day will be connected with the fact that he has redeemed his people; and he will come in order that all the appropriate honour of such a work may then be manifested. He will be "glorified" then by the numbers that shall have been redeemed; by their patience in the trials through which they have passed; by the triumphs which religion shall have made on the earth; by their praises and songs, and

11 Wherefore also we pray always for you, that our God would
count[3] you [s]worthy of *this* calling,

----
[3] or, *vouchsafe.*   [s] Col.1.12; Re.3.4.
----

by their ascent with him to the realms
of blessedness.   ¶ *And to be admired
in all them that believe.*   This may
either mean that he will be admired
among or *by* them that believe; or
that the ground of the admiration
which he will receive in that day will
be what will be seen *in* them; that is,
their graces, their numbers, their joys,
their triumphs will be the occasion of
producing admiration of *him*—for he
will be regarded as the source of it all.
Tindal renders it, "and to be made
marvellous in all them that believe."
The latter interpretation seems to me
to be the correct one.   The general
idea is, that Christ in that day will be
manifested in a glorious manner, and
that the source of his highest triumphs
will be what is seen *in* the saints.
His main honour when he returns to
the world will not be the outward
splendours which will attend his
coming, nor the angels that will accompany him, nor the manifestation
of his power over the elements, but
the church which he has redeemed.
It will then be seen that he is worthy
of universal admiration, for having redeemed that church.   He shall then
be admired or glorified in his people,
(1) for having conceived the plan of
redeeming them; (2) for being willing to become incarnate and to die to
save them; (3) for the defence of his
church in all its persecutions and trials;
(4) for raising his people from the
dead; (5) for the virtues and graces
which they will exhibit in that day.
This appropriate honour of Christ in
the church has never yet been fully
seen.   His people on earth have, in
general, most imperfectly reflected
his image.   They have in general been
comparatively few in number, and
scattered upon the earth.   They have
been poor and despised.   Often they
have been persecuted and regarded as
the "filth of the world and the off-
scouring of all things."   The honours
of this world have been withheld from
them.   The great have regarded it as

and fulfil all the good pleasure of
his goodness, and the work of faith
with power;

----

no honour to be identified with the
church, and the proud have been
ashamed to be enrolled among the followers of the Lamb.   In the last day
all this will be changed, and the assembled church will show to admiring
worlds how great and glorious is its
Redeemer, and how glorious was the
work of redemption.   ¶ *Because our
testimony among you was believed.*
The meaning of this seems to be, that
they would be among the number of
those who would in that day honour
the Saviour, because they had embraced what the apostle had preached
to them respecting these future scenes.
Thus interpreted, this clause should
be regarded as connected with ver. 7:
"And to you it is a righteous thing
that he should give rest with us, because our testimony among you was
believed."   That is, you have shown
that you are true Christians, and it is
proper that you should partake of the
triumphs and hopes of that day.

11. *Wherefore also we pray always
for you.*   Notes, 1 Thes. i. 2.   ¶ *That
our God would count you worthy of
this calling.*   Marg., "or, *vouchsafe.*"
The meaning is, "that he would regard you as worthy of this calling;"
see Notes on ver. 5.   ¶ *Of this calling.*
Notes, Eph. iv. 1.   The "calling" here,
is that which had brought them into
the kingdom, and led them to become
Christians.   ¶ *And fulfil all the good
pleasure of* his *goodness.*   That is,
make the work of salvation complete
and effectual.   Oldshausen has well
expressed the sense: "May God fill
you with all that good which is pleasing to him."   The thoughts in the
passage are, (1) that the purpose towards them on the part of God was
one of "goodness" or benevolence;
(2) that there was a state of mind
which would be regarded by him as
pleasing, or as his "good pleasure;"
and (3) that Paul wished that this
might be accomplished in them.   He
desired that there might be in them
everything which would be pleasing to
God, and which his benevolence was

12 That⁺ the name of our Lord Jesus Christ may be glorified in

t 1 Pe.1.7.

you, and ye in him, according to the grace of our God and the Lord Jesus Christ.

fitted to secure. ¶ *And the work of faith.* The work which faith is adapted to produce on the soul; see 1 John v. 4, 5. ¶ *With power.* Effectually, completely. The apostle prays that so much power may be exerted as will be sufficient to secure the object. The work of religion on the soul is always represented in the Bible as one of *power.*

12. *That the name of our Lord Jesus Christ.* That is, that the Lord Jesus himself may be honoured among you; the name often denoting the person. The idea is that the apostle wished that the Lord Jesus might be honoured among them by the fair application and development of the principles of his religion. ¶ *And ye in him.* That you may be regarded and treated as his friends when he shall come to judge the world. ¶ *According to the grace of our God and the Lord Jesus Christ.* That is, that you may experience all the honour which his grace is fitted to impart.

REMARKS.

In view of the exposition given of this chapter, we may remark:—

(1) That the wicked will certainly be punished when the Lord Jesus shall come to judgment. Words cannot reveal this truth more plainly than is done in this chapter, and if it is not to be so, then language has no meaning.

(2) The punishment of the wicked will be eternal. It is impossible for language to teach that doctrine more clearly than is done in this chapter. If it were admitted to have been the intention of God to teach the doctrine of eternal punishment, it is impossible to conceive that he could have chosen more plain and positive language to express the doctrine than has been done here. Can it be, then, that he means to trifle with men on so solemn a subject, by using words which have no meaning?

(3) It will greatly aggravate the punishment of the wicked that it will be " a *righteous* thing " for God thus to punish them. If they were to suf-

fer as martyrs; if in their sufferings they could feel that they were oppressed and crushed beneath mere power; if they could feel that they were right and that God was wrong; if they could get up a party in the universe against God, sympathizing with them as if they were wronged, the case would be changed. A man can endure suffering much more easily when he has a good conscience, and feels that he is right, than he can when he feels that what he endures is deserved. But the sinner in hell can never have this consolation. He will for ever feel that God is *right* and that he is wrong, and that every pang which he endures is deserved.

(4) If it be a "righteous thing" that the wicked shall be punished, then they never can be saved by mere justice. No one will go to heaven because he *deserves* or *merits* it. All dependence on human merit, therefore, is taken away in the matter of salvation, and if the sinner is ever saved, it will be by *grace,* and not by *justice.*

(5) If it is a "righteous thing" that the sinner should perish, he will perish. God will do right to all.

(6) It is amazing that the mass of men have so little concern about their future condition. God has plainly revealed that he will destroy the wicked for ever, and that it will be a righteous thing for him to do it; and yet the mass of mankind are wholly unconcerned, and disregard all the solemn declarations of the Bible on this subject as if they were idle tales. One would suppose that the very possibility of eternal suffering would rouse all the sensibilities of the soul, and lead to the earnest inquiry whether it is not possible to avoid it. Yet the mass of men feel no concern in this inquiry. It is impossible to get them ever to *think* of it. We cannot get them even to ask the question, seriously, whether they themselves are to be happy or miserable to all eternity. This stupidity and indifference is the most unaccount-

CHAPTER II.

NOW we beseech you, brethren, by the coming of our Lord able fact on earth, and probably distinguishes this world from all others.

(7) It is *rational* to think of religion; to reflect on eternity; to be serious; to be *anxious* about the future state. If there is even a *possibility* that we may be miserable for ever, it is proper to be *serious* about it. And if there is a solemn declaration of God that it will be a "righteous thing" for him to punish the wicked, and that he *will* "punish them with everlasting destruction," assuredly the mind *should* be concerned. Is there anything more worthy the calm and sober attention of the human soul than such solemn declarations of the infinite God?

CHAPTER II.

ANALYSIS OF THE CHAPTER.

The main object of this chapter is to correct an erroneous impression which had been made on the minds of the Thessalonians respecting the second coming of the Saviour, either by his own former letter, or by one forged in his name. They had received the impression that that event was about to take place. This belief had produced an unhappy effect on their minds, ver. 2. It became, therefore, necessary to state the truth on the subject, in order to free their minds from alarm; and this purpose of the apostle leads to one of the most important prophecies in the New Testament. The chapter comprises the following points:—

I. An exhortation that they would not be alarmed or distressed by the expectation of the speedy coming of the Saviour, ver. 1, 2.

II. A statement of the truth that he would *not* soon appear, and of the characteristics of a great apostasy which must intervene before his advent, ver. 3–12.

In this part of the chapter, the apostle shows that he did *not* mean to teach that that event would soon happen, by stating that *before* that there would occur a most melancholy

Jesus Christ, and *by* our gathering together unto him,

2 That ye be not soon shaken in apostasy, which would require a considerable time before it was matured.

(*a*) That day would not come until there should be a great apostasy, and a revelation of the man of sin, ver. 3.

(*b*) The character of this man of sin was to be such that it could not be mistaken: he would be opposed to God; would exalt himself above all that is called God; and would sit in the temple showing himself as God, ver. 4.

(*c*) There was a restraint then exercised which prevented the development of the great apostasy. There were indeed causes then at work which would lead to it, but they were then held in check, and God would restrain them until some future time, when he would suffer the man of sin to be revealed, ver. 5–7.

(*d*) When that time should come, then that "wicked" one would be revealed, with such marks that he could not be mistaken. His coming would be after the working of Satan, with power and signs and lying wonders, and under him there would be strong delusion, and the belief of a lie, ver. 8–12. This great foe of God was to be destroyed by the coming of the Saviour, and one object of his appearing would be to put an end to his dominion, ver. 8.

III. The apostle then says, that there was occasion for thankfulness to God, that he had chosen them to salvation, and not left them to be destroyed, ver. 13, 14.

IV. An exhortation to stand fast, and to maintain what they had been taught (ver. 15), and a prayer that God, who had given them a good hope, would comfort their hearts, closes the chapter, ver. 16, 17.

1. *Now we beseech you, brethren, by the coming of our Lord Jesus Christ.* The phrase "by the coming," is not here, as our translators seem to have supposed, a form of solemn adjuration. It is not common, if it ever occurs, in the Scriptures, to make a solemn adjuration in view of *an event*, and the

mind, or be troubled, neither by spirit, nor by word, nor by letter,

connection here demands that we give to the phrase a different sense. It means, *respecting his coming;* and the idea of Paul is, "In regard to that great event of which I spoke to you in my former epistle—the coming of the Saviour—I beseech you not to be troubled, as if it were soon to happen. As his views had been misunderstood or misrepresented, he now proposes to show them that there was nothing in the true doctrine which should create alarm, as if he were about to appear. ¶ *And* by *our gathering together unto him.* There is manifest allusion here to what is said in the first epistle (chap. iv. 17), "then we shall be caught up together with them in the clouds;" and the meaning is, "In reference to our being gathered unto him, I beseech you not to be shaken in mind, as if that event were near."

2. *That ye be not soon shaken in mind.* The word here used signifies, properly, to be moved as a wave of the sea, or to be tossed upon the waves, as a vessel is. Then it means to be shaken in any way; see Mat. xi. 7; xxiv. 29; Luke vi. 38; Acts iv. 31; Heb. xii. 26. The reference here is to the agitation or alarm felt from the belief that the day of judgment would soon come. It is uniformly said in the Scriptures, that the approach of the Lord Jesus to judge the world will produce a great consternation and alarm: Mat. xxiv. 30, "Then shall appear the sign of the Son of man in heaven, and then shall all the tribes of the earth mourn;" Rev. i. 7, "Behold, he cometh with clouds; and every eye shall see him, and they also which pierced him : and all kindreds of the earth shall wail because of him;" Luke xxiii. 30, "Then shall they begin to say to the mountains, Fall on us; and to the hills, Cover us;" comp. Isa. ii. 21, 22. Of the truth of this, there can be no doubt. We may *imagine* something of the effects which will be produced by the alarm caused in a community

as from us, *a*as that the day of Christ is at hand.

a Mat.24.4-6.

when a belief prevails that the day of judgment is near. In a single year (1843) seventeen persons were admitted to the Lunatic Asylum in Worcester, Mass., who had become deranged in consequence of the expectation that the Lord Jesus was about to appear. It is easy to account for such facts, and no doubt, when the Lord Jesus shall actually come, the effect on the guilty world will be overwhelming. The apostle here says, also, that those who were Christians were "shaken in mind and troubled" by this anticipation. There are, doubtless, many true Christians who would be alarmed at such an event, as there are many who, like Hezekiah (Isa. xxxviii. 1, 2), are alarmed at the prospect of death. Many real Christians might, on the sudden occurrence, of such an event, feel that they were not prepared, and be alarmed at the prospect of passing through the great trial which is to determine their everlasting destiny. It is no certain evidence of a want of piety to be alarmed at the approach of death. Our nature dreads death, and though there may be a well-founded hope of heaven, it will not always preserve a delicate physical frame from trembling when it comes. ¶ *Or be troubled.* That is, disturbed, or terrified. It would seem that this belief had produced much consternation among them. ¶ *Neither by spirit.* By any pretended spirit of prophecy. But whether this refers to the predictions of those who were false prophets in Thessalonica, or to something whioh it was alleged the apostle Paul had himself asserted there, and which was construed as meaning that the time was near, is not certain. This depends much on the question whether the phrase "as from us," refers only to the *letters* which had been sent to them, or also to the "word" and to the "spirit," here spoken of; see Oldshausen on the place. It would seem, from the connection, that *all* their consternation had been caused by some misconstruction which had been put on the sentiments of Paul himself, for if there had been any other source of alarm, he would naturally have referred to it. It is probable, therefore, that allusion is made to some representation which had been given of what he had said under the influence of the Holy Spirit, and that the expectation that the end of the world was near, was supposed to be a doctrine of inspiration. Whether, however, the Thessalonians themselves put this construction on what he said, or whether those who had caused the alarm represented him as teaching this, cannot be determined. ¶ *Nor by word.* That is, by public instruction, or in preaching. It is evident that when the apostle was among them, this subject, from such causes, was prominent in his discourses; see ver. 5. It had been inferred, it seems, from what he said, that he meant to teach that the end of the world was near. ¶ *Nor by letter.* Either the one which he had before written to them—the First Epistle to the Thessalonians—or one which had been forged in his name. ¶ *As from us.* That is, Paul, Silas, and Timothy, who are united in writing the two epistles (1 Thes. i. 1; 2 Thes. i. 1), and in whose names a letter would be forged, if one of this description were sent to them. It has been made a question, whether the apostle refers here to the former epistle which he had sent to them, or to a forged letter; and on this question critics have been about equally divided. The reasons for the former opinion may be seen in Paley's *Horæ Paulinæ, in loco.* The question is not very important, and perhaps cannot be easily settled. There are two or three circumstances, however, which seem to make it probable that he refers to an epistle which had been forged, and which had been pretended to be received from him. (1) One is found in the expression "*as from us.*" If he had referred to his own former letter, it seems to me that the allusion would have been more distinct, and that the particle "*as*" (ὡς) would not have been used. This is such an expression as would

have been employed *if* the reference were to such a forged letter. (2) A second circumstance is found in the expression in the next verse, "Let *no man deceive* you by any means," which looks as if they were not led into this belief by their own interpretation of his former epistle, but by a deliberate attempt of some one to delude them on the subject. (3) Perhaps a third circumstance would be found in the fact that it was not uncommon in early times of Christianity to attempt to impose forged writings on the churches. Nothing would be more natural for an impostor who wished to acquire influence, than to do this; and that it was often done is well known. That epistles *were* forged under the names of the apostles, appears very probable, as Benson has remarked, from chap. iii. 17; Gal. vi. 11; and Philem. 19. There are, indeed, none of those forged epistles extant which were composed in the time of the apostles, but there is extant an epistle of Paul to the Corinthians, besides the two which we have; another to the Laodiceans, and six of Paul's epistles to Seneca—all of which are undoubted forgeries; see Benson, *in loco.* If Paul, however, here refers to his former epistle, the reference is doubtless to 1 Thes. iv. 15, and v. 2, 3, 4, which might easily be understood as teaching that the end of the world was near, and to which those who maintained that opinion might appeal with great plausibility. We have, however, the authority of the apostle himself that he meant to teach no such thing. ¶ *As that the day of Christ is at hand.* The time when he would appear—called "the day of Christ," because it would be appointed especially for the manifestation of his glory. The phrase "at hand," means *near.* Grotius supposes that it denotes *that same year,* and refers for proof to Rom. viii. 38; 1 Cor. iii. 22; Gal. i. 4; Heb. ix. 9. If so, the attempt to fix the day was an early indication of the desire to determine *the very time* of his appearing—a disposition which has been so common since, and which has led into so many sad mistakes.

3 Let no man deceive you by any means: for *that day shall not come,* *b*except there come a falling

b 1 Ti.4.1.

away first, and *c*that man of sin be revealed, *d*the son of perdition:

c Da.7.25.　　　　*d* Jn.17.12.

3. *Let no man deceive you by any means.* That is, respecting the coming of the Lord Jesus. This implies that there were then *attempts* to deceive, and that it was of great importance for Christians to be on their guard. The result has shown that there is almost no subject on which caution is more proper, and on which men are more liable to delusion. The *means* then resorted to for deception appear from the previous verse to have been either an appeal to a pretended verbal message from the apostle, or a pretended letter from him. The means now, consist of a claim to uncommon wisdom in the interpretation of obscure prophecies of the Scriptures. The necessity for the *caution* here given has not ceased. ¶ *For that day shall not come, except there come a falling away first.* Until an *apostasy* (ἀποστασία) shall have occurred—*the great* apostasy. There is scarcely any passage of the New Testament which has given occasion to greater diversity of opinion than this. Though the reference seems to be plain, and there is scarcely *any* prophecy of the Bible apparently more obvious and easy in its general interpretation; yet it is proper to mention some of the opinions which have been entertained of it. Some have referred it to a great apostasy from the Christian church, particularly on account of persecution, which would occur before the destruction of Jerusalem. The "coming of the Lord" they suppose refers to the destruction of the holy city, and according to this, the meaning is, that there would be a great apostasy before that event would take place. Of this opinion was Vitringa, who refers the "apostasy" to a great defection from the faith which took place between the time of Nero and Trajan. Whitby also refers it to an event which was to take place before the destruction of Jerusalem, and supposes that the apostasy would consist in a return from the Christian to the

Jewish faith by multitudes of professed converts. The "man of sin," according to him, means the Jewish nation, so characterized on account of its eminent wickedness. Hammond explains the apostasy by the defection to the Gnostics, by the arts of Simon Magus, whom he supposes to be the man of sin, and by the "day of the Lord" he also understands the destruction of Jerusalem. Grotius takes Caius Cesar or Caligula to be the man of sin, and by the apostasy he understands his abominable wickedness. In the beginning of his government, he says, his plans of iniquity were concealed, and the hopes of all were excited in regard to his reign; but his secret iniquity was subsequently "revealed," and his true character understood. Wetstein understands by the "man of sin," "Titus and the Flavian house." He says that he does not understand it of the Roman Pontiff—who "is not one such as the demonstrative pronoun thrice repeated designates, and who neither sits in the temple of God, nor calls himself God—nor Caius, nor Simon Gioriae, nor any Jewish impostor, nor Simon Magus." Koppe refers it to the King mentioned in Dan. xi. 36. According to him, the reference is to a great apostasy of the Jews from the worship of God, and the "man of sin" is the Jewish people. Others have supposed that the reference is to Mohammed, and that the main characteristics of the prophecy may be found in him. Of the Papists, a part affirm that the apostasy is the falling away from Rome in the time of the Reformation, but the greater portion suppose that the allusion is to Antichrist, who, they say, will appear in the world before the great day of judgment, to combat religion and the saints. See these opinions stated at length, and examined, in Bishop Newton on the Prophecies, Diss. xxii. Some more recent expositors have referred it to Napoleon Bonaparte, and some (as Oldshausen) suppose that it refers to some one who has not yet appeared, in whom all the characteristics here specified will be found united. Most Protestant commentators have referred it to the great apostasy under the Papacy, and, by the "man of sin," they suppose there is allusion to the Roman Pontiff, the Pope. It is evident that we are in better circumstances to understand the passage than those were who immediately succeeded the apostles. Eighteen hundred years have passed away since the epistle was written, and the "day of the Lord" has not yet come, and we have an opportunity of inquiring, whether in all that long tract of time any one man can be found, or any series of men have arisen, to whom the description here given is applicable. If so, it is in accordance with all the proper rules of interpreting prophecy, to make such an application. If it is fairly applicable to the papacy, and cannot be applied in its great features to anything else, it is proper to regard it as having such an original reference. Happily, the expressions which are used by the apostle are, in themselves, not difficult of interpretation, and all that the expositor has to do is, to ascertain whether *in any one great apostasy all the things here mentioned have occurred.* If so, it is fair to apply the prophecy to such an event; if not so, we must wait still for its fulfilment. The word rendered "falling away" (ἀποστασία, *apostasy*), is of so *general* a character, that it may be applied to *any* departure from the faith as it was received in the time of the apostles. It occurs in the New Testament only here and in Acts xxi. 21, where it is rendered "to forsake"—"thou teachest all the Jews which are among us *to forsake* Moses"—*apostasy from Moses*—ἀποστασίαν ἀπὸ Μωϋσέως. The word means *a departing from,* or *a defection;* see the verb used in 1 Tim. iv. 1, "Some shall *depart from* the faith" —ἀποστήσονται; comp. Notes on that passage; see also Heb. iii. 12; Luke viii. 13; Acts v. 37. The reference here is evidently to some general falling away,

or to some great religious apostasy that was to occur, and which would be under one head, leader, or dynasty, and which would involve many in the same departure from the faith, and in the same destruction. The use of the article here, "*the* apostasy" (Gr.), Erasmus remarks, "signifies that great and before-predicted apostasy." It is evidently emphatic, showing that there had been a reference to this before, or that they understood well that there was to be such an apostasy. Paul says (ver. 5), that when he was with them, he had told them of these things. The writers in the New Testament often speak of such a defection under the name of Antichrist; see Rev. xiii. 14; 1 Jn. ii. 18, 22; iv. 3; 2 Jn. 7. ¶ *And that man of sin.* This is a Hebraism, meaning a man of eminent wickedness; one distinguished for depravity; comp. Jn. xvii. 12; Prov. vi. 12, in Heb. The use of the article here—ὁ ἄνθρωπος— "*the* man of sin," is also emphatic, as in the reference to "*the* falling away," and shows that there is allusion to one of whom they had before heard, and whose character was well known; who would be *the* wicked one by way of eminence; see also ver. 8, "*that* wicked"—ὁ ἄνομος. There are two general questions in regard to the proper interpretation of this appellative; the one is, whether it refers to an individual, or to a series of individuals of the same general character, aiming at the accomplishment of the same plans; and the other is, whether there has been any individual, or any series of individuals, since the time of the apostle, who, by eminence, deserved to be called, "*the* man of sin." That the phrase, "the *man* of sin," may refer to a *succession* of men of the same general character, and that it does so refer here, is evident from the following considerations: (1) The word "king" is used in Dan. vii. 25; xi. 36, to which places Paul seems to allude, to denote a succession of kings. (2) The same is true of the *beast* mentioned in Dan. vii., viii., Rev. xiii., representing a kingdom or empire through its successive changes and revolutions. (3)

The same is true of the "*woman arrayed in purple and scarlet*" (Rev. xvii. 4), which cannot refer to a single woman, but is the emblem of a continued corrupt administration. (4) It is clear that a succession is intended here, because the work assigned to "the man of sin," cannot be supposed to be that which could be accomplished by a single individual. The statement of the apostle is, that there were then tendencies to such an apostasy, and that the "man of sin" would be revealed at no distant period, and yet that he would continue his work of "lying wonders" until the coming of the Saviour. In regard to this "man of sin," it may be further observed, (1) that his appearing was to be *preceded* by "the great apostasy;" and (2) that he was to continue and perpetuate it. His rise was to be owing to a great departure from the faith, and then he was to be the principal agent in continuing it by "signs and lying wonders." He was not himself to *originate* the defection, but was to be the creation, or result of it. He was to rise upon it, or grow out of it, and, by artful arrangements adapted to that purpose, was to perpetuate it. The question then is, to whom this phrase, descriptive of a succession of individuals so eminent for wickedness that the name "*the* man of sin" could be applied, was designed by the Spirit of inspiration to refer. Bishop Newton has shown that it cannot refer to Caligula, to Simon Magus, to the revolt of the Jews from the Romans, or to the revolt of the Jews from the faith, or to the Flavian family, or to Luther, as some of the papists suppose, or to one man who will appear just before the end of the world, as others of the Romanists suppose; see his *Dissertations on the Prophecies*, xxii. pp. 393–402; comp. Oldshausen, *in loco*. The argument is too long to be inserted here. But can it be referred to the papacy? Can it denote the Pope of Rome, meaning not a single pope, but the succession? If all the circumstances of the entire passage can be shown to be fairly applicable to him, or if it can be shown

that all that is fairly implied in the *language* used here has received a fulfilment in him, then it is proper to regard it as having been designed to be so applied, and then this may be numbered among the prophecies that are in part fulfilled. The question now is on the applicability of the phrase "the man of sin" to the pope. That his rise was *preceded* by a great apostasy, or departure from the purity of the simple gospel, as revealed in the New Testament, cannot reasonably be doubted by anyone acquainted with the history of the church. That he is the *creation* or *result* of that apostasy, is equally clear. That he is the grand agent in *continuing* it, is equally manifest. Is the phrase itself one that is properly applicable to him? Is it proper to speak of the Pope of Rome, as he has actually appeared, as "*the* man of sin?" In reply to this, it might be sufficient to refer to the general character of the papacy, and to its influence in upholding and perpetuating various forms of iniquity in the world. It would be easy to show that there has been no dynasty or system that has contributed so much to uphold and perpetuate sins of various kinds on the earth, as the papacy. No other one has been so extensively and so long the patron of superstition; and there are vices of the grossest character which have all along been fostered by its system of celibacy, indulgences, monasteries, and absolutions. But it would be a better illustration of the meaning of the phrase "man of sin," as applicable to the Pope of Rome, to look at the general character of the popes themselves. Though there may have been some exceptions, yet there never has been a *succession* of men of so decidedly wicked character, as have occupied the papal throne since the great apostasy commenced. A very few references to the characters of the popes will furnish an illustration of this point. Pope Vagilius waded to the pontifical throne through the blood of his predecessor. Pope Joan —the Roman Catholic writers tell us —a female in disguise, was elected and confirmed pope, as John VIII.

4 Who opposeth and *exalteth   himself above all that is called

e Is.14.13; Re.13.6.

Platina says, that "she became with child by some of those that were round about her; that she miscarried, and died on her way from the Lateran to the temple." Pope Marcellinus sacrificed to idols. Concerning Pope Honorius, the council of Constantinople decreed, "We have caused Honorius, the late pope of Old Rome, to be *accursed;* for that in all things he followed the mind of Sergius the *heretic,* and confirmed his wicked doctrines." The council of Basil thus condemned Pope Eugenius: "We condemn and depose Pope Eugenius, a despiser of the holy canons; a disturber of the peace and unity of the church of God; a notorious offender of the whole universal church; a Simonist; a perjurer; a man incorrigible; a schismatic; a man fallen from the faith, and a wilful heretic." Pope John II. was publicly charged at Rome with incest. Pope John XIII. usurped the pontificate, spent his time in hunting, in lasciviousness, and monstrous forms of vice; he fled from the trial to which he was summoned, and was stabbed, being taken in the act of adultery. Pope Sixtus IV. licensed brothels at Rome. Pope Alexander VI. was, as a Roman Catholic historian says, "one of the greatest and most horrible monsters in nature that could scandalize the holy chair. His beastly morals, his immense ambition, his insatiable avarice, his detestable cruelty, his furious lusts, and monstrous incest with his daughter Lucretia, are, at large, described by Guicciardini Ciaconius, and other authentic papal historians." Of the popes, Platina, a Roman Catholic, says: "The chair of Saint Peter was usurped, rather than possessed, by monsters of wickedness, ambition, and bribery. They left no wickedness unpractised;" see *The New Englander,* April, 1844, pp. 285, 286. To no succession of men who have ever lived could the appellative, "*the* man of sin, be applied with so much propriety as to this succession. Yet they claim to have been

the true "successors" of the apostles, and there are *Protestants* that deem it of essential importance to be able to show that they have derived the true "succession" through such men. ¶ *Be revealed.* Be made manifest. There were, at the time when the apostle wrote, two remarkable things, (1) that there was already a *tendency* to such an apostasy as he spoke of; and (2) there was something which as yet prevented the appearance or the rise of the man of sin, ver. 7. When the hindrance which then existed should be taken out of the way, he would be manifested; see Notes on ver. 7. ¶ *The son of perdition.* This is the same appellation which the Saviour bestowed on Judas; see it explained in the Notes on John xviii. 12. It may mean either that he would be the cause of ruin to others, or that he would himself be devoted to destruction. It would seem here rather to be used in the latter sense, though this is not absolutely certain. The phrase, whichever interpretation be adopted, is used to denote one of eminent wickedness.

4. *Who opposeth.* That is, he is distinguished as an *opposer* of the great system which God has revealed for human salvation, and of those who would serve God in purity in the gospel of his Son. No Protestant will doubt that this has been the character of the papacy. The opposition of the general system to the gospel; the persecution of Wickliffe, of John Huss, of Jerome of Prague, of the Waldenses and the Reformers; the Inquisition, the cruelties in the reign of Mary, and the massacre of St. Bartholomew in France, are obvious illustrations of this. ¶ *And exalteth himself above all that is called God.* That is, whether among the heathens or the Jews; above a false God, or the true God. This could be true only of one who set aside the divine laws; who undertook to legislate where God only has a right to legislate, and whose legislation was contrary to that of God. Any claim of a

God, or that is worshipped; so that he, as God, sitteth in the

dominion over conscience; or any arrangement to set aside the divine laws, and to render them nugatory, would correspond with what is implied in this description. It cannot be supposed that anyone would openly *claim* to be superior to God, but the sense must be, that the enactments and ordinances of the "man of sin" would pertain to the province in which God only can legislate, and that the ordinances made by him would be such as to render nugatory the divine laws, by appointing others in their place. No one can reasonably doubt that all that is here affirmed may be found in the claims of the Pope of Rome. The assumptions of the papacy have related to the following things: (1) To authority above all the inferior orders of the priesthood—above all pastors, bishops, and primates. (2) Authority above all kings and emperors, "deposing some, and advancing others, obliging them to prostrate themselves before him, to kiss his toe, to hold his stirrup, to wait barefooted at his gate, treading even upon the neck, and kicking off the imperial crown with his foot" (Newton). Thus Gregory VII. made Henry IV. wait barefooted at his gate. Thus Alexander III. trod upon the neck of Alexander I. Thus Celestine kicked off the imperial crown of Henry VI. Thus the right was claimed, and asserted, of laying nations under interdict, of deposing kings, and of absolving their subjects from their oaths of allegiance. And thus the pope claimed the right over all unknown lands that might be discovered by Columbus, and apportioned the New World as he pleased—in all these things claiming prerogatives which can appertain only to God. (3) To authority over the *conscience*, in matters which can pertain only to God himself, and where he only can legislate. Thus it has been, and is, one of the claims set up for the pope that he is infallible. Thus he "forbids what God has commanded," as the marriage of the clergy, communion in both kinds, the use of the Scrip-

temple of God, showing himself that he is God.

---

tures for the common people. Thus he has set aside the second commandment by the appointment of image worship; and thus he claims the power of the remission of sins. Multitudes of things which Christ allows his people are forbidden by the papacy, and many things are enjoined, or allowed, directly contrary to the divine legislation. ¶ *Or that is worshipped*—σέβασμα. This word means *an object of worship;* see Acts xvii. 3, where it is rendered *devotions.* It may be applied to the worship of a heathen divinity, or of the true God. "It may refer to a person, an idol, or a place. Probably Paul refers here to the heroes and other subordinate divinities of the heathen mythology" (Oldshausen). No one can doubt that the pope has claimed higher honours, as the vicegerent of Christ, than was ever rendered in the ancient "hero worship." ¶ *So that he, as God.* That is, claiming the honours due to God. This expression would not imply that he actually claimed *to be* the true God, but only that he sits in the temple, and manifests himself *as if* he were God. He claims such honours and such reverence as the true God *would* if he should appear in human form. It should be observed here, however, that there is much reason to doubt the genuineness of this phrase —"*as God*"—ὡς Θεόν. Mill supposes that it was inserted from the context. It is marked with an asterisk in the Vulgate, the Coptic, and the Syriac, and is omitted by many of the fathers; see Mill and Wetstein. It is rejected by Griesbach and Lachmann, and marked as doubtful by Hahn. It is defended, however, by Matthaei, Koppe, Knapp, and Schott. The sense is not materially affected whether it be regarded as genuine or not. ¶ *Sitteth in the temple of God.* That is, in the Christian church. It is by no means necessary to understand this of the temple at Jerusalem, which was standing at the time this epistle was written, for (1) the phrase "the temple of God" is several times used with reference to the Christian church, 1 Cor. iii. 16, 17; 2 Cor. vi. 16; Eph. ii. 21; Rev. iii. 12; and (2) the temple was the proper symbol of the church, and an apostle trained amidst the Hebrew institutions would naturally speak of the church as the temple of God. The temple at Jerusalem was regarded as the peculiar dwelling-place of God on earth. When the Christian church was founded, it was spoken of as the peculiar dwelling-place of God; see the passages referred to above. He dwelt among his people. He was with them, and walked with them, and manifested himself among them—as he had done in the ancient temple. The usage in the New Testament would not lead us to restrict this language to an *edifice*, or a "church," as the word is now commonly used, but rather to suppose that it denotes the church as a society, and the idea is, that the Antichrist here referred to would present himself in the midst of that church as claiming the honours due to God alone. In the temple at Jerusalem, God himself presided. There he gave laws to his people; there he manifested himself as God; and there he was worshipped. The reign of the "man of sin" would be *as if* he should sit there. In the Christian church he would usurp the place which God had occupied in the temple. He would claim divine attributes and homage. He would give laws and responses as God did there. He would be regarded as the head of all ecclesiastical power; the source from which all authority emanated; the same in the Christian church which God himself was in the temple. This does not then refer primarily to the pope as sitting in any particular church on any particular occasion, but to his claiming *in* the church of Christ the authority and homage which God had in the temple at Jerusalem. In whatever place, whether in a cathedral or elsewhere, this authority should be exercised, all that the language here conveys would be fulfilled. No one can fail to see that the authority claimed by the Pope of Rome meets the full force of the language

used here by the apostle. ¶ *Showing himself that he is God.* This does not necessarily mean that he actually, in so many words, claimed *to be God;* but that he usurped the place of God, and claimed the prerogatives of God. If the names of God are given to him, or are claimed by him; if he receives the honours due to God; if he asserts a dominion like that of God, then all that the language fairly implies will be fulfilled. The following expressions, applied to the Pope of Rome by Catholic writers, without any rebuke from the papacy, will show how entirely applicable this is to the pretended head of the church. He has been styled "Our Lord God the pope; another God upon earth; king of kings and lord of lords. The same is the dominion of God and the pope. To believe that our Lord God the pope might not decree as he decreed, is heresy. The power of the pope is greater than all created power, and extends itself to things celestial, terrestrial, and infernal. The pope doeth whatsoever he listeth, even things unlawful, and is more than God;" see the authority for these extraordinary declarations in Bishop Newton on the Prophecies, xxii. How can it be doubted that the reference here is to the papacy? Language could not be plainer, and it is not possible to conceive that anything can ever occur which would furnish a more manifest fulfilment of this prophecy. Indeed, interpreted by the claims of the papacy, it stands among the very clearest of all the predictions in the Sacred Scriptures.

5. *Remember ye not, that, when I was yet with you, I told you these things?* The whole subject of the second advent of the Saviour seems to have constituted an important part of the instructions of Paul when at Thessalonica. He now refers them to what he had told them respecting the great apostasy, to show that his views had not changed, and that he did not mean to have them understand that the world would soon come to an end. He had stated these things to them, implying that a considerable interval *must* elapse before the Saviour

5 Remember ye not, that, when I was yet with you, I told you these things?

6 And now ye know what [1] withholdeth, that he might be revealed in his time.

[1] or, *holdeth*.

would appear. Much of the *obscurity* of this prophecy arises from the fact, that the apostle alludes to things which he had told them when with them, of which we have now no knowledge. Hence, what would be perfectly clear to them, on reading this letter, is now difficult to be understood. 6. *And now ye know what withholdeth*. Marg., *holdeth*. The reference is, to something that then operated to *constrain* or *hold back* the obvious tendency of things, so that the "man of sin" should not at once appear, or so that things should not soon so develop themselves as to give rise to this antichristian power. There were causes at work even then, which *would* ultimately lead to this; but there was also something which checked the tendency of things, so that the revelation or development of the "man of sin" was put off to a future period. The obvious meaning of this would be, that, when the apostle wrote, there was a tendency to what would occur under the great apostasy, and that this would soon develop itself if it were not restrained. If the reference is to the papacy, this would consist in corruptions already existing in the church, having a resemblance to those which afterwards existed under that system, or which were the *germ* of that system. If there was a tendency towards the concentration of all power in an individual in the church; if there was an assumption of authority by one class of ministers above another; if there was a denial of the "parity of the clergy," the tendency would have been to that ultimate assumption of authority which is found in the Romish hierarchy. But conjecture is useless as to what was the precise form in which this tendency then began to develop itself. That the corruptions early began in the church which terminated in the papacy, and which led on directly to it, we know; and that the apostle was able to fore-

see and predict such a final development, shows that he was under the influence of inspiration. It is not known precisely what is referred to by the phrase "what withholdeth," τὸ κατέχον. The phrase means, properly, something that *holds back*, or *restrains*. The word here is in the *neuter* gender, "*what* withholdeth." In the following verse it is in the *masculine* gender, ὁ κατέχων — "he that letteth," or withholdeth; and the reference would seem to be to some agency or state of things under the control of an *individual*, or of *some civil power*, that then operated as a restraint on the natural tendency of things. Of this, the apostle says, *they* had had full information; but *we* can only conjecture what it was. The restraining power of anything controlled by an individual, or of any government, or the restraining power of God, would meet all that the phrase implies. The most natural interpretation is that which refers it to civil power, meaning that there was something in the form of the existing administration which would prevent this development until that restraint should be removed. The supposition that there was even then a tendency to concentrate all ecclesiastical power at Rome, and that while the civil authority remained there it would not suffer ecclesiastical power to grow to the exorbitant height which it ultimately reached, will meet all that is implied in the language. ¶ *That he might be revealed in his time*. The man of sin. The meaning is, that there was then a restraint operating which would prevent the development of this antichristian power until the proper time; that is, till the state of the world should be such that in the divine arrangements it would be proper to permit it. It was not to be permitted until the gospel should be extensively preached, and had had an opportunity of showing its fair effects on the nations; until it

7 For the mystery of iniquity doth *already work: only he who

*1 Jn.4.3.

now letteth, *will let*, until he be taken out of the way.

---

had become so planted and established that even the rise of this antichristian power could not effectually uproot it. Had the "man of sin" been permitted to rise at once, the consequence might have been that the new religion would have been crushed, so that it could never have revived again. There was then a providential arrangement by which this growth of wickedness should be checked and restrained, until the new religion should take deep root in the earth, and its perpetuity should be secured. Then the great trial was to be permitted under the "man of sin."

7. *For the mystery of iniquity.* On the meaning of the word *mystery*, see Notes on Rom. xi. 25; comp. 1 Cor. ii. 7; Eph. i. 9; iii. 3; Col. i. 26. It means properly that which *is hidden* or *concealed;* not necessarily that which is *unintelligible.* The "mystery of iniquity" seems here to refer to some *hidden* or *concealed* depravity —some form of sin which was working secretly and silently, and which had not yet developed itself. Any secret sources of iniquity in the church— anything that tended to corrupt its doctrines, and to destroy the simplicity of the faith of the gospel, would correspond with the meaning of the word. Doddridge correctly supposes that this may refer to the pride and ambition of some ministers, the factious temper of some Christians, the imposing of unauthorized severities, the worship of angels, &c. ¶ *Doth already work.* There are elements of these corruptions already existing in the church. Bishop Newton maintains that the foundations of popery were laid in the apostle's days, and that the superstructure was raised by degrees; and this is entirely in accordance with the statements of the apostle Paul. In his own time, he says, there were things which, if not restrained, would expand and ripen into that apostasy. He has not told us particularly to what he refers, but there are several intimations in his

writings, as well as in other parts of the New Testament, that even in the apostolic age there existed the elements of those corruptions which were afterwards developed and embodied in the papacy. Even "then," says Bishop Newton, "*idolatry* was stealing into the church (1 Cor. x. 14), and a voluntary humility and worshipping of angels." [Col. ii. 18; see, however, my Note on that passage.] "There existed strife and divisions (1 Cor. iii. 3), an adulterating and handling the word of God deceitfully (2 Cor. ii. 17; iv. 2), a gain of godliness, teaching of things for filthy lucre's sake (1 Tim. vi. 5; Tit. i. 11), a vain observation of festivals (Gal. iv. 10), a vain distinction of meats (1 Cor. viii. 8), a neglecting of the body (Col. ii. 23), traditions, and commandments, and doctrines of men (Col. ii. 8, 22);" comp. 3 Jn. 9, "Diotrephes, who loveth to have the pre-eminence." These things constituted the elements of the corruptions which were afterwards developed in the papacy, and which are embodied in that system. An eye that could see all, would even then have perceived that, if there were no restraint, these incipient corruptions would grow up into that system, and would be expanded into all the corruptions and arrogant claims which have ever characterized it; comp. 1 Jn. iv. 3. ¶ *Only he who now letteth.* Who now *hinders*, or *restrains* — ὁ κατέχων. This is the same word which is used in ver. 6, and rendered "withholdeth," except that it is there in the neuter gender. There can be no doubt that there is reference to the same restraining power, or the same power under the control of an individual; but what that was, is not quite certain. It was some power which operated as a check on the growing corruptions then existing, and which prevented their full development, but which was to be removed at no distant period, and whose removal would give an opportunity for these corruptions to develop themselves, and for the full revelation of the man of sin. Such a supposition as that the civil power of Rome was such a restraint, operating to prevent the assumption of the ecclesiastical claims of supremacy which afterwards characterized the papacy, will correspond with all that is necessarily implied in the language. ¶ Will let, *until he be taken out of the way.* This will be an effectual check on these corruptions, preventing their full development, until it is removed, and then the man of sin will appear. The supposition which will best suit this language is, that there was then some civil restraint, preventing the development of existing corruptions, but that there would be a removal, or withdrawing of that restraint; and that then the tendency of the existing corruptions would be seen. It is evident, as Oldshausen remarks, that this resisting or restraining power must be something *out* of the church, and distinguished from the antichristian tendency itself—von der Kirche und vom Antichristenthum. It is necessary, therefore, to understand this of the restraints of civil power. Was there, then, any fact in history which will accord with this interpretation? The belief among the primitive Christians was, that what hindered the rise of the man of sin was the Roman empire, and therefore "they prayed for its peace and welfare, as knowing that when the Roman empire should be dissolved and broken in pieces, the empire of the man of sin would be raised on its ruins" (Bp. Newton). How this revolution was effected, may be seen by the statement of Machiavel. "The emperor of Rome, quitting Rome to dwell at Constantinople" (in the fourth century, under Constantine), "the Roman empire began to decline, but the church of Rome augmented as fast. Nevertheless, until the coming in of the Lombards, all Italy being under the dominion of either emperors or kings, the bishops assumed no more power than what was due to their doctrine and manners; in civil affairs they were subject to the civil power. But Theodoric, king of the Goths, fixing his seat at Ravenna, was that which advanced their inte-

rest, and made them more considerable in Italy, for there being no other prince left in Rome, the Romans were forced for protection to pay greater allegiance to the pope. The Lombards having invaded and reduced Italy into several cantons, the pope took the opportunity, and began to hold up his head. For being, as it were, governor and principal of Rome, the emperor of Constantinople and the Lombards bare him a respect, so that the Romans (by mediation of their pope) began to treat and confederate with Longinus [the emperor's lieutenant], and the Lombards, not as subjects, but as equals and companions; which said custom continuing, and the pope's entering into alliance sometimes with the Lombards, and sometimes with the Greeks, contracted great reputation to their dignity" (*Hist. of Florence,* b. i. p. 6, of the English translation). A more extended quotation on the same subject may be seen in Newton on the Prophecies, pp. 407, 408. To any one acquainted with the decline and fall of the Roman empire, nothing can be more manifest than the correspondence of the facts in history respecting the rise of the papacy, and the statement of the apostle Paul here. The simple facts are these: (1) There were early corruptions in the church at Rome, as there were elsewhere, but peculiarly there, as Rome was the seat of philosophy and of power. (2) There were great efforts made by the bishop of Rome to increase his authority, and there was a steady approximation to what he subsequently claimed—that of being universal bishop. (3) There was a constant tendency to yield to him deference and respect in all matters. (4) This was kept in check as long as Rome was the seat of the imperial power. Had that power remained there, it would have been impossible for the Roman bishop ever to have obtained the civil and ecclesiastical eminence which he ultimately did. Rome could not have had *two* heads, both claiming and exercising supreme power; and there never could have been a "revelation of the man of sin." (5) Constantine

8 And then shall that Wicked be revealed, whom the Lord *g*shall consume *h*with the spirit of his

mouth, and *i*shall destroy with the brightness of his coming:

removed the seat of empire to Constantinople; and this removal or "taking away" of the only restraint on the ambitious projects of the Roman bishops, gave all the opportunity which could be desired for the growth of the papal power. In all history there cannot, probably, be found a series of events corresponding more accurately with a prophetic statement than this; and there is every evidence, therefore, that these are the events to which the Spirit of inspiration referred.

8. *And then shall that Wicked be revealed.* ὁ ἄνομος—"*the* wicked one," referring to the "man of sin," and called "*the* wicked one" because of the eminent depravity of the system of which he was to be the head; see Notes on ver. 3. ¶ *Whom the Lord shall consume.* The Lord Jesus; see Notes on Acts i. 24. The word *consume* here—ἀναλώσει—means to *destroy;* see Gal. v. 15; Luke ix. 54. The word would be applicable to any kind of destruction. The *methods* by which this will be done are immediately specified—and it is of much importance to understand them, if this refers to the papacy. ¶ *With the spirit of his mouth.* What goes out of his mouth, or what he speaks; that is, *word, truth, command,* or *gospel*—all of which he may be regarded as *speaking.* In Rev. i. 16; xix. 15, 21, it is said of the Redeemer that "a sharp two-edged sword goeth out of his mouth;" that is, his word, doctrine, or command—*what he speaks* —is *like* a sharp sword. It will cut deep; will lay open the heart; will destroy his enemies. Comp. Isa. xi. 4, "With the breath of his lips shall he slay the wicked." The reference in the passage before us is to *one* of the methods which would be employed to "destroy" the man of sin; and the sense is, that it would be by what is *spoken* by the Redeemer. This may refer either to what he will say *at his coming,* or to his *truth*—already spoken; to what has gone from his

lips, by whomsoever uttered; and the meaning then is, that one of the grand agencies for destroying this antichristian power is the *truth* spoken or revealed by the Saviour—that is, his pure gospel. If this latter be the true interpretation, it may mean that the process for his destruction may have commenced long anterior to the personal appearing of the Redeemer, but that the *complete* destruction of this power will be accomplished by the splendour of his Second Advent. It cannot be denied, however, that the most obvious interpretation is that which refers both clauses in the sentence to the same period—that of his second coming. Still, it is not improper to suppose that it may be implied that his power will be weakened and diminished by the influence of the gospel, though it may not be *wholly* destroyed until the second coming of the Saviour. ¶ *And shall destroy* —καταργήσει. Shall bring to naught; cause to cease; put an end to. This is, in some respects, a stronger word than that which in the former part of the verse is rendered *consume.* It denotes a more entire *destruction* than that, though it does not refer so much to any positive *agency* by which it will be done. In the former word, the attention is directed more to the *agency* by which the destruction will be effected—to the exertion of some kind of *power* to do it; in this word the attention is directed rather to the *entireness* or *totality* of the destruction. The antichristian domination will *wholly* cease, or be *entirely* destroyed. The *words* would naturally harmonize with the idea that there would be a somewhat gradual process under the operation of *truth* toward the destruction of the man of sin, but that the *complete* annihilation of his power would be by some more manifest exhibition of the personal glory of the Saviour. ¶ *With the brightness of his coming.* This is evidently a Hebraism, meaning his splen-

9 *Even him*, whose coming is after the working of Satan, with all power and signs and lying wonders,

did or glorious appearing. The Greek word, however, rendered *"brightness"* (ἐπιφανεία—*epiphany*) means merely *an appearing* or *appearance*. So it is used in 1 Tim. vi. 4; 2 Tim. i. 10; iv. 1, 8; Tit. ii. 13, in all which places it is rendered *appearing*, and refers to the manifestation of the Saviour when he shall come to judge the world. It is used nowhere else in the New Testament. There is no necessary idea of *splendour* in the word, and the idea is not, as our translation would seem to convey, that there would be *such a dazzling light*, or *such unsufferable brightness* that all would be consumed before it, but that he would *appear*, and that this antichristian power would be destroyed *by* his appearing; that is, by *himself* when he would return. The agency in doing it would not be his *brightness*, but *himself*. It would seem to follow from this, that, however this enormous power of wickedness might be weakened by truth, the final triumph over it would be reserved for the Son of God himself on his second return to our world. Yet, if this be so, it need not lessen our zeal in endeavouring to diminish the power of these corruptions; to establish and spread the truth, or to convert the defenders of these errors to a better faith.

9. Even him, *whose coming is after the working of Satan.* Greek, κατ᾽ ἐνέργειαν τοῦ Σατανᾶ. According to the energy of Satan; that is, the energetic or efficient operation of Satan. The word rendered *after*, it need not be said to one who looks at the Greek, does not refer to *time*, but is a preposition, meaning *according to; in conformity with;* meaning that the manner of his appearing would be accompanied by such works as would show that the agency of Satan was employed, and such as he only could produce. It does not mean that *the coming of the Lord Jesus* would be *after* Satan had worked in this manner, but that the manifestation of that wicked one would be with such demonstrations of power and wonder as

Satan only could effect. The system over which he presides is originated by Satan, and sustained by those things which he alone can perform. On the word *Satan*, see Notes on Job i. 6. The idea is that it would be under the direction and control of the great enemy of God, and that the things on which it would rely for support could be traced to his agency. In all the pretended miracles to which it would appeal, there would be nothing which Satan could not accomplish. ¶ *With all power.* With all the power which Satan can exhibit; meaning also, that there would be a great exertion of power in the case. It would not be a feeble and imbecile dominion. The dominion of the papacy has been one of the *most powerful* on earth. There has been none which has been more dreaded by the nations of the earth—and there have been times when nations trembled, and kings turned pale on their thrones, at the frown of the pope. ¶ *And signs.* This word frequently denotes real miracles, but not necessarily so. It may be applied to pretended miracles as well as real, and is undoubtedly so used here, as it is connected with *"lying wonders,"* and as it is said that the thing wrought would be "after the working of Satan." There is doubtless reference to such "signs and wonders" as the Saviour mentions in Mat. xxiv. 24; see Notes on that passage. It is hardly necessary to remark that the papacy has always relied for support on its pretended miracles. Even in our own age the wonders performed by the Prince Hohenlohe, and by the pretended seamless garment of the Saviour, have been proclaimed as true miracles, and as furnishing indubitable evidence of the truth of the Roman Catholic system. The dissolving of the blood of St. Januarius, the removal of Pilate's stairs to Rome, and the transportation to Italy of the "house of our Lady," are among the miracles to which there is a constant reference in the papal communion. In addition

10 And with *all deceivableness of unrighteousness in them that perish; because they received not

k He.3.13.

the *love of the truth, that they might be saved.

11 And for this cause God shall

l 1 Co.16.22.

to these and to all similar pretensions, there is the power claimed of performing a miracle at the pleasure of the priest by the change of bread and wine into the "body and blood, the soul and divinity" of the Lord Jesus. In 1756, there was published in London a book entitled, "The Miraculous Power of the Church of Christ, asserted through each successive century, from the apostle down to the present time." The power of working miracles has been one of the standing claims of the papacy. ¶ *And lying wonders.* False or pretended miracles. They would be such as would be claimed to be miracles; such as would excite wonder; and yet such as were false and delusive. No Protestant assuredly needs to be convinced that this is just the character of the pretended miracles of the papacy. It would be impossible for language to describe them more clearly, in the apprehension of all Protestants, than is done in this language of the apostle Paul.

10. *And with all deceivableness of unrighteousness.* There are two ideas here. The first is, that there would be *deceit;* and the other is, that it would be for the purpose of promoting unrighteousness or iniquity. The iniquitous system would be maintained by fraudulent methods. No one who has read Pascal's *Provincial Letters* can ever doubt that this description is applicable to the system of the Jesuits; and no one familiar with the acts of the papacy, as they have always been practised, can doubt that the whole system is accurately described by this language. The plausible reasoning by which the advocates of that system have palliated and apologized for sins of various kinds, has been among its most remarkable features. ¶ *In them that perish. Among* those who will perish; that is, among the abandoned and wicked. The reference is to men of corrupt minds and lives, over whom this system would have power; countenancing

them in their depravity, and fitting them still farther for destruction. The idea is, that these acts would have especial reference to men who would be lost at anyrate, and who would be sustained in their wickedness by this false and delusive system. ¶ *Because they received not the love of the truth.* They prefer this system of error and delusion to the simple and pure gospel, by which they might have been saved.

11. *And for this cause.* Because they choose error, or their hearts love that more than they do truth. The original reason then of their embracing and adhering to the system was not an arbitrary decree on the part of God, but that they did not love the truth. Hence, he gave them up to this system of error. If a man strongly *prefers* error to truth, and sin to holiness, it is not wrong to allow him freely to evince his own preference. ¶ *God shall send them strong delusion.* Gr., "energy of deceit;" a Hebraism, meaning strong deceit. The agency of God is here distinctly recognized, in accordance with the uniform statements of the Scriptures, respecting evil; comp. Exod. vii. 13; ix. 12; x. 1, 20, 27; xi. 10; xiv. 8; Deut. x. 30; Isa. xlv. 7. On the nature of this agency, see Notes on Jn. xii. 40. It is not necessary here to suppose that there was any positive influence on the part of God in *causing* this delusion to come upon them, but all the force of the language will be met, as well as the reasoning of the apostle, by supposing that God withdrew all restraint, and suffered men simply *to show* that they did not love the truth. God often places men in circumstances to develop their own nature, and it cannot be shown to be wrong that he should do so. If men *have* no love of the truth, and no desire to be saved, it is not improper that they should be allowed to manifest this. How it happened that they *had* no "love of the truth," is a different question, to which the remarks

send them ^mstrong delusion, that
they should believe a lie:
12 Thatⁿ they all might be

m Eze.14.9; Ro.1.24.   n De.32.35.

of the apostle do not appertain; comp.
Notes on Rom. ix. 17, 18; i. 24.
¶ *That they should believe a lie.* This
does not affirm that God *wished* them
to believe a lie; nor that he would
not have preferred that they should
believe the truth; nor that he exerted any direct agency to cause them
to believe a lie. It means merely
that he left them, because they did
not love the truth, to believe what
was false, and what would end in their
destruction. Can anyone doubt that
this constantly occurs in the world?
Men are left to believe impostors; to
trust to false guides; to rely on unfounded information; to credit those
who live to delude and betray the innocent; and to follow those who lead
them to ruin. God does not inter-
pose by direct power to preserve
them. Can anyone doubt this? Yet
this is not peculiarly the doctrine of
revelation. The fact pertains just as
much to the infidel as it does to the
believer in Christianity, and he is
just as much bound to explain it as
the Christian is. It belongs to our
world—to us all—and it should not be
charged on Christianity as a doctrine
pertaining peculiarly to that system.
12. *That they all might be damned.*
The word *damned* we commonly apply
now exclusively to future punishment,
and it has a *harsher* signification than
the original word; comp. Notes, 1
Cor. xi. 29. The Greek word—κρίνω
—means to judge, determine, decide;
and then to condemn, Rom. ii. 27;
xiv. 22; Jam. iv. 11; John vii. 51;
Luke xix. 22; Acts xiii. 27. It may
be applied to the judgment of the last
day (John v. 22; viii. 50; Acts xvii.
31; Rom. iii. 6; 2 Tim. iv. 1), but
not necessarily. The word *judged* or
condemned, would, in this place, express all that the Greek word necessarily conveys. Yet there can be no
doubt that the *judgment* or *condemnation* which is referred to, is that which
will occur when the Saviour will appear. It does not seem to me to be

damned who believed not the
truth, but had pleasure in unrighteousness.

a necessary interpretation of this to
suppose that it teaches that God
would send a strong delusion that they
should believe a lie, *in order* that all
might be damned who did not believe
the truth; or that he *desired* that
they should be damned, and sent this
as the means of securing it; but the
sense is, that this course of events
would be allowed to occur, *so that*
(ἵνα—not εἰς τὸ) all who do not love
the truth would be condemned. The
particle here used, and rendered
"*that*" (ἵνα), in connection with the
phrase "all might be damned," is
employed in two general senses: either
as marking the end, purpose, or cause
for, or *on account of*, which anything
is done; *to the end that*, or *in order
that it may be so and so;* or as
marking simply the result, event,
or upshot of an action, *so that*,
so as that (Robinson, *Lex.*). In
the latter case it denotes merely that
something will really take place,
without indicating that such was the
design of the agent, or that what
brought it about was in order that it
might take place. It is also used,
in the later Greek, so as neither to
mark the purpose, nor to indicate that
the event would occur, but merely
to point out that to which the preceding words refer. It is not proper,
therefore, to infer, that this passage
teaches that all these things would
be brought about in the arrangements of Providence, *in order* that
they might be damned who came
under their influence. The passage
teaches that such would be the result; that the connection between
these delusions and the condemnation
of those who were deluded, would be
certain. It cannot be proved from
the Scriptures that God sends on men
strong delusions, *in order* that they
may be damned. No such construction should be put on a passage of
Scripture if it can be avoided, and it
cannot be shown that it is necessary
here. ¶ *Who believed not the truth.*

13 But *o* we are bound to give thanks alway to God for you, brethren beloved of the Lord, because God hath from the beginning *p* chosen you to salvation through sanctification of the Spirit and belief of the truth;

o ch.1.3.　　p Ep.1.4; 1 Th.1.4; 1 Pe.1.2.

The grounds or reasons why they would be damned are now stated. One would be that they did not believe the truth—not that God sent upon them delusion *in order* that they might be damned. That men will be condemned for not believing the truth, and that it will be right thus to condemn them, is everywhere the doctrine of the Scriptures, and is equally the doctrine of common sense; see Notes on Mark xvi. 16. ¶ *But had pleasure in unrighteousness.* This is the second ground or reason of their condemnation. If men have *pleasure* in sin, it is proper that they should be punished. There *can* be no more just ground of condemnation than that a man *loves to do wrong.*

13. *But we are bound to give thanks alway to God for you.* See Notes on chap. i. 3. ¶ *Because God hath from the beginning chosen you to salvation.* The following important things are affirmed or implied here: (1) That God had *chosen* or *elected* them (εἵλετο) to salvation. The doctrine of *election*, therefore, is true. (2) That this was from *the beginning* (ἀπ᾽ ἀρχῆς); that is, from eternity; see Notes on John i. 1; Eph. i. 4; iii. 9–11. The doctrine of *eternal* election is, therefore, true. (3) That this was the choice of the persons to whom Paul referred. The doctrine of *personal* election is, therefore, true. (4) That this is a reason for thanksgiving. Why should it not be? Can there be any higher ground of praise or gratitude than that God has chosen us to be eternally holy and happy, and that he has from eternity designed that we should be so? Whatever, therefore, may be the feelings with which those who are *not* chosen to salvation, regard this doctrine, it is clear that those who

14 Whereunto *q* he called you by our gospel, to the obtaining of the *r* glory of our Lord Jesus Christ.

15 Therefore, brethren, stand fast, and hold the traditions which ye have been taught, whether by word or our epistle.

q 1 Pe.5.10.　　　r Jn.17.22.

have evidence that they *are* chosen should make it a subject of grateful praise. They can have no more exalted source of gratitude than that they are chosen to eternal life. ¶ *Through sanctification of the Spirit.* Being made holy by the divine Spirit. It is not without respect to character, but it is a choice *to* holiness and then *to* salvation. No one can have evidence that he is chosen to salvation except as he has evidence that he is sanctified by the Spirit; see Notes on Eph. i. 4. ¶ *And belief of the truth.* In connection with believing the truth. No one who is not a believer in the truth can have evidence that God has chosen him.

14. *Whereunto he called you by our gospel.* He made the gospel as preached by us the means of calling you to salvation. That is, God has chosen you to salvation from eternity, and has made the gospel as preached by us the means of carrying that eternal purpose into effect. ¶ *To the obtaining of the glory of our Lord Jesus Christ.* That you may partake of the same glory as the Saviour in heaven; see Notes on John xvii. 22, 24.

15. *Therefore.* In view of the fact that you are thus chosen from eternity, and that you are to be raised up to such honour and glory. ¶ *Stand fast.* Amidst all the temptations which surround you; comp. Notes on Eph. vi. 10–14. ¶ *And hold the traditions which ye have been taught.* On the word *traditions*, see Notes on Mat. xv. 2. It means properly things delivered over from one to another; then anything orally delivered—any precept, doctrine, or law. It is frequently employed to denote that which is not written, as contradistinguished from that which is

16 Now our Lord Jesus Christ himself, and God even our Father, *which hath loved us, and

s Jn.13.1; Re.1.5.

hath given *us* everlasting consolation and *good hope through grace,

t 1 Pe.1.3.

written (comp. Mat. xv. 2), but not necessarily or always; for here the apostle speaks of the "traditions which they had been taught *by his epistle;*" comp. Notes, 1 Cor. xi. 2. Here it means the doctrines or precepts which they had received from the apostle, whether when he was with them, or after he left them; whether communicated by preaching or by letter. This passage can furnish no authority for holding the "traditions" which have come down from ancient times, and which profess to have been derived from the apostles; for, (1) there is no evidence that any of those traditions were given by the apostles; (2) many of them are manifestly so trifling, false, and contrary to the writings of the apostles, that they could not have been delivered by them; (3) if any of them are genuine, it is impossible to separate them from those which are false; (4) we have all that is necessary for salvation in the written word; and (5) there is not the least evidence that the apostle here meant to refer to any such thing. He speaks only of what had been delivered to them *by himself,* whether orally or by letter; not what was delivered from one to another as *from* him. There is no intimation here that they were to hold anything as from him which they had not received directly from him, either by his own instructions personally or by letter. With what propriety, then, can this passage be adduced to prove that we are to hold the traditions which professedly come to us through a great number of intermediate persons? Where is the evidence here that the church was to hold those unwritten traditions, and transmit them to future times? ¶ *Whether by word.* By preaching, when we were with you. It does not mean that he had sent any oral message to them by a third person. ¶ *Or our epistle.* The

former letter which he had written to them.
16. *Now our Lord Jesus Christ himself.* This expression is equivalent to this: "I pray our Lord Jesus, and our Father, to comfort you." It is really a prayer offered to the Saviour —a recognition of Christ as the source of consolation as well as the Father, and a union of his name with that of the Father in invoking important blessings. It is such language as could be used only by one who regarded the Lord Jesus as divine. ¶ *And God even our Father.* Gr., "And God, *and* (και) our Father;" though not incorrectly rendered "*even* our Father." If it should be contended that the use of the word "and"—"our Lord Jesus Christ, *and* God," proves that the Lord Jesus is a different *being* from God—the use of the same word "and" would prove that the "Father" is a different being from God. But the truth is, the apostle meant to speak of the Father *and* the Son as the *common* source of the blessing for which he prayed. ¶ *Which hath loved us.* Referring particularly to the Father. The love which is referred to is that manifested in redemption, or which is shown us through Christ; see John iii. 16; 1 John iv. 9. ¶ *And hath given* us *everlasting consolation.* Not temporary comfort, but that which will endure for ever. The joys of religion are not like other joys. *They* soon fade away;—they always terminate at death;—they cease when trouble comes, when sickness invades the frame, when wealth or friends depart, when disappointment lowers, when the senses by age refuse to minister as they once did to our pleasures. The comforts of religion depend on no such contingencies. They live through all these changes—attend us in sickness, poverty, bereavement, losses, and age; they are with us in death, and they are perpetual and unchanging beyond the grave. ¶ *And good hope through*

17 Comfort your hearts, ^uand stablish you in every good word and work.

grace. See Notes on Rom. v. 2, 5; Heb. vi. 19.

17. *Comfort your hearts.* Notes, 1 Thes. iii. 2; v. 11, 14. The Thessalonians were in the midst of trials, and Paul prayed that they might have the full consolations of their religion. ¶ *And stablish you.* Make you firm and steadfast, 1 Thes. iii. 2, 13. ¶ *In every good word and work.* In every true doctrine, and in the practice of every virtue.

REMARKS.

This chapter is very important in reference to the rise of that great antichristian power which has exerted, and which still exerts, so baleful an influence over the Christian world. Assuming now that it refers to the Papacy, in accordance with the exposition which has been given, there are a few important reflections to which it gives rise.

(1) The Second Advent of the Redeemer is an event which is distinctly predicted in the Scriptures. This is assumed in this chapter; and though Paul corrects some errors into which the Thessalonians had fallen, he does not suggest this as one of them. Their error was in regard to the *time* of his appearing—not the *fact.*

(2) The *time* when he will appear is not made known to men. The apostles did not pretend to designate it, nor did the Saviour himself, Mat. xxiv. 36; Mark xiii. 32; Acts i. 7.

(3) The course of reasoning in this chapter would lead to the expectation that a considerable time would elapse before the Saviour would appear. The apostles, therefore, did not believe that the end of the world was near, and they did not teach false doctrine on the subject, as infidels have often alleged. No one who attentively and candidly studies this chapter, it seems to me, can suppose that Paul believed that the Second Advent of the Saviour would occur within a short time, or during the generation when he lived. He has described a long series of events which were to intervene before the Saviour

would appear — events which, if the interpretation which has been given is correct, have been in fact in a process of development from that time to the present, and which, it must have been foreseen even then, would require a long period before they would be completed. There was to be a great apostasy. There were at that time subtle causes at work which would lead to it. They were, however, then held in check and restrained by some foreign influence. But the time would come when that foreign power would be withdrawn. Then these now hidden and restrained corruptions would develop themselves into this great antichristian power. That power would sustain itself by a series of pretended miracles and lying wonders — and, *after* all this, would be the second coming of the Son of man. But this would require time. Such a series of events would not be completed in a day, or in a single generation. They would require a succession—perhaps a *long* succession—of years, before these developments would be complete. It is clear, therefore, that the apostle did not hold that the Lord Jesus would return in that age, and that he did not mean to be understood as teaching it; and consequently it should not be said that he or his fellow-apostles were mistaken in the statements which they have recorded respecting the second coming of the Lord Jesus and the end of the world.

(4) The apostle Paul was inspired. He has recorded in this chapter a distinct prediction of an important series of events which were to occur at a future, and most of them at quite a remote period. They were such that they could have been foreseen by no natural sagacity, and no human skill. There were, indeed, corruptions existing then in the church, but no mere natural sagacity could have foreseen that they would grow up into that enormous system which would overshadow the Christian world, and live for so many ages.

(5) If these predictions referred to the Papacy, we may see how we are to regard that system of religion. The simple inquiry, if this interpretation is correct, is, *How did the apostle Paul regard that system to which he referred?* Did he consider it to be the true church? Did he regard it as a church at all? The language which he uses will enable us easily to answer these questions. He speaks of it as "the apostasy;" he speaks of the head of that system as "the man of sin," "the son of perdition," "the wicked one," and as "opposing and exalting himself above all that is called God;" he says that his "coming is after the working of Satan, with lying wonders, and with all deceivableness of unrighteousness." Can it be believed then that he regarded this as a true church of Jesus Christ? Are these the characteristics of the church as laid down elsewhere in the Scriptures? Wherever it may lead, it seems clear to me that the apostle did not regard that system of which he spoke as having any of the marks of a true church, and the only question which can be raised on this point is, whether the fair interpretation of the passage demands that it shall be considered as referring to the Papacy. Protestants believe that it must be so understood, and Papists have not yet disproved the reasons which they allege for their belief.

(6) If this be the fair interpretation, then we may see what is the value of the pretended "succession" of the ministry through that system. If such a regular "succession" of ministers from the apostles could be made out, what would it be worth? What is the value of a spiritual descent from Pope Alexander VI.? How would it increase the proper respect for the ministerial office, if it could be proved to be derived in a right line from those monsters of incest, ambition, covetousness, and blood, who have occupied the papal throne? A Protestant minister should blush and hang his head if it were *charged* on him that he held his office by no better title than such a derivation. Much less

should he make it a matter of glorying, and an argument to prove that he only is an authorized minister, that he has received his office through such men.

(7) From this chapter we may see the tendency of human nature to degeneracy. The elements of that great and corrupt apostasy existed even in apostolic times. Those elements grew regularly up into the system of the Papacy, and spread blighting and death over the whole Christian world. It is the tendency of human nature to corrupt the best things. The Christian church was put in possession of a pure, and lovely, and glorious system of religion. It was a religion adapted to elevate and save the race. There was not an interest of humanity which it would not have fostered and promoted; there was not a source of human sorrow which it would not have mitigated, or relieved; there were none of the race whom it would not have elevated and purified. Its influence, as far as it was seen, was uniformly of the happiest kind. It did no injury anywhere, but produced only good. But how soon was it voluntarily exchanged for the worst form of superstition and error that has ever brooded in darkness over mankind! How soon did the light fade, and how rapidly did it become more obscure, until it well-nigh went out altogether! And with what tenacity did the world adhere to the system that grew up under the great apostasy, maintaining it by learning, and power, and laws, and dungeons, and racks, and faggots! What a comment is this on human nature, thus "loving darkness more than light," and error rather than truth!

(8) The chapter teaches the importance of resisting error at the beginning. These errors had their foundation in the time of the apostles. They were then comparatively small, and perhaps to many they appeared unimportant; and yet the whole papal system was just the development of errors, the germs of which existed in their days. Had these been crushed, as Paul wished to crush them, the church might have been saved from

CHAPTER III.

FINALLY, brethren, pray for us, that the word of the

Lord may [1]have *free* course, and be glorified, even as *it is* with you;

1 *run.*

---

the corruption, and woes, and persecutions produced by the Papacy. So error now should always be opposed—no matter how small or unimportant it may appear. We have no right to connive at it; to patronize it; to smile upon it. The *beginnings* of evil are always to be resisted with firmness; and if that is done, the triumph of truth will be certain.

(9) The church is safe. It has now passed through every conceivable form of trial, and still survives, and is now more vigorous and flourishing than it ever was before. It has passed through fiery times of persecution; survived the attempts of emperors and kings to destroy it, and lived while the system of error described here by the apostle Paul has thrown its baleful shade over almost the whole Christian world. It cannot reasonably be supposed that it will be called to pass through such trials again as it has already endured; but whether it does or not, the past history of the church is a guarantee that it will survive all that it is destined to encounter. None but a religion of divine origin could have continued to live amidst so many corruptions, and so many attempts to destroy it; and in the view of the past history of that church it is impossible not to come to the conclusion that it has been founded by God himself.

CHAPTER III.

ANALYSIS OF THE CHAPTER.

is chapter is made up of exhortations and directions in regard to the performance of various Christian duties.

(1) The apostle asks their prayers, ver. 1, 2. He desires them to pray particularly that the true religion might be prospered, and that, in preaching the gospel, he might be delivered from the opposition of unreasonable and wicked men.

(2) He expresses confidence that God would incline them to do what was right, and prays that he would

keep their hearts in his love, and in patient waiting for the Saviour, ver. 3–5.

(3) He commands them to remove from their number those who were disorderly, and especially those who were idle, and addresses an earnest exhortation to this class, that they would be diligently engaged in the prosecution of the business of their appropriate callings, ver. 6–12.

(4) He exhorts them not to be weary in doing well, ver. 13.

(5) He directs that if anyone should not obey the commands given in this epistle, he should be noted, and they were to separate themselves from him. Yet they were not to regard him as an enemy, but to admonish him as a brother, ver. 14, 15.

(6) The epistle closes with the usual salutations, ver. 16–18.

1. *Finally, brethren, pray for us.* That is, for Paul, Silas, and Timothy, then engaged in arduous labours at Corinth. This request for the prayers of Christians is one which Paul often makes; see Notes, 1 Thes. v. 25. ¶ *That the word of the Lord may have* free *course.* That is, the gospel. The margin is "*run.*" So also the Greek. The idea is, that it might meet with no obstruction, but that it might be carried abroad with the rapidity of a racer out of whose way every hindrance was removed. The gospel would spread rapidly in the earth if all the obstructions which men have put in its way were removed; and that they may be removed should be one of the constant subjects of prayer. ¶ *And be glorified.* Be honoured; or appear to be glorious. ¶ *As* it is *with you.* It is evident from this that Paul met with some obstructions in preaching the gospel where he was then labouring. What they were, he mentions in the next verse. He was then at Corinth (see the Introduction), and the history in the Acts of the Apostles informs us of the difficulties which he had to encounter there; see Acts xviii.

2 And that we may be delivered from ²unreasonable and wicked men: for all *men* have not faith.

---

² *absurd.*

---

2. *And that we may be delivered from unreasonable and wicked men.* That is, from opposition in their endeavours to spread the gospel. Paul encountered such men everywhere, as all do who labour to diffuse the knowledge of the truth, but it is probable that there is particular reference here to the opposition which he encountered when in Corinth. This opposition arose mainly from the Jews; see Acts xviii. 5, 6, 12, 13. The word *unreasonable* is rendered in the margin *absurd.* The Greek word (ἄτοπος) means, properly, *out of place;* then absurd, unusual, strange; then improper, unreasonable, wicked. It is rendered in Luke xxiii. 41, *amiss;* in Acts xxviii. 6, *harm.* It does not occur elsewhere in the New Testament. It refers here to men who acted amiss or improperly; men who were not found in the right place, or who had not the right views of things; and probably does not refer so much to their being positively wicked or malicious, as *to their putting things out of their proper place.* They gave an undue prominence to certain things, and less importance to others than they deserved. They had a distorted vision of the value of objects, and in tenacious adherence to their own views, and prosecuting their own objects to the exclusion of all others, they presented a constant obstruction to the true gospel. This word would apply, and probably was designed to be applied, to Jewish teachers (see Acts xviii. 5, 6), who gave an undue prominence to the laws of Moses; but it will apply well to all who entertain distorted views of the relative importance of objects, and who put things out of their place. Men often have a *hobby.* They give more importance to some object than it deserves. They, therefore, undervalue other objects; press their own with improper zeal; denounce others who do not feel the same interest in them which they do; withdraw from those who will not go with them in their

views; form separate parties, and thus throw themselves in the way of all who are endeavouring to do good in some other method. It was from men who thus put themselves *out of place,* that the apostle prayed to be delivered. ¶ *And wicked men.* Men with bad aims and purposes. It is not always true that those who would come under the appellation of what the apostle here calls *"unreasonable,"* are *wicked.* They are sometimes well-meaning, but misguided men. But in this case, it seems, they were men of bad character, who were at heart opposed to what was good, as well as inclined to put things out of their place. ¶ *For all* men *have not faith.* Of the truth of this, no one can doubt. The only question is, as to its bearing on the case before us. Some suppose it means, "there are few men whom we can safely trust;" others, that it means that they have not that "upright and candid disposition which would engage men to receive the testimony of the apostles" (Doddridge) ; others, that "all men do not embrace the Christian faith, but many oppose it" (Benson) ; and others, that "all men do not believe, but the worthy only" (Bloomfield). The connection seems to require us to understand it as meaning that all men are not prepared to embrace the gospel. Hence they set themselves against it, and from such men Paul prayed that he might be delivered; comp. 2 Tim. iii. 8. The state of mind in which the apostle was when he wrote this, seems to have been this : He recollected the readiness with which the Thessalonians had embraced the gospel, and the firmness with which they held it, and seems to suppose that *they* would imagine the same thing must be found true everywhere. But he says all men have not the same faith; all were not prepared cordially and fully to embrace the gospel. There were unreasonable and wicked men whom he had encountered, from whom he prayed that he might be delivered.

3 But*a* the Lord is faithful, who shall stablish you, and *b*keep *you* from evil.

4 And *c*we have confidence in the Lord touching you, that ye both do and will do the things which we command you.

a 1 Co.1.9.　　*b* Jn.17.15.　　*c* 2 Co.7.16.

3. *But the Lord is faithful.* Though men cannot be trusted, God is faithful to his promises and his purposes. He may always be confided in; and when men are unbelieving, perverse, unkind, and disposed to do us wrong, we may go to him, and we shall always find in him one in whom we may confide. This is an exceedingly interesting declaration, and is a beautiful illustration of the resource which a truly pious mind will feel that it has. We often have occasion to know, to our sorrow, that "all men have not faith." We witness their infidelity. We see how they turn away from the truth. We see many who once gave some evidence that they had "faith," abandon it all; and we see many in the church who seem to have no true faith, and who refuse to lend their aid in promoting the cause of religion. In such circumstances, the heart is disposed to despond, and to ask whether religion *can* be advanced in the midst of so much indifference and opposition? At such times, how consoling is it to be able to turn, as Paul did, to One who is faithful; who never fails us; and who will certainly accomplish his benevolent purposes. Men may be faithless and false, but God never is. They may refuse to embrace the gospel, and set themselves against it, but God will not abandon his great purposes. Many who are in the church may forget their solemn and sacred vows, and may show no fidelity to the cause of their Saviour, but God himself will never abandon that cause. *To a pious mind it affords unspeakably more consolation to reflect that a faithful God is the friend of the cause which we love, than it would were all men, in and out of the church, its friends.* ¶ *Who shall stablish you, and keep you from evil.* See Notes on John xvii. 5; comp.

5 And the Lord *d*direct your hearts into the love of God, and into the [3]patient waiting for Christ.

6 Now we command you, brethren, in the name of our Lord Jesus Christ, that ye *e*withdraw yourselves from every brother

d 1 Ch.29.18.　[3] or, *patience of Christ.*　*e* 1 Ti.6.5.

Notes on Eph. vi. 16. The allusion is to *the Evil One*, or Satan, and the meaning is, that God would keep them from his wiles.

4. *And we have confidence in the Lord.* Not primarily in you, for you have hearts like others, but in the Lord. It is remarkable that when Paul expresses the utmost confidence in Christians that they will live and act as becomes their profession, his reliance is not on anything in themselves, but wholly on the faithfulness of God. He must be a stranger to the human heart who puts much confidence in it even in its best state; see Phil. i. 6; iv. 7; 2 Tim. i. 12; comp. Jude 24; Rev. iii. 10; Prov. xxviii. 26.

5. *And the Lord direct your hearts into the love of God.* So direct your hearts that you may love God. ¶*And into the patient waiting for Christ.* Marg., *patience of Christ.* The marginal reading is in accordance with the Greek, and seems best to express the apostle's meaning. The prayer of the apostle was, that they might have the love of God in their hearts, and "the patience of Christ;" that is, the same patience which Christ evinced in his trials. They were then suffering affliction and persecution. They needed patience, that they might endure their trials in a proper manner. It was natural for the apostle to refer them to the Saviour, the great example of patience, and to pray that they might have the same which he had. That it does not mean that they were to wait patiently for the *appearing* of Christ, as our translation seems to imply, is quite clear, because the apostle had just been showing them that he would *not* appear until after a long series of events had occurred.

6. *Now we command you, brethren.* The apostle now (ver. 6–12) turns to an important subject—the proper

that *walketh disorderly, and not after the tradition which ye received of us.

*1 Co. 5. 11, 13.

method of treating those who were idle and disorderly in the church. In the previous epistle he had adverted to this subject, but in the mild language of exhortation. When he wrote that epistle he was aware that there were some among them who were disposed to be idle, and he had tenderly exhorted them "to be quiet, and to mind their own business, and to work with their own hands," 1 Thes. iv. 11. But it seems the exhortation, and the example of Paul himself when there (1 Thes. ii. 9), had not been effectual in inducing them to be industrious. It became, therefore, necessary to use the strong language of *command*, as he does here, and to require that if they would not work, the church should withdraw from them. What was the original *cause* of their idleness, is not known. There seems no reason, however, to doubt that it was much increased by their expectation that the Saviour would soon appear, and that the world would soon come to an end. If this was to be so, of what use would it be to labour? Why strive to accumulate property with reference to the wants of a family, or to a day of sickness, or old age? Why should a man build a house that was soon to be burnt up, or why buy a farm which he was soon to leave? The effect of the expectation of the speedy appearing of the Lord Jesus has always been to induce men to neglect their worldly affairs, and to lead idle lives. Man, naturally disposed to be idle, wants the stimulus of hope that he is labouring for the future welfare of himself, for his family, or for society, nor will he labour if he believes that the Saviour is about to appear. ¶ *In the name of the Lord Jesus Christ.* See Notes on 1 Cor. v. 4. ¶ *That ye withdraw yourselves.* Notes on 1 Tim. vi. 5. This is the true notion of Christian discipline. It is not primarily that of cutting a man off, or denouncing him, or excommunicating him; it is that of with-

7 For yourselves know how ye ought to follow us: for we behaved not ourselves disorderly among you;

drawing from him. We cease to have fellowship with him. We do not regard him any longer as a Christian brother. We separate from him. We do not seek to affect him in any other respect; we do not injure his name or standing as a man, or hold him up to reprobation; we do not follow him with denunciation or a spirit of revenge; we simply cease to recognize him as a Christian brother, when he shows that he is no longer worthy to be regarded as such. We do not deliver him over to the civil arm; we do not inflict any positive punishment on him; we leave him unmolested in all his rights as a citizen, a man, a neighbour, a husband, a father, and simply say that he is no longer one of us as a Christian. How different is this from *excommunication*, as it has been commonly understood! How different from the anathemas fulminated by the Papacy, and the delivering of the heretic over to the civil power! ¶ *From every brother that walketh disorderly.* Comp. Notes, 1 Cor. v. 11–13. A "disorderly walk" denotes conduct that is in any way contrary to the rules of Christ. The proper idea of the word used here (ἀτάκτως), is that of soldiers who do not keep the ranks; who are regardless of order; and then who are irregular in any way. The word would include any violation of the rules of Christ on any subject. ¶ *And not after the tradition which ye received of us.* According to the doctrine which we delivered to you; see Notes on chap. ii. 15. This shows that by the word "tradition" the apostle did not mean *unwritten* doctrines handed down from one to another, for he evidently alludes to what he had himself taught them, and his direction is not that that should be *handed down* by them, but that they should *obey* it.

7. *For yourselves know how ye ought to follow us.* You know what you should do in order to imitate us. ¶ *For we behaved not ourselves dis-*

8 Neither did we eat any man's bread for nought; *g*but wrought with labour and travail night and day, that we might not be chargeable to any of you:

9 Not because we have not power,*h* but to make ourselves an ensample unto you to follow us.

g Ac.18.3; 20.34.   *h* 1 Co.9.6.

10 For even when we were with you, this we commanded you, that *i*if any would not work, neither should he eat.

11 For we hear that there are some which walk among you disorderly, *k*working not at all, but are busy-bodies.

i Ge.3.19.   *k* 1 Ti.5.13; 1 Pe.4.15.

orderly among you. See Notes on 1 Thes. ii. 10.

8. *Neither did we eat any man's bread for nought.* We were not supported in idleness at the expense of others. We gave a fair equivalent for all that we received, and, in fact, laboured for our own support; see Notes on 1 Thes. ii. 9.

9. *Not because we have not power,* &c. See Notes on 1 Cor. ix. 6, 12, 14.

10. *For even when we were with you, this we commanded you.* It would seem from this that the evil of which the apostle here complains had begun to operate even when he was with them. There were those who were disposed to be idle, and who needed the solemn command of an apostle to induce them to labour. ¶ *That if any would not work, neither should he eat.* That is, at the public expense. They should not be supported by the church. This was a maxim among the Jews (see Wetstein, *in loco*), and the same sentiment may be found in Homer, Demosthenes, and Pythagoras; see Grotius, *in loco.* The maxim is founded in obvious justice, and is in accordance with the great law under which our Creator has placed us, Gen. iii. 19. That law, in the circumstances, was benevolent, and it should be our aim to carry it out in reference to ourselves and to others. The law here laid down by the apostle extends to all who are able to work for a living, and who will not do it, and binds us *not* to contribute to their support if they will not labour for it. It should be regarded as extending—(1) To the members of a church, who, though poor, should not be supported by their brethren unless they are willing to work in any way

they can for their own maintenance. (2) To those who beg from door to door, who should never be assisted unless they are willing to do all they can do for their own support. No one can be justified in assisting a lazy man. In no possible circumstances are we to contribute to foster indolence. A man might as properly help to maintain open vice.

11. *For we hear.* It is not known in what way this was made known to Paul, whether by Timothy, or by some other one. He had no doubt of its truth, and he seems to have been prepared to believe it the more readily from what he saw when he was among them. ¶ *Which walk disorderly.* Notes, ver. 6. ¶ *But are busy-bodies.* Comp. Notes, 1 Tim. v. 13; 1 Pet. iv. 15. That is, they meddled with the affairs of others—a thing which they who have nothing of their own to busy themselves about will be very likely to do. The apostle had seen that there was a tendency to this when he was in Thessalonica, and hence he had commanded them to "do their own business," 1 Thes. iv. 11. The injunction, it seems, had availed little, for there is no class of persons who will so little heed good counsel as those who have a propensity to intermeddle with the affairs of others. One of the indispensable things to check this is, that each one should have enough to do himself; and one of the most pestiferous of all persons is he who has nothing to do but to look after the affairs of his neighbours. In times of affliction and want, we should be ready to lend our aid. At other times, we should feel that he can manage his own affairs as well as we can do it for him; or if he cannot, it is his busi-

12 Now them that are such we command and exhort by our Lord Jesus Christ, that *l* with quietness they work, and eat their own bread.

13 But ye, brethren, [4] be not weary *m* in well doing.

14 And if any man obey not our word [5] by this epistle, note that man, and *n* have no company with him, that he may be ashamed.

l Ep.4.28.   [4] or, *faint not.*   *m* 1 Co.15.58
[5] or, *signify that man by an epistle.*
n Mat.18.17; ver.6.

---

ness, not ours. The Greek word used occurs only here, and in 1 Tim. v. 13; comp. Notes on Phil. ii. 4.

12. *Now them that are such we command and exhort by our Lord Jesus,* &c. A more solemn command and appeal to do what he had before enjoined on all of them, 1 Thes. iv. 11; see Notes on that verse.

13. *But ye, brethren, be not weary in well-doing.* Marg., *faint not.* The Greek means, properly, to turn out a coward; then to be faint-hearted, to despond. The idea is, that they were not to be discouraged from doing good to the truly worthy and deserving by the idleness and improper conduct of some who asked their assistance. They were, indeed, shiftless and worthless. They would not labour; they spent their time in intermeddling with the concerns of their neighbours, and they depended for their support on the charity of others. The tendency of this, as all persons feel who have ever been applied to by such persons for aid, is, to indispose us to do good *to any.* We almost insensibly feel that all who ask for aid are of the same character; or, not being able to discriminate, we close our hands alike against all. Against this the apostle would guard us, and he says that though there may be many such persons, and though we may find it difficult to distinguish the worthy from the unworthy, we should not become so disheartened as not to give at all. Nor should we be weary though the applications for assistance are frequent. They *are* indeed frequent. God designs that they should be. But the effect should not be to dishearten us, or to make us weary in well-doing, but to fill us with gratitude—for it is a privilege to be permitted to do good. It is the great distinguishing characteristic of God that he always does

good. It was that which marked the character of the Redeemer, that he "went about doing good;" and whenever God gives us the opportunity and the means of doing good, it should be to us an occasion of special thanksgiving. A man ought to become "weary" of everything else sooner than of evincing benevolence; comp. Notes on Gal. vi. 10.

14. *And if any man obey not our word by this epistle.* Marg., or *signify that man by an epistle.* According to the marginal reading this would mean, "signify, mark out, or designate that man *to me* by an epistle." The difference is merely whether we unite the words "by the epistle" with what goes before, or what follows. The Greek would admit of either construction (Winer, p. 93), but it seems to me that the construction in the text is the correct one; for, (1) The requirement was to proceed to discipline such a man by withdrawing from him. (2) In order to do this it was not necessary that the case should be made known to Paul, for there was no supposable difficulty in it, and the effect would be only needless delay. (3) Paul regarded the right of discipline as residing in the church itself, and did not require that cases should be referred to him to determine; see Notes on 1 Cor. v. 2-4. (4) Though the Greek will admit of either construction, yet it rather favours this; see Oldshausen, *in loco.* ¶ *Note that man.* The word here used, means to mark; to sign; to note with marks; and the idea is, set such a mark upon him that he shall be shunned; that is, withdraw all Christian fellowship from him. ¶ *And have no company with him.* The Greek word here means, to mix up together; then to mingle together with; to have intercourse with. The idea is that they were not

15 Yet count *him* not as an enemy, but admonish *him* [o]as a brother.

16 Now the [p]Lord of peace himself give you peace always by all means. The Lord *be* with you all.

17 The [q]salutation of Paul with mine own hand, which is the token in every epistle: so I write.

18 The[r] grace of our Lord Jesus Christ *be* with you all. Amen.

The second *epistle* to the Thessalonians was written from Athens.

o Le.19.17. p Ro.16.20. q 1 Co.16.21. r Ro.16.24.

---

to mingle with him as a Christian brother, or as one of their own number. They were not to show that they regarded him as a worthy member of the church, or as having a claim to its privileges. The extent of their discipline was, that they were to withdraw from him; see Notes on ver. 6, and Mat. xviii. 17; comp. 2 John 10, 11.

15. *Yet count* him *not as an enemy, but admonish* him *as a brother.* This shows the true spirit in which discipline is to be administered in the Christian church. We are not to deal with a man as an adversary over whom we are to seek to gain a victory, but as an erring brother—*a brother still, though he errs.* There was necessity for this caution. There is great danger that when we undertake the work of discipline we shall forget that he who is the subject of it is a brother, and that we shall regard and treat him as an enemy. Such is human nature. We set ourselves in array against him. We cut him off as one who is unworthy to walk with us. We triumph over him, and consider him at once as an enemy of the church, and as having lost all claim to its sympathies. We abandon him to the tender mercies of a cold and unfeeling world, and let him take his course. Perhaps we follow him with anathemas, and hold him up as unworthy the confidence of mankind. Now all this is entirely unlike the method and aim of discipline as the New Testament requires. There all is kind, and gentle, though firm; the offender is a man and a brother still; he is to be followed with tender sympathy and prayer, and the hearts and the arms of the Christian brotherhood are to be open to receive him again when he gives any evidence of repenting.

16. *Now the Lord of peace.* The Lord who alone can impart peace; see Notes on Rom. xv. 33; 1 Cor. xiv. 33; Heb. xiii. 20; John xiv. 27.

17. *The salutation of Paul with mine own hand.* Notes, 1 Cor. xvi. 21. ¶ *Which is the token in every epistle.* Gr., *sign.* That is, this signature is a *sign* or *proof* of the genuineness of the epistle; comp. Notes on Gal. vi. 11. ¶ *So I write.* Referring, probably, to some mark or method which Paul had of signing his name, which was well known, and which would easily be recognized by them.

18. *The grace of our Lord Jesus Christ* be *with you all.* Notes, Rom. xvi. 20.

From the subscription to this epistle, it purports to have been "written from Athens." This is probably incorrect, as there is reason to think that it was written from Corinth. See the Introduction. At all events, this subscription is of no authority. See Notes at the end of the Epistles to the Romans and 1 Corinthians.

THE FIRST
EPISTLE OF PAUL TO TIMOTHY.

INTRODUCTION.

§ 1. *Notices of the life of Timothy.*

NEARLY all that can now be known of Timothy is to be learned from the New Testament. He was a native of either Derbe or Lystra, but it is not certainly known which, Acts xvi. 1. Paul found him there on his visit to those places, and does not appear to have been acquainted with him before. His mother, whose name was Eunice, was a Jewess, and was pious, as was also his grandmother, Lois, 2 Tim. i. 3. His father was a Greek, but was evidently not unfriendly to the Jewish religion, for Timothy had been carefully trained in the Scriptures, 2 Tim. iii. 15. Paul came to Derbe and Lystra, and became acquainted with him about A.D. 51 or 52, but there is no method now of ascertaining the exact age of Timothy at that time, though there is reason to think that he was then a youth, 1 Tim. iv. 12. It would seem, also, that he was a youth of uncommon hope and promise, and that there had been some special indications that he would rise to distinction as a religious man, and would exert an extended influence in favour of religion, 1 Tim. i. 18. At the time when Paul first met with him, he was a " disciple," or a Christian convert; but the means which had been used for his conversion are unknown. His mother had been before converted to the Christian faith (Acts xvi. 1), and Timothy was well known to the Christians in the neighbouring towns of Lystra and Iconium. The gospel had been preached by Paul and Barnabas, in Iconium, Derbe, and Lystra, some six or seven years before it is said that Paul met with Timothy (Acts xvi. 1), and it is not improbable that this youth had been converted in the interval.

Several things appear to have combined to induce the apostle to introduce him into the ministry, and to make him a travelling companion. His youth; his acquaintance with the Holy Scriptures; the " prophecies which went before on him;" his talents; his general reputation in the church, and, it would seem also, his amiableness of manners, fitting him to be an agreeable companion, attracted the attention of the apostle, and led him to desire that he might be a fellow-labourer with him. To satisfy the prejudices of the Jews, and to prevent any possible objection which might be made against his qualifications for the ministerial office, Paul circumcised him (Acts xvi. 3), and he was ordained to the office of the ministry by "the laying on of the hands of the presbytery," 1 Tim. iv. 14. *When* this ordination occurred is not known, but it is most probable that it was before he went on his travels with Paul, as it is known that Paul was present on the occasion, and took a leading part in the transaction, 2 Tim. i. 6.

Timothy having joined Paul and Silas, accompanied them on a visit to the churches of Phrygia and Galatia, in which they delivered them the decrees to keep which had been ordained at Jerusalem, Acts xvi. 4, *seq.* Having done this, they endeavoured to go together into Bithynia, a province of Asia Minor, on the north-west, but were prevented; and they then went into Mysia, and to the towns of Troas, Acts xvi. 8. Here Luke appears to have joined them, and from this place, in obedience to a vision which appeared to Paul, they went into Macedonia, and preached the gospel first at Philippi, where they established a church. In this city Paul and Silas were imprisoned; but it is remarkable that nothing is said of Timothy and Luke, and it is not known whether they shared in the sufferings of the persecution there or not. Everything, however, renders it probable that Timothy was with them at Philippi, as he is mentioned as having started with them to go on the journey (Acts xvi. 3, *seq.*); and as we find him at Berea, after the apostle had been released from prison, and had preached at Thessalonica and Berea, Acts xvii. 14. From this place Paul was conducted to Athens, but left an injunction for Silas and Timothy to join him there as soon as possible. This was done;—but when Timothy had come to Athens, Paul felt it to be important that the church at Thessalonica should be visited and comforted in its afflictions, and being prevented from doing it himself, he sent Timothy, at great personal inconvenience, back to that church. Having discharged the duty there, he rejoined the apostle at Corinth (Acts xviii. 5), from which place the first epistle to the Thessalonians was written; see Intro. to 1 Thes. and Notes on 1 Thes. i. 1, and iii. 2. These transactions occurred about A.D. 52.

Paul remained at Corinth a year and a half (Acts xviii. 11), and it is probable that Timothy and Silas continued with him; see 2 Thes. i. 1. From Corinth he sailed for Syria, accompanied by Priscilla and Aquila, whom he appears to have left on his way at Ephesus, Acts xviii. 18, 19, 26. Whether Timothy and Silas accompanied him is not mentioned, but we find Timothy again with him at Ephesus, after he had been to Cesarea and Antioch, and had returned to Ephesus, Acts xviii. 22; xix. 1, 22. From Ephesus, he sent Timothy and Erastus to Macedonia (Acts xix. 22), but for what purpose, or how long they remained, is unknown. From 1 Cor. iv. 17, it appears that Paul expected that on this journey Timothy would stop at Corinth, and would give the church there instructions adapted to its situation. Paul continued in Ephesus until he was compelled to depart by the tumult caused by Demetrius, when he left and went to Macedonia, Acts xx. Whether Timothy, during the interval, had returned to Ephesus from Macedonia, is not expressly mentioned in the history; but such a supposition is not improbable. Paul, during the early part of his residence in Ephesus, appears to have laboured quietly (Acts xix. 9, 10); and Timothy was sent away *before* the disturbances caused by Demetrius, Acts xix. 22. Paul designed to follow him soon, and then to go to Jerusalem, and then to Rome, Acts xix. 21. Paul (Acts xx. 31) was in Ephesus in all about three years; and it is not unreasonable to suppose that he remained there after Timothy was sent to Macedonia long enough for him to go and to return to him again. If so, it is *possible* that when he himself went away, he left Timothy there in his place; comp. 1 Tim. i. 3. It has been the general opinion that the First Epistle to Timothy was written at this time, either when the apostle was on his way to Macedonia, or while in Macedonia. But this opinion has not been unquestioned. The departure of Paul for Macedonia occurred about A.D. 58

or 59. In Acts xx. 4, Timothy is again mentioned as accompanying Paul, after he had remained in Greece three months, on the route to Syria through Macedonia. He went with him, in company with many others, into "Asia." Going before Paul, they waited for him at Troas (Acts xx. 5), and thence doubtless accompanied him on his way to Jerusalem. It was on this occasion that Paul delivered his farewell charge to the elders of the church of Ephesus, at Miletus, Acts xx. 17, *seq.* When in Macedonia, Paul wrote the Second Epistle to the Corinthians, and Timothy was then with him, for he unites in the salutations, 2 Cor. i. 1. Timothy was also with the apostle on this journey at Corinth, when from that city he wrote his epistle to the Romans, Rom. xvi. 21.

The subsequent events of the life of Timothy are less known. It does not appear from the Acts of the Apostles, that he was with Paul during his two years' imprisonment at Cesarea, nor during his voyage to Rome. It is certain, however, that he was at Rome with the apostle when he wrote the Epistles to the Philippians, to the Colossians, and to Philemon, Phil. i. 1; Col. i. 1; Philem. 1. From Heb. xiii. 23 it appears, also, that Timothy had been with the apostle there, but that when the epistle was written he was absent on some important embassy, and that Paul was expecting his speedy return; see Notes on that verse. Between the first and second imprisonment of Paul at Rome, no mention is made of Timothy, nor is it known where he was, or whether he accompanied him in his travels or not. When he was imprisoned there the second time, he wrote the Second Epistle to Timothy, in which he desires him to come to Rome, and bring with him several things which he had left at Troas, 2 Tim. iv. 9-13, 21. If Timothy went to Rome, agreeably to the request of the apostle, it is probable that he was a witness there of his martyrdom.

In regard to the latter part of the life of Timothy, there is nothing which can be depended on. It has been the current opinion, derived from tradition, that he was "bishop" of Ephesus; that he died and was buried there; and that his bones were subsequently removed to Constantinople. The belief that he was "bishop" of Ephesus rests mainly on the "subscription" to the Second Epistle to Timothy—which is no authority whatever; see Notes on that subscription. On the question whether he was an episcopal prelate at Ephesus, the reader may consult my *Enquiry into the Organization and Government of the Apostolic Church*, pp. 88-107. The supposition that he died at Ephesus, and was subsequently removed to Constantinople, rests on no certain historical basis.

Timothy was long the companion and the friend of the apostle Paul, and is often mentioned by him with affectionate interest. Indeed there seems to have been no one of his fellow-labourers to whom he was so warmly attached; see 1 Tim. i. 2, 18; 2 Tim. i. 2; ii. 1; 1 Cor. iv. 17, where he calls him "his own son," and "his beloved son;"—2 Tim. i. 4, where he expresses his earnest desire to see him, and makes a reference to the tears which Timothy shed at parting from him;—1 Cor. xvi. 10, 11, where he bespeaks for him a kind reception among the Corinthians;—1 Cor. xvi. 10; Rom. xvi. 21; 1 Thes. iii. 2, and especially ii. 19, 20, where he speaks of his fidelity, of his usefulness to him in his labours, and of the interest which he took in the churches which the apostle had established.

§ 2. *When and where the Epistle was written.*

The subscription at the close of the epistle states that it was written from Laodicea. But these subscriptions are of no authority, and many of them are false; see Notes at the end of 1 Corinthians. There has been much diversity of opinion in regard to the time when this epistle was written, and of course in regard to the place where it was composed. All that is certain from the epistle itself is, that it was addressed to Timothy at Ephesus, and that it was soon after Paul had left that city to go to Macedonia, 1 Tim. i. 3. Paul is mentioned in the Acts as having been at Ephesus twice, Acts xviii. 19–23; xix. 1–41. After his first visit there he went directly to Jerusalem, and of course it could not have been written at that time. The only question then is, whether it was written when Paul left the city, having been driven away by the excitement caused by Demetrius (Acts xx. 1), or whether he visited Ephesus again on some occasion *after* his first imprisonment at Rome, and of course after the narrative of Luke in the Acts of the Apostles closes. If on the former occasion, it was written about the year 58 or 59; if the latter, about the year 64 or 65. Critics have been divided in reference to this point, and the question is still unsettled, and it may be impossible to determine it with entire certainty.

Those who have maintained the former opinion, among others, are Theodoret, Benson, Zachariae, Michaelis, Schmidt, Koppe, Planck, Grotius, Lightfoot, Witsius, Lardner, Hug, and Prof. Stuart. The latter opinion, that it was written subsequently to the period of Paul's first imprisonment at Rome, is maintained by Paley, Pearson, L'Enfant, Le Clerc, Cave, Mill, Whitby, Macknight, and others.

An examination of the reasons in favour of each of these opinions in regard to the date of the epistle, may be found in Paley's *Horæ Paul.*; Macknight; Hug's *Intro.*, and Koppe, *Proleg.*

The theory of Eichhorn, which is peculiar, and which is supported by some ingenious and plausible, but not conclusive reasoning, may be seen in his *Einleitung in das neue Test.* 3 b. 314–352.

In the diversity of opinion which prevails about the time when the epistle was written, it is impossible to determine the question in such a manner as to leave no room for doubt. After the most careful examination which I have been able to give to the subject, however, it seems to me that the former opinion is correct, that it was written soon after Paul was driven from Ephesus by the tumult caused by Demetrius, as recorded in Acts xix.; xx. I. The reasons for this opinion are briefly these:—

1. This is the only *record* that occurs in the New Testament of the apostle's having gone from Ephesus to Macedonia; see above. It is natural, therefore, to suppose that this is referred to in 1 Tim. i. 3, unless there is some insuperable difficulty in the way.

2. There is no certain evidence that Paul visited the church at Ephesus after his first imprisonment at Rome. It is certainly *possible* that he did, but there is no record of any such visit in the New Testament, nor any historical record of it elsewhere. If there *had* been such a visit after his release, and if this epistle was written then, it is remarkable that the apostle

does not make any allusion to his imprisonment in this epistle, and that he does not refer at all to his own escape from this danger of death at Rome; comp. 2 Tim. iv. 16, 17.

3. The supposition that the epistle was written at the time supposed, agrees better with the character of the epistle, and with the design for which Timothy was left at Ephesus, than the others. It is manifest from the epistle that the church was in some respects in an unsettled condition, and it would seem also that one part of the duty of Timothy there was to see that it was placed under a proper organization. This Paul had evidently proposed to accomplish himself, but it is clear from chap. i. 3, that he left his work unfinished, and that he gave what *he* had proposed to do into the hands of Timothy to be perfected. After the first imprisonment of Paul at Rome, however, there is every reason to suppose that the church was completely organized. Even when Paul went from Macedonia to Jerusalem (Acts xx.), there were "elders" placed over the church at Ephesus, whom Paul assembled at Miletus, and to whom he gave his parting charge, and his final instructions in regard to the church.

4. At the time when Paul wrote this epistle, Timothy was a young man —a youth, 1 Tim. iv. 12. It is true, that if he was somewhere about twenty years of age when he was introduced into the ministry, as has been commonly supposed, this language would not be entirely inappropriate, even after the imprisonment of Paul, but still the language would more properly denote one somewhat younger than Timothy would be at that time.

5. To this may be added the declaration of Paul in 1 Tim. iii. 14, that he "hoped to come to him shortly." This is an expression which agrees well with the supposition that he had himself been driven away before he had intended to leave; that he had left something unfinished there which he desired to complete, and that he hoped that affairs would soon be in such a state that he would be permitted to return. It may be also suggested, as a circumstance of some importance, though not conclusive, that when Paul met the elders of the church of Ephesus at Miletus, he said that he had no expectation of ever seeing them again. "And now, behold, I know that ye all, among whom I have gone preaching the kingdom of God, shall see my face no more," Acts xx. 25. I do not think that this is to be understood as an inspired prediction, affirming with absolute certainty that he never would see them again, but that he rather expressed his apprehensions that it would be so from the circumstances which then existed, Acts xx. 22, 23. Still, this passage shows that when he uttered it he did not *expect* to visit Ephesus again, as he manifestly did when he wrote the epistle to Timothy.

These considerations seem so clear that they would leave no doubt on the mind, were it not for certain things which it seems to many impossible to reconcile with this supposition. The difficulties are the following :—

1. That before Paul went to Macedonia, he had sent Timothy with Erastus before him (Acts xix. 22), purposing to follow them at no distant period, and to pass through Macedonia and Achaia, and then to go to Jerusalem, and afterwards to visit Rome, Acts xix. 21. As he had sent Timothy before him but so short a time before he left Ephesus, it is asked how Timothy could be *left at Ephesus* when Paul went himself to Macedonia? To this objection we may reply, that it is not improbable by any

means that Timothy may have accomplished the object of his journey to Macedonia, and may have returned to the apostle at Ephesus before he was driven away. It does not appear, from the narrative, that Timothy was intrusted with any commission which would require a long time to fulfil it, nor that Paul expected that he would remain in Macedonia until he himself came. The purpose for which he sent Timothy and Erastus is not indeed mentioned, but it seems probable that it was with reference to the collection which he proposed to take up for the poor saints at Jerusalem; see Notes on Acts xix. 21, 22; comp, 1 Cor. xvi. 1–6. If it was the purpose to prepare the churches for such a collection, it could not have required any considerable time, nor was it necessary that Timothy should remain long in a place; and it was natural also that he *should* return to the apostle at Ephesus and apprise him of what he had done, and what was the prospect in regard to the collection. It has been clearly shown by Hug (*Intro. to the New Test.* § 104, 109), that such a journey could easily have been made during the time which the apostle remained at Ephesus after he had sent Timothy and Erastus to Macedonia.

2. The next objection—and one which is regarded by Paley as decisive against the supposition that the epistle was written on this occasion—is, that from the Second Epistle to the Corinthians (i. 1), it is evident that at the time in which this epistle is supposed to have been written, Timothy was with the apostle in Macedonia. The Second Epistle to the Corinthians was undoubtedly written during this visit of Paul to Macedonia, and at that time Timothy was with him; see the Intro. to 2 Cor. § 3. How then can it be supposed that he was at Ephesus? Or how can this fact be reconciled with the supposition that Timothy was left there, and especially with the declaration of Paul to him (1 Tim. iii. 14), that he "hoped to come to him shortly?" That Paul *expected* that Timothy would remain at Ephesus, at least for some time, is evident from 1 Tim. iii. 15, "But *if I tarry long*, that thou mayest know how thou oughtest to behave thyself in the house of God;" and from chap. iv. 13, "*Till I come*, give attendance to reading, to exhortation, to doctrine." The only solution of this difficulty is, that Timothy had left Ephesus, and had followed the apostle into Macedonia; and the only question here is, whether, since the apostle designed that he should remain at Ephesus, and expected himself to return and meet him there, Timothy would be likely to leave that place and go to Macedonia. It is certain that the history in the Acts does not make this record, but that is no material objection—since it cannot be supposed that every occurrence in the travels of the apostles was recorded. But there are two or three circumstances which may render probable the supposition that Timothy, either by the concurrence, or by the direction of Paul, privately communicated to him, may have left Ephesus sooner than was at first contemplated, and may have rejoined him in Macedonia. (1) One is, that the main business which Timothy was appointed to perform at Ephesus—to give a solemn charge to certain persons there to teach no other doctrine but that which Paul taught (1 Tim. i. 3)—might have been speedily accomplished. Paul was driven away in haste, and as he had not the opportunity of doing this himself as he wished, he left Timothy in charge of it. But this did not require, of necessity, any considerable time. (2) Another is, that the business of appointing suitable

officers over the church there, might also have been soon accomplished. In fact, the church there is known to have been supplied with proper officers not long after this, for Paul sent from Miletus for the elders to meet him there on his way to Jerusalem. This remark is made in accordance with the opinion that a part of the work which Timothy was expected to perform there was to constitute proper officers over the church. But there is no *proof* that that was a part of his business. It is not specified in what Paul mentions, in chap. i. 3, as the design for which he was left there, and it is hardly probable that the apostle would have spent so long a time as he did in Ephesus—nearly three years (Acts xx. 31)—without having organized the church with proper officers. Besides, the address of Paul to the elders at Miletus implies that they had received their appointment before he left them; see Acts xx. 18–35, particularly ver. 35. The instructions to Timothy in this epistle about the proper qualifications of the officers of the church, do not prove that he was then to appoint officers at Ephesus, for they are *general* instructions, having no particular reference to the church there, and designed to guide him in his work through life. There is, therefore, nothing in the duties which Timothy was to perform at Ephesus which would forbid the supposition that he may have soon followed the apostle into Macedonia. (3) It appears that though Paul may have intended, if possible, to visit Ephesus on his way to Jerusalem, in accordance with 1 Tim. iii. 14, 15; iv. 13, yet if that had been his intention, he subsequently changed his mind, and found it necessary to make other arrangements. Thus it is said (Acts xx. 16), that "Paul had determined to sail *by* Ephesus, because he would not spend the time in Asia;" that is, he had resolved to sail *past* Ephesus without visiting it. It would seem probable, also, that this resolution had been formed before he left Macedonia, for it is said that he "*had* determined" it ($\check{\epsilon}\kappa\rho\iota\nu\epsilon$), and if so, there is no improbability in supposing that he had in some way caused it to be intimated to Timothy that he wished him to leave Ephesus and join him before he left Macedonia. (4) In fact, and in accordance with this supposition, we find Timothy *with* Paul when he went on that occasion into "Asia," Acts xx. 4, 5. These considerations render it probable that the epistle was written to Timothy soon after Paul left Ephesus to go into Macedonia after the tumult excited by Demetrius. As Paul was driven away unexpectedly, and when he had not completed what he designed to do there, nothing is more natural than the supposition that he would embrace the earliest opportunity to give suitable instructions to Timothy, that he might know how to complete the work.

§ 3. *The occasion and design of the Epistle.*

This is specified in chap. i. 3. Paul had gone into Macedonia, having been suddenly driven away from Ephesus, before he had entirely done what he had designed to do there. He left Timothy there to "charge some that they teach no other doctrine;" that is, no other doctrine than that which he had himself taught when there. It is clear, from this, that there were certain errors prevailing there which Paul thought it of the highest importance to have corrected. In regard to those errors, see the Introduction to the Epistle to the Ephesians, and the Epistle to the Colossians. Some of the circumstances which gave occasion to this epistle can be gathered from the history in the Acts of the Apostles; others can be derived from the epistle itself. From these sources of information we learn the following things in reference to the state of the church in Ephesus, which made it proper that Timothy should be left there, and that these instructions should be given him to regulate his conduct:—

(1) There was much opposition to the apostle Paul from the Jews who resided there, Acts xix. 8, 9.

(2) There were in the church teachers who endeavoured to enforce the maxims of the Jewish law, and to represent that law as binding on Christians, 1 Tim. i. 6, 7.

(3) Some of the Jews residing there were addicted to exorcism, and endeavoured to make use of Christianity and the name of Jesus to promote their selfish ends, Acts xix. 14; comp. 1 Tim. i. 4.

(4) The Jewish teachers laid great stress on genealogies and traditions, and were much given to debates about various questions connected with the law, 1 Tim. i. 4-6.

(5) There were erroneous views prevailing respecting the rights of women, and the place which they ought to occupy in the church, 1 Tim. ii. 8-15.

(6) The organization of the officers of the church had not been effected as Paul wished it to be. It is probable that some of the officers had been appointed, and that some instructions had been given to them in regard to their duties, but the whole arrangement had not been completed, 1 Tim. iii., iv.

(7) There were certain questions in regard to the proper treatment of widows which had not yet been determined, 1 Tim. v.

(8) The apostle in his preaching had inculcated benevolent principles, and had asserted the natural equality of all men, and it would seem that certain persons had taken occasion from this to excite a spirit of discontent and insubordination among those who were servants. The doctrine seems to have been advanced, that, as all men were equal, and all had been redeemed by the same blood, therefore those who had been held in bondage were free from all obligation to serve their masters. There were those evidently who sought to excite them to insurrection; to break down the distinctions in society, and to produce a state of insubordination and disorder, 1 Tim. vi.; comp. Eph. vi. 5-10; Col. iii. 22; iv. 2.

Such appears to have been the state of things when the apostle was compelled suddenly to leave Ephesus. He had hitherto directed the affairs of the church there mainly himself, and had endeavoured to correct the errors then prevailing, and to establish the church on a right foundation. Matters appear to have been tending to the desired result; religion was acquiring a strong hold on the members of the church (Acts xix. 18-20); error was giving way; the community was becoming more and more impressed with the value of Christianity; the influence of idolatry was becoming less and less (Acts xix. 23, *seq.*), and the arrangements for the complete organization of the church were in progress. Such was the promising state of things in these respects that the apostle hoped to be able to leave Ephesus at no very distant period, and had actually made arrangements to do it, Acts xix. 21.

But his arrangements were not quite finished, and before they were completed, he was compelled to leave by the tumult excited by Demetrius. He left Timothy, therefore, to complete the arrangements, and in this first epistle, gave him all the instructions which were necessary to guide him in that work.

This view of the state of things in Ephesus at the time when the apostle was constrained to leave it, will enable us to understand the drift of the epistle, and the reasons why the various topics found in it were introduced. At the same time, the instructions are of so general a character that they would be an invaluable guide to Timothy not only at Ephesus, but through his life; and not only to him, but to all the ministers of the gospel in every age and land. A more detailed view of these topics will be furnished in the analysis prefixed to the several chapters of the epistle.

The epistles to Timothy and Titus occupy a very important place in the New Testament, and without them there would be a manifest and most material defect in the volume of inspiration. Their canonical authority has never been questioned by the great body of the church, and there is no doubt that they are the productions of the apostle Paul. If the various epistles which he wrote, and the various other books of the New Testament be attentively examined, it will be found that each one is designed to accomplish an important object, and that if any one were removed a material chasm would be made. Though the removal of any *one* of them would not so impair the volume of the New Testament as to obscure any *essential* doctrine, or prevent our obtaining the knowledge of the way of salvation from the remainder, yet it would mar the beauty and symmetry of the truth, and would render the system of instruction defective and incomplete.

This is true in regard to the epistles to Timothy and Titus, as it is of the other epistles. They fill a department which nothing else in the New Testament would enable us to supply, and without which instructions to man respecting redemption would be incomplete. They relate mainly *to the office of the ministry;* and though there are important instructions of the Saviour himself respecting the office (Mat. x., Mark xvi., and elsewhere), and though in the address of Paul to the elders of Ephesus (Acts xx.) and in the epistles to the Corinthians, there are invaluable suggestions respecting it, yet such is its importance in the organization of the church, that more full and complete instructions seem to be imperiously demanded. Those instructions are furnished in these epistles. They are as full and complete as we could desire in regard to the nature of the office, the qualifications for it, and the duties which grow out of it. They are fitted not only to direct Timothy and Titus in the work to which they were specifically appointed, but to counsel the ministry in every age and in every land. It is obvious that the character and welfare of the church depend greatly, if not entirely, on the character of the ministry. The office of the ministry is God's great appointment for the preservation of pure religion, and for spreading it abroad through the world. The church adheres to the truth; is built up in faith; is distinguished for love, and purity, and zeal, in proportion as the ministry is honoured, and shows itself qualified for its work. In every age corruption in the church has commenced in the ministry; and where the gospel has been spread abroad with zeal, and the church has arisen in her strength and beauty, it

has been pre-eminently where God has sent down his Spirit in copious measures on those who have filled the sacred office. So important, then, is this
office to the welfare of the church and the world, that it was desirable that
full instructions should be furnished in the volume of revelation in regard to
its nature and design. Such instructions we have in these epistles, and there
is scarcely *any* portion of the New Testament which the church could not
better afford to part with than the epistles to Timothy and Titus. Had the
ministry always been such as these epistles contemplate; had they who have
filled the sacred office always had the character and qualifications here described, we may believe that the church would have been saved from the
strifes that have rent it, and that the pure gospel would long ere this have
been spread through the world.

But it is not to the ministry only that these epistles are of so much value.
They are of scarcely less importance to the church at large. Its vitality; its
purity; its freedom from strife; its zeal and love, and triumph in spreading
the gospel, depend on the character of the ministry. If the church will prosper
from age to age, the pulpit must be filled with a pious, learned, laborious, and
devoted ministry, and one of the first cares of the church should be that such
a ministry should be secured. This great object cannot better be attained
than by keeping the instructions in these epistles steadily before the minds of
the members of the church; and though a large part of them is particularly
adapted to the ministers of the gospel, yet the church itself can in no better
way promote its own purity and prosperity than by a prayerful and attentive
study of the epistles to Timothy and Titus.

THE FIRST
EPISTLE OF PAUL TO TIMOTHY.

CHAPTER I.

PAUL, an ^aapostle of Jesus Christ, by the command-

a Ac.9.15.

ment of God our Saviour, and Lord Jesus Christ, *which is* ^bour hope;

2 Unto ^cTimothy *my* ^down son

b Col.1.27.   c Ac.16.1.   d Tit.1.4.

CHAPTER I.

ANALYSIS OF THE CHAPTER.

This chapter comprises the following subjects:—

(1) The salutation to Timothy, in the usual manner in which Paul introduces his epistles, ver. 1, 2.

(2) The purpose for which he had left him at Ephesus, ver. 3, 4. It was that he might correct the false instructions of some of the teachers there, and especially, as it would seem, in regard to the true use of the law. They gave undue importance to some things in the laws of Moses; they did not understand the true nature and design of his laws; and they mingled in their instructions much that was mere fable.

(3) The true use and design of the law, ver. 5–11. It was to produce *love* not vain jangling. It was not made to fetter the conscience by vain and troublesome austerities and ceremonies; it was to restrain and bind the wicked. The use of the law, according to these teachers, and according to the prevailing Jewish notions, was to prescribe a great number of formalities, and to secure outward conformity in a great variety of cumbrous rites and ceremonies. Paul instructs Timothy to teach them that *love*, out of a pure heart and a good conscience, was the elementary principle of religion, and that the "law" was primarily designed to restrain and control the wicked, and that the gospel brought to light and enforced this important truth.

(4) The mention of the gospel in this connection, leads Paul to express his thanks to God that *he* had been intrusted with this message of salvation, ver. 12–17. Once he had the same views as others. But he had obtained mercy, and he was permitted to *publish* that glorious gospel which had shed such light on the law of God, and which had revealed a plan of salvation that was worthy of universal acceptation.

(5) This solemn duty of preaching the gospel he commits now to Timothy, ver. 18–20. He says that he had been called to the work in accordance with the prophecies which had been uttered of him in anticipation of his future usefulness in the church, and in the expectation that he would not, like some others, make shipwreck of his faith.

1. *Paul, an apostle of Jesus Christ.* See Notes on Rom. i. 1. ¶ *By the commandment of God.* Notes, 1 Cor. i. 1. ¶ *Our Saviour.* The name Saviour is as applicable to God the Father as to the Lord Jesus Christ, since God is the great Author of salvation; see Notes, Luke i. 47; comp. 1 Tim. iv. 10; Tit. ii. 10; Jude 25. ¶ *And Lord Jesus Christ.* The apostle Paul had received his commission directly from him; see Notes, Gal. i. 11, 12. ¶ *Which is our hope.* See Notes, Col. i. 27.

2. *Unto Timothy.* For an account of Timothy, see Intro. § 1. ¶ *My own son in the faith.* Converted to the Christian faith by my instrumen-

in the faith: *Grace, mercy, *and* peace, from God our Father and Jesus Christ our Lord.

3 As I besought thee to abide

e Ga.1.3; 1 Pe.1.2.

still at Ephesus, *when I went into Macedonia, that thou mightest charge some that they teach no other doctrine,

f Ac.20.1,3.

tality, and regarded by me with the affection of a father; see Notes, 1 Cor. iv. 15. Paul had no children of his own, and he adopted Timothy as a son, and uniformly regarded and treated him as such. He had the same feeling also toward Titus, Tit. i. 4; comp. Notes, Gal. iv. 19; 1 Thes. ii. 7, 11; and Philem. 10. ¶ *Grace, mercy,* and *peace,* &c. See Notes, Rom. i. 7.

3. *As I besought thee to abide still at Ephesus.* It is clear from this, that Paul and Timothy had been labouring together at Ephesus, and the language accords with the supposition that Paul had been compelled to leave before he had completed what he had designed to do there. See the Intro. § 2. ¶ *When I went into Macedonia.* Having been driven away by the excitement caused by Demetrius and his fellow-craftsmen, Acts xx. 1. See the Intro. § 2, 3. ¶ *That thou mightest charge some.* The word *charge* here —παραγγειλῃς—seems to mean more than is commonly implied by the word as used by us. If it had been a single direction or command, it might have been given by Paul himself before he left, but it seems rather to refer to that *continuous instruction* which would convince these various errorists and lead them to inculcate only the true doctrine. As they may have been numerous, as they may have embraced various forms of error, and as they might have had plausible grounds for their belief, this was evidently a work requiring time, and hence Timothy was left to effect this at leisure. It would seem that the wrath which had been excited against Paul had not affected Timothy, but that he was permitted to remain and labour without molestation. It is not certainly known who these teachers were, but they appear to have been of Jewish origin, and to have inculcated the peculiar sentiments of the Jews respecting the

law. ¶ *That they teach no other doctrine.* That is, no other doctrine than that taught by the apostles. The Greek word here used is not found in the classic writers, and does not elsewhere occur in the New Testament, except in chap. vi. 3 of this epistle, where it is rendered "teach otherwise." We may learn here what was the design for which Timothy was left at Ephesus. (1) It was for a temporary purpose, and not as a permanent arrangement. It was to correct certain errors prevailing there which Paul would have been able himself soon to correct if he had been suffered to remain. Paul expected soon to return to him again, and then they would proceed unitedly with their work, chap. iv. 13; iii. 15. (2) It was not that he might be the "*Bishop*" of Ephesus. There is no evidence that he was "ordained" there at all, as the subscription to the second epistle declares (see Notes on that subscription), nor were the functions which he was to perform those of a prelatical bishop. He was not to take the charge of a "diocese," or to ordain ministers of the "second rank," or to administer the rite of confirmation, or to perform acts of discipline. He was left there for a purpose which is specified, and that is as far as possible from what are now regarded as the appropriate functions of a prelatical bishop. Perhaps no claim which has ever been set up has had less semblance of argument than that which asserts that Timothy was the "Bishop of Ephesus." See this clause examined in my *Enquiry into the Organization and Government of the Apostolic Church,* pp. 84–107.

4. *Neither give heed to fables.* That is, that *they* should not bestow their attention on fables, or regard such trifles as of importance. The "fables" here referred to were probably the idle and puerile superstitions and con-

4 Neither[g] give heed to fables and endless genealogies, which min-

g ch.6.3,4,20.

ceits of the Jewish Rabbies. The word rendered *fable* (μῦθος) means properly *speech* or *discourse*, and then fable or fiction, or a mystic discourse. Such things abounded among the Greeks as well as the Jews, but it is probable that the latter here are particularly intended. These were composed of frivolous and unfounded stories, which they regarded as of great importance, and which they seem to have desired to incorporate with the teachings of Christianity. Paul, who had been brought up amidst these superstitions, saw at once how they would tend to draw off the mind from the truth, and would corrupt the true religion. One of the most successful arts of the adversary of souls has been to mingle fable with truth; and when he cannot overthrow the truth by direct opposition, to neutralize it by mingling with it much that is false and frivolous. ¶ *And endless genealogies.* This also refers to Jewish teaching. The Hebrews kept careful genealogical records, for this was necessary in order that the distinction of their tribes might be kept up. Of course, in the lapse of centuries these tables would become very numerous, complicated, and extended—so that they might without much exaggeration be called "*endless.*" The Jews attached great importance to them, and insisted on their being carefully preserved. As the Messiah, however, had now come—as the Jewish polity was to cease — as the separation between them and the heathen was no longer necessary, and the distinction of tribes was now useless, there was no propriety that these distinctions should be regarded by Christians. The whole system was, moreover, contrary to the genius of Christianity, for it served to keep up the pride of blood and of birth. ¶ *Which minister questions.* Which afford matter for troublesome and angry debates. It was often difficult to settle or understand them. They became complicated and perplexing. Nothing is more difficult

ister questions, rather than godly edifying which is in faith; *so do.*

5 Now the [h]end of the com-

h Ro.13.8,10; Ga.5.14.

than to unravel an extensive genealogical table. To do this, therefore, would often give rise to contentions, and *when* settled, would give rise still further to questions about rank and precedence. ¶ *Rather than godly edifying which is in faith.* These inquiries do nothing to promote true religion in the soul. They settle no permanent principle of truth; they determine nothing that is really concerned in the salvation of men. They might be pursued through life, and not one soul be converted by them; they might be settled with the greatest accuracy, and yet not one heart be made better. Is not this still true of many controversies and logomachies in the church? No point of controversy is worth much trouble, which, if it were settled one way or the other, would not tend to convert the soul from sin, or to establish some important principle in promoting true religion. ¶ *So do.* These words are supplied by our translators, but they are necessary to the sense. The meaning is, that Timothy was to remain at Ephesus, and faithfully perform the duty which he had been left there to discharge.

5. *Now the end of the commandment.* See Notes on Rom. x. 4. In order that Timothy might fulfil the design of his appointment, it was necessary that he should have a correct view of the design of the law. The teachers to whom he refers insisted much on its obligation and importance; and Paul designs to say that he did not intend to teach that the law was of no consequence, and was not, when properly understood, obligatory. Its nature and use, however, was not correctly understood by them, and hence it was of great importance for Timothy to inculcate correct views of the purpose for which it was given. The word "commandment" here some have understood of the gospel (Doddridge), others of the particular command which the apostle here gives to

mandment is charity, *out of a pure heart, and *of* a good conscience, and *of* faith unfeigned:

6 From which some [1]having swerved, *k*have turned aside unto vain jangling:

7 Desiring to be teachers of the law; *l*understanding neither what they say, nor whereof they affirm.

i 2 Ti.2.22.   1 or, *not aiming at.*
k 2 Ti.4.10.   *l* Ro.1 22.

Timothy (Benson, Clarke, and Macknight); but it seems more naturally to refer to *all* that God had commanded—his whole law. As the error of these teachers arose from improper views of the nature and design of *law*, Paul says that that design should be understood. It was not to produce distinctions and angry contentions, and was not to fetter the minds of Christians with minute and burdensome observances, but it was *to produce love.* ¶ *Is charity.* On the meaning of this word, see Notes on 1 Cor. xiii. 1. ¶ *Out of a pure heart.* The love which is genuine must proceed from a holy heart. The commandment was not designed to secure merely the outward expressions of love, but that which had its seat in the heart. ¶ *And* of *a good conscience.* A conscience free from guilt. Of course there can be no genuine love to God where the dictates of conscience are constantly violated, or where a man knows that he is continually doing wrong. If a man wishes to have the evidence of love to God, he must keep a good conscience. All pretended love, where a man knows that he is living in sin, is mere hypocrisy. ¶ *And* of *faith unfeigned.* Undissembled confidence in God. This does not seem to be intended specifically of faith in the Lord Jesus, but it means that all true love to God, such as this law would produce, must be based on confidence in him. How can anyone have love to him who has no confidence in him? Can we exercise love to a professed friend in whom we have no confidence? Faith, then, is as necessary under the law as it is under the gospel.

6, *From which some having swerved.* Marg., *not aiming at.* The word here used—ἀστοχέω—means properly, to miss the mark; to err; and then, to swerve from; comp. chap. vi. 21;

2 Tim. ii. 18. It does not mean that they had ever had that from which they are said to have swerved—for it does not follow that a man who misses a mark had ever hit it—but merely that they failed of the things referred to, and had turned to vain talk. The word "which" (ὧν), in the plural, refers not to the law, but to the things enumerated—a pure heart, a good conscience, and unfeigned faith. ¶ *Have turned aside unto vain jangling.* Vain talk, empty declamation, discourses without sense. The word here used does not mean contention or strife, but that kind of discourse which is not founded in good sense. They were discourses on their pretended distinctions in the law; on their traditions and ceremonies; on their useless genealogies, and on the fabulous statements which they had appended to the law of Moses.

7. *Desiring to be teachers of the law.* That is, to have the credit and reputation of being well versed in the law of Moses, and qualified to explain it to others. This was a high honour among the Jews, and these teachers laid claim to the same distinction. ¶ *Understanding neither what they say.* That is, they do not understand the true nature and design of that law which they attempt to explain to others. This was true of the Jewish teachers, and equally so of those in the church at Ephesus, who attempted to explain it. They appear to have explained the law on the principles which commonly prevailed among the Jews, and hence their instructions tended greatly to corrupt the faith of the gospel. They made affirmations of what they knew nothing of, and though they made confident asseverations, yet they often pertained to things about which they had no knowledge. One needs only a slight acquaintance with the man-

8 But we know that *m*the law *is* good, if a man use it lawfully; 9 Knowing this, that *n*the law

m Ro.7.12.   *n* Ga.5.23.

ner of teaching among Jewish Rabbies, or with the things found in their traditions, to see the accuracy of this statement of the apostle. A sufficient illustration of this may be found in Allen's *Modern Judaism.*

8. *But we know that the law* is *good.* We admit this; it is that which we all concede. This declaration is evidently made by the apostle to guard against the supposition that he was an enemy of the law. Doubtless this charge would be brought against him, or against anyone who maintained the sentiments which he had just expressed. By speaking thus of what those teachers regarded as so important in the law, it would be natural for them to declare that he was an enemy of the law itself, and would be glad to see all its claims abrogated. Paul says that he designs no such thing. He admitted that the law was good. He was never disposed for one moment to call it in question. He only asked that it should be rightly understood and properly explained. Paul was never disposed to call in question the excellency and the utility of the law, however it might bear on him or on others; comp. Notes on Rom. vii. 12, and on Acts xxi. 21-26. ¶ *If a man use it lawfully.* In a proper manner; for the purposes for which it was designed. It is intended to occupy a most important place, but it should not be perverted. Paul asked only that it should be used *aright,* and in order to this, he proceeds to state what *is* its true design.

9. *Knowing this.* That is, "If anyone knows, or admits this, he has the proper view of the design of the law." The apostle does not refer particularly to himself as knowing or conceding this, for then he would have used the plural form of the participle (see the Greek), but he means that *anyone* who had just views of the law would see that that which he proceeds to specify was its

is not made for a righteous man, but for the lawless and disobedient, for the ungodly and for sinners,

real purpose. ¶ *The law is not made for a righteous man.* There has been great variety in the interpretation of this passage. Some suppose that the law here refers to the ceremonial laws of Moses (Clarke, Rosenmüller, Abbot); others to the denunciatory part of the law (Doddridge and Bloomfield); and others that it means that the chief purpose of the law was to restrain the wicked. It seems clear, however, that the apostle does not refer merely to the ceremonial law, for he specifies that which condemns the unholy and profane; the murderers of fathers and mothers; liars and perjured persons. It was not the *ceremonial* law which condemned these things, but the *moral* law. It cannot be supposed, moreover, that the apostle meant to say that the law was not binding on a righteous man, or that he was under no obligation to obey it—for he everywhere teaches that the moral law is obligatory on all mankind. To suppose also that a *righteous* man is released from the obligation to obey the law, that is, to do *right,* is an absurdity. Nor does he seem to mean, as Macknight supposes, that the law was not given for the purpose of justifying a righteous man—for this *was* originally one of its designs. Had man always obeyed it, he would have been justified by it. The meaning seems to be, that the purpose of the law was not to fetter and perplex those who were righteous, and who aimed to do their duty and to please God. It was not intended to produce a spirit of servitude and bondage. As the Jews interpreted it, it did this, and this interpretation appears to have been adopted by the teachers at Ephesus, to whom Paul refers. The whole tendency of their teaching was to bring the soul into a state of bondage, and to make religion a condition of servitude. Paul teaches, on the other hand, that religion was a condition of freedom, and that the main purpose of the law

for unholy and profane, for murderers of fathers and murderers of mothers, for manslayers,

was not to fetter the minds of the righteous by numberless observances and minute regulations, but that it was to restrain *the wicked* from sin. This is the case with all law. No *good* man feels himself fettered and manacled by wholesome laws, nor does he feel that the purpose of law is to reduce him to a state of servitude. It is only the wicked who have this feeling—and in this sense the law is *made* for a man who intends to do wrong. ¶ *For the lawless.* To bind and restrain them. The word here used means, properly, those who have no law, and then those who are transgressors—the wicked. It is rendered *transgressors* in Mat. xv. 28; Luke xxii. 37; and *wicked*, Acts ii. 23; 2 Thes. ii. 8. ¶ *And disobedient.* Those who are insubordinate, lawless, refractory. The word properly means those who are under no subjection or authority. It occurs in the New Testament only here, and Tit. i. 6, 10, where it is rendered *unruly*, and Heb. ii. 8, where it is translated *not put under*—that is, under Christ. ¶ *For the ungodly.* Those who have no religion; who do not worship or honour God. The Greek word occurs in the following places, in all of which it is rendered *ungodly:* Rom. iv. 5; v. 6; 1 Tim. i. 9; 1 Pet. iv. 18; 2 Pet. ii. 5; iii. 7; Jude 15. The meaning is, that the law is against all who do not worship or honour God. ¶ *And for sinners.* The word used here is the common word to denote *sinners.* It is general, and includes sins of all kinds. ¶ *For unholy.* "Those who are regardless of duty to God or man" (Robinson, *Lex.*). The word occurs in the New Testament only here, and in 2 Tim. iii. 2. It has particular reference to those who fail of their duty *towards God*, and means those who have no piety; who are irreligious. ¶ *And profane.* This does not necessarily mean that they were profane in the sense that they blasphemed the name of God, or were profane swearers—though the word

10 For whoremongers, for them that defile themselves with mankind, for menstealers, for liars, for

would include that—but it means properly those who are impious, or who are scoffers; Notes, Heb. xii. 16. The word occurs only in the following places, in all of which it is rendered *profane:* 1 Tim. i. 9; iv. 7; vi. 20; 2 Tim. ii. 16; Heb. xii. 16. A man who treats religion with contempt, mockery, or scorn, would correspond with the meaning of the word. ¶ *For murderers of fathers.* The Greek properly means *a smiter of a father* (Robinson), though here it undoubtedly means a parricide. This was expressly forbidden by the law of Moses, and was a crime punishable by death, Ex. xxi. 15. It is said to have been a crime which the Roman law did not contemplate as possible, and hence that there was no enactment against it. It is, indeed, a crime of the highest order; but facts have shown that if the Romans supposed it would *never* be committed, they did not judge aright of human nature. There is *no* sin which man will not commit if unrestrained, and there is in fact no conceivable form of crime of which he has *not* been guilty. ¶ *Murderers of mothers.* A still more atrocious and monstrous crime, if possible, than the former. We can conceive nothing superior to this in atrocity, and yet it has been committed. Nero caused his mother to be murdered, and the annals of crime disclose the names of not a few who have imbrued their own hands in the blood of those who bare them. This was also expressly forbidden by the law of Moses, Ex. xxi. 15. ¶ *For manslayers.* This word occurs nowhere else in the New Testament. It means a homicide—a murderer. The crime is expressly forbidden by the law, Ex. xx. 13; Gen. ix. 6.

10. *For whoremongers.* Lev. xix. 29; xx. 5. ¶ *For them that defile themselves with mankind.* Sodomites. See the evidence that this crime abounded in ancient times, in the Notes on Rom. i. 27. It was forbid-

perjured persons, and if there be any other thing that is contrary to sound[o] doctrine;

11 According to the glorious gospel of the [p] blessed God, [q] which was committed to my trust.

12 And I thank Christ Jesus our Lord, [r] who hath enabled me,

o 2 Ti.4.3; Tit.1.9. p ch.6.15. q 1 Co.9.17. r 1 Co.15.10.

den by the law of Moses, and was punishable with death, Lev. xx. 13. ¶ *For menstealers.* The word here used—ἀνδραποδιστής—occurs nowhere else in the New Testament. It properly means one who steals another for the purpose of making him a slave—a kidnapper. This is the common way in which men are made slaves. Some, indeed, are taken in war and sold as slaves, but the mass of those who have been reduced to servitude have become slaves by being kidnapped. Children are *stolen* from their parents, or wives from their husbands, or husbands from their wives, or parents from their children, or whole families are stolen together. None become slaves voluntarily, and consequently the whole process of making slaves partakes of the nature of *theft* of the worst kind. What theft is like that of stealing a man's children, or his wife, or his father or mother? The *guilt* of manstealing is incurred essentially by those who purchase those who are thus stolen—as the purchaser of a stolen horse, knowing it to be so, participates in the crime. A measure of that criminality also adheres to all who own slaves, and who thus maintain the system—for it is a system known to have been originated by theft. This crime was expressly forbidden by the law of God, and was made punishable with death, Ex. xxi. 16; Deut. xxiv. 7. ¶ *For liars.* Lev. vi. 2–4; xix. 11. ¶ *For perjured persons.* Those who swear falsely, Lev. xix. 12; vi. 3; Ex. xx. 7. ¶ *And if there be any other thing that is contrary to sound doctrine.* To sound or correct *teaching*—for so the word doctrine means. The meaning is, if there is anything else that is opposed to the instruction which the law of God gives.

11. *According to the glorious gospel.* The gospel is a system of divine revelation. It makes known the will of God. It states what is duty, and accords in its great principles with the law, or is in harmony with it. The law, in principle, forbids all which the gospel forbids, and in publishing the requirements of the gospel, therefore, Paul says that the law really forbade all which was prohibited in the gospel, and was designed to restrain all who would act contrary to that gospel. There is no contradiction between the law and the gospel. They forbid the same things, and in regard to morals and true piety, the clearer revelations of the gospel are but carrying out the principles stated in the law. They who preach the gospel, then,should not be regarded as arrayed against the law, and Paul says that they who preached the gospel aright really stated the true principles of the law. This he evidently intends should bear against the false teachers who professed to explain the law of Moses. He means here that if a man wished to explain the law, the best explanation would be found in that gospel which it was his office to publish; comp. Rom. iii. 31. ¶ *Of the blessed God.* Revealed by the blessed God—the same God who was the Author of the law. ¶ *Which was committed to my trust.* Not to him alone, but to him in common with others. He had received it directly from the Lord, 1 Cor. ix. 17; Notes, Gal. i. 1.

12. *And I thank Christ Jesus our Lord.* The mention of the gospel (ver. 11), and of the fact that it was committed to him, leads the apostle to express his gratitude to him who had called him to the work of preaching it. The Lord Jesus had called him when he was a blasphemer and a persecutor. He had constrained him to leave his career of persecution and blasphemy, and to consecrate himself to the defence and the propagation of the gospel. For all this, though it had required him to give up his favourite projects

for that *he counted me faithful, putting* me into the ministry;

13 Who*u* was before a blas-

s 1 Co.7.25.   *t* Col.1.25.
u Ac.8.3; 1 Co.15.9.

in life, and all the flattering schemes of ambition, he now felt that praise was due to the Redeemer. If there is anything for which a good man will be thankful, and should be thankful, it is that he has been so directed by the Spirit and providence of God as to be put into the ministry. It is indeed a work of toil, and of self-denial, and demanding many sacrifices of personal ease and comfort. It requires a man to give up his splendid prospects of worldly distinction, and of wealth and ease. It is often identified with want, and poverty, and neglect, and persecution. But it is an office so honourable, so excellent, so noble, and ennobling; it is attended with so many precious comforts here, and is so useful to the world, and it has such promises of blessedness and happiness in the world to come, that *no matter what a man is required to give up in order to become a minister of the gospel,* he should be thankful to Christ for putting him into the office. A minister, when he comes to die, feels that the highest favour which Heaven has conferred on him has been in turning his feet away from the paths of ambition, and the pursuits of ease or gain, and leading him to that holy work to which he has been enabled to consecrate his life. ¶ *Who hath enabled me.* Who has given me ability or strength for this service. The apostle traced to the Lord Jesus *the fact* that he was in the ministry at all, and all the ability which he had to perform the duties of that holy office. It is not necessary here to suppose, as many have done, that he refers to miraculous power conferred on him, but he makes the acknowledgment which any faithful minister would do, that all the strength which he has to perform the duties of his office is derived from Christ; comp. Notes, John xv. 5; 1 Cor. xv. 10. ¶ *For that he counted me faithful.* This is equivalent to saying that he reposed confidence in me. It means that there was something in the character of Paul,

and in his attachment to the Saviour, on which reliance could be placed, or that there was that which gave the assurance that he would be faithful. A sovereign, when he sends an ambassador to a foreign court, reposes confidence in him, and would not commission him unless he had reason to believe that he would be faithful. So it is in reference to all who are called by the Redeemer into the ministry. They are his ambassadors to a lost world. His putting them into the ministry is an act expressive of great confidence in them—for he commits to them great and important interests. Learn hence, (1) that no one ought to regard himself as called to the ministry who will not be "faithful" to his Master; and (2) that the office of the ministry is most honourable and responsible. Nowhere else are there so great interests intrusted to man.

13. *Who was before a blasphemer.* This does not mean that Paul before his conversion was what would now be regarded as an open blasphemer—that he was one who abused and reviled sacred things, or one who was in the habit of profane swearing. His character appears to have been just the reverse of this, for he was remarkable for treating what he regarded as sacred with the utmost respect; see Notes on Phil. iii. 4–6. The meaning is, that he had reviled the name of Christ, and opposed him and his cause—not believing that he was the Messiah; and in thus opposing he had *really* been guilty of blasphemy. The true Messiah he had in fact treated with contempt and reproaches, and he now looked back upon that fact with the deepest mortification, and with wonder that one who had been so treated by him should have been willing to put him into the ministry. On the meaning of the word *blaspheme,* see Notes on Mat. ix. 3; comp. Acts xxvi. 11. In his conduct here referred to, Paul elsewhere says, that he thought at the time that he was doing what he ought to

phemer, and a persecutor, and injurious; but I obtained mercy,

because *v*I did *it* ignorantly in unbelief.

v Lu. 23. 34.

do (Acts xxvi. 9); here he says that
he now regarded it as *blasphemy.*
Learn hence that men may have very
different views of their conduct when
they come to look at it in subsequent
life. What they now regard as harmless, or even as right and proper, may
hereafter overwhelm them with shame
and remorse. The sinner will yet
feel the deepest self - reproaches for
that which now gives us no uneasiness.
¶ *And a persecutor.* Acts ix. 1, *seq.*;
xxii. 4; xxvi. 11; 1 Cor. xv. 9; Gal. i.
13, 23. ¶ *And injurious.* The word
here used (ὑβριστής), occurs only in
one other place in the New Testament, Rom. i. 30, where it is rendered
despiteful. The word *injurious* does
not quite express its force. It does
not mean merely doing *injury*, but
refers rather to the manner or spirit
in which it is done. It is a word of
intenser signification than either the
word "blasphemer," or "persecutor,"
and means that what he did was done
with a proud, haughty, insolent spirit.
There was wicked and malicious violence, an arrogance and spirit of tyran-
ny in what he did, which greatly aggravated the wrong that was done;
comp. the Greek in Mat. xxii. 6;
Luke xi. 45; xviii. 32; Acts xiv. 5;
1 Thes. ii. 2; 2 Cor. xii. 10, for illustrations of the meaning of the word.
Tindal and Coverdale render it here
"tyrant." ¶ *But I obtained mercy,
because I did it ignorantly in unbelief.*
Comp. Notes on Luke xxiii. 34. The
ignorance and unbelief of Paul were
not such excuses for what he did that
they would wholly free him from blame,
nor did he regard them as such—for
what he did was with a violent and
wicked spirit—but they were mitigat-
ing circumstances. They served to
modify his guilt, and were among the
reasons why God had mercy on him.
What is said here, therefore, accords
with what the Saviour said in his
prayer for his murderers, "Father,
forgive them, for they know not what
they do." It is undoubtedly true
that persons who sin ignorantly, and

who regard themselves as right in
what they do, are much more likely to
obtain mercy than those who do wrong
designedly.

[Yet we cannot but regard Paul's "ignorance in unbelief" as, in itself, a *grievous sin.*
He had abundant means of knowing the truth
had he been disposed to inquire with patience
and candour. His great abilities and excellent
education are a farther aggravation of the
crime. It is, therefore, impossible to acquiesce in any solution of this clause which *seems*
to make criminal ignorance a ground of mercy.
The author, however, intends nothing of this
kind, nor would it be fair to put such construction on his words. Yet, a little more
fulness had been desirable on a subject of this
nature. It is certain that, independent of
the nature of the ignorance, whether wilful
or otherwise, the *character* of crime is affected
by it. He who should oppose truth, *knowing
it to be such*, is more guilty than he who
opposes it in ignorance, or under the conviction that it is not truth but falsehood. *In
a certain sense*, too, this ignorance may be
regarded as a reason why mercy is bestowed
on such as sin desperately or blasphemously
under it. Rather it is a reason why they
are not *excluded from* mercy. It shows why
persons *so* guilty are not beyond its pale.
This is, we think, the true key both to the
passage and that in Luke xxiii. 34. The
ignorance is not a reason why God should
bestow mercy on such persons, rather than
on others left to perish, but a reason why
they obtain mercy at all, who, by their blas-
phemies, had been supposed to have reached
the sin against the Holy Ghost.

Now consider the passage in this view. The
apostle had just been showing how great a sinner he had formerly been. His criminality had
been *so* great that it went near to shutting
him out from mercy altogether. Had he mali-
ciously persecuted and blasphemed Christ,
knowing him to be the Messiah, his had been
the unpardonable sin, and his lot that of judi-
cial, final obduracy. But he had not got that
length. He was saved from that gulf, and obtained mercy, *because*, sinning ignorantly and
in unbelief, he was not beyond its range.
That Paul should set himself to excuse his
guilt is altogether impossible. He does the
very reverse. He has but escaped the unpardonable sin. He is chief of sinners. He owes
his salvation to exceeding abundant grace.
All long-suffering has been exercised towards
him. He affirms that mercy was extended

14 And the grace of our Lord was exceeding abundant, with faith and love which is in Christ Jesus.

15 This *is* a *w*faithful saying, and worthy of all acceptation, that Christ Jesus *x* came into the world

w 2 Ti.2.11; Tit.3.8.   x Mat.9.13; Lu.19.10.

---

to him, that, to the end of time, there might be a proof or pattern of mercy to the guiltiest. Had he been assigning a reason why *he* obtained mercy, rather than others left to perish, doubtless *that* had been what he has elsewhere assigned and defended, "God will have mercy on whom he will have mercy, and he will have compassion on whom he will have compassion," Rom. ix. 15.]

14. *And the grace of our Lord was exceeding abundant.* That is, in his conversion under these circumstances, and in the aid which was afterwards imparted to him in his work. ¶ *With faith and love which is in Christ Jesus.* Accompanied with the exercise of faith and love ; or producing faith and love. The grace which was imparted to him was seen in the faith and love which it produced; see Notes, 1 Cor. xv. 10.

15. *This* is *a faithful saying.* Gr., "Faithful is the word," or doctrine— ὁ λόγος. This verse has somewhat the character of a parenthesis, and seems to have been thrown into the midst of the narrative because the mind of the apostle was full of the subject. He had said that he, a great sinner, had obtained mercy. This naturally led him to think of the purpose for which Christ came into the world—*to save sinners*—and to think how strikingly that truth had been illustrated in his own case, and how that case had shown that it was worthy the attention of all. The word rendered "saying," means in this place *doctrine, position,* or *declaration.* The word "faithful," means *assuredly true;* it was that which might be depended on, or on which reliance might be placed. The meaning is, that the doctrine that Christ came to save sinners might be depended on as certainly true ; comp. 2 Tim. ii. 11 ; Titus iii. 8. ¶ *And worthy of all acceptation.* Worthy to be embraced or believed by all. This is so, because (1) all are sinners and need a Saviour. All, therefore, ought to welcome a doctrine which shows them how they may be saved. (2)

Because Christ died for all. If he had died for only a part of the race, and could save only a part, it could not be said with any propriety that the doctrine was worthy of the acceptance of all. If that were so, what had it to do with *all?* How could all be interested in it or benefited by it? If medicine had been provided for only a part of the patients in a hospital, it could not be said that the announcement of such a fact was worthy the attention of all. It would be highly worthy the attention of those for whom it was designed, but there would be a part who would have nothing to do with it ; and why should they concern themselves about it? But if it was provided for each one, then each one would have the highest interest in it. So, if salvation has been provided for me, it is a matter claiming my profoundest attention ; and the same is true of every human being. If *not* provided for me, I have nothing to do with it. It does not concern me at all. [See this subject discussed at length in the Supplementary Note on 2 Cor. v. 14.] (3) The manner in which the provision of salvation has been made in the gospel is such as to make it worthy of universal acceptance. It provides for the complete pardon of sin, and the restoration of the soul to God. This is done in a way that is honourable to God—maintaining his law and his justice ; and, at the same time, it is in a way that is honourable to man. He is treated afterwards as a friend of God and an heir of life. He is raised up from his degradation, and restored to the favour of his Maker. If man were himself to suggest a way of salvation, he could think of none that would be more honourable to God and to himself ; none that would do so much to maintain the law and to elevate him from all that now degrades him. What higher honour can be conferred on man than to have his salvation *sought as an object of intense*

to save sinners; of whom I am chief.

16 Howbeit for this cause I

and earnest desire by one so great and glorious as the Son of God? (4) It is worthy of all acceptance, from the nature of the salvation itself. Heaven is offered, with all its everlasting glories, through the blood of Christ— and is not this worthy of universal acceptation? Men would accept of a coronet or crown; a splendid mansion, or a rich estate; a present of jewels and gold, if freely tendered to them— but what trifles are these compared with heaven! If there is anything that is worthy of *universal* acceptation, it is *heaven*—for all will be miserable unless they enter there. ¶ *That Christ Jesus came into the world to save sinners.* The great and peculiar doctrine of the gospel. He *"came* into the world." He therefore had a previous existence. He *came.* He had, therefore, an object in coming. It makes his gospel more worthy of acceptation that he had an intention, a plan, a wish, in thus coming into the world. He *"came"* when he was under no necessity of coming; he came to save, not to destroy; to reveal mercy, not to denounce judgment; to save *sinners*—the poor, the lost, the wandering, not to condemn them; he came to restore them to the favour of God, to raise them up from their degradation, and to bring them to heaven. ¶ *Of whom I am chief.* Gr., *first.* The word is used to denote eminence—and it means that he occupied the *first rank* among sinners. There were none who surpassed him. This does not mean that he had been the greatest of sinners in *all respects,* but that in some respects he had been so great a sinner, that on the whole there were none who had surpassed him. That to which he particularly refers was doubtless the part which he had taken in putting the saints to death; but in connection with this, he felt, undoubtedly, that he had by nature a heart eminently prone to sin; see Rom. vii. Except in the matter of persecuting the saints, the youthful

obtained mercy, that in me first Jesus Christ might shew forth all long-suffering, *ʸ* for a pattern to

y Ro.15.4.

Saul of Tarsus appears to have been eminently moral, and his outward conduct was framed in accordance with the strictest rules of the law, Phil. iii. 6; Acts xxvi. 4, 5. After his conversion, he never attempted to extenuate his conduct, or excuse himself. He was always ready, in all circles, and in all places, to admit to its fullest extent the fact that he was a sinner. So deeply convinced was he of the truth of this, that he bore about with him the constant impression that he was eminently unworthy; and hence he does not say merely that he *had been* a sinner of most aggravated character, but he speaks of it as something that always pertained to him—"of whom I am chief." We may remark, (1) that a true Christian will always be ready to admit that his past life has been evil; (2) that this will become the abiding and steady conviction of the soul; and (3) that an acknowledgment that we are sinners is not inconsistent with evidence of piety, and with high attainments in it. The most eminent Christian has the deepest sense of the depravity of his own heart and of the evil of his past life.

16. *Howbeit for this cause.* That is, this was *one* of the causes, or this was a leading reason. We are not to suppose that this was the only one. God had other ends to answer by his conversion than this, but this was one of the designs why he was pardoned—that there might be for all ages a permanent proof that sins of the deepest dye might be forgiven. It was well to have one such example at the outset, that a doubt might never arise about the possibility of forgiving great transgressors. The question thus would be settled for ever. ¶ *That in me first.* Not *first* in the order of time, as our translation would seem to imply, but that in me the first or chief of sinners (ἐν ἐμοὶ πρώτῳ) he might show an example. The idea is, that he sustained the first rank as a sinner, and that Jesus Christ designed to show mercy to

them which should hereafter believe on him to life everlasting.

z Ps.10.16.   a ch.6.15,16.   b Jn.1.18.

him *as such*, in order that the possibility of pardoning the greatest sinners might be evinced, and that no one might afterwards despair of salvation on account of the greatness of his crimes. ¶ *Might show forth all long-suffering.* The highest possible degree of forbearance, in order that a case might never occur about which there could be any doubt. It was shown by his example that the Lord Jesus could evince any possible degree of patience, and could have mercy on the greatest imaginable offenders. ¶ *For a pattern—ὑποτύπωσιν.* This word occurs nowhere else in the New Testament, except in 2 Tim. i. 13, where it is rendered *form.* It properly means a form, sketch, or imperfect delineation. Then it denotes a pattern or example, and here it means that the case of Paul was an example for the encouragement of sinners in all subsequent times. It was that to which they might look when they desired forgiveness and salvation. It furnished all the illustration and argument which they would need to show that they might be forgiven. It settled the question for ever that the greatest sinners might be pardoned; for as he was "the chief of sinners," it proved that a case could not occur which was beyond the possibility of mercy. ¶ *Which should hereafter believe on him to life everlasting.* All might learn from the mercy shown to him that salvation could be obtained. From this verse we may learn, (1) That no sinner should despair of mercy. No one should say that he is *so great* a sinner that he cannot be forgiven. One who regarded himself as the "chief" of sinners was pardoned, and pardoned for the very purpose of illustrating this truth, that *any* sinner might be saved. His example stands as the illustration of this to all ages; and were there no other, *any* sinner might now come and hope for mercy. But there *are* other examples. Sinners of all ranks and descriptions have

been pardoned. Indeed, there is no form of depravity of which men can be guilty, in respect to which there are not instances where just such offenders have been forgiven. The persecutor may reflect that great enemies of the cross like him have been pardoned; the profane man and the blasphemer, that many such have been forgiven; the murderer, the thief, the sensualist, that many of the same character have found mercy, and have been admitted to heaven. (2) The fact that great sinners have been pardoned, is a proof that others of the same description may be also. The same mercy that saved them can save us—for mercy is not exhausted by being frequently exercised. The blood of atonement which has cleansed so many can cleanse us—for its efficacy is not destroyed by being once applied to the guilty soul. Let no one, then, despair of obtaining mercy because he feels that his sins are too great to be forgiven. Let him look to the past, and remember what God *has* done. Let him remember the case of Saul of Tarsus; let him think of David and Peter; let him recall the names of Augustine, and Col. Gardiner, and the Earl of Rochester, and John Newton, and John Bunyan—and thousands like them, who have found mercy; and in *their* examples let him see a full proof that God is willing to save any sinner, no matter how vile, provided he is penitent and believing.

17. *Now unto the King eternal.* This ascription of praise is offered to God in view of the mercy which he had shown to so great a sinner. It is the outbreak of that grateful emotion which swelled his bosom, and which would not be denied expression, when Paul recalled his former life and the mercy of God to his soul. It somewhat interrupts, indeed, the train of his remarks, but the heart was so full that it demanded utterance. It is just an instance of the joy and gratitude which fill the soul of a Christian

wise[c] God, [d]be honour and glory for ever and ever. Amen.

c Ro.16.27.   d 1 Ch.29.11.   e ch.4.14.

when he is led along in a train of reflections which conduct him to the recollections of his former sin and danger, and to the fact that he has obtained mercy and has now the hope of heaven. The apostle Paul not unfrequently, in accordance with a mode of writing that was common among the Hebrews, interposes an expression of praise in the midst of his reasonings; comp. Rom. i. 25; 2 Cor. xi. 31. God is called *King* here, as he is often in the Scriptures, to denote that he *rules* over the universe. A literal translation of the passage would be, "To the King of ages, who is immortal," &c. The meaning of this expression—"the King of ages"—βασιλει των αιωνων—is, that he is a king who rules throughout all ages. This does not mean that he himself lives for ever, but that his dominion extends over all ages or generations. The rule of earthly monarchs does not extend into successive ages; his does. Their reign is temporary; his is enduring, and continues as one generation after another passes on, and thus embraces them all. ¶ *Immortal.* This refers to God himself, not to his reign. It means that he does not die, and it is given to him to distinguish him from other sovereigns. All other monarchs but God expire—and are just as liable to die at any moment as any other men. ¶ *Invisible.* Chap. vi. 16; see Notes on Jn. i. 18. ¶ *The only wise God.* Notes, Rom. xvi. 27. The word "*wise*" is wanting in many MSS., and in some editions of the New Testament. It is omitted by Griesbach; marked as doubtful by Tittman, and rejected in the valuable edition of Hahn. Erasmus conjectures that it was added against the Arians, who maintained that the Father only was God, and that as he is here mentioned as such, the word *wise* was interpolated to denote merely that the attribute of perfect wisdom belonged only to him. Wetstein regards the reading as genuine, and suspects that in some of the early manu-

18 This charge I commit unto thee, son Timothy, [e]according to the prophecies which went before

scripts where it is wanting it was omitted by the transcriber, because it was regarded as inelegant for two adjectives to be united in this manner. It is not easy to determine as to the genuineness of the reading. The sense is not materially affected, whichever view be adopted. It is true that Jehovah is the only God; it is also true that he is the only *wise* God. The gods of the heathen are "vanity and a lie," and they are wholly destitute of wisdom; see Ps. cxv. 3–8; cxxxv. 15–18; Isa. xl. 18–20; xliv. 10–17. ¶ Be *honour.* Let there be all the respect and veneration shown to him which is his due. ¶ *And glory.* Praise. Let him be praised by all for ever. ¶ *Amen.* So be it; an expression of strong affirmation, Jn. iii. 3. Here it is used to denote the solemn assent of the heart to the sentiment conveyed by the words used; see Notes on Mat. vi. 13; 1 Cor. xiv. 16.

18. *This charge.* This command or injunction. It does not refer to any "charge," or "cure," which he had as bishop or minister, as the word is sometimes used now, but to the commands or injunctions which he was delivering to him. The command particularly referred to is that in ver. 8. ¶ *According to the prophecies which went before on thee.* The general meaning of this is plain. It is, that Paul was committing to him an important trust, and one that required great wisdom and fidelity; and that in doing it he was acting in conformity with the hopes which had been cherished respecting Timothy, and with certain expressed anticipations about his influence in the church. From early life the hope had been entertained that he would be a man to whom important trusts might be committed; and it had been predicted that he would be distinguished as a friend of religion. These hopes seem to have been cherished in consequence of the careful training in religion which he had had (2 Tim. ii.

on thee, that thou by them mightest war a good warfare;

19 Holding[f] faith, and a good conscience, which some having put

1; iii. 15), and probably from the early indications of seriousness, prudence, and piety which he manifested. It was natural to entertain such hopes, and it seems, from this place, that such hopes had even assumed the form of predictions. It is not absolutely necessary to suppose that these predictions referred to by the word *prophecies* were inspired, for the word *may* be used in a popular sense, as it is often now. We speak now familiarly of *predicting* or *foretelling* the future usefulness of a serious, prudent, studious, and pious youth. We argue from what he is, to what he will be, and we do not deem it unsafe or improper to hazard the prediction that, if he lives, he will be a man to whom important interests may be intrusted. As there were, however, prophets in the Christian church (Notes, Acts xi. 27; 1 Cor. xiv.), and as it is possible that in some cases they were inspired to foretell future events, it cannot be regarded as improper to suppose that some of them had foretold the future usefulness of this religiously educated youth. — Whatever may be meant by the expression, this general observation may be made, that when a young man enters on the active duties of life, and when great interests are intrusted to him, it is not improper to remind him of the hopes which had been cherished of him; of the anticipations which had been formed of his future usefulness; and of the expressions which have been used by the pious and the discerning respecting his future character. This is a kind of reminiscence which will rather increase his sense of responsibility than flatter his vanity; and it may be made a means of exciting him to diligence and fidelity. A virtuous young man will not willingly disappoint the long-cherished hopes of his friends. He will be likely to be made more diligent by the remembrance of all their fond anticipations of his future success. ¶ *That thou by them.* By those pro-

phecies. That is, that being stimulated and excited by those predictions and hopes, you might be led to fidelity and usefulness. ¶ *Mightest war a good warfare.* The Christian life is often compared to a warfare or struggle for victory (comp. Eph. vi. 10-17; 1 Cor. ix. 7; 2 Cor. iv. 4), and the services of the Christian ministry especially are likened to those of a soldier, 2 Tim. ii. 3, 4; iv. 7. The meaning here is, that he should contend with earnestness as a Christian and a minister in that holy service in which he was engaged, and endeavour to secure the victory. He "wars a good warfare" who is engaged in a righteous cause; who is faithful to his commander and to his post; who is unslumbering in observing the motions of the enemy, and fearless in courage in meeting them; who never forsakes his standard, and who continues thus faithful till the period of his enlistment has expired, or till death. *Such* a soldier the Christian minister should be.

19. *Holding faith.* Fidelity to the cause in which you are enlisted—as a good soldier should do. This does not mean, as it seems to me, that Timothy should hold to the system of doctrines revealed in the gospel, but that he should have that fidelity which a good soldier should have. He should not betray his trust. He should adhere to the cause of his master with unwavering steadfastness. This would include, of course, a belief of the truth, but this is not the leading idea in the phrase. ¶ *And a good conscience.* See Notes, Acts xxiii. 1. A good conscience, as well as fidelity, is necessary in the service of the Redeemer. A good conscience is that which is well informed in regard to what is right, and where its dictates are honestly followed. ¶ *Which some having put away.* That is, *which good conscience* some have put from them, or in other words, have not followed its dictates. The truth thus taught is, that men make

away, concerning faith have made shipwreck:

20 Of whom is Hymeneus and

shipwreck of their faith by not keeping a good conscience. They love sin. They follow the leadings of passion. They choose to indulge in carnal propensities. As a matter of course, they must, if they will do this, reject and renounce the gospel. Men become infidels because they wish to indulge in sin. No man can be a sensualist, and yet love that gospel which enjoins purity of life. If men would keep a good conscience, the way to a steady belief in the gospel would be easy. If men will not, they must expect sooner or later to be landed in infidelity. ¶ *Concerning faith.* In respect to the whole subject of faith. They are unfaithful to God, and they reject the whole system of the gospel. "Faith" is sometimes used to denote the gospel—as faith is the principal thing *in* the gospel. ¶ *Have made shipwreck.* There is an entire destruction of faith—as a ship is wholly ruined that strikes on a rock and sinks.

20. *Of whom is Hymeneus and Alexander.* Hymeneus is nowhere else mentioned in the New Testament, except in 2 Tim. ii. 17, where he is mentioned in connection with Philetus as a very dangerous man. An Alexander is mentioned in Acts xix. 33, which some have supposed to be the same as the one referred to here. It is not certain, however, that the same person is intended; see Notes on that verse. In 2 Tim. iv. 14, Alexander the coppersmith is mentioned as one who had done the apostle "much evil," and there can be little doubt that he is the same person who is referred to here. One of the doctrines which Hymeneus held was, that the "resurrection was past already" (2 Tim. ii. 18); but what doctrine Alexander held is unknown. It is not improbable, as he is mentioned here in connection with Hymeneus, that he maintained the same opinion, and in addition to that he appears to have been guilty of some personal injury to the apostle. Both also were guilty of blasphemy.

Alexander; *g* whom I have delivered unto Satan, that they may learn not to blaspheme.

g 1 Co.5.5.

¶ *Whom I have delivered unto Satan.* On the meaning of this expression, see Notes on 1 Cor. v. 5. ¶ *That they may learn not to blaspheme.* It cannot be supposed that Satan would undertake to *teach* them not to blaspheme, or that Paul put them under him as an *instructor* on that subject. The instructions of Satan tend rather to teach his followers to blaspheme, and none in his school fail to be apt scholars. The meaning here is, that Paul excommunicated them, and not improbably brought upon them, by giving them over to Satan, some physical maladies, that they might be reformed; comp. Notes on 1 Cor. v. 5. It is not entirely clear what is meant by *blaspheme* in this place; comp. Notes on ver. 13. It cannot be supposed that they were open and bold blasphemers, for such could not have maintained a place in the church, but rather that they held doctrines which the apostle regarded as amounting to blasphemy; that is, doctrines which were *in fact* a reproach on the divine character. There are many doctrines held by men which are in fact a reflection on the divine character, and which amount to the same thing as blasphemy. A blasphemer openly expresses views of the divine character which are a reproach to God; an errorist expresses the same thing in another way—by teaching as true about God that which represents him in a false light, and to suppose which, in fact, is a reproach. The spirit with which this is done in the two cases may be different; the thing itself may be the same. Let us be careful that we hold no views about God which are reproachful to him, and which, though we do not express it in words, may lead us to blaspheme him in our hearts.

CHAPTER II.

ANALYSIS OF THE CHAPTER.

This chapter is occupied mainly in directions about the mode of conduct-

CHAPTER II.

I ¹EXHORT, therefore, that, first of all, supplications,

prayers, intercessions, *and* giving of thanks, be made for all men;

1 or, *desire.*

---

ing public worship. . Timothy had been left at Ephesus to complete the plans which the apostle had commenced in reference to the church there, but from completing which he had been unexpectedly prevented (see the Intro.); and it was important to state the views which he entertained on this subject to Timothy. It was important also that general directions on these subjects should be given, which would be useful to the church at large. The directions in this chapter relate to the following subjects:—

I. Public prayer, ver. 1–8.

(1) It was to be offered for all classes of men, without distinction of rank, sect, party, country, or name, especially for all that were in authority, ver. 1, 2. The reasons for this were:

(*a*) That God desired all men to be saved, and it was acceptable to him that prayer should be offered for all, ver. 3, 4.

(*b*) There is but one God over all the human race, and all are alike his children, ver. 5.

(*c*) There is one and the same Mediator between God and all men, ver. 5.

(*d*) The same atonement has been made for all, ver. 6, 7.

(2) The way in which prayer should be offered. It should be with holy hands, and without the intermingling of any bad passion, ver. 8.

II. The duties of women, ver. 9–15.

(1) Modesty in their demeanour and apparel, ver. 9.

(2) Good works—the chief ornament of women professing piety, ver. 10.

(3) The duty of learning from others with a gentle and quiet spirit, ver. 11.

(4) The duty of a proper subordination and submission to man, ver. 12.

(5) The reasons for this subordination and submission are then stated. They are:

(*a*) That Adam was first formed, ver. 13.

(*b*) That the woman had been deceived, and should be willing to occupy a subordinate place, as she was first in the transgression and was the means of leading him into sin, ver. 14.

(6) Yet, as if to make a kind remark in favour of woman—to show that he did not intend to teach that she was degraded and abandoned of God—the apostle says that she would be under the divine protection, and that in the special sorrow and peril which had been brought upon her for her transgression, God would sustain her if she continued in faith, and evinced the spirit of a Christian in her life, ver. 15.

1. *I exhort, therefore.* Marg., *desire.* The word *exhort,* however, better expresses the sense of the original. The exhortation here is not addressed particularly to Timothy, but relates to all who were called to lead in public prayer, ver. 8. This exhortation, it may be observed, is inconsistent with the supposition that a *liturgy* was then in use, or with the supposition that there ever would be a liturgy—since, in that case, the objects to be prayed for would be prescribed. How singular would it be now for an Episcopal bishop to "exhort" his presbyters to pray "for the President of the United States and for all who are in authority!" When the prayer is prescribed, do they not do this as a matter of course? ¶ *First of all.* That is, as the first duty to be enjoined; the thing that is to be regarded with primary concern; comp. Luke xii. 1; 2 Pet. i. 20. It does not mean that this was to be the first thing in public worship in the order of time, but that it was to be regarded as a duty of primary importance. The duty of praying for the salvation of the whole world was not to be regarded as a subordinate and secondary thing. ¶ *Supplications.* It is not entirely

2 For ^akings, and *for* all that are in ²authority: that we may

lead a quiet and peaceable life in all godliness and honesty.

a Ro.13.1, &c.

² or, *eminent place.*

easy to mark the difference in the meaning of the words used here, and it is not essential. They all relate to *prayer*, and refer only to the different parts of prayer, or to distinct classes of thought and desire which come before the mind in pleading for others. On the difference between the words *supplications* and *prayers*, see Notes on Heb. v. 7. ¶ *Intercessions.* The noun used occurs only in this place, and in chap. iv. 5 of this epistle. The *verb*, however (εντιγχανω), occurs in Acts xxv. 4; Rom. viii. 27, 34; xi. 2; Heb. vii. 25. See the meaning explained in the Notes on Rom. viii. 26; Heb. vii. 25. There is one great Intercessor between God and man, who pleads for our salvation on the ground of what he himself has done, but we are permitted to intercede for others, not on the ground of any merit which they or we possess, but on the ground of the merit of the great Advocate and Intercessor. It is an inestimable privilege to be permitted to plead for the salvation of our fellow-men. ¶ *Giving of thanks.* That is, in behalf of others. We ought to give thanks for the mercy of God to ourselves; it is right and proper also that we should give thanks for the goodness of God to others. We should render praise that there is a way of salvation provided; that no one is excluded from the offer of mercy; and that God is using so many means to call lost sinners to himself. ¶ *For all men.* Prayers should be made for all men—for all need the grace and mercy of God; thanks should be rendered for all, for all may be saved. Does not this direction imply that Christ died for all mankind? How could we give thanks in their behalf if there were no mercy for them, and no way had been provided by which they could be saved? It may be observed here, that the direction to pray and to give thanks for all men, showed the large and catholic nature of Christianity. It was opposed entirely to the narrow and bigoted feelings of the Jews, who regarded the

whole Gentile world as excluded from covenant mercies, and as having no offer of life. Christianity threw down all these barriers, and all men are on a level; and since Christ has died for all, there is ample ground for thanksgiving and praise in behalf of the whole human race. [See Supplementary Note, 2 Cor. v. 14.] 2. *For kings.* On the respect due to rulers, see Notes on Rom. xiii. 1-7. The meaning here is, that while all men should be the subjects of prayer, those should be particularly remembered before the throne of grace who are in authority. The reason is, that so much depends on their character and plans; that the security of life, liberty, and property depends so much on them. God has power to influence their hearts, and to incline them to what is just and equal; and hence we should pray that a divine influence may descend upon them. The salvation of a king is of itself of no more importance than that of a peasant or a slave; but the welfare of thousands may depend on him, and hence he should be made the special subject of prayer. ¶ *All that are in authority.* Marg., or, "*eminent place.*" This does not necessarily mean those who hold office, but refers to any of elevated rank. The happiness of all who are under their control depends greatly on them, and hence we should pray for them that they may be converted men, and inclined to do that which is right. ¶ *That we may lead a quiet and peaceable life.* That their hearts may be so inclined to what is right that they may protect us in the enjoyment of religion, and that we may not be opposed or harassed by persecution. This does not mean that their protection would *dispose* us to lead quiet and peaceful lives, but that under their protection we may be saved from oppression on account of our religion. Christians are disposed of themselves to be peaceful and orderly; they ask of their rulers only that they may not

3 For this *is* good and acceptable in the sight of God our Saviour;

4 Who[b] will have all men to be saved, and to come unto the knowledge of the truth.

b Jn.3.15,16; 2 Pe.3.9.

be harassed in the enjoyment of their rights. ¶ *In all godliness and honesty.* In the practice of all our duties towards God, and of all the duties which we owe to men. The word *godliness* here denotes *piety*—or the duty which we owe to God; the word *honesty* refers to our duties to our fellow-men. The Christian asks from civil rulers such protection that he may be enabled quietly to perform both these classes of duties.

3. *For this* is *good and acceptable.* That is, it is good and acceptable to God that we should pray for all men. The reason is, that he desires their salvation, and hence it is agreeable to him that we should pray for it. If there were no provision made for their salvation, or if he was unwilling that they should be saved, it could not be agreeable to him that we should offer prayer for them.

4. *Who will have all men to be saved.* That is, it is in accordance with his nature, his feelings, his desires. The word *will* cannot be taken here in the absolute sense, denoting a decree like that by which he willed the creation of the world, for then it would certainly be done. But the word is often used to denote a desire, wish, or what is in accordance with the nature of anyone. Thus it may be said of God that he "wills" that his creatures may be happy—because it is in accordance with his nature, and because he has made abundant provision for their happiness—though it is not true that he *wills* it in the sense that he exerts his absolute power to make them happy. God wills that sickness should be relieved, and sorrow mitigated, and that the oppressed should go free, because it is agreeable to his nature; though it is not true that he wills it in the sense that he exerts his absolute power to produce it. A parent wills the welfare of his child. It is in accordance with his nature, his feelings, his desires; and he makes every needful arrangement

for it. If the child is not virtuous and happy, it is his own fault. So God wills that all men should be saved. It would be in accordance with his benevolent nature. He has made ample provision for it. He uses all proper means to secure their salvation. He uses *no* positive means to prevent it, and if they are *not* saved it will be their own fault. For places in the New Testament where the word here translated "will" (θέλω), means *to desire* or *wish,* see Luke viii. 20; xxiii. 8; Jn. xvi. 19; Gal. iv. 20; Mark xvii. 24; 1 Cor. vii. 7; xi. 3; xiv. 5; Mat. xv. 28. This passage cannot mean, as many have supposed, that God wills that all *kinds* of men should be saved, or that some sinners of every rank and class may be saved, because, (1) The natural and obvious interpretation of the language is opposed to such a sense. The language expresses the desire that "*all men*" should be saved, and we should not depart from the obvious sense of a passage unless necessity requires it. (2) Prayer and thanksgiving (ver. 1) are directed to be offered, not for *some* of all ranks and conditions, but for all mankind. No exception is made, and no direction is given that we should exclude any of the race from the expressions of our sympathy, and from an interest in our supplications. The reason given *here* for that prayer is, that God desires that all men should be saved. But how could this be a reason for praying for *all,* if it means that God desired only the salvation of some of *all* ranks? (3) In ver. 5 and 6, the apostle gives reasons showing that God wished the salvation of all men, and those reasons are such as to prove that the language here is to be taken in the most unlimited sense. Those reasons are, (*a*) that there is one God over all, and one Mediator between God and men—showing that God is the Father of all, and has the same interest in all; and (*b*) that Christ gave himself a ransom for all

5 For *there is* ^cone God, and one^d mediator between God and men, the man Christ Jesus;

c Ro.3 30.   d He.9.15.

6 Who gave himself ^ea ransom for all, to be ³testified in due time.

e Mat.20.28.   3 or, *a testimony.*

—showing that God desired their salvation. This verse proves (1) that salvation is provided for all—for if God wished all men to be saved, he would undoubtedly make provision for their salvation; and if he had *not* made such provision, it could not be said that he desired their salvation, since no one can doubt that he has *power* to provide for the salvation of all; (2) that salvation should be offered to all men —for if God desires it, it is right for his ministers to announce that desire, and if he desires it, it is *not* proper for them to announce anything contrary to this; (3) that men are to blame if they are not saved. If God did not wish their salvation, and if he had made no provision for it, they could not be to blame if they rejected the gospel. If God wishes it, and has made provision for it, and they are *not* saved, the sin must be their own—and it is a *great* sin, for there is no greater crime which a man can commit than to destroy his own soul, and to make himself the eternal enemy of his Maker. ¶ *And to come unto the knowledge of the truth.* The truth which God has revealed; the "truth as it is in Jesus." Notes, Eph. iv. 21.

5. *For* there is *one God.* This is a reason for offering prayer for all men, and for the declaration (ver. 4) that God desires that all men should be saved. The reason is founded in the fact that he is the common Father of all the race, and that he must have the same desire for the welfare of all his children. He has made them of one blood (Acts xvii. 26), and he must have the same interest in the happiness of all; comp. Notes, Eph. iv. 6; Rom. iii. 30. ¶ *And one Mediator between God and men.* See Notes on Gal. iii. 19, 20; Heb. ix. 15. This also is given as a reason why prayer should be offered for all, and a proof that God desires their salvation. The argument is, that there is the same Mediator between God and *all* men. He is not the Mediator between God and *a part* of the human race, but between "God and *men*," implying that He desired the salvation of the race. Whatever love there was in giving the Mediator at all, was love for all the race; whatever can be argued from that about the interest which God has in man, is proof of his interest in the race at large. It is proper, therefore, to pray for all. It may be remarked here that there is but *one* Mediator. There is not one for kings and another for their subjects; one for the rich and another for the poor; one for the master and another for the slave. All are on the same level, and the servant may feel that, in the gift of a Mediator, God regarded him with the same interest that he did his master. It may be added also that the doctrine of the Papists, that the saints or the Virgin Mary may act as mediators to procure blessings for us, is false. There is but "one Mediator;" and but one is necessary. Prayer offered to the "saints," or to the "Virgin," is idolatry, and at the same time removes the one great Mediator from the office which he alone holds, of making intercession with God. ¶ *The man Christ Jesus.* Jesus was truly and properly a man, having a perfect human body and soul, and is often called *a man* in the New Testament. But this does not prove that he was not also divine—any more than his being called *God* (John i. 1; xx. 28; Rom. ix. 5; 1 John v. 20; Heb. i. 8), proves that he was not also a man. The use of the word *man* here was probably designed to intimate that though he was divine, it was in his human nature that we are to consider him as discharging the office (Doddridge).

6. *Who gave himself a ransom for all.* This also is stated as a reason why prayer should be offered for all, and a proof that God desires the salvation of all. The argument is, that as Christ died for all, it is proper to pray for all, and that the fact that he died

7 Whereunto I am ordained a preacher, and an apostle, (I speak the truth in Christ, *and* lie not;)

for all is proof that God desired the salvation of all. Whatever proof of his desire for their salvation can be derived from this in relation to *any* of the race, is proof in relation to all. On the meaning of the phrase "he gave himself a ransom," see Notes on Mat. xx. 28; Rom. iii. 25; on the fact that it was for "*all*," see Notes on 2 Cor. v. 14.

[See also the Supp. Note on the same passage.] ¶ *To be testified in due time.* Marg., *a testimony.* The Greek is, "the testimony in its own times," or in proper times — τὸ μαρτύριον καιροῖς ἰδίοις. There have been very different explanations of this phrase. The common interpretation, and that which seems to me to be correct, is, that "the testimony of this will be furnished in the proper time; that is, in the proper time it shall be made known through all the world;" see Rosenmüller. Paul affirms it as a great and important truth that Christ gave himself a ransom for all mankind — for Jews and Gentiles; for all classes and conditions of men alike. This truth had not always been understood. The Jews had supposed that salvation was designed exclusively for their nation, and denied that it could be extended to others, unless they became Jews. According to them, salvation was not provided for, or offered to heathens *as such*, but only on condition that they became Jews. In opposition to this, Paul says that it was a doctrine of revelation that redemption was to be provided for all men, and that it was intended that the testimony to this should be afforded at the proper time. It was not fully made known under the ancient dispensation, but now the period had come when it should be communicated to all; comp. Notes on Rom. v. 6, and Gal. iv. 4.

7. *Whereunto.* Gr., "Unto which;" that is, to the bearing of which testimony I am appointed. ¶ *I am ordained.* Gr., "I am placed or constituted" — ἐτέθην. The word "ordain"

a teacher of the Gentiles in faith and verity.

8 I will therefore that men

has now acquired a technical signification, meaning to set apart solemnly to a sacred office by the imposition of hands; but it has not that meaning here. It does not refer to the *manner* in which he was set apart, or to any act of others in consecrating him to this work, but merely to the fact that he had been placed in this office or appointed to it. He refers doubtless to the fact that the Lord Jesus had designated him to this work. ¶ *A preacher and an apostle.* See Notes on 1 Cor. ix. 1–6; Gal. i. 11, 12. ¶ *I speak the truth in Christ, and lie not.* That is, *by* Christ; or I solemnly appeal to Christ — a form of an oath; Notes, Rom. ix. 1. Paul makes a solemn declaration similar to this in regard to his call to the apostleship, in Gal. i. 20. For the *reasons* why he did it, see Notes on that verse. It is probable that there were those in Ephesus who denied that he *could* be an apostle, and hence his solemn declaration affirming it. ¶ *A teacher of the Gentiles.* Specially appointed to carry the gospel to the Gentiles or the heathen; see Notes on Rom. xi. 13; Gal. ii. 7. ¶ *In faith and verity.* These words mean that he was appointed to instruct the Gentiles in faith and the knowledge of the truth.

8. *I will therefore.* The Greek word here (βούλομαι) is different from the word rendered *will* — θέλω — in ver. 4. The distinction is, that the word there used — θέλω — denotes an active volition or purpose; the word here used — βούλομαι — a mere passive desire, propensity, willingness (Rob. *Lex.*). The meaning here is, "it is my will" — expressing his wish in the case, or giving direction — though using a milder word than that which is commonly employed to denote an act of will. ¶ *That men pray every where.* Not merely in the temple, or in other sacred places, but in all places. The Jews supposed that there was special efficacy in prayers offered at the temple in Jerusalem; the heathen also had the same view in regard to

pray*f* every where, *g* lifting up

f Jn.4.21.　　　*g* He.10.22.

their temples—for both seemed to suppose that they came *nearer* to God by approaching his sacred abode. Christianity teaches that God may be worshipped in any place, and that we are at all times equally near him; see Notes on John iv. 20-24; Acts xvii. 25. The direction here given that *men* should pray, in contradistinction from the duties of *women*, specified in the next verse, may be intended to imply that men should conduct the exercises of public worship. The duties of women pertain to a different sphere; comp. ver. 11, 12. ¶ *Lifting up holy hands.* To lift up the hands denotes supplication, as it was a common attitude of prayer to spread abroad the hands towards heaven; comp. Ps. lxviii. 31; Ex. xix. 29, 33; 1 Kings viii. 22; 2 Chron. vi. 12, 13; Isa. i. 15; see also Horace, *Odes,* III. xxiii. 1; Ovid, *M.* ix. 701; Livy, v. 21; Seneca, *Ep.* 21. "Holy hands" here, mean hands that are not defiled by sin, and that have not been employed for any purpose of iniquity. The idea is, that when men approach God they should do it in a pure and holy manner. ¶ *Without wrath.* This is, without the intermingling of any evil passion; with a calm, peaceful, benevolent mind. There should be nothing of the spirit of contention; there should be no anger towards others; the suppliant should be at peace with all men. It is impossible for a man to pray with comfort, or to suppose that his prayers will be heard, if he cherishes anger. The following exquisite and oft-quoted passage from Jeremy Taylor is a more beautiful and striking illustration of the effect of anger in causing our prayers to return unanswered than was probably ever penned by anyone else. Nothing could be more true, beautiful, and graphic. "Anger sets the house on fire, and all the spirits are busy upon trouble, and intend propulsion, defence, displeasure, or revenge. It is a short madness, and an eternal enemy to discourse and a fair conversation; it intends its own ob-

holy hands, without wrath and doubting.

ject with all the earnestness of perception or activity of design, and a quicker motion of a too warm and distempered blood; it is a fever in the heart, and a calenture in the head, and a fire in the face, and a sword in the hand, and a fury all over; and therefore can never suffer a man to be in a disposition to pray. For prayer is the peace of our spirit, the stillness of our thoughts, the evenness of recollection, the seat of meditation, the rest of our cares, and the calm of our tempest; prayer is the issue of a quiet mind, of untroubled thoughts; it is the daughter of charity and the sister of meekness; and he that prays to God with an angry, that is, with a troubled and discomposed spirit, is like him that retires into a battle to meditate, and sets up his closet in the out-quarters of an army, and chooses a frontier garrison to be wise in. Anger is a perfect alienation of the mind from prayer, and therefore is contrary to that attention which presents our prayers in a right line to God. For so have I seen a lark rising from his bed of grass, and soaring upwards, and singing as he rises, and hopes to get to heaven, and rise above the clouds; but the poor bird was beaten back with the loud sighings of an eastern wind, and his motion made irregular and inconsistent, descending more at every breath of the tempest than it could recover by the libration and frequent weighing of his wings, till the little creature was forced to sit down and pant, and stay till the storm was over; and then it made a prosperous flight, and did rise and sing, as if it had learned music and motion from an angel" (*The Return of Prayers,* Works, vol. i. 638, ed. Lond. 1835). ¶ *And doubting.* This word, as used here, does not mean, as our translation would seem to imply, that we are to come before God without any doubts of our own piety, or in the exercise of perfect faith. The word used (διαλογισμός) means, properly, computation, adjustment of accounts; then reflection, thought; then reason-

9 In like manner also, that women adorn themselves in modest apparel, with shamefacedness and sobriety; not with [4] broidered hair, or gold, or pearls, or costly array;

[4] or, *plaited*, 1 Pe.3.3.

ing, opinion; then debate, contention, strife, Luke ix. 46; Mark ix. 33, 34; Phil. ii. 14. This is the sense evidently in this place. They were not to approach God in prayer in the midst of clamorous disputings and angry contentions. They were not to come when the mind was heated with debate, and irritated by strife for victory. Prayer was to be offered in a calm, serious, sober state of mind, and they who engaged in polemical strife, or in warm contention of any kind, are little fitted to unite in the solemn act of addressing God. How often are theologians, when assembled together, so heated by debate, and so anxious for party victory, that they are in no suitable state of mind to pray! How often do even good men, holding different views on the disputed points of religious doctrine, suffer their minds to become so excited, and their temper so ruffled, that they are conscious they are in an unfit state of mind to approach the throne of grace together! That theological debate has gone too far; that strife for victory has become too warm, when the disputants are in such a state of mind that they cannot unite in prayer; when they could not cease their contentions, and with a calm and proper spirit bow together before the throne of grace.

9. *In like manner also.* That is, with the same propriety; with the same regard to what religion demands. The apostle had stated particularly the duty of *men* in public worship (ver. 8), and he now proceeds to state the duty of *women.* All the directions here evidently refer to the proper manner of conducting public worship, and not to private duties; and the object here is to state the way in which he would have the different sexes appear. He had said that he would have prayers offered for all men (ver. 1, *seq.*), and that in offering such petitions he would have the men on whom devolved the duty of con-ducting public devotion, do it with holy hands, and without any intermingling of passion, and with entire freedom from the spirit of contention. In reference to the duty of females in attendance on public worship, he says that he would have *them* appear in apparel suitable to the place and the occasion—adorned not after the manner of the world, but with the zeal and love in the cause of the Redeemer which became Christians. He would not have a woman become a public teacher (ver. 12), but would wish her ever to occupy the place in society for which she was designed (ver. 11), and to which she had shown that she was adapted, ver. 13, 14. The direction in ver. 9–12, therefore, is to be understood particularly of the proper deportment of females in the duties of public worship. At the same time, the principles laid down are doubtless such as were intended to apply to them in the other situations in life, for if modest apparel is appropriate in the sanctuary, it is appropriate everywhere. If what is here prohibited in dress is *wrong* there, it would be difficult to show that it is *right* elsewhere. ¶ *That women adorn themselves.* The words "I will" are to be understood here as repeated from ver. 8. The apostle, by the use of the word *adorn* (κοσμεῖν), shows that he is not opposed to *ornament* or *adorning,* provided it be of the right kind. The world, as God has made it, is full of beauty, and he has shown in each flower that he is not opposed to true ornament. There are multitudes of things which, so far as we can see, appear to be designed for *mere* ornament, or are made merely *because* they are beautiful. Religion does not forbid true adorning. It differs from the world only on the question what *is* true ornament, or what it becomes us, all things considered, to do in the situation in which we are placed, the character which we sustain, the duties which we have

to perform, and the profession which we make. It may be that there are ornaments in heaven which would be anything but appropriate for the condition of a poor, lost, dying sinner on earth. ¶ *In modest apparel.* The word here rendered *modest* (κόσμιος), properly relates to ornament, or decoration, and means that which is *well-ordered, decorous, becoming.* It does not, properly, mean *modest* in the sense of being opposed to that which is *immodest*, or which tends to excite improper passions and desires, but that which is *becoming* or *appropriate.* The apostle does not positively specify what this would be, but he mentions some things which are to be excluded from it, and which, in his view, are inconsistent with the true adorning of Christian females—"broidered hair, gold, pearls, costly array." The sense here is, that the apparel of females should be such as becomes them, or is appropriate to them. The word here used (κόσμιος), shows that there should be due attention that it may be *truly* neat, fit, decorous. There is no religion in a negligent mode of apparel, or in inattention to personal appearance—any more than there is in wearing gold and pearls; and a female may as truly violate the precepts of her religion by neglecting her personal appearance as by excessive attention to it. The true idea here is, that her attention to her appearance should be such that she will be offensive to no class of persons; such as to show that her mind is supremely fixed on higher and more important things, and such as to interfere with no duty which she owes, and no good which she can do, either by spending her time needlessly in personal adorning, or by lavishing that money for dress which might do good to others, or by neglecting the proprieties of her station, and making herself offensive to others. ¶ *With shamefacedness.* With modesty of appearance and manner—an eminent female virtue, whether in the sanctuary or at home. ¶ *And sobriety.* The word here used means, properly, *sanity;* then sober-mindedness, moderation of the desires and passions. It is opposed to all that is frivolous, and to all undue excitement of the passions. The idea is, that in their apparel and deportment they should not intrench on the strictest decorum (Doddridge). ¶ *Not with broidered hair.* Marg., *plaited.* Females in the East pay much more attention to the hair than is commonly done with us. It is plaited with great care, and arranged in various forms, according to the prevailing fashion, and often ornamented with spangles or with silver wire or tissue interwoven; see Notes on Isa. iii. 24. The sense here is, that Christian females are not to imitate those of the world in their careful attention to the ornaments of the head. It cannot be supposed that the mere *braiding* of the hair is forbidden, but only that careful attention to the manner of doing it, and to the ornaments usually worn in it, which characterized worldly females. ¶ *Or gold, or pearls.* It is not to be supposed that *all* use of gold or pearls as articles of dress is here forbidden; but the idea is, that the Christian female is not to seek these as the adorning which she desires, or is not to imitate the world in these personal decorations. It may be a difficult question to settle how *much* ornament is allowable, and when the true line is passed. But though this cannot be settled by any exact rules, since much must depend on age, and on the relative rank in life, and the means which one may possess, yet there is one general rule which is applicable to all, and which might regulate all. It is, that the true line is passed when more is thought of this external adorning, than of the ornament of the heart. Any external decoration which occupies the mind more than the virtues of the heart, and which engrosses the time and attention more, we may be certain is wrong. The apparel should be such as not to attract attention; such as becomes our situation; such as will not be particularly singular; such as shall leave the impression that the heart is not fixed on it. It is a poor ambition to decorate a dying body with gold and pearls. It

10 But (which becometh women professing godliness) with good works.

11 Let[h] the woman learn in silence with all subjection.

h 1 Co.14.34.

should not be forgotten that the body thus adorned will soon need other habiliments, and will occupy a position where gold and pearls would be a mockery. When the *heart* is right; when there is true and supreme love for religion, it is usually not difficult to regulate the subject of dress. ¶ *Costly array.* Expensive dress. This is forbidden—for it is foolish, and the money thus employed may be much more profitably used in doing good. "Costly array" includes that which can be ill afforded, and that which is inconsistent with the feeling that the principal ornament is that of the heart.

10. *But (which becometh women professing godliness) with good works.* That is, it is not appropriate for women who profess to be the followers of the Saviour, to seek to be distinguished for personal, external decorations. If they are Christians, they have seen the vanity of these things, and have fixed the heart on more substantial realities. They are professed followers of Him "who went about doing good," and the performance of good works especially becomes them. They profess to have fixed the affections on God their Saviour, and to be living for heaven; and it is not becoming in them to seek such ornaments as would indicate that the heart is supremely attached to worldly things. There is great beauty in this direction. Good works, or deeds of benevolence, eminently become a Christian female. The nature of woman seems to be adapted to the performance of all deeds demanding kindness, tenderness, and gentleness of feeling; of all that proceeds from pity, sympathy, and affection; and we feel instinctively that while acts of hardy enterprise and daring in a good cause peculiarly become a Christian man, there is something exquisitely appropriate to the female

12 But I suffer not a woman to teach, nor to usurp authority over the man, but to be in silence.

13 For Adam was first formed, then Eve.

14 And Adam was not deceived,

character in deeds of humble and unobtrusive sympathy and benevolence. God seems to have formed her mind for just such things, and in such things it occupies its appropriate sphere rather than in seeking external adorning.

11. *Let the woman learn in silence.* Listen attentively to instruction, without attempting to teach in public; see Notes on 1 Cor. xiv. 35. ¶ *With all subjection.* With due subjection to those who are in authority, and who are appointed to minister in holy things; Notes, 1 Cor. xiv. 34.

12. *But I suffer not a woman to teach.* See Notes on 1 Cor. xiv. 34. ¶ *Nor to usurp authority over the man.* Notes, 1 Cor. xi. 3.

13. *For Adam was first formed, then Eve.* The apostle, in this verse, and the following, gives reasons why a woman should occupy a subordinate situation, and not usurp authority. The first is, that she was second in the act of creation, or was made subsequent to man. The reason here assigned cannot be understood to be *merely* that of priority of existence—for then it would give every old person authority over a younger one; but it must refer to the circumstances of the case as detailed in the history of the creation, Gen. i., ii. Man was made as the lord of this lower creation and placed in the garden, and then the woman was made of a rib taken from his side, and given to him, not as a lord, but as a companion. All the circumstances combine to show the subordinate nature of her rank, and to prove that she was not designed to exert authority over the man; comp. Notes on 1 Cor. xi. 8, 9.

14. *And Adam was not deceived.* This is the second reason why the woman should occupy a subordinate rank in all things. It is, that in the most important situation in which she was ever placed, she had shown that she

but the woman being deceived, was in the transgression.

15 Notwithstanding she shall be saved in childbearing, if they continue in faith and charity and holiness with sobriety.

---

was not qualified to take the lead. She had evinced a readiness to yield to temptation; a feebleness of resistance; a pliancy of character, which showed that she was not adapted to the situation of headship, and which made it proper that she *should* ever afterwards occupy a subordinate situation. It is not meant here that Adam did not sin, nor even that he was not deceived by the tempter, but that the woman opposed a feebler resistance to the temptation than he would have done, and that the temptation as actually applied to *her* would have been ineffectual on *him.* To tempt and seduce *him* to fall, there were needed all the soft persuasions, the entreaties, and example of his wife. Satan understood this, and approached man not with the specious argument of the serpent, but through the allurements of his wife. It is undoubtedly implied here that man in general has a power of resisting certain kinds of temptation superior to that possessed by woman, and hence that the *headship* properly belongs to him. This is, undoubtedly, the general truth, though there may be many exceptions, and many noble cases, to the honour of the female sex, in which they evince a power of resistance to temptation superior to man. In many traits of character, and among them those which are most lovely, woman is superior to man; yet it is undoubtedly true that, as a general thing, temptation will make a stronger impression on her than on him. When it is said that "Adam was not deceived," it is not meant that when he partook actually of the fruit he was under no deception, but that he was not deceived by the serpent; he was not first deceived, or first in the transgression. The woman should remember that sin *began* with her, and she should therefore be willing to occupy an humble and subordinate situation. ¶ *But the woman being deceived.* She was made to suppose that the fruit would not injure her, but would make

her wise, and that God would not fulfil his threatening of death. Sin, from the beginning, has been a process of delusion. Every man or woman who violates the law of God is deceived as to the happiness which is expected from the violation, and as to the consequences which will follow it.

15. *Notwithstanding she shall be saved.* The promise in this verse is designed to alleviate the apparent severity of the remarks just made about the condition of woman, and of the allusion to the painful facts of her early history. What the apostle had just said would carry the mind back to the period in which woman introduced sin into the world, and, by an obvious and easy association, to the sentence which had been passed on her in consequence of her transgression, and to the burden of sorrows which she was doomed to bear. By the remark in this verse, however, Paul shows that it was not his intention to overwhelm her with anguish. He did not design to harrow up her feelings by an unkind allusion to a melancholy fact in her history. It was necessary for him to state, and for her to know, that her place was secondary and subordinate, and he wished this truth ever to be kept in memory among Christians. It was not unkind or improper also to state the reasons for this opinion, and to show that her own history had demonstrated that she was not designed for *headship.* But she was not to be regarded as degraded and abandoned. She was not to be overwhelmed by the recollection of what "the mother of all living" had done. There were consolations in her case. There was a special divine interposition which she might look for, evincing tender care on the part of God in those deep sorrows which had come upon her in consequence of her transgression; and instead of being crushed and brokenhearted on account of her condition, she should remember that the everlasting arms of God would sustain her

in her condition of sorrow and pain. Paul, then, would speak to her the language of consolation, and while he would have her occupy her proper place, he would have her feel that *God was her Friend.* In regard to the *nature* of the consolation referred to here, there has been a considerable variety of opinion. Some have held, that by the expression "she shall be saved in child-bearing," the apostle designs to include all the duties of the maternal relation, meaning that she should be saved through the faithful performance of her duties as a mother (Robinson, *Lex.*). Rosenmüller regards the words rendered "child-bearing" (τεκνογονία), as synonymous with *education,* and supposes that the meaning is, that a woman, by the proper training of her children, can obtain salvation as well as her husband, and that her appropriate duty is not public teaching, but the training of her family. Wetstein supposes that it means, "she shall be saved from the arts of impostors, and from the luxury and vice of the age, if, instead of wandering about, she remains at home, cultivates modesty, is subject to her husband, and engages carefully in the training of her children." This sense agrees well with the connection. Calvin supposes that the apostle designs to console the woman by the assurance that, if she bears the trials of her condition of sorrow with a proper spirit, abiding in faith and holiness, she will be saved. She is not to regard herself as cut off from the hope of heaven. Doddridge, Macknight, Clarke, and others, suppose that it refers to the promise in Gen. iii. 15, and means that the woman shall be saved through, or by means of bearing a child, to wit, the Messiah; and that the apostle means to sustain the woman in her sorrows, and in her state of subordination and inferiority, by referring to the honour which has been put upon her by the fact that a woman gave birth to the Messiah. It is supposed, also, that he means to say that special honour is thus conferred on her over the man, inasmuch as the Messiah had no human father (Doddridge). The objections to this interpretation, however, though it is sustained by most respectable names, seem to me to be insuperable. They are such as these: (1) The interpretation is too refined and abstruse. It is not that which is obvious. It depends for its point on the fact that the Messiah had no human father, and if the apostle had intended to refer to that, and to build an argument on it, it may be doubted whether he would have done it in so obscure a manner. But it may reasonably be questioned whether he would have made that fact a point on which his argument would turn. There would be a species of refinement about such an argument, such as we should not look for in the writings of Paul. (2) It is not the obvious meaning of the word "child-bearing." There is nothing in the word which requires that it should have any reference to the birth of the Messiah. The word is of a general character, and properly refers to child-bearing in general. (3) It is not true that woman would be "saved" merely by having given birth to the Messiah. She will be saved, as man will be, as a consequence of his having been born; but there is no evidence that the *mere fact* that woman gave birth to him, and that he had no human father, did anything to save Mary herself, or anyone else of her sex. If, therefore, the word refers to the "bearing" of the Messiah, or to the fact that he was born, it would be no more proper to say that this was connected with the salvation of *woman* than that of *man.* The true meaning, it seems to me, has been suggested by Calvin, and may be seen by the following remarks. (1) The apostle designed to comfort woman, or to alleviate the sadness of the picture which he had drawn respecting her condition. (2) He had referred, incidentally, as a proof of the subordinate character of her station, to the first apostasy. This naturally suggested the sentence which was passed on her, and the condition of sorrow to which she was doomed, particularly in child-birth. *That* was the standing demonstration of her guilt; that the condition in which she suffered most; that the situation in which she was in greatest peril. (3) Paul assures her, therefore, that though she *must* thus suffer, yet that she ought not to regard herself in her deep sorrows and dangers, though on account of sin, as necessarily under the divine displeasure, or as excluded from the hope of heaven. The way of salvation was open to her as well as to men, and was to be entered in the same manner. If *she* had faith and holiness, even *in* her condition of sorrow brought on by guilt, she might as well hope for eternal life as man. The object of the apostle seems to be to guard against a *possible* construction which might be put on his words, that he did not regard the woman as in circumstances as favourable for salvation as those of man, or as if he thought that salvation for her was more difficult, or perhaps that she could not be saved at all. The general sentiments of the Jews in regard to the salvation of the female sex, and their exclusion from the religious privileges which men enjoy; the views of the Mohammedans in reference to the inferiority of the sex; and the prevalent feelings in the heathen world, degrading the sex and making their condition, in regard to salvation, far inferior to that of man, show the propriety of what the apostle here says, and the fitness that he should so guard himself that his language could not possibly be construed so as to give countenance to such a sentiment. According to the interpretation of the passage here proposed, the apostle does not mean to teach that a Christian female would be certainly saved from death in childbirth—for this would not be true, and the proper construction of the passage does not require us to understand him as affirming this. Religion is not designed to make any immediate and direct change in the laws of our physical being. It does not of itself guard us from the pestilence; it does not arrest the progress of disease; it does not save us from death; and, as a matter of fact, woman, by the highest degree of piety, is not necessarily saved from the perils of that condition to which she has been subjected in consequence of the apostasy. The apostle means to show this—that in all her pain and sorrow; amidst all the evidence of apostasy, and all that reminds her that she was *"first"* in the transgression, she may look up to God as her Friend and strength, and may hope for acceptance and salvation. ¶ *If they continue.* If woman continues—it being not uncommon to change the singular form to the plural, especially if the subject spoken of have the character of a noun of multitude. Many have understood this of children, as teaching that if the mother were faithful, so that her children continued in faith, she would be saved. But this is not a necessary or probable interpretation. The apostle says nothing of children, and it is not reasonable to suppose that he would make the prospect of *her* salvation depend on *their* being pious. This would be to add a hard condition of salvation, and one nowhere else suggested in the New Testament. The object of the apostle evidently is, to show that woman must *continue* in the faithful service of God if she would be saved—a doctrine everywhere insisted on in the New Testament in reference to all persons. She must not imitate the example of the mother of mankind, but she must faithfully yield obedience to the laws of God till death. ¶ *Faith.* Faith in the Redeemer and in divine truth, or a life of fidelity in the service of God. ¶ *Charity.* Love to all; comp. Notes on 1 Cor. xiii. ¶ *Holiness.* She must be truly righteous. ¶ *With sobriety.* All these things must be united with a becoming soberness or seriousness of deportment; Notes, ver. 9. In such a life, woman may look to a world where she will be for ever free from all the sadnesses and sorrows of her condition here; where, by unequalled pain, she will be no more reminded of the time when

"her rash hand in evil hour
Forth reaching to the fruit, she pluck'd, she ate;

and when before the throne she shall be admitted to full equality with all the redeemed of the Lord. Religion meets all the sadnesses of her condition here; pours consolation into the

CHAPTER III.

T HIS *is* a true saying, If a man

cup of her many woes; speaks kindly to her in her distresses; utters the language of forgiveness to her heart when crushed with the remembrance of sin—for "she loves much" (Luke vii. 37-48); and conducts her to immortal glory in that world where all sorrow shall be unknown.

CHAPTER III.

ANALYSIS OF THE CHAPTER.

The object of this chapter is to give directions respecting the qualifications and duties of the officers of the Christian church. As it is evident that Timothy was to be partly employed in the appointment of suitable officers for the church at Ephesus, and as the kinds of officers here referred to were to be permanent in the church, it was important that a full statement should be put on record, under the influence of inspiration, respecting their qualifications and duties. The chapter embraces the following subjects:—

I. The qualifications of a bishop, ver. 1-7. The enumeration of his qualifications is preceded by a general statement that the office was an honourable one, and that he who aspired to it sought an employment that was, in itself, to be regarded as desirable, ver. 1. The qualifications specified for this office are the following:—

(1) He must be a man of good private character; possessing and illustrating the Christian virtues; or, as we would say now, an upright man, and a Christian gentleman, ver. 2, 3.

(2) He must be a man who ruled his own house well, and who thus showed that he was qualified to preside as the first officer in the church of God, ver. 4, 5.

(3) He must be a man of suitable age and experience—one who would not be likely to fall into the temptations that are laid for the young, ver. 6.

(4) He must have a fair reputation among those who were not Christians —as it is intended that the influence

desire the office of a *a*bishop, he desireth a good work.

of his ministry shall reach them, and as it is impossible to do them good unless he is believed to be a man of integrity, ver. 7.

II. The qualifications of deacons, ver. 8-10, 12, 13. They must be—

(1) Men of fair character—serious, temperate, candid, ver. 8.

(2) Men who hold to the doctrines of the gospel with a pure conscience, ver. 9.

(3) Men who have been proved, and who have shown that they are qualified to serve the church, ver. 10.

(4) Men whose wives are of such a character that their example will contribute to the promotion of the common cause, ver. 11.

(5) Men not living in polygamy, and who exercise exemplary family government, ver. 12, 13.

III. The reason why Paul gave these instructions to Timothy, ver. 14, 15. It was, that he might know how he ought to demean himself in the important station which he was called to occupy. Paul hoped to be able to come to him before long, and to complete the work which he had commenced at Ephesus, but, in the meantime, he gave him these written counsels, that he might understand particularly the duty which was required of him.

IV. The chapter closes with a statement which seems to have been intended to impress the mind of Timothy with the importance of the duties in which he was engaged, ver. 15, 16. The statement is, that the church is the great defender of the truth in the world (ver. 15), and that the truth which the church is to maintain is of the greatest importance. It relates to the incarnation of the Son of God, and to the work which he accomplished on earth—a work which excited the deepest interest in heaven, and the true doctrine respecting which it was of the utmost importance to keep up among men, ver. 16. This reason is further urged in the following chapter, by showing that the time would come when, under the influence of

Satan, these great doctrines would be denied, and the truth be corrupted and perverted.

1. *This* is *a true saying.* Gr., "Faithful is the word"—the very phrase which is used in chap. i. 15; see Notes on that verse. The idea here is, that it was worthy of credence; it was not to be doubted. ¶ *If a man desire.* Implying that there would be those who would wish to be put into the ministry. The Lord, undoubtedly, by his Spirit, often excites an earnest and irrepressible desire to preach the gospel—a desire so strong, that he in whom it exists can be satisfied in no other calling. In such a case, it should be regarded as one evidence of a call to this work. The apostle, however, by the statements which follow, intimates that wherever this desire exists, it is of the utmost importance to have just views of the nature of the office, and that there should be other qualifications for the ministry than a mere desire to preach the gospel. He proceeds, therefore, to state those qualifications, and no one who "desires" the office of the ministry should conclude that he is *called* to it, unless these qualifications substantially are found in him. The word rendered *desire* here (ὀρέγω), denotes properly, *to reach* or *stretch out*—and hence to reach after anything, to long after, to try to obtain, Heb. xi. 16. ¶ *The office of a bishop.* The Greek here is a single word—ἐπισκοπῆς. The word ἐπισκοπή—*episcope*—whence the word *Episcopal* is derived—occurs but four times in the New Testament. It is translated *visitation* in Luke xix. 44, and in 1 Pet. ii. 12; *bishoprick,* Acts i. 20; and in this place *office of a bishop.* The verb from which it is derived (ἐπισκοπέω), occurs but twice. In Heb. xii. 15, it is rendered *looking diligently,* and in 1 Pet. v. 2, *taking the oversight.* The noun rendered *bishop* occurs in Acts xx. 28; Phil. i. 1; 1 Tim. iii. 2; Tit. i. 7; 1 Pet. ii. 25. The verb means, properly, to look upon, behold; to inspect, to look after, see to, take care of; and the noun denotes the office of overseeing, inspecting, or looking to. It is used to denote the care of the sick, Xeno.

Oec. 15, 9; comp. Passow; and is of so general a character that it may denote any office of overseeing, or attending to. There is nothing in the word itself which would limit it to any class or grade of the ministry, and it is, in fact, applied to nearly all the officers of the church in the New Testament, and, indeed, to Christians who did not sustain *any* office. Thus it is applied (*a*) to believers in general, directing them to "*look diligently,* lest any one should fail of the grace of God," Heb. xii. 15; (*b*) to the elders of the church at Ephesus, "over the which the Holy Ghost hath made you *overseers,*" Acts xx. 28; (*c*) to the elders or presbyters of the church in 1 Pet. v. 2, "Feed the flock of God, *taking the oversight thereof;* (d) to the officers of the church in Philippi, mentioned in connection with deacons as the only officers of the church there, "to the saints at Philippi, with the *bishops* and deacons," Phil. i. 1; (*e*) to Judas the apostate, Acts i. 20; and (*f*) to the great Head of the church, the Lord Jesus Christ, 1 Pet. ii. 25, "the Shepherd and *Bishop* of your souls." From this use of the term it follows, (1) That the word is never used to designate the *peculiarity* of the apostolic office, or so as to have any special applicability to the apostles. Indeed, the term *bishop* is *never* applied to any of them in the New Testament; nor is the word in any of its forms ever used with reference to them, except in the single case of *Judas,* Acts i. 20. (2) It is never employed in the New Testament to designate an order of men superior to presbyters, regarded as having any other functions than presbyters, or being in any sense "successors" to the apostles. It is so used now by the advocates of prelacy; but this is a use wholly unknown to the New Testament. It is so undeniable that the name is never given in the New Testament to those who are now called "bishops," that even Episcopalians concede it. Thus, Dr. Onderdonk (Tract on Episcopacy, p. 12) says, "ALL that we read in the New Testament concerning 'bishops' is to be regarded as pertaining to the 'middle

2 .A [b] bishop then must be

ō Tit.1.6,&c.

blameless, the husband of one wife,

---

grade;' that is, to those who are now regarded as 'priests.'" This is not strictly correct, as is clear from the remarks above respecting what is called the "middle grade;" but it *is* strictly correct, so far as it affirms that it is *never* applied to prelates. (3) It is used in the New Testament to denote ministers of the gospel who had the care or oversight of the churches, without any regard to grade or rank. (4) It has now, as used by Episcopalians, a sense which is wholly unauthorized by the New Testament, and which, indeed, is entirely at variance with the usage there. To apply the term to a pretended superior order of clergy, as designating their peculiar office, is wholly to depart from the use of the word as it occurs in the Bible. (5) As it is never used in the Scriptures with reference to *prelates*, it *should* be used with reference to the pastors, or other officers of the church; and to be a *pastor*, or *overseer* of the flock of Christ, should be regarded as being a scriptural *bishop.* ¶ *He desireth a good work.* An honourable office; an office which it is right for a man to desire. There are some stations in life which ought never to be desired; it is proper for anyone to desire the office of a bishop who has the proper qualifications; comp. Notes on Rom. xi. 13.

2. *A bishop.* A minister of religion, according to the foregoing remarks, who has the charge or oversight of any Christian church. The reference here is doubtless to one who had the government of the church intrusted to him (ver. 4, 5), and who was also a preacher of the gospel. ¶ *Must be blameless.* This is a different word (ἀνεπίληπτος) from that rendered *blameless* in Luke i. 6; Phil. ii. 15; iii. 6 (ἄμεμπτος); comp. however, Notes on Luke i. 6; Phil. iii. 6. The word here used does not mean that, as a necessary qualification for office, a bishop should be *perfect;* but that he should be a man against whom no charge of immorality, or of holding false doctrine, is alleged. His con-

duct should be irreprehensible or irreproachable. Undoubtedly it means that if *any* charge could be brought against him implying moral obliquity, he is not fit for the office. He should be a man of irreproachable character for truth, honesty, chastity, and general uprightness. ¶ *The husband of one wife.* This need not be understood as requiring that a bishop *should be* a married man, as Vigilantius, a presbyter in the church at Barcelona in the fourth century, supposed, however desirable in general it may be that a minister of the gospel should be married. But, while this interpretation is manifestly to be excluded as false, there has been much difference of opinion on the question whether the passage means that a minister should not have more than one wife at the same time, or whether it prohibits the marriage of a second wife after the death of the first. On this question, the Notes of Bloomfield, Doddridge, and Macknight may be consulted. That the former is the correct opinion, seems to me to be evident from the following considerations: (1) It is the most obvious meaning of the language, and it would doubtless be thus understood by those to whom it was addressed. At a time when polygamy was not uncommon, to say that a man should "have but *one wife*" would be naturally understood as prohibiting polygamy. (2) The marriage of a second wife, after the death of the first, is nowhere spoken of in the Scriptures as wrong. The marriage of a widow to a second husband is expressly declared to be proper (1 Cor. vii. 39); and it is not unfair to infer from that permission that it is equally lawful and proper for a man to marry the second time. But if it is lawful for any man, it is right for a minister of the gospel. No reason can be assigned against such marriages in his case, which would not be equally valid in any other. Marriage is as honourable for a minister of the gospel as for any other man (comp. Notes on Heb. xiii. 4);

vigilant, sober, of [1]good behaviour, | given to hospitality, apt to teach:

1 or, *modest.*

and, as Doddridge has well remarked, "Circumstances may be so adjusted that there may be as much reason for a second marriage as for the first, and as little inconvenience of any kind may attend it." (3) There was a special propriety in the prohibition, if understood as prohibiting polygamy. It is known that it was extensively practised, and was not regarded as unlawful. Yet one design of the gospel was to restore the marriage relation to its primitive condition; and though it might not have seemed absolutely necessary to require of every man who came into the church to divorce his wives, if he had more than one, yet, in order to fix a brand on this irregular practice, it might have been deemed desirable to require of the ministers of the gospel that they should have but one wife. Thus the practice of polygamy would gradually come to be regarded as dishonourable and improper, and the example and influence of the ministry would tend to introduce correct views in regard to the nature of this relation. One thing is clear from this passage, that the views of the Papists in regard to the celibacy of the clergy are directly at variance with the Bible. The declaration of Paul in Heb. xiii. 4, is, that "marriage is honourable in *all;*" and here it is implied that it was proper that a minister should be married. If it were not, why did not Paul prohibit it altogether? Instead of saying that it was improper that a bishop should have more than one wife, why did he not say that it was improper that he should be married at all? Would not a Romanist say so now? ¶ *Vigilant.* This word (νηφάλεος) occurs only here and in 1 Tim. iii. 11; Tit. ii. 2. It means, properly, *sober, temperate, abstinent,* especially in respect to wine; then *sober-minded, watchful, circumspect* (Robinson). A minister should have a watchful care over his own conduct. He should be on his guard against sin in any form. ¶ *Sober—σώφρονα.* Properly, a man of *a sound mind;* one who follows

sound reason, and who is not under the control of passion. The idea is, that he should have his desires and passions well regulated. Perhaps the word *prudent* would come nearer to the meaning of the apostle than any single word which we have. ¶ *Of good behaviour.* Marg., *modest.* Coverdale renders it, *mannerly.* The most correct rendering, according to the modern use of language, would be, that he should be *a gentleman.* He should not be slovenly in his appearance, or rough and boorish in his manners. He should not do violence to the usages of refined intercourse, nor be unfit to appear respectable in the most refined circles of society. Inattention to personal neatness, and to the rules which regulate refined intercourse, is indicative neither of talent, learning, nor religion; and though they are occasionally—not often—connected with talent, learning, and religion, yet they are never the fruit of either, and are always a disgrace to those who exhibit such incivility and boorishness, for such men *ought* to know better. A minister of the gospel should be a finished gentleman in his manners, and there is no excuse for him if he is not. His religion, if he has any, is adapted to make him such. He has usually received such an education as ought to make him such, and in all cases *ought* to have had such a training. He is admitted into the best society, and has an opportunity of becoming familiar with the laws of refined intercourse. He should be an example and a pattern in all that goes to promote the welfare of mankind, and there are few things so easily acquired that are fitted to do this, as refinement and gentility of manners. No man can do good, on the whole, or in the "long run," by disregarding the rules of refined intercourse; and, other things being equal, the refined, courteous, polite gentleman in the ministry, will always do more good than he who neglects the rules of good-breeding. ¶ *Given to hospitality.*

3 Not[2] given to wine, no striker, not greedy of filthy lucre; but

[2] or, *Not ready to quarrel and offer wrong, as one in wine.*

[c]patient, not a brawler not covetous.

[c] 2 Ti.2.24.

This is often enjoined on all Christians as a duty of religion. For the reasons of this, and the nature of the duty, see Notes on Rom. xii. 13; Heb. xiii. 2. It was a special duty of the ministers of religion, as they were to be examples of every Christian virtue. ¶ *Apt to teach.* Gr., *didactic;* that is, capable of instructing, or qualified for the office of a teacher of religion. As the principal business of a preacher of the gospel is to *teach,* or to communicate to his fellow-men the knowledge of the truth, the necessity of this qualification is obvious. No one should be allowed to enter the ministry who is not qualified to impart *instruction* to others on the doctrines and duties of religion; and no one should feel that he ought to continue in the ministry, who has not industry, and self-denial, and the love of study enough to lead him constantly to endeavour to *increase* in knowledge, that he may be qualified to teach others. A man who would *teach* a people, must himself keep in *advance* of them on the subjects on which he would instruct them.

3. *Not given to wine.* Marg., "*Not ready to quarrel and offer wrong, as one in wine.*" The Greek word (πάροινος) occurs in the New Testament only here and in Titus i. 7. It means, properly, *by wine;* i.e., spoken of what takes place *by* or *over* wine, as revelry, drinking songs, &c. Then it denotes, as it does here, one who sits *by* wine; that is, who is in the habit of drinking it. It cannot be inferred, from the use of the word here, that wine was absolutely and entirely prohibited; for the word does not properly express that idea. It means that one who is in the *habit* of drinking wine, or who is accustomed to sit with those who indulge in it, should not be admitted to the ministry. The way in which the apostle mentions the subject here would lead us fairly to suppose that he did not mean to commend its use in any sense; that he regarded its use as dangerous, and that he would wish the ministers of religion to avoid it altogether. In regard to its use at all, except at the communion or as a medicine, it may be remarked, that a minister will do no injury to himself or others by letting it entirely alone; he *may* do injury by indulging in it. No man is under any *obligation* of courtesy or Christian duty to use it; thousands of ministers of the gospel have brought ruin on themselves, and disgrace on the ministry, by its use; comp. Notes on Mat. xi. 9, and 1 Tim. v. 23. ¶ *No striker.* He must be a peaceable, not a quarrelsome man. This is connected with the caution about the use of wine, probably, because that is commonly found to produce a spirit of contention and strife. ¶ *Not greedy of filthy lucre.* Not contentious or avaricious. Gr., Not desirous of base gain. The desire of this is condemned everywhere in the New Testament; but it is especially the duty of a minister of the gospel to be free from it. He has a right to a support (see Notes on 1 Cor. ix.); but there is nothing that more certainly paralyses the usefulness of a minister of the gospel than the love of money. There is an instinctive feeling in the human bosom that such a man ought to be actuated by a nobler and a purer principle. As avarice, moreover, is the great sin of the world—the sin that sways more hearts, and does more to hinder the progress of the gospel, than all others combined—it is important in the highest degree that the minister of religion should be an example of what men *should* be, and that he, by his whole life, should set his face against that which is the main obstruction to the progress of that gospel which he is appointed to preach. ¶ *But patient.* Modest, mild, gentle. See the word (Gr.) in Phil. iv. 5; Titus iii. 2; James iii. 17, and 1

4 One that *ruleth well his own house, having his children in subjection with all gravity:

d Ps.101.2.

5 (For if a man know not how to rule his own house, how shall he take care of the church of God?)

Pet. ii. 18, where it is rendered *gentle*. The word means that the minister of the gospel should be a man of mild and kind demeanour, such as his Master was. ¶ *Not a brawler.* Comp. 2 Tim. ii. 24. That is, he should not be a man given to contention, or apt to take up a quarrel. The Greek is, literally, *Not disposed to fight*. ¶ *Not covetous.* Gr., *Not a lover of silver;* that is, of money. A man should not be put into the ministry who is characteristically a lover of money. Such a one, no matter what his talents may be, has no proper qualification for the office, and will do more harm than good.

4. *One that ruleth well his own house.* This implies that a minister of the gospel would be, and ought to be, a married man. It is everywhere in the New Testament supposed that he would be a man who could be an example in all the relations of life. The position which he occupies in the church has a strong resemblance to the relation which a father sustains to his household; and a qualification to govern a family well, would be an evidence of a qualification to preside properly in the church. It is probable that, in the early Christian church, ministers were not unfrequently taken from those of mature life, and who were, at the time, at the head of families; and, of course, such would be men who had had an opportunity of showing that they had this qualification for the office. Though, however, this cannot be insisted on now as a *previous* qualification for the office, yet it is still true that, if he has a family, it *is* a necessary qualification, and that a man in the ministry *should be* one who governs his own house well. A want of this will always be a hindrance to extensive usefulness. ¶ *Having his children in subjection with all gravity.* This does not mean that his *children* should evince gravity, whatever may be true on that point; but it refers *to the*

father. He should be a grave or serious man in his family; a man free from levity of character, and from frivolity and fickleness, in his intercourse with his children. It does not mean that he should be severe, stern, morose—which are traits that are often mistaken for gravity, and which are as inconsistent with the proper spirit of a father as frivolity of manner—but that he should be a serious and sober-minded man. He should maintain proper *dignity* ($\sigma\epsilon\mu\nu\delta\tau\eta s$); he should maintain self-respect, and his deportment should be such as to inspire others with respect for him.

5. *For if a man know not how to rule.* This is a beautiful and striking argument. A church resembles a family. It is, indeed, larger, and there is a greater variety of dispositions in it than there is in a family. The authority of a minister of the gospel in a church is also less absolute than that of a father. But still there is a striking resemblance. The church is made up of an assemblage of brothers and sisters. They are banded together for the same purposes, and have a common object to aim at. They have common feelings and common wants. They have sympathy, like a family, with each other in their distresses and afflictions. The government of the church also is designed to be *paternal.* It should be felt that he who presides over it has the feelings of a father; that he loves all the members of the great family; that he has no prejudices, no partialities, no selfish aims to gratify. Now, if a man cannot govern his own family well; if he is severe, partial, neglectful, or tyrannical at home, how can he be expected to take charge of the more numerous "household of faith" with proper views and feelings? If, with all the natural and strong ties of affection which bind a father to his own children; if, when they are few comparatively in number, and where

6 Not ³a novice, lest being lifted up ᵉwith pride he fall into

³ or, *one newly come to the faith.*   e Pr.16.18.

/the condemnation of the devil.

7 Moreover he must have a

ƒ Jude 6.

his eye is constantly upon them, he is unable to govern them aright, how can he be expected to preside in a proper manner over the larger household where he will be bound with comparatively feebler ties, and where he will be exposed more to the influence of passion, and where he will have a much less constant opportunity of supervision? Confucius, as quoted by Doddridge, has a sentiment strikingly resembling that before us: "It is impossible that he who knows not how to govern and reform his own family, should rightly govern and reform a people." We may remark, also, in this verse, a delicate and beautiful use of words by the apostle to prevent the possibility of misapprehension. While he institutes a comparison between the government of a family and that of the church, he guards against the possibility of its being supposed that he would countenance *arbitrary* authority in the church, even such authority as a father must of necessity employ in his own family. Hence he uses different words. He speaks of the father as "*ruling*" over his own family, or *presiding over it*—προστῆναι; he describes the minister of religion as *having a tender care for the church*—ἐπιμελήσεται.

6. *Not a novice.* Marg., *one newly come to the faith.* The Greek word, which occurs nowhere else in the New Testament, means, properly, that which is *newly planted.* Thus it would mean a plant that was not strong, or not fitted to bear the severity of storms; that had not as yet struck its roots deep, and could not resist the fierceness of a cold blast. Then the word comes to mean a new convert; one who has had little opportunity to test his own faith, or to give evidence to others that he would be faithful to the trust committed to him. The word does not refer so much to one who is young *in years*, as one who is young *in faith.* Still, all the reasons which apply against introducing a very recent convert into the

ministry, will apply commonly with equal force against introducing one young in years. ¶ *Lest being lifted up with pride.* We are not to suppose that this is the *only* reason against introducing a recent convert into the ministry, but it is a *sufficient* reason. He would be likely to be elated by being intrusted at once with the highest office in the church, and by the commendations and flattery which he might receive. No condition is *wholly* proof against this; but he is much less likely to be injured who has had much experience of the depravity of his own heart, and whose mind has been deeply imbued with the spirit of the gospel. ¶ *He fall into the condemnation of the devil.* That is, the same kind of condemnation which the devil fell into; to wit, condemnation on account of pride. It is here intimated that the cause of the apostasy of Satan was pride—a cause which is as likely to have been the true one as any other. Who can tell but it may have been produced by some new honour which was conferred on him in heaven, and that his virtue was not found sufficient for the untried circumstances in which he was placed? Much of the apostasy from eminent virtue in this world, arises from this cause; and possibly the case of Satan may have been the most signal instance of this kind which has occurred in the universe. The idea of Paul is, that a young convert should not suddenly be raised to an exalted station in the church. Who can doubt the wisdom of this direction? The word rendered *lifted up* (τυφωθεὶς), is from a verb which means to smoke, to fume, to surround with smoke; then to *inflate*—as a bladder is with air; and then to be conceited or proud; that is, to be *like* a bladder filled, not with a solid substance, but with air.

7. *Moreover he must have a good report of them which are without.* Who are without the church; that is, of those who are not Christians.

good report of *g*them which are without; lest he fall into reproach, and *h*the snare of the devil.

8 Likewise *must* the *i*deacons

g Ac.22.12; 1 Th.4.12.　　*h* ch.6.9; 2 Ti.2.26.

This includes, of course, *all* classes of those who are not Christians— heathens, infidels, Jews, moral men, and scoffers. The idea is, that he must have a fair reputation with them for integrity of character. His life must be in their view upright. He must not be addicted to anything which they regard as inconsistent with good morals. His deportment must be such that they shall regard it as not inconsistent with his profession. He must be true and just and honest in his dealings with his fellow-men, and so live that they cannot say that he has wronged them. He must not give occasion for scandal or reproach in his intercourse with the other sex, but must be regarded as a man of a pure life and of a holy walk. The *reason* for this injunction is obvious. It is his business to endeavour to do such men good, and to persuade them to become Christians. *But no minister of the gospel can possibly do such men good, unless they regard him as an upright and honest man.* No matter how he preaches or prays; no matter how orthodox, learned, or apparently devout he may be, all his efforts will be in vain unless *they* regard him as a man of incorruptible integrity. If they hate religion themselves, they insist justly that since *he* has professed it he shall be governed by its principles; or if they feel its importance, they will not be influenced to embrace it by a man that they regard as hypocritical and impure. Go to a man whom you have defrauded, or who regards you as having done or attempted wrong to any other one, and talk to him about the necessity of religion, and he will instinctively say that he does not *want* a religion which will not make its professor true, honest, and pure. It is impossible, therefore, for a minister to over-estimate the importance of having a fair character in the view of the world, and no man should be introduced into

be grave, not double-tongued, *k*not given to much wine, not greedy of filthy lucre;

i Ac.6.3.
k ver.3; Le.10.9; Eze.44.21.

the ministry, or sustained in it, who has not a fair reputation; comp. Notes on Col. iv. 5; 1 Thes. iv. 12. ¶ *Lest he fall into reproach.* That is, in such a way as to bring dishonour on the ministerial character. His life will be such as to give men occasion to reproach the cause of religion. ¶ *And the snare of the devil.* The snare which the devil lays to entrap and ruin the ministers of the gospel and all good men. The snare to which reference is here made, is that of *blasting the character and influence of the minister of the gospel.* The idea is, that Satan lays this snare so to entangle him as to secure this object, and the means which he uses is the vigilance and suspicion of those who are out of the church. If there is anything of this kind in the life of a minister which they can make use of, they will be ready to do it. Hence the necessity on his part of an upright and blameless life. Satan is constantly aiming at this thing; the world is watching for it, and if the minister has any *propensity* which is not in entire accordance with honesty, Satan will take advantage of it and lead him into the snare.

8. *Likewise* must *the deacons.* On the meaning of the word *deacons,* see Notes on Phil. i. 1. On their appointment, see Notes, Acts vi. 1. The word here evidently denotes those who had charge of the temporal affairs of the church, the poor, &c. No qualifications are mentioned, implying that they were to be preachers of the gospel. In most respects, except in regard to preaching, their qualifications were to be the same as those of the *bishops.* ¶ *Be grave.* Serious, sober-minded men. In Acts vi. 3, it is said that they should be men *of honest report.* On the meaning of the word *grave,* see Notes on ver. 4. They should be men who by their serious deportment will inspire respect. ¶ *Not double-tongued.* The word here used

9 Holding¹ the ᵐmystery of the faith in a pure conscience.

10 And let these also first be

l Ep.1.9.   *m* ver.16.

proved; then let them use the office of a deacon, being *found* blameless.

—δίλογος—does not occur elsewhere in the New Testament. It means, properly, uttering the same thing twice (from δίς and λέγω), and then deceitful, or speaking one thing and meaning another. They should be men who can be relied on for the exact truth of what they say, and for the exact fulfilment of their promises. ¶ *Not given to much wine.* See ver. 3. The word *much* is added here to what is said (ver. 2) of the qualification of a bishop. It is not affirmed that it would be proper for the deacon, any more than the bishop, to indulge in the use of wine in small quantities, but it *is* affirmed that a man who is much given to the use of wine ought not, on any consideration, to be a deacon. It may be remarked here, that this qualification was everywhere regarded as necessary for a minister of religion. Even the heathen priests, on entering a temple, did not drink wine (Bloomfield). The use of wine, and of strong drinks of all kinds, was absolutely prohibited to the Jewish ministers of every rank when they were about to engage in the service of God, Lev. x. 9. Why should it then be any more proper for a Christian minister to drink wine than for a Jewish or a heathen priest? Shall a minister of the gospel be less holy than they? Shall he have a feebler sense of the purity of his vocation? Shall he be less careful lest he expose himself to the possibility of conducting the services of religion in an irreverent and silly manner? Shall he venture to approach the altar of God under the influence of intoxicating drinks, when a sense of propriety restrained the heathen priest, and a solemn statute of Jehovah restrained the Jewish priest from doing it? ¶ *Not greedy of filthy lucre.* Notes, ver. 3. The special reason why this qualification was important in the deacon was, that he would be intrusted with the funds of the church, and might be tempted to appropriate them

to his own use instead of the charitable purposes for which they were designed; see this illustrated in the case of Judas, John xii. 6.

9. *Holding the mystery of the faith.* On the word *mystery*, see Notes on 1 Cor. ii. 7. It means that which had been concealed, or hidden, but which was now revealed. The word *faith* here, is synonymous with *the gospel;* and the sense is, that he should hold firmly the great doctrines of the Christian religion which had been so long concealed from men, but which were now revealed. The reason is obvious. Though not a preacher, yet his influence and example would be great, and a man who held material error ought not to be in office. ¶ *In a pure conscience.* A mere orthodox faith was not all that was necessary, for it was possible that a man might be professedly firm in the belief of the truths of revelation, and yet be corrupt at heart.

10. *And let these also be first proved.* That is, tried or tested in regard to the things which were the proper qualifications for the office. This does not mean that they were to be employed as *preachers*, but that they were to undergo a proper trial in regard to their fitness for the office which they were to fill. They were not to be put into it without any opportunity of knowing what they were. It should be ascertained that they were grave, serious, temperate, trustworthy men—men who were sound in the faith, and who would not dishonour the office. It is not said here that there should be a *formal* trial, as if they were candidates for this office; but the meaning is, that they should have had an opportunity of making their character known, and should have gained such respect for their piety, and their other qualifications, that there would be reason to believe that they would perform the functions of the office well. Thus, in Acts vi. 3, when deacons were first appointed,

11 Even so *must* *their* wives *be* grave, not slanderers, sober, faithful in all things.

12 Let the deacons be the husbands of one wife, *ruling* their children and their own houses well.

13 For they that have [4]used the office of a deacon *well*, purchase to themselves a good degree, *and* great boldness in the faith which is in Christ Jesus.

n Tit. 2.3.　　　*o* ver. 4.
[4] or, *ministered*.　　*p* Mat. 25.21.　　*q* 2 Ti. 2.1.

---

the church was directed to "look out seven men *of honest report,*" who might be appointed to the office. ¶ *Then let them use the office of a deacon.* Let them be appointed to this office, and fulfil its duties. ¶ *Being* found *blameless.* If nothing can be alleged against their character; see Notes on ver. 2.

11. *Even so* must their *wives* be *grave.* Chrysostom, Theophylact, Grotius, Bloomfield, and many others, suppose that by the word *wives,* here (γυναῖκας), the apostle means *deaconesses.* Clarke supposes that it refers to women in general. The reason assigned for supposing that it does not refer to the wives of deacons, as such, is, that nothing is said of the qualifications of the wives of bishops—a matter of as much importance as that of the character of the wife of a deacon; and that it cannot be supposed that the apostle would specify the one without some allusion to the other. But that the common interpretation, which makes it refer to the wives of deacons, as such, is to be adhered to, seems to me to be clear. For, (1) It is the obvious and natural interpretation. (2) The word here used—*wives*—is never used of itself to denote deaconesses. (3) If the apostle had meant deaconesses it would have been easy to express it without ambiguity; comp. Notes, Rom. xvi. 1. (4) What is here mentioned is important, whether the same thing is mentioned of bishops or not. (5) In the qualifications of bishops, the apostle had made a statement respecting his family, which made any specification about the particular members of the family unnecessary. He was to be one who presided in a proper manner over his own house, or who had a well-regulated family, ver. 4, 5. By a comparison of this passage, also,

with Tit. ii. 3, 4, which bears a strong resemblance to this, it would seem that it was supposed that the deacons would be taken from those who were advanced in life, and that their wives would have some superintendence over the younger females of the church. It was, therefore, especially important that they should be persons whose influence would be known to be decidedly favourable to piety. No one can doubt that the character of a woman may be such, that it is not desirable that her husband should be an officer in the church. A bad woman ought not to be intrusted with any additional power or influence. ¶ *Grave.* Notes, ver. 4. ¶ *Not slanderers.* Comp. Tit. ii. 3, "Not false accusers." The Greek word is διαβόλους—*devils.* It is used here in its original and proper sense, to denote a *calumniator, slanderer,* or *accuser.* It occurs in the same sense in 2 Tim. iii. 3, and Tit. ii. 3. Elsewhere in the New Testament, it is uniformly rendered *devil* (comp. Notes, Mat. iv. 1), and is given to Satan, the prince of the fallen angels (Mat. ix. 34), by way of eminence, as *the accuser;* comp. Notes on Job i. 6–11, and Rev. xii. 10. Here it means that they should not be women who were in the habit of calumniating others, or aspersing their character. Mingling as they would with the church, and having an opportunity to claim acquaintance with many, it would be in their power, if they chose, to do great injury to the character of others. ¶ *Sober.* Notes, ver. 2. ¶ *Faithful in all things.* To their husbands, to their families, to the church, to the Saviour.

12. *Let the deacons be the husbands of one wife.* Notes, ver. 2. ¶ *Ruling their children and their own houses well.* Notes, ver. 4, 5.

13. *For they that have used the*

14 These things write I unto thee, hoping to come unto thee shortly:

15 But if I tarry long, that thou mayest know how thou oughtest to

behave thyself in ʳthe house of God, which is the church of the living God, the pillar and ⁵ground of the truth.

r 2 Ti.2.20.   5 or, *stay.*

office of a deacon well. Marg., *ministered.* The Greek word is the same as deacon, meaning ministering, or serving in this office. The sense would be well expressed by the phrase, *deaconizing well.* The *word* implies nothing as to the exact nature of the office. ¶ *Purchase to themselves.* Procure for themselves. See this word explained in the Notes on Acts xx. 28. ¶ *A good degree.* The word here used (βαϑμός) occurs nowhere else in the New Testament. It means, properly, *a step,* as of a stair; and the fair meaning is that of going up higher, or taking an additional step of dignity, honour, or standing. So far as the *word* is concerned, it may mean either an advance in office, in dignity, in respectability, or in influence. It cannot certainly be inferred that the apostle referred to a higher grade of *office;* for all that the word essentially conveys is, that, by exercising this office well, a deacon would secure additional respectability and influence in the church. Still, it is possible that those who had performed the duties of this office well were appointed to be preachers. They may have shown so much piety, prudence, good sense, and ability to preside over the church, that it was judged proper that they should be advanced to the office of bishops or pastors of the churches. Such a course would not be unnatural. This is, however, far from teaching that the office of a deacon is a subordinate office, *with a view* to an ascent to a higher grade. ¶ *And great boldness in the faith.* The word here rendered *boldness* properly refers to boldness *in speaking;* see it explained in the Notes on Acts iv. 13; 2 Cor. iii. 12; Phil. i. 20. But the word is commonly used to denote boldness of any kind —openness, frankness, confidence, assurance, Jn. viii. 13, 26; Mark viii. 32; 2 Cor. vii. 4. As it is here connected with *faith*—"boldness in the faith"—it means, evidently, not so

much public speaking, as a manly and independent exercise of faith in Christ. The sense is, that by the faithful performance of the duties of the office of a deacon, and by the kind of experience which a man would have in that office, he would establish a character of firmness in the faith, which would show that he was a decided Christian. This passage, therefore, cannot be fairly used to prove that the deacon was *a preacher,* or that he belonged to a grade of ministerial office from which he was regularly to rise to that of a presbyter.

14. *These things write I unto thee, hoping to come unto thee shortly.* That is, he hoped to come there to give instructions personally, or to finish, himself, the work which he had commenced in Ephesus, and which had been interrupted by his being driven so unexpectedly away. This verse PROVES that the apostle Paul did not regard Timothy as the permanent diocesan bishop of Ephesus. Would any Episcopal bishop write this to another bishop? If Timothy were the permanent prelate of Ephesus, would Paul have intimated that he expected soon to come and take the work of completing the arrangements there into his own hands? In regard to his expectation of going soon to Ephesus, see Notes on chap. i. 3; comp. the Introduction to the epistle.

15. *But if I tarry long.* Paul appears to have been uncertain how long circumstances would require him to be absent. He expected to return, but it was possible that his hope of returning soon would be disappointed. ¶ *That thou mayest know how thou oughtest to behave thyself.* That is, that he might have just views about settling the affairs of the church. ¶ *In the house of God.* This does not mean in a place of public worship, nor does it refer to propriety of deportment there. It refers rather to the

church as a body of believers, and to intercourse with them. The church is called the "house of God," because it is that in which he dwells. Formerly, his peculiar residence was in the temple at Jerusalem; now that the temple is destroyed, it is the church of Christ, among his people. ¶ *Which is the church of the living God.* This seems to have been added to impress the mind of Timothy with the solemn nature of the duty which he was to perform. What he did pertained to the honour and welfare of the church of the living God, and hence he should feel the importance of a correct deportment, and of a right administration of its affairs. ¶ *The pillar and ground of the truth.* There has been no little diversity of opinion among critics whether this phrase is to be taken in connection with the preceding, meaning that *the church* is the pillar and ground of the truth; or whether it is to be taken in connection with what follows, meaning that the principal support of the truth was the doctrine there referred to—that God was manifest in the flesh. Bloomfield remarks on this: "It is surprising that any who have any knowledge or experience in Greek literature could tolerate so harsh a construction as that which arises from the latter method." The more natural interpretation certainly is, to refer it to the former; and this is supported by the consideration that it would then fall in with the object of the apostle. His design here seems to be, to impress Timothy with a deep sense of the importance of correct conduct in relation to the church; of the responsibility of those who presided over it; and of the necessity of care and caution in the selection of proper officers. To do this, he reminded him that the truth of God—that revealed truth which he had given to save the world—was intrusted to the church; that it was designed to preserve it pure, to defend it, and to transmit it to future times; and that, therefore, every one to whom the administration of the affairs of the church was intrusted, should engage in this duty with a deep conviction of his responsibility. On the construction of the passage, Bloomfield, Rosenmüller, and Clarke may be consulted. The word "pillar" means a column, such as that by which a building is supported, and then any firm prop or support, Gal. ii. 9; Rev. iii. 12. If it refers to the church here, it means that that is the support of the truth, as a pillar is of a building. It sustains it amidst the war of elements, the natural tendency to fall, and the assaults which may be made on it, and preserves it when it would otherwise tumble into ruin. Thus it is with the church. It is intrusted with the business of maintaining the truth, of defending it from the assaults of error, and of transmitting it to future times. The truth *is*, in fact, upheld in the world by the church. The people of the world feel no interest in defending it, and it is to the church of Christ that it is owing that it is preserved and transmitted from age to age. The word rendered " ground " — ἑδραίωμα — means, properly, a basis, or foundation. The figure here is evidently taken from architecture, as the use of the word pillar is. The proper meaning of the one expression would be, that truth is supported by the church, as an edifice is by a pillar; of the other, that the truth rests *on* the church, as a house does on its foundation. It is that which makes it fixed, stable, permanent; that on which it securely stands amidst storms and tempests; that which renders it firm when systems of error are swept away as a house that is built on the sand; comp. Notes on Mat. vii. 24–27. The meaning then is, that the stability of the truth on earth is dependent on the church. It is owing to the fact that the church is itself founded on a rock, that the gates of hell cannot prevail against it, that no storms of persecution can overthrow it, that the truth is preserved from age to age. Other systems of religion are swept away; other opinions change; other forms of doctrine vanish; but the knowledge of the great system of redemption is preserved on earth unshaken, because the church is pre-

16 And, without controversy,
great is the *mystery of godli-

s 1 Co.2.7.

served, and because its foundations
cannot be moved. This does not refer, I suppose, to creeds and confessions, or to the decisions of synods and
councils; but to the living spirit of
truth and piety *in* the church itself.
As certainly as the church continues
to live, so certain it will be that the
truth of God will be perpetuated
among men.

16. *And, without controversy.* Undeniably, certainly. The object of
the apostle is, to say that the truth
which he was about to state admitted
of no dispute. ¶ *Great is the mystery.* On the meaning of the word
mystery, see Notes on 1 Cor. ii. 7.
The word means that which had been
hidden or concealed. The meaning
here is, not that the proposition which
he affirms was mysterious in the sense
that it was unintelligible, or impossible to be understood; but that the
doctrine respecting the incarnation
and the work of the Messiah, which
had been so long *kept hidden* from the
world, was a subject of the deepest importance. This passage, therefore,
should not be used to prove that there
is anything unintelligible, or anything
that surpasses human comprehension,
in that doctrine, whatever may be the
truth on that point; but that the doctrine which he now proceeds to state,
and which had been so long concealed
from mankind, was of the utmost consequence. ¶ *Of godliness.* The
word *godliness* means, properly, piety,
reverence or religiousness. It is
used here, however, for the gospel
scheme, to wit, that which the apostle
proceeds to state. This "mystery,"
which had "been hidden from ages
and from generations, and which was
now manifest" (Col. i. 26), was the
great doctrine on which depended *religion* everywhere, or was that which
constituted the Christian scheme.
¶ *God.* Probably there is no passage
in the New Testament which has excited so much discussion among critics
as this, and none in reference to which
it is so difficult to determine the true

ness: God was ⁶manifest ᵗin the
flesh, ᵘjustified in the Spirit,

6 *manifested.*　　　t Jn.1.14; 1 Jn.1.2.
u Mat.3.16; Jn.16.8,9; Ro.1.4; 1 Pe.3.18; 1 Jn.5.6.

reading. It is the only one, it is believed, in which the microscope has
been employed to determine the lines
of the letters used in a manuscript;
and, after all that has been done to
ascertain the exact truth in regard to
it, still the question remains unde-
cided. It is not the object of these
Notes to enter into the examination
of questions of this nature. A full in-
vestigation may be found in Wetstein.
The question which has excited so
much controversy is, whether the
original Greek word was Θεὸς, *God*,
or whether it was ὅς, *who*, or ὁ, *which*.
The controversy has turned, to a considerable degree, on the reading in
the *Codex Alexandrinus;* and a remark or two on the method in which
the manuscripts in the New Testament were written, will show the true
nature of the controversy. Greek
manuscripts were formerly written entirely in capital letters, and without
breaks or intervals between the words,
and without accents; see a full description of the methods of writing
the New Testament, in an article by
Prof. Stuart in Dr. Robinson's *Bibliotheca Sacra*, No. 2, pp. 254, *seq.*
The small, cursive Greek letters which
are now used, were not commonly employed in transcribing the New Testament, if at all, until the ninth or tenth
centuries. It was a common thing
to abridge or contract words in the
manuscript. Thus, πρ would be used
for πατερ, *father;* κs for κυριος, *Lord;*
Ꝋs for Ꝋeos, *God*, &c. The words thus
contracted were designated by a faint
line or dash over them. In this
place, therefore, if the original were
ΘC, standing for Θεὸς, *God*, and the
line in the Θ, and the faint line over
it, were obliterated from any cause,
it would easily be mistaken for OC—
ὅς, *who*. To ascertain which of these
is the true reading, has been the great
question; and it is with reference to
this that the microscope has been resorted to in the examination of the
Alexandrian manuscript. It is now

seen[v] of angels, [w]preached unto the Gentiles, [x]believed on in the world, [y]received up into glory.

v Mat.4.11; Lu.2.13; Ep.3.10; 1 Pe.1.12.
w Ac.13.46,48; Ro.10.12,18.　　x Col.1.6.

y Lu.24.51; Ac.1.9.

generally admitted that the faint line *over* the word has been added by some later hand, though not improbably by one who found that the line was nearly obliterated, and who meant merely to restore it. Whether the letter O was originally written with a line *within* it, making the reading *God*, it is now said to be impossible to determine, in consequence of the manuscript at this place having become so much worn by frequent examination. The Vulgate and the Syriac read it, *who* or *which*. The Vulgate is, "Great is the sacrament of piety which was manifested in the flesh." The Syriac, "Great is the mystery of godliness, that he was manifested in the flesh." The *probability* in regard to the correct reading here, as it seems to me, is, that the word, as originally written, was Θεὸς, *God*. At the same time, however, the evidence is not so clear that it can be properly used in an argument. But the passage is not *necessary* to prove the doctrine which is affirmed, on the supposition that that is the correct reading. The same truth is abundantly taught elsewhere; comp. Mat. i. 23; Jn. i. 14. ¶ *Was manifest.* Marg., *manifested.* The meaning is, *appeared* in the flesh. ¶ *In the flesh.* In human nature; see this explained in the Notes on Rom. i. 3. The expression here looks as though the true reading of the much-disputed word was *God.* It could not have been, it would seem evident, ὃ, *which*, referring to "mystery;" for how could a mystery "be manifested in the flesh?" Nor could it be ὅς, *who*, unless that should refer to one who was more than a man; for how absurd would it be to say that "a man was manifested, or appeared in the flesh?" How else could a man appear? The phrase here means that God appeared in human form, or with human nature; and this is declared to be the "great" truth so long concealed from human view, but now revealed as constituting the funda-

mental doctrine of the gospel. The expressions which follow in this verse refer to God as thus manifested in the flesh; to the Saviour as he appeared on earth, regarded as a divine and human being. It was the fact that he thus appeared and sustained this character, which made the things which are immediately specified so remarkable, and so worthy of attention. ¶ *Justified in the Spirit.* That is, the incarnate person above referred to; the Redeemer, regarded as God and man. The word *Spirit*, here, it is evident, refers to the Holy Spirit; for, (1) it is not possible to attach any intelligible idea to the phrase, "he was justified by his own spirit, or soul;" (2) as the Holy Spirit performed so important a part in the work of Christ, it is natural to suppose there would be some allusion here to him; and (3) as the "angels" are mentioned here as having been with him, and as the Holy Spirit is often mentioned in connection with him, it is natural to suppose that there would be some allusion to Him here. The word *justified*, here, is not used in the sense in which it is when applied to Christians, but in its more common signification. It means to *vindicate*, and the sense is, that he was shown to be the Son of God by the agency of the Holy Ghost; he was thus vindicated from the charges alleged against him. The Holy Spirit furnished the evidence that he was the Son of God, or *justified* his claims. Thus he descended on him at his baptism, Mat. iii. 16; he was sent to convince the world of sin because it did not believe on him, Jn. xvi. 8, 9; the Saviour cast out devils by him, Mat. xii. 28; the Spirit was given to him without measure, Jn. iii. 34; and the Spirit was sent down in accordance with his promise, to convert the hearts of men, Acts ii. 33. All the manifestations of God to him; all the power of working miracles by his agency; all the influences imparted to the man Christ Jesus, endowing him with such wisdom as man never had before, may be regarded as an attestation of the Holy Ghost to the divine mission of the Lord Jesus, and of course as a vindication from all the charges against him. In like manner, the descent of the Holy Ghost on the day of Pentecost, and his agency in the conversion of every sinner, prove the same thing, and furnish the grand argument in vindication of the Redeemer that he was sent from God. To this the apostle refers as a part of the glorious truth of the Christian scheme now revealed —the "mystery of religion;" as a portion of the amazing records, the memory of which the church was to preserve as connected with the redemption of the world. ¶ *Seen of angels.* They were attendants on his ministry, and came to him in times of distress, peril, and want; comp. Luke ii. 9–13; xxii. 43; xxiv. 4; Heb. i. 6; Mat. iv. 11. They felt an interest in him and his work, and they gladly came to him in his sorrows and troubles. The design of the apostle is to give an impressive view of the grandeur and glory of that work which attracted the attention of the heavenly hosts, and which drew them from the skies that they might proclaim his advent, sustain him in his temptations, witness his crucifixion, and watch over him in the tomb. The work of Christ, though despised by men, excited the deepest interest in heaven; comp. Notes on 1 Pet. i. 12. ¶ *Preached unto the Gentiles.* This is placed by the apostle among the "great" things which constituted the "mystery" of religion. The meaning is, that it was a glorious truth that salvation might be, and should be, proclaimed to all mankind, and that this was a part of the important truths made known in the gospel. Elsewhere this is called, by way of eminence, "*the* mystery of the gospel;" that is, the grand truth which had not been known until the coming of the Saviour; see Notes on Eph. vi. 19; Col. i. 26, 27; iv. 3. Before his coming, a wall of partition had divided the Jewish and Gentile world. The Jews regarded the rest of mankind as excluded from the

covenant mercies of God, and it was one of the principal stumbling-blocks in their way, in regard to the gospel, that it proclaimed that all the race was on a level, that that middle wall of partition was broken down, and that salvation might now be published to all men; comp. Acts xxii. 21; Eph. ii. 14, 15; Rom. iii. 22; x. 11–20. The Jew had no peculiar advantage for salvation by being a Jew; the Gentile was not excluded from the hope of salvation. The plan of redemption was adapted *to man* as such—without regard to his complexion, country, customs, or laws. The blood of Christ was shed for all, and wherever a human being could be found salvation might be freely offered him. This *is* a glorious truth; and taken in all its bearings, and in reference to the views which then prevailed, and which have always more or less prevailed, about the distinctions made among men by caste and rank, there is scarcely any more glorious truth connected with the Christian revelation, or one which will exert a wider influence in promoting the welfare of man. It is a great privilege to be permitted to proclaim that all men, in one respect—and that the most important—are on a level; that they are all equally the objects of the divine compassion; that Christ died for one as really as for another; that birth, wealth, elevated rank, or beauty of complexion, contribute nothing to the salvation of one man; and that poverty, a darker skin, slavery, or a meaner rank, do nothing to exclude another from the favour of his Maker. ¶ *Believed on in the world.* This also is mentioned among the "great" things which constitute the mystery of revealed religion. But why is this regarded as so remarkable as to be mentioned thus? In point of importance, how can it be mentioned in connection with the fact that God was manifest in the flesh; that he was vindicated by the Holy Ghost; that he was an object of intense interest to angelic hosts, and that his coming had broken down the walls which had separated the world, and placed them now on a level? I answer, perhaps the following circumstances may have induced the apostle to place this among the remarkable things evincing the greatness of this truth:—(1) The strong *improbability* arising from the greatness of the "mystery," that the doctrines respecting the incarnate Deity *would be* believed. Such is the incomprehensible nature of many of the truths connected with the incarnation; so strange does it seem that God *would* become incarnate; so amazing that he should appear in human flesh and blood, and that the incarnate Son of God should die, that it might be regarded as a wonderful thing that such a doctrine had in fact obtained credence in the world. But it was a glorious truth that all the natural improbabilities in the case had been overcome, and that men had accredited the announcement. (2) The strong improbability that his message would be believed, arising from the *wickedness of the human heart.* Man, in all his history, had shown a strong reluctance to believe *any* message from God, or *any* truth whatever revealed by him. The Jews had rejected his prophets and put them to death (Mat. xxiii., Acts vii.); and had at last put his own Son—their Messiah—to death. Man everywhere had shown his strong inclination to unbelief. There is in the human soul no elementary principle or germ of faith in God. Every man is an unbeliever by nature—an infidel first, a Christian afterwards; an infidel as he comes into the world, a believer only as he is made so by grace. The apostle, therefore, regarded it as a glorious fact that the message respecting the Saviour *had been* believed in the world. It overcame such a strong and universal reluctance to confide in God, that it showed that there was more than human power in operation to overcome this reluctance. (3) The *extent* to which this had been done may have been a reason why he thought it worthy of the place which he gives it here. It had been embraced, not by a few, but by thousands in all lands where the gospel had been published; and it was proof of the truth of the doctrine, and of the great power of God, that such high mysteries as those relating to redemption, and so much opposed to the natural feelings of the human heart, should have been embraced by so many. The same thing occurs now. The gospel makes its way against the native incredulity of the world, and every new convert is an additional demonstration that it is from God, and a new illustration of the greatness of this mystery. ¶ *Received up into glory.* To heaven; comp. John xvii. 5; see Notes on Acts i. 9. This is mentioned as among the "great" or remarkable things pertaining to "godliness," or the Christian revelation, because it was an event which had not elsewhere occurred, and was the crowning grandeur of the work of Christ. It was an event that was fitted to excite the deepest interest in heaven itself. No event of more importance has ever occurred in the universe, of which we have any knowledge, than the re-ascension of the triumphant Son of God to glory after having accomplished the redemption of a world.

REMARKS.

In view of the instructions of this chapter, we may make the following remarks.

1. The word *bishop* in the New Testament never means what is now commonly understood by it—a *prelate.* It does not denote here, or anywhere else in the New Testament, one who has charge over a *diocese* composed of a certain district of country, embracing a number of churches with their clergy.

2. There are not "three orders" of clergy in the New Testament. The apostle Paul in this chapter expressly designates the characteristics of those who should have charge of the church, but mentions only two, "bishops" and "deacons." The former are ministers of the word, having charge of the spiritual interests of the church; the other are deacons, of whom there is no evidence that they were appointed to preach. There is no "third" order. There is no allusion to any one who was to be "superior" to the "bishops" and "deacons." As the apostle Paul was expressly giving in-

structions in regard to the organization of the church, such an omission is unaccountable if he supposed there was to be an order of "prelates" in the church. Why is there no allusion to them? Why is there no mention of their qualifications? If Timothy was himself a prelate, was he to have nothing to do in transmitting the office to others? Were there no peculiar qualifications required in such an order of men which it would be proper to mention? Would it not be *respectful*, at least, in Paul to have made some allusion to such an office, if Timothy himself held it?

3. There is only one order of preachers in the church. The qualifications of that order are specified with great minuteness and particularity, as well as beauty, ver. 2–7. No man really needs to know more of the qualifications for this office than could be learned from a prayerful study of this passage.

4. A man who enters the ministry *ought* to have high qualifications, ver. 2–7. No man *ought*, under any pretence, to be put into the ministry who has not the qualifications here specified. Nothing is gained, in any department of human labour, by appointing incompetent persons to fill it. A farmer gains nothing by employing a man on his farm who has no proper qualifications for his business; a carpenter, a shoemaker, or a blacksmith, gains nothing by employing a man who knows nothing about his trade; and a neighbourhood gains nothing by employing a man as a teacher of a school who has no qualifications to teach, or who has a bad character. Such a man would do more mischief on a farm, or in a workshop, or in a school, than all the good which he could do would compensate. And so it is in the ministry. The true object is not to increase the *number* of ministers, it is to increase the number of those who are *qualified* for their work, and if a man has *not* the qualifications laid down by the inspired apostle, he had better seek some other calling.

5. The church is the guardian of the truth, ver. 15. It is appointed to preserve it pure, and to transmit

it to future ages. The world is dependent on it for any just views of truth. The church has the power, and is intrusted with the duty, of preserving on earth a just knowledge of God and of eternal things; of the way of salvation; of the requirements of pure morality;—to keep up the knowledge of that truth which tends to elevate society and to save man. It is intrusted with the Bible, to preserve uncorrupted, and to transmit to distant ages and lands. It is bound to maintain and assert the truth in its creeds and confessions of faith. And it is to preserve the truth by the holy lives of its members, and to show in their walk what is the appropriate influence of truth on the soul. Whatever religious truth there is now on the earth, has been thus preserved and transmitted, and it still devolves on the church to bear the truth of God on to future times, and to diffuse it abroad to distant lands.

6. The closing verse of this chapter (ver. 16) gives us a most elevated view of the plan of salvation, and of its grandeur and glory. It would be difficult, if not impossible, to condense more interesting and sublime thought into so narrow a compass as this. The great mystery of the incarnation; the interest of angelic beings in the events of redemption; the effect of the gospel on the heathen world; the tendency of the Christian religion to break down every barrier among men, and to place all the race on a level; its power in overcoming the unbelief of mankind; and the re-ascension of the Son of God to heaven, present a series of most wonderful facts to our contemplation. These things are found in no other system of religion, and these are worthy of the profound attention of every human being. The manifestation of God in the flesh! What a thought! It was worthy of the deepest interest among the angels, and it *claims* the attention of men, for it was *for* men and not for angels that he thus appeared in human form; comp. Notes on 1 Pet. i. 12.

7. How strange it is that *man* feels no more interest in these things! God was manifest in the flesh for his

CHAPTER IV.

NOW the Spirit speaketh expressly, that *a*in the latter

a Da.11.35; Mat.24.5-12; 2 Pe.2.1.

salvation, but he does not regard it. Angels looked upon it with wonder; but man, for whom he came, feels little interest in his advent or his work! The Christian religion has broken down the barrier among nations, and has proclaimed that all men may be saved; yet the mass of men look on this with entire unconcern. The Redeemer ascended to heaven, having finished his great work; but how little interest do the mass of mankind feel in this! He will come again to judge the world; but the race moves on, regardless of this truth; unalarmed at the prospect of meeting him; feeling no interest in the assurance that he *has* come and died for sinners, and no apprehension in view of the fact that he *will* come again, and that they must stand at his bar. All heaven was moved with his first advent, and will be with his second; but the earth regards it with unconcern. Angelic beings look upon this with the deepest anxiety, though they have no personal interest in it; man, though all his great interests are concentrated on it, regards it as a fable, disbelieves it all, and treats it with contempt and scorn. Such is the difference between heaven and earth—angels and men!

CHAPTER IV.
ANALYSIS OF THE CHAPTER.

There is, in many respects, a strong resemblance between the first part of this chapter and 2 Thes. ii.; comp. Notes on that chapter. The leading object of this chapter is to state to Timothy certain things of which he was constantly to remind the church; and having done this, the apostle gives him some directions about his personal deportment. The chapter may be conveniently divided into three parts:

I. Timothy was to put the church constantly in remembrance of the great apostasy which was to occur, and to guard them against the doctrines which would be inculcated under that apostasy, ver. 1-6.

times some shall depart from the faith, *b*giving heed to seducing spirits, and doctrines of devils;

b Re.16.14.

(*a*) There was to be, in the latter days, a great departing from the faith, ver. 1.

(*b*) Some of the characteristics of that apostasy were these: There would be a giving heed to seducing spirits and doctrines of devils, ver. 1. Those who taught would hypocritically speak what they knew to be falsehood, having their own consciences seared, ver. 2. They would forbid to marry, and forbid the use of certain articles of food which God had appointed for man, ver. 3-5.

II. Timothy was to warn the churches against trifling and superstitious views, such as the apostle calls "old wives'" fables, ver. 7-11.

(*a*) He was not to allow himself to be influenced by such fables, but at once to reject them, ver. 7.

(*b*) The bodily exercise which the friends of such "fables" recommended was of no advantage to the soul, and no stress ought to be laid on it, as if it were important, ver. 8.

(*c*) That which was truly profitable, and which ought to be regarded as important, was godliness; for *that* had promise of the present life, and of the life to come, ver. 8.

(*d*) Timothy must expect, in giving these instructions, to endure labour and to suffer reproach; nevertheless, he was faithfully to inculcate these important truths, ver. 10, 11.

III. Various admonitions respecting his personal deportment, ver. 12-16.

(*a*) He was so to live that no one would despise him or his ministry because he was young, ver. 12.

(*b*) He was to give a constant attention to his duties until the apostle should himself return to him, ver. 13.

(*c*) He was carefully to cultivate

the gift which had been conferred by his education, and by his ordination to the work of the ministry, ver. 14.

(d) He was to meditate on these things, and to give himself wholly to the work, so that his profiting might appear to all, ver. 15.

(e) He was to take good heed to himself, and to the manner and matter of his teaching, that he might save himself and those who heard him, ver. 16.

1. *Now the Spirit.* Evidently the Holy Spirit; the Spirit of inspiration. It is not quite certain, from this passage, whether the apostle means to say that this was a revelation *then* made to him, or whether it was a well-understood thing as taught by the Holy Spirit. He himself elsewhere refers to this same prophecy, and John also more than once mentions it; comp. 2 Thes. ii.; 1 John ii. 18; Rev. xx. From 2 Thes. ii. 5, it would seem that this was a truth which had before been communicated to the apostle Paul, and that he' had dwelt on it when he preached the gospel in Thessalonica. There is no improbability, however, in the supposition that so important a subject was communicated directly by the Holy Ghost to others of the apostles. ¶ *Speaketh expressly.* In express words—ῥητῶς. It was not by mere hints, and symbols, and shadowy images of the future; it was in an open and plain manner—in so many words. The object of this statement seems to be to call the attention of Timothy to it in an emphatic manner, and to show the importance of attending to it. ¶ *That in the latter times.* Under the last dispensation, during which the affairs of the world would close; see Notes on Heb. i. 2. It does not mean that this would occur *just before* the end of the world, but that it would take place during *that last dispensation,* and that the end of the world would not happen *until* this should take place; see Notes on 2 Thes. ii. 3. ¶ *Some shall depart from the faith.* The Greek word here—ἀποστήσονται, *apostesontai*—is that from which we have derived the word *apostatize,* and

would be properly so rendered here. The meaning is, that they would *apostatize* from the belief of the truths of the gospel. It does not mean that, as individuals, they would have been true Christians; but that there would be a departure from the great doctrines which constitute the Christian faith. The *ways* in which they would do this are immediately specified, showing what the apostle meant here by departing from the faith. They would give heed to seducing spirits, to the doctrines of devils, &c. The use of the word "*some,*" here—τινες—does not imply that the number would be small. The meaning is, that *certain persons* would thus depart, or that *there would be* an apostasy of the kind here mentioned, in the last days. From the parallel passage in 2 Thes. ii. 3, it would seem that this was to be an extensive apostasy. ¶ *Giving heed to seducing spirits.* Rather than to the Spirit of God. It would be a part of their system to yield to those spirits that led astray. The spirits here referred to are any that cause to err, and the most obvious and natural construction is to refer it to the agency of fallen spirits. Though it *may* apply to false teachers, yet, if so, it is rather to them as under the influence of evil spirits. This may be applied, so far as the phraseology is concerned, to *any* false teaching; but it is evident that the apostle had a specific apostasy in view — some great *system* that would greatly corrupt the Christian faith; and the words here should be interpreted with reference to that. It is true that men in all ages are prone to give heed to seducing spirits; but the thing referred to here is some grand apostasy, in which the characteristics would be manifested, and the doctrines held which the apostle proceeds immediately to specify; comp. 1 Jn. iv. 1. ¶ *And doctrines of devils.* Gr., "teachings of demons"—διδασκαλίαις δαιμονίων. This may either mean teachings *respecting* demons, or teachings *by* demons. The particular sense must be determined by the connection. Ambiguity of this kind in the construction of words, where one is in the genitive case, is not uncommon; comp. John xv. 9, 10; xxi. 15. Instances of the construction where the genitive denotes the *object*, and should be translated *concerning*, occur in Mat. ix. 25, "The gospel *of* the kingdom," *i.e.* concerning the kingdom; Mat. x. 1, "Power *of* unclean spirits," *i.e.* over or concerning unclean spirits; so, also, Acts iv. 9; Rom. xvi. 15; 2 Cor. i. 5; Eph. iii. 1; Rev. ii. 13. Instances of construction where the genitive denotes the *agent*, occur in the following places: Luke i. 69, "A horn *of* salvation," *i.e.* a horn which produces or causes salvation; John vi. 28; Rom. iii. 22; 2 Cor. iv. 10; Eph. iv. 18; Col. ii. 11. Whether the phrase here means that, in the apostasy, they would give heed to doctrines *respecting* demons, or to doctrines which demons *taught*, cannot, it seems to me, be determined with certainty. If the previous phrase, however, means that they would embrace doctrines taught by evil spirits, it can hardly be supposed that the apostle would immediately repeat the same idea in another form; and then the sense would be, that one characteristic of the time referred to would be the prevalent teaching *respecting* demons. They would "give heed to," or embrace, some peculiar views respecting demons. The word here rendered *devils* is δαιμονία—*demons*. This word, among the Greeks, denoted the following things: (1) A *god* or *goddess*, spoken of the heathen gods; comp. in New Testament, Acts xvii. 18. (2) A divine being, where no particular one was specified, the agent or author of good or evil fortune; of death, fate, &c. In this sense it is often used in Homer. (3) The souls of men of the golden age, which dwelt unobserved upon the earth to regard the actions of men, and to defend them—tutelary divinities, or geniuses—like that which Socrates regarded as his constant attendant (Xen. *Mem.* 4. 8. 1. 5; Apol. Soc. 4. See Passow). (4) To this may be added the common use in the New Testament, where the word denotes a demon in the Jewish sense—

a bad spirit, subject to Satan, and under his control; one of the host of fallen angels—commonly, but not very properly rendered *devil* or *devils*. These spirits were supposed to wander in desolate places, Mat. xii. 43; comp. Isa. xiii. 21; xxxiv. 14; or they dwell in the air, Eph. ii. 2. They were regarded as hostile to mankind, John viii. 44; as able to utter heathen oracles, Acts xvi. 17; as lurking in the idols of the heathen, 1 Cor. x. 20; Rev. ix. 20. They are spoken of as the authors of evil, James ii. 19; comp. Eph. vi. 12, and as having the power of taking *possession* of a person, of producing diseases, or of causing mania, as in the case of the demoniacs, Luke iv. 33; viii. 27; Mat. xvii. 18; Mark vii. 29, 30; and often elsewhere. The doctrine, therefore, which the apostle predicted would prevail, might, *so far as the word used is concerned*, be either of the following: (1) Accordance with the prevalent notions of the heathen respecting false gods; or a falling into idolatry similar to that taught in the Grecian mythology. It can hardly be supposed, however, that he designed to say that the common notions of the heathen would prevail in the Christian church, or that the worship of the heathen gods *as such* would be set up there. (2) An accordance with the Jewish views respecting demoniacal possessions and the power of exorcising them. If this view should extensively prevail in the Christian church, it would be in accordance with the language of the prediction. (3) Accordance with the prevalent heathen notions respecting the departed spirits of the good and the great, who were exalted to the rank of demi-gods, and who, though invisible, were supposed still to exert an important influence in favour of mankind. To these beings, the heathen rendered extraordinary homage. They regarded them as demi-gods. They supposed that they took a deep interest in human affairs. They invoked their aid. They set apart days in honour of them. They offered sacrifices, and performed rites and ceremonies to propitiate their favour. They were regarded as a sort of mediators or intercessors between man and the superior divinities. If these things are found anywhere in the Christian church, they may be regarded as a fulfilment of this prediction, for they were not of a nature to be foreseen by any human sagacity. Now it so happens, that they are in fact found in the Papal communion, and in a way that corresponds fairly to the meaning of the phrase, as it would have been understood in the time of the apostle. There is, *first*, the worship of the Virgin and of the saints, or the extraordinary honours rendered to them—corresponding almost entirely with the reverence paid by the heathen to the spirits of heroes or to demi-gods. The saints are supposed to have extraordinary power with God, and their aid is implored as intercessors. The Virgin Mary is invoked as "the mother of God," and as having power still to command her Son. The Papists do not, indeed, offer the same homage to the saints which they do to God, but they ask their aid; they offer prayer to them. The following extracts from the Catechism of Dr. James Butler, approved and recommended by Dr. Kenrick, "Bishop of Philadelphia," expresses the general views of Roman Catholics on this subject:—"Q. How do Catholics distinguish between the honour they give to God, and the honour they give to the saints, when they pray to God and the saints? A. Of God alone they beg grace and mercy; and of the saints they only ask the assistance of their prayers? Q. Is it lawful to recommend ourselves to the saints, and ask their prayers? A. Yes; as it is lawful and a very pious practice to ask the prayers of our fellow-creatures on earth, and to pray for them." In the "Prayer to be said before mass," the following language occurs: "In union with the holy church and its minister, and invoking the blessed Virgin Mary, Mother of God, and all the angels and saints, we now offer the adorable sacrifice of the mass," &c. In the General Confession, it is said—"I confess to almighty God, to the blessed Mary, ever Virgin, to blessed

Michael the archangel, to blessed John the Baptist, to the holy apostles Peter and Paul, and to all the saints, that I have sinned exceedingly." So also, the Council of Trent declared, sess. 25, *Concerning the invocation of the saints,* "that it is good and useful to supplicate them, and to fly to their prayers, power, and aid; but that they who deny that the saints are to be invoked, or who assert that they do not pray for men, or that their invocation of them is idolatry, hold an impious opinion." See also Peter Dens' *Moral Theology,* translated by the Rev. J. F. Berg, pp. 342–356. *Secondly,* in the Papal communion the doctrine of *exorcism* is still held —implying a belief that evil spirits or demons have power over the human frame—a doctrine which comes fairly under the meaning of the phrase here—"*the doctrine respecting demons.*" Thus in Dr. Butler's Catechism: "Q. What do you mean by exorcism? A. The rites and prayers instituted by the church for the casting out devils, or restraining them from hurting persons, disquieting places, or abusing any of God's creatures to our harm. Q. Has Christ given his church any such power over devils? A. Yes, he has; see St. Mat. x. 1; St. Mark iii. 15; St. Luke ix. 1. And that this power was not to die with the apostles, nor to cease after the apostolic age, we learn from the perpetual practice of the church, and the experience of all ages." The characteristic here referred to by the apostle, therefore, is one that applies precisely to the Roman Catholic communion, and cannot be applied with the same fitness to any other association calling itself Christian on earth. There can be no doubt, therefore, that the Holy Spirit designed to designate that apostate church.

2. *Speaking lies in hypocrisy—* Ἐν ὑποκρισει ψευδολόγων. Or rather, "by, or through the hypocrisy of those speaking lies." So it is rendered by Whitby, Benson, Macknight, and others. Our translators have rendered it as if the word translated "speaking lies"—ψευδολόγων— referred to *demons,* or *devils*—δαι-

2 Speaking[c] lies in hypocrisy;
    c Mat.7.15; Ro.16.18.

μονίων—in the previous verse. But there are two objections to this. One is, that then, as Koppe observes, the words would have been inverted— ψευδολόγων ἐν ὑποκρίσει. The other is, that if that construction is adopted, it must be carried through the sentence, and then all the phrases "speaking lies," "having their conscience seared," "forbidding to marry," &c., must be referred to demons. The preposition ἐν, in, may denote by or through, and is often so used. If this be the true construction, then it will mean that those who departed from the faith did it by or through the hypocritical teachings of those who spoke lies, or who knew that they were inculcating falsehoods; of those whose conscience was seared; of those who forbade to marry, &c. The meaning then will be, "In the last days certain persons will depart from the faith of the gospel. This apostasy will essentially consist in their giving heed to spirits that lead to error, and in embracing corrupt and erroneous views on demonology, or in reference to invisible beings between us and God. This they will do through the hypocritical teaching of those who inculcate falsehood; whose consciences are seared," &c. The series of characteristics, therefore, which follow, are those of the *teachers*, not of *the taught;* of the ministers of the church, not of the great body of the people. The apostle meant to say that this grand apostasy would occur under the influence of a hypocritical, hardened, and arbitrary ministry, teaching their own doctrines instead of the divine commands, and forbidding that which God had declared to be lawful. In the clause before us—"*speaking lies in hypocrisy*"—two things are implied: *first*, that the characteristic of those referred to would be that they would "*speak lies;*" *second*, that this would be done *hypocritically*. In regard to the first, there can be no doubt among Protestants of its applicability to the Papal communion. The entire series of

having their conscience seared with a hot iron;

doctrines respecting the authority of the pope, purgatory, the mass, the invocation of the saints, the veneration of relics, the seven sacraments, the authority of tradition, the doctrine of merit, &c., is regarded as false. Indeed, the system could not be better characterized than by saying that it is a system "speaking lies." The entire scheme attempts to palm falsehood upon the world, in the place of the simple teaching of the New Testament. The only question is, whether this is done "in hypocrisy," or hypocritically. In regard to this, it is not necessary to maintain that there is *no* sincerity among the ministers of that communion, or that *all* are hypocritical in their belief and their teaching. The sense is, that this is the general characteristic, or that this is understood by the leaders or prime movers in that apostasy. In regard to the applicability of this to the ministers of the Papal communion, and the question whether they teach what they know to be false, we may observe, (1) That many of them are men of eminent learning, and there can be no reason to doubt that they *know* that many of the Catholic legends are false, and many of the doctrines of their faith contrary to the Bible. (2) Not a few of the things in that communion *must* be known by them to be false, though not known to be so by the people. Such are all the pretended miracles wrought by the relics of the saints; the liquefying of the blood of St. Januarius, &c.; see Notes on 2 Thes. ii. 9. As the working of these tricks depends wholly on the priesthood, they must know that they are "speaking lies in hypocrisy." (3) The matter of fact seems to be, that when young men who have been trained in the Catholic church first turn their attention to the ministry, they are sincere. They have not yet been made acquainted with the "mysteries of iniquity" in the communion in which they have been trained, and

3 Forbidding to marry, *and com-* | *manding* to abstain from meats,

they do not suspect the deceptions that are practised there. When they pass through their course of study, however, and become acquainted with the arts and devices on which the fabric rests, and with the scandalous lives of many of the clergy, they are shocked to find how corrupt and false the whole system is. But they are now committed. They have devoted their lives to this profession. They are trained now to this system of imposture, and they must continue to practise and perpetuate the fraud, or abandon the church, and subject themselves to all the civil and ecclesiastical disabilities which would now follow if they were to leave and reveal all its frauds and impostures. A gentleman of high authority, and who has had as good an opportunity as any man living to make accurate and extensive observations, stated to me that this was a common thing in regard to the Catholic clergy in France and Italy. No one can reasonably doubt that the great body of that clergy *must* be apprised that much that is relied on for the support of the system is mere legend, and that the miracles which are pretended to be wrought are mere trick and imposture. ¶ *Having their conscience seared with a hot iron.* The allusion here is doubtless to the effect of applying a hot iron to the skin. The cauterized part becomes rigid and hard, and is dead to sensibility. So with the conscience of those referred to. It has the same relation to a conscience that is sensitive and quick in its decisions, that a cauterized part of the body has to a thin, delicate, and sensitive skin. Such a conscience exists in a mind that will practise delusion without concern; that will carry on a vast system of fraud without wincing; that will incarcerate, scourge, or burn the innocent without compassion; and that will practise gross enormities, and indulge in sensual gratifications under the mask of piety. While there are many eminent exceptions to an application of this to the Papal com-

munion, yet this description will apply better to the Roman priesthood in the time of Luther—and in many other periods of the world—than to any other *body of men* that ever lived.

3. *Forbidding to marry.* That is, "They will depart from the faith through the hypocritical teaching—of those who forbid to marry;" see Notes on ver. 2. This does not necessarily mean that they would prohibit marriage altogether, but that it would be a characteristic of their teaching that marriage *would be forbidden,* whether of one class of persons or many. They would *commend* and *enjoin* celibacy and virginity. They would regard such a state, for certain persons, as more holy than the married condition, and would consider it as *so* holy that they would absolutely prohibit those who wished to be most holy from entering into the relation. It is needless to say how accurately this applies to the views of the Papacy in regard to the comparative purity and advantages of a state of celibacy, and to their absolute prohibition of the marriage of the clergy. The tenth article of the decree of the Council of Trent, in relation to marriage, will show the general view of the Papacy on that subject. "Whosoever shall say that the married state is to be preferred to a state of virginity, or celibacy, and that it is not better and more blessed to remain in virginity, or celibacy, than to be joined in marriage; let him be accursed!" Comp. Peter Dens' *Moral Theology,* pp. 497–500. ¶ And commanding *to abstain from meats,* &c. The word *meat* in the Scriptures, commonly denotes *food* of all kinds, Mat. iii. 4; vi. 25; x. 10; xv. 37. This was the meaning of the word when the translation of the Bible was made. It is now used by us, almost exclusively, to denote animal food. The word here used—βρῶμα—means, properly, whatever is eaten, and may refer to animal flesh, fish, fruit, or vegetables. It is often, however, in the New Testament, employed particularly to denote the flesh

which God hath created to be received [d] with thanksgiving of

d Ec.5.18.

of animals, Heb. ix. 10; xiii. 9; Rom. xiv. 15, 20; 1 Cor. viii. 8, 13. As it was animal food particularly which was forbidden under the Jewish code, and as the questions on this subject among Christians would relate to the same kinds of prohibition, it is probable that the word has the same limited signification here, and should be taken as meaning the same thing that the word *meat* does with us. To forbid the use of certain meats, is here described as one of the characteristics of those who would instruct the church in the time of the great apostasy. It is not necessary to suppose that there would be an *entire* prohibition, but only a prohibition of certain kinds, and at certain seasons. That *this* characteristic is found in the Papacy more than anywhere else in the Christian world, it is needless to prove. The following questions and answers from Dr. Butler's Catechism, will show what is the sentiment of Roman Catholics on this subject:—"Q. Are there any other commandments besides the Ten Commandments of God? A. There are the commandments or precepts of the church, which are chiefly six. Q. What are we obliged to do by the second commandment of the church? A. To give part of the year to fast and abstinence. Q. What do you mean by fast-days? A. Certain days on which we are allowed but one meal, *and forbidden flesh meat.* Q. What do you mean by days of abstinence? A. Certain days on which *we are forbidden to eat flesh meat;* but are allowed the usual number of meals. Q. Is it strictly forbidden by the church to eat flesh meat on days of abstinence? A. Yes; and to eat flesh meat on any day on which it is forbidden, without necessity and leave of the church, is very sinful." Could there be a more impressive and striking commentary on what the apostle says here, that "in the latter days some would depart from the faith, under the hypocritical teach-

them which believe and know the truth.

ing of those who *commanded to abstain from meats?*" The authority claimed by the Papacy to issue *commands* on this subject, may be seen still further by the following extract from the same catechism, showing the gracious permission of the church to the "faithful." "The abstinence on Saturday is dispensed with, for the faithful throughout the United States, for the space of ten years (from 1833), except when a fast falls on a Saturday. The use of flesh meat is allowed at present by dispensation in the diocess of Philadelphia, on all the Sundays of Lent, except Palm Sunday, and once a day on Monday, Tuesday, and Thursday in each week, except the Thursday after Ash Wednesday, and also excepting Holy-week." Such is the Roman Catholic religion! See also Peter Dens' *Moral Theology,* pp. 321–330. It is true that what is said here *might* apply to the Essenes, as Koppe supposes, or to the Judaizing teachers, but it applies more appropriately and fully to the Papal communion than to any other body of men professing Christianity; and taken in connection with the other characteristics of the apostasy, there can be no doubt that the reference is to that. ¶ *Which God hath created.* The articles of food which he has made, and which he has designed for the nourishment of man. The fact that God had *created* them was proof that they were not to be regarded as evil, and that it was not to be considered as a religious duty to abstain from them. All that *God* has made is good in its place, and what is adapted to be food for man is not to be refused or forbidden; comp. Eccl. v. 18. There can be no doubt that in the apostasy here referred to, those things would be forbidden, not because they were injurious or hurtful in their nature, but because it might be made a part of a system of religion of self-righteousness, and because there might be connected with such a prohibition the belief of special merit.

4 For every creature of God *is* good, and nothing to be refused, if it be received with thanksgiving:

5 For it is sanctified by the word of God and prayer.

6 If thou put the brethren in remembrance of these things, thou shalt be a good minister of Jesus Christ, *e*nourished up in the words of faith and of good doctrine, whereunto thou hast attained.

e Je.15.16; 1 Pe.2.2.

---

4. *For every creature of God is good.* Gr., *all the creatures,* or *all that God has created* — πᾶν κτίσμα: that is, as he made it; comp. Gen. i. 10, 12, 18, 31. It does not mean that every moral agent *remains* good as long as he is *a creature of God,* but moral agents, men and angels, *were* good as they were made at first, Gen. i. 31. Nor does it mean that all that God has made is good *for every object to which it can be applied.* It is good in its place; good for the purpose for which he made it. But it should not be inferred that a thing which is poisonous in its nature is good for food, *because* it is a creation of God. It is good only in its place, and for the ends for which he intended it. Nor should it be inferred that what God has made is necessarily good *after* it has been perverted by man. As God made it originally, it might have been used without injury. Apples and peaches were made good, and are still useful and proper as articles of food; rye and Indian corn are good, and are admirably adapted to the support of man and beast, but it does not follow that all that *man* can make of them is necessarily good. He extracts from them a poisonous liquid, and then says that " *every creature* of God is good, and nothing to be refused." But is this a fair use of this passage of Scripture? True, they *are* good—they *are* to be received with gratitude as he made them, and as applied to the uses for which he designed them; but why apply this passage to prove that a deleterious beverage, which *man* has extracted from what God has made, is good also, and good for all the purposes to which it can be applied? As *God* made these things, they are good. As man perverts them, it is no longer proper to call them the "creation of God," and they may be injurious in the

highest degree. This passage, therefore, should not be adduced to vindicate the use of intoxicating drinks. As employed by the apostle, it had no such reference, nor does it contain any *principle* which can properly receive any such application. ¶ *And nothing to be refused.* Nothing that God has made, for the purposes for which he designed it. The necessity of the case—the "exigency of the passage" — requires this interpretation. It *cannot* mean that we are not to refuse poison if offered in our food, or that we are never to refuse food that is to us injurious or offensive; nor can it any more mean that we are to receive *all* that may be offered to us as a beverage. The sense is, that as God made it, and for the purposes for which he designed it, it is not to be held to be evil; or, which is the same thing, it is not to be prohibited as if there were merit in abstaining from it. It is not to be regarded as a religious duty to abstain from food which God has appointed for the support of man. ¶ *If it be received with thanksgiving.* See Notes on 1 Cor. x. 31; Eph. v. 20; Phil. iv. 6.

5. *For it is sanctified by the word of God.* By the authority or permission of God. It would be profane or unholy if he had forbidden it; it is made holy or proper for our use by his permission, and no command of *man* can make it unholy or improper; comp. Gen. i. 29; ix. 3. ¶ *And prayer.* If it is partaken of with prayer. By prayer we are enabled to receive it with gratitude, and everything that we eat or drink may thus be made a means of grace.

6. *If thou put the brethren in remembrance of these things.* Of the truths just stated. They are, therefore, proper subjects to preach upon. It is the duty of the ministry to show to the people of their charge what *is*

7 But' refuse profane and old wives' fables, and exercise thyself *rather* unto godliness.

8 For bodily exercise profiteth

f Tit 1 14.

error and where it may be apprehended, and to caution them to avoid it. ¶ *Nourished up in the words of faith.* That is, you will be then "a good minister of Jesus Christ, as becomes one who has been nourished up in the words of faith, or trained up in the doctrines of religion." The apostle evidently designs to remind Timothy of the manner in which he had been trained, and to show him how he might act in accordance with that. From one who had been thus educated, it was reasonable to expect that he would be a faithful and exemplary minister of the gospel. ¶ *Whereunto thou hast attained.* The word used here means, properly, to accompany side by side; to follow closely; to follow out, trace, or examine. It is rendered *shall follow,* in Mat. xvi. 17; *having had understanding,* in Luke i. 3; and *hast fully known,* in 2 Tim. iii. 10. It does not elsewhere occur in the New Testament. The meaning here seems to be, that Timothy had followed out the doctrines in which he had been trained to their legitimate results; he had accurately seen and understood their bearing, as leading him to embrace the Christian religion. His early training in the Scriptures of the Old Testament (2 Tim. i. 5; iii. 15), he had now fully carried out, by embracing the Lord Jesus as the Messiah, and by evincing the proper results of the early teaching which he had received in connection with that religion. If he now followed the directions of the apostle, he would be a minister of the Lord Jesus, worthy of the attainments in religious knowledge which he had made, and of the expectations which had been formed of him. No young man should, by neglect, indolence, or folly, disappoint the reasonable expectations of his friends. Their cherished hopes are a proper ground of appeal to him, and it may be properly demanded of everyone that he shall carry out to

¹little; but *g* godliness is profitable unto all things, *h* having promise of the life that now is, and of that which is to come.

¹ or, *for a little time.* *g* ch.6.6.   *h* Ps.84.11.

their legitimate results all the principles of his early training, and that he shall be in his profession all that his early advantages make it reasonable to *expect* that he will be.

7. *But refuse.* That is, refuse to pay attention to them, or reject them. Do not consider them of sufficient importance to occupy your time. ¶ *Profane.* The word here used does not mean that the fables here referred to were blasphemous or impious in their character, but that they had not the character of true religion, 2 Tim. ii. 16. ¶ *And old wives'.* Old women's stories; or such as old women held to be important. The word is used here, as it is often with us, in the sense of silly. ¶ *Fables.* Fictions, or stories that were not founded on fact. The heathen religion abounded with fictions of this kind, and the Jewish teachers were also remarkable for the number of such fables which they had introduced into their system. It is probable that the apostle referred here particularly to the Jewish fables, and the counsel which he gives to Timothy is, to have nothing to do with them. ¶ *And exercise thyself* rather *unto godliness.* Rather than attempt to understand those fables. Do not occupy your time and attention with them, but rather cultivate piety, and seek to become more holy.

8. *For bodily exercise profiteth little.* Marg., *for a little time.* The Greek will admit of either interpretation, and what is here affirmed is true in either sense. The bodily exercise to which the apostle refers is of little advantage compared with that piety which he recommended Timothy to cultivate, and whatever advantage could be derived from it, would be but of short duration. "Bodily exercise" here refers, doubtless, to the mortifications of the body by abstinence and penance which the ancient devotees, and particularly the Essenes, made so important as a part of their religion.

The apostle does not mean to say that bodily exercise is in itself improper, or that no advantage can be derived from it in the preservation of health, but he refers to it solely as a means of religion; as supposed to promote holiness of heart and of life. By these bodily austerities it was supposed that the corrupt passions would be subdued, the wanderings of an unholy fancy fettered down, and the soul brought into conformity to God. In opposition to this supposition, the apostle has here stated a great principle which experience has shown to be universally correct, that such austerities do little to promote holiness, but much to promote superstition. There must be a deeper work on the soul than any which can be accomplished by the mere mortification of the body; see Notes on Col. ii. 23, and comp. 1 Cor. ix. 25-27. ¶ *But godliness.* Piety or religion. ¶ *Is profitable unto all things.* In every respect. There is not an interest of man, in reference to this life, or to the life to come, which it would not promote. It is favourable to health of body, by promoting temperance, industry and frugality; to clearness and vigour of intellect, by giving just views of truth, and of the relative value of objects; to peace of conscience, by leading to the faithful performance of duty; to prosperity in business, by making a man sober, honest, prudent, and industrious; to a good name, by leading a man to pursue such a course of life as shall deserve it; and to comfort in trial, calmness in death, and immortal peace beyond the grave. Religion injures no one. It does not destroy health; it does not enfeeble the intellect; it does not disturb the conscience; it does not pander to raging and consuming passions; it does not diminish the honour of a good name; it furnishes no subject of bitter reflection on a bed of death. It makes no one the poorer; it prompts to no crime; it engenders no disease. If a man should do that which would most certainly make him happy, he would be decidedly and conscientiously religious; and though piety promises no

earthly possessions directly as its reward, and secures no immunity from sickness, bereavement, and death, yet there is nothing which so certainly secures a steady growth of prosperity in a community as the virtues which it engenders and sustains, and there is nothing else that will certainly meet the ills to which man is subject. I have no doubt that it is the real conviction of every man, that if he ever becomes certainly *happy,* he will be a Christian; and I presume that it is the honest belief of every one that the true and consistent Christian is the most happy of men. And yet, with this conviction, men seek everything else rather than religion, and in the pursuit of baubles, which they know cannot confer happiness, they defer religion—the only certain source of happiness at any time—to the last period of life, or reject it altogether. ¶ *Having promise of the life that now is.* That is, it furnishes the promise of whatever is really necessary for us in this life. The promises of the Scriptures on this subject are abundant, and there is probably not a want of our nature for which there might not be found a specific promise in the Bible; comp. Ps. xxiii. 1; lxxxiv. 11; Phil. iv. 19. Religion promises us needful food and raiment, Mat. vi. 25-33; Isa. xxxiii. 16; comfort in affliction, Deut. xxxiii. 27; Job v. 19; Ps. xlvi.; Heb. xiii. 5; support in old age and death, Isa. xlvi. 4; Ps. xxiii. 4; comp. Isa. xliii. 2; and a good reputation, an honoured name when we are dead; Ps. xxxvii. 1-6. There is nothing which man really *needs* in this life, which is not promised by religion; and if the inquiry were made, it would be surprising to many, even with our imperfect religion, how literally these promises are fulfilled. David, near the close of a long life, was able to bear this remarkable testimony on this subject: "I have been young, and now am old; yet have I not seen the righteous forsaken, nor his seed begging bread," Ps. xxxvii. 25. And now, of the beggars that come to our doors, to how few of them can we give a cup of cold water, feeling that we are giving

9 This *is* a faithful saying, and worthy of all acceptation.

10 For therefore we both labour and suffer reproach, because we

it to a disciple? How rare is it that a true Christian becomes a beggar! Of the inmates of our alms-houses, how very few give any evidence that they have religion! They have been brought there by vice, not by religion. True piety sends none to the alms-house; it would have saved the great mass of those who are there from ever needing the charity of their fellow-men. ¶ *And of that which is to come.* Eternal life. And it is the only thing that *promises* such a life. Infidelity makes no *promise* of future happiness. Its business is to take away all the comforts which religion gives, and to leave men to go to a dark eternity with no promise or hope of eternal joy. Vice *promises* pleasures in the present life, but only to disappoint its votaries here; it makes no promise of happiness in the future world. There is nothing that furnishes any certain *promises* of happiness hereafter, in this world or the next, but religion. God makes no promise of such happiness to beauty, birth, or blood; to the possession of honours or wealth; to great attainments in science and learning, or to the graces of external accomplishment. All these, whatever flattering hopes of happiness they may hold out here, have no assurance of future eternal bliss. It is not by such things that God graduates the rewards of heaven, and it is only *piety* or *true religion* that furnishes any assurance of happiness in the world to come.

9. *This* is *a faithful saying.* See Notes on chap. i. 15.

10. *For therefore we both labour and suffer reproach.* In making this truth known, that all might be saved, or that salvation was offered to all. The *labour* was chiefly experienced in carrying this intelligence abroad among the Gentiles; the *reproach* arose chiefly from the Jews for doing it. ¶ *Because we trust in the living God.* This does not mean, as our translation would seem to imply, that

trust in the living God, who is the ᵸ Saviour of all men, specially of those that believe.

ᵸ Is.45.17,22.

he laboured and suffered *because* he confided in God, or that this was the *reason* of his sufferings, but rather that this trust in the living God was his *support* in these labours and trials. "We labour and suffer reproach, *for* we have hope in God. Through him we look for salvation. We believe that he has made this known to men, and believing this, we labour earnestly to make it known, even though it be attended with reproaches." The sentiment is, that the belief that God has revealed a plan of salvation for all men, and invites all men to be saved, will make his friends willing to *labour* to make this known, though it be attended with reproaches. ¶ *Who is the Saviour of all men.* This must be understood as denoting that he is the Saviour of all men in some sense which differs from what is immediately affirmed—"*especially* of those that believe." There is something pertaining to *them* in regard to salvation which does not pertain to "*all* men." It cannot mean that he brings all men to heaven, *especially* those who believe —for this would be nonsense. And if he brings all men actually to heaven, how can it be *especially* true that he does this in regard to those who believe? Does it mean that he saves others *without* believing? But this would be contrary to the uniform doctrine of the Scriptures; see Mark xvi. 16. When, therefore, it is said that he "is the Saviour of *all* men, *especially* of those who believe," it must mean that there is a sense in which it is true that he may be called the Saviour of all men, while, at the same time, it is *actually* true that those only are saved who believe. This may be true in two respects: (1) As he is the *Preserver* of men (Job vii. 20), for in this sense he may be said to *save* them from famine, and war, and peril—keeping them from day to day; comp. Ps. cvii. 28. (2) As he has *provided* salvation for all men. He is thus their Saviour—and

11 These things command and teach.

12 Let *i* no man despise thy

i Tit.2.7,15.

youth; but be thou an example of the believers, in word, in conversation, in charity, in spirit, in faith, in purity.

may be called the common Saviour of all; that is, he has confined the offer of salvation to no one class of men; he has not limited the atonement to one division of the human race; and he actually saves all who are willing to be saved by him. [See Supplementary Note, 2 Cor. v. 24. This passage, however, is not regarded a proof text now on the extent of the atonement, as the fair rendering of *σωτὴρ* is "Preserver." Dr. Wardlaw has accordingly excluded it in his work on the Atonement.]

¶ *Specially of those that believe.* This is evidently designed to limit the previous remark. If it had been left there, it might have been inferred that he would *actually save* all men. But the apostle held no such doctrine, and he here teaches that salvation is *actually* limited to those who believe. This is the speciality or the peculiarity in the salvation of those who actually reach heaven, that they are *believers;* see Notes on Mark xvi. 16. All men, therefore, do not enter heaven, unless all men have faith. But is this so? What evidence is there that the great mass of mankind die believing on the Son of God?

11. *These things command and teach.* As important doctrines, and as embracing the sum of the Christian system. It follows from this, that a minister of the gospel is solemnly bound to teach that there is a sense in which God is the Saviour of all men. He is just as much bound to teach this, as he is that only those will be saved who believe. It is a glorious truth—and it is a thing for which a man should unceasingly give thanks to God, that he may go and proclaim that he has provided salvation for all, and is willing that all should come and live.

12. *Let no man despise thy youth.* That is, do not act in such a manner that any shall despise you on account of your youth. Act as becomes a minister of the gospel in all things, and in such a way that men will re-

spect you as such, though you are young. It is clear from this that Timothy was then a young man, but his exact age there is no means of determining. It is implied here, (1) that there was danger that, by the levity and indiscretion to which youth are so much exposed, the ministry might be regarded with contempt; and (2) that it was possible that his deportment should be so grave, serious, and every way appropriate, that the ministry would not be blamed, but honoured. The *way* in which Timothy was to live so that the ministry would not be despised on account of his youth, the apostle proceeds immediately to specify. ¶ *But be thou an example of the believers.* One of the constant duties of a minister of the gospel, no matter what his age. A minister should so live, that if all his people should closely follow his example, their salvation would be secure, and they would make the highest possible attainments in piety. On the meaning of the word rendered *example*, see Notes on Phil. iii. 17; 1 Thes. i. 7. ¶ *In word.* In *speech;* that is, your manner of conversation. This does not refer to his *public teaching*—in which he could not probably be an *example* to them—but to his usual and familiar conversation. ¶ *In conversation.* In general deportment. See this word explained in the Notes on Phil. i. 27. ¶ *In charity.* Love to the brethren, and to all; see Notes on 1 Cor. xiii. ¶ *In spirit.* In the government of your passions, and in a mild, meek, forgiving disposition. ¶ *In faith.* At all times, and in all trials, show to believers by your example how they ought to maintain unshaken confidence in God. ¶ *In purity.* In chasteness of life; see chap. v. 2. There should be nothing in your intercourse with the other sex that would give rise to scandal. The Papists, with great impropriety, understand this as enjoining celibacy —as if there could be no *purity* in

13 Till I come, give attendance to reading, to exhortation, to doctrine.

14 Neglect[k] not the gift that is

[k] 2 Ti.1 6.

in thee, [l]which was given thee by prophecy, [m]with the laying on of the hands of the presbytery.

[l] ch.1.18.　　　[m] Ac.13.3.

that holy relation which God appointed in Eden, and which he has declared to "be honourable in all" (Heb. xiii. 4), and which he has made so essential to the well-being of mankind. If the apostle had wished to produce the highest possible degree of corruption in the church, he would have enjoined the celibacy of the clergy and the celibacy of an indefinite number of nuns and monks. There are no other institutions on the earth which have done so much to corrupt the chastity of the race, as those which have grown out of the doctrine that celibacy is more honourable than marriage.

13. *Till I come.* Notes, chap. iii. 14, 15. ¶ *Give attendance to reading.* The word here used may refer either to public or to private reading; see Acts xiii. 15; 2 Cor. iii. 14; comp. Esdr. ix. 48. The more obvious interpretation here is to refer it to private reading, or to a careful perusal of those books which would qualify him for his public work. The then written portions of the sacred volume —the Old Testament—are doubtless specially intended here, but there is no reason to doubt that there were included also such other books as would be useful, to which Timothy might have access. Even those were then few in number, but Paul evidently meant that Timothy should, as far as practicable, become acquainted with them. The apostle himself, on more than one occasion, showed that he had some acquaintance with the classic writings of Greece, Acts xvii. 28; Titus i. 12. ¶ *To exhortation.* See Notes on Rom. xii. 8. ¶ *To doctrine.* To teaching—for so the word means; comp. Notes on Rom. xii. 7.

14. *Neglect not the gift that is in thee.* An important question arises here, to what the word *gift* refers;—whether to natural endowment; to office; or to some supposed virtue which had been conferred by ordination—some transmitted influence which made

him holy as a minister of religion, and which was to continue to be transmitted by the imposition of apostolic hands. The word which is here used, is rendered *gift* in every place in which it occurs in the New Testament. It is found in the following places, and with the following significations:— Deliverance from peril, 2 Cor. i. 11; a gift or quality of the mind, 1 Cor. vii. 7; gifts of Christian knowledge or consolation, Rom. i. 11; 1 Cor. i. 7; redemption or salvation through Christ, Rom. v. 15, 16; vi. 23; xi. 29; the miraculous endowments conferred by the Holy Spirit, Rom. xii. 6; 1 Cor. xii. 4, 9, 28, 30, 31; and the special gift or endowment for the work of the ministry, 1 Tim. iv. 14; 2 Tim. i. 6; 1 Pet. iv. 10. The *gift* then referred to here was that by which Timothy was qualified for the work of the ministry. It relates to his office and qualifications — to *every thing* that entered into his fitness for the work. It does not refer *exclusively* to any influence that came upon him in virtue of his ordination, or to any new grace that was infused into him by that act, making him either officially or personally more holy than other men, or than he was before; or to any efficacy in the mere act of ordination: but it comprised *the whole train of circumstances* by which he had been qualified for the sacred office and recognized as a minister of religion. All this was regarded as a *gift,* a *benefit,* or a *favour*—χαρισμα— and he was not to neglect or disregard the responsibilities and advantages growing out of it. In regard to the manner in which this gift or favour was bestowed, the following things are specified. (1) It was the gift of God, 2 Tim. i. 6. He was to be recognized as its source; and it was not therefore conferred merely by human hands. The call to the ministry, the qualifications for the office, and the whole arrangement by which one is endowed for the work, are primarily to be traced to him as the source. (2) It was given to Timothy in accordance with certain predictions which had existed in regard to him—the expectations of those who had observed his qualifications for such an office, and who had expressed the hope that he would one day be permitted to serve the Lord in it. (3) It was sanctioned by the laying on of the hands of the presbytery. The call of God to the work thus recognized by the church, and the approbation of the presbytery expressed by setting him apart to the office, should be regarded by Timothy as a part of the "gift" or *benefit* (*charisma*) which had been conferred on him, and which he was not to neglect. (4) An additional circumstance which might serve to impress the mind of Timothy with the value of this endowment, and the responsibility of this office, was, that Paul himself had been concerned in his ordination, 2 Tim. i. 6. He who was so much more aged (Philem. 9; comp. 2 Tim. iv. 6, 7); he who had been a father to him, and who had adopted him and treated him as a son, had been concerned in his ordination; and this fact imposed a higher obligation to perform aright the functions of an office which had been conferred on him in this manner. We are not to suppose, therefore, that there was any mysterious influence—any *virtus* —conveyed by the act of ordination, or that that act imparted any additional degree of holiness. The endowment for the ministry; the previous anticipations and hopes of friends; and the manner in which he had been inducted into the sacred office, should all be regarded as a *benefit* or *favour* of a high order, and as a reason why the gift thus bestowed should not be neglected—and the same things now should make a man who is in the ministry deeply feel the solemn obligations resting on him to cultivate his powers in the highest degree, and to make the most of his talents. ¶ *Which was given thee by prophecy.* That is, the prophetic declarations and the hopes of pious friends in regard to your future usefulness, have been among the means by which you have been introduced to the ministry, and should be a reason why you should cultivate your powers, and perform faithfully the duties of your office; see Notes on chap. i. 18. ¶ *With the laying on of the hands of the presbytery.* It was common to lay on the hands in imparting a blessing, or in setting apart to any office; see Mat. xix. 15; Mark vi. 5; Luke iv. 40; xiii. 13; Lev. viii. 14; Num. xxvii. 23; Acts xxviii. 8; vi. 6; viii. 17; xiii. 3. The reference here is undoubtedly to the act by which Timothy was set apart to the office of the ministry. The word rendered *presbytery* — πρεσβυτέριον — occurs only in two other places in the New Testament: Luke xxii. 66, where it is rendered *elders;* and Acts xxii. 5, where it is rendered "*estate of the elders.*" It properly means, *an assembly of aged men; council of elders.* In Luke xxii. 66, and Acts xxii. 5, it refers to the Jewish *sanhedrim;* see Notes on Mat. v. 22. In the passage before us, it cannot refer to that body —for they did not ordain men to the Christian ministry—but to some association, or council, or body of elders of the Christian church. It is clear from the passage, (1) That there was more than *one person* engaged in this service, and taking part in it, when Timothy was ordained, and therefore it could not have been by a *prelate* or *bishop* alone. (2) That the power conferred, whatever it was, was conferred by the whole body constituting the presbytery — since the apostle says that the "gift" was imparted, not in virtue of any particular power or eminence in any one individual, but by the "laying on of the hands *of the presbytery.*" (3) The statement here is just such a one as would be made now respecting a Presbyterian ordination; it is not one which would be made of an Episcopal ordination. A Presbyterian would choose *these very words* in giving an account of an ordination to the work of the ministry; an Episcopalian *would not.* The former speaks of an ordination by a *presbytery;* the latter of ordination by a *bishop.* The former can use the account of the apostle Paul here as applicable to an ordination, without

15 Meditate upon these things: give thyself wholly to them; that thy profiting may appear [2]to all.

2 or, in all things.

16 Take[n] heed unto thyself, and unto the doctrine; continue in them: for in doing this[o]thou shalt both save thyself, and them that hear thee.

n 1 Pe.5.2,3.   *o* Ja.5.20.

explanations, comments, new versions or criticisms; the latter cannot. The passage, therefore, is full proof that, in one of the most important ordinations mentioned in the New Testament, it was performed by an association of men, and not by a prelate, and *therefore*, that this was the primitive mode of ordination. Indeed, there is not a single instance of ordination to an office mentioned in the New Testament which was performed *by one man alone.* See this passage examined at greater length in my *Enquiry into the Organization and Government of the Apostolic Church*, pp. 208-221.

15. *Meditate upon these things.* Upon the train of events by which you have been led into the ministry, and upon the responsibilities and duties of the office. Let your mind be deeply impressed with these things; make them the subject of profound and serious thought. ¶ *Give thyself wholly to them.* Gr., "Be in them"—a phrase similar to that of Horace— *totus in illis.* The meaning is plain. He was to devote his life wholly to this work. He was to have no other grand aim of living. His time, attention, talents, were to be absorbed in the proper duties of the work. He was not to make that subordinate and tributary to any other purpose, nor was he to allow any other object to interfere with the appropriate duties of that office. He was not to live for money, fame, or pleasure; not to devote his time to the pursuits of literature or science for their own sakes; not to seek the reputation of an elegant or profound scholar; not to aim to be distinguished merely as an accomplished gentleman, or as a skilful farmer, teacher, or author. Whatever was done in any of these departments, was to be wholly consistent with the direction, ἐν τούτοις ἴσθι—"*be in these things*"—be absorbed in the appropriate duties of the ministerial office. It may be remarked here, that no man will ever make much of himself, or accomplish much in any profession, who does not make this the rule of his life. He who has one great purpose of life to which he patiently and steadily devotes himself, and to which he makes everything else bend, will uniformly rise to high respectability, if not to eminence. He who does not do this can expect to accomplish nothing. ¶ *That thy profiting.* Gr., thy going forward; that is, thy advancement or progress. A minister of the gospel ought to make steady improvement in all that pertains to his office. No man ought to be satisfied with present attainments. ¶ *To all.* Marg., *in all things.* The margin is the more correct rendering, but either of them makes good sense. It *should be* apparent to all persons who attend on the stated preaching of a minister of the gospel, that he is making steady advances in knowledge, wisdom, and piety, and in *all* things that pertain to the proper performance of the duties of his office. If a man really makes progress, it will be seen and appreciated by others; if he does not, *that* will be as well understood by his hearers.

16. *Take heed unto thyself.* This may be understood as relating to everything of a personal nature that would qualify him for his work. It may be applied to personal piety; to health; to manners; to habits of living; to temper; to the ruling purposes; to the intercourse with others. In relation to personal religion, a minister should take heed (1) that he has true piety; and (2) that he is advancing in the knowledge and love of God. In relation to morals, he should be upright; to his intercourse with others, and his personal habits, he should be correct, consistent, and gentlemanly, so as to give needless offence to none. The person of a

minister should be neat and cleanly; his manners such as will show the fair influence of religion on his temper and deportment; his style of intercourse such as will be an example to the old and the young, and such as will not offend against the proper laws of courtesy and urbanity. There is no religion in a filthy person; in uncouth manners; in an inconvenient and strange form of apparel; in bad grammar, and in slovenly habits—and to be a real gentleman should be as much a matter of conscience with a minister of the gospel as to be a real Christian. Indeed, under the full and fair influence of the gospel, the one always implies the other. Religion refines the manners—it does not corrupt them; it makes one courteous, polite, and kind—it never produces boorish manners, or habits that give offence to the well-bred and the refined. ¶ *And unto the doctrine.* The kind of *teaching* which you give, or to your public instructions. The meaning is, that he should hold and teach only the truth. He was to "take heed" to the whole business of public instruction; that is, both to the matter and the manner. The great object was to get as much truth as possible before the minds of his hearers, and in such a way as to produce the deepest impression on them. ¶ *Continue in them.* That is, in *these things* which have been specified. He was ever to be found perseveringly engaged in the performance of these duties. ¶ *For so doing thou shalt both save thyself.* By holding of the truth, and by the faithful performance of your duties, you will secure the salvation of the soul. We are not to suppose that the apostle meant to teach that this would be the meritorious cause of his salvation, but that these faithful labours would be regarded as an evidence of piety, and would be accepted as such. It is equivalent to saying that an unfaithful minister of the gospel cannot be saved; one who faithfully performs all the duties of that office with a right spirit, *will be.* ¶ *And them that hear thee.* That is, you will be the *means* of their salvation. It is not

necessary to suppose that the apostle meant to teach that he would save *all* that heard him. The declaration is to be understood in a popular sense, and it is undoubtedly true that a faithful minister will be the means of saving many sinners. This assurance furnishes a ground of encouragement for a minister of the gospel. He may hope for success, and should look for success. He has the promise of God that if he is faithful he shall see the fruit of his labours, and this result of his work is a sufficient reward for all the toils and sacrifices and self-denials of the ministry. If a minister should be the means of saving but one soul from the horrors of eternal suffering and eternal sinning, it would be worth the most self-denying labours of the longest life. Yet what minister of the gospel is there, who is at all faithful to his trust, who is not made the honoured instrument of the salvation of many more than one? Few are the devoted ministers of Christ who are not permitted to see evidence even here, that their labour has not been in vain. Let not, then, the faithful preacher be discouraged. A single soul rescued from death will be a gem in his eternal crown brighter by far than ever sparkled on the brow of royalty.

CHAPTER V.

ANALYSIS OF THE CHAPTER.

This chapter embraces the following subjects:—

(1) The proper method of admonition when others err—to wit, an aged man should be *entreated* as a father, younger men as brethren, the aged women as mothers, and the younger with the pure feelings which one has for a sister, ver. 1, 2.

(2) Instructions respecting the proper treatment of widows, ver. 3-16.

(a) Those who were true widows were to be regarded with honour and respect.

(b) Who sustained this character, ver. 4 – 7. Those who had evinced piety at home in taking charge of those who were dependent on them, and who were steady in their devotions.

CHAPTER V.

REBUKE not an elder, but entreat *him* as a father;

No one was to be received into this number who was not of the age of sixty, who had been married to more than one man, and who had not given evidence, in all the duties of domestic fidelity and charity, that she was imbued with the spirit of religion, ver. 9, 10.

(c) Those who were young were not to be admitted into this class, ver. 11-15. The reasons given are, that they would marry again, or that they would be idle, and would be intermeddlers in the affairs of others. It was better, therefore, that they should marry, and have charge of a family of their own, ver. 14, 15.

(d) The duty of the individual members of the church to sustain helpless and dependent widows, if they had such among their relations, ver. 16. In these verses (3-16) it is evident that the apostle had his eye on a *class* of widows that sustained some such relation to other females as the elders did to the whole church. They were aged women to whom was intrusted the superintendence of the females of the church—probably because, from the customs then prevalent, men had much less liberty of access to the other sex, and much less freedom of intercourse was allowable, than now.

(3) The duty of supporting and honouring those who ruled in the church, ver. 17, 18.

(4) The suitable guarding of the rights of the elders in the church. No accusation was to be received unless it was sustained by two or three witnesses, ver. 19.

(5) No one who was guilty was to be spared. All who sinned were to be publicly rebuked, ver. 20.

(6) A solemn charge is given to Timothy to keep these commandments, ver. 21.

and the younger men as brethren;

2 The elder women as mothers;

(7) The statement of his duty not to ordain any person rashly or hastily to the sacred office, ver. 22.

(8) To guard his health, ver. 23.

(9) A declaration respecting sin—that sometimes it is open beforehand, and sometimes it is concealed till it is revealed at the judgment, closes the chapter, ver. 24, 25. The design of this closing statement seems to be, to show Timothy that he should not judge men by appearances, but that he should evince great caution in forming his estimate of their character.

1. *Rebuke not an elder.* The word *elder* here is not used in the sense in which it often is, to denote an officer of the church, a *presbyter*, but in its proper and usual sense, to denote *an aged man.* This is evident, because the apostle immediately mentions in contradistinction from the *elder*, "the younger men," where it cannot be supposed that he refers to them as officers. The command to treat the "elder" as a "father," also shows the same thing. By the direction not to *rebuke*, it is not to be supposed that the minister of the gospel is not to admonish the aged, or that he is not to show them their sins when they go astray, but that he is to do this as he would to a father. He is not to assume a harsh, dictatorial, and denunciatory manner. The precepts of religion always respect the proprieties of life, and never allow us to transgress them, even when the object is to reclaim a soul from error, and to save one who is wandering. Besides, when this *is* the aim, it will always be most certainly accomplished by observing the respect due to others on account of office, relation, rank, or age. ¶ *But entreat* him *as a father.* As you would a father. That is, do not harshly denounce him. Endeavour to *persuade* him to lead a more holy life. One of the things for which the ancients were remarkable above most of the moderns, and for which the Orientals

the younger as sisters, with all purity.

3 Honour widows that are *widows indeed.

a ver.5,16.

are still distinguished, was respect for age. Few things are enjoined with more explicitness and emphasis in the Bible than this, Lev. xix. 32; Job xxix.; Prov. xx. 20; xxx. 17; comp. Dan. vii. 9, 10; Rev. i. 14, 15. The apostle would have Timothy, and, for the same reason, every other minister of the gospel, a model of this virtue. ¶ And *the younger men as brethren.* That is, treat them as you would your own brothers. Do not consider them as aliens, strangers, or enemies, but entertain towards them, even when they go astray, the kindly feelings of a brother. This refers more particularly to his private intercourse with them, and to his personal efforts to reclaim them when they had fallen into sin. When these efforts were ineffectual, and they sinned openly, he was to "rebuke them before all" (ver. 20), that others might be deterred from following their example.

2. *The elder women as mothers.* Showing still the same respect for age, and for the proprieties of life. No son who had proper feelings would *rebuke* his own mother with severity. Let the minister of religion evince the same feelings if he is called to address a "mother in Israel" who has erred. ¶ *The younger as sisters.* With the feelings which you have towards a sister. The tender love which one has for a beloved sister would always keep him from using harsh and severe language. *The same* mildness, gentleness, and affection should be used towards a sister in the church. ¶ *With all purity.* Nothing could be more characteristic of Paul's manner than this injunction; nothing could show a deeper acquaintance with human nature. He knew the danger which would beset a youthful minister of the gospel when it was his duty to admonish and entreat a youthful female; he knew, too, the scandal to which he might be exposed if, in the performance of the necessary duties of his office, there should be the slightest

departure from purity and propriety. He was therefore to guard his heart with more than common vigilance in such circumstances, and was to indulge in no word, or look, or action, which could by any possibility be construed as manifesting an improper state of feeling. On nothing else do the fair character and usefulness of a youthful minister more depend, than on the observance of this precept. Nowhere else does he more need the grace of the Lord Jesus, and the exercise of prudence, and the manifestation of incorruptible integrity, than in the performance of this duty. A youthful minister who fails here, can never recover the perfect purity of an unsullied reputation, and never in subsequent life be wholly free from suspicion; comp. Notes, Mat. v. 28.

3. *Honour widows.* The particular attention and respect which are enjoined here, seem to refer to the *class* of widows who were supported by the church, and who were intrusted with the performance of certain duties towards the other female members; see ver. 9. It is to be remembered that the intercourse of the sexes was much more circumscribed in Oriental countries than it is among us; that access to the female members of the church would be much less free than it is now, and that consequently there might have been a special propriety in intrusting the duty of watching over the younger among them to the more aged. This duty would be naturally intrusted to those who had not the care of families. It would also be natural to commit it, if they were qualified, to those who had not the means of support, and who, while they were maintained by the church, might be rendering a valuable service to it. It would seem, therefore, that there was a *class* of this description, who were intrusted with these duties, and in regard to whose qualifications it was proper that Timothy should be instructed. The change of customs

4 But if any widow have children or nephews, let them learn first to show [1] piety at home, and to requite their parents: for that is good and acceptable before God.

5 Now she that is a widow indeed, and desolate, trusteth in God, and continueth in supplications and prayers night and day.

1 or, *kindness.*

---

in society has made this class less necessary, and probably the arrangement was never designed to be permanent, but still it may be a question whether such an arrangement would not now be wise and useful in the church. On this subject, see Notes on Rom. xvi. 1. ¶ *That are widows indeed.* Who are *truly* widows. We associate with the word *widow*, commonly, not only the idea of the loss of a husband, but many other things that are the usual accompaniments of widowhood—a poor and dependent condition; care and solicitude; sadness and sorrow. This idea is implied in the use of the word employed here—χήρα—which means properly one who is *bereaved* (from the adjective χῆρος, *bereaved*), and which, as Calvin says, conveys the idea of one in distressed circumstances. What Paul regarded as constituting true widowhood, he specifies in verses 4, 5, 9, 10. He connects with it the idea that she had no persons dependent on her; that she was desolate, and evinced true trust in God; that she was so aged that she would not marry again; and that by her life she had given evidence of possessing a heart of true benevolence, ver. 10.

4. *But if any widow have children.* Who would be dependent on her care, and who might themselves contribute to her support. ¶ *Or nephews.* The word *nephew* now commonly means the son of a brother or sister. Formerly the English word also meant grandchildren, or descendants of any description (Webster). The Greek word here—ἔκγονα—has the latter meaning. It denotes those *sprung from* or *born of;* and then descendants of any kind—sons, daughters, grandchildren. The Greek word would not, in fact, properly include *nephews* and *nieces.* It embraces only those in a direct line. ¶ *Let them learn first to show piety at home.* Marg., "or

kindness." That is, let the *children* and *grandchildren* learn to do this. Let them have an opportunity of performing their duty toward their aged parent or grandparent. Do not receive such a widow among the poor and dependent females of the church, to be maintained at public expense, but let her children support her. Thus they will have an opportunity of evincing Christian kindness, and of requiting her for her care. This the apostle calls "*showing piety*"—εὐσεβεῖν—that is, *filial piety;* piety towards a parent, by providing for the wants of that parent in advanced age. The word is commonly used to denote piety towards God, but it is also used to denote proper reverence and respect for a parent (Robinson). ¶ *And to requite their parents.* To repay them, as far as possible, for all *their* kindness. This debt can *never* be wholly repaid, but still a child should feel it a matter of sacred obligation to do as much towards it as possible. ¶ *For that is good and acceptable before God.* It is a duty everywhere enjoined; comp. Notes on Mat. xv. 5–7; Eph. vi. 1, 2.

5. *A widow indeed and desolate.* The word rendered *desolate* means *solitary, alone.* It does not necessarily imply the idea of *discomfort* which we attach to the word *desolate.* The sense is, that she had no children or other descendants; none on whom she could depend for support. ¶ *Trusteth in God.* She has no one else to look to but God. She has no earthly reliance, and, destitute of husband, children, and property, she feels her dependence, and steadily looks to God for consolation and support. ¶ *And continueth in supplications and prayers night and day.* Continually; comp. Notes on chap. ii. 1; see also the description of Anna in Luke ii. 36, 37. The apostle regards this as one of the characteristics of those who were

6 But she that liveth ²in pleasure *b* is dead while she liveth.

7 And these things give in charge,
that they may be blameless.

2 or, *delicately.*   *b* Re.3.1.

"widows indeed," whom he would
have received into the *class* to be
maintained by the church, and to
whom the charge of younger members
of the church might be intrusted.

6. *But she that liveth in pleasure.*
Marg., *delicately.* The Greek word
(σπαταλάω) occurs nowhere else in
the New Testament, except in James
v. 5, " *Ye have lived in pleasure* on
the earth." It properly means to
live in luxury, voluptuously; to indulge freely in eating and drinking;
to yield to the indulgence of the appetites. It does not indicate grossly
criminal pleasures; but the kind of
pleasure connected with luxurious
living, and with pampering the appetites. It is probable that in the time
of the apostle, there were professedly
Christian widows who lived in this
manner—as there are such professing
Christians of all kinds in every age of
the world. ¶ *Is dead while she
liveth.* To all the proper purposes of
life she is as if she were dead. There
is great emphasis in this expression,
and nothing could convey more forcibly the idea that true happiness is not
to be found in the pleasures of sense.
There is nothing in them that answers
the purposes of life. They are not
the objects for which life was given,
and as to the great and proper designs
of existence, such persons might as
well be dead.

7. *And these things give in charge.*
Announce, or declare these things, to
wit, particularly respecting the duty
of children to their widowed mothers,
and the proper duty of those who are
widows.

8. *But if any provide not for his
own.* The apostle was speaking
(ver. 4) particularly of the duty of
children towards a widowed mother.
In enforcing that duty, he gives the
subject, as he often does in similar
cases, a *general* direction, and says
that *all* ought to provide for those

8 But if any provide not for his
own, *c* and specially for those of
his own ³house, he hath denied
the faith, and is worse than an
infidel.

c Is.58.7.   3 or, *kindred.*

who were dependent on them, and that
if they did not do this, they had a less
impressive sense of the obligations of
duty than even the heathen had. On
the duty here referred to, comp. Notes,
Rom. xii. 17; 2 Cor. viii. 21. The
meaning is, that the person referred
to is to *think beforehand* (προνοεῖ) of
the probable wants of his own family,
and make arrangements to meet them.
God thus *provides* for our wants;
that is, he sees *beforehand* what we
shall need, and makes arrangements
for those wants by long preparation.
The food that we eat, and the raiment that we wear, he foresaw that
we should need, and the arrangement for the supply was made years
since, and to meet these wants he has
been carrying forward the plans of his
providence in the seasons; in the
growth of animals; in the formation
of fruit; in the bountiful harvest. So,
according to *our* measure, *we* are to
anticipate what will be the probable
wants of our families, and to make
arrangements to meet them. The
words "*his own,*" refer to those who
are naturally dependent on him, whether living in his own immediate
family or not. There may be many
distant relatives naturally dependent
on our aid, besides those who live in
our own house. ¶ *And specially for
those of his own house.* Marg., *kindred.* The word *house,* or *household,*
better expresses the sense than the
word *kindred.* The meaning is, those
who live in his own family. They
would naturally have higher claims on
him than those who did not. They
would commonly be his nearer relatives, and the fact, from whatever
cause, that they constituted his own
family, would lay the foundation for a
strong claim upon him. He who neglected his own immediate family
would be more guilty than he who
neglected a more remote relative.
¶ *He hath denied the faith.* By

9 Let not a widow be [4]taken into the number under threescore

years old, having been the wife of one man,

---

his *conduct*, perhaps, not openly. He may be still a *professor* of religion and do this; but he will show that he is imbued with none of the spirit of religion, and is a stranger to its real nature. The meaning is, that he would, by such an act, have practically renounced Christianity, since it enjoins this duty on all. We may hence learn that it is possible to deny the faith by *conduct* as well as by words; and that a *neglect* of doing our duty is as real a denial of Christianity as it would be openly to renounce it. Peter denied his Lord in one way, and thousands do the same thing in another. He did it in *words;* they by neglecting their duty to their families, or their duty in their closets, or their duty in attempting to send salvation to their fellow-men, or by an openly irreligious life. *A neglect of any duty is so far a denial of the faith.* ¶ *And is worse than an infidel.* The word here does not mean an *infidel*, technically so called, or one who openly professes to disbelieve Christianity, but anyone who does *not believe;* that is, anyone who is not a sincere Christian. The word, therefore, would include the heathen, and it is to them, doubtless, that the apostle particularly refers. *They* acknowledged the obligation to provide for their relatives. This was one of the great laws of nature written on their hearts, and a law which they felt bound to obey. Few things were inculcated more constantly by heathen moralists than this duty. Galgacus, in Tacitus, says, "Nature dictates that to everyone, his own children and relatives should be most dear." Cicero says, "Every man should take care of his own family"—suos quisque debet tueri; see Rosenmüller, *in loco*, and also numerous examples of the same kind quoted from Apuleius, Cicero, Plutarch, Homer, Terence, Virgil, and Servius, in Pricæus, *in loco.* The doctrine here is, (1) that a Christian ought not to be inferior to an unbeliever in respect to any virtue;

(2) that in all that constitutes true virtue he ought to surpass him; (3) that the duties which are taught by nature ought to be regarded as the more sacred and obligatory from the fact that God has given us a better religion; and (4) that a Christian ought never to give occasion to an enemy of the gospel to point to a man of the world and say, "There is one who surpasses you in *any* virtue."

9. *Let not a widow be taken into the number.* Marg., *chosen.* The margin expresses the sense of the Greek more accurately, but the meaning is not materially different. Paul does not here specify into *what* "number" the widow is to be "taken," or for what purpose she is to be "chosen," but he speaks of this as a thing that was well understood. There can be no doubt, however, what he means. In the Acts of the Apostles (chap. vi. 1) we have this account: "And in those days, when the number of the disciples was multiplied, there arose a murmuring of the Grecians against the Hebrews, *because their widows were neglected in the daily ministration.*" "It appears that from the first formation of the Christian church, provision was made out of the public funds of the society for the indigent *widows* who belonged to it;" see Paley's *Horæ Paulinæ*, on 1 Tim., No. 11. To this, as to a well-known practice, Paul here evidently refers. The *manner* in which he refers to it is such as to show that the custom had an existence. All that was necessary in the case, was, not to speak of it as if it were a *new* arrangement, but to mention those who ought to be regarded as proper subjects of the charity. It would seem, also, that it was understood that such widows, according to their ability, should exercise a proper watch over the younger females of the church. In this way, while they were supported by the church, they might render themselves useful. ¶ *Under threescore years old.* For such reasons as those mentioned

10 Well reported of for good works; if she have brought up children, if she have ᵃlodged

ᵈ Ac.16.15.

in ver. 11–14. ¶ *Having been the wife of one man.* There has been much diversity of opinion whether this means that she had never had but one husband, or whether she had been the wife of but one man at a time; that is, whether [she had cast off one and married another; see Whitby, *in loco.* The same difficulty has been felt in regard to this as on the passage in chap. iii. 2; see Notes on that verse. Doddridge, Clarke, and others, suppose that it means, "who had lived in conjugal fidelity to her husband." The reason assigned for this opinion by Doddridge is, that the apostle did not mean to condemn second marriages, since he expressly (ver. 14) commends it in the younger widows. The correct interpretation probably is, to refer it to one who had been married *but once,* and who, after her husband had died, had remained a widow. The reasons for this opinion briefly are—(1) That this is the interpretation most naturally suggested by the phrase; (2) that it agrees better with the description of the one that was to be enrolled among the "number"—those who were "*widows indeed*"—as we should more naturally apply this term to one who had remained unmarried after the death of her husband, than to one who had been married again; (3) that, while it was not unlawful or improper in itself for a widow to marry a second time, there was a degree of respect and honour attached to one who did not do it, which would not be felt for one who did; comp. Luke ii. 36, 37, " She was a widow of great age, and had lived with an husband seven years from her virginity; *and she was a widow of about fourscore and four years.*" The same is true now. There is a higher degree of respect felt for *such* a widow than there is for one who has been married again, though she may be again a widow. (4) Among the heathens, it was regarded as especially honourable to have been married to

strangers, if she have washed the saints' feet, if she have relieved the afflicted, if she have diligently followed every good work.

but one man, and such widows wore the *pudicitiæ coronam,* or crown of chastity; Val. Max. lib. i. c. ii.; comp. Livy, lib. x. c. 23; see Whitby. (5) As these persons were not only to be maintained by the church, but appear also to have been intrusted with an office of guardianship over the younger females, it was of importance that they should have such a character that no occasion of offence should be given, even among the heathen; and, in order to that, Paul gave direction that only those should be thus enrolled who were in all respects *widows,* and who would be regarded, on account of their age and their whole deportment, as "widows indeed." I cannot doubt, therefore, that he meant to exclude those from the number here referred to who had been married the second time.

10. *Well reported of for good works.* Of good character or reputation; see Notes on chap. iii. 7. ¶ *If she have brought up children.* Either her own or others. The idea is, if she has done this in a proper manner. ¶ *If she have lodged strangers.* If she has been characterized by hospitality— a virtue greatly commended in the Scriptures; comp. Notes on chap. iii. 2. ¶ *If she have washed the saints' feet.* It is not certain whether this is to be understood literally, or whether it merely denotes that she had performed offices of a humble and self-denying kind, — such as would be shown by washing the feet of others. It was one of the rites of hospitality in the East to wash the feet of the guest (Gen. xviii. 4), and Paul *might* have spoken of this as having been literally performed. There is not the slightest evidence that he refers to it as a *religious rite* or *ordinance,* any more than he does to the act of bringing up children as a religious rite; comp. Notes on John xiii. 1–10. ¶ *If she have relieved the afflicted.* If it has been her character that she was ready to furnish relief to those who

11 But the younger widows refuse: for when they have begun to wax wanton against Christ, they will marry;

12 Having damnation, because they have cast off their first faith.

were in distress. ¶ *If she have diligently followed every good work.* This is one of the characteristics of true piety. A sincere Christian will, like God, be the friend of all that is good, and will be ready to promote every good object according to his ability. He will not merely be the friend of *one* good cause, to the neglect of others, but he will endeavour to promote every good object, and though from peculiar circumstances, and peculiar dealings of Providence, he may have been *particularly* interested in some one object of charity, yet every good object will find a response in his heart, and he will be ready to promote it by his influence, his property, and his prayers.

11. *But the younger widows refuse.* That is, in respect to the matter under discussion. Do not admit them into the class of widows referred to. It cannot mean that he was to reject them as members of the church, or not to treat them with respect and kindness. ¶ *For when they have begun to wax wanton against Christ.* There is probably a thought conveyed by these words to most minds which is by no means in the original, and which does injustice both to the apostle and to the "younger widows" referred to. In the Greek there is no idea of *wantonness* in the sense of lasciviousness or lewdness; nor was this, though now a common idea attached to the word, by any means essential to it when our translation was made. The word *wanton* then meant *wandering* or *roving in gaiety or sport; moving* or *flying loosely; playing in the wind;* then, *wandering from moral rectitude, licentious, dissolute, libidinous* (Webster). The Greek word here used, καταστηνιάζω, occurs nowhere else in the New Testament. The word στρηνιάω—*streniao*, however, is used twice, and is in both cases translated *lived deliciously,* Rev. xviii. 7, 9. The word is derived

from στρῆνος—*strenos* (whence *strenuous*), properly meaning *rudeness, insolence, pride,* and hence, *revel, riot, luxury;* or from στρηνής—*strenes,* the adjective—*strong, stiff, hard, rough.* The verb then means *"to live strenuously, rudely,"* as in English, *"to live hard;"* also, to live wild, or without restraint; to run riot, to live luxuriously. The idea of *strength* is the essential one, and then of strength that is not subordinate to law, that is wild and riotous; see Passow and Robinson, *Lex.* The sense here is, that they would not be subordinate to the restraints implied in that situation; they would become impatient, and would marry again. The idea is not that of wantonness or lewdness, but it is that of a mind not subdued by age and by trials, and that would be impatient under the necessary restraints of the condition which was contemplated. They could not be depended on with certainty, but they might be expected again to enter into the married relation. ¶ *They will marry.* It is clear, from this, that the apostle did not contemplate any *vows* which would prevent their marrying again; nor does he say that it would be absolutely wrong for them to marry, even if they were admitted into that rank; or as if there were any vows to restrain them from doing it. This passage, therefore, can never be adduced in favour of that practice of taking the veil in nunneries, and of a vow of perpetual seclusion from the world.

12. *Having damnation.* Or, rather, having *condemnation;* or incurring guilt. This does not mean of necessity that they would lose their souls; see the phrase explained in the Notes on 1 Cor. xi. 29. The meaning is, that they would contract guilt, if they had been admitted among this class of persons, and then married again. The apostle does not say that that would be wrong in itself (comp. Notes on ver. 14), or that they would be absolutely prohibited from it, but

13 And withal they learn *to be* idle, wandering about from house to house; and *e*not only idle, but tattlers also, and busy-bodies, speaking things which they ought not.

e 2 Th.3.11.

that injury would be done if they were admitted among those who were "widows indeed"—who were supported by the church, and who were intrusted with a certain degree of care over the more youthful females —and then should leave that situation. It might give occasion for scandal; it might break in upon the arrangements; it would show that there was a relaxing of the faith, and of the deadness to the world, which they were supposed to have; and it was better that they should be married (ver. 14), without having been thus admitted. ¶ *Because they have cast off their first faith.* This does not mean that they would lose all their religion, or wholly fall away, but that this would show that they had not the strong faith, the deadness to the world, the simple dependence on God (ver. 5), and the desire which they had to be weaned from worldly cares and influences, which they once had. When they became widows, all their earthly hopes seemed to be blasted. They were then dead to the world, and felt their sole dependence on God. But if, under the influence of these strong emotions, they were admitted to the "class of widows" in the church, there was no certainty that they would continue in this state of mind. Time would do much to modify their grief. There would be a reviving love of the world, and under the influence of this they would be disposed to enter again into the marriage relation, and thus show that they had not the strong and simple *faith* which they had when the blow which made them widows fell heavily upon them.

13. *And withal.* In addition to the prospect that they may marry again, there are other disadvantages which might follow from such an arrangement, and other evils to be feared, which it is desirable to avoid. ¶ *They learn* to be *idle.* That is, if supported by the church, and if without the settled principles which might be expected in those more aged and experienced, it may be feared that they will give themselves up to an indolent life. There would be a security in the age and established habits of those more advanced in life, which there could *not* be in their case. The apostle does not mean that widows are naturally *disposed* to be idle, but that in the situation referred to there would be danger of it. ¶ *Wandering about from house to house.* A natural consequence of supposing that they had nothing to do, and a practice not only profitless, but always attended with mischief. ¶ *Tattlers also.* Literally, *overflowing;* then overflowing with talk; praters, triflers. They would learn all the news; become acquainted with the secrets of families, and of course indulge in much idle and improper conversation. Our word *gossippers* would accurately express the meaning here. The *noun* does not occur elsewhere in the New Testament. The *verb* occurs in John iii. 10; rendered, *prating against.* ¶ *And busy-bodies.* See Notes on 2 Thes. iii. 11. The word means, probably, *working all round, overdoing,* and then *an intermeddler.* Persons who have nothing to do of their own, commonly find employment by interesting themselves in the affairs of their neighbours. No one likes to be wholly idle, and if anyone is not found doing what he *ought* to do, he will commonly be found engaged in doing what he ought *not.* ¶ *Speaking things which they ought not.* Revealing the concerns of their neighbours; disclosing secrets; magnifying trifles, so as to exalt themselves into importance, as if they were intrusted with the secrets of others; inventing stories and tales of gossip, that they may magnify and maintain their own consequence in the community. No persons are commonly more dangerous to the peace of a neighbourhood than those who have nothing to do.

14 I will therefore that the younger women marry, bear children, guide the house, give none occasion to the adversary [5]to speak reproachfully.

[5] *for their railing.*

14. *I will therefore.* I give it as my opinion; or this is my counsel; comp. Notes, 1 Cor. vii. 6, 10, 40. ¶ *That the younger women marry.* The word *women* is not expressed or necessarily implied in the original—*νεωτέρας*—and it is evident that the apostle here had particular reference to *widows*, and that the injunction should be understood as relating to them. We are not to suppose that he gives this as an absolute and universal command, for it might not always be at the option of the widow to marry again, and it cannot be doubted that there may be cases where it would be unadvisable. But he speaks of this as a general rule. It is better for such persons to have domestic concerns that require their attention, than it is to be exposed to the evils of an idle life.—We may learn from this, (1) that second marriages are not improper or unlawful, but that in some circumstances they may be preferable to widowhood; (2) that marriage itself is in a high degree honourable. How different are the views of the inspired apostle Paul about marriage from those of the Papists ! ¶ *Bear children, guide the house.* These words signify, says Bloomfield, to "exercise and occupy themselves in the duties of a wife." It is better to be employed in the duties growing out of the cares of a family than to lead a life of celibacy. ¶ *Give none occasion to the adversary.* The enemy of religion—the heathen or the infidel. ¶ *To speak reproachfully.* Marg., *for their railing.* That is, on account of a life which would do no honour to religion. In the performance of domestic duties, when fully employed, they would avoid the evils specified in ver. 13. Every one who professes religion should so live as to give no occasion to an infidel or a man of the world to speak reproachfully of the cause of the Redeemer.

15 For some are already turned aside after Satan.

16 If any man or woman that believeth have widows, let them relieve them, and let not the church be charged; that it may

15. *For some are already turned aside after Satan.* That is, some young widows. The meaning is, that in the respects above mentioned (ver. 13), they had followed the great Tempter, rather than the Lord Jesus. This is stated as a reason why they should not be admitted into the number of the widows who were to be maintained at the expense of the church, and to whom the care of the younger female members was to be committed.

16. *If any man or woman that believeth.* Christians are often simply called *believers*, because faith is the leading and most important act of their religion. ¶ *Have widows.* Widowed mothers, or grandmothers, or any other widows whose support would naturally devolve on them. ¶ *Let them relieve them.* That is, let them support them. This was an obvious rule of duty; see Notes on ver. 8. Nothing can be more unreasonable than to leave those who are properly dependent on us to be supported by others, when we are able to maintain them ourselves. ¶ *That it may relieve*, &c. That it may have the means of supporting those who are truly dependent. To require or expect the church, therefore, to support those whom *we* ought ourselves to support, is, in fact, to rob the poor and friendless.—In regard to these directions respecting widows (ver. 3–16), we may remark in general, as the result of the exposition which has been given, (1) They were to be *poor* widows, who had not the means of support themselves. (2) They were, probably, to be not merely *supported*, but to be usefully employed in the service of the church, particularly in overseeing the conduct, and imparting instruction to the female members. (3) They were to be of such age and character that there would be security of stability and correctness

relieve them that are widows indeed.

17 Let* the elders that rule

*1 Th.5.12,13.

of deportment; such that they would not be tempted to leave the situation, or to act so as to give occasion of reproach. (4) It is by no means certain that this was intended to be a permanent arrangement. It grew, probably, out of the peculiar customs respecting intercourse between the sexes in the Oriental world, and would undoubtedly be proper now in similar circumstances. But it by no means follows that this arrangement is binding on the churches where the customs of society are different. Yet (5) the passage inculcates the general principle, that the poor widows of the church are to be assisted when they have no relatives on whom they can naturally depend. No class of people are more helpless than aged widows, and for that class God has always shown a special concern, and his people should do so likewise.

17. *Let the elders that rule well.* Gr., πρεσβύτεροι, *presbyters.* The apostle had given full instructions respecting bishops (chap. iii. 1–7); deacons (chap. iii. 8–13); widows (chap. v. 3–16); and he here proceeds to prescribe the duty of the church towards those who sustain the office of elder. The word used— *elder* or *presbyter*—properly refers to *age,* and is then used to denote the officers of the church, probably because the *aged* were at first intrusted with the administration of the affairs of the church. The word was in familiar use among the Jews to denote the body of men that presided in the synagogue; see Notes on Mat. xv. 2; Acts xi. 30; xv. 2. ¶ *That rule well.* Presiding well, or well managing the spiritual interests of the church. The word rendered *rule*— προεστῶτες—is from a verb meaning to be over; to preside over; to have the care of. The word is used with reference to bishops, Tit. i. 5, 7; to an apostle, 1 Pet. v. 1; and is such a word as would apply to any officers to whom the management and govern-

well be counted worthy of double honour, especially they who labour in the word and doctrine.

ment of the church was intrusted. On the general subject of the rulers in the church, see Notes on 1 Cor. xii. 28. It is probable that not precisely the same organization was pursued in every place where a church was established; and where there was a Jewish synagogue, the Christian church would be formed substantially after that model, and in such a church there would be a bench of presiding elders; see, on this subject, Whately's *Kingdom of Christ Delineated,* pp. 84–86. The language here seems to have been taken from such an organization. On the Jewish synagogue, see Notes on Mat. iv. 23. ¶ *Be counted worthy of double honour.* Of double respect; that is, of a high degree of respect; of a degree of respect becoming their age and office; comp. 1 Thes. v. 12, 13. From the quotation which is made in ver. 18, in relation to this subject, it would seem probable that the apostle had some reference also to their support, or to what was necessary for their maintenance. There is no improbability in supposing that *all* the officers of the church, of whatever grade or rank, may have had some compensation, corresponding to the amount of time which their office required them to devote to the service of the church. Nothing would be more reasonable than that, if their duties in the church interfered with their regular employments in their secular calling, their brethren should contribute to their support; comp. Notes on 1 Cor. ix. ¶ *Especially they who labour in word and doctrine.* In preaching and instructing the people. From this it is clear that, while there were "elders" who laboured "in the word and doctrine," that is, in preaching, there were also those who did *not* labour "in the word and doctrine," but who were nevertheless appointed to rule in the church. Whether, however, they were regarded as a separate and distinct class of officers, does not appear from this passage. It may have

18 For the scripture saith, Thou[g] shalt not muzzle the ox that treadeth out the corn: And, [h]The labourer is worthy of his reward.

g De.25.4.   h Lu.10.7.

been that there was a bench of elders to whom the general management of the church was confided, and that a part of them were engaged in preaching; a part may have performed the office of "teachers" (see Notes on Rom. xii. 7; 1 Cor. xii. 28); and a part may have been employed in managing other concerns of the church; and yet all were regarded as the προεστῶτες πρεσβύτεροι, or "elders presiding over the church." It cannot, I think, be certainly concluded from this passage that the ruling elders who did not teach or preach were regarded as a separate class or order of permanent officers in the church. There seems to have been a bench of elders selected on account of age, piety, prudence, and wisdom, to whom was intrusted the whole business of the instruction and government of the church, and they performed the various parts of the duty as they had ability. Those among them who "laboured in the word and doctrine," and who gave up all their time to the business of their office, would be worthy of special respect, and of a higher compensation.

18. *For the Scripture saith.* This is adduced as a reason why a church should show all due respect and care for its ministers. The reason is, that as God took care to make provision for the labouring ox, much more should due attention be paid to those who labour for the welfare of the church. ¶ *Thou shalt not muzzle the ox.* See this passage explained, and its bearing on such an argument shown, in the Notes on 1 Cor. ix. 8–10. ¶ *And, The labourer is worthy of his reward.* This expression is found substantially in Mat. x. 10, and Luke x. 7. It does not occur in so many words in the Old Testament, and yet the apostle adduces it evidently as a quotation from the Scriptures, and as authority in the case. It would seem probable, there-

19 Against an elder receive not an accusation, but [6]before [i]two or three witnesses.

6 or, under.   i De.19.15.

fore, that he had seen the Gospel by Matthew or by Luke, and that he quoted this as a part of Scripture, and regarded the Book from which he made the quotation as of the same authority as the Old Testament. If so, then this may be regarded as an attestation of the apostle to the inspiration of the "Gospel" in which it was found.

19. *Against an elder.* The word elder here seems to be used in the sense in which it is in the previous verse as relating to *office*, and not in the sense of an aged man, as in ver. 1. The connection demands this interpretation. ¶ *Receive not an accusation.* He was not to regard such a charge as well-founded unless sustained by two or three witnesses. It is clear from this, that Paul supposed that Timothy would be called on to hear charges against others who were in the ministerial office, and to express his judgment on such cases. There is no reason, however, to suppose that he meant that he should hear them *alone,* or as a "bishop," for this direction does not make the supposition improper that others would be associated with him. It is just such counsel as would now be given to a Presbyterian or Congregational minister, or such as would be given to an associate justice in a court, on the supposition that a brother judge was at any time to be tried by him and his colleagues. ¶ *But before two or three witnesses.* Marg., *under.* The meaning is, unless supported by the testimony of two or three persons. He was not to regard an accusation against a presbyter as proved, if there was but one witness in the case, however positive he might be in his testimony. The *reasons* for this direction were probably such as these: (1) This was the requirement of the Jewish law in all cases, which had thus settled a *principle* which the apostle seems to have regarded as important, if not obligatory, under

20 Them that sin *rebuke before all, *that others also may fear.

k Le.19.17.   l De.13.11.

21 I *m* charge *thee* before God, and the Lord Jesus Christ, and

m 2 Ti.4.1.

the Christian dispensation; see Deut. xvii. 6; xix. 15; comp. Notes on John viii. 17; 2 Cor. xiii. 1. (2) There would be much greater reason to apprehend that one person might be deceived in the manner on which he bore witness, or might do it from malignant motives, or might be bribed to give false testimony, than that two or three would give such testimony; and the arrangement, therefore, furnished important security for the innocent. (3) There might be reason to apprehend that evil-minded persons might be disposed to bring charges against the ministers of the gospel or other officers of the church, and it was important, therefore, that their rights should be guarded with anxious care. The ministers of religion often give offence to wicked men by their rebukes of sin (comp. Mark vi. 17–20); wicked men would rejoice to see an accusation against them sustained; the cause of religion would be liable to suffer much when its ministers were condemned as guilty of gross offences, and it is right, therefore, that the evidence in the case should be as free as possible from all suspicion that it is caused by malignity, by hatred of religion, or by conspiracy, or by a desire to see religion disgraced. (4) The character of a minister of the gospel is of value, not only to himself and family, as is the case with that of other men, but is of special value to the church, and to the cause of religion. It is the property of the church. The interests of religion depend much on it, and it should not be wantonly assailed; and every precaution should be adopted that Christianity should not be deprived of the advantage which may be derived in its favour from the piety, experience, and talents of its public defenders. At the same time, however, the wicked, though in the ministry, should not be screened from the punishment which they deserve. The apostle gave no injunction to attempt to cover up their faults, or to save

them from a fair trial. He only demanded such security as the nature of the case required, that the trial *should be fair.* If a minister of the gospel has been proved to be guilty of crime, the honour of religion, as well as simple justice, requires that he shall be punished as he deserves. He sins against great light; he prostitutes a holy office, and makes use of the very reputation which his office gives him, that he may betray the confidence of others; and such a man *should not escape.* There should be no " benefit of clergy," and neither a black coat, nor bands, nor the lawn should save a villain.

20. *Them that sin.* That have been proved to have committed sin—referring probably to the elders mentioned in the previous verse, but giving the direction so general a form that it might be applicable to others. ¶ *Rebuke before all.* Before all the church or congregation. The word *rebuke* properly denotes to reprove or reprehend. It means here that there should be a public statement of the nature of the offence, and such a censure as the case demanded. It extends only to *spiritual* censures. There is no power given of inflicting any punishment by fine or imprisonment. The power of the church, in such cases, is only to express its strong and decided disapprobation of the wrong done, and, if the case demands it, of disowning the offending member or minister. This direction to "rebuke an offender before all," may be easily reconciled with the direction in ver. 1, "Rebuke not an elder." The latter refers to the private and pastoral intercourse with an elder, and to the method in which he should be treated in such intercourse—to wit, with the feelings due to a father; the direction here refers to the manner in which an offender should be treated who has been *proved* to be guilty, and where the case has become public. Then there is to be a public expression of disapprobation. ¶ *That*

the *elect angels, that thou ob- serve these things without 7 pre-

n Re.12.7-9.　　　7 or, *prejudice.*

others also may fear. That they may be kept from committing the same offence; comp. 1 Pet. ii. 14. The end of punishment is not the gratifi- cation of the private feelings of him who administers it, but the prevention of crime.

21. *I charge* thee *before God.* Comp. Luke xvi. 28; Acts ii. 2**0**. The word rendered *charge* means, properly, to call to witness; then to affirm with solemn attestations; and then to admonish solemnly, to urge upon earnestly. It is a word which implies that the subject is of great importance. Paul gives *this* charge as in the presence of God, of the Re- deemer, and of the elect angels, and wishes to secure that sense of its solemnity which must arise from the presence of such holy witnesses. ¶ *And the Lord Jesus Christ.* As in the presence of the Lord Jesus; with his eye resting upon you. ¶ *And the elect angels.* It is not uncommon in the Scriptures to speak as if we were in the presence of holy angels, and of the disembodied spirits of the good; comp. Notes on Heb. xii. 1. No one can *prove* that the angels, and that the departed spirits of holy men, are *not* witnesses of what we do. At all events, it is right to urge on others the performance of duty *as if* the eye of a departed father, mother, or sister were fixed upon us, and *as if* we were encompassed by all the holy beings of heaven. Sin, too, should be avoided *as if* every eye in the uni- verse were upon us. How many things do we do which we would not; how many feelings do we cherish which we would at once banish from our minds, if we felt that the heavens above us were as transparent as glass, and that all the holy beings around the throne were fixing an intense gaze upon us! The word "elect" here seems to imply that there had been some influence used to keep them, and some purpose respect- ing them, which had not existed in regard to those who had fallen.

ferring *o* one before another, doing nothing by partiality.

o De.1.17.

Saints are called *elect* because they are chosen of God unto salvation (Notes on Eph. i. 4, 5), and it would appear that it is a great law extending through the universe, that both those who *remain* in a state of holiness, and those who are *made* holy, are the subjects of purpose and choice on the part of God. The *fact* only is stated; the *reasons* which led to the choice, alike in regard to angels and men, are unknown to us; comp. Notes on Mat. xi. 25. ¶ *That thou observe these things.* Probably referring to *all* the things which he had enjoined in the previous parts of the epistle. ¶ *Without preferring one before another.* Marg., *prejudice.* The meaning is, *without previous judgment*— χωρὶς προκρίματος —with- out any prejudice on account of rank, wealth, personal friendship, or predi- lection of any sort. Let there be en- tire impartiality in all cases. Justice was beautifully represented by the ancients as holding a pair of scales equally balanced. It is as important that there should be entire impartiality in the church as in civil transactions, and though it is not wrong for a min- ister of the gospel to have his per- sonal friends, yet in the administration of the affairs of the church he should remember that all are brethren, and all, of whatever rank, colour, sex, or age, have equal rights. ¶ *Partiality.* Gr., *inclination,* or *proclivity*—that is, without being *inclined* to favour one party or person more than an- other. There should be no *purpose* to find one guilty and another inno- cent; no *inclination* of heart towards one which would lead us to resolve to find him innocent; and no *aversion* from another which would make us resolve to find him guilty.

22. *Lay hands suddenly on no man.* Some have understood this of laying on of hands to heal the sick (Koppe); others of the laying on of hands to absolve penitents; but the obvious meaning is to refer it to ordination. It was usual to lay the hands on the

22 Lay[p] hands suddenly on no man, [q]neither be partaker of other men's sins: keep thyself pure.

    p Ac.13.3.   *q* 2 Jn.11.

23 Drink no longer water, [r]but use a little wine for thy stomach's sake and thine often infirmities.

    r Pr.31.6.

heads of those who were ordained to a sacred office, or appointed to perform an important duty; Notes, chap. iv. 14; comp. Acts vi. 6; viii. 17. The idea here is, that Timothy should not be *hasty* in an act so important as that of introducing men to the ministry. He should take time to give them a fair trial of their piety; he should have satisfactory evidence of their qualifications. He should not at once introduce a man to the ministry because he gave evidence of piety, or because he burned with an ardent zeal, or because he thought himself qualified for the work. It is clear from this that the apostle regarded Timothy as having the right to *ordain* to the ministry; but not that he was to ordain alone, or *as a prelate.* The injunction would be entirely proper on the supposition that others were to be associated with him in the act of ordaining. It is just such as a Presbyterian father in the ministry would give in a charge to his son now; it is in fact just the charge which is now given *by* Presbyterians and Congregationalists to those who are set apart to the sacred office, in reference to ordaining others. ¶ *Neither be partakers of other men's sins.* This is evidently to be interpreted in connection with the injunction "to lay hands suddenly on no man." The meaning, in this connection, is, that Timothy was not to become a participant in the sins of another by introducing him to the sacred office. He was not to invest one with a holy office who was a wicked man or a heretic, for this would be to sanction his wickedness and error. If we ordain a man to the office of the ministry who is known to be living in sin, or to cherish dangerous error, we become the patrons of the sin and of the heresy. We lend to it the sanction of our approbation; and give to it whatever currency it may acquire from the reputation which *we* may have, or which it may acquire from the influence of the sacred office

of the ministry. Hence the importance of caution in investing anyone with the ministerial office. But while Paul meant, doubtless, that this should be applied particularly to ordination to the ministry, he has given it a *general* character. *In no way* are we to participate in the sins of other men. We are not to be engaged with them in doing wrong; we are not to patronize them in a wicked business; we are not to be known as their companions or friends; and we are not to partake of their unlawful gains. We are not to lend money, or a boat, or a horse, or a pistol, or a bowie-knife, for an unlawful business; we are not to furnish capital for the slave-trade, or for manufacturing intoxicating drinks, or for an enterprise that contemplates the violation of the Sabbath. ¶ *Keep thyself pure.* Particularly, in regard to participation in the sins of others; generally, in all things—in heart, in word, in conduct.

23. *Drink no longer water.* There has been much difficulty felt in regard to the *connection* which this advice has with what precedes and what follows. Many have considered the difficulty to be so great that they have supposed that this verse has been displaced, and that it should be introduced in some other connection. The true connection and the reason for the introduction of the counsel here, seems to me to be this : Paul appears to have been suddenly impressed with the thought—a thought which is very likely to come over a man who is writing on the duties of the ministry —of the arduous nature of the ministerial office. He was giving counsels in regard to an office which required a great amount of labour, care, and anxiety. The labours enjoined were such as to demand all the time; the care and anxiety incident to such a charge would be very likely to prostrate the frame, and to injure the health. Then he remembered that Timothy was yet but a youth; he re-

called his feebleness of constitution and his frequent attacks of illness; he recollected the very abstemious habits which he had prescribed for himself; and, in this connection, he urges him to a careful regard for his health, and prescribes the use of a small quantity of wine, mingled with his water, as a suitable medicine in his case. Thus considered, this direction is as worthy to be given by an inspired teacher as it is to counsel a man to pay a proper regard to his health, and not needlessly to throw away his life; comp. Mat. x. 23. The phrase, "drink no longer water," is equivalent to, "drink not water *only;*" see numerous instances in Wetstein. The Greek word here used does not elsewhere occur in the New Testament. ¶ *But use a little wine.* Mingled with the water—the common method of drinking wine in the East; see Robinson's *Bibliotheca Sacra,* i. 512, 513. ¶ *For thy stomach's sake.* It was not for the pleasure to be derived from the use of wine, or because it would produce hilarity or excitement, but solely because it was regarded as necessary for the promotion of health; that is, as a medicine. ¶ *And thine often infirmities.* ἀσθενείας—weaknesses or sicknesses. The word would include all infirmities of body, but seems to refer here to some attacks of sickness to which Timothy was liable, or to some feebleness of constitution; but beyond this we have no information in regard to the *nature* of his maladies. In view of this passage, and as a further explanation of it, we may make the following remarks: (1) The use of wine, and of all intoxicating drinks, was solemnly forbidden to the priests under the Mosaic law, when engaged in the performance of their sacred duties, Lev. x. 9, 10. The same was the case among the Egyptian priests (Clarke); comp. Notes on chap. iii. 3. It is not improbable that the same thing would be regarded as proper among those who ministered in holy things under the Christian dispensation. The natural feeling would be, and not improperly, that a Christian minister should not be less holy than a Jewish priest, and especially when it is remembered

that the *reason* of the Jewish law remained the same—"that ye may put difference between holy and unholy, and clean and unclean." (2) It is evident from this passage that *Timothy* usually drank water *only,* or that, in modern language, he was a "*teetotaller.*" He was, evidently, not in the *habit* of drinking wine, or he could not have been exhorted to do it. (3) He must have been a remarkably temperate youth to have required the authority of an apostle to induce him to drink even a *little* wine; see Doddridge. There are few young men so temperate as to require *such* an authority to induce them to do it. (4) The exhortation extended only to a *very moderate* use of wine. It was not to drink it *freely;* it was not to drink it at the tables of the rich and the great, or in the social circle; it was not even to drink it by itself; it was to use "a *little,*" mingled with water—for this was the usual method; see Athenæus, *Deipno.,* lib. ix. x. c. 7. (5) It was not as a common drink, but the exhortation or command extends *only* to its use as a medicine. All the use which can be legitimately made of this injunction—whatever conclusion may be drawn from other precepts—is, that it is proper to use a small quantity of wine for medicinal purposes. (6) There are many ministers of the gospel now, alas! to whom under no circumstances could an apostle apply this exhortation—"Drink no longer water only." They would ask, with surprise, what he meant? whether he intended it in irony, and for banter—for they need no apostolic command to drink wine. Or if he should address to them the exhortation, "Use a *little* wine," they could regard it only as a reproof for their usual habit of drinking much. To many, the exhortation would be appropriate, if they ought to use wine at all, only because they are in the habit of using so *much* that it would be proper to restrain them to a much smaller quantity. (7) This whole passage is one of great value to the cause of temperance. Timothy was undoubtedly in the habit of abstaining wholly from the use of wine. Paul

24 Some men's sins *are open beforehand, going before to judgment: and some *men* they follow after.

8 Ga.5.19.

25 Likewise also the good works *of some* are manifest beforehand; and they that are otherwise cannot be hid.

knew this, and he did not reprove him for it. He manifestly favoured the general habit, and only asked him to depart in some small degree from it, in order that he might restore and preserve his health. So far, and no farther, is it right to apply this language in regard to the use of wine; and the minister who should follow this injunction would be in no danger of disgracing his sacred profession by the debasing and demoralizing sin of intemperance.

24. *Some men's sins are open beforehand.* This declaration, though it assumes a general form, is to be taken evidently in connection with the general subject of introducing men to the ministry (ver. 22); and ver. 23 is to be regarded as a parenthesis. The apostle had given Timothy a charge (ver. 22) respecting the character of those whom he should ordain. He here says, in reference to that, that the character of some men was manifest. There was no disguise. It was evident to all what it was, and there could be no danger of mistake respecting it. Their conduct was apparent to all. About *such* men he ought not to hesitate a moment, and, no matter what their talents, or learning, or rank in the community, he ought to have no participation in introducing them to the ministry. ¶ *Going before to judgment.* Their character is well understood. There is no need of waiting for the day of judgment to know what they are. Their deeds so precede their own appearance at the judgment-bar, that the record and the verdict can be made up before they arrive there, and there will be scarcely need even of the formality of a trial. The meaning here is, that there could be no doubt about the character of such men, and Timothy should not be accessory to their being introduced into the office of the ministry. ¶ *And some* men *they follow after.* That is, their character is not fully understood

here. They conceal their plans. They practise deception. They appear different from what they really are. But the character of such men will be developed, and they will be judged according to their works. They cannot hope to escape with impunity. Though they have endeavoured to hide their evil deeds, yet they will follow after them to the judgment-bar, and will meet them there. The meaning, in this connection, seems to be, that there ought to be circumspection in judging of the qualifications of men for the office of the ministry. It ought not to be inferred from favourable appearances at once, or on slight acquaintance, that they are qualified for the office—for they may be of the number of those whose characters, now concealed or misunderstood, will be developed only on the final trial.

25. *Likewise also the good works of some are manifest beforehand.* The character of some men is clear, and accurately understood. There can be no doubt, from their works, that they are good men. We need not wait for the day of judgment to determine that, but may treat them here *as* good men, and introduce them to offices which only good men can fill. The idea here is, that their character may be so certain and undoubted that there need be no hesitation in setting them apart to the office of the ministry. ¶ *And they that are otherwise cannot be hid.* That is, they cannot be ultimately concealed or misunderstood. There are arrangements in the divine government for bringing out the character of every man so that it may be clearly understood. The expression here refers to good men. The idea is, that there are *some* good men whose character is known to all. Their deeds spread a glory around them, so that no one can mistake what they are. *They* correspond, in respect to the publicity of their character, with those mentioned

in ver. 24, whose "*sins* are open beforehand;" for the good deeds of the one are as manifest as the sins of the other. But there are those who are "*otherwise.*" They are modest, retiring, unobtrusive, unknown. They may live in obscurity; may have slender means for doing good; may be constitutionally so diffident that they never appear on the stage of public action. What they do is concealed from the world. *These* correspond in respect to publicity with those mentioned in ver. 24, "whose deeds follow after them." Yet, says the apostle, *these* cannot always be hid. There are arrangements for developing every man's character, and it will be ultimately known what he is. The connection here seems to be this. As Timothy (ver. 24) was to be on his guard, in introducing men into the ministry, against those whose character for evil was not developed, but who might be concealing their plans and practising secret sins, so he was to endeavour to search out the modest, the unobtrusive, and those who, though now unknown, were among the excellent of the earth, and bring them forward to a station of usefulness where their virtues might shine on the world.

REMARKS.

Apart from the reference of this beautiful passage (ver. 24, 25) to the ministry, it contains truth important to all.

(1) The character of many wicked men is now clearly known. No one has any doubt of it. Their deeds have gone before them, and are recorded in the books that will be open at the judgment. They might even *now* be judged without the formality of appearing there, and the universe would acquiesce in the sentence of condemnation.

(2) The character of many wicked men is concealed. They hide their plans. They are practising secret iniquity. They do not mean that the world shall know what they are. More than half the real depravity of the world is thus concealed from human view, and in regard to more than half the race who are going up to the judgment there is an entire mistake as to their real character. If all the *secret* wickedness of the earth were disclosed, no one would have any doubt about the doctrine of human depravity.

(3) There is a process steadily going forward for bringing out the real character of men, and showing what they are. This process consists, *first*, in the arrangements of Providence for developing their character *here*. Many a man who was supposed to be virtuous, is shown, by some sudden trial, to have been all along a villain at heart. Many a minister of the gospel, a lawyer, a physician, an officer in a bank, a merchant, whose character was supposed to stand fair, has been suffered to fall into open sin, that he might develop the long-cherished secret depravity of his soul. *Secondly,* the process will be completed on the final trial. Then *nothing* will be concealed. Every man will be seen as he is. All they whose characters were understood to be wicked here, will be seen then also to be wicked, and many who were supposed on earth to have a good character, will be seen there to have been hollow-hearted and base hypocrites.

(4) Every man in the last day will be judged according to his real character. No one, however successful he may have been here, can hope to practise a deception on his final Judge.

(5) There is a fitness and propriety in the fact that there will be a final judgment. Indeed, there *must* be such a judgment, in order that God may be just. The characters of men are not fully developed here. The process is not completed. Many are taken away before their schemes of iniquity are accomplished, and before their real characters are understood. If they were to live long enough on the earth their characters would be ultimately developed here, but the divine arrangement is, that man shall *not* live long here, and the development, therefore, must be in the future world.

(6) The modest, the retiring, the humble, and those here unknown, will not be overlooked in the last great

CHAPTER VI.

L ET as many *a*servants as are
under the yoke count their

a Ep.6.5.

day. There is much *good*, as there is
much *evil* in the world, that is now
concealed. There are many plans of
benevolence formed which they who
formed them are not permitted to
complete; many desires of benefiting
others are cherished which there are
no means of gratifying; many a deed
of kindness is performed which is not
blazoned abroad to the world; and
many a wish is entertained for the
progress of virtue, the freedom of the
enslaved, the relief of the oppressed,
and the salvation of the world, which
can find expression only in prayer.
We are not to suppose, then, that all
that is concealed and unknown in the
world is *evil*.

(7) There will be amazing developments in the last great day; and as it
will then be seen in the revelations
of the secret deeds of evil that human
nature is corrupt, so it will be seen
that there was much more good in the
world than was commonly supposed.
As a large portion of the wickedness
of the earth is concealed, so, from the
necessity of the case, it is true that no
small portion of the goodness on earth
is hidden. *Wickedness* conceals itself
from shame, from a desire better to
effect its purposes, from the dread of
punishment; *goodness*, from its modesty, its retiring nature, and from the
want of an opportunity of acting out
its desires; but whatever may have
been the cause of the concealment, in
all cases all will be made known on
the final trial—to the shame and confusion of the one class; to the joy and
triumph of the other.

CHAPTER VI.

ANALYSIS OF THE CHAPTER.

This chapter embraces the following subjects of counsel and exhortation:—

(1) The kind of instruction which
was to be given to servants, ver. 1–
5. They were to treat their masters
with all proper respect, ver. 1; if

own masters worthy of all honour,
that the name of God and *his* doctrine be not blasphemed.

their masters were Christians, they
were, on that account, to serve them
with the more fidelity, ver. 2; and
any opposite kind of teaching would
tend only to stir up strife and produce
dissatisfaction and contention, and
could proceed only from a proud and
self-confident heart.

(2) The advantage of piety and of
a contented mind, ver. 6–8. The
argument for this is, that we brought
nothing into the world, and can carry
nothing out; that our essential wants
here are food and raiment, and that,
having enough to make us comfortable,
we should be content.

(3) The evils of a desire to be
rich (ver. 9, 10)—evils seen in the
temptations to which it leads; the
passions which it fosters, and the
danger to religion itself.

(4) An exhortation to Timothy, as
a minister of religion, to pursue
higher and nobler objects, ver. 11–16.
He was (*a*) to avoid these worldly
things; he was (*b*) to pursue nobler
objects. He was to follow after
righteousness, and to fight the good
fight of faith. To do this, he was to
be encouraged by the assurance that
the Great and only Potentate would,
in due time, place the crown on his
head.

(5) The duty of those who were
rich—for it is supposed that some
Christians will be rich—either by
inheritance or by prosperous business,
ver. 17–19. They are (*a*) not to be
proud; (*b*) nor to trust in their riches
so as to forget their dependence on
God; (*c*) to do good with their property; and (*d*) to make their wealth
the means of securing eternal life.

(6) A solemn charge to Timothy
to observe these things, and not to be
turned from them by any of the arguments and objections of pretended
science, ver. 20, 21.

1. *Let as many servants.* On the
word here rendered *servants*—δοῦλοι—
see Notes on Eph. vi. 5. The word is
that which was commonly applied in
a *slave*, but it is so extensive in its

2 And they that have believing masters, let them not despise *them*, because they are brethren; but rather do *them* service, because

they are [1]faithful and beloved, partakers of the benefit. These things teach and exhort.

[1] or, *believing.*

signification as to be applicable to *any* species of servitude, whether voluntary or involuntary. If slavery existed in Ephesus at the time when this epistle was written, it would be applicable to slaves; if any other kind of servitude existed, the word would be equally applicable to that. There is nothing *in the word itself* which essentially limits it to *slavery;* examine Mat. xiii. 27; xx. 27; Mark x. 44; Luke ii. 29; John xv. 15; Acts ii. 18; iv. 29; xvi. 17; Rom. i. 1; 2 Cor. iv. 5; Jude 1; Rev. i. 1; ii. 20; vii. 3. The addition of the phrase "under the yoke," however, shows undoubtedly that it is to be understood here of slavery. ¶ *As are under the yoke.* On the word *yoke*, see Notes on Mat. xi. 29. The phrase here properly denotes slavery, as it would not be applied to any other species of servitude; see Lev. xxvi. 13; Dem. 322, 12; ζεῦγος δουλοσύνης, Rob. *Lex.* It sometimes denotes the bondage of the Mosaic law, as being a severe and oppressive burden, Acts xv. 10; Gal. v. 1. It may be remarked here, that the apostle did not regard slavery as a *light* or *desirable* thing. *He would not have applied this term to the condition of a wife or of a child.* ¶ *Count their own masters worthy of all honour.* Treat them with all proper respect. They were to manifest the *right spirit themselves*, whatever their masters did; they were not to do anything that would dishonour religion. The injunction *here* would seem to have particular reference to those whose masters were not Christians. In the following verse, the apostle gives particular instructions to those who had pious masters. The meaning here is, that the slave ought to show the Christian spirit towards his master who was not a Christian; he ought to conduct himself so that his religion would not be dishonoured; he ought not to give his master occasion to say that the only effect of the Christian religion on the mind of a

servant was to make him restless, discontented, dissatisfied, and disobedient. In the humble and trying situation in which he confessedly was —*under the yoke of bondage*—he ought to evince patience, kindness, and respect for his master, and as long as the relation continued he was to be obedient. This command, however, was by no means inconsistent with his desiring his freedom, and securing it, if the opportunity presented itself; see Notes on 1 Cor. vii. 21; comp., on the passage before us, the Notes on Eph. vi. 5–8, and 1 Pet. ii. 18. ¶ *That the name of God and his doctrine be not blasphemed.* That religion be not dishonoured and reproached, and that there may be no occasion to say that Christianity tends to produce discontent and to lead to insurrection. If the effect of religion had been to teach all who were servants that they should no longer obey their masters, or that they should rise upon them and assert their freedom by violence, or that their masters were to be treated with indignity on account of their usurped rights over others, the effect would have been obvious. There would have been a loud and united outcry against the new religion, and it could have made no progress in the world. Instead of this, Christianity taught the necessity of patience, and meekness, and forbearance in the endurance of *all wrong*—whether from private individuals (Mat. v. 39–41; 1 Cor. vi. 7), or under the oppressions and exactions of Nero (Rom. xiii. 1–7), or amidst the hardships and cruelties of slavery. These peaceful injunctions, however, did not demonstrate that Christ approved the act of him "that smote on the one cheek," or that Paul regarded the government of Nero as a good government; and as little do they prove that Paul or the Saviour approved of slavery.

2. *And they that have believing masters.* Masters who are Christians. It is clear from this, that Paul sup-

posed that, at that time, and under those circumstances, a man might *become* a Christian who had slaves under him. How long he might *continue* to hold his fellow-men in bondage, and yet be a Christian, is, however, quite a different question. It is quite clear, from the New Testament, as well as from facts now, that God may convert men when pursuing any kind of wickedness. The effect of religion, however, in all cases, will be to lead them to cease to do wrong. It is by no means improbable that many of those who *had* owned slaves, in accordance with the prevailing custom in the Roman empire, may have been converted—for the fact that a man has been living a life of sin does not prevent the possibility of his conversion. There is no evidence that Paul refers here to any who had *bought* slaves *after* they were converted; nor is there any intimation of any such transaction among Christians in the New Testament. Nor is there any intimation that he regarded it as right and best that they should *continue* to hold slaves; nor that he would approve their making arrangements to persevere in this as a permanent institution. Nor is it to be fairly inferred from this passage that he meant to teach that they might *continue* this, and yet be entitled to all the respect and confidence due to the Christian name, or be regarded as maintaining a good standing in the church. Whatever may be true on these points, the passage before us only proves that Paul considered that a man who was a slaveholder *might* be converted, and be spoken of as a "believer," or a Christian. Many have been converted in similar circumstances, as many have in the practice of all other kinds of iniquity. What was their duty *after* their conversion, was another question; and what was the duty of their "servants" or slaves, was another question still. It is only this latter question which the apostle is here considering. ¶ *Not despise* them, *because they are brethren.* Not treat them with any want of the respect which is due to their station. The word here used sometimes denotes *to neglect,* or *not*

to care for, Mat. vi. 24; Luke xvi. 13. Here it is not necessary to suppose that it denotes actual *contempt,* but only that want of respect which might possibly spring up in the mind if not well instructed, or not on its guard, among those who were servants or slaves. It was to be apprehended that the effect of the master and the slave having both embraced religion, would be to produce in the mind of the servant a want of respect and deference for his master. This danger was to be apprehended from the following causes:—(1) Christianity taught that all men were made of "one blood," and were by nature *equal,* Acts xvii. 26. It was natural, therefore, for the slave to infer, that by nature he was equal to his master, and it would be easy to pervert this truth to make him disrespectful and insubordinate. (2) They were equal to them as Christians. Christianity taught them that they were all "brethren" in the Lord, and that there was no distinction before God. It might be natural to infer from this, that *all* distinctions in society were to be abolished, and that, *in all respects,* the slave was to regard himself as on a level with his master. (3) Some, who did not well understand the nature of Christianity, or who might have been disposed to cause trouble, may have taken advantage of the undeniable truths about the equality of men by nature and by redemption, to produce discontent on the part of the slave. They may have endeavoured to embitter the feelings of the slaves towards their masters who held them in bondage. The effect, it is easy to see, may have been to lead those who were in a state of servitude to manifest open and marked disrespect. In opposition to this, the apostle would have Timothy teach that Christianity did not rudely assail the existing institutions of society, and especially did not teach those who were in subordinate ranks to be disrespectful to those above them. ¶ *But rather do* them *service.* That is, serve them with more cheerfulness and alacrity than they did before the master was converted; or serve them with the more cheerfulness *because* they

3 If any man teach otherwise, and consent not to *b* wholesome words, *even* the words of our

Lord Jesus Christ, and to the doctrine which is *c* according to godliness,

were Christians. The reasons for this were, because the master was now more worthy of affectionate regard, and because the servant might look for better treatment at his hands; comp. Notes on Eph. vi. 6. ¶ *Because they are faithful.* That is, *because* they are *believers,* or are Christians—πιστοί; the same word which in the beginning of the verse is rendered *believing.* It does not here mean that they were "faithful" to their servants or their God, but merely that they were *Christians.* ¶ *And beloved.* Probably, "beloved *of God;*" for so the word is often used. As they are the friends of God, they who are servants should show them the more respect. The idea is, simply, that one whom God loves should be treated with more respect than if he were *not* thus beloved; or, a good man deserves more respect than a wicked man. In all the relations of life, we should respect those above us the more in proportion to the excellency of their character. ¶ *Partakers of the benefit.* That is, the benefit which the gospel imparts—for so the connection requires us to understand it. It cannot mean, as many have supposed, that they were "partakers of the benefit of the labours of the servant," or enjoyed the fruits of their labours—for how could this be a reason for their treating them with the more respect? It would be rather a reason for treating them with *less* respect, because they were living on the avails of unrequited toil. But the true reason assigned is, that the master had been, by the grace of God, permitted to participate in the same benefits of salvation as the servant; he had received, like him, the pardon of sin, and he was to be regarded as a fellow-heir of the grace of life. The expression here might be rendered, "they are *partakers of,* or are *devoted to, the good cause*" (Rob. *Lex.*). The argument is, that they were not infidels, or strangers to religion, or those who would

try to hinder the progress of that which was dear to the heart of the servant, but were united with them in that same good work; they participated in the blessings of the same salvation, and they were really endeavouring to further the interests of religion. There ought, therefore, to be the more respect shown to them, and the more cheerful service rendered them.

3. *If any man teach otherwise.* Any otherwise than that respect should be shown to masters; and that a more cheerful and ready service should be rendered *because* they were Christians. It is evidently implied here that some might be disposed to inculcate such views of religion as would produce discontent and a spirit of insubordination among those who were held to servitude. *Who* they were is not known, nor is it known what arguments they would employ to do it. It would seem probable that the arguments which would be employed would be such as these:—that God made all men equal; that all had been redeemed by the same blood; that all true Christians were fellow-heirs of heaven; and that it was wrong to hold a Christian brother in bondage, &c. From undeniable principles it would seem that they drew the inference that slaves ought at once to assert their freedom; that they should refuse obedience to their masters; and that the tendency of their teaching was, instead of removing the evil by the gradual and silent influence of Christian principles, to produce discontent and insurrection. From some of the expressions here used by the apostle, as characteristic of these teachers, it would seem to be probable that these persons were Jews. They were men given to subtle disputations, and those who doted about questions and verbal disputes, and who were intent on gain, supposing that that which conduced to mere worldly prosperity was of course religion. These characteristics apply well to Jewish

4 He is proud, [2]knowing [d]no-
thing, but [3]doting about questions
and strifes of words, whereof com-

2 or, *a fool.*　　*d* 1 Co.8.2.　　3 or, *sick.*

eth envy, strife, railings, evil sur-
misings,

5 Perverse[4] disputings of men

4 or, *Gallings one of another.*

---

teachers. ¶ *And consent not to wholesome words.* Words conducing to a
healthful state of the church; that is,
doctrines tending to produce order
and a due observance of the proprieties
of life; doctrines leading to contentment, and sober industry, and the
patient endurance of evils. ¶ *Even
the words of our Lord Jesus Christ.*
The doctrines of the Saviour—all of
which tended to a quiet life, and to a
patient endurance of wrongs. ¶ *And
to the doctrine which is according to
godliness.* Which tends to produce
piety or religion; that is, the doctrine which would be most favourable
to an easy and rapid propagation of
the gospel. The idea seems to be,
that such a state of insubordination
and discontent as they would produce,
would be unfavourable to the promotion of religion. Who can doubt it?
4. *He is proud.* That is, he is lifted
up with his fancied superior acquaintance with the nature of religion.
The Greek verb means, properly, *to
smoke, to fume;* and then *to be inflated, to be conceited,* &c. The idea
is, that he has no proper knowledge of
the nature of the gospel, and yet he
values himself on a fancied superior
acquaintance with its principles.
¶ *Knowing nothing.* Marg., *a fool.*
That is, that he does not understand
the nature of religion as he supposes
he does. His views in regard to the
relation of masters and servants, and
to the bearing of religion on that relation, show that he does not understand the genius of Christianity. The
apostle expresses this in strong language, by saying that he knows *nothing;*
see Notes on 1 Cor. viii. 2. ¶ *But
doting.* Marg., *sick.* The Greek
word—*νοσέω*—means properly to be
sick; then to languish, to pine after.
The meaning here is, that such persons had a *sickly* or *morbid* desire for
debates of this kind. They had not a
sound and healthy state of mind on
the subject of religion. They were
like a sickly man, who has no desire

for solid and healthful food, but for
that which will gratify a diseased
appetite. They desired not sound
doctrine, but controversies about unimportant and unsubstantial matters
—things that bore the same relation
to important doctrines which the
things that a sick man pines after do
to substantial food. ¶ *Questions and
strifes of words.* The Jews abounded
much in disputes of this sort, and it
would seem probable that the persons
here referred to were Jewish teachers;
comp. Notes, chap. i. 6, 7, and Acts
xviii. 15. ¶ *Whereof cometh envy.*
The only fruit of which is to produce
envy. That is, the appearance of
superior knowledge; the boast of being
profoundly acquainted with religion,
and the show of an ability for subtle
argumentation, would produce in a
certain class *envy.* Envy is uneasiness, pain, mortification, or discontent,
excited by another's prosperity, or by
his superior knowledge or possessions;
see Notes on Rom. i. 29. ¶ *Strife.*
Or contentions with those who will
not readily yield to their opinions.
¶ *Railings.* Harsh and abusive language towards those who will not
concede a point—a common effect of
disputes, and more commonly of disputes about small and unimportant
matters, than of those which are of
magnitude. Such railings often attend disputes that arise out of nice
and subtle distinctions. ¶ *Evil sur-
misings.* Suspicions that they are
led to hold their views, not by the
love of the truth, but from sordid or
worldly motives. Such suspicions are
very apt to attend an angry debate of
any kind. It might be expected peculiarly to exist on such a question as
the apostle refers to here—the relation of a master and a slave. It is
always very hard to do justice to the
motives of one who seems to *us* to be
living in sin, or to believe it to be
possible that he acts from right motives.

5. *Perverse disputings.* Marg.,

of corrupt minds, and destitute of the truth, supposing that gain is

Gallings one of another. In regard to the correct *reading* of this passage, see *Bib. Repository*, vol. iii. pp. 61, 62. The word which is here used in the Received Text—παραδιατρίβη—occurs nowhere else in the New Testament. It properly means *misemployment;* then *idle occupation* (Rob. *Lex.*). The verb from which this is derived means *to rub in pieces, to wear away;* and hence the word here used refers to what was a mere *wearing away* of time. The idea is that of employments that merely consumed time without any advantage. The notion of *contention* or *dispute* is not necessarily implied in this passage, but the allusion is to inquiries or discussions that were of no practical value, but were a mere consumption of *time;* comp. Koppe on the passage. The reading in the margin is derived from the common usage of the verb *to rub,* and hence our translators attached the idea of *rubbing against* each other, or of *galling* each other, as by rubbing. This is not, however, the idea in the Greek word. The phrase "*idle employments*" would better suit the meaning of the Greek than either of the phrases which our translators have employed. ¶ *Of men of corrupt minds.* That is, of wicked hearts. ¶ *And destitute of the truth.* Not knowing the truth; or not having just views of truth. They show that they have no correct acquaintance with the Christian system. ¶ *Supposing that gain is godliness.* That that which contributes to an increase of property is of course true religion; or that it is proper to infer that any course which contributes to worldly prosperity must be sanctioned by religion. They judge of the consistency of any course with religion by its tendency to promote outward prosperity. This they have exalted into a maxim, and this they make the essential thing in religion. But how could any man do this? And what connection would this have with the subject under consideration—the kind of instruction

godliness; *from such withdraw thyself.

e 2 Ti.3.5.

that was to be given to servants? The *meaning* of the maxim seems to be, that religion must necessarily promote prosperity by its promoting temperance, and industry, and length of days; and that since this was the case, it was fair to infer that anything which would *not* do this could not be consistent with religion. They adopted it, therefore, as a general rule of judging, and one in entire accordance with the wishes of their own hearts, that any course of life that would *not* do this must be contrary to the true spirit of religion. This maxim, it would seem, they applied to the relation of the slave and his master, and as the tendency of the system was always to keep the servant poor and in an humble condition, they seem to have inferred that the relation was contrary to Christianity, and hence to have excited the servant to disaffection. In their *reasoning* they were not far out of the way, for it *is* fair to infer that a system that tends to produce uniform poverty, and to perpetuate a degraded condition in society, is contrary to the genius of Christianity. They were *wrong* (1) in making this a *general* maxim by which to judge of everything in religion; and (2) in so applying it as to produce insubordination and discontent in the minds of servants towards their masters; and (3) in supposing that *everything* which produced gain was consistent with religion, or that they could infallibly judge of the moral quality of any course of life by its contributing to outward prosperity. Religion will uniformly lead to that which conduces to prosperity, but it does not follow that every way of making money is therefore a part of piety. It is possible, also, that in some way they hoped for "gain" to themselves by inculcating those principles. It may be remarked here, that this is not an uncommon maxim practically among men—that "gain is godliness." The whole object of life with them is to make money; the rule by which they judge of everything is by its tendency to produce gain; and their whole religion may be summed up in this, that *they live for gain.* Wealth is the real object of pursuit; but it is often with them cloaked under the pretence of piety. They have no more religion than they suppose will contribute to this object; they judge of the nature and value of every maxim by its tendency to make men prosperous in their worldly business; they have as much as they suppose will promote their pecuniary interest, and they sacrifice every principle of religion which they suppose would conflict with their earthly advancement. ¶ *From such withdraw thyself.* That is, have no communion or fellowship with them. Do not recognize them as religious teachers; do not countenance their views. Timothy was in no way to show that he regarded them as inculcating truth, or to patronize their doctrines. From such men, as having any claim to the character of Christians, every man *should* withdraw with feelings of unutterable pity and loathing.—This passage (ver. 1–5) is often appealed to by the advocates and apologists for slavery to prove that Christianity countenances that institution, and that no direct attempt should be made by the ministers of the gospel, or other Christians, to show the evil of the institution, and to promote its abolition, and to prove that we have no right to interfere in any way with what pertains to these "domestic relations." It is of importance, therefore, in view of the exposition which has been given of the words and phrases in the passage, to sum up the truths which it inculcates. From it, therefore, the following lessons may be derived: (1) That those who are slaves, and who have been converted to Christianity, should not be indolent or disorderly. If their masters are Christians, they should treat them with respect, and all the more because they are fellow-heirs of the grace of life. If they are *not* Christians, they should yet show the nature of religion on *themselves,* and bear the evils of their condition with patience—showing how religion teaches them to endure wrong. In either case, they are to be quiet, industrious, kind, meek, respectful. This Christianity everywhere enjoins while the relation continues. At the same time, however, it does not forbid the slave earnestly to desire his freedom, or to use all proper measures to obtain it; see 1 Cor. vii. 21. (2) That the ministers of religion should not labour to produce a spirit of discontent among slaves, or excite them to rise upon their masters. This passage would undoubtedly forbid all *such* interference, and all agencies or embassies sent *among slaves themselves* to inflame their minds against their masters, in view of their wrongs; to put arms into their hands; or to induce them to form combinations for purposes of insurrection. It is not so much in the true spirit of Christianity to go to those who *are wronged,* as to those who *do the wrong.* The primary message in such cases is to the latter; and when it does go to the former, it is to teach them to be patient under their wrongs, to evince the Christian spirit there, and to make use only of those means which are consistent with the gospel to free themselves from the evils under which they suffer. At the same time, nothing in this passage, or in any other part of the New Testament, forbids us to go to the *master himself,* and to show him the evil of the system, and to enjoin upon him to let the oppressed go free. Nothing in this passage can be reasonably construed as teaching that an appeal of the most earnest and urgent kind may not be made to him; or that the wrongs of the system may not be fully set before him, or that any man or set of men may not lawfully lift up in his hearing a loud and earnest voice in favour of the freedom of all. And in like manner there is nothing which makes it improper that the slave himself should be put fully in possession of that gospel which will apprise him of his rights as a man, and as redeemed by the blood of Jesus. Every human being, whether held in bondage or not, has a *right* to be made acquainted with all the provisions and truths of that gospel, nor has any man or class of men a right to withhold such knowledge from him. No *system* of things *can* be right which contemplates that that gospel shall be withheld, or under which it is necessary to withhold it in order to the perpetuity of the system. (3) The passage teaches that it is possible that a man who is a slaveholder may become a Christian. But it does *not* teach that, though he may become a Christian while he is a slaveholder, that it is proper for him to continue this relation after he becomes such. It does *not* teach that a man can be a Christian and yet go into the business of buying and selling slaves. It does not teach that a man can be a Christian and *continue* to hold others in bondage, whatever may be true on that point. It does not teach that he ought to be considered as maintaining a "good standing" in the church, if he *continues* to be a slaveholder; and whatever may be the truth on these points, *this* passage should not be adduced as demonstrating them. It settles one point only in regard to these questions—that a case was supposable in which a slave had a Christian master. It settles the duty *of the slave* in such a case; it says nothing about the duty *of the master.* (4) This passage does *not* teach that slavery is either a *good* thing, or a *just* thing, a *desirable* relation in life, or an institution that God wishes to be *perpetuated* on the earth. The injunctions to slaves to be patient, meek, industrious, and respectful, no more demonstrate this, than the command to subjects to be obedient to the laws proves that God regarded the government of Nero as such an administration as he wished to be perpetuated on the earth. To exhort a slave to manifest a Christian spirit under his oppressions and wrongs, is not to justify the system that does him wrong, nor does it prohibit us from showing to masters that the system is contrary to the gospel, and that it ought to be abandoned. (5) This passage, therefore, furnishes no real support for slavery. It can no more be adduced in favour of it than

any exhortation to those who are oppressed, or in any degrading situation in life, to be patient, proves that the system which oppresses and degrades them is a good one. Nor does the fact that a man might be converted who was a slaveholder, and might be spoken of as a πιστός, or *believer*, prove that it would be right and desirable that he should *continue* that relation, any more than the fact that Saul of Tarsus became a Christian when engaged in persecution, proves that it would have been right for him to continue in that business, or than the conversion of the Ephesians who "used curious arts" (Acts xix. 19), proved that it would have been proper for them to continue in that employment. Men who are doing wrong are converted in order to turn them *from* that course of life, not to justify them *in* it.

6. *But godliness.* Piety; religion. The meaning is, that real religion should be regarded as the greatest and most valuable acquisition. ¶ *With contentment.* This word, as now used, refers to a state of mind; a calm and satisfied feeling; a freedom from murmuring and complaining. The idea is, that "piety, connected with a contented mind—or a mind acquiescing in the allotments of life—is to be regarded as the *real* gain." Tindal gives substantially the same interpretation: "Godliness is great riches, if a man be content with that he hath." Coverdale: "Howbeit, it is of great advantage, who is so godly, and holdeth him content with that he hath." The word which is used here—αὐτάρκεια—means, properly, *self-sufficiency,* and is used here, in a good sense, to denote a mind satisfied with its lot. If there be true religion, united with its proper accompaniment, peace of mind, it is to be regarded as the true riches. The object of the apostle seems to be, to rebuke those who supposed that *property* constituted everything that was worth living for. He tells them, therefore, that the true gain, the real riches which we ought to seek, is religion, with a contented mind. This does more to promote happiness than

6 But godliness with contentment is great gain.

7 For we brought nothing into *this* world, *g and it is* certain we can carry nothing out.

f Pr.15.16.   *g* Ps.49.17.

wealth can ever do, and this is what should be regarded as the great object of life.

7. *For we brought nothing into* this *world*, &c. A sentiment very similar to this occurs in Job i. 21, and it would seem probable that the apostle had that passage in his eye; see Notes on that passage. Numerous expressions of this kind occur in the classic writers; see Wetstein, *in loco,* and Pricæus, *in loco,* in the *Critici Sacri.* Of the *truth* of what is here said, there can be nothing more obvious. It is apparent to all. We bring no property with us into the world—no clothing, no jewels, no gold—and it is equally clear that we can take nothing with us when we leave the earth. Our coming into the world introduces no additional property to that which the race before possessed, and our going from the world removes none that we may have helped the race to accumulate. This is said by the apostle as an obvious reason why we should be contented if our actual wants are supplied—for this is really all that we need, and all that the world is toiling for. ¶ *We can carry nothing out.* Comp. Ps. xlix. 17, "For when he [the rich man] dieth, he shall carry nothing away; his glory shall not descend after him."

8. *And having food and raiment.* "Food and raiment," here, seem to be used to denote supplies for our wants in general. It is not uncommon to denote the whole by a part, and, as these are the *principal* things which we really need, and without which life could not be sustained, the apostle uses the phrase to denote all that is really necessary for us. We cannot suppose that he would forbid a desire of a comfortable habitation, or of the means of knowledge, or of conveniences for worshipping God, &c. The idea is, that having those things which

8 And having food and raiment, *h* let us be therewith content.

9 But *i* they that will be rich, fall into temptation, and a snare, and *into* many foolish and hurtful

h Ge.28.20.   *i* Pr.28.20.

meet the actual necessities of our nature, and save us from distress, we should not strive after "uncertain riches," or make wealth the object of our anxious pursuit; comp. Notes on Phil. iv. 11, 12.

9. *But they that will be rich.* Further to enforce the duty of contentment, the apostle refers to some of the evils which necessarily attend a desire to be rich. Those evils have been so great and uniform in all ages, and are so necessary accompaniments of that desire, that, even amidst many inconveniences which may attend the opposite condition, we should be contented with our lot. Indeed, if we could see all, it would only be necessary to see the evils which the desire of wealth produces in the world, to make us contented with a most lowly condition of life. Perhaps nothing more would be necessary to make a poor man satisfied with his lot, and grateful for it, than to be acquainted with the perplexities and cares of a rich man. There is more emphasis to be placed on the word *will*, here, in the phrase, "*will* be rich," than might be supposed from our translation. It is not the sign of the future tense, but implies an actual *purpose* or *design* to become rich—οἱ βουλόμενοι. The reference is to those in whom this becomes the object of earnest desire, and who lay their plans for it. ¶ *Fall into temptation.* That is, they are tempted to do wicked things in order to accomplish their purposes. It is *extremely* difficult to cherish the desire to be rich, as the leading purpose of the soul, and to be an honest man. ¶ *And a snare.* Birds are taken in a snare, and wild beasts were formerly; see Notes on Job xviii. 8, 9. The net was sprung suddenly upon them, and they could not escape. The idea here is, that they who have this desire become so *entangled*, that they cannot easily escape. They be-

lusts, which drown men in destruction and perdition.

10 For^k the love of money is the root of all evil; which while

k Ex.23.8.

come involved in the meshes of worldliness and sin; their movements are so fettered by cares, and inordinate desires, and by artificial wants, that they are no longer freemen. They become so involved in these things, that they cannot well break away from them if they would; comp. Prov. xxviii. 20. ¶ *And into many foolish and hurtful lusts.* Desires, such as the love of wealth creates. They are *foolish*—as being not such as an intelligent and immortal being should pursue; and they are *hurtful*—as being injurious to morals, to health, and to the soul. Among those desires, are the fondness for display; for a magnificent dwelling, a train of menials, and a splendid equipage; for sumptuous living, feasting, the social glass, company, and riotous dissipation. ¶ *Which drown men in destruction and perdition.* The word which is here rendered *drown* — βυθίζω—means, *to sink in the deep,* or, *to cause to sink;* and the meaning here is, that they become submerged as a ship that sinks. The idea of *drowning* is not properly that of the apostle, but the image is that of a wreck, where a ship and all that is in it go down together. The destruction is complete. There is a total ruin of happiness, of virtue, of reputation, and of the soul. The ruling desire to be rich leads on a train of follies which ruins everything here, and hereafter. — How many of the human family have thus been destroyed!

10. *For the love of money is the root of all evil.* That is, of all *kinds* of evil. This is evidently not to be understood as *literally* true, for there *are* evils which cannot be traced to the love of money—the evils growing out of ambition, and intemperance, and debasing lusts, and of the hatred of God and of goodness. The expression here is evidently a popular saying—"All sorts of evils grow

some coveted after, they have ^{5}erred from the faith, and pierced themselves through with many sorrows.

^{5} or, *been seduced.*

out of the love of money." Similar expressions often occur in the classic writers; see Wetstein, *in loco,* and numerous examples quoted by Pricæus. Of the *truth* of this, no one can doubt. No small part of the crimes of the world can be traced to the love of gold. But it deserves to be remarked here, that the apostle does not say that "*money* is the root of all evil," or that it is an evil at all. It is the "*love*" of it which is the source of evil. ¶ *Which while some coveted after.* That is, some who were professing Christians. The apostle is doubtless referring to persons whose history was known to Timothy, and warning him, and teaching him to warn others, by their example. ¶ *They have erred from the faith.* Marg., *been seduced.* The Greek is, they have been led astray from; that is, they have been so deceived as to depart from the faith. The notion of *deception* or *delusion* is in the word, and the sense is, that, deceived by the promises held out by the prospect of wealth, they have apostatized from the faith. It is not implied of necessity that they were ever real Christians. They have been led off from truth and duty, and from all the hopes and joys which religion would have imparted. ¶ *And have pierced themselves through with many sorrows.* With such sorrows as remorse, and painful reflections on their folly, and the apprehension of future wrath. Too late they see that they have thrown away the hopes of religion for that which is at best unworthy the pursuit of an immortal mind; which leads them on to a life of wickedness; which fails of imparting what it promised when its pursuit is successful, and which, in the great majority of instances, disappoints its votaries in respect to its attainment. The word rendered "pierced themselves through"—περιέπειραν—occurs nowhere else in the New Testament,

11 But thou, *l*O man of God, flee these things; and follow after righteousness, godliness, faith, love, patience, meekness.

12 Fight *m* the good fight of

l De.33.1.   *m* 2 Ti.4.7.

faith, lay hold on eternal life, whereunto thou art also called, and hast *n*professed a good profession before many witnesses.

13 I *o* give thee charge in the

n He.10.23.   *o* ch.5.21.

and is a word whose force and emphasis cannot be well expressed in a translation. It is from πείρω, *peiro*, and is made more emphatic by the addition of the preposition περι, *peri*. The word πείρω, *peiro*, means, properly, *to pierce through from one end to another*, and is applied to meat that is *pierced through* by the spit when it is to be roasted (Passow); then it means to pierce through and through. The addition of the preposition (περι) to the word, conveys the idea of doing this *all round;* of piercing everywhere. It was not a single thrust which was made, but they are gashed all round with penetrating wounds. Such is the effect on those who cast off religion for the sake of gold. None can avoid these consequences who do this. Every man is in the hands of a holy and just God, and sooner or later he *must* feel the effects of his sin and folly.

11. *But thou, O man of God, flee these things.* These allurements of wealth, and these sad consequences which the love of gold produces. ¶ *But follow after righteousness,* &c. Make these the grand object of your pursuit. On the virtues here enumerated, see Notes on Gal. v. 22, 23.

12. *Fight the good fight of faith.* The noble conflict in the cause of religion; see Notes on Eph. vi. 10–17; comp. Notes on 1 Cor. ix. 26, 27. The allusion is to the contests at the Grecian games. ¶ *Lay hold on eternal life.* As the crown of victory that is held out to you. Seize this as eagerly as the competitors at the Grecian games laid hold on the prize; see Notes on 1 Cor. ix. 25. ¶ *Whereunto thou art also called.* That is, by the Spirit of God, and by the very nature of your profession. God does not "*call*" his people that they may become rich; he does not convert them in order that they may devote themselves to the business of gain.

They are "called" to a higher and nobler work. Yet how many professing Christians there are who seem to live *as if* God had "called" them to the special business of making money, and who devote themselves to it with a zeal and assiduity that would do honour to such a calling, if this had been the grand object which God had in view in converting them! ¶ *And hast professed a good profession before many witnesses.* That is, either when he embraced the Christian religion, and made a public profession of it in the presence of the church and of the world; or when he was solemnly set apart to the ministry; or as he in his Christian life had been enabled publicly to evince his attachment to the Saviour. I see no reason to doubt that the apostle may have referred to the former, and that in early times a profession of religion may have been openly made before the church and the world. Such a method of admitting members to the church would have been natural, and would have been fitted to make a deep impression on others. It is a good thing often to remind professors of religion of the feelings which they had when they made a profession of religion; of the fact that the transaction was witnessed by the world; and of the promises which they then made to lead holy lives. One of the best ways of stimulating ourselves or others to the faithful performance of duty, is the remembrance of the vows then made; and one of the most effectual methods of reclaiming a backslider is to bring to his remembrance that solemn hour when he publicly gave himself to God.

13. *I give thee charge in the sight of God.* See Notes on chap. v. 21. ¶ *Who quickeneth all things.* Who gives *life* to all; Notes on Eph. ii. 1. It is not quite clear why the apostle refers to this attribute of God as en-

sight of God, who quickeneth all things, and *before* Christ Jesus, who *p* before Pontius Pilate witnessed a good [6] confession; 14 That thou keep *this* commandment without spot,[q] unrebuk-

p Jn.18.36,37.   6 or, *profession.*   q Phi.2.15.

forcing the charge which he here makes. Perhaps he means to say that God is the source of life, and that as he had given life to Timothy —natural and spiritual—he had a right to require that it should be employed in his service; and that, if, in obedience to this charge and in the performance of his duties, he should be required to lay down his life, he should bear in remembrance that God had power to raise him up again. This is more distinctly urged in 2 Tim. ii. 8–10. ¶ *And* before *Christ Jesus.* As in the presence of Christ, and stimulated by his example. ¶ *Who before Pontius Pilate witnessed a good confession.* Marg., *profession.* The same Greek word is used which in ver. 12 is translated *profession.* The reference is to the fact that the Lord Jesus, when standing at the bar of Pilate who claimed to have power over his life, did not shrink from an open avowal of the truth, John xviii. 36, 37. Nothing can be better fitted to preserve our minds steadfast in the faith, and to enable us to maintain our sacred vows in this world when allured by temptation, or when ridiculed for our religion, than to remember the example of the Lord Jesus. Let us place him before us as he stood at the bar of Pilate—threatened with death in its most appalling form, and ridiculed for the principles which he maintained; let us look on him, friendless and alone, and see with what seriousness, and sincerity, and boldness he stated *the simple truth* about himself, and we shall have one of the best securities that we can have that we shall not dishonour our profession. A clear view of the example of Christ our Saviour, in those circumstances, and a deep conviction that his eye is upon us to discern whether we are steadfast as he was, will do more than all abstract pre-

able *r* until the appearing of our Lord Jesus Christ: 15 Which in his times he shall show *who is* *s* the blessed and only Potentate, *r* the King of kings, and Lord of lords;

r 1 Th.5.23.   s ch.1.17.   t Re.17.14.

cepts to make us faithful to our Christian calling. 14. *That thou keep* this *commandment.* Referring particularly to the solemn injunction which he had just given him, to "fight the good fight of faith," but perhaps also including all that he had enjoined on him. ¶ *Without spot.* It seems harsh, and is unusual, to apply the epithet, "*without spot*" — ἄσπιλος — to a *command* or *doctrine,* and the passage may be so construed that this may be understood as referring to Timothy himself—"That thou keep the commandment so that thou mayest be without spot and unrebukable." See Bloomfield, *Crit. Dig., in loco.* The word here rendered "without spot," occurs in the New Testament only here and in James i. 27; 1 Pet. i. 19; 2 Pet. iii. 14. It means without any *stain* or *blemish; pure.* If applied here to *Timothy,* it means that he should so keep the command that there would be no stain on his moral character; if to the *doctrine,* that that should be kept pure. ¶ *Unrebukable.* So that there be no occasion for reproach or reproof; see Notes on Phil. ii. 15. ¶ *Until the appearing of our Lord Jesus Christ.* See Notes on 1 Thes. ii. 19; iv. 16; v. 23. 15. *Which in his times he shall show.* Which God will reveal at such times as he shall deem best. It is implied here that the time is unknown to men; see Notes on Acts i. 7. ¶ *Who is the blessed and only Potentate.* God, who is the ruler over all. The word used here—δυνάστης—means one who is *mighty* (Luke i. 22), then a prince or ruler; comp. Acts viii. 27. It is applied here to God as the mighty ruler over the universe. ¶ *The King of kings.* Who claims dominion over all the kings of the earth. In Rev. vii. 14, the same appellation is

16 Who only hath immortality, dwelling in *u*the light which no man can approach unto; *v*whom no man hath seen nor can see: *w*to whom *be* honour and power everlasting. Amen.

u Re.1.16,17   v Ex.33.20.
w Jude 25; Re.1.6.

17 Charge them that are rich in this world, that they be not high-minded, *x*nor trust in [7]uncertain riches, but in the living God, *y*who giveth us richly all things to enjoy;

x Ps.62.10.   7 the uncertainty of.
y Ec.5.18,19.

applied to the Lord Jesus, ascribing to him universal dominion. ¶ *Lord of lords.* The idea here is, that all the sovereigns of the earth are under his sway; that none of them can prevent the accomplishment of his purposes; and that he can direct the winding up of human affairs when he pleases.

16. *Who only hath immortality.* The word here—ἀθανασία—properly means *exemption from death,* and seems to mean that God, in his own nature, enjoys a perfect and certain exemption from death. Creatures have immortality only as they derive it from him, and of course are dependent on him for it. He has it by his very nature, and it is in his case underived, and he cannot be deprived of it. It is one of the essential attributes of his being, that he will always exist, and that *death* cannot reach him; comp. the expression in John v. 26, "The Father hath life in himself," and the Notes on that passage. ¶ *Dwelling in the light which no man can approach unto.* Gr., "inhabiting inapproachable light." The light where he dwells is so brilliant and dazzling that mortal eyes could not endure it. This is a very common representation of the dwelling place of God. See examples quoted in Pricæus, *in loco.* Heaven is constantly represented as a place of the most pure and brilliant light, needing not the light of the sun, or the moon, or the stars (Rev. xxi. 23, 24; xxii. 5), and God is represented as dwelling in that light, surrounded by amazing and inapproachable glory; comp. Rev. iv. 6; Ezek. i. 4; Heb. i. 3. ¶ *Whom no man hath seen nor can see.* Notes on John i. 18. ¶ *To whom be honour and power everlasting. Amen.* See Notes on Rom. xi. 36.

17. *Charge them that are rich in*

this world, that they be not high-minded. One of the evils to which they are particularly exposed. The idea is, that they should not value themselves on account of their wealth, or look down with pride and arrogance on their inferiors. They should not suppose that they are any better men, or any nearer heaven, because they are wealthy. Property really makes no distinction in the great things that pertain to character and salvation. It does not necessarily make one wise, or learned, or great, or good. In all these things, the man who has not wealth may be vastly the superior of him who has; and for so slight and unimportant a distinction as gold can confer, no man should be proud. Besides, let such a man reflect that his property is the gift of God; that he is made rich because God has chosen to arrange things so that he should be; that it is not primarily owing to any skill or wisdom which he has; that his property only increases his responsibility, and that it must all soon be left, and he be as poor as the "beggar that lies at his gate;" and he will see ample reason why he should not be proud. ¶ *Nor trust in uncertain riches.* Marg., *the uncertainty of.* The margin expresses the meaning of the Greek more accurately than the text, but the sense is not materially varied. Riches are uncertain because they may soon be taken away. No dependence can be placed on them in the emergencies of life. He who is rich to-day, has no security that he will be to-morrow; and if he *shall* be rich to-morrow, he has no certainty that his riches will meet his necessities then. A man whose house is in flames, or who is shipwrecked, or whose child lies dying, or who is himself in the agonies of death, can derive no advantage

18 That they do good, that they be rich in good works, ready to distribute, [8]willing to communicate;

19 Laying up in store for them-

[8] or, *sociable.*

---

from the fact that he is richer than other men; see Notes on Luke xii. 16–21. That against which Paul here directs Timothy to caution the rich, is that to which they are most exposed. A man who is rich, is very liable to "trust" in his riches, and to suppose that he needs nothing more; comp. Luke xii. 19. He feels that he is not dependent on his fellow-men, and he is very likely to feel that he is not dependent on God. It is for this cause that God has recorded so many solemn declarations in his word respecting the instability of riches (comp. Prov. xxiii. 5), and that he is furnishing so many instructive lessons in his providence, showing how easily riches may suddenly vanish away. ¶ *But in the living God.* (1) He is able to supply *all* our wants, and to do for us what riches cannot do; and (2) he never changes, or leaves those who put their trust in him. He is able to meet our wants if in the flames, or in a storm at sea, or when a friend dies, or when we lie down on a bed of death, or wherever we may be in the eternal world. ¶ *Who giveth us richly all things to enjoy.* The meaning of this seems to be, that God permits us to enjoy everything. Everything in the works of creation and redemption he has given to man for his happiness, and he should therefore trust in him. He has not merely given wealth for the comfort of men, but he has given everything, and he on whom so many and so great blessings have been bestowed for his comfort should trust in the great Benefactor himself, and not rely merely on one of his gifts; comp. Notes on 1 Cor. iii. 21–23.

18. *That they do good.* On the duty enjoined in this verse, see Notes on Gal. vi. 10; Heb. xiii. 16. ¶ *That they be rich in good works.* "That their good works may be as abundant as their riches." ¶ *Ready to distribute.* To divide with others; comp.

selves a good foundation against the time to come, that they may [z]lay hold on eternal life.

20 O Timothy, keep that which is committed to thy trust, avoiding

[z] Phi.3.14.

Acts iv. 34. The meaning is, that they should be liberal, or bountiful. ¶ *Willing to communicate.* Marg., or *sociable.* The translation in the text is a more correct rendering of the Greek. The idea is, that they should be willing to share their blessings with others, so as to make others comfortable; see Notes on Heb. xiii. 16; comp. the argument of Paul in 2 Cor. viii. 13–15, and the Notes on that passage.

19. *Laying up in store for themselves,* &c. The meaning of this verse is, that they were to make such a use of their property that it would contribute to their eternal welfare. It might be the means of exalted happiness and honour in heaven, if they would so use it as not to interfere with religion in the soul, and so as to do the most good possible. See the sentiment in this verse explained at length in the Notes on Luke xvi. 9.

20. *Keep that which is committed to thy trust. All* that is intrusted to you, and to which reference has been particularly made in this epistle. The honour of the gospel, and the interests of religion, had been specially committed to him; and he was sacredly to guard this holy trust, and not suffer it to be wrested from him. ¶ *Avoiding profane* and *vain babblings.* Gr., "profane, empty words." The reference is to such controversies and doctrines as tended only to produce strife, and were not adapted to promote the edification of the church; see Notes on chap. i. 4; iv. 7. ¶ *And oppositions of science falsely so called.* Religion has nothing to fear from *true* science, and the minister of the gospel is not exhorted to dread that. Real science, in all its advances, contributes to the support of religion; and just in proportion as that is promoted will it be found to sustain the Bible, and to confirm the claims of religion to the faith of mankind. See

profane[a] *and* vain babblings, and oppositions of science falsely so called:

21 Which some professing [b] have

a Tit.1.14.   b 2 Ti.2.18.

this illustrated at length in Wiseman's Lectures on the connection between science and religion. It is only false or pretended science that religion has to dread, and which the friend of Christianity is to avoid. The meaning here is, that Timothy was to avoid everything which *falsely* laid claim to being "knowledge" or "science." There was much of this in the world at the time the apostle wrote; and this, more perhaps than anything else, has tended to corrupt true religion since.

21. *Which some professing.* Evi-

erred concerning the faith. Grace *be* with thee. Amen.

The first to Timothy was written from Laodicea, which is the chiefest city of Phrygia Pacatiana.

dently some who professed to be true Christians. They were attracted by false philosophy, and soon, as a consequence, were led to deny the doctrines of Christianity. This result has not been uncommon in the world. ¶ *Have erred concerning the faith.* See Notes on chap. i. 6, 7; vi. 10. ¶ *Grace* be *with thee.* See Notes, Rom. i. 7.

On the subscription at the close of this epistle, see Intro. § 2. It is, like the other subscriptions at the close of the epistles, of no authority.

THE SECOND
EPISTLE OF PAUL TO TIMOTHY.

INTRODUCTION.

§ 1. *Time and place of writing the Epistle.*

THERE has been much diversity of sentiment on the question when this epistle was written. That it was written at Rome, and when the apostle was imprisoned there, is the unanimous opinion of all who have written on the epistle, and indeed is apparent on the face of it; see chap. i. 8, 16; iv. 6. But whether it was written during his first imprisonment there, or during a second imprisonment, is a question on which critics even now are by no means agreed. The most respectable names may be found on each side of this question, though the common opinion has been that it was during a second imprisonment. Of this opinion are Mosheim, Michaelis, Benson, Mill, Macknight, Le Clerc, Paley, Stuart, Clarke, and Doddridge. The reasons for this may be seen at length in Hug's *Introduction*, pp. 761–763, Macknight, and in Paley's *Horæ Paulinæ*. Dr. Lardner, Baronius, Witsius, Lightfoot, Hammond, Hug, Hemsen, and others, maintain that it was written during the first imprisonment, and that it was sent about the same time as the epistles to the Ephesians, Colossians, Philippians, and Philemon. The reasons for this opinion may be found in Hug's *Introduction*, pp. 556–559, and in Lardner, vol. vi. pp. 38–72. It is not consistent with the design of these Notes to go at length into an examination of this question, and it is not material in order to an exposition of the epistle.

After considering the reasonings of Lardner and Hug to prove that this epistle was written during Paul's first imprisonment at Rome—that is, as they suppose, during his *only* imprisonment there, and not long after the first epistle was written—it seems to me still that there are insuperable difficulties in such a view, and that the evidence is clear that it was during a second imprisonment. The reasons for this are briefly the following :—

(1) In the epistles to the Philippians and to Philemon, written during his first imprisonment, Paul confidently looked forward to a release, and to a speedy departure from Rome. In this, he had no such expectation. Thus, he tells the Philippians (ii. 24), "I trust in the Lord, that I myself shall come shortly;" see also chap. i. 24. In the Epistle to Philemon (ver. 22), he says, "But withal prepare me also a lodging': for I trust that through your prayers I shall be given unto you." In this epistle, however, the author had no such expectation; chap. iv. 6, "For I am now ready to be offered, and the time of my departure is at hand. I have fought a good fight, I have finished my course, I have kept the faith; henceforth there is laid up for me a crown of righteousness."

(2) In chap. iv. 16, the apostle uses the following language : "At my first answer, no man stood with me, but all forsook me." It is true that this *may*

refer to a hearing which he had had before Nero during the same imprisonment at Rome in which this second epistle was written; but the most natural interpretation is to suppose that he had had one hearing, and had been discharged, and that the imprisonment of which he speaks in this epistle was a second one. This seems to me to be confirmed by what he says in the next verse: "Notwithstanding, the Lord stood with me, and strengthened me; that by me the preaching might be fully known, and that all the Gentiles might hear; and I was delivered out of the mouth of the lion." Here it appears (a) that he had been delivered, on that occasion, from death—"I was delivered out of the mouth of the lion," which is equivalent to saying that he was discharged; (b) that after that discharge he was permitted to preach the gospel—"that by me the preaching might be fully known;" (c) that he had been permitted after that to travel and preach—"and that all the Gentiles might hear," which is just such an expression as he would use on the supposition that he had been discharged, and been permitted to go abroad and preach the gospel extensively, and is *not* such an expression as he could have used if he had been imprisoned but once.

(3) The expression occurring in chap. iv. 20, "Erastus *abode* at Corinth," implies that he had made a second journey to Rome. The word rendered "abode"—ἔμεινεν—is such as would be used where two were travelling together, and where one of them chose to *remain* at a certain place. It implies that, at the time referred to, the two were together, and that one chose to go on, and the other to remain. But it is capable of very clear proof that, when Paul was sent to Rome by Festus (Acts xxvi. xxvii.), he did not stop at Corinth; and if Erastus had been with him then, he would have passed by that place with him on his way to Rome. Further, when Paul left Corinth, as related in Acts xx., on his way to Jerusalem, Timothy was with him. This is the last time that Paul is mentioned as having been at Corinth before coming to Rome, and there could have been no need of informing Timothy of the fact that Erasmus remained there, if this were so, because that fact would be known to Timothy as well as Paul. Besides, that departure from Corinth took place some five years before Paul wrote this Second Epistle to Timothy; and what would be the use of his reminding Timothy of this after so long an interval? It is clear, moreover, that Paul refers to some *recent* transaction. He is urging Timothy to use all diligence to come to him before winter; that is, as soon as possible, chap. iv. 21. But how could it be a reason for this urgency to say that, *some five years before*, he had been forsaken by one fellow-labourer, and had been obliged to leave another one sick on the way?

(4) Similar remarks may be made respecting what Paul says in the close of the same verse (chap. iv. 20): "Trophimus have I left at Miletum sick." Paul, when sent by Festus to Rome, did not stop at Miletus; for the course which the ship took on that occasion is minutely described (Acts xxvii.), and there is every certainty that there can be that it did not put in at that place. The time, then, to which Paul must refer here, unless he made a second journey to Rome after he had been once discharged, must have been several years before; certainly as far back as when he took leave of the elders of the church of Ephesus, as recorded in Acts xx. But this was about five years before; and what would have been the pertinency of informing

Timothy that, some five years before, he had left a fellow-labourer sick there, as a reason why he should then hasten to Rome as soon as possible? It was evidently a recent occurrence to which the apostle refers here; and the only natural supposition is, that, not long before his arrival at Rome, he had parted with both these friends, and now needed, in consequence, especially the presence of Timothy. Of course, if this be so, Paul must have made another circuit through these countries, of which the Acts of the Apostles gives us no account, and which must have been after his first imprisonment. It is true that Hug suggests that the word rendered "I have left"—ἀπέλιπον—may be in the third person plural, and may be rendered "they have left." But, who left him there? We are not told; and as "nothing is suggested in the context which would supply us with a subject of the verb in the *third person plural*, we are led naturally to construe it of the *first* person singular, and, consequently, to apply it to Paul" (Prof. Stuart, in Hug's *Intro.*).

(5) With this supposition of a second and recent journey, agrees the passage in 2 Tim. iv. 13, "The cloak which I left at Troas with Carpus, when thou comest, bring with thee, and the books, but especially the parchments." This evidently refers to some recent affair. Can it be believed that these had been there for some five years, and that Paul had not needed them before? He was two years at Cæsarea. He had abundant opportunity of sending for them. An article of wearing apparel, or books to study, or his own writings, he would be likely to need long before, and it is highly improbable that he should have suffered them to remain during this long period without sending for them.

(6) In the epistles which were written during Paul's first imprisonment, certain persons are referred to as being then with him, who are in this epistle mentioned as absent. It is almost beyond a doubt that the epistles to the Ephesians, Philippians, Colossians, and to Philemon, were written during Paul's first imprisonment at Rome; see the Introduction to those epistles. In the Epistle to the Colossians (i. 1), Timothy is mentioned as being then with the apostle. When this was written, of course he was absent. In the same epistle, Mark is mentioned as with Paul, and unites with him in the salutation to the Colossians (chap. iv. 10); when this epistle was written, he was absent, for Timothy is ordered to bring him with him (chap. iv. 11). Demas was then with him (Col. iv. 14); now he was absent, for Paul say, "Demas hath forsaken me, having loved this present world, and is departed unto Thessalonica," chap. iv. 10. These circumstances make it quite clear that the Second Epistle to Timothy was not written during the imprisonment at Rome in which the epistles to the Colossians, to Philemon, &c., were written, unless a change had taken place in the circumstances of the apostle, which we have no reason to suppose occurred. The probability, then, seems to be strong, that the apostle was imprisoned there a second time, and that the things referred to in this epistle occurred then.

(7) To these circumstances should be added the fact, that many of the Fathers say that Paul was liberated from his *first* imprisonment, and afterwards travelled extensively in preaching the gospel. This testimony is borne by Eusebius, Chrysostom, Theodoret, and others; see Calmet's *Dictionary*, and *Lives of the Apostles*, by D. F. Bacon, New Haven, pp. 619-

621.—If the supposition of a second imprisonment at Rome, during which this epistle was written, is correct, then it was written probably not far from the year 65. Lardner, however, who supposes it was written during the first imprisonment, places its date in May, A.D. 61; Hug, also, in the same year.

§ 2. *The place where Timothy was when the Epistle was addressed to him.*

There can be little doubt that Timothy was at Ephesus at the time when this epistle was addressed to him. The evidence for this opinion is thus stated by Lightfoot and others:—(1) Paul directs Timothy to salute the household of Onesiphorus, chap. iv. 19. But it is evident, from chap. i. 18, that Onesiphorus was an Ephesian, and, as the direction is to salute his "*household*," it may be argued with the more certainty that Timothy was then at Ephesus, the ordinary residence of the family of Onesiphorus. (2) He directs Timothy to take Troas in the way as he came to him at Rome (chap. iv. 13), which was the way that Paul had gone to Ephesus (2 Cor. ii. 12; Acts xx. 5), thus showing that this was the usual route of travel, and was a way which Timothy would naturally take in passing from Ephesus to Rome. It is true that this does not absolutely prove that he was at *Ephesus*—since, if he had been in any other part of the western portion of Asia Minor, the direction would have been the same—but it is a slight circumstance corroborating others. (3) He warns him to beware of Alexander (chap. iv. 14), who we know was an Ephesian, 1 Tim. i. 20; Acts xix. 33. (4) In chap. iv. 9, he gives direction to Timothy to come to him as soon as possible, and then adds (ver. 12), "Tychicus have I sent to Ephesus." From this it would seem that one reason why he wished him then to come was, that he had appointed one to occupy his place there, so that he could leave without injury to the cause. But it would seem also probable that Paul was not in the habit of calling away a labourer from an important station without supplying his place. Thus, in Titus iii. 12, he says, "When I shall send Artemas unto thee, or Tychicus, be diligent to come unto me." It may thence be inferred that Timothy was at Ephesus at the time when Paul wrote to him, and that he had taken care that his place should not be left vacant, by the appointment of Tychicus to fill it when he should leave. (5) It may be added, that the errors and vices which Timothy is directed to oppose, are the same which are referred to in the first epistle, and it may be hence inferred that he was at the same place.

How long Timothy had been in Ephesus is not certainly known, and is not material to be known in order to a proper understanding of the epistle. It does not appear, from the Acts, that he was with Paul during the two years in which he was in Cæsarea, nor during his voyage to Rome; yet it is certain that he was in Rome when Paul wrote to the Philippians, to the Colossians, and to Philemon, because he is named in the titles to those epistles. In Heb. xiii. 23, Paul says that Timothy was "set at liberty," or, more probably, "sent away" (see Notes on that verse), but to what place he had gone is not mentioned. Nothing would be more natural, however, than that he should visit Ephesus again, and it is not improbable that Paul would leave him there when he again visited Rome.

§ 3. *The occasion on which the Epistle was written.*

The epistle was evidently written when the apostle was expecting soon to be put to death, chap. iv. 6–8. The main object of writing it seems to have been to request Timothy to come to him as speedily as possible, chap. iv. 9. But, in doing this, it was natural that Paul should accompany the request with such counsel as Timothy needed, and such as it was proper for Paul to give in probably the last letter that he would write to him. The particular *reason* why the apostle desired the presence of Timothy seems to have been, that nearly all the others on whom he might have supposed he could rely in à time of trial, had left him. Thus he says that Demas had forsaken him; Crescens had gone to Galatia; Titus to Dalmatia, and Tychicus he had himself sent to Ephesus, chap. iv. 10–12. No one remained with him but Luke (chap. iv. 11), and he was, therefore, desirous that Timothy and Mark should be with him, chap. iv. 11. He did not ask their presence merely that they might sustain him in his trials, but that they might aid him in the work of the ministry (chap. iv. 11), for it would seem that all hope of doing good in Rome was not closed.

If the view of the time when this epistle was written which has been taken in this introduction is correct, and if this is the last epistle which was written by the Apostle Paul before his martyrdom, then it occupies a very important place in the sacred canon, and is invested with great interest. It may be regarded as the dying counsels of the most eminent of the apostles to one who had just entered on the ministerial life. We should read it with the interest with which we do the last words of the great and the good. Then we feel that every word which they utter has a weight which demands attention. We feel that, whatever a man might do at other times, he will not trifle then. We feel that, having little time to express his wishes, he will select topics that lie nearest his heart, and that he deems most important. There is no more interesting position in which we can be placed, than when we sit down at such a man's feet, and listen to his parting counsels. To a young minister of the gospel, therefore, this epistle is invaluable; to any and every Christian, it cannot fail to be a matter of interest to listen to the last words of the great apostle of the Gentiles, and to ponder his last written testimony in favour of that religion to the promulgation of which he had devoted his talents and his life.

THE SECOND

EPISTLE OF PAUL TO TIMOTHY.

CHAPTER I.

PAUL, an apostle of Jesus Christ by the will of God, according

CHAPTER I.

ANALYSIS OF THE CHAPTER.

The principal design of this chapter is to exhort Timothy to steadfastness and fidelity as a Christian and a minister; and to entreat him to adhere to the truth, and live as became a Christian, in the midst of all the temptations by which he was surrounded, and while so many were turning away from the Christian faith. Timothy was young; he was exposed, like others, to trials; he could not be unaware that not a few had apostatized; he knew that his father in Christ was in bonds, and he was liable to become disheartened, or to be led astray. In these circumstances, the apostle seems to have resolved to place before him strong reasons to induce him to devote himself steadfastly to the cause of religion, and not to allow those things which might tend to alienate him from Christianity to have any effect on his mind. After the usual salutations, therefore (ver. 1, 2), he proceeds to present these considerations to the mind of Timothy: (1) He commences the chapter with *delicate praise* of his young friend —one of the most happy methods of inducing him to persevere in the course of life on which he had entered, ver. 3–5. We naturally desire to perfect that in which we already excel; we feel encouraged for future efforts in a cause in which we have already been successful. The apostle, therefore, reminds Timothy of the manner in which he had

to [a] the promise of life which is in Christ Jesus,

been trained; of the piety of his mother and grandmother, and assures him of his belief that their efforts to train him up in the ways of religion had not been in vain. (2) He urges various considerations to induce him not to turn away from that holy purpose to which he had devoted himself. The considerations which he urges, are these: (*a*) he had been solemnly consecrated to the work of preaching the gospel, ver. 6; (*b*) God had imparted to him, as to others, a spirit of love and power, and a sound mind, ver. 7; (*c*) the grace of God had called him to his great work, and he possessed that gospel by which life and immortality are brought to light, ver. 8–11; (*d*) Paul urges his own example, and says that, amidst all his own trials, he had never seen occasion to be ashamed of the gospel, ver. 12–14; and (*e*) he reminds Timothy that all his other friends in Asia had turned away from him, specifying two of them, and urges him, therefore, to maintain a steadfast attachment to the principles which he had professed, ver. 15. (3) The chapter closes with the expression of an earnest prayer that the Lord would bless the family of Onesiphorus, and with a grateful mention of his kindness to him, ver. 16–18.

1. *Paul, an apostle of Jesus Christ.* Notes, Rom. i. 1. ¶ *By the will of God.* Called to be an apostle in accordance with the divine will and purpose; Notes, Gal. i. 1. ¶ *According to the promise of life which is in Christ Jesus.* In accordance with the great promise of eternal life through the Saviour; that is, he was called to be

2 To Timothy, *my* dearly be-loved son: Grace, mercy, *and* peace, from God the Father and Christ Jesus our Lord.

3 I thank God, *c* whom I serve from *my* forefathers *d* with pure conscience, that without ceasing I

have remembrance of thee in my prayers night and day;

4 Greatly *e* desiring to see thee, being mindful of thy tears, that I may be filled with joy;

5 When I call to remembrance *f* the unfeigned faith that is in thee,

b 1 Ti.1,2.   *c* Ac.23.1.   *d* He.13.18.

e ch.4.9,21.   *f* 1 Ti.4.6.

an apostle to carry out the great pur-pose of human salvation; comp. Eph. iii. 6. God has made a promise of life to mankind through faith in the Lord Jesus, and it was with reference to this that he was called to the apos-tleship.

2. *To Timothy, my dearly beloved son.* Notes, 1 Tim. i. 2. ¶ *Grace, mercy, and peace*, &c. See Notes on Rom. i. 7.

3. *I thank God, whom I serve from my forefathers.* Paul reckoned among his forefathers the patriarchs and the holy men of former times, as being of the same nation with himself, though it may be that he also included his more immediate ancestors, who, for anything known to the contrary, may have been distinguished examples of piety. His own parents, it is certain, took care that he should be trained up in the ways of religion; comp. Notes on Phil. iii. 4, 5; Acts xxvi. 4, 5. The phrase "from my forefathers," probably means, after the *example* of my ancestors. He worshipped the same God; he held substantially the same truths; he had the same hope of the resurrection and of immortality; he trusted to the same Saviour *having come*, on whom they relied as *about to come*. His was not, therefore, a different religion from theirs; it was the same religion carried out and perfected. The religion of the Old Testament and the New is essentially the same; see Notes on Acts xxiii. 6. ¶ *With pure conscience.* See Notes on Acts xxiii. 1. ¶ *That without ceasing.* Comp. Notes on Rom. xii. 12; 1 Thes. v. 17. ¶ *I have remembrance of thee in my prayers night and day.* See Notes, Phil. i. 3, 4.

4. *Greatly desiring to see thee.* See chap. iv. 9, 21. It was probably on account of this earnest desire that

this epistle was written. He wished to see him, not only on account of the warm friendship which he had for him, but because he would be useful to him in his present circumstances; see Intro. § 3. ¶ *Being mindful of thy tears.* Alluding probably to the tears which he shed at parting from him. The occasion to which he re-fers is not mentioned; but nothing is more probable than that Timothy would weep when separated from *such* a father and friend. It is not wrong thus to weep, for religion is not in-tended to make us stoics or savages. ¶ *That I may be filled with joy.* By seeing you again. It is easy to im-agine what joy it would give Paul, then a prisoner, and forsaken by nearly all his friends, and about to die, to see a friend whom he loved as he did this young man. Learn hence, that there *may be* very pure and warm friendship between an old and young man, and that the warmth of true friendship is not diminished by the near prospect of death.

5. *When I call to remembrance the unfeigned faith that is in thee.* Notes, 1 Tim. i. 5. On the faith of Timothy, see Notes on 1 Tim. iv. 6. ¶ *Which dwelt first in thy grandmother Lois.* That is, the same faith dwelt in her; or, she was a sincere believer in Christ. It would seem probable, from this, that she was the first of the family who had been converted. In the Acts of the Apostles (xvi. 1), we have an account of the family of Timothy:—"Then came he to Derbe and Lystra; and behold a certain disciple was there, named Timotheus, the son of a certain woman which was a Jewess, and believed; but his father was a Greek." In this account no mention is made of the grandmother Lois, but there is no improbability in

which dwelt first in thy grandmother Lois, *g* and thy mother
Eunice; and I am persuaded that
in thee also.

g Ac.16.1.

supposing that Paul was better acquainted with the family than Luke.
There is, at anyrate, no contradiction between the two accounts; but
the one confirms the other, and the
"undesigned coincidence" furnishes
an argument for the authenticity of
both. See Paley's *Horæ Paulinæ*,
in loco. As the mother of Timothy
was a Hebrew, it is clear that his
grandmother was also. Nothing more
is known of her than is here mentioned. ¶ *And in thy mother Eunice.*
In Acts xvi. 1, it is said that the
mother of Timothy was "a Jewess,
and believed;" but her name is not
mentioned. This shows that Paul
was acquainted with the family, and
that the statement in the Epistle to
Timothy was not forged from the account in the Acts. Here is another
"undesigned coincidence." In the
history in the Acts, nothing is said of
the father, except that he was "a
Greek," but it is implied that he
was not a believer. In the epistle
before us, nothing *whatever* is said of
him. But the piety of his mother
alone is commended, and it is fairly
implied that his father was *not* a believer. This is one of those coincidences on which Paley has constructed
his beautiful argument in the *Horæ
Paulinæ* in favour of the genuineness
of the New Testament.

6. *That thou stir up the gift of
God.* Gr., That thou *kindle up* as a
fire. The original word used here
denotes the kindling of a fire, as by
bellows, &c. It is not uncommon to
compare piety to a flame or a fire,
and the image is one that is obvious
when we speak of causing that to
burn more brightly. The idea is,
that Timothy was to use all proper
means to keep the flame of pure religion in the soul burning, and more
particularly his zeal in the great cause
to which he had been set apart. The
agency of man himself is needful to
keep the religion of the heart warm

6 Wherefore I put thee in remembrance that thou stir up *h* the
gift of God, which is in thee by
the putting on of my hands.

h 1 Ti.4 14.

and glowing. However rich the gifts
which God has bestowed upon us,
they do not grow of their own accord,
but need to be cultivated by our own
personal care. ¶ *Which is in thee
by the putting on of my hands.* In
connection with the presbytery; see
Notes on 1 Tim. iv. 14. This proves
that Paul took part in the ordination
of Timothy; but it does *not* prove
either that he performed the duty
alone, or that the "ordaining virtue,"
whatever that was, was imparted by
him only; for (1) it is expressly said
(1 Tim. iv. 14), that he was ordained
by the laying on of the hands of the
presbytery, of which Paul was doubtless one; and (2) the language here
used, "by the putting on of *my* hands,"
is just such as Paul, or any other one
of the presbytery, would use in referring to the ordination of Timothy,
though they were all regarded as on
a level. It is such an expression as
an aged Presbyterian, or Congregational, or Baptist minister would address to a son whom he had assisted
to ordain. Nothing would be more
natural than to remind him that *his
own* hands had been laid on him when
he was set apart to the work of the
ministry. It would be in the nature
of a tender, pathetic, and solemn appeal, bringing all that there was in
his own character, age, and relation
to the other, to bear on him, in order
to induce him to be faithful to his
trust. On other occasions he would
naturally remind him that *others* had
united with him in the act, and that
he had derived his authority through
the presbytery, just as Paul appeals
to Timothy, 1 Tim. iv. 14. But no
one would now think of inferring from
this, that he meant to be understood
as saying that he alone had ordained
him, or that all the authority for
preaching the gospel had been imparted through *his* hands, and that
those who were associated with him
only expressed "*concurrence;*" that

7 For[i] God hath not given us the spirit of fear; [k]but of power, and of love, and of a sound mind.

8 Be not thou therefore ashamed of the testimony of our Lord, nor

i Ro.8.15; 1 Jn.4.18.   k Lu.24.49.

is, that their presence there was only an unmeaning ceremony. . What *was* the "gift of God" which had been conferred in this way, Paul specifies in the next verse. It is "the spirit of power, and of love, and of a sound mind." The meaning is, that these had been conferred by God, and that the gift had been recognized by his ordination. It does not imply that any mysterious influence had gone from the hands of the ordainers, imparting any holiness to Timothy which he had not before. 7. *For God hath not given us the spirit of fear.* A timorous and servile spirit. This is said in order to encourage Timothy, who was not improbably modest and diffident. ¶ *But of power.* Power to encounter foes and dangers; power to bear up under trials; power to triumph in persecutions. That is, it is the nature of the gospel to inspire the mind with holy courage; comp., however, Luke xxiv. 49. ¶ *And of love.* Love to God and to the souls of men. The tendency of *this*, also, is to "cast out fear" (1 John iv. 18), and to make the mind bold and constant. Nothing will do more to inspire courage, to make a man fearless of danger, or ready to endure privation and persecution, than *love.* The love of country, and wife, and children, and home, makes the most timid bold when they are assailed; and the love of Christ and of a dying world nerves the soul to great enterprises, and sustains it in the deepest sorrows. ¶ *And of a sound mind.* The Greek word denotes one of sober mind; a man of prudence and discretion. The state referred to here is that in which the mind is well balanced, and under right influences; in which it sees things in their just proportions and relations; in which it is not feverish and excited, but when everything is in its

of me his prisoner: [l]but be thou partaker of the afflictions of the gospel according to the power of God:

9 Who[m] hath saved us, [n]and called us with an holy calling,

l Col.1.24.   m Mat.1.21.   n Ro.8.28,30.

proper place. It was this state of mind which Timothy was exhorted to cultivate; this which Paul regarded as so necessary to the performance of the duties of his office. It is as needful now for the minister of religion as it was then.

8. *Be not thou therefore ashamed of the testimony of our Lord.* Do not be ashamed to bear your testimony to the doctrines taught by the Lord Jesus, John iii. 11, 32, 33; vii. 7; comp. Acts x. 22; xx. 24; 1 Cor. i. 6; Rev. xxii. 16. Paul seems to have apprehended that Timothy was in some danger of being ashamed of this gospel, or of shrinking back from its open avowal in the trials and persecutions to which he now saw it exposed him. ¶ *Nor of me his prisoner.* Of the testimony which I have borne to the truth of the gospel. This passage proves that, when Paul wrote this epistle, he was in confinement; comp. Eph. iii. 1; vi. 20; Phil. i. 13, 14, 16; Col. iv. 3, 18; Philem. 9. Timothy knew that he had been thrown into prison on account of his love for the gospel. To avoid that himself, there might be some danger that a timid young man might shrink from an open avowal of his belief in the same system of truth. ¶ *But be thou partaker of the afflictions of the gospel.* The sufferings to which the profession of the gospel may expose you; comp. Notes on Col. i. 24. ¶ *According to the power of God.* That is, according to the power which God gives to those who are afflicted on account of the gospel. The apostle evidently supposes that they who were subjected to trials on account of the gospel, might look for divine strength to uphold them, and asks him to endure those trials, relying on that strength, and not on his own.

9. *Who hath saved us.* Notes, Mat.

not*o* according to our works, but according*p* to his own purpose and grace, which was given us

o Tit.3.5.   *p* De.7.7,8; Ep.1.9,11.

in Christ Jesus, *q*before the world began;

10 But is *r*now made manifest

q Ep.1.4.   *r* 1 Pe.1.20.

i. 21. He has brought us into a state in which salvation is so certain, that Paul could speak of it as if it were already done. ¶ *And called us.* Notes, Rom. viii. 28, 30. ¶ *With an holy calling.* A calling which is in its own nature holy, and which leads to holiness; comp. Notes on Eph. iv. 1; Phil. iii. 14; Heb. iii. 1. ¶ *Not according to our works.* Titus iii. 5; Notes, Eph. ii. 8, 9. The idea is, that our own works have nothing to do in inducing God to call us. As, when we *become* Christians, he does not choose us *because* of our works, so the eternal purpose in regard to our salvation could not have been formed because he foresaw that we *would* perform such works as would be a reason why he should choose us. The whole arrangement was irrespective of our deserts. ¶ *But according to his own purpose and grace.* See Notes on Rom. ix. 11–13, 16; Eph. i. 4, 5. ¶ *Which was given us in Christ Jesus, before the world began.* That is, which he *intended* to give us, for it was not then *actually* given. The thing was so certain in the divine purposes, that it might be said to be already done; comp. Notes, Rom. iv. 17.

10. *But is now made manifest.* The purpose to save us was long concealed in the divine mind, but the Saviour came that he might make it known. ¶ *Who hath abolished death.* That is, he has made it so certain that death *will be* abolished, that it may be spoken of as already done. It is remarkable how often, in this chapter, Paul speaks of what God *intends* to do as so certain, that it may be spoken of as a thing that is already done. On the meaning of the expression here, see Notes on 1 Cor. xv. 54; comp. Notes on Heb. ii. 14. The meaning is, that, through the gospel, death will cease to reign, and over those who are saved there will be no such thing as we now understand by dying. ¶ *And hath brought*

life and immortality to light through the gospel. This is one of the great and glorious achievements of the gospel, and one of the things by which it is distinguished from every other system. The word rendered "hath brought to light"—φωτίζω—means to give light, to shine; then to give light to, to shine upon; and then to bring to light, to make known (Rob. *Lex.*). The sense is, that these things were before obscure or unknown, and that they have been disclosed to us by the gospel. It is, of course, not meant that there were *no* intimations of these truths before, or that *nothing* was known of them—for the Old Testament shed some light on them; but that they are fully disclosed to man in the gospel. It is there that all ambiguity and doubt are removed, and that the evidence is so clearly stated as to leave no doubt on the subject. The intimations of a future state, among the wisest of the heathen, were certainly very obscure, and their hopes very faint. The hope of a future state is styled by Cicero, Futurorum quoddam augurium sæculorum—*a conjecture* or *surmise of future ages* (*Tusc. Q.* 1). Seneca says it is "that which our wise men do promise, but they do not prove" (*Epis.* 102). Socrates, even at his death, said, "I hope to go hence to good men, but of that I am not very confident; nor doth it become any wise man to be positive that so it will be. I must now die, and you shall live; but which of us is in the better state, the living or the dead, God only knows." Pliny says, "Neither soul nor body has any more sense after death, than before it was born." Cicero begins his discourse on the subject with a profession that he intended to deliver nothing as fixed and certain, but only as probable, and as having some likelihood of truth. And, having mentioned the different sentiments of philosophers, he concludes —"Which of these opinions is true,

by the appearing of our Saviour Jesus Christ, *who hath abolished death, *and hath brought life and immortality to light through the gospel :

s 1 Co.15.54.   *t* Jn.5.24-29.

some god must tell us; which is most like to truth, is a great question." See Whitby, *in loco.* Such doubts existed in regard to the immortality of the *soul;* but of the resurrection and future life of the *body*, they had no conception whatever; comp. Acts xvii. 32. With what propriety, then, may it be said that these doctrines were brought to light through the gospel! Man would never have known them if it had not been for revelation. The word "*life*," here, refers undoubtedly to life in the future world. The question was, whether man would live at all; and that question has been determined by the gospel. The word "immortality" means, properly, *incorruption, incapacity of decay;* and may be applied either to the body or the soul. See it explained in the Notes on 1 Cor. xv. 42. It is used in reference to the *body*, in 1 Cor. xv. 42, 53, 54; in Rom. ii. 7, it is applied to the future state of rewards, without special reference to the body or soul. Here it seems to refer to the future state as that in which there will be no corruption or decay. Many suppose that the phrase "life and immortality," here, is used by hendiadys (two things for one), as meaning' immortal or incorruptible life. The gospel thus has truths not found in any other system, and contains what man never would have discovered of himself. As fair a trial had been made among the philosophers of Greece and Rome as could be made to determine whether the unaided powers of the human mind could arrive at these great truths; and their most distinguished philosophers confessed that they could arrive at no certainty on the subject. In this state of things, the gospel comes and reveals truths worthy of all acceptation; sheds light where man had desired it; solves the great problems which had for ages perplexed the

11 Whereunto I am appointed a preacher, and an apostle, and a teacher of the Gentiles.

12 For the which cause I also suffer these things : nevertheless

human mind, and discloses to man all that he could wish—that not only the soul will live for ever, but that the body will be raised from the grave, and that the entire man will become immortal. How strange it is that men will not embrace the gospel! Socrates and Cicero would have hailed its light, and welcomed its truths, as those which their whole nature panted to know.

11. *Whereunto I am appointed a preacher.* That is, I am appointed to make these truths known; see Notes on Eph. iii. 7, 8.

12. *For the which cause I also suffer these things.* That is, I suffer on account of my purpose to carry the gospel to the Gentiles; see Notes on Col. i. 24. ¶ *Nevertheless I am not ashamed.* Comp. Notes on Rom. i. 16. ¶ *For I know whom I have believed.* Marg., *trusted.* The idea is, that he understood the character of that Redeemer to whom he had committed his eternal interests, and knew that he had no reason to be ashamed of confiding in him. He was able to keep all that he had intrusted to his care, and would not suffer him to be lost; see Isa. xxviii. 16. ¶ *And am persuaded that he is able to keep that which I have committed unto him.* That is, the soul, with all its immortal interests. A man has nothing of higher value to intrust to another than the interests of his soul, and there is no other act of confidence like that in which he intrusts the keeping of that soul to the Son of God. Learn hence, (1) That religion consists in committing the soul to the care of the Lord Jesus; because, (*a*) we feel that we cannot secure its salvation ourselves; (*b*) it is by nature in danger; (*c*) if not saved by him, it will not be saved at all. (2) That it is a great and invaluable treasure which is committed to him. (*a*) No higher treasure can be committed to another;

I*u* am not ashamed: for I know whom I have ¹believed, and am persuaded that he is able to keep

that *v*which I have committed unto him against that day.

13 Hold *w* fast *x* the form of

u Ro.1.16.   ¹ or, *trusted.*

v 1 Pe.4.19.   *w* Re.2.25.   *x* Ro.6.17.

(*b*) in connection with that the whole question of our happiness on earth and in heaven is intrusted to him, and all depends on his fidelity. (3) It is done by the true Christian with the most entire confidence, so that the mind is at rest. The *grounds* of this confidence are—(*a*) what is said of the mighty *power* of the Saviour; (*b*) his promises that he *will* keep all who confide in him (comp. John x. 27-29); (*c*) experience—the fact that those who *have* trusted in him have have found that he is able to keep them. (4) This act of committing the soul, with all its interests, to the Saviour, is the true source of peace in the trials of life. This is so because, (*a*) having done this, we feel that our *great* interests are secure. If the *soul* is safe, why need we be disturbed by the loss of health, or property, or other temporal comforts? Those are secondary things. A man who is shipwrecked, and who sees his son or daughter safe with him on the shore, will be little concerned that a casket of jewels fell overboard, however valuable it might be. (*b*) All those trials will soon pass away, and he will be safe in heaven. (*c*) These very things *may* further the great object—the salvation of the soul. A man's great interests *may* be more safe when in a prison than when in a palace; on a pallet of straw than on a bed of down; when *constrained* to say, "Give us this day our daily bread," than when encompassed with the wealth of Crœsus. ¶ *Against that day.* The day of judgment—called "*that* day," without anything further to designate it, because it is *the* great day; "the day for which all other days were made." It seems to have been so much the object of thought and conversation among the early Christians, that the apostle supposed that he would be understood by merely referring to it as "*that* day;" that is, the day which they

were always preaching about, and talking about, and thinking about. 13. *Hold fast the form of sound words.* See Notes, 1 Tim. i. 3. On the Greek word here rendered "*form*," see Notes on 1 Tim. i. 16, where it is rendered *pattern.* The word means a form, sketch, or imperfect delineation—an outline. Grotius says that it here means "an exemplar, but an exemplar fixed in the mind—an idea." Calvin says that the command is that he should adhere to the doctrine which he had learned, not only in its substance but in its form. Archbishop Tillotson explains this as meaning the profession of faith which was made by Christians at baptism. There seems to be an allusion to some summary or outline of truth which Paul had given to Timothy, though there is no evidence that it was written. Indeed, there is every presumption that, if it refers to such a summary, it was *not* committed to writing. If it had been, it would have been regarded as inspired, and would have taken its place in the canon of Scripture. It may be presumed that almost none of the sacred writings would have been more sacredly preserved than such a condensed summary of Christian truth. But there is no improbability in supposing that Paul, either at his ordination, or on some other occasion, may have stated the outlines of the Christian religion to Timothy, that he might have a clear and connected view of the subject. The passage, therefore, may be used as an argument for the propriety of some brief summary of doctrine as a matter of convenience, though not as having binding authority on the consciences of others. ¶ *Of sound words.* Comp. Notes on 1 Tim. vi. 3. The Greek is the same in both places. ¶ *Which thou hast heard of me.* This proves that he does not refer to a *written* creed, since what he refers to was something which he had *heard.* ¶ *In faith and love which*

sound[y] words, which thou hast heard of me, in faith and love which is in Christ Jesus.

14 That[z] good thing which was committed unto thee, keep by the Holy Ghost which dwelleth in us.

15 This thou knowest, that

[y] 1 Ti.6.3.　　[z] 1 Ti.6.20.　　[a] Ac.19.10.

[a]all they which are in Asia be [b]turned away from me; of whom are Phygellus and Hermogenes.

16 The Lord give mercy unto the house of [c]Onesiphorus; for he oft refreshed me, and was not ashamed of [d]my chain.

[b] ch.4.10,16.　　[c] ch.4.19.　　[d] Ac.28.20.

---

is in Christ Jesus. Hold these truths with sincere faith in the Lord Jesus, and with that love which is the best evidence of attachment to him.

14. *That good thing which was committed unto thee.* See Notes, 1 Tim. vi. 20. The reference here in the phrase, "that good thing committed to thee," is to the sound Christian doctrine with which he had been intrusted, and which he was required to transmit to others. ¶ *Keep by the Holy Ghost.* By the aid of the Holy Ghost. One of the best methods of preserving the knowledge and the love of truth is to cherish the influences of the Holy Spirit.

15. *This thou knowest, that all they which are in Asia be turned away from me.* That is, in that part of Asia Minor of which Ephesus was the capital. The name Asia was often given particularly to that part of Asia Minor; see Notes on Acts ii. 9; xvi. 6. This passage proves that Timothy was somewhere in that region when this epistle was written to him, for otherwise he could not be supposed to "know" what is here said. When Paul says that "*all*" were turned away from him, he must use the word in a general sense, for he immediately specifies *one* who had been faithful and kind to him. ¶ *Of whom are Phygellus and Hermogenes.* We know nothing of these individuals but what is here mentioned. It would seem that they were prominent persons, and those from whom the apostle had a right to expect other treatment. "The ecclesiastical traditions allege that they were of the seventy disciples, and in the end became followers of Simon Magus. We imagine that this is little more than conjecture" (*Pict. Bib.*). It is a sad thing when the *only* record made of a man—the

only evidence which we have that he ever lived at all—is, that he turned away from a friend, or forsook the paths of true religion. And yet, there are many men of whom the only thing to be remembered of them is, that they lived to do wrong.

16. *The Lord give mercy unto the house of Onesiphorus.* The *family* of Onesiphorus—for so the word *house* is often used. He was himself still living (ver. 18), but not improbably then absent from his home; comp. chap. iv. 19. He was evidently of Asia, and is the only one who is mentioned from that region who had showed the apostle kindness in his trials. He is mentioned only in this epistle, and nothing more is known of him. The record is entirely honourable to him, and for his family the apostle felt a warm interest on account of the kindness which he had showed to him in prison. The ecclesiastical traditions also state that *he* was one of the seventy disciples, and was ultimately Bishop of Corone. But there is no evidence of this. There is much force in the remark of the editor of the *Pictorial Bible*, that "the pretended lists of the seventy disciples seem to have been made out on the principle of including all the names incidentally mentioned in the sacred books, and not otherwise appropriated." ¶ *For he oft refreshed me.* That is, showed me kindness and ministered to my wants. ¶ *And was not ashamed of my chain.* Was not ashamed to be known as a friend of one who was a prisoner on account of religion. Paul was bound with a chain when a prisoner at Rome, Phil. i. 13, 14, 16; Col. iv. 3, 18; Philem. 10; Notes, Acts xxviii. 20.

17. *But when he was in Rome.* What was the employment of One-

17 But when he was in Rome, he sought me out very diligently, and found *me*.

18 The Lord grant unto him that he may find mercy of the

siphorus is not known. It may have been that he was a merchant, and had occasion to visit Rome on business. At all events, he was at pains to search out the apostle, and his attention was the more valuable because it cost him trouble to find him. It is not every one, even among professors of religion, who in a great and splendid city would be at the trouble to search out a Christian brother, or even a minister, who was a prisoner, and endeavour to relieve his sorrows. This man, so kind to the great apostle, will be among those to whom the Saviour will say, at the final judgment, "I was in prison, and ye came unto me," Mat. xxv. 36.

18. *The Lord grant unto him that he may find mercy of the Lord in that day.* The day of judgment; Notes on ver. 12. This proves that Onesiphorus was then alive, as Paul would not offer prayer for him if he was dead. The Papists, indeed, argue from this in favour of praying for the dead—*assuming* from chap. iv. 19 that Onesiphorus was then dead. But there is no evidence of that. The passage in chap. iv. 19 would prove only that he was then absent from his family. ¶ *And in how many things he ministered unto me at Ephesus.* This was the home of Onesiphorus, and his family was still there, chap. iv. 19. When Paul was at Ephesus, it would seem that Onesiphorus had showed him great kindness. His affection for him did not change when he became a prisoner. True friendship, and especially that which is based on religion, will live in all the vicissitudes of fortune, whether we are in prosperity or adversity; whether in a home of plenty, or in a prison.

REMARKS.

This chapter is full of interest, and may suggest many interesting reflections. We see,

(1) A holy man imprisoned and

Lord *e*in that day: and in how many things *f*he ministered unto me at Ephesus, thou knowest very well.

e Mat. 25. 34-40.   *f* He. 6. 10.

about to die. He had nearly finished his course, and had the prospect of soon departing.

(2) He was forsaken by his friends, and left to bear his sorrows alone. They on whom he might have relied, had left him; and to all his outward sufferings, there was added this, one of the keenest which his Master endured before him, that his friends forsook him, and left him to bear his sorrows alone.

(3) Yet his mind is calm, and his faith in the gospel is unshaken. He expresses no regret that he had embraced the gospel; no sorrow that he had been so zealous in it as to bring these calamities upon himself. That gospel he still loves, and his great solicitude is, that his young friend may never shrink from avowing it, though it may call him also to pass through scenes of persecution and sorrow.

(4) In the general apostasy, the turning away of those on whom he might have relied, it is refreshing and interesting to find mention made of *one* unshaken friend, ver. 16. He never swerved in his affections. He had been kind to him in former years of comparative honour, and he did not leave him now in the dark day of adversity. It is always interesting to find true friendship in this world—friendship that survives all reverses, and that is willing to manifest itself when the great mass turn coldly away. There *is* such a thing as friendship, and there *is* such a thing as religion, and when they meet and mingle in the same heart, the one strengthens the other; and *then* neither persecution, nor poverty, nor chains, will prevent our doing good to him who is in prison and is about to die; see Notes on chap. iv. 16.

CHAPTER II.

ANALYSIS OF THE CHAPTER.

This chapter is made up of vari-

CHAPTER II.

THOU therefore, my son, *a*be strong in the grace that is in Christ Jesus.

ous exhortations and encouragements to duty. The apostle exhorts Timothy to be strong in the Christian graces (ver. 1); to commit the great trust which he had received to faithful men (ver. 2); to endure hardships like a good soldier (ver. 3–7), and refers him (*a*) to the case of one who goes to war, whose great business it is to please him in whose service he is (ver. 4); (*b*) to the case of one who strives for a crown at the games (ver. 5); and (*c*) to the husbandman who looks onward for the reward of his labour, ver. 6. He then, in order to encourage him to be patient in enduring the trials to which he would be exposed, refers him (*a*) to the certainty of the truth of that religion in whose cause he would suffer (ver. 8); (*b*) to his own case, reminding him how much *he* had endured in that cause (ver. 9, 10); (*c*) to the fact that our sufferings here will be crowned with certain glory hereafter (ver. 11, 12); and (*d*) to the assurance that the Lord Jesus will be faithful to all his promises to his people, ver. 13. These things the apostle then exhorts him to press upon the hearts of others, that they might not waste their time in unprofitable pursuits, but might engage in the same great and arduous struggle for securing the reward, ver. 14. He then exhorts Timothy to study to perform his duties in such a way that he would not be ashamed, and to avoid the unimportant strifes which were then raging; and to enforce this, he refers to a real case with which Timothy was acquainted—that of Hymeneus and Philetus, who, by unprofitable speculations, had been led to deny a fundamental doctrine of religion, ver. 15–18. Yet, Paul says, he should not be discouraged because some had been led into dangerous errors. The foundation of God remained firm. Those that were truly his were known, and would not apostatize, ver. 19. In illustration of this, and to show that it was to be

2 And the things that thou hast heard of me [1]among many witnesses, *b*the same commit thou to

a Jos.1.7; Ep.6.10.   [1] or, *by*.   *b* 1 Ti.1.18.

expected that *all* would not honour religion, the apostle refers to a house in which there were all sorts of vessels, some to honour and some to dishonour, and says that, if anyone would endeavour to free himself from all that was base and impure, he would be a vessel meet for the use of the Master, ver. 20, 21. To accomplish this, he gives Timothy various directions respecting his conduct. He was to flee from youthful lusts; he was to follow righteousness, faith, charity, and peace; he was to avoid foolish questions; he was to be an example of gentleness and meekness, and he was patiently to instruct those that were of a different character, ver. 22–26.

1. *Thou therefore.* In view of the fact stated in the previous chapter, that many had turned away from the apostle, and had forsaken the paths of truth. ¶ *Be strong in the grace which is in Christ Jesus.* Comp. Notes on Eph. vi. 10. The meaning is, Be strong, relying on the grace which the Lord Jesus only can impart.

2. *And the things which thou hast heard of me among many witnesses.* Marg., *by.* Before, or in the presence of, many witnesses. Perhaps he refers to a solemn charge which he gave him, in the presence of the church, when he was ordained. It is by no means improbable that such a charge was given then to a newly ordained minister, as it is now. On such an occasion, the apostle would be likely to state a summary of Christian doctrine (comp. Notes on chap. i. 13), and to exhort Timothy to a faithful adherence to it. ¶ *The same commit thou to faithful men.* In the same way as those things have been committed to you. The reference is undoubtedly to ordination to the ministerial office. Timothy was to see that those only were admitted to the ministry who were qualified to understand the truths of religion, and to

faithful men, ^cwho shall be able to teach others also.

3 Thou therefore ^dendure hardness, as a good soldier of Jesus Christ.

c Tit.1.9.   *d* ch.4.5.

4 No^e man that warreth entangleth himself with the affairs of *this* life; that he may please him who hath chosen him to be a soldier.

e 1 Co.9.25,26.

communicate them to others. This is a clear warrant for ministers to set apart others to the same sacred office. It does not prove that the people are not at liberty to choose their own pastor, but only that those in the ministry are to set apart others to the same office with themselves. There is, doubtless, to be a "succession" of ministers in the church; but the true line of the "succession" is to be found in good men who are qualified to teach, and who have the spirit of Christ, and not merely in those who have been ordained. ¶ *Who shall be able to teach others also.* On the qualifications of ministers, see Notes on 1 Tim. iii. 2–7.

3. *Thou therefore endure hardness, as a good soldier of Jesus Christ.* Such hardships as a soldier is called to endure. The apostle supposes that a minister of the gospel might be called to endure hardships, and that it is reasonable that he should be as ready to do it as a soldier is. On the hardships which *he* endured himself, see Notes on 2 Cor. xi. 23–29. Soldiers often endure great privations. Taken from their homes and friends; exposed to cold, or heat, or storms, or fatiguing marches; sustained on coarse fare, or almost destitute of food, they are often compelled to endure as much as the human frame can bear, and often, indeed, sink under their burdens, and die. If, for reward or their country's sake, they are willing to do this, the soldier of the cross should be willing to do it for his Saviour's sake, and for the good of the human race. Hence, let no man seek the office of the ministry as a place of ease. Let no one come into it merely to enjoy himself. Let no one enter it who is not prepared to lead a soldier's life, and to welcome hardship and trial as his portion. He would make a bad soldier, who, at his enlistment, should make it a condition that he should be

permitted to sleep on a bed of down, and always be well clothed and fed, and never exposed to peril, or compelled to pursue a wearisome march. Yet do not some men enter the ministry making these the conditions? and *would* they enter the ministry on any other terms?

4. *No man that warreth entangleth himself with the affairs of* this *life.* Having alluded to the soldier, and stated one thing in which the Christian minister is to resemble him, another point of resemblance is suggested to the mind of the apostle. Neither the minister nor the soldier is to be encumbered with the affairs of this life, and the one should not be more than the other. This is always a condition in becoming a soldier. He gives up his own business during the time for which he is enlisted, and devotes himself to the service of his country. The farmer leaves his plough, and the mechanic his shop, and the merchant his store, and the student his books, and the lawyer his brief; and neither of them expect to pursue these things while engaged in the service of their country. It would be wholly impracticable to carry on the plans of a campaign, if each one of these classes should undertake to prosecute his private business. See this fully illustrated from the *Rules of War among the Romans,* by Grotius, *in loco.* Roman soldiers were not allowed to marry, or to engage in any husbandry or trade; and they were forbidden to act as tutors to any person, or curators to any man's estate, or proctors in the cause of other men. The general principle was, that they were excluded from those relations, agencies, and engagements, which it was thought would divert their minds from that which was to be the sole object of pursuit. So with the ministers of the gospel. It is *equally* improper for them to

5 And if a man also strive for masteries, *yet* is he not crowned, except he strive lawfully.

6 The husbandman ²that laboureth must be first partaker of the fruits.

² or, *labouring first, must be partaker.*

"entangle" themselves with the business of a farm or plantation; with plans of speculation and gain, and with any purpose of worldly aggrandizement. The minister of the gospel accomplishes the design of his appointment only when he can say in sincerity, that he "is not entangled with the affairs of this life;" comp. Notes, 1 Cor. ix. 25–27. ¶ *That he may please him who hath chosen him to be a soldier.* That is, him who has enlisted him, or in whose employ he is. His great object is to approve himself to him. It is not to pursue his own plans, or to have his own will, or to accumulate property or fame for himself. His will is absorbed in the will of his commander, and his purpose is accomplished if he meet with his approbation. Nowhere else is it so true that the will of one becomes lost in that of another, as in the case of the soldier. In an army it is contemplated that there shall be but one mind, one heart, one purpose —that of the commander; and that the whole army shall be as obedient to that as the members of the human body are to the one will that controls all. The application of this is obvious. The grand purpose of the minister of the gospel is to please Christ. He is to pursue no separate plans, and to have no separate will of his own; and it is contemplated that the whole *corps* of Christian ministers and members of the churches shall be as entirely subordinate to the will of Christ, as an army is to the orders of its chief.

5. *And if a man also strive for masteries.* As in the Grecian games. See this favourite illustration of Paul explained in the Notes on 1 Cor. ix. 24, *seq.* ¶ *Yet is he not crowned, except he strive lawfully.* In conformity with the rules of the games. See Grotius, *in loco.* No one could obtain the prize unless he had complied with all the laws of the games, and had thus given to those with whom he contended, a fair opportunity to succeed. "In those contests, he who transgressed the rules in the least matter, not only failed of the prize, even though the apparent victor, but was sometimes disgraced and punished" (*Pict. Bib.*). So the apostle here represents the Christian minister as engaged in a struggle or conflict for the crown. He says that he could not hope to win it unless he should comply with all the laws by which it is conferred; unless he should subdue every improper propensity, and make an effort like that evinced by the combatants at the Olympic games; comp. Notes on 1 Cor. ix. 26, 27.

6. *The husbandman that laboureth.* The margin is, "*labouring first, must be partaker.*" The idea, according to the translation in the text, is, that there is a fitness or propriety (δει) that the man who cultivates the earth, should enjoy the fruits of his labour. See the same image explained in the Notes on 1 Cor. ix. 10. But if this be the meaning here, it is not easy to see why the apostle introduces it. According to the marginal reading, the word "*first*" is introduced in connection with the word *labour*— "*labouring first, must be partaker.*" That is, it is a great law that the husbandman must work before he receives a harvest. This sense will accord with the purpose of the apostle. It was to remind Timothy that *labour* must precede reward; that if a man would reap, he must sow; that he could hope for no fruits, unless he toiled for them. The point was not that the husbandman would be *the first one* who would partake of the fruits; but that he must *first labour* before he obtained the reward. Thus understood, this would be an encouragement to Timothy to persevere in his toils, looking onward to the reward. The Greek will bear this construction, though it is not the most obvious one.

7 Consider what I say; *and the Lord give thee understanding in all things.

8 Remember that Jesus Christ,

f 1 Ti.4.15.   *g* Pr.2.6.

h of the seed of David, was raised from the dead according to my gospel:

9 Wherein I suffer trouble,

h Ro.1.3,4.

---

7. *Consider what I say.* See Notes, 1 Tim. iv. 15. The sense is, "Think of the condition of the soldier, and the principles on which he is enlisted; think of the aspirant for the crown in the Grecian games; think of the farmer, patiently toiling in the prospect of the distant harvest; and then go to *your* work with a similar spirit." These things *are* worth attention. When the minister of the gospel thinks of his hardships, of his struggles against an evil world, and of his arduous and constant discouraging toil, let him think of the soldier, of the man who struggles for this world's honours, and of the patient farmer— *and be content.* How patiently do they bear all, and yet for what inferior rewards! ¶ *And the Lord give thee understanding in all things.* Enable you to see the force of these considerations, and to apply them to your own case. Such are often the discouragements of the ministry; so prone is the mind to despondency, that we need the help of the Lord to enable us to apply the most obvious considerations, and to derive support from the most plain and simple truths and promises.

8. *Remember that Jesus Christ, of the seed of David, was raised from the dead.* Or rather, perhaps, "Remember Jesus Christ; him who was raised from the dead." The idea seems not to be, as our translators supposed, that he was to reflect on the fact that he was raised from the dead; but rather that he was to think of the Saviour himself. "Think of the Saviour, now raised up from the dead after all the sorrows of this life, and let this encourage you to bear *your* trials." There is nothing better fitted to enable us to endure the labours and trials of this life, than to think of the Saviour. On the phrase "seed of David," see Notes on Rom. i. 3. ¶ *According to my gospel.* The

gospel which I preach; Notes, 2 Thes. ii. 14.

9. *Wherein I suffer trouble, as an evil-doer. As if* I were a violator of the laws. That is, I am treated as if I were a criminal. ¶ *Even unto bonds.* As if I were one of the worst kind of malefactors; Notes, Eph. vi. 20. During the apostle's first imprisonment at Rome, he was permitted to "dwell in his own hired house," though guarded by a soldier, and probably chained to him; see Notes on Acts xxviii. 16, 30. What was his condition in his second imprisonment, during which this epistle was written, we have no means of knowing with certainty. It is probable, however, that he was subjected to much more rigid treatment than he had been in the first instance. The tradition is, that he and Peter were together in the Mamertine prison at Rome; and the place is still shown in which it is said that they were confined. The Mamertine prisons are of great antiquity. According to Livy, they were constructed by Ancus Martius, and enlarged by Servius Tullius. The lower prison is supposed to have been once a quarry, and to have been at one time occupied as a granary. These prisons are on the descent of the Capitoline Mount, towards the Forum. They consist of two apartments, one over the other, built with large, uncemented stones. There is no entrance to either, except by a small aperture in the roof, and by a small hole in the upper floor, leading to the cell below, without any staircase to either. The upper prison is twenty-seven feet long, by twenty wide; the lower one is elliptical, and measures twenty feet by ten. In the lower one is a small spring, which is said at Rome to have arisen at the command of Peter, to enable him to baptize his keepers, Processus and Martianus, with forty-seven companions, whom

as an evil-doer, ⁱ*even* unto bonds; but the word of God is not bound.

10 Therefore I endure all things for ᵏ the elect's sakes, that they may also obtain the salvation which is in Christ Jesus with eternal glory.

11 *It is* a faithful saying: ˡFor

if we be dead with *him*, we shall also live with *him:*

12 If we suffer, we shall also reign with *him:* ᵐif we deny *him*, he also will deny us:

13 If ⁿ we believe not, *yet* he abideth faithful: ᵒhe cannot deny himself.

i Ep.6.20.   *k* 2 Co.1.6.   *l* Ro.6.5,8.   *m* Mat.10.33.   *n* Ro.3.3.   *o* Nu.23.19.

---

he converted. No certain reliance can be placed on any part of this tradition, though in itself there is no improbability in supposing that these prisons may have been used for confining Christians, and the apostle Paul among others. Dr. Burton says that a more horrible place for the confinement of a ʰuman being can scarcely be conceived. ¶ *But the word of God is not bound.* This is one of Paul's happy turns of thought; comp. Acts xxvi. 29. The meaning is plain. The gospel was prospered. *That* could not be fettered and imprisoned. It circulated with freedom, even when he who was appointed to preach it was in chains; see Phil. i. 13, 14. As this was the great matter, his own imprisonment was of comparatively little consequence. What may befall *us* is of secondary importance. The grand thing is the triumph of truth on the earth; and well may *we* bear privations and sorrows, if the gospel moves on in triumph.

10. *Therefore I endure all things for the elect's sakes.* See Notes on 2 Cor. i. 6. The sense is, What I suffer is in the cause of the church, spoken of here, as it is often, as *chosen,* or *elected;* Notes on Eph. i. 4. ¶ *That they may also obtain the salvation,* &c. Their salvation, though they were elected, could not be secured without proper efforts. The meaning of the apostle here is, that he was willing to suffer if he might save others; and anyone *ought* to be willing to suffer in order to secure the salvation of the elect—for it was an object for which the Redeemer was willing to lay down his life.

11. It is *a faithful saying.* Or, rather, that which he was about to

say was worthy of entire credence and profound attention; see Notes on 1 Tim. i. 15. The object is to encourage Timothy to bear trials by the hope of salvation. ¶ *For if we be dead with* him. See Notes on Rom. vi. 8. ¶ *We shall also live with* him. This was a sort of maxim, or a settled point, which is often referred to in the Bible; see Notes on Rom. vi. 3, 4, 5; John xi. 25; 1 Thes. iv. 14.

12. *If we suffer, we shall also reign with* him. The meaning is, that the members will be treated as the Head is. We become united with him by faith, and, if we share his treatment on earth, we shall share his triumphs in heaven; see Notes, Rom. viii. 17. ¶ *If we deny* him, *he also will deny us.* See Notes on Mat. x. 32, 33.

13. *If we believe not, yet he abideth faithful.* This cannot mean that, if we live in sin, he will certainly save us, as if he had made any promise to the elect, or formed any purpose that he would save them, whatever might be their conduct; for (1) he had just said that if we deny him he will deny us; and (2) there is no such promise in the Bible, and no such purpose has been formed. The promise is, that he that is a believer shall be saved, and there is no purpose to save any but such as lead holy lives. The meaning must be, that if we are unbelieving and unfaithful, Christ will remain true to his word, and we cannot hope to be saved. The object of the apostle evidently is, to excite Timothy to fidelity in the performance of duty, and to encourage him to bear trials, by the assurance that we cannot hope to escape if we are not faithful to the cause of the Saviour. This interpretation accords

14 Of these things ᵖput *them* in remembrance, charging *them* before the Lord that they ᑫstrive not about words to no profit, *but* to the subverting of the hearers.

p 2 Pe.1.13.　　　*q* Tit.3.9,10.

15 Study ʳ to show thyself approved unto God, a workman that needeth not to be ashamed, ˢrightly dividing the word of truth.

16 But shun profane *and* vain

r 2 Pe.1.10.　　　*s* Mat.13.52.

with the design which he had in view. ¶ *He cannot deny himself.* Implying that it would be a denial of his very nature to save those who are unfaithful. He is holy: and how can he save one who is unholy? His very nature is purity; and how can he save one who has no purity? Let no one, then, suppose that, because he is elected, he is safe, if he lives in sin. The electing purpose of God, indeed, makes salvation sure; but it is only for those who lead righteous lives. Nothing would be more dishonourable for God than to resolve to save a man that lived habitually in sin; and if that were the doctrine of election, it would deserve all the opprobrium that has ever been heaped upon it.

14. *Of these things put* them *in remembrance.* These great principles in regard to the kingdom of Christ. They would be as useful to others as they were for Timothy, to whom they were specially addressed. ¶ *Charging* them *before the Lord.* In the presence of the Lord, implying that it was a very important matter; Notes, 1 Tim. i. 18. ¶ *That they strive not about words to no profit.* See Notes, 1 Tim. i. 6; vi. 4. ¶ But *to the subverting of the hearers.* Turning them away from the simplicity of faith. It is rare, indeed, that a religious controversy does not produce this effect, and this is commonly the case, where, as often happens, the matter in dispute is of little importance.

15. *Study to show thyself approved unto God.* Give diligence (2 Pet. ii. 10), or make an effort so to discharge the duties of the ministerial office as to meet the divine approbation. The object of the ministry is not to please men. Such doctrines should be preached, and such plans formed, and such a manner of life pursued, as God will approve. To do this demands *study* or *care*—for there are many

temptations to the opposite course; there are many things the tendency of which is to lead a minister to seek popular favour rather than the divine approval. If *any* man please God, it will be as the result of deliberate intention and a careful life. ¶ *A workman that needeth not to be ashamed.* A man faithfully performing his duty, so that when he looks over what he has done, he may not blush. ¶ *Rightly dividing the word of truth.* The word here rendered "rightly dividing," occurs nowhere else in the New Testament. It means, properly, *to cut straight, to divide right;* and the allusion here may be to a steward who makes a proper distribution to each one under his care of such things as his office and their necessities require; comp. Notes on Mat. xiii. 52. Some have supposed that there is an allusion here to the Jewish priest, cutting or dividing the sacrifice into proper parts; others, that the allusion is to the scribes dividing the law into sections; others, to a carver distributing food to the guests at a feast. Robinson (*Lex.*) renders it, "rightly proceeding as to the word of truth;" that is, rightfully and skilfully teaching the word of truth. The idea seems to be, that the minister of the gospel is to make a proper distribution of that word, adapting his instructions to the circumstances and wants of his hearers, and giving to each that which will be fitted to nourish the soul for heaven.

16. *But shun profane and vain babblings.* Notes, 1 Tim. vi. 20. ¶ *For they will increase unto more ungodliness.* Their tendency is to alienate the soul from God, and to lead to impiety. Such kinds of disputation are not merely a waste of time, they are productive of positive mischief. A man fond of contention in religious things is seldom one who

babblings; for they will increase unto more ungodliness;

17 And their word will eat as doth a ³canker; of whom is Hymenæus and Philetus;

³ *gangrene.*

18 Who *t* concerning the truth have erred, *u* saying that the resurrection is past already; and overthrow the faith of some.

19 Nevertheless *v* the foundation

t 1 Ti.6.21.　　*u* 1 Co.15.12.　　*v* Pr.10.25.

has much love for the practical duties of piety, or any very deep sense of the distinction between right and wrong. You will not usually look for him in the place of prayer, nor can you expect his aid in the conversion of sinners, nor will you find that he has any very strict views of religious obligation.

17. *And their word.* The word, or the discourses of those who love vain and idle disputations. ¶ *Will eat as doth a canker.* Marg., *gangrene.* This word — γάγγραινα — occurs nowhere else in the New Testament. It is derived from γραιω, γραινω—*graio* or *graino*—to devour, corrode, and means *gangrene* or *mortification*—the death of a part, spreading, unless arrested, by degrees over the whole body. The words rendered "will eat," mean *will have nutriment;* that is, will spread over and consume the healthful parts. It will not merely destroy the parts immediately affected, but will extend into the surrounding healthy parts and destroy them also. So it is with erroneous doctrines. They will not merely eat out the truth in the particular matter to which they refer, but they will also spread over and corrupt other truths. The doctrines of religion are closely connected, and are dependent on each other—like the different parts of the human body. One cannot be corrupted without affecting those adjacent to it, and unless checked, the corruption will soon spread over the whole. ¶ *Of whom is Hymenæus and Philetus.* In regard to Hymenæus, see Notes on 1 Tim. i. 20. Of Philetus nothing more is known. They have gained an undesirable immortality, destined to be known to the end of time only as the advocates of error.

18. *Who concerning the truth have erred.* To what extent they had erred is unknown. Paul mentions only one

point—that pertaining to the resurrection; but says that this was like a gangrene. It would certainly, unless checked, destroy all the other doctrines of religion. No man can safely hold a single error, any more than he can safely have one part of his body in a state of mortification. ¶ *Saying that the resurrection is past already.* It is not known in what *form* they held this opinion. It may have been, as Augustine supposes, that they taught that there was no resurrection but that which occurs in the soul when it is recovered from the death of sin, and made to live anew. Or it may be that they held that those who had died had experienced all the resurrection which they ever would, by passing into another state, and receiving at death a spiritual body fitted to their mode of being in the heavenly world. Whatever was the form of the opinion, the apostle regarded it as a most dangerous error, for just views of the resurrection undoubtedly lie at the foundation of correct apprehensions of the Christian system; comp. Notes on 1 Cor. xv. 12–19. ¶ *And overthrow the faith of some.* That is, on this point, and as would appear on all the correlative subjects of Christian belief; comp. 1 Tim. i. 19, 20.

19. *Nevertheless the foundation of God is sure.* Marg., *steady.* The meaning is, that though some had been turned away by the arts of these errorists, yet the foundation of the church which God had laid remained firm; comp. Eph. ii. 20, "And are built upon the foundation of the apostles and prophets, Jesus Christ himself being the chief corner-stone." As long as this foundation remained firm, there was no reason to be troubled from the few instances of apostasy which had occurred; comp. Ps. xi. 3. It is not uncommon to com-

of God standeth ⁴sure, having this seal, ʷThe Lord knoweth them that are his. And, ˣLet every one that nameth the name of Christ depart from iniquity.

4 or, *steady.* w Na.1.7; Jn.10.14,27. x Ps.97.10.

20 But in a great house there are not only ʸvessels of gold and of silver, but also of wood and of earth; and some to honour, and some to dishonour.

y Ro.9.21.

pare the church to a building erected on a solid foundation; Eph. ii. 20, 21; 1 Cor. iii. 9, 10; Mat. xvi. 18. ¶ *Having this seal.* Or rather a seal with this inscription. The word *seal* is sometimes used to denote the instrument by which an impression is made, and sometimes the impression or inscription itself. A seal is used for security (Mat. xxvii. 66), or as a mark of genuineness, Rev. ix. 4. The seal here is one that was affixed to the *foundation,* and seems to refer to some inscription *on* the foundation-stone which always remained there, and which denoted the character and design of the edifice. The allusion is to the custom, in rearing an edifice, of inscribing the name of the builder and the design of the edifice on the corner-stone. See Rosenmüller, *Alte und neue Morgenland,* No. 405. So the church of Christ is a building reared by the hands of God. Its foundation has been firmly and securely laid, and *on* that foundation there is an inscription always remaining which determines the character of the edifice. ¶ *The Lord knoweth them that are his.* This is one of the inscriptions on the foundation-stone of the ·church, which seems to mark the character of the building. It always stands there, no matter who apostatizes. It is at the same time a fearful inscription—showing that no one can deceive God; that he is intimately acquainted with all who enter that building; and that in the multitudes which enter there, the friends and the foes of God are intimately known. He can separate his own friends from all others, and his constant care will be extended to all who are truly his own, to keep them from falling. This has the *appearance* of being a quotation, but no such passage is found in the Old Testament in so many words. In Nahum i. 7,

the following words are found: "And he knoweth them that trust in him;" and it is possible that Paul may have had that in his eye; but it is not necessary to suppose that he designed it as a quotation. A phrase somewhat similar to this is found in Num. xvi. 5, "The Lord will show who are his;" rendered in the Septuagint, "God knoweth who are his; and Whitby supposes that this is the passage referred to. But whether Paul had these passages in view or not, it is clear that he meant to say that it was one of the fundamental things in religion, that God knew who were his own people, and that he would preserve them from the danger of making shipwreck of their faith. ¶ *And, Let every one that nameth the name of Christ depart from iniquity.* This is the other seal or inscription which is made on the foundation which God has laid. The foundation has two inscriptions—the first implying that God knows all who are his own people; the other, that all who are his professed people should depart from evil. This is not found in so many words in the Old Testament, and, like the former, it is not to be regarded as a quotation. The meaning is, that it is an elementary principle in the true church, that all who become members of it should lead holy lives. It was also true that they *would* lead holy lives, and amidst all the defections of errorists, and all their attempts to draw away others from the true faith, those might be known to be the true people of God who *did* avoid evil.

20. *But in a great house.* Still keeping up the comparison of the church with a building. The idea is, that the church is a *large* edifice, and that in such a building we are not to expect entire uniformity in all the articles which it contains. ¶ *There*

21 If[z] a man therefore purge himself from these, he shall be a vessel unto honour, sanctified, and meet for the master's use, [a]*and* prepared unto every good work.

z Je.15.19.　　*a* ch.3.17.

22 Flee[b] also youthful lusts: but [c]follow righteousness, faith, charity, peace, with [d]them that call on the Lord out of a pure heart.

23 But foolish and unlearned

b Ec.11.9,10.　*c* He.12.14.　*d* 1 Co.1.2.

are not only vessels of gold and of silver, &c. You are not to expect to find all the articles of furniture alike, or all made of the same material. Variety in the form, and use, and material, is necessary in furnishing such a house. ¶ *And some to honour, and some to dishonour.* Some to most honourable uses—as drinking-vessels, and vessels to contain costly viands, and some for the less honourable purposes connected with cooking, &c. The same thing is to be expected in the church. See this idea illustrated at greater length under another figure in the Notes on 1 Cor. xii. 14–26; comp. Notes, Rom. ix. 21. The *application* here seems to be, that in the church it is to be presumed that there will be a great variety of gifts and attainments, and that we are no more to expect that all will be alike, than we are that all the vessels in a large house will be made of gold.

21. *If a man therefore purge himself from these, he shall be a vessel unto honour.* If a man *cleanse* or *purify* himself; comp. Notes on John xv. 2. The word *"these"* refers, here, to the persons represented by the vessels of wood and of earth—the vessels made to dishonour, as mentioned in the previous verse. The idea is, that if one would preserve himself from the corrupting influence of such men, he would be fitted to be a vessel of honour, or to be employed in the most useful and honourable service in the cause of his Master. On the word *vessel,* see Notes on Acts ix. 15. ¶ *And meet for the master's use.* Fit to be employed by the Lord Jesus in promoting his work on earth.

22. *Flee also youthful lusts.* Such passions as youth are subject to. On the word *flee,* and the pertinency of its use in such a connection, see Notes

on 1 Cor. vi. 18. Paul felt that Timothy, then a young man, was subject to the same passions as other young men; and hence his repeated cautions to him to avoid all those things, arising from his youth, which might be the occasion of scandal; comp. Notes on 1 Tim. iv. 12; v. 2. It is to be remembered that this epistle is applicable to other ministers, as well as to Timothy; and, to a young man in the ministry, no counsel could be more appropriate than to "FLEE *from youthful lusts;"* not to indulge for a moment in those corrupt passions to which youth are subject, but to cultivate the pure and sober virtues which become the ministerial office. ¶ *But follow righteousness,* &c. Comp. Notes on Heb. xii. 14. The general meaning here is, that he was to practise all that is good and virtuous. He was to practise *righteousness,* or justice and equity, in all his dealings with men; *faith,* or fidelity in his duties; *charity,* or love to all men (Notes, 1 Cor. xiii.); *peace,* or harmony and concord with all others. What virtues could be more appropriate for a minister of the gospel? ¶ *With them that call on the Lord out of a pure heart.* That is, with all Christians, who are often characterized as those who call on the Lord, 1 Cor. i. 2; comp. Acts ix. 11. In all his intercourse with them, Timothy was to manifest the virtues above recommended. But not with them alone. It would be incumbent on him to exhibit the same virtues in his intercourse with all.

23. *But foolish and unlearned questions avoid.* See Notes on ver. 16; comp. Notes on 1 Tim. i. 4, 6; iv. 7. The word *unlearned,* here, means *trifling; that which does not tend to edification; stupid.* The Greeks and the Hebrews were greatly given to controversies of various

questions *avoid, knowing that they do gender strifes.

24 And the servant of the Lord

e ver. 16.

must not strive; but be gentle unto all *men,* apt to teach, [5] patient,

25 In *f* meekness instructing

[5] or, *forbearing.*   *f* Ga. 6. 1.

kinds, and many of the questions discussed pertained to points which could not be settled, or which, *if* settled, were of no importance. Such has been the character of no small part of the disputes which have agitated the world. Paul correctly says that the only effect of such disputes is to engender harsh contention. Points of *real* importance can be discussed with no injury to the temper; but men cannot safely dispute about trifles.

24. *And the servant of the Lord.* Referring here primarily to the Christian minister, but applicable to all Christians; for all profess to be the servants of the Lord. ¶ *Must not strive.* He may calmly inquire after truth; he may discuss points of morals, or theology, if he will do it with a proper spirit; he may "contend earnestly for the faith once delivered to the saints" (Jude 3); but he may *not* do that which is here mentioned as *strife.* The Greek word—μάχεσθαι—commonly denotes, *to fight, to make war, to contend.* In John vi. 52; Acts vii. 26; 2 Tim. ii. 24, it is rendered *strove* and *strive;* in James iv. 2, *fight.* It is not elsewhere used in the New Testament. The meaning is, that the servant of Christ should be a man of peace. He should not indulge in the feelings which commonly give rise to contention, and which commonly characterize it. He should not struggle for mere victory, even when endeavouring to maintain truth; but should do this, in all cases, with a kind spirit, and a mild temper; with entire candour; with nothing designed to provoke and irritate an adversary; and so that, whatever may be the result of the discussion, "the bond of peace" may, if possible, be preserved; comp. Notes, Rom. xii. 18. ¶ *But be gentle unto all* men. Notes, 1 Thes. ii. 7. The word rendered *gentle,* does not occur elsewhere in the New Testament. It means that the Christian minister is to be meek and mild towards all, not

disputatious and quarrelsome. ¶ *Apt to teach.* Notes, 1 Tim. iii. 2. ¶ *Patient.* Marg., *forbearing.* The Greek word here used does not elsewhere occur in the New Testament. It means, patient under evils and injuries (Robinson, *Lex.*). Comp. Notes on Eph. iv. 2; Col. iii. 13.

25. *In meekness instructing those that oppose themselves.* That is, those who embrace error, and array themselves against the truth. We are not to become angry with such persons, and denounce them at once as heretics. We are not to hold them up to public reproach and scorn; but we are to set about the business of patiently *instructing them.* Their grand difficulty, it is supposed in this direction, is, that they are ignorant of the truth. Our business with them is, *calmly to show them what the truth is.* If *they* are angry, *we* are not to be. If they oppose the truth, we are still calmly to state it to them. If they are slow to see it, we are not to become weary or impatient. Nor, if they do not embrace it at all, are we to become angry with them, and denounce them. We may pity them, but we need not use hard words. This is the apostolic precept about the way of treating those who are in error; and can anyone fail to see its beauty and propriety? Let it be remembered, also, that this is not only beautiful and proper in itself; it is the *wisest* course, if we would bring others over to our opinions. You are not likely to convince a man that you are right, and that he is wrong, if you first make him angry; nor are you very likely to do it, if you enter into harsh contention. You then put him on his guard; you make him a party, and, from self-respect, or pride, or anger, he will endeavour to defend his own opinions, and will *not* yield to yours. *Meekness* and *gentleness* are the very best things, if you wish to convince another that he is wrong. Win his *heart* first, and

those that oppose themselves; *g*if God peradventure will give them repentance *h*to the acknowledging of the truth;

then modestly and kindly show him *what the truth is,* in as few words, and with as unassuming a spirit, as possible, *and you have him.* ¶ *If God peradventure will give them repentance,* &c. Give them such a view of the error which they have embraced, and such regret for having embraced it, that they shall be willing to admit the truth. After all our care in teaching others the truth, our only dependence is on God for its success. We cannot be absolutely certain that they will see their error; we cannot rely certainly on any power which argument will have; we can only hope that *God* may show them their error, and enable them to see and embrace the truth; comp. Acts xi. 18. The word rendered *peradventure,* here—μήποτε—means, usually, *not even, never;* and then, *that never, lest ever*—the same as *lest perhaps.* It is translated *lest at any time,* Mat. iv. 6; Mark iv. 12; Luke xxi. 34; *lest,* Mat. vii. 6; xiii. 29; xv. 32, *et al.; lest haply,* Luke xiv. 12; Acts v. 39. It does not imply that there was *any chance* about what is said, but rather that there was uncertainty in the mind of the speaker, and that there was need of caution *lest* something should occur; or, that anything was done, or should be done, to prevent something from happening. It is not used elsewhere in the New Testament in the sense which our translators, and all the critics, so far as I have examined, give to it here—as implying *a hope* that God *would* give them repentance, &c. But I may be permitted to suggest another interpretation, which will accord with the uniform meaning of the word in the New Testament, and which will refer the matter to those who had embraced the error, and not to God. It is this: "In meekness instructing *those that oppose themselves* (ἀντιδιατιθεμένους) *lest* —μήποτε—God should give them re-

26 And *that* they may [6]recover themselves out of *i*the snare of the devil, who are taken [7]captive by him at his will.

pentance, and they should recover themselves out of the snare of the devil," &c. That is, they put themselves in this posture of opposition so that they shall not be brought to repentance, and recover themselves. They do it with a precautionary view that they *may not* be thus brought to repentance, and be recovered to God. They take this position of opposition to the truth, intending not to be converted; and this is the reason why they are not converted.

26. *And* that *they may recover themselves.* Marg., *awake.* The word which is rendered *recover* in the text, and *awake* in the margin—ἀνανήψωσιν—occurs nowhere else in the New Testament. It properly means, to become sober again, as from inebriation; to awake from a deep sleep; and then, to come to a right mind, as one does who is aroused from a state of inebriety, or from sleep. The representation in this part of the verse implies that, while under the influence of error, they were like a man intoxicated, or like one in deep slumber. From this state they were to be roused as one is from sleep, or as a man is recovered from the stupor and dulness of intoxication. ¶ *Out of the snare of the devil.* The snare which the devil has spread for them, and in which they have become entangled. There is a little confusion of metaphor here, since, in the first part of the verse, they are represented as asleep, or intoxicated; and here, as taken in a snare. Yet the general idea is clear. In one part of the verse, the influence of error is represented as producing sleep, or stupor; in the other, as being taken in a snare, or net; and in both the idea is, that an effort was to be made that they might be rescued from this perilous condition. ¶ *Who are taken captive by him at his will.* Marg., *alive.* The Greek word means, properly, to take alive; and then, to

CHAPTER III.

THIS know also, that *a*in the

a 1 Ti.4.1; 2 Pe.3.3; 1 Jn.2.18; Jude 17,18.

last days *b*perilous times shall come.

b Re. vi. viii. ix. xi.-xiii. xviii.

---

take captive, to win over (Luke v. 10); and then, to ensnare, or seduce. Here it means that they had been ensnared by the arts of Satan *unto* (εἰς) *his will;* that is, they were so influenced by him, that they complied with his will. Another interpretation of this passage should be mentioned here, by which it is proposed to avoid the incongruousness of the metaphor of *awaking* one from a *snare.* It is adopted by Doddridge, and is suggested also by Burder, as quoted by Rosenmüller, *A. u. n. Morgenland.* According to this, the reference is to an artifice of fowlers, to scatter seeds impregnated with some intoxicating drugs, intended to lay birds asleep, that they may draw the snare over them more securely. There can be no doubt that such arts were practised, and it is possible that Paul may have alluded to it. Whatever is the allusion, the general idea is clear. It is an affecting representation of those who have fallen into error. They are in a deep slumber. They are as if under the fatal influence of some stupefying potion. They are like birds taken alive in this state, and at the mercy of the fowler. They will remain in this condition, unless they shall be roused by the mercy of God; and it is the business of the ministers of religion to carry to them that gospel call, which God is accustomed to bless in showing them their danger. That message should be continually sounded in the ears of the sinner, with the prayer and the *hope* that God will make it the means of arousing him to seek his salvation.

CHAPTER III.

ANALYSIS OF THE CHAPTER.

In the first part of this chapter (ver. 1-8), Paul reminds Timothy of the great apostasy which was to be expected in the church, and states some of the characteristics of it. In ver. 9, he says that that apostasy would not always continue; but would

be at some time arrested, and so arrested as to show to all men the folly of those who were concerned in it. In ver. 11, 12, he refers Timothy to his own manner of life in the midst of persecutions, as an encouragement to him to bear the trials which might be expected to occur to him in a similar manner. " Perilous times " were to come, and Timothy might be expected to be called to pass through trials similar to those which Paul himself had experienced. *In* those times the remembrance of his example would be invaluable. In ver. 12, 13, he assures Timothy that persecutions were to be expected by *all* who aimed to lead holy lives, and that it was as certainly to be expected that evil men would become worse and worse. And in ver. 14-17, he exhorts him to be steadfast in maintaining the truth; and, to encourage him to do this, reminds him of his early training in the Holy Scriptures, and of the value of those Scriptures. To the Scriptures he might repair in all times of trial, and find support in the divine promises. What he had learned there was the inspired truth of God, and was able to make him wise, and to furnish him abundantly for all that he was to do or to suffer.

1. *This know also.* The *object* of this reference to the perilous times which were to occur, was evidently to show the necessity of using every precaution to preserve the purity of the church, from the fact that such sad scenes were to open upon it. The apostle had dwelt upon this subject in his first epistle to Timothy (chap. iv.), but its importance leads him to advert to it again. ¶ *In the last days.* Under the gospel dispensation; some time in that period during which the affairs of the world will be closed up; see Notes, 1 Tim. iv. 1, and Heb. i. 2. ¶ *Perilous times shall come.* Times of danger, of persecution, and of trial. On the general meaning of this passage, and the general characteristics

2 For[c] men shall be lovers of their own selves, covetous, boasters, proud, blasphemers, disobedient to parents, unthankful, unholy,

c Ro.1.29-31.

3 Without natural affection, truce-breakers, [1]false accusers, incontinent, fierce, despisers of those that are good,

4 Traitors,[d] heady, high-minded,

1 or, *makebates.*   *d* 2 Pe.2.10, &c.

of those times, the reader may consult the Notes on 2 Thes. ii. 1–12, and 1 Tim. iv. 1–3. There can be no doubt that in all these passages the apostle refers to the same events.

2. *For men shall be lovers of their own selves.* It shall be one of the characteristics of those times that men shall be eminently selfish—evidently under the garb of religion, ver. 5. The word here used—φίλαυτος—does not elsewhere occur in the New Testament. It means a lover of one's self, *selfish.* Such a love of *self* as to lead us to secure our salvation, is proper. But this interferes with the rights and happiness of no other persons. The selfishness which is condemned, is that regard to our own interests which interferes with the rights and comforts of others; which makes *self* the central and leading object of living; and which tramples on all that would interfere with that. As such, it is a base, and hateful, and narrow passion; but it has been so common in the world that no one can doubt the correctness of the prophecy of the apostle that it would exist " *in the last times.*" ¶ *Covetous.* Gr., lovers of silver; *i.e.* of money, Luke vi. 14; Notes, 1 Tim. vi. 20. ¶ *Boasters.* Notes, Rom. i. 30. ¶ *Proud.* Notes, Rom. i. 30. ¶ *Blasphemers.* See Notes, Mat. ix. 3. ¶ *Disobedient to parents.* See Notes on Rom. i. 30. ¶ *Unthankful.* See Luke vi. 35. The word here used occurs in the New Testament only in these two places. Ingratitude has always been regarded as one of the worst of crimes. It is said here that it would characterize that wicked age of which the apostle speaks, and its prevalence would, as it always does, indicate a decline of religion. Religion makes us grateful to every benefactor—to God, and to man. ¶ *Unholy.* Notes, 1 Tim. i. 9.

3. *Without natural affection.* See

Notes on Rom. i. 31. ¶ *Truce-breakers.* The same word in Rom. i. 31, is rendered *implacable;* see Notes on that verse. It properly means *without treaty;* that is, those who are averse to any treaty or compact. It may thus refer to those who are unwilling to enter into any agreement; that is, either those who are unwilling to be reconciled to others when there is a variance—*implacable;* or those who *disregard* treaties or agreements. In either case, this marks a very corrupt condition of society. Nothing would be more indicative of the lowest state of degradation, than that in which all compacts and agreements were utterly disregarded. ¶ *False accusers.* Marg., *makebates.* The word *makebate* means one who excites contentions and quarrels (Webster). The Greek here is διάβολοι—*devils*—the primitive meaning of which is, *calumniator, slanderer, accuser;* comp. Notes on 1 Tim. iii. 11, where the word is rendered *slanderers.* ¶ *Incontinent.* 1 Cor. vii. 5. Literally, *without strength;* that is, without strength to resist the solicitations of passion, or who readily yield to it. ¶ *Fierce.* The Greek word used here—ἀνήμερος—does not elsewhere occur in the New Testament. It means *ungentle, harsh, severe,* and is the opposite of gentleness and mildness. Religion produces gentleness; the want of it makes men rough, harsh, cruel; comp. Notes on chap. ii. 24. ¶ *Despisers of those that are good.* In Titus i. 8, it is said of a bishop that he must be " a lover of good men." This, in every condition of life, is a virtue, and hence the opposite of it is here set down as one of the characteristics of that evil age of which the apostle speaks.

4. *Traitors.* This word is used in the New Testament only here and in

lovers *e* of pleasures more than lovers of God;

5 Having *f* a form of godliness,

e Phi.3.19.　　　　*f* Tit.1.16.

but denying the power thereof: from such turn away.

6 For of this sort are they

Luke vi. 16; Acts vii. 52. It means anyone who betrays—whether it be a friend or his country. *Treason* has been in all ages regarded as one of the worst crimes that man can commit. ¶ *Heady.* The same word in Acts xix. 36, is rendered *rashly.* It occurs only there and in this place in the New Testament. It properly means *falling forwards; prone, inclined, ready to do anything;* then *precipitate, headlong, rash.* It is opposed to that which is deliberate and calm, and here means that men would be ready to do anything without deliberation, or concern for the consequences. They would engage in enterprises which would only disturb society, or prove their own ruin. ¶ *High-minded.* Literally, *puffed up;* comp. Notes on 1 Tim. iii. 6, where the same word is rendered *lifted up with pride.* The meaning is, that they would be inflated with pride or self-conceit. ¶ *Lovers of pleasures more than lovers of God.* That is, of sensual pleasures, or vain amusements. This has been, and is, the characteristic of a great part of the world, and has often distinguished even many who profess religion. Of a large portion of mankind it may be said that this is their characteristic, that they live for pleasure; they have no serious pursuits; they brook no restraints which interfere with their amusements, and they greatly prefer the pleasures to be found in the gay assembly, in the ball-room, or in the place of low dissipation, to the friendship of their Creator.

5. *Having a form of godliness.* That is, they profess religion, or are in connection with the church. This shows that the apostle referred to some great corruption in the church; and there can be little doubt that he had his eye on the same great apostasy to which he refers in 2 Thes. ii. and 1 Tim. iv. All these things to which he refers here have been practised and tolerated in that apostate church, while no body of men, at any time, have been more zealous in maintaining *a form of godliness;* that is, in keeping up the *forms* of religion. ¶ *But denying the power thereof.* Opposing the real power of religion; not allowing it to exert any influence in their lives. It imposes no restraint on their passions and carnal propensities, but in all respects, except in the *form* of religion, they live as if they had *none.* This has been common in the world. The most regular and bigoted adherence to the *forms* of religion furnishes no evidence in itself that there is any true piety at heart, or that true religion has any actual control over the soul. It is much easier for men to observe the forms of religion than it is to bring the heart under its controlling influence. ¶ *From such turn away.* Have no intercourse with them as if they were Christians; show no countenance to their religion; do not associate with them; comp. 2 John 10, 11; Notes, 2 Cor. vi. 17.

6. *For of this sort are they which creep into houses.* Who go slyly and insidiously into families. They are not open and manly in endeavouring to propagate their views, but they endeavour by their address to ingratiate themselves first with weak women, and through them to influence men; comp. Titus i. 11. The word translated "creep into," is rendered by Doddridge *insinuate themselves;* by Bloomfield, *wind their way into,* in the manner of serpents; by Bretschneider, *deceitfully enter;* by Robinson and Passow, *go in, enter in.* It is not certain that the idea of *deceit* or *cunning* is contained in this *word,* yet the whole complexion of the passage implies that they made their way by art and deceitful tricks. ¶ *And lead captive silly women.* One of the tricks always played by the advocates of error, and one of the ways by which they seek to promote their purposes. Satan began his work of temptation

which *g* creep into houses, and lead captive silly women laden with sins, led away with divers lusts,

7 Ever learning, and never able

g Tit.1.11.

to come to the knowledge of the truth.

8 Now as Jannes and Jambres *h* withstood Moses, so do these also resist the truth: *i* men of corrupt

h Ex.7.11.   *i* 1 Ti.6.5.

with Eve rather than with Adam, and the advocates of error usually follow his example. There are always weak-minded women enough in any community to give an opportunity of practising these arts, and often the aims of the impostor and deceiver can be best secured by appealing to them. Such women are easily flattered; they are charmed by the graceful manners of religious instructors; they lend a willing ear to anything that has the appearance of religion, and their hearts are open to anything that promises to advance the welfare of the world. At the same time, they are just such persons as the propagators of error can rely on. They have leisure; they have wealth; they are busy; they move about in society, and by their activity they obtain an influence to which they are by no means entitled by their piety or talents. There *are*, indeed, very many women in the world who cannot be so easily led away as men; but it cannot be denied also that there are those who are just adapted to the purposes of such as seek to spread plausible error. The word rendered *silly women*, means properly *little women*, and then *weak women*. ¶ *Laden with sins*. With so many sins that they seem to be *burdened* with them. The idea is, that they are under the influence of sinful desires and propensities, and hence are better adapted to the purposes of deceivers. ¶ *Led away with divers lusts*. With various kinds of passions or desires—ἐπιϑυμίας—such as pride, vanity, the love of novelty, or a susceptibility to flattery, so as to make them an easy prey to deceivers.

7. *Ever learning*. That is, these "silly women;" for so the Greek demands. The idea is, that they *seem* to be disciples. They put themselves wholly under the care of these professedly religious teachers, but they

never acquire the true knowledge of the way of salvation. ¶ *And never able to come to the knowledge of the truth*. They may learn many things, but the true nature of religion they do not learn. There are many such persons in the world, who, whatever attention they may pay to religion, never understand its nature. Many obtain much speculative acquaintance with the *doctrines* of Christianity, but never become savingly acquainted with the system; many study the constitution and government of the church, but remain strangers to practical piety; many become familiar with the various philosophical theories of religion, but never become truly acquainted with what religion is; and many embrace visionary theories, who never show that they are influenced by the spirit of the gospel. Nothing is more common than for persons to be very busy and active in religion, and even to *learn* many things about it, who still remain strangers to the saving power of the gospel.

8. *Now as Jannes and Jambres withstood Moses*. The names of these two men are not elsewhere mentioned in the Bible. They are supposed to have been two of the magicians who resisted Moses (Ex. vii. 11, *et al.*), and who opposed their miracles to those of Moses and Aaron. It is not certain where the apostle obtained their names; but they are frequently mentioned by the Hebrew writers, and also by other writers; so that there can be no reasonable doubt that their names were correctly handed down by tradition. Nothing is more probable than that the names of the more distinguished magicians who attempted to imitate the miracles of Moses, would be preserved by tradition; and though they are not mentioned by Moses himself, and the Jews have told many ridiculous stories respecting them, yet this should not

minds, ²reprobate concerning the faith.

² or, *of no judgment.*

9 But they shall proceed no further: for their folly shall be

---

lead us to doubt the truth of the tradition respecting their names. A full collection of the Jewish statements in regard to them may be found in Wetstein, *in loco.* They are also mentioned by Pliny, *Nat. Hist.* xxx. 7; and by Numenius, the philosopher, as quoted by Eusebius, ix. 8; and Origen, against Celsus, p. 199. See Wetstein. By the rabbinical writers, they are sometimes mentioned as Egyptian magicians who opposed Moses in Egypt, and sometimes as the sons of Balaam. The more common account is, that they were the princes of the Egyptian magicians. One of the Jewish rabbins represents them as having been convinced by the miracles of Moses, and as having become converts to the Hebrew religion. There is no reason to doubt that these were in fact the leading men who opposed Moses in Egypt, by attempting to work counter-miracles. The *point* of the remark of the apostle here is, that they resisted Moses by attempting to *imitate* his miracles, thus *neutralizing* the evidence that he was sent from God. In like manner, the persons here referred to opposed the progress of the gospel by setting up a similar claim to that of the apostles; by pretending to have as much authority as they had; and by thus neutralizing the claims of the true religion, and leading off weak-minded persons from the truth. This is often the most dangerous kind of opposition that is made to religion. ¶ *Men of corrupt minds.* Comp. Notes, 1 Tim. vi. 5. ¶ *Reprobate concerning the faith.* So far as the Christian faith is concerned. On the word rendered *reprobate,* see Notes on Rom. i. 28; 1 Cor. ix. 27, rendered *cast-away;* 2 Cor. xiii. 5. The margin here is, "of no judgment." The meaning is, that in respect to the Christian faith, or the doctrines of religion, their views could not be approved, and they were not to be regarded as true teachers of religion.

9. *But they shall proceed no further.* There is a certain point beyond which they will not be allowed to go. Their folly will become manifest, and the world will understand it. The apostle does not say *how far* these false teachers would be allowed to go, but that they would not be suffered always to prosper and prevail. They might be plausible at first, and lead many astray; they might, by art and cunning, cover up the real character of their system; but there would be a fair development of it, and it would be seen to be folly. The apostle here may be understood as declaring a general truth in regard to error. It often is so plausible at first, that it seems to be true. It wins the hearts of many persons, and leads them astray. It flatters them personally, or it flatters them with the hope of a better state of things in the church and the world. But the time will *always* come when men will see the folly of it. Error will advance only to a certain point, when it will be *seen* to be falsehood and folly, and when the world will arise and cast it off. In some cases this point may be slower in being reached than in others; but there *is* a point beyond which error will not go. At the reformation under Luther, that point had been reached, when the teachings of the great apostasy were seen to be "folly," and when the awakened intellect of the world would allow it to "proceed no farther," and aroused itself and threw it off. In the workings of society, as well as by the direct appointment of God, there *is* a point beyond which error cannot prevail; and hence there is a certainty that truth will finally triumph. ¶ *For their folly shall be manifest unto all* men. The world will see and understand what they are, and what they teach. By smooth sophistry, and cunning arts, they will not be able always to deceive mankind. ¶ *As their's also was.* That

manifest unto all *men,* as their's also was.

10 But thou hast ³fully known

³ or, *been a diligent follower of.*

of Jannes and Jambres. That is, it became manifest to all that they could not compete with Moses and Aaron; that their claims to the power of working miracles were the mere arts of magicians, and that they had set up pretensions which they could not sustain; comp. Ex. viii. 18, 19. In regard to the *time* to which the apostle referred in this description, it has already been observed (Notes on ver. 1), that it was probably to that great apostasy of the "latter days," which he has described in 2 Thes. ii. and 1 Tim. iv. But there seems to be no reason to doubt that he had his eye immediately on some persons who had appeared then, and who had evinced some of the traits which would characterize the great apostasy, and whose conduct showed that the great "falling away" had already commenced. In 2 Thes. ii. 7, he says that the "mystery of iniquity" was already at work, or was even then manifesting itself; and there can be no doubt that the apostle saw that there had then commenced what he knew must yet grow up into the great defection from the truth. In some persons, at that time, who had the form of godliness, but who denied its power; who made use of insinuating arts to proselyte the weak and the credulous; who endeavoured to imitate the true apostles, perhaps by attempting to work miracles, as Jannes and Jambres did, he saw the *germ* of what was yet to grow up into so gigantic a system of iniquity as to overshadow the world. Yet he consoled Timothy with the assurance that there was a point beyond which the system of error would not be allowed to go, but where its folly must be seen, and where it would be arrested.

10. *But thou hast fully known my doctrine,* &c. Marg., *been a diligent follower of.* The margin is more in accordance with the usual meaning of the Greek word, which means, properly, to accompany side

my doctrine, manner of life, purpose, faith, long-suffering, charity, patience,

by side; to follow closely; to trace out; to examine (Luke i. 3), and to conform to. The meaning here, however, seems to be, that Timothy had an opportunity to follow out, *i.e.* to examine closely, the manner of life of the apostle Paul. He had been so long his companion, that he had had the fullest opportunity of knowing how he had lived and taught, and how he had borne persecutions. The *object* of this reference to his own life and sufferings is evidently to encourage Timothy to bear persecutions and trials in the same manner; comp. ver. 14. He saw, in the events which began already to develop themselves, that trials must be expected; he knew that all who would live holy lives must suffer persecution; and hence he sought to prepare the mind of Timothy for the proper endurance of trials, by a reference to his own case. The word *doctrine,* here, refers to his *teaching,* or manner of giving instruction. It does not refer, as the word now does, to the *opinions* which he held; see Notes on 1 Tim. iv. 16. In regard to the opportunities which Timothy had for knowing the manner of Paul's life, see the introduction to the epistle, and Paley. *Hor. Paul., in loco.* Timothy had been the companion of Paul during a considerable portion of the time after his conversion. The *persecutions* referred to here (ver. 11) are those which occurred in the vicinity of Timothy's native place, and which he would have had a particular opportunity of being acquainted with. This circumstance, and the fact that Paul did not refer to *other* persecutions in more remote places, is one of the "*undesigned coincidences,*" of which Paley has made so much in his incomparable little work—the *Horæ Paulinæ.* ¶ *Manner of life.* Literally, *leading, guidance;* then, the method in which one is led—his manner of life; comp. Notes, 1 Thes. ii. 1. ¶ *Purpose.* Plans, or designs.

11 Persecutions, afflictions, which came unto me *k* at Antioch, *l* at Iconium, at Lystra; what perse-

k Ac.13.45,50.   *l* Ac.14.5,6,19.

¶ *Faith.* Perhaps fidelity, or faithfulness. ¶ *Long-suffering.* With the evil passions of others, and their efforts to injure him. See the word explained in the Notes on 1 Cor. xiii. 4. ¶ *Charity.* Notes, 1 Cor. xiii. ¶ *Patience.* "A calm temper, which suffers evils without murmuring or discontent" (Webster). 11. *Persecutions.* On the meaning of this word, see Notes on Mat. v. 10. ¶ *Afflictions.* Trials of other kinds than those which arose from persecutions. The apostle met them everywhere; comp. Notes, Acts xx. 23. ¶ *Which came unto me at Antioch.* The Antioch here referred to is not the place of that name in Syria (Notes, Acts xi. 19); but a city of the same name in Pisidia, in Asia Minor; Notes, Acts xiii. 14. Paul there suffered persecution from the Jews, Acts xiii. 45. ¶ *At Iconium.* Notes, Acts xiii. 50. On the persecution there, see Notes on Acts xiv. 3–6. ¶ *At Lystra.* Acts xiv. 6. At this place, Paul was stoned; Notes, Acts xiv. 19. Timothy was a native of either Derbe or Lystra, cities near to each other, and was doubtless there at the time of this occurrence, Acts xvi. 1. ¶ *But out of them all the Lord delivered me.* See the history in the places referred to in the Acts.

12. *Yea, and all that will live godly in Christ Jesus shall suffer persecution.* Paul takes occasion from the reference to his own persecutions, to say that his case was not peculiar. It was the common lot of all who endeavoured to serve their Redeemer faithfully; and Timothy himself, therefore, must not hope to escape from it. The apostle had a particular reference, doubtless, to his own times; but he has put his remark into the most general form, as applicable to all periods. It is undoubtedly true at all times, and will ever be, that they who are devoted Christians—who live as the Saviour

cutions I endured: *m* but out of *them* all the Lord delivered me. 12 Yea, and all that will live

m Ps.34.19.

did—and who carry out his principles always, will experience some form of persecution. The *essence* of persecution consists in *subjecting a person to injury or disadvantage on account of his opinions.* It is something more than meeting his opinions by argument, which is always right and proper; it is inflicting some injury on him; depriving him of some privilege, or right; subjecting him to some disadvantage, or placing him in less favourable circumstances, on account of his sentiments. This may be either an injury done to his feelings, his family, his reputation, his property, his liberty, his influence; it may be by depriving him of an office which he held, or preventing him from obtaining one to which he is eligible; it may be by subjecting him to fine or imprisonment, to banishment, torture, or death. If, in any manner, or in any way, he is subjected to disadvantage on account of his religious opinions, and deprived of any immunities and rights to which he would be otherwise entitled, this is persecution. Now, it is doubtless as true as it ever was, that a man who will live as the Saviour did, will, like him, be subjected to some such injury or disadvantage. On account of his opinions, he may be held up to ridicule, or treated with neglect, or excluded from society to which his attainments and manners would otherwise introduce him, or shunned by those who might otherwise value his friendship. These things may be expected in the best times, and under the most favourable circumstances; and it is known that a large part of the history of the world, in its relation to the church, is nothing more than a history of persecution. It follows from this, (1) That they who make a profession of religion, should come prepared to be persecuted. It should be considered as one of the proper qualifications for membership in the church, to be *willing* to bear persecu-

godly in Christ Jesus shall suffer persecution.

13 But evil men and seducers

shall wax worse and worse, deceiving, and ^{n} being deceived.

n 2 Th.2.11.

tion, and to *resolve* not to shrink from any duty in order to avoid it. (2) They who *are* persecuted for their opinions, should consider that this *may be* one evidence that they have the spirit of Christ, and are his true friends. They should remember that, in this respect, they are treated as the Master was, and are in the goodly company of the prophets, apostles, and martyrs; for they were *all* persecuted. Yet, (3) if we are persecuted, we should carefully inquire, before we avail ourselves of this consolation, whether we are persecuted *because* we "live godly in Christ Jesus," or for some other reason. A man may embrace some absurd opinion, and call it religion; he may adopt some mode of dress irresistibly ludicrous, from the mere love of singularity, and may call it *conscience;* or he may be boorish in his manners, and uncivil in his deportment, outraging all the laws of social life, and may call this "deadness to the world;" and for these, and similar things, he may be contemned, ridiculed, and despised. But let him not infer, *therefore,* that he is to be enrolled among the martyrs, and that he is certainly a real Christian. That persecution which will properly furnish any evidence that we are the friends of Christ, must be *only* that which is "for righteousness' sake" (Mat. v. 10), and must be brought upon us in an honest effort to obey the commands of God. (4) Let those who have never been persecuted in any way, inquire whether it is not an evidence that they have no religion. If they had been more faithful, and more like their Master, would they have always escaped? And may not their freedom from it prove that they have surrendered the principles of their religion, where they should have stood firm, though the world were arrayed against them? It is easy for a professed Christian to avoid persecution, if he *yields* every point in which religion is opposed to the world. But

let not a man who will do this suppose that he has any claim to be numbered among the martyrs, or even entitled to the Christian name.

13. *But evil men and seducers shall wax worse and worse.* That is, it is the character of such men to do this; they may be expected to do it. This is the general law of depravity — that if men are not converted, they are always growing worse, and sinking deeper into iniquity. Their progress will be certain, though it may be gradual, since *nemo repentè turpissimus.* The *connection* here is this: that Timothy was not to expect that he would be exempt from persecution (ver. 12), by any change for the better in the wicked men referred to. He was to anticipate in them the operation of the general law in regard to bad men and seducers—that they would grow worse and worse. From this fact, he was to regard it as certain that he, as well as others, would be liable to be persecuted. The word rendered *seducers*—γόης—occurs nowhere else in the New Testament. It means, properly, a *juggler,* or *diviner;* and then, a *deceiver,* or *impostor.* Here it refers to those who, by seductive arts, lead persons into error. ¶ *Deceiving.* Making others believe that to be true and right, which is false and wrong. This was, of course, done by seductive arts. ¶ *And being deceived.* Under delusion themselves. The advocates of error are often themselves as really under deception, as those whom they impose upon. They are often sincere in the belief of error, and then they are under a delusion; or, if they are insincere, they are equally deluded in supposing that they can make error pass for truth before God, or can deceive the Searcher of hearts. The worst victims of delusion are those who attempt to delude others.

14. *But continue thou in the things which thou hast learned and hast been assured of.* To wit, the truths of religion. Timothy had been taught

14 But *continue thou in the things which thou hast learned and hast been assured of, know-

o ch. 1. 13.

those truths when a child, and he had been confirmed in them by the instructions of Paul. Amidst the errors and seductions of false teachers, Paul now exhorts him to hold fast those doctrines, whoever might oppose them, or whatever might be the consequence; comp. Notes, chap. i. 13. ¶ *Knowing of whom thou hast learned* them. To wit, of his mother (chap. i. 5), and of Paul, chap. i. 13. The reference seems to be particularly to the fact that he had learned these truths first from the lips of a mother (see ver. 15); and the *doctrine* taught here is, *that the fact that we have received the views of truth from a parent's lips, is a strong motive for adhering to them.* It is not to be supposed, indeed, that this is the *highest* motive, or that we are always to adhere to the doctrines which have been taught us, if, on maturer examination, we are convinced they are erroneous; but that this is a strong reason for adhering to what we have been taught in early life. It is so, because, (1) a parent has no motive for deceiving a child, and it cannot be supposed that he would teach him what he knew to be false; (2) a parent usually has had much more experience, and much better opportunities of examining what is true, than his child has; (3) there is a degree of respect which nature teaches us to be due to the sentiments of a parent. A child should depart very slowly from the opinions held by a father or mother; and, when it *is* done, it should be only as the result of prolonged examination and prayer. These considerations should have the greater weight, if a parent has been eminent for piety, and especially if that parent has been removed to heaven. A child, standing by the grave of a pious father or mother, should reflect and pray much, before he deliberately adopts opinions which he knows that father or mother would regard as wrong.

15. *And that from a child thou*

ing of whom thou hast learned *them;*

15 And that from a child thou hast known the holy Scriptures,

hast known the holy Scriptures. That is, the Old Testament; for the New Testament was not then written; Notes, John v. 39. The mother of Timothy was a pious Hebrewess, and regarded it as one of the duties of her religion to train her son in the careful knowledge of the word of God. This was regarded by the Hebrews as an important duty of religion, and there is reason to believe that it was commonly faithfully performed. The Jewish writings abound with lessons on this subject. Rabbi Judah says, "The boy of five years of age ought to apply to the study of the sacred Scriptures." Rabbi Solomon, on Deut. xi. 19, says, "When the boy begins to talk, his father ought to converse with him in the sacred language, and to teach him the law; if he does not do that, he seems to bury him." See numerous instances referred to in Wetstein, *in loco.* The expression used by Paul—*from a child* (ἀπὸ βρέφους)—does not make it certain at precisely *what* age Timothy was first instructed in the Scriptures, though it would denote an *early* age. The word used—βρέφος—denotes, (1) a babe unborn, Luke i. 41, 44; (2) an infant, babe, suckling. In the New Testament, it is rendered *babe* and *babes,* Luke i. 41, 44; ii. 12, 16; 1 Pet. ii. 2; *infants,* Luke viii. 15; and *young children,* Acts vii. 19. It does not elsewhere occur, and its current use would make it probable that Timothy had been taught the Scriptures as soon as he was capable of learning anything. Dr. Doddridge correctly renders it here "*from infancy.*" It may be remarked then, (1) That it is proper to teach the Bible to children at as early a period of life as possible. (2) That there is reason to hope that such instruction will not be forgotten, but will have a salutary influence on their future lives. The piety of Timothy is traced by the apostle to the fact that he had been early taught to read the Scrip-

which[p] are able to make thee wise unto salvation through faith which is in Christ Jesus.

16 All[q] Scripture *is* given by

p Jn.5.39.   q 2 Pe.1.21.

tures, and a great proportion of those who are in the church have been early made acquainted with the Bible. (3) It is proper to teach the *Old* Testament to children—since this was all that Timothy had, and this was made the means of his salvation. (4) We may see the utility of Sabbath-schools. The great, and almost the sole object of such schools is to teach the Bible, and from the view which Paul had of the advantage to Timothy of having been early made acquainted with the Bible, there can be no doubt that if Sunday-schools had then been in existence, he would have been their hearty patron and friend. ¶ *Which are able to make thee wise unto salvation.* So to instruct you in the way of salvation, that you may find the path to life. Learn, hence, (1) That the plan of salvation may be learned from the Old Testament. It is not as clearly revealed there as it is in the New, but *it is there;* and if a man had only the Old Testament, he might find the way to be saved. The Jew, then, has no excuse if he is not saved. (2) The Scriptures have *power.* They are "*able* to make one wise to salvation." They are not a cold, tame, dead thing. There is no book that has so much *power* as the Bible; none that is so efficient in moving the hearts, and consciences, and intellects of mankind. There is no book that *has* moved so many minds; none that has produced so deep and permanent effects on the world. (3) To find the way of salvation, is the best kind of wisdom; and none are wise who do not make that the great object of life. ¶ *Through faith which is in Christ Jesus.* Notes, Mark xvi. 16; Rom. i. 17. Paul knew of no salvation, except through the Lord Jesus. He says, therefore, that the study of the Scriptures, valuable as they were, would not save the soul unless there

inspiration of God, [r]and *is* profitable for doctrine, for reproof, for correction, for instruction in righteousness;

r Ro.15.4.

was faith in the Redeemer; and it is implied, also, that the proper effect of a careful study of the *Old* Testament, would be to lead one to put his trust in the Messiah.

16. *All Scripture.* This properly refers to the Old Testament, and should not be applied to any part of the New Testament, unless it can be shown that that part was then written, and was included under the general name of *the Scriptures;* comp. 2 Pet. iii. 15, 16. But it includes the *whole* of the Old Testament, and is the solemn testimony of Paul that it was *all* inspired. If now it can be proved that Paul himself was an inspired man, this settles the question as to the inspiration of the Old Testament. ¶ *Is given by inspiration of God.* All this is expressed in the original by one word—θεόπνευστος—*theopneustos.* This word occurs nowhere else in the New Testament. It properly means, *God-inspired*—from Θεός, *God,* and πνέω, *to breathe, to breathe out.* The idea of *breathing upon,* or *breathing into the soul,* is that which the word naturally conveys. Thus God breathed into the nostrils of Adam the breath of life (Gen. ii. 7), and thus the Saviour breathed on his disciples, and said, "Receive ye the Holy Ghost," John xx. 22. The idea seems to have been, that the life was in the breath, and that an intelligent spirit was communicated with the breath. The expression was used among the Greeks, and a similar one was employed by the Romans. Plutarch ed. R. ix. p. 383. 9: τοὺς ὀνείρους τοὺς θεοπνεύστους. Phocylid.121: τῆς δὲ θεοπνεύστου σοφίης λόγος ἐστὶν ἄριστος. Perhaps, however, this is not an expression of Phocylides, but of the pseudo Phocylides. So it is understood by Bloomfield. Cicero, pro Arch. 8: *poetam—quasi divino quodam spiritu inflari.* The word does not occur in the Septuagint, but is found in Josephus, *C. Ap.* i. 7:

17 That[s] the man of God may

[s] Ps.119.98-100.   [4] or, *perfected.*

"The Scripture of the prophets who were taught according to the inspiration of God"—κατὰ τὴν ἐπίπνοιαν τὴν ἀπὸ τοῦ Ͽεοῦ. In regard to the manner of inspiration, and to the various questions which have been started as to its nature, nothing can be learned from the use of this word. It asserts a *fact*—that the Old Testament was composed under a divine influence, which might be represented by *breathing on one,* and so imparting life. But the language *must* be figurative; for God does not *breathe,* though the fair inference is, that those Scriptures are as much the production of God, or are as much to be traced to him, as life is; comp. Mat. xxii. 43; 2 Pet. i. 21. The question as to the *degree* of inspiration, and whether it extends to the *words* of Scripture, and how far the sacred writers were left to the exercise of their own faculties, is foreign to the design of these Notes. All that is necessary to be held is, that the sacred writers were kept from error on those subjects which were matters of their own observation, or which pertained to memory; and that there were truths imparted to them directly by the Spirit of God, which they could never have arrived at by the unaided exercise of their own minds. Comp. Intro. to Isaiah and Job. ¶ *And* is *profitable.* It is useful; it is adapted to give instruction, to administer reproof, &c. If "*all*" Scripture is thus valuable, then we are to esteem no part of the Old Testament as worthless. There is no portion of it, even now, which may not be fitted, in certain circumstances, to furnish us valuable lessons, and, consequently, no part of it which could be spared from the sacred canon. There is no part of the human body which is not useful in its place, and no part of it which can be spared without sensible loss. ¶ *For doctrine.* For teaching or communicating instruction; comp. Notes on 1 Tim. iv. 16. ¶ *For reproof.* On the meaning of the word here rendered *reproof*—ἔλεγχος—see

be perfect, thoroughly [4]furnished unto all good works.

Notes on Heb. xi. 1. It here means, probably, for *convincing;* that is, convincing a man of his sins, of the truth and claims of religion, &c.; see Notes on John xvi. 8. ¶ *For correction.* The word here used—ἐπανόρθωσις—occurs nowhere else in the New Testament. It means, properly, a *setting to rights, reparation, restoration* (from ἐπανορϿόω, to right up again, to restore); and here means, the leading to a correction or amendment of life—*a reformation.* The meaning is, that the Scriptures are a powerful means of reformation, or of putting men into the proper condition in regard to morals. After all the means which have been employed to reform mankind; all the appeals which are made to them on the score of health, happiness, respectability, property, and long life, the word of God is still the most powerful and the most effectual means of recovering those who have fallen into vice. No reformation can be permanent which is not based on the principles of the word of God. ¶ *For instruction in righteousness.* Instruction in regard to the principles of justice, or what is right. Man needs not only to be made acquainted with truth, to be convinced of his error, and to be reformed; but he needs to be taught what is right, or what is required of him, in order that he may lead a holy life. Every reformed and regenerated man needs instruction, and should not be left merely with the evidence that he is *reformed,* or *converted.* He should be followed with the principles of the word of God, to show him how he may lead an upright life. The Scriptures furnish the rules of holy living in abundance, and thus they are adapted to the whole work of recovering man, and of guiding him to heaven.

17. *That the man of God may be perfect.* The object is not merely to convince and to convert him; it is to furnish all the instruction needful for his entire perfection. The idea here is, not that anyone *is* ab-

16

solutely perfect, but that the Scriptures have laid down the way which leads to perfection, and that, if any one *were* perfect, he would find in the Scriptures all the instruction which he needed in those circumstances. There is no deficiency in the Bible for man, in any of the situations in which he may be placed in life; and the whole tendency of the book is to make him who will put himself fairly under its instructions, absolutely perfect. ¶ *Thoroughly furnished unto all good works.* Marg., *perfected.* The Greek means, to bring to an end; to make complete. The idea is, that whatever good work the man of God desires to perform, or however perfect he aims to be, he will find no deficiency in the Scriptures, but will find there the most ample instructions that he needs. He can never advance so far, as to become forsaken of his guide. He can never make such progress, as to have gone in advance of the volume of revealed truth, and to be thrown upon his own resources in a region which was not thought of by the Author of the Bible. No new phase of human affairs can appear in which it will not direct him; no new plan of benevolence can be started, for which he will not find principles there to guide him; and he can make no progress in knowledge or holiness, where he will not feel that his holy counsellor is in advance of him still, and that it is capable of conducting him even yet into higher and purer regions. Let us, then, study and prize the Bible. It is a holy and a safe guide. It has conducted millions along the dark and dangerous way of life, and has never led one astray. The human mind, in its investigations of truth, has never gone beyond its teachings; nor has man ever advanced into a region so bright that its light has become dim, or where it has not thrown its beams of glory on still far distant objects. We are often in circumstances in which we feel that we have reached the outer limit of what man can teach us; but we never get into such circumstances in regard to the word of God.

How precious is the book divine,
 By inspiration given!
Bright as a lamp its doctrines shine,
 To guide our souls to heaven.

It sweetly cheers our drooping hearts
 In this dark vale of tears;
Life, light, and joy it still imparts,
 And quells our rising fears.

This lamp, through all the tedious night
 Of life, shall guide our way;
Till we behold the clearer light
 Of an eternal day.

CHAPTER IV.

ANALYSIS OF THE CHAPTER.

This chapter comprises the following subjects:—

(1) A solemn charge to Timothy, to be faithful in preaching the gospel, and in the whole work of the ministry, ver. 1–5. The particular *reason* given for this charge was, that the time was approaching when men would not endure sound doctrine, but would turn away from the truth. Hence, Timothy is exhorted to be faithful in his work, and to be prepared to endure the trials which, in such circumstances, a faithful minister must be expected to meet.

(2) A statement of Paul that his own work was nearly done, and that the hour of his departure drew near, ver. 6–8. This statement, also, seems to be made in order to excite Timothy to increased fidelity in the ministry. His teacher, guide, father, and friend, was about to be withdrawn, and the great work of preaching was to be committed to other hands. Hence, in view of his own departure, Paul exhorts Timothy to fidelity when he himself should be removed.

(3) An exhortation to Timothy to come to him as soon as practicable, ver. 9–15. Paul was then in bonds, and was expecting soon to die. He was alone. For various reasons, those who had been with him had left him, and he needed some companion and friend. He therefore exhorts Timothy to come to him as soon as possible.

(4) Paul refers now to his first trial before the emperor, and to the fact that then no one stood by him, ver. 16–19. The *reason* of his referring to this seems to be, to induce Timothy to come to him in view of his an-

CHAPTER IV.

I ^aCHARGE *thee* therefore before God, and the Lord Jesus

a 1 Ti.5.21; 6.13.

ticipated *second* trial. The *Lord,* he says, *then* stood by him, and he had confidence that he would continue to do it; yet who is there that does not feel it desirable to have some dear earthly friend to be with him when he dies?

(5) The epistle is closed, in the usual manner, with various salutations, and with the benediction, ver. 19–22.

1. *I charge* thee *therefore before God.* Notes on 1 Tim. v. 21. ¶ *Who shall judge the quick and the dead.* That is, the Lord Jesus; for he is to be the judge of men, Mat. xxv. 31–46; 2 Cor. v. 10. The word *quick* means *living* (Notes, Acts x. 42; Eph. ii. 1); and the idea is, that he would be alike the judge of all who were alive when he should come, and of all who had died; see Notes on 1 Thes. iv. 16, 17. In view of the fact that *all,* whether preachers or hearers, must give up their account to the final Judge, Paul charges Timothy to be faithful; and what is there which will more conduce to fidelity in the discharge of duty, than the thought that we must soon give up a solemn account of the manner in which we have performed it? ¶ *At his appearing.* That is, the judgment shall then take place. This must refer to a judgment yet to take place, for the Lord Jesus has not yet "appeared" the second time to men; and, if this be so, then there is to be a resurrection of the dead. On the meaning of the word rendered *appearing,* see Notes on 2 Thes. ii. 8. It is there rendered *brightness;* comp. 1 Tim. vi. 14; 2 Tim. i. 10; Tit. ii. 13. ¶ *And his kingdom.* Or, at the setting up of his kingdom. The idea of his *reigning,* or setting up his kingdom, is not unfrequently associated with the idea of his *coming;* see Mat. xvi. 28. The meaning is, that, at his second advent, the extent and majesty of his kingdom will be fully displayed. It will be seen that he has control over the

Christ, ^bwho shall judge the quick and the dead at his appearing and his kingdom;

2 Preach the word; be instant

b Re.20.12,13.

elements, over the graves of the dead, and over all the living. It will be seen that the earth and the heavens are under his sway, and that all things there acknowledge him as their sovereign Lord. In order to meet the full force of the language used by Paul here, it is not necessary to suppose that he will set up a visible kingdom on the earth, but only that there will be an illustrious display of himself as a king, and of the extent and majesty of the empire over which he presides; comp. Notes on Rom. xiv. 11; Phil. ii. 10.

2. *Preach the word.* The word of God; the gospel. This was to be the main business of the life of Timothy, and Paul solemnly charges him, in view of the certain coming of the Redeemer to judgment, to be faithful in the performance of it. ¶ *Be instant.* See Notes, Rom. xii. 12. The meaning here is, that he should be constant in this duty. Literally, *to stand by,* or *to stand fast by;* that is, he was to be pressing or urgent in the performance of this work. He was always to be at his post, and was to embrace every opportunity of making known the gospel. What Paul seems to have contemplated was, not merely that he should perform the duty at stated and regular times; but that he should press the matter as one who had the subject much at heart, and never lose an opportunity of making the gospel known. ¶ *In season—εὐκαίρως.* In good time; opportunely; comp. Mat. xxvi. 16; Luke xxii. 6; Mark xiv. 11. The sense is, when it could be *conveniently* done; when all things were favourable, and when there were no obstructions or hindrances. It may include the *stated* and *regular* seasons for public worship, but is not confined to them. ¶ *Out of season—ἀκαίρως.* This word does not elsewhere occur in the New Testament. It is the opposite of the former, and means that a

in season, out of season; ^creprove, rebuke, exhort with all long-suffering and doctrine.

3 For the time will come when

c Tit.2.15.

minister is to seek opportunities to preach the gospel even at such periods as might be inconvenient to himself, or when there might be hindrances and embarrassments, or when there was no stated appointment for preaching. He is not to confine himself to the appointed times of worship, or to preach only when it will be perfectly convenient for himself, but he is to have such an interest and earnestness in the work, that it will lead him to do it in the face of embarrassments and discouragements, and whenever he can find an opportunity. A man who is greatly intent on an object will seek every opportunity to promote it. He will not confine himself to stated times and places, but will present it everywhere, and at all times. A man, therefore, who merely confines himself to the stated seasons of preaching the gospel, or who merely preaches when it is convenient to himself, should not consider that he has come up to the requirement of the rule laid down by the apostle. He should preach in his private conversation, and in the intervals of his public labours, at the side of the sick-bed, and wherever there is a prospect of doing good to anyone. If his heart is full of love to the Saviour and to souls, he cannot help doing this. ¶ *Reprove.* Or, *convince;* Notes, chap. iii. 16. The meaning is, that he was to use such arguments as would *convince* men of the truth of religion, and of their own need of it. ¶ *Rebuke.* Rebuke offenders, Titus ii. 15; see the use of the word in Mat. viii. 26; xii. 16 (rendered *charged*); xvi. 22; xvii. 18; xix. 13; xx. 31; Luke iv. 35, 39; xvii. 13; xviii. 15; Jude 9. In the New Testament the word is used to express a judgment of what is wrong or contrary to one's will, and hence to admonish or reprove. It implies our conviction that there is something evil, or some fault in him who is re-

they will not endure sound doctrine; but after their own lusts shall they heap to themselves teachers, having itching ears;

buked. The word in this verse rendered *reprove,* does not imply this, but merely that one may be in error, and needs to have *arguments* presented to convince him of the truth. That word also implies no superior *authority* in him who does it. He presents *reasons,* or *argues* the case, for the purpose of *convincing.* The word here rendered *rebuke,* implies authority or superiority, and means merely that we may *say* that a thing is wrong, and administer a rebuke for it, as if there were no doubt that it was wrong. The propriety of the rebuke rests on our *authority* for doing it, not on the *arguments* which we present. This is based on the presumption that men often *know* that they are doing wrong, and need no arguments to *convince* them of it. The idea is, that the minister is not merely to *reason* about sin, and *convince* men that it is wrong, but he may solemnly admonish them not to do it, and warn them of the consequences. ¶ *Exhort.* Notes, Rom. xii. 8. ¶ *With all long-suffering.* That is, with a patient and persevering spirit if you are opposed; see Notes on chap. ii. 25; comp. Notes, Rom. ii. 4; comp. Rom. ix. 22; 2 Cor. vi. 6; Gal. v. 22; Eph. iv. 2; Col. i. 11; iii. 12; 1 Tim. i. 16. ¶ *And doctrine.* Teaching, or patient instruction.

3. *For the time will come,* &c. Probably referring to the time mentioned in chap. iii. 1, *seq.* ¶ *When they will not endure sound doctrine.* Greek, *healthful doctrine; i.e.* doctrine contributing to the health of the soul, or to salvation. At that time they would seek a kind of instruction more conformable to their wishes and feelings. ¶ *But after their own lusts.* They will seek such kind of preaching as will accord with their carnal desires; or such as will palliate their evil propensities, and deal gently with their vices; comp. Isa. xxx. 10, "Speak unto us smooth things; pro-

4 And they shall turn away *their* ears from the truth, and shall be *d* turned unto fables.

5 But watch thou in all things,

d 1 Ti.1.4.

phesy deceits." ¶ *Shall they heap to themselves teachers, having itching ears.* The word rendered *heap*— ἐπισωρεύω—does not occur elsewhere in the New Testament. It means *to heap up upon, to accumulate;* and here *to multiply.* The word rendered *itching*—κνήθω—also occurs only in this place in the New Testament. It means *to rub, to scratch;* and then *to tickle,* and here to feel an *itching* for something pleasing or gratifying. The image is derived from the desire which we have, when there is an itching sensation, to have it rubbed or scratched. Such an uneasiness would these persons have to have some kind of instruction that would allay their restless and uneasy desires, or would gratify them. In explanation of this passage we may observe, (1) That there will be always religious teachers of some kind, and that in proportion as error and sin abound, they will be multiplied. The apostle here says, that by turning away from Timothy, and from sound instruction, they would not abandon *all* religious teachers, but would rather increase and multiply them. Men often declaim much against a regular ministry, and call it *priestcraft;* and yet, if they were to get rid of *such* a ministry, they would by no means escape from *all* kinds of religious teachers. The deeper the darkness, and the more gross the errors, and the more prevalent the wickedness of men, the more will a certain kind of religious teachers abound, and the more it will cost to support them. Italy and Spain swarm with priests, and in every heathen nation they constitute a very numerous class of the population. The *cheapest* ministry on the earth is a well-educated Protestant clergy, and if society wishes to free itself from swarms of preachers, and prophets, and exhorters, it should secure the regular services of an educated and pious ministry. (2) In such

e endure afflictions, do the work of an evangelist, [1] make *f* full proof of thy ministry.

e ch.2.3.   1 or, *fulfil.*   f 1 Ti.4.12,15.

classes of persons as the apostle here refers to, there is a restless, uneasy desire to *have* some kind of preachers. They have "itching ears." They will be ready to run after all kinds of public instructors. They will be little pleased with any, and this will be one reason why they will have so many. They are fickle, and unsettled, and never satisfied. A desire to hear the *truth,* and to learn the way of salvation, is a good desire. But this can be better gratified by far under the patient and intelligent labour of a single religious teacher, than by running after many teachers, or than by frequent changes. How much would a child learn if he was constantly running from one school to another? (3) Such persons would have teachers according to "their own lusts;" that is, their own tastes, or wishes. They would have those who would coincide with their whims; who would foster every vagary which might enter their imagination; who would countenance every wild project for doing good; who would be the advocates of the errors which they held; and who would be afraid to rebuke their faults. These are the principles on which many persons choose their religious teachers. The *true* principle should be, to select those who will faithfully declare the truth, and who will shrink from exposing and denouncing sin, wherever it may be found.

4. *And they shall turn away their ears from the truth.* That is, the people themselves will turn away from the truth. It does not mean that the teachers would turn them away by the influence of their instructions. ¶ *And shall be turned unto fables.* Notes, 1 Tim. i. 4.

5. *But watch thou in all things.* Be vigilant against error and against sin, and faithful in the performance of duty; Notes, Mat. xxv. 13; 1 Cor. xvi. 13. ¶ *Endure afflictions.* Notes, chap. ii. 3. The Greek word here is

6 For I am now ready to be
g Phi.1.23; 2 Pe.1.14.

offered, g and the time of my departure is at hand.

the same which is there rendered "*endure hardness.*" ¶ *Do the work of an evangelist.* On the word *evangelist*, see Notes on Acts xxi. 8. The phrase here means, *do the work of preaching the gospel*, or of one appointed to proclaim the glad tidings of salvation. This is the proper business of all ministers, whatever other rank they may maintain. Whether it was ever regarded as the proper duty of a separate class of men to do this, see Notes on Eph. iv. 11. ¶ *Make full proof of thy ministry.* Marg., *fulfil;* comp. Notes, Rom. xiv. 5. The word here used denotes, properly, to bear or bring fully; then to persuade fully; and then to make fully assured of, to give full proof of. The meaning here seems to be, *to furnish full evidence of what is the design of the Christian ministry, and of what it is adapted to accomplish*, by the faithful performance of all its duties. Timothy was so to discharge the duties of his office as to furnish *a fair illustration* of what the ministry could do, and thus to show the wisdom of the Saviour in its institution. This should be the aim of all the ministers of the gospel. Each one should resolve, by the blessing of God, that the ministry, in his hands, shall be allowed, *by a fair trial*, to show to the utmost what it is adapted to do for the welfare of mankind.

6. *For I am now ready to be offered.* This conviction of the apostle that he was about to die, is urged as a reason why Timothy should be laborious and faithful in the performance of the duties of his office. His own work was nearly done. He was soon to be withdrawn from the earth, and whatever benefit the world might have derived from his experience or active exertions, it was now to be deprived of it. He was about to leave a work which he much loved, and to which he had devoted the vigour of his life, and he was anxious that they who were to succeed him should carry on the work with all the energy and zeal in their power. This expresses

the common feeling of aged ministers as death draws near. The word "*ready*" in the phrase "ready to be offered," conveys an idea which is not in the original. It implies a *willingness* to depart, which, whether true or not, is not the idea conveyed by the apostle. His statement is merely of *the fact* that he was *about* to die, or that his work was drawing to a close. No doubt he *was* "ready," in the sense of being willing and prepared, but this is not the idea in the Greek. The single Greek word rendered, "I am ready to be offered"—σπένδομαι—occurs nowhere else in the New Testament, except in Phil. ii. 17, where it is translated "if I *be offered;*" see it explained in the Notes on that place. The allusion here, says Burder (in Rosenmüller's *A. u. n. Morgenland*), is to the custom which prevailed among the heathen generally, of pouring wine and oil on the head of a victim when it was about to be offered in sacrifice. The idea of the apostle then is, that he was in the condition of the victim on whose head the wine and oil had been already poured, and which was just about to be put to death; that is, he was about to die. Every preparation had been made, and he only awaited the blow which was to strike him down. The meaning is not that he was to be a *sacrifice;* it is that his death was about to occur. Nothing more remained to be done but to die. The victim was all ready, and he was sure that the blow would soon fall. What was the *ground* of his expectation, he has not told us. Probably there were events occurring in Rome which made it morally certain that though he had once been acquitted, he could not now escape. At all events, it is interesting to contemplate an aged and experienced Christian on the borders of the grave, and to learn what were his feelings in the prospect of his departure to the eternal world. Happily, Paul has in more places than one (comp. Phil. i. 23), stated his views in such circumstances, and we know

7 I have [h]fought a good fight,
I have [i]finished *my* course, [k]I
have kept the faith:

8 Henceforth there is laid up
for me [l]a crown of righteousness,

h 1 Ti.6.12.　*i* Ac.20.24.　*k* Pr.23.23; Re.3.10.

which the Lord, the righteous
judge, shall give me at that day;
and not to me only, but unto
[m]all them also that love his appearing.

l 1 Co.9.25; 1 Pe.5.4; Re.2.10.　　*m* 1 Co.2.9.

that his religion then did not fail him.
He found it to be in the prospect of
death what he had found it to be
through all his life—the source of unspeakable consolation; and he was
enabled to look calmly onward to the
hour which should summon him into
the presence of his Judge. ¶ *And
the time of my departure is at hand.*
Gr., *dissolving,* or *dissolution.* So we
speak of the *dissolution* of the soul
and body. The verb from which the
noun (ἀνάλυσις) is derived (ἀναλύω),
means to loosen again; to undo. It
is applied to the act of unloosing or
casting off the fastenings of a ship,
preparatory to a departure. The
proper idea in the use of the word
would be, that he had been bound to
the present world, like a ship to its
moorings, and that death would be a
release. He would now spread his
sails on the broad ocean of eternity.
The true idea of death is that of
loosening the bands that confine us to
the present world; of setting us free,
and permitting the soul to go forth,
as with expanded sails, on its eternal
voyage. With such a view of death,
why should a Christian fear to die?
7. *I have fought a good fight.* The
Christian life is often represented as
a conflict, or warfare; see Notes on
1 Tim. vi. 12. That noble conflict
with sin, the world, the flesh, and the
devil, Paul now says he had been
able to maintain. ¶ *I have finished*
my *course.* The Christian life, too,
is often represented as a *race* to be
run; comp. Notes, 1 Cor. ix. 24–26.
¶ *I have kept the faith.* I have steadfastly maintained the faith of the
gospel; or, have lived a life of fidelity
to my Master. Probably the expression means that he had kept his
plighted faith to the Redeemer, or
had spent a life in faithfully endeavouring to serve his Lord.
8. *Henceforth there is laid up for*

me. At the end of my race, as there
was a crown in reserve for those who
had successfully striven in the Grecian
games; comp. Notes on 1 Cor. ix.
25. The word *henceforth*—λοιπὸν—
means *what remains,* or *as to the rest;*
and the idea is, that that was what
remained of the whole career. The
race had been run; the conflict had
been waged; and all which was now
necessary to complete the whole transaction, was merely that the crown be
bestowed. ¶ *A crown of righteousness.* That is, a crown won in the
cause of righteousness, and conferred
as the reward of his conflicts and efforts in the cause of holiness. It was
not the crown of ambition; it was
not a garland won in struggles for
earthly distinction; it was that which
was the appropriate reward of his
efforts to be personally holy, and to
spread the principles of holiness as far
as possible through the world. ¶ *Which
the Lord, the righteous judge, shall
give me.* The Lord Jesus, appointed
to judge the world, and to dispense
the rewards of eternity. It will be
seen in the last day that the rewards
of heaven are not conferred in an arbitrary manner, but that they are bestowed because they *ought* to be, or
that God is righteous and just in
doing it. No man will be admitted
to heaven who *ought not,* under all
the circumstances of the case, to be
admitted there; no one will be excluded who *ought* to have been saved.
¶ *At that day.* That is, the time
when he will come to judge the world,
Mat. xxv. ¶ *And not to me only.*
"Though my life has been spent in
laboriously endeavouring to spread
his religion; though I have suffered
much, and laboured long; though I
have struggled hard to win the prize,
and now have it full in view, yet I do
not suppose that it is to be conferred on
me alone. It is not like the wreath of

9 Do thy diligence to come shortly unto me:

10 For Demas hath forsaken me, ⁿhaving loved this present

world, and is departed unto Thessalonica; Crescens to Galatia, Titus unto Dalmatia.

n 1 Jn.2.15.

olive, laurel, pine, or parsley (Notes, 1 Cor. ix. 25), which could be conferred only on one victor (Notes, 1 Cor. ix. 24); but here every one may obtain the crown who strives for it. The struggle is not between me and a competitor in such a sense that, if *I* obtain the crown, *he* must be excluded; but it is a crown which *he* can obtain as well as *I*. As many as run—as many as fight the good fight—as many as keep the faith—as many as love his appearing, may win the crown as well as I." Such is religion, and such is the manner in which its rewards differ from all others. At the Grecian games, but one could obtain the prize, 1 Cor. ix. 24. All the rest who contended in those games, no matter how numerous they were, or how skilfully they contended, or how much effort they made, were of course subjected to the mortification of a failure, and to all the ill-feeling and envy to which such a failure might give rise. So it is in respect to all the prizes which this world can bestow. In a lottery, but one can obtain the highest prize; in a class in college, but one can secure the highest honour; in the scramble for office, no matter how numerous the competitors may be, or what may be their merits, but one can obtain it. All the rest are liable to the disappointments and mortifications of defeat. Not so in religion. No matter how numerous the competitors, or how worthy any one of them may be, or how pre-eminent above his brethren, yet all may obtain the prize, all may be crowned with a diadem of life, of equal brilliancy. No one is excluded because another is successful; no one fails of the reward because another obtains it. Who, then, would not make an effort to win the immortal crown? ¶ *Unto all them also that love his appearing.* That is, unto all who *desire* his second coming. To believe in the second advent of the Lord Jesus to judge the world, and to

desire his return, became a kind of a criterion by which Christians were known. No others but true Christians were supposed to believe in that, and no others truly desired it; comp. Rev. i. 7; xxii. 20. It is so now. It is one of the characteristics of a true Christian that he sincerely *desires* the return of his Saviour, and would *welcome* his appearing in the clouds of heaven.

9. *Do thy diligence to come shortly unto me.* As soon as possible. Timothy had been Paul's travelling companion, and was his intimate friend. The apostle was now nearly forsaken, and was about to pass through severe trials. It is not certainly known for what purpose he wished him to come to him, but perhaps he desired to give him some parting counsels; perhaps he wished him to be near him when he died. It is evident from this that he did not regard him as the prelatical "bishop of the church of the Ephesians," or consider that he was so confined to that place in his labours, that he was not also to go to other places if he was called in the providence of God. It is probable that Timothy would obey such a summons; and there is no reason to believe that he ever returned to Ephesus.

10. *For Demas hath forsaken me.* Demas is honourably mentioned in Col. iv. 14; but nothing more is known of him than what can be gathered from that place and this—that he was at first a friend and fellow-labourer of Paul, but that, under the influence of a desire to live, he afterwards forsook him, even in circumstances where he greatly needed the presence of a friend. ¶ *Having loved this present world.* This does not mean, necessarily, that he was an avaricious man, or that, in itself, he loved the honours or wealth of this world; but it means that he desired to live. He was not willing to stay with Paul, and subject him-

11 Only Luke is with me. Take Mark, and bring him with thee; for he is profitable to me for the ministry.

self to the probabilities of martyrdom; and, in order to secure his life, he departed to a place of safety. The Greek is, ἀγαπήσας τὸν νῦν αἰῶνα—having loved the world that now is; that is, this world as it is, with all its cares, and troubles, and comforts; having desired to remain in this world, rather than to go to the other. There is, perhaps, a slight censure here in the language of Paul—*the censure of grief;* but there is no reason why Demas should be held up as an example of a worldly man. That he desired to live longer; that he was unwilling to remain and risk the loss of life, is indeed clear. That Paul was pained by his departure, and that he felt lonely and sad, is quite apparent; but I see no evidence that Demas was influenced by what are commonly called *worldly* feelings, or that he was led to this course by the desire of wealth, or fame, or pleasure. ¶ *And is departed unto Thessalonica.* Perhaps his native place (Calmet). ¶ *Crescens.* Nothing more is known of Crescens than is here mentioned. " He is thought by Eusebius and others to have preached in Gaul, and to have founded the church in Vienne, in Dauphiny " (Calmet). ¶ *To Galatia.* See Intro. to the Epistle to the Galatians, § 1. It is not known to what part of Galatia he had gone, or why he went there. ¶ *Titus unto Dalmatia.* Dalmatia was a part of Illyricum, on the Gulf of Venice, or the Adriatic Sea. On the situation of Illyricum, see Notes on Rom. xv. 19. Paul does not mention the reason why Titus had gone there; but it is not improbable that he had gone to preach the gospel, or to visit the churches which Paul had planted in that region. The apostle does not suggest that he was deserving of blame for having gone, and it can hardly be supposed that *Titus* would have left him at this time without his concurrence. Perhaps, when he permitted him to go, he did not know how soon events would come to a crisis with him; and as a letter would more readily reach Timothy

at Ephesus, than Titus in Dalmatia, he requested him to come to him, instead of directing Titus to return.
　11. *Only Luke is with me.* Luke, the author of the gospel which bears his name, and of the Acts of the Apostles. For a considerable part of the ministry of Paul, he was his travelling companion (comp. Notes on Acts xvi. 10), and we know that he went with him to Rome, Acts xxvii. 1. ¶ *Take Mark.* John Mark; Notes, Acts xv. 37. He was the son of a sister of Barnabas, and had been the travelling companion of Barnabas and Paul. There had been a temporary alienation between Paul and him (Acts xv. 38); but this passage proves that that had been removed, and that Paul was reconciled to him. ¶ *For he is profitable to me for the ministry.* In what way he would be profitable, he does not say; nor is it known why Mark was at that time with Timothy. It may be observed, however, that this is such language as Paul might be expected to use of Mark, after what had occurred, as recorded in Acts xv. 38. He felt that he was now about to die. If he suspected that there was on the part of Mark any lingering apprehension that the great apostle was not entirely reconciled to him, or retained a recollection of what had formerly occurred, nothing would be more natural than that, at this trying time of his life, Paul should summon him to his side, and express towards him the kindest emotions. It would soothe *any* lingering irritation in the mind of Mark, to receive such a message.
　12. *And Tychicus.* See Acts xx. 4. In Eph. vi. 21, Paul calls him " a beloved brother, and faithful minister in the Lord." But it may be asked why he did not retain him with him, or why should he have sent him away, and then called Timothy to him? The probability is, that he had sent him before he had seen reason to apprehend that he would be put to death; and now, feeling the need of a friend to be with him, he sent to Timothy, rather

12 And *Tychicus have I sent to Ephesus.

13 The cloak that I left at

o Tit. 3. 12.

Troas with Carpus, when thou comest, bring *with thee*, and the books, *but* especially the parchments.

---

than to him, because Tychicus had been employed to perform some service which he could not well leave, and because Paul wished to give some special instructions to Timothy before he died. ¶ *Have I sent to Ephesus.* Why, is not certainly known; comp. Intro. § 2.

13. *The cloak that I left at Troas.* On the situation of Troas, see Notes on Acts xvi. 8. It was not on the most direct route from Ephesus to Rome, but was 'a route frequently taken; comp. the Map in the Notes on the Acts of the Apostles. See also the Intro. § 2. In regard to what the "cloak" here mentioned was, there has been considerable difference of opinion. The Greek word used (φελόνης—variously written φαιλόνης, φελόνης, and φελώνης), occurs nowhere else in the New Testament. It is supposed to be used for a similar Greek word (φαινόλης), to denote a cloak, or great-coat, with a hood, used chiefly on journeys, or in the army: Latin, *penula.* It is described by Eschenberg (*Man. Class. Lit.*, p. 209) as a "cloak without sleeves, for cold or rainy weather." See the uses of it in the quotations made by Wetstein, *in loco.* Others, however, have supposed that the word means a travelling-case for books, &c. So Hesychius understands it. Bloomfield endeavours to unite the two opinions by suggesting that it may mean a *cloak-bag,* and that he had left his books and parchments in it. It is impossible to settle the precise meaning of the word here, and it is not material. The common opinion, that it was a wrapper or travelling-cloak, is the most probable; and such a garment would not be undesirable for a prisoner. It should be remembered, also, that winter was approaching (ver. 21), and such a cloak would be particularly needed. He had probably passed through Troas in summer, and, not needing the cloak, and not choosing

to encumber himself with it, had left it at the house of a friend. On the meaning of the word, see Wetstein, Robinson, *Lex.*, and Schleusner, *Lex.* Comp., also, Suic. Thess. ii. 1422. The doubt in regard to what is here meant, is as old as Chrysostom. He says (Hom. x. on this epistle), that "the word (φελόνην) denotes a garment—τὸ ἱμάτιον. But some understood by it a capsula, or bag—γλωσσόκομον" (comp. Notes on John xii. 6), "in which books, &c., were carried." ¶ *With Carpus.* Carpus is not elsewhere mentioned. He was evidently a friend of the apostle, and it would seem probable that Paul had made his house his home when he was in Troas. ¶ *And the books.* It is impossible to determine what books are meant here. They may have been portions of the Old Testament, or classic writings, or books written by other Christians, or by himself. It is worthy of remark that even *Paul* did not travel without *books,* and that he found them in some way necessary for the work of the ministry. ¶ *Especially the parchments.* The word here used (μεμβράνας, whence our word *membrane*), occurs only in this place in the New Testament, and means skin, membrane, or parchment. Dressed skins were among the earliest materials for writing, and were in common use before the art of making paper from rags was discovered. These "parchments" seem to have been something different from "books," and probably refer to some of his own writings. They may have contained notes, memorandums, journals, or unfinished letters. It is, of course, impossible now to determine what they were. Benson supposes they were letters which he had received from the churches; Macknight, that they were the originals of the letters which he had written; Bishop Bull, that they were a kind of commonplace book, in which he inserted hints

14 Alexander the coppersmith did me much evil: *p* the Lord reward him according to his works:

p Ps. 28. 4.

15 Of whom be thou ware also; for he hath greatly withstood our ² words.

² or, *preachings*.

and extracts of the most remarkable passages in the authors which he read. All this, however, is mere conjecture. 14. *Alexander the coppersmith.* Or, rather, *the brazier* — ὁ χαλκεὺς. The word is used, however, to denote a worker in any kind of metals. This is probably the same person who is mentioned in 1 Tim. i. 20, and perhaps the same as the one mentioned in Acts xix. 33; see Notes on 1 Tim. i. 20. ¶ *Did me much evil.* In what way this was done, is not mentioned. If this is the same person who is referred to in 1 Tim. i. 20, it is probable that it was not evil to Paul personally, so much as embarrassment to the cause of religion which he advocated; comp. 2 Tim. ii. 17, 18. ¶ *The Lord reward him according to his works.* Comp. Notes, 1 Tim. i. 20. This need not be regarded as an expression of private feeling; still less should it be understood as expressing a desire of revenge. It is the language of one who wished that God would treat him exactly as he ought to be treated, and might be in accordance with the highest benevolence of any heart. It is the aim of every just government that everyone should be treated exactly as he deserves; and every good citizen should desire and pray that exact justice may be done to all. It is the business of a police officer to ferret out the guilty, to bring them to trial, to secure a just sentence; and any police officer might *pray*, with the utmost propriety, that God would assist him in his endeavours, and enable him to perform his duty. This might be done with no malevolent feeling toward any human being, but with the purest love of country, and the most earnest desire for the welfare of all. *If* such a police officer, or *if* a judge, or a juryman, were heard thus to pray, who would dare to accuse him of having a vindictive spirit, or a malevolent heart? And

why should Paul be so charged, when his prayer amounts to no more than this? For it remains yet to be proved that he refers to any *private* wrong which Alexander had done him, or that he was actuated by any other desire than that the sacred interests of truth should be guarded, and equal justice done to all. Why is it wrong to desire or to pray that universal justice may be done, and that every man may be treated as, under all the circumstances of the case, he *ought* to be treated? On the subject of the "Imprecations in the Scriptures," the reader may consult an article in the *Bibliotheca Sacra,* vol. i. pp. 97–110. It should be added here, that some manuscripts, instead of ἀποδῴη, "*may* the Lord reward," read it in the future—ἀποδώσει, "*will* reward." See Wetstein. The future is also found in the Vulgate, Coptic, and in Augustine, Theodoret, and Chrysostom. Augustine says (on the Sermon on the Mount), "He does not say, may he reward (*reddat*); but, he will reward (*reddet*), which is a verb of prophecy, not of imprecation. The authority, however, is not sufficient to justify a change in the present reading. These variations have doubtless arisen from a belief that the common reading expresses a sentiment inconsistent with the true spirit of a Christian, and a desire to find a better. But there is no reason *for desiring* a change in the text.

15. *Of whom be thou ware also.* It would seem from this that Alexander was still a public teacher, and that his discourses were plausible and artful. The best and the wisest of men need to be on their guard against the efforts of the advocates of error. ¶ *For he hath greatly withstood our words.* Marg., *preachings.* The Greek is, *words;* but the reference is doubtless to the public teachings of Paul. This verse makes it clear that it was no *private* wrong that Paul re-

16 At my first answer no man stood with me, but *q* all *men* forsook me; *r* 1 *pray God* that it may not be laid to their charge.

q ch.1.15.

r Ac.7.60.

ferred to, but the injury which he was doing to the cause of truth as a professed public teacher.

16. *At my first answer.* Gr., *apology* (*ἀπολογία*), *plea*, or *defence.* This evidently refers to some trial which he had had before the Roman emperor. He speaks of a *first* trial of this kind; but whether it was on some former occasion, and he had been released and permitted again to go abroad, or whether it was a trial which he had already had during his second imprisonment, it is not easy to determine. The former is the most natural supposition; for if he had had a trial during his present imprisonment, it is difficult to see why he was still held as a prisoner. See this point examined in the Intro. § 1. ¶ *No man stood with me.* Paul had many friends in Rome (ver. 21; comp. Rom. xvi.); but it seems that they did not wish to appear as such when he was put on trial for his life. They were doubtless afraid that they would be identified with him, and would endanger their own lives. It should be said that some of the friends of the apostle, mentioned in Rom. xvi., and who were there when that epistle was written, may have died before the apostle arrived there, or, in the trials and persecutions to which they were exposed, may have left the city. Still, it is remarkable that those who *were* there should have all left him on so trying an occasion. But to forsake a friend in the day of calamity is not uncommon, and Paul experienced what thousands before him and since have done. Thus Job was forsaken by friends and kindred in the day of his trials; see his pathetic description in Job xix. 13–17:

He hath put my brethren far from me,
And mine acquaintance verily are estranged from
　me.
My kinsfolk have failed,
And my familiar friends have forgotten me.
They that dwell in my house, and my maids, count
　me for a stranger,
I am an alien in their sight.
I called my servant, and he gave me no answer; I
　entreated him with my mouth.

My breath is strange to my wife,
Though I entreated for the children's sake of
　mine own body.

Thus the Psalmist was forsaken by his friends in the time of calamity, Ps. xxxv. 12–16; xxxviii. 2; xli. 9; lv. 12. And thus the Saviour was forsaken in his trials, Mat. xxvi. 56; comp., for illustration, Zec. xiii. 6. The world is full of instances in which those who have been overtaken by overwhelming calamities have been forsaken by professed friends, and have been left to suffer alone. This has arisen, partly from the circumstance that many *sincere* friends are timid, and their courage fails them when their attachment for another would expose them to peril; but more commonly, from the circumstance that there is much professed friendship in the world which is false, and that calamity becomes a test of it which it cannot abide. There is professed friendship which is caused by wealth (Prov. xiv. 20; xix. 4); there is that which is cherished for those in elevated and fashionable circles; there is that which is formed for beauty of person, or graceful manners, rather than for the solid virtues of the heart; there is that which is created in the sunshine of life—the affection of those "swallow friends, who retire in the winter, and return in the spring." Comp. the concluding remarks on the book of Job. Such friendship is always tested by calamity; and when affliction comes, they who in the days of prosperity were surrounded by many flatterers and admirers, are surprised to find how few there were among them who truly loved them.

" In the wind and tempest of his frown,
　Distinction, with a broad and powerful fan,
　Puffing at all, winnows the light away;
　And what hath mass or matter by itself,
　Lies, rich in virtue and unmingled."
　　　　　　　　Troilus and Cressida.

So common has this been—so little confidence can be placed in professed friends in time of adversity, that we are sometimes disposed to believe

17 Notwithstanding *the Lord stood with me,and strengthened me; that by me the preaching might be

s Mat.10.19; Ac.23.11.

that there is more truth than fancy in the representation of the poet when he says—

 "And what is friendship but a name,
 A charm that lulls to sleep;
 A shade that follows wealth or fame,
 But leaves the wretch to weep?"

Yet *there is* true friendship in the world. It existed between Damon and Pythias, and its power and beauty were still more strikingly illustrated in the warm affection of David and Jonathan. In the trials of David—though raised from the condition of a shepherd boy, and though having no powerful friends at court—the son of Saul never forsook him, and never gave him occasion to suspect the sincerity or the depth of his affection. With what exquisite beauty he sang of that attachment when Jonathan was dead!

"I am distressed for thee, my brother Jonathan:
Very pleasant hast thou been unto me:
Thy love to me was wonderful,
Passing the love of women."
    2 Sam. i. 26.

True friendship, founded on sincere love, so rare, so difficult to be found, so little known among the gay and the great, is one of the richest of Heaven's blessings to man, and *when* enjoyed, should be regarded as more than a compensation for all of show, and splendour, and flattery that wealth can obtain.

"Though choice of follies fasten on the great,
None clings more obstinate, than fancy fond
That sacred friendship is their easy prey;
Caught by the wafture of a golden lure,
Or fascination of a high-born smile.
Their smiles, the great, and the coquette, throw out
For other's hearts, tenacious of their own,
And we no less of ours, when such the bait.
Ye fortune's cofferers! ye powers of wealth!
Can gold gain friendship? Impudence of hope!
As well mere man an angel might beget.
Love, and love only, is the loan for love.
Lorenzo! pride repress; nor hope to find
A friend, but what has found a friend in thee.
All like the purchase; few the price will pay,
And this makes friends such miracles below.
A friend is worth all hazards we can run.
Poor is the friendless master of a world;
A world in purchase of a friend is gain."
    Night Thoughts, Night 2.

fully known, and *that* all the Gentiles might hear : *t*and I was delivered out of the mouth of the lion.

t Ps.22.21.

¶ I pray God *that it may not be laid to their charge.* That it may not be *reckoned,* or imputed to them—λογισθείη. On the meaning of this word, see Notes on Rom. iv. 3, and Philem. 18. The prayer of the apostle here breathes the very spirit of Christ; see Notes on Luke xxiii. 34; comp. Acts vii. 60.

17. *Notwithstanding the Lord stood with me.* Though all *men* forsook me, yet *God* did not. This expresses a universal truth in regard to the faithfulness of God; see Ps. xxvii. 10; comp. Job v. 17–19; Isa. xliii. 1, 2. ¶ *That by me the preaching might be fully known.* The word *preaching* here probably means *the gospel as preached by him.* The word rendered "might be fully known"—πληροφορηθῇ—means *might obtain full credence;* that is, might be fully confirmed, so that others might be assured of its truth. The apostle doubtless means, that on his trial, though forsaken by all men, he was enabled to be so steadfast in his profession of the truth, and so calm in the prospect of death, that all who witnessed his trial saw that there was a reality in religion, and that the gospel was founded in truth. He had maintained as a preacher that the gospel was able to support the soul in trial, and he was now able to illustrate its power in his own case. He had proclaimed the gospel as the true system of religion, and he was now able to bear testimony to it with the prospect of approaching martyrdom. The sentiment of this passage then is, that the truth of the gospel is made known, or that men may become fully assured of it, by the testimony which is borne to it by its friends in the near prospect of death. One of the most important means of establishing the truth of the gospel in the world has been the testimony borne to it by martyrs, and the spirit of unwavering confidence in God which they have evinced. And now, one of the most important methods

18 And[u] the Lord shall deliver me from every evil work, and will preserve *me* unto his heavenly

kingdom: to whom *be* glory for ever and ever. Amen.

19 Salute Prisca and Aquila, and the household of Onesiphorus.

of keeping up the knowledge of the value of religion in the world, and of convincing men of the truth of Christianity, is the spirit evinced by its friends when they are about to die. Men judge much, and justly, of the value of a system of religion by its power to comfort in the day of calamity, and to sustain the soul when about to enter on an untried state of being. That system is of little value to mankind which leaves us in the day of trial; that is of inestimable worth, which will enable us to die with the firm hope of a brighter and better world. A Christian, having served his God faithfully in life, may, therefore, be eminently useful when he comes to die. ¶ *And that all the Gentiles might hear.* Paul was at this time in Rome. His trial was before a heathen tribunal, and he was surrounded by Pagans. Rome, too, was then the centre of the world, and at all times there was a great conflux of strangers there. His trial, therefore, gave him an opportunity of testifying to the truth of Christianity before Gentile rulers, and in such circumstances that the knowledge of his sufferings, and of the religion for which he suffered, might be conveyed by the strangers who witnessed it to the ends of the world. His main object in life was to make the gospel known to the Gentiles, and he had thus an opportunity of furthering that great cause, even on what he supposed might be the trial which would determine with him the question of life or death; comp. Notes on Rom. i. 10. ¶ *And I was delivered out of the mouth of the lion.* This may either mean that he was delivered from Nero, compared with a lion, or literally that he was saved from being thrown to lions in the amphitheatre, as was common in Rome; see Notes on 1 Cor. xv. 32, (3). It is not uncommon in the Scriptures to compare tyrants and persecutors with ravenous wild beasts; comp. Ps. xxii. 13, 21; Jer.

ii. 30. Nero is called a *lion* by Seneca, and it was usual among heathen writers to apply the term in various senses to princes and warriors; see Grotius, *in loco.* The common interpretation here has been, that this refers to Nero, and there is no improbability in the interpretation. Still, it is quite as natural to suppose that the punishment which had been appointed for him, or to which he would have been subjected, was to be thrown to lions, and that in some way, now unknown to us, he had been delivered from it. Paul attributes his deliverance entirely to the Lord—but what instrumental agency there may have been, he does not specify. It seems probable that it was his own defence; that he was enabled to plead his own cause with so much ability that he found favour even with the Roman emperor, and was discharged. If it had been through the help of a friend at court, it is hardly to be supposed that he would not have mentioned the name of him to whom he owed his deliverance.

18. *And the Lord shall deliver me from every evil work.* He does not say from *death,* for he expected now to die; see ver. 6. But he was assured that God would keep him from shrinking from death when the hour approached; from apostasy, and from the manifestation of an improper spirit when he came to die. ¶ *And will preserve* me *unto his heavenly kingdom.* So keep me from evil that I shall reach his heavenly kingdom; see ver. 8. ¶ *To whom* be *glory for ever and ever.* Paul was accustomed to introduce a doxology in his writings when his heart was full (comp. Rom. ix. 5), and in no place could it be more appropriate than here, when he had the fullest confidence that he was soon to be brought to heaven. If man is ever disposed to ascribe glory to God, it is on such an occasion.

19. *Salute Prisca and Aquila.* Prisca, or Priscilla, was the wife of

20 Erastus abode at Corinth: but Trophimus have I left at Miletum sick.

21 Do thy diligence to come before winter. Eubulus greeteth thee, and Pudens, and Linus, and Claudia, and all the brethren.

22 The Lord Jesus Christ *be* with

thy spirit.   Grace *be* with you. Amen.

The second *epistle* unto Timotheus, ordained the first bishop of the church of the Ephesians, was written from Rome, when Paul was brought before [3]Nero the second time.

[3] *Cæsar Nero,* or *the Emperor Nero.*

Aquila, though her name is sometimes mentioned first. In regard to their history, see Notes, Rom. xvi. 3. They were at Rome when Paul wrote his Epistle to the Romans, but afterwards went into Asia Minor, which was the native place of Aquila (Acts xviii. 2), and where they probably died. ¶ *And the household of Onesiphorus.* Notes, chap. i. 16.

20. *Erastus.* See Notes on Rom. xvi. 23. ¶ *Abode at Corinth.* This was his home, where he filled an important office; Notes, Rom. xvi. 23. It would seem ¡that when Paul went to Rome, there was some expectation that he would accompany him, but that reasons had occurred for his remaining in Corinth. His doing so is referred to without blame. ¶ *But Trophimus.* See Acts xx. 4. He was a native of Asia Minor. ¶ *Have I left at Miletum sick.* Probably he designed to accompany him to Rome, as he had been often with him in his journeys. On the situation of Miletus, or Miletum, see Notes on Acts xx. 15.

21. *Do thy diligence.* Ver. 9. ¶ *To come before winter.* Probably be-

cause of the dangers of the navigation then, and because the circumstances of the apostle were such as to demand the presence of a friend. ¶ *Eubulus,* &c. These names are of common occurrence in the works of the classic writers, but of the persons here referred to we know nothing.

22. *The Lord Jesus Christ* be *with thy spirit.* See Gal. vi. 18; Rom. xv. 20.

The subscription to this epistle was not added by Paul himself, nor is there any evidence that it was by an inspired man, and it is of no authority. There is not the slightest evidence that Timothy was "ordained the first bishop of the church of the Ephesians," or that he was a "bishop" there at all. There is no reason to believe that he was even a *pastor* there, in the technical sense; see Notes on 1 Tim. i. 3. Compare the remarks on the subscriptions to the Epistle to the Romans, 1 Corinthians, and especially Titus.

THE
EPISTLE OF PAUL TO TITUS.

INTRODUCTION.

§ 1. *The history of Titus.*

OF Titus nothing more is certainly known than what we find in the epistles of Paul. It is somewhat remarkable that there is no mention of him in the Acts of the Apostles, nor does his name occur in the New Testament anywhere, except in the writings of the apostle Paul. From his incidental allusions to him, we learn the following particulars respecting him.

(1) He was by birth a Gentile. In Gal. ii. 3, he is called a Greek, and it is certain from that passage that he had not been circumcised, and the probability is, that up to the time of his conversion he had lived as other Gentiles, and had not been converted to the Jewish faith. His father and mother were, doubtless, both Greeks, and thus he was distinguished from Timothy, whose mother was a Jewess, but whose father was a Greek, Acts xvi. 3; comp. Notes on Gal. ii. 3. If Titus had been proselyted to the Jewish faith, it is to be presumed that he would have been circumcised.

(2) He had been converted to Christianity by the instrumentality of Paul himself. This is clear from the epistle, chap. i. 4, "To Titus, *mine own son,* after the common faith;" see Notes on 1 Tim. i. 2. This is language which the apostle would not have used of one who had been converted by the instrumentality of another. But where he lived, and when or how he was converted, is wholly unknown. As to *the time* when he was converted, it is known only that this occurred before the fourteenth year after the conversion of Paul, for at that time Titus, a Christian, was with Paul at Jerusalem, Gal. ii. 1. As to *the place* where he lived, there seems some reason to suppose that it was in some part of Asia Minor—for the Greeks abounded there; Paul laboured much there; and there were numerous converts made there to the Christian faith. Still this is not by any means certain.

(3) Titus went with Paul to Jerusalem, when he was deputed by the church at Antioch with Barnabas, to lay certain questions before the apostles and elders there in reference to the converts from the Gentiles, Acts xv.; comp. Gal. ii. 1. It is not known *why* he took Titus with him on that occasion, and the reasons can be only conjectural; see Notes on Gal. ii. 1. It is possible that he was taken with him to Jerusalem because his was *a case in point* in regard to the question which was to come before the apostles and elders there. It is not improbable, from an expression which Paul uses in describing his visit there—"neither was Titus *compelled* to be circumcised" —that the case came up for discussion, and that strenuous efforts were made by the judaizing portion there (comp. Gal. ii. 4), to have him circumcised. Paul and Barnabas, however, so managed the cause that the principle was

settled that it was not necessary that converts from the heathen should be circumcised, Acts xv. 19, 20.

(4) After the council at Jerusalem, it seems probable that Titus returned with Paul and Barnabas, accompanied by Silas and Judas (Acts xv. 23), and that afterwards he attended the apostle for a considerable time in his travels and labours. This appears from a remark in 2 Cor. viii. 23, "Whether any do inquire of Titus, he is my partner and fellow-helper concerning you." From this it would seem, that he had been with Paul; that he was as yet not well known; and that the fact that he had been seen with him had led to inquiry who he was, and what was the office which he sustained. That he was also a companion of Paul, and quite essential to his comfort in his work, is apparent from the following allusions to him in the same epistle—2 Cor. vii. 6, "God, that comforteth those who are cast down, comforted us by the coming of Titus;" ii. 13, "I had no rest in my spirit because I found not Titus my brother;" vii. 13, "Yea and exceedingly the more joyed we for the joy of Titus;" comp. 2 Tim. iv. 10; 2 Cor. xii. 18.

(5) There is reason to believe that Titus spent some time with the apostle in Ephesus. For the First Epistle to the Corinthians was written at Ephesus, and was sent by the hand of Titus; Intro. to 1 Cor. §§ 3, 6. It is to be presumed, also, that he would on such an occasion send some one with the epistle in whom he had entire confidence, and who had been so long with him as to become familiar with his views. For Titus, on this occasion, was sent not only to bear the epistle, but to endeavour to heal the divisions and disorders there, and to complete a collection for the poor saints in Jerusalem which the apostle had himself commenced; comp. Notes on 2 Cor. ii. 13; vii. 6; viii. 6. After this he met Paul in Macedonia (2 Cor. vii. 5, 6), but whether he was with him when he went with the collection to Jerusalem, and during his imprisonment in Cesarea, or on his voyage to Rome, we have no information.

(6) We next hear of him as being left by the apostle in the island of Crete, that he might "set in order the things that were wanting, and ordain elders in every city," Titus i. 5. This is supposed to have occurred about the year 62, and after the first imprisonment of the apostle at Rome. It is evidently implied that the apostle had been himself there with him, and that he had undertaken to accomplish some important object there, but that something had prevented his completing it, and that he had left Titus to finish it. This was clearly a temporary arrangement, for there is no evidence that it was designed that Titus should be a permanent "bishop" of Crete, or that he remained there long. That he did not design that he should be a permanent bishop of that island, is clear from chap. iii. 12, where the apostle directs him, when he should send Artemas to take his place, to come to him to Nicopolis. If Titus was a prelatical bishop, the apostle would not in this summary manner have superseded him, or removed him from his diocese.

(7) He was with Paul in Rome during his second imprisonment there. He did not, however, remain with him until his trial, but left him and went into Dalmatia, 2 Tim. iv. 10. For the probable reason why he had gone there, see Notes on that place. What became of him afterward, we are not

informed. The tradition is, that he returned to Crete, and preached the gospel there and in the neighbouring islands, and died at the age of ninety-four. But this tradition depends on no certain evidence.

§ 2. The island of Crete.

As Paul (chap. i. 5) says that he had left Titus in Crete to perform an important service there, and as the instructions in this epistle doubtless had some peculiar applicability to the state of things existing there, it is of importance, in order to a correct understanding of the epistle, to have some knowledge of that island, and of the circumstances in which the gospel was introduced there.

The island of Crete, now Candia, is one of the largest islands in the Mediterranean, at the south of all the Cyclades. See the Map of Asia Minor, prefixed to the Acts of the Apostles. Its name is said by some to have been derived from the Curetes, who are supposed to have been its first inhabitants; by others, from the nymph Crete, daughter of Hesperus; and by others, from Cres, a son of Jupiter and the nymph Idæa. The ancient authors in general say that Crete was originally peopled from Palestine. According to Bochart (lib. 5, c. 15), that part of Palestine which lies by the Mediterranean was called by the Arabs *Keritha*, and by the Syrians *Creth;* and the Hebrews called the inhabitants *Crethi*, or *Crethim*, which the LXX. have rendered Κρητας—*Cretans*, Ezek. xxv. 16; Zep. ii. 5. It would be easy to pass from Palestine to the island of Crete. Sir Isaac Newton, also, is of opinion that Crete was peopled from Palestine. He says, "Many of the Phœnicians and Syrians, in the year before Christ 1045, fled from Zidon, and from King David, into Asia Minor, *Crete*, Greece, and Libya, and introduced letters, music, poetry, the *Octæteris*, metals and their fabrication, and other arts, sciences, and customs of the Phœnicians. Along with these Phœnicians came a sort of men skilled in religious mysteries, arts, and sciences of Phœnicia, and settled in several places, under the names of Curetes, Idæi, Dactyli," &c. According to Pliny, the extent of Crete from east to west is about 270 miles, but its breadth nowhere exceeds fifty miles. The early inhabitants are generally supposed to be the Eteocretes of Homer; but their origin is unknown. Minos, who had expelled his brother Sarpedon from the throne, first gave laws to the Cretans, and, having conquered the pirates who infested the Ægean Sea, established a powerful navy. In the Trojan war, Idomeneus, sovereign of Crete, led its forces to war in eighty vessels—a number little inferior to those commanded by Agamemnon himself. At this period the island appears to have been inhabited by a mixed population of Greeks and barbarians. After the Trojan war, the principal cities formed themselves into several republics, for the most part independent, while some of them were connected with federal ties. The Cretan code of laws was supposed by many to have furnished Lycurgus with the model of his most salutary regulations. It was founded on the just basis of liberty and an equality of rights, and its great aim was to promote social harmony and peace, by enforcing temperance and frugality. In regard to this code, see Anthon's *Class. Dic.*, art. "Creta." In the time of Polybius (B. C. 203), the Cretans had much degenerated from their ancient character; for he charges them repeatedly with the grossest immorality and the basest vices (Polyb. iv. 47, 53; vi. 46). We know, also, with what severity they are reproved by Paul, in the words of Epimenides; see Notes on chap. i. 12. Crete was subdued by the Romans, and became a part of a Roman province. The interior of the island is very hilly and woody, and intersected with fertile valleys. Mount Ida, in the centre of the island, is the principal mountain, and surpasses all the others in elevation. The island contains no lakes, and its rivers are mostly mountain torrents, which are dry during the summer season. The valleys, or sloping plains, in the island are represented as very fertile. The greater portion of the land is not cultivated; but it might produce sugar-cane, excellent wine, and the best kind of fruit. It has a delightful climate, and is remarkably healthful. The ancients asserted that this delightful island, the birth-place of Jupiter, was freed, by the indulgence of the gods, from every noxious animal. No quadrupeds of a ferocious character belong to it. The wild goat is the only inhabitant of the forest and the lofty mountains, and sheep overspread the plains, and graze undisturbed by ravenous enemies. The island now is under Turkish rule, and is divided into three pashalics; but the inhabitants are mostly Greeks, who are kept in a state of great depression. The native Candians are of the Greek Church, and are allowed the free exercise of their religion. The island is divided into twelve bishoprics, the bishop of one of which assumes the title of archbishop, and is appointed by the patriarch of Constantinople. The situation of this island for commerce can scarcely be surpassed. It is at an almost equal distance from Asia, Europe, and Africa, and might be made the emporium for the manufactures and agricultural productions of each; but, from the oppressive nature of the government, the indolence of the Turks, and the degraded state of the Greeks, those advantages are not improved, and its condition partakes of that of the general condition of the Turkish empire.

This island was formerly famous for its hundred cities; it is distinguished in the ancient fabulous legends for the arrival there of Europa, on a bull, from Phœnicia; for the laws of Minos; for the labyrinth, the work of Dædalus; and, above all, as the place where Jupiter was born and was buried. According to the fables of mythology, he was born in a cavern near Lyctus, or Cnosus; was rocked in a golden cradle; was fed with honey, and with the milk of the goat Amalthea, while the Curetes danced around him, clashing their arms, to prevent his cries from being heard by Saturn. He became, according to the legend, the King of Crete, and was buried on the island. See Anthon, *Class. Dic.*, art. "Jupiter."

§ 3. *The introduction of the Gospel into Crete.*

We have no certain information in regard to the time when the gospel was first preached in Crete, nor by whom it was done. There are some circumstances mentioned, however, which furnish all the light which we need on this point, in order to an understanding of the epistle before us. Among the persons who were in Jerusalem on the day of Pentecost, and who were converted there, *Cretans* are mentioned (Acts ii. 11); and it is highly probable that, when they returned to their homes, they made the gospel known to their countrymen. Yet history is wholly silent as to the method by which it was done, and as to the result on the minds of the inhabitants. As no visit of any of the apostles to that island is mentioned by Luke in the Acts of the Apostles, it may be presumed that the gospel there had not produced any very marked success; and the early history of Christianity there is to us unknown.

It is clear from the epistle before us (chap. i. 5), that the apostle Paul was there on some occasion, and that the gospel, either when he was there or before, was attended with success—"For this cause left I thee in Crete, that thou shouldest set in order the things that are wanting, and ordain elders in every city." Here it is manifest that Paul had been there with Titus; that he had commenced some arrangements which he had not been able himself to complete; and that the gospel had had an effect extensively on the island, since he was to ordain elders "*in every city.*"

It is not certainly known, however, when Paul was there. There is no mention in the Acts of the Apostles of his having been there, except when he was on his way to Rome (Acts xxvii. 7, 8); and this was in such circumstances as to preclude the supposition that that was the time referred to in this epistle; for, (1) Titus was not then with him; (2) there is no reason to suppose that he remained there long enough to preach the gospel to any extent, or to establish churches. He was sailing to Rome as a prisoner, and there is no probability that he would be permitted to go at large and preach for any considerable time. There is, therefore, a moral certainty that it must have been on some other occasion. "It is striking," says Neander (*History of the Planting of the Christian Church*, vol. i. pp. 400, 401), "that while Luke in the Acts reports so fully and circumstantially the occurrences of the apostle's last voyage to Rome, and mentions his stay in Crete, he says not a word (contrary to his usual practice in such cases) of the friendly reception given to him by the Christians there, or even of his meeting them at all. Hence we may conclude that no Christian churches existed in that island, though that transient visit would naturally give rise to the intention of planting the gospel there, which he probably fulfilled soon after he was set at liberty, when he came into these parts."

There is reason to believe that Paul, after his first imprisonment at Rome, was released, and again visited Asia Minor and Macedonia. See Intro. to 2 Timothy. On this journey, it is not improbable that he may have visited Crete, having, as Neander supposes, had his attention called to this island as a desirable place for preaching the gospel, when on his way to Rome. "If we may be allowed to suppose," says Dr. Paley (*Hor. Paul.*), "that St. Paul, after his liberation at Rome, sailed into Asia, taking Crete in his way; that from Asia, and from Ephesus, the capital of that country, he proceeded into Macedonia, and, crossing the peninsula in his progress, came into the neighbourhood of Nicopolis, we have a route which falls in with everything. It executes the intention expressed by the apostle of visiting Colosse and Philippi, as soon as he should be set at liberty at Rome. It allows him to leave 'Titus at Crete,' and 'Timothy at Ephesus as he went into Macedonia,' and to write to both, not long after, from the peninsula of Greece, and probably from the neighbourhood of Nicopolis, thus bringing together the dates of these two letters" (1 Tim. and Titus), "and thereby accounting for that affinity between them, both in subject and language, which our remarks have pointed out. I confess that the journey which we have thus traced out for St. Paul is in a great measure hypothetic; but it should be observed that it is a species of consistency which seldom belongs to falsehood, to admit of an hypothesis which includes a great number of remote and independent circumstances without contradiction." See Neander, *History of the Planting of the Churches,* i. 401. Comp., however, Intro. to 1 Tim. § 2.

Why Paul left Crete without completing the work which was to be done, and especially without ordaining the elders himself, is not certainly known. There is evidently a striking resemblance between the circumstances which induced him to leave Titus there, and those which existed at Ephesus when he left Timothy there to complete an important work, 1 Tim. i. 3, 4. We know that Paul was driven away from Ephesus before he had finished the work there which he had purposed to accomplish (Acts xix.; xx. 1); and it is not at all improbable that some such disturbance took place in Crete. Comp. Koppe, *Proleg.* p. 194. When he thus left, he committed to Titus the work which he had designed to accomplish, with instructions to finish it as soon as possible, and then to come to him at Nicopolis, chap. iii. 12.

§ 4. *The place, time, and occasion of writing the Epistle.*

There has been much diversity of opinion as to the time and place of writing this epistle.

In regard to the *place,* there can be little doubt that it was at *a* Nicopolis; for the apostle in chap. iii. 12, directs Titus to come to him at that place. But it is not easy to determine *what* Nicopolis is meant, for there were many cities of that name. The person who affixed the subscription at the end of the epistle, affirms that it was "Nicopolis of Macedonia;" but, as has been frequently remarked in these Notes, these subscriptions are of no authority. The name *Nicopolis* (meaning properly, *a city of victory—νίκη* and *πόλις*) was given to several places. There was a city of this name in Thrace, on the river Nessus, now called Nikopi. There was also a city of the same name in Epirus, two in Mœsia, another in Armenia, another in Cilicia, and another in Egypt, in the vicinity of Alexandria. It is by no means easy to ascertain which of these cities is meant, though, as Paul was accustomed to travel in Greece and Asia Minor, there seems to be a probability that one of those cities is intended. The only way of determining this with any degree of probability, is, to ascertain what city was *best known* by that name at the time when the epistle was written, or what city one would be likely to go to, if he were directed to go to Nicopolis, without any further specification—as if one were directed to go to Philadelphia, London, or Rome. In such a case, he would go to the principal city of that name, though there might be many other smaller places of that name also. But even this would not be absolutely certain, for Paul may have specified to Titus the place where he *expected* to go before he left him, so that he would be in no danger of doubt where the place was. But if we were to allow this consideration to influence us in regard to the place, there can be little doubt that the city which he meant was Nicopolis in Epirus, and the common opinion has been that the apostle alludes to this city. This Nicopolis was situated in Epirus, in Greece, north-west of Corinth and Athens, on the Ambracian Gulf, and near its mouth. See the Map prefixed to the Acts of the Apostles. On the same gulf, and directly opposite to Nicopolis, is Actium, the place where Augustus achieved a signal victory over Mark Antony; and the city of Nicopolis he built in honour of that victory. Augustus was anxious to raise this city to the highest rank among the cities of Greece, and caused games to be celebrated there, with great pomp, every few years. Having afterwards fallen into decay, the city was restored by the Emperor Julian. Modern travellers describe the remains of Nicopolis as very extensive; the site which they now occupy is called *Prevesa Vecchia.* See Anthon's *Class. Dic.* It should be said, however, that there is no absolute certainty about the place where the epistle was written. Macknight and Benson suppose it was at Colosse; Lardner supposes it was in or near Macedonia; Hug, at Ephesus.

If the epistle was written from the Nicopolis referred to, then it was probably after Paul's first imprisonment at Rome. If so, it was written about the year 63 or 64. But there is great diversity of opinion as to the time. Lardner and Hug place it in the year 56. It is of no material importance to be able to determine the exact time.

The occasion on which it was written is specified by the apostle himself, with such clearness, that there can be no doubt on that point. Paul had left Titus in Crete, to "set in order the things which were wanting, and to ordain elders in every city" (chap. i. 5); and as he had himself, perhaps, been called to leave suddenly, it was important that Titus should have more full instructions than he had been able to give him on various points of duty, or, at anyrate, that he should have *permanent* instructions to which he could refer. The epistle is occupied, therefore, mainly with such counsels as were appropriate to a minister of the gospel engaged in the duties which Titus was left to discharge.

The principal difficulties which it was apprehended Titus would meet with in the performance of his duties there, and which in fact made his labours there desirable, arose from two sources: (1) the character of the Cretans themselves; and (2) the influence of judaizing teachers.

(1) The character of the Cretans themselves was such as to demand the vigilance and care of Titus. They were a people characterized for insincerity, falsehood, and gross living, chap. i. 12. There was great danger, therefore, that their religion would be hollow and insincere, and great need of caution lest they should be corrupted from the simplicity and purity required in the gospel, chap. i. 13.

(2) The influence of judaizing teachers was to be guarded against. It is evident from Acts ii. 11, that there were Jews residing there; and it is probable that it was by those who had gone from that island to Jerusalem to attend the feast of the Pentecost, and who had been converted on that occasion, that the gospel was first introduced there. From this epistle, also, it is clear that one of the great dangers to piety in the churches of Crete, arose from the efforts of such teachers, and from the plausible arguments which they would use in favour of the Mosaic law; see chap. i. 10, 14–16; iii. 9. To counteract the effect of their teaching, it was necessary to have ministers of

the gospel appointed in every important place, who should be qualified for their work. To make these arrangements, was the great design for which Titus was left there; and to give him full information as to the kind of ministers which was needed this epistle was written.

There is a very striking resemblance between this epistle and the First Epistle to Timothy. See Paley's *Horæ Paulinæ.* "Both letters were addressed to persons left by the writer to preside in their respective churches during his absence. Both letters are principally occupied in describing the qualifications to be sought for in those whom they should appoint to offices in the church; and the ingredients of this description are, in both letters, nearly the same. Timothy and Titus, likewise, are cautioned against the same prevailing corruptions, and, in particular, against the same misdirection of their cares and studies" (Paley). This similarity is found, not only in the general structure of the epistles, but also in particular phrases and expressions; comp. I Tim. i. 2, 3, with Tit. i. 4, 5; 1 Tim. i. 4, with Tit. i. 14, iii. 9; 1 Tim. iv. 12, with Tit. iii. 7, and ii. 15; 1 Tim. iii. 2-4, with Tit. i. 6-8.

It is evident from this that the epistles were written by the same person, and to those who were in substantially the same circumstances. They are incidental proofs that they are genuine, and were written by the person, and to the persons, whose names appear, and on the occasions which are said in the epistle to have existed. On the subjects in this introduction, the reader may consult Macknight's Introduction to the Epistle, Michaelis's *Introduction*, Benson, Koppe, and especially Paley's *Horæ Paulinæ*—a work which will never be consulted without profit.

THE
EPISTLE OF PAUL TO TITUS.

CHAPTER I.

PAUL, a servant of God, and an apostle of Jesus Christ, according to the faith of God's elect, *a*and the acknowledging of the truth *b*which is after godliness;

a 2 Ti.2.25.   b 1 Ti.6.3.

CHAPTER I.

ANALYSIS OF THE CHAPTER.

This chapter embraces the following points:—

(1) The usual inscription and salutation, ver. 1-4. In this Paul declares himself to be the author of the epistle, and asserts in the strongest manner his claims to the apostleship. He alludes to the great cause in which, as an apostle, he was engaged—as acting under the eternal plan of God for the salvation of the elect, and appointed to communicate the glorious truths of that system which had been now revealed to mankind. The object of this seems to be to impress the mind of Titus with his right to give him instruction.

(2) A statement of the object for which Titus had been left in Crete, and the general character of the work which he was to perform there, ver. 5.

(3) The qualifications of those who were to be ordained to the ministry, ver. 6-9. The characteristics laid down are substantially the same as in 1 Tim. iii.

(4) Reasons for great caution and prudence in thus appointing elders over the churches, ver. 10-13. Those reasons arose from the character of the Cretans. There were many deceivers there, and the character of the Cretans was such that there was great danger that they who professed to be Christians would be hypocritical, and if put into the eldership that they would do great injury to the cause.

(5) A solemn charge to Titus to rebuke them faithfully for their prevailing and characteristic vices, and to avoid giving any countenance to that for which they were so much distinguished, ver. 13-16.

1. *Paul a servant of God, and an apostle of Jesus Christ.* See Notes, Rom. i. 1; comp. Notes, 1 Cor. ix. 1-5. ¶ *According to the faith of God's elect.* Comp. Notes, Rom. viii. 33; Eph. i. 4; 2 Tim. ii. 10. The meaning of the word rendered here, "according to"—*κατὰ*—is, probably, *with reference to;* that is, he was appointed to be an apostle *with respect to the faith of* those whom God had chosen, or, *in order* that they might be led to believe the gospel. God had chosen them to salvation, but he intended that it should be in connection with their believing, and *in order to that,* he had appointed Paul to be an apostle that he might go and make known to them the gospel. It is the purpose of God to save his people, but he does not mean to save them as infidels, or unbelievers. He intends that they shall be believers first—and hence he sends his ministers that they may become such. ¶ *And the acknowledging of the truth.* In order to secure the acknowledgment or recognition of the truth. The object of the apostleship, as it is of the ministry in general, is to secure the proper acknowledgment of the *truth* among men. ¶ *Which is after godliness.* Which tends to promote piety towards God. On the word rendered *godliness,* see Notes on 1 Tim. ii. 2; iii. 16. The truth, the acknowledg-

2 [1]In hope of eternal life, which God, [c]that cannot lie, [d]promised before the world began;

3 But[e] hath in due times manifested his word [f]through preaching, which is committed unto me, according to the commandment of God our Saviour;

[1] or, *For.*　c 1 Sa.15.29; He.6.18.　d Mat.25.34.

ment of which Paul was appointed to secure, was not scientific, historical, or political truth; it was that of religion—that which was adapted to lead men to a holy life, and to prepare them for a holy heaven.

2. *In hope of eternal life.* Marg., *For.* Gr., Ἐπ’ ἐλπίδι. This does not mean that Paul cherished the hope of eternal life, but that the "faith of the elect," which he aimed to secure, was *in order* that men might have the hope of eternal life. The whole system which he was appointed to preach was designed to secure to man a well-founded hope of salvation; comp. Notes, 2 Tim. i. 10. ¶ *Which God, that cannot lie.* On the phrase "cannot lie," see Notes on Heb. vi. 18. The fact that God cannot lie; that it is his nature always to speak the truth; and that no circumstances can ever occur in which he will depart from it, is the foundation of all our hopes of salvation. ¶ *Promised.* The only hope of salvation is in the *promise* of God. It is only as we can have evidence that he has assured us that we may be saved, that we are authorized to cherish any hope of salvation. That promise is not made to us as individuals, or by name, but it becomes ours, (1) because he has made a general promise that they who repent and believe shall be saved; and (2) because we may have evidence that we have repented, and do believe the gospel. If this be so, we fairly come under the promise of salvation, and may apply it to ourselves. ¶ *Before the world began.* That is, the purpose was then formed, and the promise may be considered as in fact then made—for a purpose in the mind of God, though it is not as yet made known, is equivalent to a promise; comp. Notes on Mat. xxv. 34; 2 Tim. i. 9.

4 To Titus, [g]mine own son after the common faith: Grace, mercy, *and* peace, from God the Father and the Lord Jesus Christ our Saviour.

5 For this cause left I thee in Crete, that thou shouldest set in

e 2 Ti.1.10.　　f Ro.10.14,15.
g 1 Ti.1.1,2.

3. *But hath in due times.* At the proper time; the time which he had intended; the best time; see Notes on 1 Tim. ii. 6; comp. Notes on Mat. ii. 2. ¶ *Manifested his word through preaching.* See Notes on 2 Tim. ii. 10. The meaning here is, that he has made known his eternal purpose through the preaching of the gospel; comp. Notes on Rom. x. 14, 15. ¶ *Which is committed unto me.* Not exclusively, but in common with others; see Notes on 2 Tim. i. 11. ¶ *According to the commandment of God our Saviour.* Paul always claimed to be divinely commissioned, and affirmed that he was engaged in the work of preaching by the authority of God; see Gal. i. 1, 11, 12; 1 Cor. i. 1; Rom. i. 1–5.

4. *To Titus.* See the Intro. § 1. ¶ *Mine own son.* Notes, 1 Tim. i. 2. ¶ *After the common faith.* The faith of all Christians; equivalent to saying "my son in the gospel." That is, Paul had been the means of converting him by preaching that gospel which was received by all who were Christians. ¶ *Grace, mercy,* and *peace,* &c. See Notes on Rom. i. 7.

5. *For this cause left I thee in Crete.* Comp. Notes, 1 Tim. i. 3. On the situation of Crete, see the Intro. § 2. ¶ *That thou shouldest set in order the things that are wanting.* Marg., *left undone.* The Greek is, "the things that are left;" that is, those which were left unfinished; referring, doubtless, to arrangements which had been commenced, but which for some cause had been left incomplete. Whether this had occurred because he had been driven away by persecution, or called away by important duties demanding his attention elsewhere, cannot now be determined. The word rendered

order^h the things that are ² want-

h 1 Co.11.34.   ² or, *left undone.*
i Ac.14.23; 2 Ti.2.2.

ing, and ⁱordain elders in every city as I had appointed thee:

_____

"set in order"—ἐπιδιορϑώσῃ—occurs nowhere else in the New Testament. It means, properly, *to make straight upon,* and then to put further to rights, to arrange further (Robinson, *Lex.*). There were things left unfinished which he was to complete. One of these things, and perhaps the principal, was, to appoint elders in the various cities where the gospel had been preached. ¶ *And ordain.* The word *ordain* has now acquired a technical signification which it cannot be shown that it has in the New Testament. It means, in common usage, to "invest with a ministerial function or sacerdotal power; to introduce, and establish, and settle in the pastoral office with the customary forms and solemnities" (Webster); and, it may be added, with the idea always connected with it of the imposition of hands. But the word used here does not necessarily convey this meaning, or imply that Titus was to go through what would now be called *an ordination service.* It means to set, place, or constitute; then, to set over anything, as a steward or other officer (see Mat. xxiv. 45; Luke xii. 42; Acts vi. 3), though without reference to any particular mode of investment with an office; see the word *ordain* explained in the Notes on Acts i. 22; xiv. 23. Titus was to appoint or set them over the churches, though with what ceremony is now unknown. There is no reason to suppose that he did this except as the result of the choice of the people; comp. Notes on Acts vi. 3. ¶ *Elders.* Gr., presbyters; see the word explained in the Notes on Acts xiv. 23. These *elders,* or *presbyters,* were also called *bishops* (comp. Notes on 1 Tim. iii. 1), for Paul immediately, in describing their qualifications, calls them bishops:— "ordain elders in every city—if any be blameless—FOR a *bishop* must be blameless," &c. If the elders and bishops in the times of the apostles were of different ranks, this direction would be wholly unmeaning. It would

be the same as if the following direction were given to one who was authorized to appoint officers over an army: "Appoint *captains* over each company, who shall be of good character, and acquainted with military tactics, FOR *a brigadier-general* must be of good character, and acquainted with the rules of war." That the same rank is denoted also by the terms *presbyter* and *bishop* here, is further apparent, because the qualifications which Paul states as requisite for the "bishop" are not those which pertain to a prelate or a diocesan bishop, but to one who was a pastor of a church, or an evangelist. It is clear, from ver. 7, that those whom Titus was to appoint were "bishops," and yet it is absurd to suppose that the apostle meant *prelatical* bishops, for no one can believe that such bishops were to be appointed in "every city" of the island. According to all modern notions of Episcopacy, one such bishop would have been enough for such an island as Crete, and indeed it has been not unfrequently maintained that Titus himself was in fact the bishop of that diocese. But if these were not prelates who were to be ordained by Titus, then it is clear that the term "bishop" in the New Testament is given to the presbyters or elders; that is, to all ministers of the gospel. That usage should never have been departed from. ¶ *In every city.* Crete was anciently celebrated for the number of its cities. In one passage Homer ascribes to the island an hundred cities (*Il.* ii. 649), in another ninety (*Od.* xix. 174). It may be presumed that many of these cities were towns of no very considerable size, and yet it would seem probable that each one was large enough to have a church, and to maintain the gospel. Paul, doubtless, expected that Titus would travel over the whole island, and endeavour to introduce the gospel in every important place. ¶ *As I had appointed thee.* As I commanded thee, or gave thee direction

6 If any be blameless, the husband of one wife, having faithful children, not accused of riot, or unruly.

7 For[k] a bishop must be blame-

k 1 Ti.3.2, &c.

—διεταξάμην. This is a different word from the one used in the former part of the verse, and rendered *ordain*—καθίστημι. It does not mean that Titus was to ordain elders in the same manner as Paul had ordained him, but that he was to set them over the cities as he had *directed* him to do. He had, doubtless, given him oral instructions, when he left him, as to the way in which it was to be done.

6. *If any be blameless, the husband of one wife.* Notes, 1 Tim. iii. 2. ¶ *Having faithful children.* Notes, 1 Tim. iii. 4, 5. That is, having a family well-governed, and well-trained in religion. The word here—πιστὰ—applied to the children, and rendered *faithful*, does not necessarily mean that they should be truly pious, but it is descriptive of those who had been well-trained, and were in due subordination. If a man's family were not of his character—if his children were insubordinate, and opposed to religion —if they were decided infidels or scoffers, it would show that there was such a deficiency in the head of the family that he could not be safely intrusted with the government of the church; comp. Notes on 1 Tim. iii. 5. It is probably true, also, that the preachers at that time would be selected, as far as practicable, from those whose families were all Christians. There might be great impropriety in placing a man over a church, a part of whose family were Jews or heathens. ¶ *Not accused of riot.* That is, whose *children* were not accused of riot. This explains what is meant by *faithful*. The word rendered *riot*—ἀσωτία—is translated *excess* in Eph. v. 18, and *riot* in Tit. i. 6; 1 Pet. iv. 4. It does not elsewhere occur in the New Testament, though the word *riotous* is found in Luke xv. 13; but it is explained in the Notes on Eph. v. 18. The meaning here is, that they should not be *justly* accused of this; this should not be

less, as the steward of God; not self-willed, not soon angry, not given to wine, no striker, not given to filthy lucre;

8 But a lover of hospitality, a

their character. It would, doubtless, be a good reason now why a man should not be ordained to the ministry, that he had a dissipated and disorderly family. ¶ *Or unruly.* Insubordinate; ungoverned; see Notes, 1 Tim. i. 9; and iii. 4.

7. *For a bishop must be blameless.* 1 Tim. iii. 2. ¶ *As the steward of God.* See Notes, 1 Cor. iv. 1, 2. A man, in order to perform the duties of such an office, should be one against whom no accusation could lie. ¶ *Not self-willed.* Comp. 2 Pet. ii. 10. The word—αὐθάδης—does not elsewhere occur in the New Testament. It means, properly, *self-complacent;* and then, *assuming, arrogant, imperious* (Rob. *Lex.*). The *gist* of the offence— the very "head and front"—is that of being *self-complacent;* a trait of character which, of necessity, makes a man imperious, dogmatical, impatient of contradiction, and unyielding. Such a man, evidently, is not fit for the office of a minister of the gospel. ¶ *Not soon angry.* See Notes, 1 Tim. iii. 2, and the margin there. ¶ *Not given to wine.* Notes, 1 Tim. iii. 3. ¶ *No striker.* Notes, 1 Tim. iii. 3. ¶ *Not given to filthy lucre.* In 1 Tim. iii. 3, "not *greedy* of filthy lucre." The same Greek word is used.

8. *But a lover of hospitality.* Notes, 1 Tim. iii. 2. ¶ *A lover of good men.* Marg., "or *things.*" The Greek (φιλάγαθος) means, *a lover of good,* and may apply to anything that is good. It may refer to good men, as included under the general term *good;* and there is no more essential qualification of a bishop than this. A man who sustains the office of a minister of the gospel, should love every good object, and be ever ready to promote it; and he should love every good man, no matter in what denomination or country he may be found—no matter what his complexion, and no matter what his rank in life; comp. Notes

lover of good ³men, sober, just, holy, temperate;

9 Holding*fast the faithful word, as⁴ he hath been taught, that he may be able by sound doctrine both to exhort and to convince the gainsayers.

³ or, *things.* *l* 2 Th.2.15. ⁴ or, *in teaching.*

on Phil. iv. 8. ¶ *Sober.* Notes, 1 Tim. i. 2. ¶ *Just.* Upright in his dealings with all. A minister can do little good who is not; comp. Notes on Phil. iv. 8. ¶ *Holy.* Pious, or devout. Faithful in all his duties to God; Notes, 1 Tim. ii. 8. ¶ *Temperate*—εγκρατῆ. Having power or control over all his passions. We apply the term, now, with reference to abstinence from intoxicating liquors. In the Scriptures, it includes not only that, but also much more. It implies control over *all* our passions and appetites. See it explained in the Notes on Acts xxiv. 25; comp. 1 Cor. vii. 9; ix. 25; Gal. v. 23.

9. *Holding fast the faithful word.* That is, the true doctrines of the gospel. This means that he is to hold this fast, in opposition to one who would wrest it away, and in opposition to all false teachers, and to all systems of false philosophy. He must be a man who is firm in his belief of the doctrines of the Christian faith, and a man who can be relied on to maintain and defend those doctrines in all circumstances; comp. Notes, 2 Thes. ii. 15. ¶ *As he hath been taught.* Marg., *in teaching.* Gr., "according to the teaching." The sense is, according to that doctrine as taught by the inspired teachers of religion. It does not mean as *he* had individually been taught; but he was to hold the faith as it was delivered by those whom the Saviour had appointed to make it known to mankind. The phrase "*the* doctrine," or "*the* teaching," had a sort of technical meaning, denoting the gospel as that which had been communicated to mankind, not by human reason, but by *teaching.* ¶ *That he may be able by sound doctrine.* By sound *teaching,* or *instruction;* Notes, 1 Tim. i. 10; iv. 16. He was not to *dictate,* or to *denounce;* but to seek to

10 For there are many unruly and ᵐvain talkers and deceivers, specially they of the circumcision :

11 Whose mouths must be stopped ; ⁿwho subvert whole houses, teaching things which

m Ja.1.26.   *n* Mat.23.14.

convince by the statement of the truth; see Notes, 2 Tim. ii. 25. ¶ *Both to exhort and to convince.* To persuade them, or to bring them over to your views by kind exhortation, and by the instruction which shall convince. The former method is to be used where men *know* the truth, but need encouragement to follow it ; the latter, where they are ignorant, or are opposed to it. Both exhortation and argument are to be used by the ministers of religion. ¶ *The gainsayers.* Opposers. Literally, *those who speak against;* that is, against the truth; Notes, Rom. x. 21.

10. *For there are many unruly and vain talkers and deceivers.* There are many persons who are indisposed to submit to authority (see the word *unruly* in ver. 6); many who are *vain talkers*—who are more given to *talk* than to the duties of practical religion (see the character of "Talkative," in the *Pilgrim's Progress*); and many who live to deceive others under the mask of religion. They make great pretensions to piety; they are fluent in argument, and they urge their views in a plausible manner. ¶ *Specially they of the circumcision.* Jews, spoken of here as "of the circumcision" particularly, because they urged the necessity of circumcision in order that men might be saved; Notes, Acts xv. 1. This proves that there were not a few Jews in the island of Crete.

11. *Whose mouths must be stopped.* The word here rendered *stopped*—ἐπιστομίζειν--occurs nowhere else in the New Testament. It means, properly, to check, or curb, as with a bridle; to restrain, or bridle in; and then, to put to silence. It is, of course, implied here that this was to be done in a proper way, and in accordance with the spirit of the gospel. The apostle gives Timothy no *civil* power to do it,

they ought not, for filthy lucre's sake.

12 One*o* of themselves, *even a*

nor does he direct him to call in the aid of the civil arm. All the agency which he specifies as proper for this, is that of argument and exhortation. These are the proper means of silencing the advocates of error; and the history of the church shows that the ministers of religion can be safely intrusted with no other; comp. Ps. xxxii. 8, 9. ¶ *Who subvert whole houses.* Whole families; comp. Mat. xxiii. 14; 2 Tim. iii. 6. That is, they turn them aside from the faith. ¶ *Teaching things which they ought not, for filthy lucre's sake.* For gain. That is, they inculcate such doctrines as will make themselves popular, and as will give them access to the confidence of the people. They make it their first object to acquire influence as ministers of religion, and then abuse that in order to obtain money from the people. This they would doubtless do under many pretences; such as that it was needful for the support of the gospel, or for the relief of the poor, or perhaps for the assistance of distant Christians in persecution. Religion is the most powerful principle that ever governs the mind; and if a man has the control of *that*, it is no difficult thing to induce men to give up their worldly possessions. In all ages there have been impostors who have taken advantage of the powerful principle of religion to obtain money from their deluded followers. No people can be too vigilant in regard to pretended religious teachers; and while it is undoubtedly their duty to contribute liberally for the support of the gospel, and the promotion of every good cause, it is *no less* their duty to examine with care every proposed object of benevolence, and to watch with an eagle eye those who have the disbursement of the charities of the church. It is very rare that ministers ought to have much to do with disposing of the funds given for benevolent purposes; and *when* they do, they should in all cases be associated with

prophet of their own, said, The Cretians *are* always liars, evil beasts, slow bellies.

their lay brethren; see Paley's *Horæ Paulinæ*, chap. iv., No. 1, 3, note; comp. 1 Cor. xvi. 3. On the phrase "filthy lucre," see Notes, 1 Tim. iii. 3. 12. *One of themselves.* That is, one of the Cretans. The quotation here shows that Paul had his eye not only on the *Jewish* teachers there, but on the native Cretans. The meaning is, that, alike in reference to Jewish teachers and native-born Cretans, there was need of the utmost vigilance in the selection of persons for the ministry. They all had well-known traits of character, which made it proper that no one should be introduced into the ministry without extreme caution. It would seem, also, from the reasoning of Paul here, that the trait of character here referred to pertained not only to the native Cretans, but also to the character of the Jews residing there; for he evidently means that the caution should extend to all who dwelt on the island. ¶ *Even a prophet of their own.* Or, a *poet;* for the word *prophet*—προφήτης—like the Latin word *vates*, was often applied to poets, because they were supposed to be *inspired* of the muses, or to write under the influence of inspiration. So Virgil, *Ecl.* 9. 32 : Et me fecere poetam Pierides . . . me quoque dicunt vatem pastores. Varro, *Ling. Lat.* 6. 3: Vates poetæ dicti sunt. The term *prophet* was also given by the Greeks to one who was regarded as the *interpreter* of the gods, or who explained the obscure responses of the oracles. As such an interpreter—as one who thus saw future events, he was called a *prophet;* and as the poets claimed much of this kind of knowledge, the name was given to them. It was also given to one who was regarded as eminently endowed with *wisdom*, or who had that kind of sagacity by which the results of present conduct might be foreseen, as if he was under the influence of a kind of inspiration. The word might have been applied to the person here referred to—Epimenides—in this latter sense, because he was eminently endowed with wisdom. He was one of the seven wise men of Greece. He was a contemporary of Solon, and was born at Phæstus, in the island of Crete, B.C. 659, and is said to have reached the age of 157 years. Many marvellous tales are told of him (see Anthon, *Class. Dic.*), which are commonly supposed to be fabulous, and which are to be traced to the invention of the Cretans. The event in his life which is best known is, that he visited Athens, at the request of the inhabitants, to prepare the way by sacrifices for the introduction of the laws of Solon. He was supposed to have intercourse with the gods, and it was presumed that a peculiar sacredness would attend the religious services in which he officiated. On this account, also, as well as because he was a poet, the name *prophet* may have been given him. Feuds and animosities prevailed at Athens, which it was supposed such a man might allay, and thus prepare them for the reception of the laws of Solon. The Athenians wished to reward him with wealth and public honours; but he refused to accept of any remuneration, and only demanded a branch of the sacred olive tree, and a decree of perpetual friendship between Athens and his native city. After his death divine honours were paid to him by the Cretans. He wrote a poem on the Argonautic expedition, and other poems, which are now entirely lost. The quotation here is supposed to be made from a treatise on oracles and responses, which is also lost. ¶ *The Cretians are always liars.* This character of the Cretans is abundantly sustained by the examples adduced by Wetstein. *To be a Cretan,* became synonymous with being a liar, in the same way as *to be a Corinthian,* became synonymous with living a licentious life; comp. Intro. to 1 Cor. § 1. Thus the scholiast says, παροιμία ἐστι τὸ κρητίζειν ἐπὶ τοῦ ψεύδεσθαι—to act the Cretan, is a proverb for to lie. The particular *reason* why they had this character abroad, rather than other people, is unknown. Bishop Warburton supposes that they acquired it by claiming

to have among them the tomb of Jupiter, and by maintaining that *all* the gods, like Jupiter, were only mortals who had been raised to divine honours. Thus the Greeks maintained that they *always* proclaimed a falsehood by asserting this opinion. But their reputation for falsehood seems to have arisen from some deeper cause than this, and to have pertained to their general moral character. They were only more eminent in what was common among the ancient heathen, and what is almost universal among the heathen now; comp. Notes on Eph. iv. 25. ¶ *Evil beasts.* In their character, beasts or brutes of a ferocious or malignant kind. This would imply that there was a great want of civilization, and that their want of refinement was accompanied with what commonly exists in that condition—the unrestrained indulgence of wild and ferocious passions. See examples of the same manner of speaking of barbarous and malicious men in Wetstein. ¶ *Slow bellies.* Mere gormandizers. Two vices seem here to be attributed to them, which indeed commonly go together—*gluttony* and *sloth.* An industrious man will not be likely to be a gormandizer, and a gormandizer will not often be an industrious man. The mind of the poet, in this, seems to have conceived of them first as an indolent, worthless people; and then immediately to have recurred to the cause—that they were a race of gluttons, a people whose only concern was the stomach; comp. Phil. iii. 19. On the connection between gluttony and sloth, see the examples in Wetstein. Seldom have more undesirable, and, in some respects, incongruous qualities, been grouped together in describing any people. They were false to a proverb, which was, indeed, consistent enough with their being ferocious—though ferocious and wild nations are sometimes faithful to their word; but they were at the same time ferocious and lazy, fierce and gluttonous—qualities which are not often found together. In some respects, therefore, they surpassed the common depravity of human nature, and blended in themselves ignoble properties which,

13 This witness is true. Wherefore *p*rebuke them sharply; that
they may be sound in the faith.
14 Not giving heed to Jewish

p 2 Ti.4.2.

among the worst people, are usually
found existing alone. To mingle apparently contradictory qualities of
wickedness in the same individual or
people, is the height of depravity; as
to blend in the same mind apparently
inconsistent traits of virtuous character, or those which exist commonly
in their highest perfection only alone,
is the highest virtue.

13. *This witness is true.* That is,
this testimony long before borne by
one of their own number, was true
when the apostle wrote to Titus. The
fact that this was the general character of the people, was a reason why he
should be on his guard in introducing
men into the ministry, and in the arrangement of affairs pertaining to the
church. That it *was* true, see proofs
in Wetstein. ¶ *Wherefore rebuke
them.* Notes, 2 Tim. iv. 2. ¶ *Sharply.*
ἀποτόμως—*cuttingly, severely*—from
ἀποτέμνω, *to cut off.* The word is used
here in the sense of severity, meaning
that the reproof should be such as
would be understood, and would show
them plainly the wickedness of such
traits of character. He was not to
be *mealy-mouthed,* but he was to call
things by their right names, and not
to spare their faults. When men
know that they are doing wrong, we
should tell them so in few words; if
they do not know it, it is necessary to
teach them, in order to convince them
of their error. ¶ *That they may be
sound in the faith.* That they may
not allow the prevailing vices to corrupt their views of religion.

14. *Not giving heed to Jewish fables,*
&c. See Notes, 1 Tim. i. 4. ¶ *And
commandments of men that turn from
the truth.* Notes, Mat. xv. 3-5.

15. *Unto the pure all things* are
pure. See Notes on Rom. xiv. 14, 20.
There is probably an allusion here to
the distinctions made in respect to
meats and drinks among the Jews.
Some articles of food were regarded
as "clean," or allowed to be eaten,

*q*fables, and commandments of men
that turn from the truth.
15 Unto *r* the pure all things *are*
pure: but unto them that are defiled

q 1 Ti.1.4.   *r* Ro.14.14,20.

and some as "unclean," or forbidden.
Paul says that those distinctions ceased
under the Christian dispensation, and
that to those who had a conscience
not easily troubled by nice and delicate questions about ceremonial observances, all kinds of food might be
regarded as lawful and proper; comp.
Notes, 1 Tim. iv. 4, 5. If a man
habitually maintains a good conscience
in the sight of God, it will be accepted
of him whether he do or do not abstain from certain kinds of food;
comp. Notes on Col. ii. 16. This
passage, therefore, should not be interpreted as proving that all things
are right and lawful for a Christian,
or that whatever he may choose to do
will be regarded as pure, but as primarily referring to distinctions in
food, and meaning that there was no
sanctity in eating one kind of food,
and no sin in another, but that the
mind was equally pure whatever was
eaten. The phrase has a proverbial
cast, though I know not that it was so
used. The *principle* of the declaration is, that a pure mind—a truly
pious mind—will not regard the distinctions of food and drink; of festivals, rites, ceremonies, and days, as
necessary to be observed in order to
promote its purity. The conscience
is not to be burdened and enslaved by
these things, but is to be controlled
only by the moral laws which God has
ordained. But there may be a somewhat higher application of the words
—that *every* ordinance of religion,
every command of God, every event
that occurs in divine providence,
tends to promote the holiness of one
who is of pure heart. He can see a
sanctifying tendency in everything,
and can derive from all that is commanded, and all that occurs, the
means of making the heart more holy.
While a depraved mind will turn every
such thing to a pernicious use, and
make it the means of augmenting its
malignity and corruption, to the pure

and unbelieving *is* nothing pure;
but even their mind and conscience
is defiled.

16 They *s* profess that they know

s 2 Ti.3.5,7.

mind it will be the means of increasing
its confidence in God, and of making
itself more holy. To such a mind
everything may become a means of
grace. ¶ *But unto them that are defiled and unbelieving is nothing pure.*
Everything is made the means of increasing their depravity. No matter
what ordinances of religion they observe; what distinctions of meats, or
drinks, or days they regard, and what
events of providence occur, all are
the occasion of augmented depravity.
Such distinctions in food they make
the means of fostering their pride and
producing self-righteousness; the mercies of God they abuse to pamper
their own lusts, and the afflictive
events of divine providence they make
the occasion of murmuring and re-
bellion. Naturally corrupt at heart,
no ordinances of religion, and no
events of providence, make them any
better, but all tend to deepen their
depravity. A sentiment similar to
this is found in the classic writers.
Thus Seneca, Epis. 98: Malus animus omnia in malum vertit, etiam
quæ specie optimi venerunt. So
again (*de Beneficiis*, v. 12): Quemad-
modum stomachus morbo vitiatus, et
colliques bilem, quoscunque acceperit
cibos mutat—ita animus cæcus, quic-
quid illi commiseris, id onus suum et
perniciem facit. ¶ *But even their
mind and conscience is defiled.* It is
not a mere external defilement—a
thing which they so much dread—but
a much worse kind of pollution, that
which extends to the soul and the
conscience. Everything which they
do tends to corrupt the inner man
more and more, and to make them
really more polluted and abominable
in the sight of God. The wicked,
while they remain impenitent, are
constantly becoming worse and worse.
They make everything the means of
increasing their depravity, and even
those things which seem to pertain
only to outward observances are made

God; but in works they deny *him*,
being abominable, and disobedient,
and unto every good work *5* reprobate.

5 or, *void of judgment.*

the occasion of the deeper corruption
of the heart.

16. *They profess that they know
God.* That is, the Jewish teachers
particularly, who are referred to in
ver. 14. All those persons were professors of religion, and claimed that
they had a peculiar knowledge of
God. ¶ *But in works they deny* him.
Their conduct is such as to show that
they have no real acquaintance with
him. ¶ *Being abominable.* In their
conduct. The word here used —
βδελυκτοί—occurs nowhere else in the
New Testament. It means that which
is detestable, or to be held in abhor-
rence. ¶ *And disobedient, and unto
every good work reprobate.* Marg.,
void of judgment. On the word here
used—ἀδόκιμος—see Notes on Rom. i.
28; 2 Cor. xiii. 5. It means here
that in reference to everything that
was good, their conduct was such that
it could not be approved, or deserved
disapprobation. It was for this
reason—from the character of the
people of the island of Crete, and of
those who claimed to be teachers
there enforcing the obligation of the
Mosaic law—that it was so important
for Titus to exercise special care in
introducing men into the ministry,
and in completing the arrangements
contemplated in the organization of
the churches there. Yet is this character confined to them? Are there
none now who profess that they know
God, but in works deny him; whose
conduct is such that it ought to be
abhorred; who are disobedient to the
plain commands of God, and whose
character in respect to all that pertains to true piety is to be disap-
proved by the truly pious, and will
be by God at the last day? Alas,
taking the church at large, there are
many such, and the fact that there are
such persons is the grand hindrance to
the triumphs of religion on the earth.
" *The way to heaven is blocked up by
dead professors of religion.*"

18

CHAPTER II.

BUT speak thou the things which become sound doctrine:

2 That the *a*aged men be [1]sober, grave, temperate, sound in faith, in charity, in patience.

a Pr.16.31.   [1] or, *vigilant.*

CHAPTER II.

ANALYSIS OF THE CHAPTER.

In the previous chapter, the apostle had directed Titus what to do in the organization of churches in the various cities of Crete, and had put him on his guard in doing it, by showing the character of the people he had to deal with. In this chapter he gives him various instructions as to his *own* method of teaching, showing what kind of doctrines he should inculcate, and what kind of instructions he should give to the various *classes* of his hearers. He was, in general, to speak only such things as became sound doctrine, ver. 1. In particular he was to instruct aged men to be sober, grave, and temperate—acting in a manner that became their time of life, ver. 2; the aged women to be a proper example to the younger females, and to exercise a proper care over them, ver. 3–5; the young men to be sober-minded, ver. 6; Titus himself, who evidently came under the class of young men, was to be an example to them in all things, ver. 7, 8; and servants were to be instructed to perform their duty to their masters with fidelity, ver. 9, 10. The duty of giving these instructions is then enforced by a reference to the nature and design of the gospel, ver. 11–15. That grace which brings salvation has appeared to all mankind, and its design is to make all holy who embrace it, and to teach all to live for a higher and a better world.

1. *But speak thou.* In thine own ministry. In the previous chapter he had given him instructions as to the kind of persons who were to be put into the sacred office. Here he gives him special instructions in regard to his own preaching. ¶ *The things which become sound doctrine.* To wit, those which he proceeds immediately to specify. On the phrase *sound doctrine,* see Notes, 1 Tim. i. 10; comp. 2 Tim. iv. 3.

2. *That the aged men.* All aged men—for there is no reason to suppose that the apostle refers particularly to those who were in office, or who were technically *elders,* or *presbyters.* If he had, he would have used the common word—πρεσβύτερος, *presbyter* (see Mat. xv. 2; xvi. 21; xxi. 23; xxvi. 3, 47, 57, 59; 1 Tim. v. 1, 17, 19; Tit. i. 5; Jam. v. 14; 1 Pet. v. 1), instead of the unusual word πρεσβύτης, an old or aged man—a word which occurs nowhere else in the New Testament except in Luke i. 18, "For I am *an old man,*" and Philem. 9, "being such an one as Paul *the aged.*" It is in no instance applied to *an office.* Besides, the instructions which Titus was to give to such men was not that which peculiarly pertained to *elders* as officers in the church, but to *all* old men. The idea is, that he was to adapt his instructions to the peculiar character of different classes of his hearers. The *aged* needed special instructions, and so did the *young.* ¶ *Be sober.* Marg., *vigilant.* See the word explained in the Notes on 1 Tim. iii. 2, where it is rendered *vigilant.* In 1 Tim. iii. 11, the same word is rendered *sober.* ¶ *Grave.* Serious; see Notes on 1 Tim. iii. 8; comp. Notes on Phil. iv. 8, where the same word is rendered *honest.* ¶ *Temperate*—σώφρονας. Rather, *prudent,* or *sober-minded.* See it explained in the Notes, 1 Tim. iii. 2, where it is rendered *sober.* Also Tit. i. 8. ¶ *Sound in faith.* Notes, 1 Tim. i. 10; Tit. i. 13. ¶ *In charity.* In love; Notes, 1 Cor. xiii. The meaning is, that an old man should evince love for all, especially for those who are good. He should have overcome, at his time of life, all the fiery, impetuous, envious, wrathful passions of his early years, and his mind should be subdued into sweet benevolence to all mankind. ¶ *In patience.* In the infirmities of old age—in the trials resulting from the loss of the friends of their early years—in

3 The aged women likewise, that
they be in behaviour as becometh
holiness,[2] not [3]false accusers, not
given to much wine, teachers of
good things;

2 or, *holy women.*　　3 or, *make-bates.*

their loneliness in the world, they
should show that the effect of all God's
dealings with them has been to produce patience. The aged should submit to the trials of their advanced
years, also, with resignation—for they
will soon be over. A few more sighs,
and they will sigh no more; a little
longer bearing up under their infirmities, and they will renew their youth
before the throne of God.

3. *The aged women likewise.* Not
only those who may have the office of
deaconesses, but all aged females.
¶ *That* they be *in behaviour as becometh holiness.* Marg., *holy women.*
The Greek word is not found elsewhere in the New Testament. It
means appropriate to a sacred place
or person, or becoming to religion.
Their conduct should be such as the
gospel requires. ¶ *Not false accusers.*
Marg., *make-bates.* Gr. διαβόλου—
the word commonly applied to the
devil *as the accuser.* See it explained
in the Notes on 1 Tim. iii. 11, where
it is rendered *slanderers.* ¶ *Not given
to much wine.* Notes, 1 Tim. iii. 3.
¶ *Teachers of good things.* That is,
instructing the younger — whether
their own children, or whether they
sustain the office of deaconess, and
are appointed to give instruction to
younger females; comp. Notes on
1 Tim. v. 2–6.

4. *That they may teach the young
women to be sober.* Marg., *wise*—a
word similar to that which in ver. 2
is rendered *temperate,* and in 1 Tim.
iii. 2, *sober.* The meaning is, that
they should instruct them to have
their desires and passions well regulated, or under proper control. ¶ *To
love their husbands—φιλάνδρους.* This
word occurs nowhere else in the New
Testament. In Eph. v. 25, Paul directs husbands to love their wives,
and in ver. 33, the wife to reverence
her husband, and here he says that it
should be one of the first duties en-

4 That they may teach the
[b]young women to be [4]sober, to
love their husbands, to love their
children,

5 *To be* discreet, chaste, keepers

b 1 Ti.5.14.　　4 or, *wise.*

joined on the wife that she should love
her husband. All happiness in the marriage relation is based on mutual love.
When that departs, happiness departs.
No wealth or splendour in a dwelling
—no gorgeousness of equipage or apparel—no magnificence of entertainment or sweetness of music—and no
forms of courtesy and politeness, can
be a compensation for the want of affection. Mutual love between a husband and wife will diffuse comfort
through the obscurest cottage of poverty; the want of it cannot be supplied by all that can be furnished in the
palaces of the great. ¶ *To love their
children.* Nature prompts to this,
and yet there are those so depraved
that they have no maternal affection;
Notes, Rom. i. 31. Religion repro-
duces natural affection when sin has
weakened or destroyed it, and it is
the design of Christianity to recover
and invigorate all the lost or weakened
sensibilities of our nature.

5. To be *discreet.* The same word
rendered, in ver. 2, *temperate,* and
explained in ver. 4. ¶ *Chaste.* Pure
—in heart, and in life. ¶ *Keepers at
home.* That is, characteristically attentive to their domestic concerns, or
to their duties in their families. A
similar injunction is found in the precepts of the Pythagoreans—τὰν γὰρ
γύναικα δεῖ οἰκουρεῖν καὶ ἔνδον μένειν.
See Creuzer's *Symbolik,* iii. 120. This
does not mean, of course, that they
are *never* to go abroad, but they are
not to neglect their domestic affairs;
they are not to be better known
abroad than at home; they are not to
omit their own duties and become
"busybodies" in the concerns of
others. Religion is the patron of the
domestic virtues, and regards the appropriate duties in a family as those
most intimately connected with its
own progress in the world. It looks
benignly on all which makes *home* a
place of contentment, intelligence,

at home, good, obedient to their own husbands, that the word of God be not blasphemed.

6 Young men likewise exhort to be [5]sober-minded:

7 In [c]all things showing thyself a pattern of good works: in doctrine *showing* uncorruptness, gravity, sincerity,

5 or, *discreet.*　　　　c 1 Ti.4.12.

and peace. It does not flourish when domestic duties are neglected;—and whatever may be done abroad, or whatever self-denial and zeal in the cause of religion may be evinced there, or whatever call there may be for the labours of Christians there, or however much good may be actually done abroad, religion has *gained nothing*, on the whole, if, in order to secure these things, the duties of a wife and mother at home have been disregarded. Our first duty is *at home*, and all other duties will be well performed just in proportion as that is. ¶ *Good.* In all respects, and in all relations. To a wife, a mother, a sister, there can be no higher characteristic ascribed, than to say that she is *good*. What other trait of mind will enable her better to perform her appropriate duties of life? What other will make her more like her Saviour? ¶ *Obedient to their own husbands.* Notes, Eph. v. 22–24; Col. iii. 18. ¶ *That the word of God be not blasphemed.* That the gospel may not be *injuriously spoken of* (Notes, Mat. ix. 3), on account of the inconsistent lives of those who profess to be influenced by it. The idea is, that religion *ought* to produce the virtues here spoken of, and that when it does not, it will be reproached as being of no value.

6. *Young men likewise exhort to be sober-minded.* Marg., *discreet.* On the meaning of the Greek word used here (σωφρονεῖν), see Notes on ver. 2 and 4. The idea is, that they should be entreated to be prudent, discreet, serious in their deportment; to get the mastery over their passions and appetites; to control the propensities to which youth are subject; and that there should be such self-government, under the influence of religion, as to avoid excess in every-thing. A well-governed mind, superior to the indulgence of those passions to which the young are prone, will express the meaning of the word here.

They should be "steady in their behaviour, superior to sensual temptations, and constant in the exercise of every part of self-government" (Doddridge). The *reasons* for this are obvious: (1) The hopes of the church depend much on them. (2) A young man who cannot govern himself, gives little promise of being useful or happy. (3) Indulgence in the propensities to which young men are prone, will, sooner or later, bring ruin to the body and the soul. (4) They are just at the period of life when they are exposed to peculiar temptations, and when they need to exercise a peculiar guardianship over their own conduct. (5) Like others, they may soon die; and they should be habitually in such a frame of mind as to be prepared to stand before God. A young man who feels that he may be soon in the eternal world, cannot but be sensible of the propriety of having a serious mind, and of living and acting as in the immediate presence of his Maker and Judge.

7. *In all things showing thyself a pattern of good works.* Not merely *teaching* others, but showing them by *example* how they ought to live. On the word rendered *pattern* (τύπον, *type*), see Notes on Heb. ix. 5; 1 Cor. x. 6; Phil. iii. 17. ¶ *In doctrine.* In your manner of teaching; Notes, 1 Tim. iv. 16. ¶ Showing *uncorruptness.* The word here used does not occur elsewhere in the New Testament. It means, here, the same as *purity*—that which is not erroneous, and which does not tend to corrupt or vitiate the morals of others, or to endanger their salvation. Everything in his teaching was to be such as to make men purer and better. ¶ *Gravity.* See this word explained in the Notes on 1 Tim. ii. 2, where it is rendered *honesty;* comp. Notes on 1 Tim. iii. 4, where it is rendered *gravity.* It does not elsewhere occur; see the use of the adjective, however, in

8 Sound[d] speech that cannot be condemned; that he that is of the contrary part may be ashamed, having no evil thing to say of you.

d 1 Ti.6.3.

Phil. iv. 8; 1 Tim. iii. 8, 11; Tit. ii. 2. The word properly means *venerableness;* then, whatever will ensure respect, in character, opinions, deportment. The sense here is, that the manner in which a preacher delivers his message, should be such as *to command respect.* He should evince good sense, undoubted piety, an acquaintance with his subject, simplicity, seriousness, and earnestness, in his manner. ¶ *Sincerity.* See this word (ἀφθαρσία) explained in the Notes on Eph. vi. 24. It is rendered *immortality* in Rom. ii. 7; 2 Tim. i. 10; *incorruption,* in 1 Cor. xv. 42, 50, 53, 54; and *sincerity,* Eph. vi. 24, and in the place before us. It does not elsewhere occur in the New Testament. It means *incorruption, incapacity of decay;* and, therefore, would be here synonymous with *purity.* It should be said, however, that it is wanting in many MSS., and is rejected in the later editions of the New Testament by Wetstein, Tittman, and Hahn.

8. *Sound speech.* Notes, 1 Tim. i. 10. He was to use language that would be spiritually *healthful* (ὑγιῆ); that is, true, pure, uncorrupted. This word, and its correlatives, is used in this sense, in the New Testament, only by the apostle Paul. It is commonly applied to the body, meaning that which is *healthful,* or *whole;* see Luke v. 31; vi. 10; vii. 10; xv. 27; Mat. xii. 13; xv. 31; Mark iii. 5; v. 34; John v. 4, 6, 9, 11, 14, 15; vii. 23; Acts iv. 10; 3 John 2. For *Paul's* use of the word, see 1 Tim. i. 10; vi. 3; 2 Tim. i. 13; iv. 3; Tit. i. 9, 13; ii. 1, 2, 8. It does not elsewhere occur. ¶ *That cannot be condemned.* Such as cannot be shown to be weak, or unsound; such that no one could find fault with it, or such as an adversary could not take hold of and blame. This direction would imply purity and seriousness of language, solidity of argument,

9 *Exhort*[e] servants to be obedient unto their own masters, *and* to please *them* well in all *things;* not [6]answering again; 10 Not purloining, but showing

e Ep.6.5,&c.   6 or, *gainsaying.*

and truth in the doctrines which he maintained. ¶ *That he that is of the contrary part may be ashamed,* &c. Ashamed that he has opposed such views.

9. Exhort *servants to be obedient to their own masters.* See this explained in the Notes on Eph. vi. 5, *seq.,* and 1 Tim. vi. 1–4. ¶ And *to please* them *well in all* things. That is, so far as they lawfully may, or in those things which are not contrary to the will of God; comp. Eph. vi. 6. It should be an object with one who is a servant, to meet the approbation of his master, as long as this relation continues. This rule would not, however, go to the extent to require him to please his master in doing anything that is contrary to the law of God, or that is morally wrong. ¶ *Not answering again.* Marg., *gainsaying.* Not contradicting, or not disobeying. They were to do what the master required, if it did not interfere with the rights of conscience, without attempting to argue the matter—without disputing with the master—and without advancing their own opinions. Where this relation exists, no one can doubt that this is a proper frame of mind for a servant. It may be observed, however, that all that is here said would be equally appropriate, whether the servitude was voluntary or involuntary. A man who becomes voluntarily a servant, binds himself to obey his master cheerfully and quietly, without gainsaying, and without attempting to reason the matter with him, or propounding his own opinions, even though they may be much wiser than those of his employer. He makes a contract to *obey* his master, not to *reason* with him, or to *instruct* him.

10. *Not purloining.* Not to appropriate to themselves what belongs to their masters. The word *purloin* means, literally, to take or carry away for one's self; and would be ap-

all good fidelity; *f*that they may
adorn the doctrine of God our
Saviour in all things.

11 For*g* the grace of God that

f Mat.5.16.   *g* Ro.5.15.

bringeth salvation [7]hath appeared
to all men,

12 Teaching us, that, *h*denying
ungodliness and *i*worldly lusts,

7 or, *to all men, hath appeared.*
h Ro.8.13.   *i* 1 Pe.2.11.

plied to an appropriation to one's self
of what pertained to a common stock,
or what belonged to one in whose employ we are—as the embezzlement of
public funds. Here it means that the
servant was not to apply to his own
use what belonged to his master; that
is, was not to *pilfer*—a vice to which,
as all know, servants, and especially
slaves, are particularly exposed; see
the word explained in the Notes on
Acts v. 2. ¶ *But showing all good
fidelity.* In labouring, and in taking
care of the property intrusted to them.
¶ *That they may adorn the doctrine
of God our Saviour in all things.*
That they may show the fair influence
of religion on them, in all respects,
making them industrious, honest, kind,
and obedient. They were to show
that the effect of the religion which
they professed was to make them better
fitted to discharge the duties of their
station in life, however humble; or
that its influence on them was desirable in every respect. In this way
they might hope also that the minds of
their masters might be reached, and
that they might be brought to respect
and love the gospel. Learn hence,
(1) That one in the most humble walk
of life *may* so live as to be an *ornament* to religion, as well as one favoured with more advantages. (2)
That servants *may* do much good, by
so living as to show to all around
them that there is a reality in the
gospel, and to lead others to love it.
(3) If, in this situation of life, it is a
duty so to live as to adorn religion, it
cannot be less so in more elevated
situations. A master should feel the
obligation not to be surpassed in religious character by his servant.

11. *For the grace of God.* The
favour of God, shown to the unde-
serving; see Notes on Rom. i. 7.
¶ *That bringeth salvation.* Marg.,
to all men, hath appeared. That is,
in the margin, "the grace which

brings salvation to all men has been
revealed." The marginal reading is
most in accordance with the Greek,
though it will bear either construction.
If that which is in the text be adopted,
it means that the plan of salvation has
been revealed to all classes of men;
that is, that it is *announced* or *revealed* to all the race that they may
be saved; comp. Notes on Col. i. 23.
If the other rendering be adopted, it
means that that plan was fitted to secure the salvation of *all men;* that
none were excluded from the offer;
that provision had been made for all,
and all might come and be saved.
Whichever interpretation be adopted,
the sense here will not be essentially
varied. It is, that the gospel was
adapted *to man as man,* and therefore might include servants as well as
masters; subjects, as well as kings;
the poor, as well as the rich; the
ignorant, as well as the learned; see
Notes on 1 Tim. ii. 1, 2; Acts xvii.
26.

12. *Teaching us.* That is, the
"grace of God" so teaches us; or that
system of religion which is a manifestation of the grace of God, inculcates the great and important duties
which Paul proceeds to state. ¶ *That
denying ungodliness and worldly lusts.*
"That by denying ourselves of these,
or refusing to practise them, we should
lead a holy life." The word *ungodliness* here means all that would be included under the word *impiety;* that
is, all failure in the performance of
our proper duties towards God; see
Notes, Rom. i. 18. The phrase
"worldly lusts" refers to all improper
desires pertaining to this life—the
desire of wealth, pleasure, honour,
sensual indulgence. It refers to such
passions as the men of this world are
prone to, and would include all those
things which cannot be indulged in
with a proper reference to the world
to come. The gross passions would

we*should live soberly, righteously, and godly, in this present world;

k Lu.1.75.

be of course included, and all those more refined pleasures also which constitute the characteristic and peculiar enjoyments of those who do not live unto God. ¶ *We should live soberly.* See the word *soberly* (σωφρόνως) explained in the Notes on ver. 2, 4. It means that we should exercise a due restraint on our passions and propensities. ¶ *Righteously.* Justly—δικαίως. This refers to the proper performance of our duties to our fellow-men; and it means that religion teaches us to perform those duties with fidelity, according to all our relations in life; to all our promises and contracts; to our fellow-citizens and neighbours; to the poor, and needy, and ignorant, and oppressed; and to all those who are providentially placed in our way who need our kind offices. *Justice* to them would lead us to act as we would wish that they would towards us. ¶ *And godly.* Piously; that is, in the faithful performance of our duties to God. We have here, then, an epitome of all that religion requires: (1) Our duty to ourselves—included in the word "soberly" and requiring a suitable control over our evil propensities and passions; (2) our duty to our fellow-men in all the relations we sustain in life; and (3) our duty to God—evinced in what will be properly regarded as *a pious life.* He that does these things, meets all the responsibilities of his condition and relations; and the Christian system, requiring the faithful performance of these duties, shows how admirably it is adapted to man. ¶ *In this present world.* That is, as long as we shall continue in it. These are the duties which we owe in the present life.

13. *Looking for.* Expecting; waiting for. That is, in the faithful performance of our duties to ourselves, to our fellow-creatures and to God, we are patiently to wait for the coming of our Lord. (1) We are to believe that he will return; (2) we are to be in a posture of expectation, not knowing *when* he will come; and (3)

13 Looking*l* for that blessed hope, and the glorious appearing

l 2 Pe.3.12.

we are to be ready for him whenever he shall come; see Notes on Mat. xxiv. 42–44; 1 Thes. v. 4; Phil. iii. 20. ¶ *That blessed hope.* The fulfilment of that hope so full of blessedness to us. ¶ *The glorious appearing.* Notes, 2 Thes. ii. 8; comp. 1 Tim. vi. 14; 2 Tim. i. 10; iv. 1, 8. ¶ *Of the great God.* There can be little doubt, if any, that by "the great God" here, the apostle referred to the Lord Jesus, for it is not a doctrine of the New Testament, that God himself *as such,* or in contradistinction from his incarnate Son, will appear at the last day. It is said, indeed, that the Saviour will come "in the glory of his Father, with his angels" (Mat. xvi. 27), but that God as such will appear is not taught in the Bible. The doctrine there is, that God will be manifest in his Son; that the divine approach to our world will be through him to judge the race; and that though he will be accompanied with the appropriate symbols of the divinity, yet it will be the Son of God who will be visible. No one accustomed to Paul's views can well doubt that when he used this language he had his eye throughout on the Son of God, and that he expected no other manifestation than what would be made through him. In no place in the New Testament is the phrase ἐπιφάνειαν τοῦ Θεοῦ —"the manifestation or appearing of God"—applied to any other one than Christ. It is true that this is spoken of here as the "appearing of *the glory* —τῆς δόξης—of the great God," but the idea is that of such a manifestation as *became* God, or would appropriately display his glory. It is known to most persons who have attended to religious controversies, that this passage has given rise to much discussion. The ancients, in general, interpreted it as meaning, "the glorious appearing of our great God and Saviour Jesus Christ." This sense has been vindicated by the labours of Beza, Whitby, Bull, Matthæi, and Middleton (on the Greek article), and

of [m]the great God and our Saviour Jesus Christ;

14 Who[n] gave himself for us, that he might [o]redeem us from all

m Re.1.7.　　n Ep.5.2.　　o Ps.130.8.

is the common interpretation of those who claim to be orthodox; see Bloomfield, *Rec. Syn.*, and Notes, *in loco*. He contends that the meaning is, "the glorious appearance of *that* GREAT BEING *who is our* GOD AND SAVIOUR." The arguments for this opinion are well summed up by Bloomfield. Without going into a critical examination of this passage, which would not be in accordance with the design of these Notes, it may be remarked in general, (1) That no plain reader of the New Testament, accustomed to the common language there, would have any doubt that the apostle referred here to the coming of the Lord Jesus. (2) That the "coming" of God, as such, is not spoken of in this manner in the New Testament. (3) That the expectation of Christians was directed to the advent of the ascended Saviour, not to the appearing of God as such. (4) That this is just such language as one would use who believed that the Lord Jesus is divine, or that the name God might properly be applied to him. (5) That it would naturally and obviously convey the idea that he was divine, to one who had no theory to defend. (6) That if the apostle did *not* mean this, he used such language as was fitted to lead men into error. And (7) that the fair construction of the Greek here, according to the application of the most rigid rules, abundantly sustains the interpretation which the plain reader of the New Testament would affix to it. The names above referred to are abundant proof that no violation is done to the rules of the Greek language by this interpretation, but rather that the fair construction of the original demands it. If this be so, then this furnishes an important proof of the divinity of Christ.

14. *Who gave himself for us.* See Notes, Eph. v. 2. ¶ *That he might redeem us from all iniquity.* The word here rendered *redeem*—λυτρόω,

iniquity, and [p]purify unto himself [q]a peculiar people, [r]zealous of good works.

15 These things speak, and exhort;

p He.9.14.　　q De.7.6; 1 Pe.2.9.　　r Ep.2.10.

lutroō—occurs only here and in Luke xxiv. 21; 1 Pet. i. 18. The *noun*, however—λύτρον, *lutron*—occurs in Mat. xx. 28; and Mark x. 45; where it is rendered *ransom;* see it explained in the Notes on Mat. xx. 28. It is here said that the *object* of his giving himself was to save his people from all iniquity; see this explained in the Notes on Mat. i. 21. ¶ *And purify unto himself.* (1) *Purify* them, or make them holy. This is the first and leading object; see Notes, Heb. ix. 14. (2) *Unto himself;* that is, they are no longer to be regarded as their own, but as redeemed for his own service, and for the promotion of his glory; Notes, 1 Cor. vi. 19, 20. ¶ *A peculiar people.* 1 Pet. ii. 9. The word here used (περιούσιος) occurs nowhere else in the New Testament. It means, properly, *having abundance;* and then *one's own, what is special,* or *peculiar* (Rob. *Lex.*), and here means that they were to be regarded as *belonging* to the Lord Jesus. It does not mean, as the word would *seem* to imply—and as is undoubtedly true —that they are to be a *peculiar people* in the sense that they are to be *unlike others,* or to have views and principles *peculiar to themselves;* but that they belong to the Saviour in contradistinction from belonging to themselves —"peculiar" or his own in the sense that a man's property is his own, and does not belong to others. This passage, therefore, should not be used to prove that Christians should be *unlike others* in their manner of living, but that *they belong to Christ* as his redeemed people. From that it may indeed be *inferred* that they should be unlike others, but that is not the direct teaching of the passage. ¶ *Zealous of good works.* As the result of their redemption; that is, this is one object of their having been redeemed; Notes, Eph. ii. 10.

15. *These things speak and exhort.* Notes, 1 Tim. vi. 2. ¶ *And rebuke*

and rebuke with all authority. *Let no man despise thee.

CHAPTER III.

PUT them in mind *a* to be subject to principalities and powers,

s 1 Ti.4.12.   a Ro.13.1.

with all authority. Notes, 1 Tim. v. 1, 20; 2 Tim. iv. 2. The word _authority_ here means _command—ἐπιταγὴ_; 1 Cor. vii. 6, 25; 2 Cor. viii. 8; 1 Tim. i. 1; Tit. i. 3. The sense here is, he was to do it decidedly, without ambiguity, without compromise, and without keeping anything back. He was to state these things not as being advice or counsel, but as the requirement of God. ¶ _Let no man despise thee._ That is, conduct yourself, as you may easily do, so as to command universal respect as a minister of God; see Notes on 1 Tim. iv. 12.

CHAPTER III.
ANALYSIS OF THE CHAPTER.

This chapter comprises the following subjects :—

(1) Titus was to instruct his hearers to be subject to lawful authority, and in general to manifest meekness and gentleness towards all classes of men, ver. 1, 2.

(2) A _reason_ is assigned why they should do this, ver. 3-8. They who were Christians were once, indeed, like others, disobedient and unholy; they were regardless of law, and gave free indulgence to their evil propensities, but they had been redeemed for a better purpose, and it was the design of God in redeeming them, that they should manifest every kind of virtue.

(3) Titus was to avoid foolish questions, and contentions, and strifes about the law, ver. 9.

(4) He who was a heretic was to be rejected after suitable admonitions, ver. 10, 11.

(5) Paul directs Titus to come to him at Nicopolis, and to bring Zenas and Apollos with him, ver. 12–14.

(6) He closes with the customary salutations, ver. 15.

1. _Put them in mind to be subject,_ &c. See the duty here enjoined explained in the Notes on Rom. xiii. 1, _seq._ ¶ _Principalities and powers._

to obey magistrates, to be ready to every good work,

2 To speak evil of no man, to be no brawlers, _but_ gentle, *b* showing all meekness unto all men.

b Ep.4.2.

See these words explained in the Notes on Rom. viii. 38. The word here rendered _powers_ (ἐξουσίαις), is not, indeed, the same as that which is found there (δυνάμεις), but the same idea is conveyed; comp. Notes on Eph. i. 21. ¶ _To obey magistrates._ That is, to obey them in all that was not contrary to the word of God; Notes, Rom. xiii. 1, _seq._; Acts iv. 19, 20. ¶ _To be ready to every good work._ To be _prepared for_ (ἑτοίμους); prompt to perform all that is good; Notes, Phil. iv. 8. A Christian should be always _ready_ to do good as far as he is able. He should not need to be urged, or coaxed, or persuaded, but should be so ready always to do good that he will count it a privilege to have the opportunity to do it.

2. _To speak evil of no man._ Gr., "to _blaspheme_ (βλασφημεῖν; comp. Notes on Mat. ix. 3) no one." Doddridge renders it, "calumniate no one." The idea is, that we are not to slander, revile, or defame anyone. We are not to say anything _to_ anyone, or _of_ anyone, which will do him injury. We are never to utter anything which we know to be false about him, or to give such a colouring to his words or conduct as to do him wrong in any way. We should always so speak _to_ him and _of_ him in such a way that he will have no reason to complain that he is an injured man. It may be necessary, when we are called to state what we know of his character, to say things which are not at all in his favour, or things which he has said or done that were wrong; but (1) we should never do this _for the purpose_ of doing him injury, or so as to find a pleasure in it; and (2) where it is necessary to make the statement, it should be so as to do him no injustice. We should give no improper colouring. We should exaggerate no circumstances. We should never attempt to express ourselves about his

3 For[c] we ourselves also were sometime foolish, disobedient, de-

c 1 Co.6.11; 1 Pe.4.3.

motives, or charge on him bad motives —for we know not what his motives were. We should state every palliating circumstance of which we have knowledge, and *do entire justice to it.* We should not make the bad traits of his character prominent, and pass over all that is good. In a word, we should show that we would rather find him to be a good man than a bad man—*even if the result should be that we had been mistaken in our opinions.* It is better that *we* should have been mistaken, than that he should be a bad man. ¶ *To be no brawlers.* See Notes, 1 Tim. iii. 3. The same Greek word occurs in both places. It is not elsewhere found in the New Testament. ¶ But *gentle.* The word here used is rendered *moderation* in Phil. iv. 5, *patient* in 1 Tim. iii. 3, and elsewhere *gentle;* see Notes on 1 Tim. iii. 3. ¶ *Showing all meekness unto all men.* In the reception of injuries; see Notes on Mat. v. 5; Eph. iv. 2.

3. *For we ourselves.* We who are Christians. There is no reason for supposing, as Benson does, that this is to be understood as confined to Paul himself. There are some things mentioned here which were not probably true of him before his conversion, and the connection does not require us to suppose that he referred particularly to himself. He is stating a reason why those to whom Titus was appointed to preach should be urged to lead holy lives, and especially to manifest a spirit of order, peace, kindness, and due subordination to law. In enforcing this, he says, that those who were now Christians had formerly been wicked, disorderly, and sensual, but that, under the influence of the gospel, they had been induced to lead better lives. The same gospel which had been effectual in their case, might be in others. To others it would be an encouragement to show that there were cases in which the gospel *had* been thus efficacious, and they who were appointed to preach it

ceived, serving divers lusts and pleasures, living in malice and envy, hateful, *and* hating one another.

might refer to their own example as a reason why others should be persuaded to lead holy lives. In preaching to others, also, they were not to be proud or arrogant. They were to remember that they were formerly in the same condition with those whom they addressed, and whom they exhorted to reformation. They were not to forget that what they had that was superior to others they owed to the grace of God, and not to any native goodness. He will exhort the wicked to repentance most effectually who remembers that his own former life was wicked; he will evince most of the proper spirit in doing it who has the deepest sense of the errors and folly of his own past ways. ¶ *Foolish.* See this word explained in the Notes on Luke xxiv. 25, where it is rendered *fools;* comp. Rom. i. 14, where it is rendered *unwise,* and Gal. iii. 1, 3; 1 Tim. vi. 9, where it is rendered *foolish.* ¶ *Disobedient.* To law, to parents, to civil authority, to God. This is the natural character of the human heart; see Luke i. 17; Rom. i. 30; 2 Tim. iii. 2; Tit. i. 16, where the same word occurs. ¶ *Deceived.* By the great enemy, by false teachers, by our own hearts, and by the flattery of others. It is a characteristic of man by nature that he sees nothing in its true light, but walks along amidst constant, though changing and very beautiful illusions; comp. Mat. xxiv. 4, 5, 11; 2 Tim. iii. 13; 1 Pet. ii. 25; Rev. xii. 9; xviii. 23, where the same word occurs; see also Rev. xx. 3, 8, 10, where the same word is applied to that great deceiver who has led the world astray. Every one who is converted feels, and is ready to confess, that before conversion he was deceived as to the comparative value of things, as to the enjoyment which he expected to find in scenes of pleasure and riot, and often in what seemed to him well-formed plans. ¶ *Serving divers lusts and pleasures.* Indulging in the various corrupt passions and propensities of

4 But after that the kindness and love[1] of God our Saviour toward man appeared,

5 Not[d] by works of righteous-

[1] or, *pity.*

ness which we have done, but according to his mercy he saved us, by the washing of regeneration, and renewing of the Holy Ghost;

[d] Ep.2.4,8,9.

the soul. We were so under their influence that it might be said we were their *servants,* or were *slaves* to them (δουλεύοντες); that is, we implicitly obeyed them; see Notes, Rom. vi. 16, 17. ¶ *Living in malice.* Gr., *in evil*—ἐν κακίᾳ; that is, in all kinds of evil; see Notes on Rom. i. 29, where the word is rendered *maliciousness.* ¶ *And envy.* Displeasure at the happiness and prosperity of others; Notes, Rom. i. 29. ¶ *Hateful*—στυγητοί. This word does not elsewhere occur in the New Testament. It means that our conduct was such as to be worthy of the hatred of others. Of whom, before his conversion, is not this true? ¶ *And hating one another.* There was no brotherly love; no true affection for others. There was ill-will felt in the heart, and it was evinced in the life. This is an apt description of the state of the heathen world before the gospel shines on it, and it may be regarded as the characteristic of all men before conversion. They have no true love for one another, such as they ought to cherish, and they are liable constantly to give indulgence to feelings which evince hatred. In contentions, and strifes, and litigations, and wars, this feeling is constantly breaking out. All this is suggested here as a *reason* why Christians should now be gentle and mild toward those who are evil. Let us remember what we were, and we shall not be disposed to treat others harshly. When a Christian is tempted to unkind thoughts or words towards others, nothing is more appropriate for him than to reflect on his own past life.

4. *But after that.* Gr., *when*—ὅτε. The meaning is, that "when the love of God was manifested in the plan of salvation, he saved us from this state by our being washed and purified." The idea is not, that "the love of God appeared" *after* we had sinned

in this way, but that *when* his mercy was thus displayed we were converted from our sins, and made pure in his sight. ¶ *The kindness*—χρηστότης. *The goodness,* or *the benignity.* The word is. rendered *goodness* and *good* in Rom. ii. 4; iii. 12; xi. 22, thrice; *kindness,* 2 Cor. vi. 6; Eph. ii. 7; Col. iii. 12; Tit. iii. 4; and *gentleness,* Gal. v. 22. The act of redeeming us was one *of great kindness,* or *goodness.* ¶ *And love of God.* Marg., *pity.* The Greek word is φιλανθρωπία, *philanthropy, the love of man.* The plan of salvation was founded on love to man, and was the highest expression of that love; Notes on John iii. 16. The Greek of this verse is, "When the kindness and love of God our Saviour to man was manifested, he saved us" (ver. 5), to wit, from those sins of which we had before been guilty.

5. *Not by works of righteousness which we have done.* The plan was not based on our own good works, nor are our own good works now the cause of our salvation. If men could have been saved by their own good works, there would have been no need of salvation by the Redeemer; if our own deeds were now the basis of our title to eternal life, the work of Christ would be equally unnecessary. It is a great and fundamental principle of the gospel that the good works of men come in for no share in the justification of the soul. They are in no sense a *consideration* on account of which God pardons a man, and receives him to favour. The only basis of justification is the merit of the Lord Jesus Christ, and in the matter of justification before God, all the race is on a level; see Notes on Eph. ii. 8, 9. ¶ *But according to his mercy.* (1) It had its origin in mercy; (2) it is by *mere* mercy or compassion, and not by justice; (3) it is an expression of *great* mercy, and (4) it is now *in fact* conferred only by mercy.

Whatever we have done or can do, when we come to receive salvation from the hand of God, there is no other element which enters into it *but* mercy. It is not because our deeds deserve it; it is not because we have by repentance and faith wrought ourselves into such a state of mind that we can *claim* it; but, after all our tears, and sighs, and prayers, and good deeds, it is a mere favour. Even then God might justly withhold it if he chose, and no blame would be attached to him if he should suffer us to sink down to ruin. ¶ *He saved us.* That is, he *began* that salvation in us which is to be *completed* in heaven. A man who is already renewed and pardoned may be spoken of as *saved*—for (1) the work of salvation is *begun*, and (2) when begun it will certainly be completed; see Notes on Phil. i. 6. ¶ *By the washing of regeneration.* In order to a correct understanding of this important passage, it is necessary to ascertain whether the phrase here used refers to *baptism*, and whether anything different is intended by it from what is meant by the succeeding phrase—"renewing of the Holy Ghost." The word rendered *washing* (λουτρὸν, *loutron*) occurs in the New Testament only in this place and in Eph. v. 26, where also it is rendered *washing*—"That he might sanctify and cleanse it [the church] with the *washing* of water by the word." The word properly means *a bath;* then water for bathing; then the act of bathing, washing, ablution (Passow and Robinson). It is used by Homer to denote a warm or cold bath; then a washing away, and is thus applied to the drink-offerings in sacrifice, which were supposed to purify or wash away sin (Passow). The word here does not mean *laver*, or the vessel for washing in, which would be expressed by λουτὴρ, *loutēr*, and this word cannot be properly applied to the baptismal font. The word in itself would naturally be understood as referring to baptism (comp. Notes on Acts xxii. 16), which was regarded as the emblem of washing away sins, or of cleansing from them. I say it was

the *emblem*, not the *means* of purifying the soul from sin. If this be the allusion, and it seems probable, then the phrase "washing of regeneration" would mean "that outward washing or baptism which is the *emblem* of regeneration," and which is appointed as one of the ordinances connected with salvation; see Notes, Mark xvi. 16, "He that believeth and *is baptized* shall be saved." It is not affirmed in this phrase that baptism is the *means* of regeneration; or that grace is *necessarily* conveyed by it; and still less that baptism *is* regeneration, for no one of these is a *necessary* interpretation of the passage, and should not be *assumed* to be the true one. The full force of the language will be met by the supposition that it means that baptism is the *emblem* or *symbol* of regeneration, and, if this is the case, no one has a right to assume that the other *is* certainly the meaning. And that this *is* the meaning is further clear, because it is nowhere taught in the New Testament that baptism *is* regeneration, or that it is *the means* of regeneration. The word rendered *regeneration* (παλιγγενεσία, *palingenesia*) occurs in the New Testament only here and in Mat. xix. 28, "In the *regeneration* when the Son of man," &c. It means, properly, a new birth, reproduction, or renewal. It would probably be applied to one who should be begotten again in this sense, that a new life was commenced in him in some way corresponding to his being made to live at first. To the proper idea of the word, it is essential that there should be connected the notion of the commencement of life in the man, so that he may be said to live anew; and as religion is in the Scriptures represented as *life*, it is properly applied to the *beginning* of that kind of life by which man may be said to live anew. This word, occurring only here and in Mat. xix. 28, and there indubitably *not* referring to baptism, should not be here understood as referring to that, or be applied to that; for, (1) that is not the proper meaning of the word; (2) there is no Scripture usage to sanction it; (3) the connection here does

6 Which he shed on us ²abundantly through Jesus Christ our Saviour:

² or, *richly.*

7 That *ᵉbeing justified by his grace, we should be made heirs according to the hope of eternal life.

e Ro.3.24.

not demand it; (4) the correlatives of the word (see John iii. 3, 5, 6, 8; 1 Pet. i. 3) are applied only to that great moral change which is produced by the Holy Ghost; and (5) it is a dangerous use of the word. Its use in this sense leaves the impression that the *only* change needful for man is that which is produced by being regularly baptized. On almost no point has so much injury been done in the church as by the application of the word *regeneration* to baptism. It affects the beginning of religion in the soul, and if a mistake is made there, it is one which must pervade all the views of piety. ¶ *And renewing of the Holy Ghost.* This is an important clause, added by Paul apparently to save from the possibility of falling into error. If the former expression, "the washing of regeneration," had been left to stand by itself, it might have been supposed possibly that *all* the regeneration which would be needed would be that which would accompany baptism. But he avoids the possibility of this error, by saying that the "renewing of the Holy Ghost" is an indispensable part of that by which we are saved. It is necessary that this should exist *in addition* to that which is the mere emblem of it —the washing of regeneration—for without this the former would be unmeaning and unavailing. It is important to observe that the apostle by no means says that this *always* follows from the former, nor does he affirm that it *ever* follows from it— whatever may be the truth on that point—but he asserts that this is that on which our salvation depends. The word rendered *renewing* (ἀνα- καίνωσις, *anakainosis*) occurs only here and in Rom. xii. 2, where it is also rendered *renewing;* comp. Note on that place. The *verb* (ανακαινόω, *anakainoō*) occurs in 2 Cor. iv. 15, and Col. iii. 19, in both which places it is rendered *renewed,* and the corresponding word (ἀνακαινίζω, *ana-*

kainidzo) in Heb. vi. 6. The noun properly means *making new again; a renewing; a renovation;* comp. H. Planck in *Bib. Repos.,* i. 677. It is a word which is found only in the writings of Paul, and in ecclesiastical Greek writers. It would be properly applied to such a change as the Holy Spirit produces in the soul, making one a *new* man; that is, a man *new,* so far as religion is concerned—new in his views, feelings, desires, hopes, plans, and purposes. He is so far different from what he was before, that it may be said he enters on a new life; see Notes on Eph. iv. 23, 24. The "renewing *of the Holy Ghost*" of course means that which the Holy Ghost produces, recognizing the fact, everywhere taught in the Scriptures, that the Holy Spirit is the Author of the new creation. It cannot mean, as Koppe supposes, the renewing of the mind itself, or producing *a* holy spirit in the soul.

6. *Which he shed on us.* Gr., "Which he *poured out* on us"— ἐξέχεεν; see Notes on Acts ii. 17. The same Greek word is used there as here. It occurs also in the same sense in Acts ii. 18, 33. ¶ *Abundantly.* Marg., as in Gr., *richly.* The meaning is, that the Holy Spirit had been imparted in copious measure in order to convert them from their former wickedness. There is no particular allusion here to the day of Pentecost, but the sense is, that the Holy Spirit had been imparted richly to *all* who were converted, at any time or place, from the error of their ways. What the apostle says here is true of all who become Christians, and can be applied to all who become believers in any age or land. ¶ *Through Jesus Christ our Saviour.* See Notes, Acts ii. 33.

7. *That being justified by his grace.* Not by our own works, but by his favour or mercy; see Notes, Rom. iii. 24. ¶ *We should be made heirs.* See Notes, Rom. viii. 15, 17. ¶ *Ac-*

8 *This is* a faithful saying,
and these things I will that thou
affirm constantly, that they which
have believed in God might *ᶠ*be
careful to maintain good works.
These things are good and profitable unto men.

* f* ver.1,14.

9 But*ᵍ* avoid foolish questions,
and genealogies, and contentions,
and strivings about the law; for
they are unprofitable and vain.

10 A man that is an heretic,
*ʰ*after the first and second admonition reject;

g 2 Ti.2.23.   *h* Mat.18.17.

---

cording to the hope of eternal life. In
reference to the hope of eternal life;
that is, we have that hope in virtue of
our being adopted with the family of
God, and being made heirs. He has
received us as his children, and permits us to hope that we shall live with
him for ever.
8. *This is a faithful saying.* See
Notes on 1 Tim. i. 15. The reference
here is to what he had been just saying, meaning that the doctrine which
he had stated about the method of
salvation was in the highest degree important, and entirely worthy of belief.
¶ *And these things I will that thou
affirm constantly.* Make them the
constant subject of your preaching.
¶ *That they which have believed in
God might be careful to maintain
good works.* This shows that Paul
supposed that the doctrines of the
gospel were fitted to lead men to holy
living; comp. ver. 1, and Notes, Phil.
iv. 8. The "good works" here refer not merely to acts of benevolence
and charity, but to all that is upright
and good—to an honest and holy life.
¶ *These things are good and profitable unto men.* That is, these doctrines which he had stated were not
mere matters of speculation, but they
were fitted to promote human happiness, and they should be constantly
taught.
9. *But avoid foolish questions and
genealogies.* See Notes on 1 Tim. i.
4; 2 Tim. ii. 16, 23. ¶ *And contentions, and strivings about the law.*
Such as the Jews started about various matters connected with the law—
about meats and drinks, &c.; Notes
on 1 Tim. i. 4; comp. Notes on Acts
xviii. 15. ¶ *For they are unprofitable
and vain.* They disturb and embitter
the feelings; they lead to the indulgence of a bad spirit; they are often

difficult to be settled, and are of no
practical importance if they could be
determined. The same thing might
be said of multitudes of things about
which men dispute so earnestly now.
10. *A man that is an heretic.* The
word *heretic* is now commonly applied
to one who holds some fundamental
error of doctrine, " a person who holds
and teaches opinions repugnant to the
established faith, or that which is
made the standard of orthodoxy"
(Webster). The Greek word here used
(αἱρετικὸς, *haireticos*) occurs nowhere
else in the New Testament. The
corresponding noun (αἵρεσις, *hairesis*)
occurs in the following places: Acts
v. 17; xv. 5; xxiv. 5; xxvi. 5; xxviii.
22, where it is rendered *sect;* and
Acts xxv. 14; 1 Cor. xi. 19; Gal. v.
20; 2 Pet. ii. 1, where it is rendered
heresy, and *heresies;* see Notes on
Acts xxiv. 14. The true notion of
the word is that of one who is a pro-
moter of a sect or party. The man
who makes divisions in a church, instead of aiming to promote unity, is
the one who is intended. Such a
man may form sects and parties on
some points of doctrine on which he
differs from others, or on some custom,
religious rite, or peculiar practice;
he may make some unimportant matter a ground of distinction from his
brethren, and may refuse to have fellowship with them, and endeavour to
get up a new organization. Such a
man, according to the Scripture usage, is *a heretic,* and not merely one
who holds a different doctrine from
that which is regarded as orthodoxy.
The spirit of the doctrine here is the
same as in Rom. xvi. 17, and the
same class of persons is referred to—
"Mark them which cause divisions
and offences contrary to the doctrine
which ye have received; and avoid

11 Knowing that he that is such

is subverted, and sinneth, *i*being condemned of himself.

them." See Notes on that passage. The word here used is defined by Robinson (*Lex.*), " one who creates dissensions, introduces errors, a factious person." It is not found in classic Greek, but often in ecclesiastical writers; see Suicer's *Thesau.* ¶ *After the first and second admonition.* Comp. Mat. xviii. 15–17. That is, do not do it hastily and rashly. Give him an opportunity to explain himself, and to repent and abandon his course. No man is to be cut off without giving him a proper opportunity to vindicate his conduct, and to repent if he has done wrong. If, after the first and second admonition, a man who is undoubtedly doing wrong will not repent, then he is to be cut off. The apostle does not say in what *way* this admonition is to be given, or whether it should be public or private. The language which he uses would justify either, and the method which is to be adopted is doubtless to be determined by circumstances. The *thing* which is to be reached is, that *his fault is to be fairly set before his mind.* ¶ *Reject*—παραιτοῦ. This word is rendered *excuse* in Luke xiv. 18, 19; *refuse*, Acts xxv. 11; 1 Tim. iv. 7; v. 11; Heb. xii. 25; *avoid*, 2 Tim. ii. 23, and *entreated*, Heb. xii. 19. Its prevailing meaning, as used in connections like the one before us, is to reject *in relation to an office;* that is, to decline appointing one to an office. It probably had a primary reference to that here, and meant that a man who was given to making dissensions, or who was a factious person, should not be admitted to an office in the church. The general direction would also include this,—that he should not be admitted to the church. He is neither to be owned as a member, nor admitted to office; comp. Mat. xviii. 17, " Let him be unto thee as a heathen man and a publican." In regard to this passage, then, we may observe, (1) That the utmost limit which this allows is *mere exclusion.* It does not allow us to follow the offender with injury. (2) It does

not authorize us to oppose one on account of his mere private opinions. The essential idea is that of a *factious, division-making man;* a man who aims to form sects and parties, whether on account of opinions, or from any other cause. (3) It does not make it right to deliver such a man over to the " secular arm," or to harm him in body, soul, property, or reputation. It gives no power to torture him on the rack, or with thumb-screws, or to bind him to the stake. It authorizes us *not* to recognize him as a Christian brother, or to admit him to an office in the church—but beyond this it gives us no right to go. He has a right to his own opinion still, so far as *we* are concerned, and we are not to molest him in the enjoyment of that right. (4) It demands that, when a man is undoubtedly a heretic in the sense here explained, there should be the utmost kindness towards him, in order if possible to reclaim him. We should not *begin* by attacking and denouncing his opinions; or by formally arraigning him; or by blazoning his name *as* a heretic; but he is to be dealt with in all Christian kindness and brotherly fidelity. He is to be admonished *more than once* by those who have the right to admonish him; and then, and then only, if he does not repent, he is *to be simply avoided.* That is to be an end of the matter so far as we are concerned. The power of the church there ceases. It has no power to deliver him over to anyone else for persecution or punishment, or *in any way to meddle with him.* He may live where he pleases, pursue his own plans, entertain his own opinions or company, provided he does not interfere with us; and though we have a right to examine the *opinions* which he may entertain, yet our work with *him* is done. If these plain principles had been observed, what scenes of bloody and cruel persecution in the church would have been avoided!

11. *Knowing that he that is such is subverted.* Literally, *is turned out;* or, *is changed, i.e.* for the worse. He has

12 When I shall send Artemas unto thee, or Tychicus, be diligent to come unto me to Nicopolis: for I have determined there to winter.

13 Bring Zenas the lawyer, and Apollos, on their journey dili-

gently, that nothing be wanting unto them.

14 And let ours also learn to ³maintain ᵏgood works for necessary uses, that they be not unfruitful.

<hr>

³ or, *profess honest trades.*   k ver.8.

<hr>

gone from the right way, and therefore he should be rejected. ¶ *And sinneth, being condemned of himself.* His own conscience condemns him. He will approve the sentence, for he knows that he is wrong; and his self-condemnation will be punishment sufficient. His own course, in attempting a division or schism in the church, shows him that it is right that *he* should be separated from the communion of Christians. He that attempts to rend the church without a good reason, should himself be separated from it.

12. *When I shall send Artemas unto thee.* This person is not elsewhere mentioned in the New Testament, and nothing more is known of him. ¶ *Or Tychicus.* Notes, Acts xx. 4. ¶ *Be diligent.* Notes, 2 Tim. iv. 9. ¶ *To come unto me to Nicopolis.* It was at this place, probably, that this epistle was written. In regard to its situation, see Intro. § 4. ¶ *For I have determined there to winter.* Why Paul designed to spend the winter there, or what he purposed to do there, are questions on which no light can now be thrown. There is no *evidence* that he organized a church there, though it may be *presumed* that he preached the gospel, and that he did not do it without success. His requesting Titus to leave his important post and to come to him, looks as if his aid were needed in the work of the ministry there, and as if Paul supposed there was a promising field of labour there.

13. *Bring Zenas the lawyer.* This person is not elsewhere mentioned in the New Testament, and nothing more is known of him. He belonged doubtless to that class of persons so often mentioned in the New Testament as *lawyers;* that is, who were regarded as qualified to expound the Jewish

laws; see Notes, Mat. xxii. 35. It does not mean that he practised law, in the modern sense of that phrase. He had doubtless been converted to the Christian faith, and it is not improbable that there were Jews at Nicopolis, and that Paul supposed he might be particularly useful among them. ¶ *And Apollos.* Notes, Acts xviii. 24. He was also well-skilled in the laws of Moses, being "mighty in the Scriptures" (Acts xviii. 24), and he and Zenas appear to have been travelling together. It would seem that they had been already on a journey, probably in preaching the gospel, and Paul supposed that they would be in Crete, and that Titus could aid them. ¶ *Diligently.* 2 Tim. iv. 9. Gr., speedily ; *i.e.* facilitate their journey as much as possible. ¶ *That nothing be wanting unto them.* Nothing necessary for their journey. Paul desired that they might meet with hospitable treatment from Christians in Crete, and might not be embarrassed for the want of that which was needful for their journey. It would seem most probable that they had been *sent* by Paul on a visit to the churches.

14. *And let ours.* Our friends ; that is, those who were Christians. Paul had just directed Titus to aid Zenas and Apollos himself, and he here adds that he wished that others who were Christians would be characterized by good works of all kinds. ¶ *To maintain good works.* Marg., *profess honest trades.* The Greek will admit of the interpretation in the margin, or will *include* that, but there is no reason why the direction should be supposed to have any peculiar reference to an honest mode of livelihood, or why it should be confined to that. It rather means, that they should be distinguished for good works, includ-

15 All that are with me salute thee. Greet them that love us in the faith. Grace *be* with you all. Amen.

It was written to Titus, ordained the first bishop of the church of the Cretians, from Nicopolis of Macedonia.

ing benevolent deeds, acts of charity, honest toil, and whatever would enter into the conception of an upright life; see Notes on ver. 8. ¶ *For necessary uses.* Such as are required by their duty to their families, and by the demands of charity; see ver. 8. ¶ *That they be not unfruitful.* That it may be seen that their religion is not barren and worthless, but that it produces a happy effect on themselves and on society; comp. Notes on John xv. 16; Eph. iv. 28.

15. *All that are with me salute thee.* Notes, Rom. xvi. 3. Paul, at the close of his epistles, usually mentions the *names* of those who sent affectionate salutations. Here it would seem to be implied that Titus knew who were with Paul, and also that he himself had been travelling with him. He evidently refers, not to those who were *residing* in the place where he was, but to those who had gone with him from Crete as his companions. ¶ *Greet them that love us in the faith.* In the faith of the gospel, or as Christians. No names are here mentioned; comp. 1 Thes. v. 26; Col. iv. 15. ¶ *Grace* be *with you all.* Notes, Rom. i. 7; xvi. 20.

The subscription, "It was written to Titus," &c., is, like the other subscriptions at the close of the epistles, of no authority whatever; see the close of the Notes on 1 Cor. In this subscription there are probably two errors: (1) In the statement that Titus was "ordained the first bishop of the church of the Cretians;" for, (*a*) there is no evidence that there was a church there called "*the* church

of the Cretians," as there were doubtless many churches on the island; (*b*) there is no evidence that Titus was the *first* bishop of the church there, or that he was the first one there to whom might be properly applied the term *bishop* in the scriptural sense. Indeed, there is positive evidence that he was *not* the first, for Paul was there with him, and Titus was "*left*" there to complete what he had begun. (*c*) There is no evidence that Titus was "bishop" there at all in the prelatical sense of the term, or even that he was a settled pastor; see Notes on ver. 1, 5. (2) That the epistle was written "from Nicopolis of Macedonia;" for, (*a*) there is no certain evidence that it was written at Nicopolis at all, though this is probable; (*b*) there is no reason to believe that the Nicopolis referred to was in Macedonia; see Intro. § 4. These subscriptions are so utterly destitute of authority, and are so full of mistakes, that it is high time they were omitted in the editions of the Bible. They are no part of the inspired writings, but are of the nature of "notes and comments," and are constantly doing something, perhaps much, to perpetuate error. *The opinion that Timothy and Titus were prelatical bishops, the one of Ephesus and the other of Crete, depends far more on these worthless subscriptions than on anything in the epistles themselves.* Indeed, there is *no* evidence of it in the epistles; and, if these subscriptions were removed, no man from the New Testament would ever suppose that they sustained this office at all.

THE
EPISTLE OF PAUL TO PHILEMON.

INTRODUCTION.

§ 1. *The history of Philemon.*

Of Philemon, to whom this epistle was addressed, almost nothing more is known than can be ascertained from the epistle itself. It is short, and of a private character; but it is a bright and beautiful *gem* in the volume of inspiration.

From Col. iv. 9, it may be inferred that the person to whom it was addressed was an inhabitant of Colosse, since Onesimus, concerning whom this epistle was written, is there mentioned as "one of them." See Notes on that verse; comp. the ingenious remarks of Paley, *Hor. Paul.*, on Colossians, No. IV. He is said by Calmet and Michaelis to have been wealthy; but this cannot be determined with certainty, though it is not improbable. The only circumstances which seem to indicate this, are, that Onesimus had been his "servant," from which it has been inferred that he was an owner of slaves; and that he appears to have been accustomed to show hospitality to strangers, or, as Michaelis expresses it, "travelling Christians;" see ver. 22 of the epistle. But these circumstances are not sufficient to determine that he was a man of property. There is no evidence, as we shall see, that he was a slave-holder; and Christians in moderate circumstances were accustomed to show hospitality to their brethren. Besides, it is not said in ver. 22 that he was accustomed to show *general* hospitality; but Paul merely asks him to provide for *him* a lodging. It is probable that he had been accustomed to remain with him when he was in Colosse.

It is quite clear that he had been converted under the ministry of the apostle himself. This appears from what is said in ver. 19: "I do not say to thee how thou owest unto me even thine own self." This cannot be understood otherwise than as implying that he had been converted under his preaching, unless the apostle, on some former occasion, had been the means of saving his life, of which there is no evidence. Indeed, it is manifest, from the general tone of the epistle, that Philemon had been converted by the labours of the author. It is just such a letter as it would be natural and proper to write on such a supposition; it is not one which the apostle would have been likely to write to anyone who did not sustain such a relation to him. But where and when he was converted, is unknown. It is *possible* that Paul may have met with him at Ephesus; but it is much more probable that he had himself been at Colosse, and that Philemon was one of his converts there. See Intro. to the Epistle to the Colossians.

It is evident from the epistle that Paul regarded him as a sincere Christian; as a man of strict integrity; as one who could be depended on to do right. Thus (ver. 5-7), he says that he had heard of his "love and faith

toward the Lord Jesus, and toward all saints;" thus he confidently asks him
to provide for him a lodging when he should come (ver. 22); and thus he expresses the assured belief that he would do what was right towards one who
had been his servant, who, having been formerly unfaithful, was now converted, and, in the estimation of the apostle, was worthy of the confidence
and affection of his former master.

In regard to his rank in the Christian church, nothing whatever is known.
Paul calls him (ver. 1) his "fellow-labourer;" but this appellation is so
general, that it determines nothing in regard to the *manner* in which he
co-operated with him in promoting religion. It is a term which might be
applied to *any* active Christian, whether a preacher, an elder, a deacon,
or a private member of the church. It would seem clear, however, that
he was not a *travelling* preacher, for he had a home in Colosse (ver. 2, 22);
and the presumption is, that he was an active and benevolent member of
the church, who did not sustain any office. There are many private members of the churches, to whom all that is said of Philemon in the epistle
would apply. Yet there have been various conjectures in regard to the
office which he held. Hoffmann (*Intro. ad Lection. Ep. ad Colossenses,*
§ 18) supposes that he was *bishop* of Colosse; Michaelis supposes that he
was a *deacon* in the church; but of either of these, there is no evidence
whatever.

Nothing is known of his age, his profession, or of the time and circumstances of his death. Neither is it certainly known what effect this epistle
had on him, or whether he again received Onesimus under his roof. It may
be presumed, however, that *such* a letter, addressed to *such* a man, would not
fail of its object.

§ 2. *The occasion on which the Epistle was written.*

This can be learned only from the epistle itself, and there the circumstances are so marked as to make a mistake impossible.

(1) Philemon had had a servant of the name of Onesimus. Of the
character of this servant, before Paul became acquainted with him, nothing
more is known than that he had been "unprofitable" to Philemon (ver. 11),
and that he had probably done him some wrong, either by taking his property, or by the fact that he had escaped from him, ver. 18. It is not
necessary to suppose that he was a *slave;* for all that is implied of necessity in the word which is employed to designate his condition in ver. 16
(δοῦλος), and all that is stated of him in the epistle, would be met by the
supposition that he was bound to Philemon, either by his parents or
guardians, or that he had bound himself to render voluntary service; see
Notes on ver. 16.

(2) For some cause, this servant had fled from his master, and had gone
to Rome. The *cause* of his escaping is unknown. It may be that he had
purloined the property of his master, and dreaded detection; or that he had,
by his base conduct in some other way, exposed himself to punishment; or
that he merely desired freedom from oppression; or that he disregarded the
bonds into which he himself, or his parents or guardians, had entered, and
had therefore escaped. Nothing can be inferred about his condition, or his
relation to Philemon, from the fact that he ran away. It is perhaps quite

as common for *apprentices* to run away, as it is for *slaves;* and they who enter into voluntary bonds to render service to another, do not always regard them.

(3) In some way, when at Rome, this servant had found out the apostle Paul, and had been converted by his instrumentality.   Paul says (ver. 10) that he had "begotten him *in his bonds*"—ἐν τοῖς δεσμοῖς μου; which seems to imply that Onesimus had come *to him,* and not that Paul had searched him out.   It does not appear that Paul, when a prisoner at Rome, was allowed to go at large (comp. Acts xxviii. 30), though he was permitted to receive all who came *to* him.   *Why* Onesimus came to the apostle, is not known.   It may have been because he was in want, and Paul was the only one in Rome whom he had ever seen; or it may have been because his mind had become distressed on account of sin, and he sought him out to obtain spiritual counsel. Conjecture on these points is useless, where there is not even a *hint* that can serve as a clue to find out the truth.

(4) From some cause, equally unknown, Onesimus, when converted, was desirous of returning to his former master.   It is commonly *assumed* that his returning again was at the *instigation* of the apostle, and that this furnishes an instance of his belief that runaway slaves should be sent back to their masters.   But, besides that there is no certain evidence that he ever was *a slave,* there is as little proof that he returned at the instigation of Paul, or that his return was not wholly voluntary on his part.   For the only expression which the apostle uses on this subject (ver. 12), "whom I have sent again"— ἀνέπεμψα—does not necessarily imply that he even *proposed* it to him, still less that he *commanded* it.   It is a word of such general import, that it would be employed on the supposition that Onesimus *desired* to return, and that Paul, who had a strong wish to retain him, to aid him in the same way that Philemon himself would do if he were with him (comp. ver. 13), had, on the whole, concluded to part with him, and to send him again with a letter to his friend Philemon.   It is just such language as he would have used of Timothy, Titus, or Epaphroditus, if employed on an important embassy at the request of the apostle; comp. Luke vii. 6, 10, 19; xx. 13; Acts x. 5; xv. 22; 1 Cor. iv. 17; 2 Cor. ix. 3; Eph. vi. 22; Phil. ii. 19, 23, 25, 28; 1 Thes. iii. 2, 5; Tit. iii. 12, for a similar use of the word *send* (πέμπω).   There is nothing in the statement which forbids us to suppose that Onesimus was himself *disposed* to return to Philemon, and that Paul "sent" him at his own request.   To this, Onesimus might have been inclined from many causes.   He may have repented that he left his master, and had forsaken the comforts which he had enjoyed under his roof.   It is no uncommon thing for a runaway apprentice, or servant, when he has seen and felt the misery of being among strangers and in want, to wish himself well back again in the house of his master.   Or he may have felt that he had wronged his master in some way (comp. Notes on ver. 18), and, being now converted, was desirous of repairing the wrong.   Or he may have had friends and kindred in Colosse whom he was desirous of seeing again.   Since any one of these, or of many other supposable causes, may have induced him to *desire* to return to his master, it should not be *assumed* that Paul sent him *against his will, and thence be inferred that he was in favour of sending back runaway slaves to their masters* AGAINST *their will.*   There are many

points to be proved, which cannot be proved, to make that a legitimate inference; see Notes on ver. 12.

(5) Whatever were the reasons why Onesimus desired to return to Philemon, it is clear that he was apprehensive of some trouble if he went back. What those reasons were, it is impossible now to determine with absolute certainty, but it is not difficult to conjecture what they may have been, and any of the following will account for his apprehensions—either, (*a*) that he had done his master wrong by the mere act of leaving him, depriving him of valuable services which he was bound to render; or, (*b*) that he may have felt that the *mere act* of running away had injured the *character* of his master, for such an act always implies that there is something in the dealings of a master which makes it desirable to leave him; or, (*c*) that he had in some way injured him in respect to property, by taking that which did not belong to him, ver. 18; or, (*d*) that he owed his master, and he may have inferred from his leaving him that he meant to defraud him, ver. 18; or, (*e*) that the laws of Phrygia were such that Onesimus apprehended that if he returned, even penitent, it would be judged by his master necessary to punish him, in order to deter others from committing a similar offence. The laws of Phrygia, it is said, allowed the master to punish a slave without applying to a magistrate. See Macknight. It should be said also that the Phrygians were a severe people (Curtius, lib. v. c. 1), and it is not improbable that, from the customs there, Onesimus may have apprehended harsh treatment if he returned.—It is not proper to assume that any *one* of these was certainly the reason why he feared to return, for this cannot be absolutely determined. We should not take it for granted that he had defrauded his master—for that is not necessarily implied in what is said in ver. 18, and we should not impute crimes to men without proof; nor should we take it for granted that he feared to be punished as a runaway *slave*—for *that* cannot be proved; but some one or more of these reasons doubtless operated to make him apprehensive that if he returned he would meet with, at least, a cold reception.

(6) To induce his master to receive him kindly again, was the main object of this courteous and kind epistle. For a view of the *arguments* on which he urges this, see the Analysis of the Epistle. The arguments are such, that we should suppose they could not be resisted, and we may presume, without impropriety, that they had the desired effect on the mind of Philemon—but of that we have no certain evidence.

§ 3. *The time and place of writing the Epistle.*

There can be no doubt that this letter was written from Rome about the time when the Epistle to the Colossians was written; comp. Intro. to that epistle. The circumstances which conduct to this conclusion are such as the following : (1) Paul at the time when it was written was a prisoner, ver. 1, "Paul, a prisoner of Jesus Christ;" ver. 10, "Whom I have begotten in my bonds;" comp. ver. 23, "Epaphras, my fellow-prisoner in Christ Jesus." (2) It was written when he had hopes of obtaining his liberty, or when he had such a prospect of it that he could ask Philemon with confidence to "prepare him a lodging," ver. 22. (3)

Timothy was with him at the time when it was written (ver. 1), and we know that Paul desired him to come to him to Rome when he was a prisoner there as soon as possible, 2 Tim. iv. 9, " Do thy diligence to come shortly unto me." (4) We know that Onesimus was actually sent by Paul to Colosse while he was a prisoner at Rome, and it would be morally certain that, under the circumstances of the case, he would send the letter to his master at that time. No other instance is mentioned in which he sent him to Colosse, and the evidence is as certain as the nature of the case admits, that that was the time when the epistle was written; see Col. iv. 9. (5) The same persons are mentioned in the salutations in the two epistles, at least they are so far the same as to make it probable that the epistles were written at the same time, for it is not very probable that the same persons would in another place, and on another occasion, have been with the apostle. Thus Aristarchus, Mark, Epaphras, Luke, and Demas, join in the salutations both to the church at Colosse and to Philemon. Probably at no other time in the life of Paul were all these persons with him, than when he was a prisoner at Rome. These considerations make it clear that the epistle was written while Paul was a prisoner at Rome, and at about the same time with the Epistle to the Colossians. If so, it was about A.D. 62.

§ 4. *The character of this Epistle.*

This letter is almost wholly of a private character, and yet there is scarcely any portion of the New Testament of equal length which is of more value. It is exquisitely beautiful and delicate. It is a model of courtesy and politeness. It presents the character of the author in a most amiable light, and shows what true religion will produce in causing genuine refinement of thought and language. It is gentle and persuasive, and yet the argument is one that we should suppose would have been, and probably was, irresistible. It is very easy to conceive that the task which the apostle undertook to perform was one which it would be difficult to accomplish—that of reconciling an offended master to a runaway servant. And yet it is done with so much kindness, persuasiveness, gentleness, and true affection, that, as the letter was read, it is easy to imagine that all the hostility of the master was disarmed, and we can almost see him desiring to embrace him who bore it, not now as a servant, but as a Christian brother, ver. 16. "It is impossible," says Doddridge, "to read over this admirable epistle without being touched with the delicacy of sentiment, and the masterly address, that appear in every part of it. We see here, in a most striking light, how perfectly consistent true politeness is,—not only with all the warmth and sincerity of a friend, but even with the dignity of the Christian and the Apostle. And if this letter were to be considered in no other view than as a mere human composition, it must be allowed to be a master-piece in its kind. As an illustration of this remark, it may not be improper to compare it with an epistle of Pliny, that seems to have been written on a similar occasion (lib. ix. let. 21); which, though penned by one that was reckoned to excel in the epistolary style, though it has undoubtedly many beauties, yet must be acknowledged by every impartial reader vastly inferior to this animated composition of the apostle." As a specimen of the courtesy and politeness which the Christian ought to practise at all times, as well as furnishing many valuable lessons on Christian duty (see the Remarks at the close), it deserves a place in the volume of inspiration; and a material chasm would be produced in the instructions which are needful for us, if it were withdrawn from the sacred canon.

THE

EPISTLE OF PAUL TO PHILEMON.

PAUL, a *prisoner of Jesus Christ, and Timothy *our* brother, unto Philemon our dearly beloved, and *b*fellow-labourer,

2 And to *our* beloved Apphia, and *c*Archippus our fellow-soldier, and to *d*the church in thy house:

3 Grace*e* to you, and peace, from

a Ep.3.1.   b Phi.2.25.

c Col.4.17.   d Ro.16.5.   e Ep.1.2.

it would give him if Philemon would receive his former servant again; and with the expression of his conviction that he *would* do more than he asked in the matter, and then asks that, while he showed favour to Onesimus, he would also prepare a lodging for him, for he hoped soon to be with him, ver. 20–22. *Perhaps* by this last suggestion he hoped also to do much to favour the cause of Onesimus—for Philemon could hardly turn him away when he expected that Paul himself would soon be with him. Such an argument would be likely to be effectual in the case. We do not like to deny the request which a friend makes in a letter, if we expect soon to see the writer himself. It would be much more easy to do it if we had no expectations of seeing him very soon.

IV. The epistle closes with affectionate salutations from certain persons who were with Paul, and who were probably well known to Philemon, and with the customary benediction, ver. 23–25.

1. *Paul, a prisoner of Jesus Christ.* A prisoner at Rome in the cause of Jesus Christ; Notes, Eph. iii. 1; 2 Tim. i. 8. ¶ *And Timothy our brother.* Timothy, it seems, had come to him agreeably to his request, 2 Tim. iv. 9. Paul not unfrequently joins his name with his own in his epistles, 2 Cor. i. 1; Phil. i. 1; Col. i. 1; 1 Thes. i. 1; 2 Thes. i. 1. As Timothy was of that region of country, and as he had accompanied Paul in his travels, he was doubtless acquainted with Philemon. ¶ *Unto Philemon our dearly beloved, and fellow-labourer.* See Intro. § 1. The word rendered *fellow-labourer* (συνεργὸς), does not determine what office he held, if he held any, or in what respects he was

a fellow-labourer with Paul. It means a co-worker, or helper, and doubtless here means that he was a helper or fellow-worker in the great cause to which Paul had devoted his life, but whether as a preacher, or deacon, or a private Christian, cannot be ascertained. It is *commonly*, in the New Testament, applied to ministers of the gospel, though by no means exclusively, and in several instances it cannot be determined whether it denotes ministers of the gospel, or those who furthered the cause of religion, and co-operated with the apostle in some other way than preaching. See the following places, which are the only ones where it occurs in the New Testament: Rom. xvi. 3, 9, 21; 1 Cor. iii. 9; 2 Cor. i. 24; viii. 23; Phil. ii. 25; iv. 3; Col. iv. 11; 1 Thes. iii. 2; Philem. 1, 24; 3 John 8.

2. *And to* our *beloved Apphia.* This was a female (Gr. ἀγαπητῇ), and was probably the wife of Philemon. ¶ *And Archippus our fellow-soldier.* See Notes, Col. iv. 17. It has been supposed that he was a son of Philemon, and this would appear not to be improbable, as he was one of his family. On the term "fellow-soldier," see Notes, Phil. ii. 25. It is applied here to one who was a minister of the gospel, and who is spoken of in connection with Paul as *enlisted* under the banners of the Captain of salvation, and waging a warfare with the wickedness of the world; comp. Notes, 2 Tim. ii. 3, 4. That Archippus was a minister of the gospel, is clear from Col. iv. 17. ¶ *And to the church in thy house.* Either the church that commonly met in his house, or more probably that was composed of his own family; comp. Notes, Rom. xvi. 5.

3. *Grace to you, and peace, &c.* See Notes on Rom. i. 7.

4. *I thank my God.* That is, for what I hear of you. ¶ *Making men-*

God our Father and the Lord Jesus Christ.

4 I⸍ thank my God, making mention of thee always in my prayers,

f Ep.1.16.

tion of thee always in my prayers. See a similar declaration respecting the church at Ephesus, Eph. i. 16. It would appear from this that Paul, in his private devotions, was in the habit of mentioning churches and individuals by name. It would seem, also, that though he was a prisoner, yet he somehow found opportunity for secret devotion. And it would appear further, that, though encompassed with many cares and sorrows, and about to be put on trial for his life, he did not forget to remember a Christian brother though far distant from him, and to bear him on his heart before the throne of grace. To remember with affectionate concern these churches and individuals, as he did, Paul must have been a man of much prayer.

5. _Hearing of thy love and faith._ Either by Onesimus, who, after his conversion, would be disposed to state all that he knew that was favourable of Philemon, or hearing it by some other persons who had come from Colosse to Rome. The _faith_ which is mentioned here refers to the Lord Jesus; the _love,_ to the saints. The order in the Greek is indeed the same as in our version, but it is not unusual by _synthesis,_ or uniting two or more things together, to arrange words in that manner. Thus Mat. xii. 22, "The blind and dumb both spake and saw;" that is, the blind saw, and the dumb spake. The meaning is, that he had strong faith in the Lord Jesus, and ardent love towards all who were Christians. See a similar declaration in Col. i. 4.

6. _That the communication of thy faith._ That is, this was a subject of prayer on the part of the apostle, that the "communication of his faith" might receive from all the proper acknowledgment of the good which he did in the Christian cause. The phrase translated "communication of thy faith," means the making of thy faith

5 Hearing of thy love and faith, which thou hast toward the Lord Jesus, and toward all saints;

6 That*g* the communication of thy faith may *h* become effectual by

g Phi.1.9-11.　　　*h* Ja.2.14,17.

common to others; that is, enabling others to partake of the fruits of it, to wit, by good deeds. On the meaning of the word here rendered "communication" (κοινωνία, _koinonia_), see Notes on Eph. iii. 9; comp. Phil. ii. 1; iii. 10. Calvin has well expressed the sense of this passage. "It is to be observed that the apostle here does not proceed in the commendation of Philemon, but rather expresses what he desires for him from the Lord. These words are connected with those in which he says that he remembered him in his prayers. What, therefore, did he desire for Philemon? That his faith, expressing itself by good fruits, might be shown to be true and not vain. For he calls that the communication of his faith when it does not remain inoperative within, but bears itself forth to benefit men by its proper effects. For although faith has its proper seat in the heart, yet it communicates itself to men by good works." The meaning is, that he desired that Philemon would so _make common_ the proper fruits of faith by his good deeds towards others, that all might acknowledge it to be genuine and efficacious. ¶ _May become effectual._ Gr., "may be energetic" (ἐνεργὴς); may become operative, active, effective. ¶ _By the acknowledging._ That is, so as to secure from others the proper recognition of the existence of faith in your heart. In other words, so that others may see that you are truly pious, and understand to what extent you have faith. ¶ _Of every good thing which is in you._ Of every good principle, and of every benevolent trait, which is in your character. That is, the proper outward expression of his faith in Christ, by doing good to others, would be a development of the benevolence which existed in his heart. ¶ _In Christ Jesus._ Or "_towards_ (εἰς) Christ Jesus." The goodness in his heart had respect to

the acknowledging of *every good thing which is in you in Christ Jesus.

7 For we have great joy and consolation in thy love, *because the bowels of the saints are refreshed by thee, brother.

i Phi.4.8; 2 Pe.1.5-8.   *k* 2 Co.7.13; 2 Ti.1.16.

the Lord Jesus as its proper object, but would be made manifest by his kindness to men. The *truth* which is taught in this passage, therefore, is, that when faith exists in the heart, it is very desirable that it should impart its proper fruits towards others in such a way that all may see that it is operative, and may recognize its power; or in other words, it is desirable that when true religion exists it should be fairly developed, that its possessor may be acknowledged to be under its influence. We should wish that he may have all the credit and honour which the goodness of his heart is entitled to. Paul supposed that a case had now occurred in which an opportunity was furnished to Philemon to show the world how much he was governed by the faith of the gospel.

7. *For we have great joy and consolation in thy love.* In thy love towards Christians. The word here rendered *joy* (χάριν), properly means *grace.* A large number of manuscripts, however, instead of this word, have χαράν (*charan*), *joy.* See Wetstein. This reading has been adopted by Griesbach, Tittman, and Hahn. ¶ *Because the bowels of the saints are refreshed by thee, brother.* For your kindness to them. The word *bowels* here probably means *minds, hearts,* for it is used in the Scriptures to denote the affections. The sense is, that the kindness which he had shown to Christians had done much to make them happy. On the word *refreshed,* see 2 Cor. vii. 13; 2 Tim. i. 16.

8. *Wherefore, though I might be much bold in Christ.* Though I might have much boldness as an apostle of Christ. He means that he was invested with authority by the Lord Jesus, and would have a right, as an apostle, to enjoin what ought to be done in the case which he is about to

8 Wherefore, *though I might be much bold in Christ to enjoin thee that which is convenient,

9 Yet for love's sake I rather beseech *thee,* being such an one as Paul the aged, and now also a prisoner of Jesus Christ.

l 1 Th.2.6.

lay before him; comp. 1 Thes. ii. 6, 7. ¶ *To enjoin thee that which is convenient.* To command what is proper to be done. The word *convenient* here (τὸ ἀνῆκον), means that which would be fit or proper in the case; comp. Notes, Eph. v. 4. The apostle implies here that what he was about to ask, was *proper to be done* in the circumstances, but he does not put it on that ground, but rather asks it as a personal favour. It is usually not best to *command* a thing to be done if we can as well secure it by *asking* it as a favour; comp. Dan. i. 8, 11, 12.

9. *Yet for love's sake.* For the love which you bear me, and for the common cause. ¶ *I rather beseech* thee. Rather than *command* thee. ¶ *Being such an one as Paul the aged.* πρεσβύτης, *an old man.* We have no means of ascertaining the exact age of Paul at this time, and I do not recollect that he ever alludes to his age, though he often does to his infirmities, in any place except here. Doddridge supposes that at the time when Stephen was stoned, when he is called "a young man" (νεανίας, Acts vii. 58), he was twenty-four years of age, in which case he would now have been about fifty-three. Chrysostom supposes that he may have been thirty-five years old at the time of his conversion, which would have made him about sixty-three at this time. The difficulty of determining with any degree of accuracy the age of the apostle at this time, arises from the indefinite nature of the word used by Luke, Acts vii. 58, and rendered *a young man.* That word, like the corresponding word νεανίσκος (*neaniskos*), was applied to men in the vigour of manhood up to the age of forty years (Robinson, *Lex.*). Phavorinus says a man is called νεανίσκος(*neaniskos*), a young man, till he is twenty-eight; and πρεσβύτης (*presbytēs*) from forty-

10 I beseech thee for my son Onesimus,[m] whom I have begotten in [n]my bonds:

m Col.4.9.   n 1 Co.4.15.

nine till he is fifty-six. Varro says that a man is young (*juvenis*) till he is forty-five, and aged at sixty (Whitby). These periods of time, however, are very indefinite; but it will accord well with the usual meaning of the words to suppose that Paul was in the neighbourhood of thirty when he was converted, and that he was now not far from sixty. We are to remember, also, that the constitution of Paul may have been much broken by his labours, his perils, and his trials. Not advanced, probably, to the usual limit of human life, he may have had all the characteristics of a very aged man; comp. the note of Benson. The argument here is, that we feel that it is proper, as far as we can, to grant the request of an old man. Paul thus felt that it was reasonable to suppose that Philemon would not refuse to gratify the wishes of an aged servant of Christ, who had spent the vigour of his life in the service of their common Master. It should be a very strong case when we refuse to gratify the wishes of an aged Christian in anything, especially if he has rendered important services to the church and the world. ¶ *And now also a prisoner of Jesus Christ.* In the *cause* of Jesus Christ; or a prisoner for endeavouring to make him known to the world; comp. Notes on Eph. iii. 1; iv. 1; vi. 20; Col. iv. 10. The argument here is, that it might be presumed that Philemon would not refuse the request of one who was suffering in prison on account of their common religion. For such a prisoner we should be ready to do all that we can to mitigate the sorrows of his confinement, and to make his condition comfortable.

10. *I beseech thee for my son Onesimus.* That is, my son in the gospel; one to whom I sustain the relation of a spiritual father; comp. Notes on 1 Tim. i. 2. The address and *tact* of Paul here are worthy of particular observation. Any other mode of bringing the case before the mind of Phile-

11 Which[o] in time past was to thee unprofitable, but now profitable to thee and to me:

o 1 Pe.2.10.

mon might have repelled him. If he had simply said, " I beseech thee *for Onesimus;*" or, " I beseech thee for *thy servant* Onesimus," he would at once have reverted to his former conduct, and remembered all his ingratitude and disobedience. But the phrase "*my son,*" makes the way easy for the mention of his name, for he had already found the way to his heart before his eye lighted on his name, by the mention of the relation which he sustained to himself. Who could refuse to such a man as Paul—a laborious servant of Christ, an aged man, exhausted with his many sufferings and toils, and a prisoner—a request which he made for one whom he regarded *as his son?* It may be added, that the delicate address of the apostle in introducing the subject, is better seen in the original than in our translation. In the original, the name Onesimus is reserved to come in last in the sentence. The order of the Greek is this: " I entreat thee concerning a son of mine, whom I have begotten in my bonds—Onesimus." Here the name is not suggested, until he had mentioned that he sustained to him the relation of a son, and also till he had added that his conversion was the fruit of his labours *while he was a prisoner.* Then, when the name of Onesimus *is* mentioned, it would occur to Philemon not primarily as the name of an ungrateful and disobedient servant, but as the interesting case of one converted by the labours of his own friend in prison. Was there ever more delicacy evinced in preparing the way for disarming one of prejudice, and carrying an appeal to his heart? ¶ *Whom I have begotten in my bonds.* Who has been converted by my efforts while I have been a prisoner. On the phrase " whom I have begotten," see 1 Cor. iv. 15. Nothing is said of the way in which he had become acquainted with Onesimus, or why he had put himself under the teaching of Paul; see the Intro. § 2. (3).

11. *Which in time past was to thee*

12 Whom I have sent again: thou therefore receive him, that is, mine own bowels:

13 Whom I would have retained with me, *that in thy stead he might

p 1 Co.16.17; Phi.2.30.

unprofitable. Either because he was indolent; because he had wronged him (comp. Notes on ver. 18), or because he had run away from him. It is *possible* that there may be an allusion here to the meaning of the name *Onesimus,* which denotes *profitable* (from ὀνίνημι, fut. ὀνήσω, *to be useful, to be profitable, to help*), and that Paul means to say that he had hitherto not well answered to the meaning of his own name, but that now he would be found to do so. ¶ *But now profitable to thee.* The Greek here is εὔχρηστον (*euchrēston*), but the meaning is about the same as that of the word Onesimus. It denotes *very useful.* In 2 Tim. ii. 21, it is rendered *meet for use;* in 2 Tim. iv. 11, and here, *profitable.* It does not elsewhere occur in the New Testament. ¶ *And to me.* Paul had doubtless found him useful to him as a Christian brother in his bonds, and it is easy to conceive that, in his circumstances, he would greatly desire to retain him with him.

12. *Whom I have sent again.* That is, to Philemon. This was, doubtless, at his own request; for, (1) There is not the slightest evidence that he *compelled* him, or even *urged* him to go. The language is just such as would have been used on the supposition either that he *requested* him to go and bear a letter to Colosse, or that Onesimus desired to go, and that Paul sent him agreeably to his request; comp. Phil. ii. 25, "Yet I supposed it necessary *to send* to you Epaphroditus my brother, and companion in labour," &c.; Col. iv. 7, 8, "All my state shall Tychicus declare unto you, who is a beloved brother, and a faithful minister and fellow-servant in the Lord: whom I have *sent* unto you for the same purpose, that he might know your estate," &c. But Epaphroditus and Tychicus were not sent against their own will—nor is there any more reason to think that Onesimus was; see Intro. § 2. (4). (2) Paul had no power to send Onesimus back to his master unless he chose

to go. He had no civil anthority; he had no guard to accompany him; he could intrust him to no sheriff to convey him from place to place, and he had no means of controlling him, if he chose to go to any other place than Colosse. He could indeed have sent him away from himself; he could have *told* him to go to Colosse, but there his power ended. Onesimus then could have gone where he pleased. But there is no evidence that Paul even *told* him to go to Colosse against his own inclination, or that he would have sent him away at all unless he had himself requested it. (3) There may have been many reasons why Onesimus desired to return to Colosse, and no one can prove that he did not express that desire to Paul, and that his "sending" him was not in consequence of such a request. He may have had friends and relatives there; or, being now converted, he may have been sensible that he had wronged his former master, and that he ought to return and repair the wrong; or he may have been poor, and a stranger in Rome, and may have been greatly disappointed in what he had expected to find there when he left Philemon, and may have desired to return to the comparative comforts of his former condition. (4) It may be added, therefore, (*a*) That this passage should not be adduced to prove that we *ought* to send back runaway slaves to their former masters against their own consent; or to justify the laws which require magistrates to do it; or to show that they who have escaped should be arrested and forcibly detained; or *to justify any sort of influence over a runaway slave to induce him to return to his former master.* There is not the least evidence that any of these things occurred in the case before us, and if this instance is ever appealed to, it should be to justify *what Paul did*—AND NOTHING ELSE. (*b*)·The passage shows that it is right to aid a servant of any kind to return to his master *if* he desires it. It is right to give him

have ministered unto me in the bonds of the gospel:

14 But without thy mind would

a "letter," and to plead earnestly for his favourable reception if he has in any way wronged his master—for Paul did this. On the same principle it would be right to give him pecuniary assistance to enable him to return— for there *may be* cases where one who has fled from servitude might wish to return. There *may* be instances where one has had a kind master, with whom he would feel that on the whole he could be more happy than in his present circumstances. Such cases, however, are exceedingly rare. Or there may be instances where one may have relatives that are in the neighbourhood or in the family of his former master, and the desire to be with them may be so strong that on the whole he would choose to be a servant as he was before, rather than to remain as he is now. In all such cases it is right to render aid—for the example of the apostle Paul goes to sustain this. But it goes no further. So far as appears, he neither *advised* Onesimus to return, nor did he *compel* him; nor did he say one word to *influence* him to do it;—nor did he *mean* or *expect* that he would be a *slave* when he should have been received again by his master; see Notes on ver. 16. ¶ *Thou therefore receive him, that is, mine own bowels.* There is great delicacy also in this expression. If he had merely said, "receive *him*," Philemon might have thought only of him as he formerly was. Paul, therefore, adds, "that is, *mine own bowels*"—"one whom I so tenderly love that he seems to carry my heart with him wherever he goes" (Doddridge).

13. *Whom I would have retained with me, that in thy stead.* "That he might render me the service which I know you would if you were here." The Greek is, "for thee" (ὑπὲρ σοῦ); that is, what he should do for Paul might be regarded as done by Philemon himself. ¶ *He might have ministered unto me.* He might have ren-

I do nothing; *q*that thy benefit should not be as it were of necessity, but willingly.

q 2 Co.9.7.

dered me assistance (διακονῇ); to wit, in such a way as one who was in bonds would need.

14. *But without thy mind would I do nothing.* Nothing in the matter referred to. He would not retain Onesimus in his service, much as he needed his assistance, without the cordial consent of Philemon. He would not give him occasion for hard feeling or complaint, *as if* Paul had induced him to leave his master, or *as if* he persuaded him to remain with him when he wished to return— or *as if* he kept him away from him when he owed him or had wronged him. All that is said here is entirely consistent with the supposition that Onesimus was *disposed* to return to his master, and with the supposition that Paul did not compel or urge him to do it. For it is probable that *if* Onesimus had proposed to return, it would have been easy for Paul to have retained him with him. He might have represented his own want of a friend. He might have appealed to his gratitude on account of his efforts for his conversion. He might have shown him that he was under no moral obligation to go back. He might have refused to give him this letter, and might have so represented to him the dangers of the way, and the probability of a harsh reception, as effectually to have dissuaded him from such a purpose. But, in that case, it is clear that this might have caused hard feeling in the bosom of Philemon, and rather than do that he preferred to let him return to his master, and to plead for him that he might have a kind reception. It is, therefore, by no means necessary to suppose that Paul felt that Onesimus was under *obligation* to return, or that he was disposed to *compel* him, or that Onesimus was not inclined to return voluntarily; but all the circumstances of the case are met by the supposition that, if Paul retained him, Philemon might conceive that he had

15 For*r* perhaps he therefore departed for a season, that thou shouldest receive him for ever;
16 Not now as a servant, but

r Ge.45.5-8.

injured *him.* Suppose, as seems to have been the case, that Onesimus "owed" Philemon (ver. 18), and then suppose that Paul had chosen to retain him with himself, and had dissuaded him from returning to him, would not Philemon have had reason to complain of it? There was, therefore, on every account, great propriety in his saying that he did not wish to use any influence over him to retain him with him when he purposed to return to Colosse, and that he felt that it would be wrong for him to keep him, much as he needed him, without the consent of Philemon. Nor is it necessary, by what is said here, to suppose that Onesimus was *a slave,* and that Paul believed that Philemon had a right to him and to his services *as* such. All that he says here would be met by the supposition that he was a hired servant, and would be in fact equally proper even on the supposition that he was an apprentice. In either case he would feel that he gave just ground of complaint on the part of Philemon if, when Onesimus desired to return, he used any influence to dissuade him from it, and to retain him with himself. It would have been a violation of the rule requiring us to do to others as we would wish them to do unto us, and Paul therefore felt unwilling, much as he needed the services of Onesimus, to make use of any influence to retain him with him without the consent of his master. ¶ *That thy benefit.* The favour which I might receive from thee by having the services of Onesimus. If Onesimus should remain with him and assist him, he would feel that the benefit which would be conferred by his services would be in fact bestowed by Philemon, for he had a right to the service of Onesimus, and, while Paul enjoyed it, he would be deprived of it. The word rendered *benefit* here— ἀγαθόν —means *good,* and the sense is, "the *good* which you

above a servant, *s* a brother beloved, specially to me, but how much more unto thee, *t* both in the flesh, and in the Lord?

s Mat.23.8; 1 Ti.6.2.   *t* Col.3.22.

would do me;" to wit, by the service of Onesimus. ¶ *Should not be as it were of necessity.* As it would be if Paul should detain Onesimus with him without affording Philemon an opportunity of expressing his assent. Paul would even then have felt that he was in fact receiving a "good" at the expense of Philemon, but it would not be a *voluntary* favour on his part. ¶ *But willingly.* As it would be if he had given his consent that Onesimus should remain with him.

15. *For perhaps he therefore departed for a season.* Perhaps on this *account,* or *for this reason*—διὰ τοῦτο —he left you for a little time. Greek, "for an hour"—πρὸς ὥραν. The meaning is, that it was possible that this was permitted in the providence of God *in order* that Onesimus might be brought under the influence of the gospel, and be far more serviceable to Philemon as a Christian, than he could have been in his former relation to him. What appeared to Philemon, therefore, to be a calamity, and what seemed to him to be wrong on the part of Onesimus, might have been permitted to occur in order that he might receive a higher benefit. Such things are not uncommon in human affairs. ¶ *That thou shouldest receive him for ever.* That is, in the higher relation of a Christian friend and brother; that he might be united to thee in eternal affection; that he might not only be with thee in a far more endearing relation during the present life than he was before, but in the bonds of love in a world that shall never end.

16. *Not now as a servant.* The adverb rendered "*not now*" (οὐκέτι), means *no more, no further, no longer.* It implies that he had been before in this condition, but was not to be now; comp. Mat. xix. 6, "They are *no more* twain." They were once so, but they are not to be regarded as such now, Mat. xxii. 46, "Neither

durst any man, from that day forth, ask him *any more* questions." They once did it, but now they did not dare to do it; Luke xv. 19, "And am *no more* worthy to be called thy son," though I once was; John vi. 66, "And walked *no more* with him," though they once did; see also John xi. 54; xiv. 19; xvii. 11; Acts viii. 39; Gal. iv. 7; Eph. ii. 19. This passage then proves that he had been before *a servant*—δοῦλος (*doulos*). But still, it is not certain what *kind* of a servant he was. The word does not necessarily mean *slave*, nor can it be proved from this passage, or from any other part of the epistle, that he was at any time a slave; see Notes on Eph. vi. 5, and 1 Tim. vi. 1. The word denotes *servant* of any kind, and it should never be assumed that those to whom it was applied were slaves. It is true that slavery existed in the heathen nations when the gospel was first preached, and it is doubtless true that many slaves were converted (comp. Notes on 1 Cor. vii. 21), but the mere use of *the word* does not necessarily prove that he to whom it is applied was a slave. If Onesimus was a slave, there is reason to think that he was of a most respectable character (comp. Notes on Col. iv. 9); and indeed *all* that is implied in the use of the term here, and *all* that is said of him, would be met by the supposition that he was a *voluntary servant*, and that he had been in fact intrusted with important business by Philemon. It would seem from ver. 18 ("or *oweth thee ought*"), that he was in a condition which made it possible for him to hold property, or at least to be intrusted. ¶ *But above a servant, a brother beloved.* A Christian brother; comp. Notes, 1 Tim. vi. 2. He was especially dear to Paul himself as a Christian, and he trusted that he would be so to Philemon. ¶ *Specially to me.* That is, I feel a special or particular interest in him, and affection for him. This he felt not only on account of the traits of character which he had evinced since his conversion, but because he had been converted under his instrumentality when he was a prisoner. A convert made in such circumstances

would be particularly dear to one. ¶ *But how much more unto thee.* Why, it may be asked, would he then be particularly dear to Philemon? I answer, because (1) of the former relation which he sustained to him—a member of his own family, and bound to him by strong ties; (2) because he would receive him as a penitent, and would have joy in his returning from the error of his ways; (3) because he might expect him to remain long with him and be of advantage to him as a Christian brother; and (4) because he had voluntarily returned, and thus shown that he felt a strong attachment to his former master. ¶ *In the flesh.* This phrase is properly used in reference to *any* relation which may exist pertaining to the present world, as contradistinguished from that which is formed primarily by religion, and which would be expressed by the subjoined phrase, "in the Lord." It might, in itself, refer to any natural relation of blood, or to any formed in business, or to any constituted by mere friendship, or to family alliance, or to any relation having its origin in voluntary or involuntary servitude. It is not necessary to suppose, in order to meet the full force of the expression, either that Onesimus had been a slave, or that he would continue to be regarded as such. *Whatever* relation of the kind, referred to above, may have existed between him and Philemon, would be appropriately denoted by this phrase. The new and more interesting relation which they were now to sustain to each other, which was formed by religion, is expressed by the phrase "in the Lord." In *both* these, Paul hoped that Onesimus would manifest the appropriate spirit of a Christian, and be worthy of his entire confidence. ¶ *In the Lord.* As a Christian. He will be greatly endeared to your heart as a consistent and worthy follower of the Lord Jesus.—On this important verse, then, in relation to the use which is so often made of this epistle by the advocates of slavery, to show that Paul sanctioned it, and that it is a duty to send back those who have escaped from their masters that they may again be held in bondage, we may remark, (1) There is no certain evidence that Onesimus was ever a *slave* at all. *All* the proof that he was, is to be found in the word δοῦλος (*doulos*) in this verse. But, as we have seen, the mere use of this word by no means proves that. All that is necessarily implied by it is, that he was in some way the *servant* of Philemon —whether hired or bought cannot be shown. (2) At all events, even supposing that he had been a slave, Paul did not mean that he should return *as* such, or to be regarded as such. He meant, whatever may have been his former relation, and whatever subsequent relation he may have sustained, that he should be regarded *as a beloved Christian brother;* that the leading conception in regard to him should be that he was a fellow-heir of salvation, a member of the same redeemed church, a candidate for the same heaven. (3) Paul did not send him back *in order* that he might be a slave, or with a view that the shackles of servitude should be riveted on him. There is not the slightest evidence that he *forced* him to return, or that he *advised* him to do it, or even that he expressed a *wish* that he would; and when he did send him, it was not *as a slave*, but *as a beloved brother in the Lord.* It cannot be shown that the motive for sending him back was in the slightest degree that he should be a slave. No such thing is intimated, nor is any such thing necessary to be supposed in order to a fair interpretation of the passage. (4) It is clear that, even *if* Onesimus had been a slave before, it would have been contrary to the wishes of Paul that Philemon should now hold him as such. Paul wished him to regard him "*not* as a servant," but as a "beloved brother." If Philemon complied with his wishes, Onesimus was never afterwards regarded or treated as a slave. If he *did* so regard or treat him, it was contrary to the expressed intention of the apostle, and it is certain that he could never have shown this letter in justification of it. It cannot fail to strike anyone that, if Philemon fol-

lowed the spirit of this epistle, he would not consider Onesimus to be a slave, but if he sustained the relation of a servant at all, it would be as a voluntary member of his household, where, in all respects, he would be regarded and treated, not as a "chattel," or a "thing," but as a Christian brother. (5) This passage, therefore, may be regarded as full proof that it is *not* right to send a slave back, against his will, to his former master, *to be a slave.* It is right to help one if he wishes to go back; to give him a letter to his master, as Paul did to Onesimus; to furnish him money to help him on his journey if he desires to return; and to commend him as a Christian brother, if he is such; but beyond that, the example of the apostle Paul does not go. It is perfectly clear that he would *not* have sent him back to be regarded and treated as a slave, but being able to commend him as a Christian, he was willing to do it, and he expected that he *would be* treated, not as a slave, but as a Christian. The case before us does not go at all to prove that Paul would have ever sent him back to be a chattel or a thing. If, with his own consent, and by his own wish, we can send a slave back to his master, to be treated *as a Christian* and *as a man*, the example of Paul may show that it would be right to do it, but it does not go beyond that. (6) In confirmation of this, and as a guide in duty now, it may be observed, that Paul had been educated as a Hebrew; that he was thoroughly imbued with the doctrines of the Old Testament, and that one of the elementary principles of that system of religion was, that a runaway slave was *in no circumstances* to be returned by force to his former master. "*Thou shalt* NOT *deliver unto his master the servant that is escaped from his master unto thee,*" Deut. xxiii. 15. It cannot be supposed that, trained as he was in the principles of the Hebrew religion—of which this was a positive and unrepealed law—and imbued with the benevolent spirit of the gospel—a system so hostile to oppression—the apostle Paul would have constrained a slave

17 If thou count me therefore a "partner, receive him as myself.

u 2 Co.8.23.

18 If he hath wronged thee, or oweth *thee* ought, put that on mine account.

who had escaped from bondage to return to servitude against his will. (7) It may be added, that if the principles here acted on by Paul were carried out, slavery would speedily cease in the world. Very soon would it come to an end if masters were to regard those whom they hold, "not as slaves," but *as beloved Christian brothers;* not as *chattels* and *things,* but as the redeemed children of God. Thus regarding them, they would no longer feel that they might chain them, and task them, and sell them as property. They would feel that, as Christians and as men, they were on a level with themselves, and that they who were made in the image of God, and who had been redeemed with the blood of his Son, *ought to be* FREE.

17. *If thou count me therefore a partner.* The word rendered *partner* (κοινωνὸς), means *a partaker, a companion.* The idea in the word is that of having something *in common* (κοινὸς) with anyone—as common principles, common attachments, a common interest in an enterprise, common hopes. It may be applied to those who hold the same principles of religion, and who have the same hope of heaven, the same views of things, &c. Here the meaning is, that if Philemon regarded Paul as sharing with him in the principles and hopes of religion, or as a brother in the gospel, so that he would receive *him,* he ought to receive Onesimus in the same way. He was actuated by the same principles, and had the same hopes, and had a claim to be received as a Christian brother. His receiving Onesimus would be interpreted by Paul as proof that he regarded him as a partaker of the hopes of the gospel, and as a companion and friend. For a plea in behalf of another strongly resembling this, see Horace, *Epis.* lib. i. ep. 9.

18. *If he hath wronged thee.* Either by escaping from you, or by failing to perform what he had agreed to, or by unfaithfulness when he was with you as a servant, or by taking your property when he went away. Any of these methods would meet all that is said here, and it is impossible to determine in which of them he had done Philemon wrong. It may be observed, however, that the apostle evinces much delicacy in this matter. He does not say that he *had* wronged him, but he makes *a supposition* that he might have done it. Doubtless Philemon would suppose that he *had* done it, even if he had done no more than to escape from him, and, whatever Paul's views of that might be, he says that even *if it were so,* he would wish him to set that over to his account. He took the blame on himself, and asked Philemon not to remember it against Onesimus. ¶ *Or oweth* thee *ought.* It appears from this, that Onesimus, whatever may have been his former condition, was capable of holding property, and of contracting debts. It is possible that he might have borrowed money of Philemon, or he may have been regarded as a tenant, and may not have paid the rent of his farm, or the apostle may mean that he had owed him service which he had not performed. Conjecture is useless as to the way in which the debt was contracted. ¶ *Put that on mine account.* Reckon, or impute that to me —ἐμοὶ ἐλλόγει. This word occurs nowhere else in the New Testament, except in Rom. v. 13, where it is rendered *imputed.* See Notes on that passage. It means to reckon; to put to one's account, to wit, what properly belongs to him, or what he assumes. It never implies that that is to be charged on one which does not properly belong to him, either as his own act, or as that which he has assumed. In this case it would have been manifestly unjust for Philemon to charge the wrong which Onesimus had done, or what he owed him,

19 I Paul have written *it* with mine own hand, I will repay *it:* albeit I

do not say to thee how thou owest unto me even thine own self besides.

to the apostle Paul without his consent; and it cannot be inferred from what Paul says here that it would have been right to do so. The *steps* in the case were these: (1) Onesimus, not Paul, had done the wrong. (2) Paul was not guilty of it, or blameworthy for it, and never in any way, or by any process, could be made to be, or conceived to be. It would be true for ever that Onesimus and not he had done the wrong. (3) Paul *assumed* the debt and the wrong to himself. He was willing, by putting himself in the place of Onesimus, to bear the consequences, and to have Onesimus treated *as if* he had not done it. When he had voluntarily assumed it, it was right to treat him *as if* he had done so; that is, to hold him responsible. A man may *assume* a debt if he pleases, and then he may be held answerable for it. (4) If he had *not* assumed this himself, it never could have been right for Philemon to charge it on him. No possible supposition could make it right. No agency which he had in the conversion of Onesimus, no friendship which he had for him, no favour which he had shown him, could make it right. The *consent,* the *concurrence* on the part of Paul was absolutely *necessary* in order that he should be in anyway responsible for what Onesimus had done. (5) The same principle prevails in imputation everywhere. (*a*) What we have done is chargeable upon us. (*b*) If we have not done a thing, or have not assumed it by a voluntary act, it is not right to charge it upon us. (*c*) God reckons things as they are. The Saviour voluntarily *assumed* the place of man, and God *reckoned,* or considered it so. He did not hold him guilty or blameworthy in the case; but as he had voluntarily taken the place of the sinner, he was treated *as if* he had been a sinner. God, in like manner, does not charge on man crimes of which he is not guilty. He does not hold him to be blameworthy, or ill-deserving for the sin of Adam, or any other sin but his own. He

reckons things as they are. Adam sinned, and *he* alone was held to be blameworthy or ill-deserving for the act. By a divine constitution (comp. Notes, Rom. v. 12, *seq.*), he had appointed that *if* he sinned, the consequences or results should pass over and terminate on his posterity—as the consequences of the sin of the drunkard pass over and terminate on his sons—and God *reckons* this to be so, and treats the race accordingly. He never reckons those to be guilty who are not guilty; or those to be ill-deserving who are not ill-deserving; nor does he punish one for what another has done. When Paul, therefore, voluntarily *assumed* a debt or an obligation, what he did should not be urged as an argument to prove that it would be right for God to charge on all the posterity of Adam the sin of their first father, or to hold them guilty for an offence committed ages before they had an existence. The case should be adduced to demonstrate *one point* only—that when a man *assumes* a debt, or voluntarily takes a wrong done upon himself, it is right to hold him responsible for it.

[See the subject of imputation discussed in the Supplementary Notes, Rom. v. 12, 19; 2 Cor. v. 19, 21; Gal. iii. 13.]

19. *I Paul have written* it *with mine own hand.* It has been inferred from this, that Paul wrote this entire epistle with his own hand, though this was contrary to his usual practice; comp. Notes on Rom. xvi. 22; 1 Cor. xvi. 21; Gal. vi. 11. He undoubtedly meant to refer to this as a mark of special favour towards Philemon, and as furnishing security that he would certainly be bound for what he had promised. ¶ *I will repay* it. I will be security for it. It is not probable that Paul supposed that Philemon would rigidly exact it from him, but if he did, he would feel himself bound to pay it. ¶ *Albeit I do not say to thee how thou owest unto me even thine own self besides.* Paul had doubtless been the means

20 Yea, brother, let me have joy of thee in the Lord: *v*refresh my bowels in the Lord.

21 Having*w* confidence in thy obedience I wrote unto thee, knowing that thou wilt also do more than I say.

v ver.7.　　　　　*w* 2 Co.7.16.

of the conversion of Philemon, and whatever hope he cherished of eternal life, was to be traced to his instrumentality. Paul says that this was equivalent to his owing *himself* to him. His very life—his eternal welfare—was to be traced to his labours. What he asked now of him was a small matter compared with this, and he seems to have supposed —what was probably true—that for this consideration, Philemon would not think of exacting of him what he had voluntarily obligated himself to pay.

20. *Yea, brother, let me have joy of thee in the Lord.* "By showing me this favour in receiving my friend and brother as I request." The phrase "in the Lord," here seems to mean that, if this request was granted, he would recognize the hand of the Lord in it, and would receive it as a favour from him. ¶ *Refresh my bowels in the Lord.* The bowels, in the Scriptures, are uniformly spoken of as the seat of the affections—meaning commonly the upper viscera, embracing the heart and the lungs; comp. Notes on Isa. xvi. 11. The reason is, that in any deep emotion this part of our frame is peculiarly affected, or we *feel* it there. Comp. Robinson's *Lex.* on the word σπλάγχνον. See this illustrated at length in Sir Charles Bell's *Anatomy of Expression*, p. 85, seq., ed. London, 1844. The idea here is, that Paul had such a tender affection for Onesimus as to give him great concern and uneasiness. The word rendered "*refresh*"—ἀνάπαυσόν —means *to give rest to, to give repose, to free from sorrow or care;* and the sense is, that by receiving Onesimus, Philemon would cause the deep and anxious feelings of Paul to cease, and he would be calm and happy; comp. Notes on ver. 7.

22 But withal prepare me also a lodging: *x*for I trust that*y*through your prayers I shall be given unto you.

23 There salute thee *z*Epaphras, my fellow-prisoner in Christ Jesus;

x Phi.2.24.　　*y* 2 Co.1.11.　　*z* Col.1.7.

21. *Having confidence in thy obedience.* That you would comply with all my expressed desires. ¶ *I wrote unto thee.* "I have written to you;" to wit, in this epistle. ¶ *Knowing that thou wilt also do more than I say.* In all the respects which he had mentioned—in receiving Onesimus, and in his kind treatment of him. He had asked a great favour of him, but he knew that he would go even beyond what he had asked.

22. *But withal.* Or, *at the same time*—Ἅμα. While you are granting this favour, do me also another by preparing a lodging for me. ¶ *Prepare me also a lodging.* Philemon had been accustomed to show kindness to the saints (ver. 5), and not improbably Paul had before shared his hospitality. The word rendered *lodging* (ξενία), means properly, *guest-right, hospitality, entertainment;* and then, *a place for a guest;* comp. Acts xxviii. 23. ¶ *For I trust.* Paul had some hope of being released—an event which probably occurred; see Notes on Phil. i. 25; ii. 23, 24; comp. Intro. to 2 Timothy. ¶ *Through your prayers.* Notes, 2 Cor. i. 11. He expected release in answer to the petitions of those who loved him, and the cause in which he was engaged; comp. Notes on Acts xii. 5. ¶ *I shall be given unto you.* I shall be permitted to return to you, as a favour— χαρισθήσομαι. Paul had no doubt that Philemon would so regard it, and he had no apprehension that his abiding with him would be considered as a burden.

23. *There salute thee Epaphras.* The same persons who are here mentioned as greeting Philemon, are mentioned in the close of the epistle to the Colossians—furnishing a high degree of evidence that Philemon resided at Colosse. Epaphras was a

24 *a*Marcus, *b*Aristarchus, *c*Demas, Lucas, my fellow-labourers.

25 The*d* grace of our Lord

a Ac.12.12,25. *b* Ac.19.29. *c* 2 Ti.4.11. *d* 2 Ti.4.22.

member of the church there; Notes on Col. iv. 12. ¶ *My fellow-prisoner in Christ Jesus.* In the cause of Christ; Notes, ver. 1. The circumstance of his being a prisoner is not mentioned in the parallel place in the Epistle to the Colossians, but nothing is more probable.

24. *Marcus, Aristarchus, Demas, and Lucas.* See Notes on the Epistle to the Colossians, iv. 10, 14.

25. *The grace of our Lord Jesus Christ,* &c. Notes, 2 Tim. iv. 22.

The subscription to the epistle is of no authority, but in this case is undoubtedly correct. Compare the Remarks at the close of 1 Corinthians, and Titus.

REMARKS.

Having now passed through with the exposition of this epistle, it may be proper to copy, for comparison with it, one of the most beautiful specimens of epistolary composition to be found in profane literature, an epistle of Pliny, written on a similar occasion, and having a strong resemblance to this. As a matter of taste, it is of importance to show that the sacred writers do not fall behind the most favourable specimens of literary composition to be found in uninspired writings. The epistle of Pliny was directed to his friend Sabinianus, in behalf of his manumitted slave who had offended him, and who was consequently cast out of his favour. It is in the following words:—

C. Plinius Sabiniano, S.

Libertus tuus, cui succensere te dixeras, venit ad me, advolutusque pedibus meis, tanquam tuis, hæsit : flevit multùm, multùm rogavit, multùm etiam tacuit : in summâ, fecit mihi fidem pœnitentiæ. Verè credo emendatum, quia deliquisse sentit. Irasceris scio; et irasceris meritó, id quoque scio : sed tunc præcipua mansuetudinis laus, cum iræ causa justissima est. Amâsti hominem; et

Jesus Christ *be* with your spirit. Amen.

Written from Rome to Philemon, by Onesimus a servant.

spero amabis : interim sufficit ut exorari te sinas. Licebit rursus irasci, si meruerit; quòd exoratus excusatiùs facies.

Remitte aliquid adolescentiæ ipsius ; remitte lachrymis; remitte indulgentiæ tuæ; ne torseris illum, ne torseris etiam te. Torqueris enim cùm tam lenis irasceris. Vereor, ne videar non rogare, sed cogere, si precibus ejus meas junxero. Jungam tamen tanto plenius et effusiùs quanto ipsum acriùs severiùsque corripui, destrictè minatus, nunquam me postea rogaturum. Hoc illi, quem terreri oportebat ; tibi non idem. Nam fortasse iterum rogabo, impetrabo iterum : sit modo tale, ut rogare me, ut præstare te, deceat. Vale. (*Epistolar.* lib. ix. ep. 21.)

"Caius Pliny to Sabinianus, health:

"Thy freed man, with whom thou didst say thou wert incensed, came to me, and having thrown himself at my feet, grasped them as if they had been thine. He wept much ; pleaded much ; and yet pleaded more by his silence. In short, he fully convinced me that he was a penitent. I do sincerely believe that he is reformed, because he perceives that he has done wrong. I know that thou art incensed against him ; and I know also that thou art justly so ; but then clemency has its chief praise when there is the greatest cause for anger. Thou hast loved the man; and I hope that thou wilt love him again. In the meantime, it may suffice that thou dost suffer thyself to be entreated for him. It will be right for thee again to be offended if he deserves it; because, having allowed thyself to be entreated, you will do it with greater propriety.

"Forgive something for his youth; forgive on account of his tears; forgive on account of thine own kindness: do not torment him; do not torment thyself—for thou wilt be tormented when thou, who art of so gentle a disposition, dost suffer thyself to be angry. I fear, if I should unite my prayers to his, that I should seem not to ask, but to compel. Yet I will write them, and the more largely and earnestly, too, as I have sharply and severely reproved him; solemnly threatening him, should he offend again, never more to intercede for him. This I said to him, because it was necessary to alarm him; but I will not say the same to thee. For perhaps I may again entreat thee, and again obtain, if now that shall be done which it is fit that I should ask and you concede. Farewell."

Those who compare these two epistles, much as they may admire that of Pliny as a literary composition and as adapted to secure the end which he had in view, will coincide with the remark of Doddridge, that it is much inferior to the letter of Paul. There is less courtesy—though there is much; there is less that is touching and tender—though there is much force in the pleading; and there is much less that is affecting in the manner of the appeal than in the epistle of the apostle.

The Epistle to Philemon, though the shortest that Paul wrote, and though pertaining to a private matter in which the church at large could not be expected to have any direct interest, is nevertheless a most interesting portion of the New Testament, and furnishes some invaluable lessons for the church.

I. It is a model of courtesy. It shows that the apostle was a man of refined sensibility, and had a delicate perception of what was due in friendship, and what was required by true politeness. There are turns of thought in this epistle which no one would employ who was not thoroughly under the influence of true courtesy of feeling, and who had not an exquisite sense of what was proper in intercourse with a Christian gentleman.

II. The epistle shows that he had great tact in argument, and great skill in selecting just such things as would be adapted to secure the end in view. It would be hardly possible to accumulate, even in a letter of fiction, more circumstances which would be fitted to accomplish the object which he contemplated, than he has introduced into this short letter, or to arrange them in a way better fitted to secure the desired result. If we remember the state of mind in which it is reasonable to suppose Philemon was in regard to this runaway servant, and the little probability that a man in his circumstances would receive him with kindness again, it is impossible not to admire the address with which Paul approaches him. It is not difficult to imagine in what state of mind Philemon may have been, or the obstacles which it was necessary to surmount in order to induce him to receive Onesimus again—*and especially to receive him as a Christian brother.* If, as has been commonly supposed, Onesimus had been a slave; if he had run away from him; if he had been formerly intractable and disobedient; if he had wronged him by taking property with him that did not belong to him, or if he had owed him, and had run off without paying him, it is not difficult for anyone to imagine how great was the difficulty to be overcome in his mind before the object of Paul could be accomplished. This will be felt to be especially so if we bear in remembrance the repugnance necessarily felt by a slaveholder to receive one who has been a slave as an equal in any respect, or to regard and treat such an one as a Christian brother on the same level with himself. Or if we suppose that Onesimus had been a voluntary servant in the employ of Philemon, and had failed to render the service which he had contracted to perform, or had embezzled property, or had gone off in debt, greatly irritating the mind of his master, the difficulty to be overcome before he received him again would be little less. In either case it would be necessary to soothe his irritated feelings, and to inspire confidence in one who hitherto had evinced little claim to it, and to persuade him now to receive one who had shown that he was not to be trusted as a Christian brother. If the epistle be examined with reference to either of these suppositions, it will be found to be composed with the most finished tact and art.

III. This epistle has been frequently appealed to by the friends and advocates of slavery as furnishing a support or apology for that institution. Indeed, it would seem to be regarded by the advocates of that system as so clear on the point, that all that they need to do is to *name* it as settling the whole matter in debate. The points which it is supposed by the advocates of that system to prove are two: *first*, that slavery is right—since it is assumed that Onesimus was a slave, and that Paul does not intimate to Philemon that the relation was contrary to the spirit of Christianity; and *second*, that it is our duty to send back a runaway slave to his master—since it is assumed that Paul did this in the case of Onesimus.—It cannot be denied that this view of the matter would be sustained by most of the *commentaries* on the epistle, but it is time to inquire whether such an exposition is the true one, and whether this epistle really gives countenance to *slavery* in respect to these points. In order to this, it is important to know exactly what was the state of the case in reference to these points—for in interpreting the New Testament it should not be *assumed* that anything is in favour of slavery, nor should anything be *admitted* to be in favour of it without applying the most rigid principles of interpretation—any more than in the case of profaneness, adultery, or any other sin. As the result of the examination of the epistle, we are now prepared to inquire what countenance the epistle gives to slavery in these respects, and whether it can be fairly appealed to either in justification of the system, or in showing that it is a duty to return a runaway slave against his consent to his former master. To make out these points from the epistle, it would be necessary to demonstrate that Onesimus was certainly a slave; that Paul so treats the subject as to show that he approved of the institution; that he sent back Onesimus against his own will; that he

returned him because he supposed he had done wrong by escaping from servitude; and that he meant that he should continue to be regarded as a slave, and held as a slave, after his return to Philemon. Now, in regard to these points, I would make the following remarks in view of the exposition which has been given of the epistle:—

(1) There is no positive evidence that Onesimus was a *slave* at all; see Notes on ver. 16. Even if it should be admitted to be *probable* that he was, it would be necessary, in order that this epistle should be adduced in favour of slavery, that that fact should be made out without any ground of doubt, or the argument is worthless. It is clear that the epistle, under any circumstances, can be adduced in favour of slavery only *so far* as it is certain that Onesimus was a slave. But that is *not* certain. It cannot be made to be certain. It should not be taken for granted. Either of the suppositions, that he was bound to service till he was of age by a parent or guardian, or that he had voluntarily bound himself to service for wages, will meet all that is *necessarily* implied in the epistle.

(2) There is not the least evidence that Paul used any force or even persuasion to induce him to return to his master. It cannot be proved from the epistle that he even *advised* him to return. It is certain that he did not *compel* him to do it—for Paul had no power to do this, and no guard or civil officer accompanied Onesimus to secure him if he had chosen to escape. Every one of the circumstances mentioned in the epistle will be met by the supposition that Onesimus *desired* to return, but that there were circumstances which made him apprehensive that if he did, he would not be kindly received, and that, at his request, Paul wrote the epistle to induce Philemon to receive him kindly. Nothing more can be *proved;* nothing more is necessary to be believed, in order to a fair interpretation of the epistle. Nothing is more natural than the supposition that, when Onesimus was

truly converted, he would *desire* to return to Philemon if he had in any way done him wrong. But to make it proper to adduce this epistle to show that it is a *duty* to return a runaway slave to his master, even on the supposition that Onesimus was a slave, it is necessary to *prove* either that Paul *advised* him to return, or that he *compelled* him to do it against his will. No one doubts that it would be right to help one who had escaped from slavery, if, on any proper account, he should *wish* to go back to his former master: if he felt that he had wronged him, or if he had a wife and children in the neighbourhood, or if he was satisfied that he could be more happy in his service than he could be elsewhere. To this point, and this only, this epistle goes.

(3) There is no evidence that Paul meant that Onesimus should return *as* a slave, or with a view to be retained and treated *as* a slave. Even supposing he had been so formerly, there is not the slightest intimation in the epistle that, when he sent him back to his master, he meant that he should throw himself into the chains of bondage again. Nor is there the slightest evidence that, *if* he had supposed that this would be the result, he would have even *consented* that he should return to his master. No man can take this epistle and prove from it that Paul *would* have sent him at all, if he had supposed that the effect would be that he would be reduced to slavery, and held in bondage. If *such* had been his expectation, he would never have written such a letter as this. The expression of such a desire would have found a place in the epistle; or, at least, the epistle would not have been so framed as almost of necessity to lead to a different result.

(4) There is very satisfactory evidence, besides this, that he did *not* mean that Onesimus should be regarded and treated by Philemon as a slave. It would be impossible for Philemon to comply with the wishes breathed forth in this letter, and meet exactly the desires of Paul in the case, and yet retain him as a slave, or regard him as property—as a "chattel," as a "thing." For, (*a*) *If* he had been formerly a slave; if this is the fair meaning of the word δοῦλος (*doulos*), then this is expressly declared. Thus, in ver. 16, he is commanded to receive him "NOT *now* as a *servant*"—οὐκέτι ὡς δοῦλον. *If* he had been a slave before, he did not *wish* that he should be received as such now, or regarded as such any longer. How *could* Philemon comply with the wish of the apostle, and yet regard Onesimus as a slave? The very attempt to do it would be directly in the face of the expressed desire of Paul, and every moment he held him as such he would be disregarding his wishes. (*b*) He desired him to receive and treat him, in all respects, as a Christian brother—as one redeemed—as a man—"*above* a servant, *a brother beloved.*" How could he do this, and yet regard and treat him as a slave? *Is* it treating one as a Christian brother to hold him as property; to deprive him of freedom; to consider him an article of merchandise; to exact his labour without compensation? Would the man himself who makes another a slave suppose that *he* was treated as a Christian brother, if *he* were reduced to that condition? Would he feel that his son was so regarded if *he* was made a slave? There are no ways of reconciling these things. It is *impossible* for a master to regard his slave as, in the proper and full sense of the phrase, "*a Christian brother.*" He may, indeed, esteem him highly as a Christian; he may treat him with kindness; he may show him many favours; *but* —*he regards him also* AS HIS SLAVE; and this fact makes a difference wide "as from the centre thrice to the utmost pole" in his feelings towards him and other Christians. He is *not* on a level with them *as* a Christian. The notion of his being *his slave* mingles with all his feelings towards him, and gives a colouring to all his views of him. He cannot but feel, if he himself is under the influence of religion, that that slave, if he were treated in all respects *as* a Christian, would be as free as himself; would

have a right to his time, and skill, and liberty; would be permitted to form his own plans, and to enjoy the avails of his own labour; and would be secure from the possibility of being *sold*. (*c*) Suppose now that Paul, after a short interval, had actually come to the residence of Philemon, as he expected to (ver. 22), and had found him regarding and treating Onesimus *as a slave;* would he have felt that Philemon had complied with his wishes? Did he ask this of him? Did he not request just the contrary? ver. 16. Would it not be natural for him to say to him that he had NOT received him as he wished him to? And how would Philemon reply to this?

(5) The principles laid down in this epistle would lead to the universal abolition of slavery. If all those who are now slaves were to become Christians, and their masters were to treat them "not as slaves, but as brethren beloved," the period would not be far distant when slavery would cease. This probably will be admitted by all. But a state of things which would be destroyed by the widest prevalence of Christianity is not right at any time. Christianity, in its highest influences, interferes with nothing that is good, and would annihilate nothing which is not wrong. That which is true, and best for the welfare of man, will survive when the true religion spreads all over the world; and to say, as is commonly admitted even by the advocates of slavery, that Christianity will ultimately destroy the system, is to say that *it is now wrong*—for Christianity destroys nothing which is in itself right, and which is desirable for the highest good of man. It will destroy intemperance, and idolatry, and superstition, and war—because they are evil and wrong—and *only* because they are so; and for the same reason, and that only, will it abolish slavery. When a man, therefore, admits that the gospel will ultimately destroy slavery, he at the same time admits that it is now an *evil* and a *sin*. The gospel is adapted and designed to put an end to the system. It *did* annihilate it in the Roman empire, and its tendency everywhere is to secure its final abolition. The system, *therefore*, is evil. It is opposed to the spirit of religion. It is destructive of the welfare of society. It is a violation of human rights. It is contrary to the will of God. The gospel everywhere teaches us to regard the slave "no longer as a slave, but as a brother;" and when this is secured, the system must speedily come to an end. For this, and for all its other anticipated influences, we should labour and pray that the gospel may be diffused as speedily as possible all over the world; that it may raise man everywhere from his degradation, and invest every human being with the dignity of a freeman; that it "may undo the heavy burden, break every yoke, and bid the oppressed go free," Isa. lviii. 6.